A Dictionary for the Modern Flutist

Reviews for *A Dictionary for the Modern Flutist*

"The art of flutemaking, like any art form, has a language all its own, filled with contradictions and potential contentiousness among its users. Susan Maclagan took on an immense and delicate task, and has shown great success. Her extraordinary patience, curiosity, and endurance have produced a volume [that] will be a tremendous asset for years to come. Furthermore, her hard work and absolute objectivity have been an inspiration throughout this long process."
—David Shorey, author, lecturer, historian, dealer of old flutes, Los Angeles

"Susan Maclagan's flute dictionary is truly a labor of love. I have been privileged to watch it develop from a dream to a comprehensive work that is thorough, accurate, and wonderfully informative. My admiration and congratulations for creating a book that is a must in any flute lover's library."—Leonard E. Lopatin, flutist, flutemaker, flute designer, Asheville, North Carolina

"An astounding amount of work, this ten-year project of Sue Maclagan will prove of great value to flutists, especially teachers who need to answer their students' prying questions and students who do not want to bother their teachers. I found information in her book [that] was new to me. Ms. Maclagan's labor of love provides answers to every conceivable question about the instrument."—Robert Aitken, flutist, composer, conductor, teacher, Freiburg, Toronto

"By owning this book you will have access to the most comprehensive knowledge base on the flute currently in existence. Encyclopedic in scope, exhaustively researched and written in an engagingly accessible style, the dictionary will be an indispensable reference for players, teachers, makers, repairers, and anyone else whose passion is the flute."—Stephen Wessel, flutemaker, engineer, England

"Authoritative, readable, complete. A must for every flutist's library."—Jim Phelan, flutemaker, engineer, Burkart-Phelan, Inc., Boston

"I'm delighted that Susan Maclagan, in scouring every nook and cranny of the flute world, has taken into full consideration historical members of the flute family, including the recorder. In dealing with the modern flute, she has managed to answer countless questions that I didn't even realize I had. Bravo!"—Dr. David Lasocki, researcher of wind instruments, Indiana University

"*A Dictionary for the Modern Flutist* is a truly definitive work. Susan Maclagan has tirelessly delved into every corner of the flute and its world, from the humblest cleaning rod to the most profound issues of flute design and performance and emerged with clear, accurate, and fascinating definitions throughout. My copy shall be well worn, indeed!"—Robert Dick, flutist, composer, author, inventor, teacher, New York City

A Dictionary for the Modern Flutist

Susan J. Maclagan

THE SCARECROW PRESS
Lanham, Maryland • Toronto • Plymouth, UK
2009

SCARECROW PRESS, INC.

Published in the United States of America
by Scarecrow Press, Inc.
A wholly owned subsidary of The Rowman & Littlefield Publishing Group, Inc.
4501 Forbes Boulevard, Suite 200, Lanham, Maryland 20706
www.scarecrowpress.com

Estover Road
Plymouth PL6 7PY
United Kingdom

Brögger Mekanik is a trademark licensed to Brannen Brothers Flutemakers, Inc.
and covered by patent rights issued and/or pending.

British Library Cataloguing in Publication Information Available

Library of Congress Cataloging-in-Publication Data

Maclagan, Susan J., 1952–
  A dictionary for the modern flutist / Susan J. Maclagan.
     p. cm.
  Includes bibliographical references.
  ISBN-13: 978-0-8108-6711-6 (hardcover : alk. paper)
  ISBN-13: 978-0-8108-6728-4 (ebook)
  ISBN-10: 0-8108-6711-7 (hardcover : alk. paper)
  ISBN-10: 0-8108-6728-1 (ebook)
  1. Flute—Dictionaries. 2. Flute players—Biography—Dictionaries. I. Title.
  ML102.F58M33 2009
  788.3'1903—dc22   2008047439

∞™ The paper used in this publication meets the minimum requirements of
American National Standard for Information Sciences—Permanence of Paper
for Printed Library Materials, ANSI/NISO Z39.48-1992.
Manufactured in the United States of America.

To my husband, Dwight Vincent,
my parents, and my children,
Tess and Trevor Vincent

A journey of a thousand miles begins with a single step.

—Lao Tzu

Contents

Foreword

I have known Susan Maclagan for some years, during which time she has relentlessly bothered me, and I am sure others as well, in her efforts to collect accurate flute information. At busy times, this was difficult, but as the years passed, I became increasingly interested in her commitment, and more tolerant towards her aim, as I realized that here was an important book in the making. It takes a special kind of person to probe, delve, collect, and prepare for publication flute facts—especially so when there are critics waiting to correct and complain!

The Internet has made gathering information easier, though sifting through the vast quantity of this is daunting and it can be time consuming to sort out the excellent from the untrustworthy. Though some will continue to use the Internet, many still prefer a hard copy, not just for conveniently finding a topic but also for the enjoyment of armchair browsing. Susan has had the patience and resolve to tackle this huge task so that student and professional alike can turn to this work with confidence in its credibility. Any book that spreads flute information and at the same time reduces misconceptions is even more helpful. Particularly valuable is the amount of information on flute construction, acoustics, and other technical subjects rarely found in other flute books, and this together with new information makes it particularly useful. I am certain it will both add to our knowledge and remove myths, legends, and misinformation in a clear, concise, and accurate way.

Collecting and compiling such a book of flute facts is a long process, and anyone willing to take this on with such dedication and determination deserves the praise and thanks of the flute community worldwide for doing so. Susan Maclagan's hard work, careful research, and clear objectivity will surely guarantee the success of this labor of love, and I warmly wish it every success.

Trevor Wye

Acknowledgments

This book could not have been written without the most generous assistance and encouragement of the following people, who helped with any or all of the following: research, editing, writing, and illustrating many of the definitions. In alphabetical order, these people are:

- Flutist Helen Bledsoe has been a member of the Cologne-based contemporary music ensemble musikFabrik since 1997 and teaches at the Hochschule der Künste in Bremen. She was the 1996 first-prize winner of the International Gaudeamus Competition for Contemporary Music. See www.helenbledsoe.com.
- Joe W. Butkevicius Jr. is a Pearl Flutes product specialist and technician, a flute player, and a national clinician for NAPBIRT and has been a consultant for various instrument manufacturers.
- John W. Coltman, a physicist and retired research executive of the Westinghouse Electric Corporation, has devoted much of his spare time to the study of the flute in its musical, historical, and acoustical aspects. His research in musical acoustics has contributed significantly to what is known today about the behavior of flute-like instruments. Several of his forty papers on this subject are recognized as standard reference material. See http://ccrma.stanford.edu/marl/.
- Pierre Csillag is a pianist and composer living in southern France. Formerly he was a professor of digital electronics. See www.geocities.com/pcsillag.geo/.
- Jon Landell Sr. is the founder of the Vermont Guild of Flute Making and the principal teacher of flute building and repair at his Landell Flute Workshops. Landell has written several articles and a book about his techniques, "The Landell Flute Tune-up Manual."
- Dr. David Lasocki is head of reference services in the Cook Music Library at Indiana University, Bloomington. As a scholar, he has specialized in the history of woodwind instruments, particularly the flute and recorder, about which he has written or edited a dozen books and published almost 200 articles. In his earlier days, he edited exactly 100 editions of 18th-century woodwind music. See http://mypage.iu.edu/~lasocki/.
- Leonard Lopatin is a professional flutist, orchestral player, flutemaker, recording artist, and designer of the SquareONE family of flutes, which features the Lopatin Scale. More about Lenny's groundbreaking work can be found at his website, www.lopatinflutes.com.
- Terry McGee is a maker, restorer, and researcher of flutes from Canberra, Australia. He is one of the developers of the modern Irish flute and is also investigating the development of 19th-century London-made flutes. See www.mcgee-flutes.com.
- Dean Stallard is a flute player and flute teacher at Oslo Music and Culture School in Norway. He has authored many articles on flute playing and teaching in international periodicals. See www.fluteped.org.
- Charles C. Stevens was a senior systems engineer, architect, and consultant at Unisys Corporation involved in support and development for the company's programming-languages products and is an amateur flutist with a thorough knowledge of flute mechanics.
- David Tanner is a saxophonist, flutist, woodwind doubler, composer, arranger, and producer involved in a broad variety of musical styles. Formerly, he was instructor at the University of Toronto and the Royal Conservatory of Music of Toronto, a Yamaha clinician, and a librarian and

sometime saxophonist with the Toronto Symphony Orchestra.

- Maarten Visser is a woodwind maker and repair technician. In 1986, he started his own business, specializing in flutes and adaptive wind instruments such as a one-handed flute and recorder. His work on ergonomic flutes started in 1993 and resulted in the Swan-Neck headjoint and the Vertical Headjoint. See http://flutelab.com.

- David Welans is a flute player and teacher from Boston who specializes in flute restoration, customization, and headjoint design.

- Stephen Wessel is an English flutemaker of 22 years' standing. His unconventional techniques and choice of keywork materials have resulted in almost a hundred highly distinctive instruments, many of which are in the hands of distinguished players. With a solid background of professional mechanical engineering, clarinet playing, and harpsichord building, Stephen's wide understanding and experience of engineering materials and acoustics have enabled him to bring a much-needed fresh angle to flutemaking. See www.wessel-flutes.co.uk.

- Rick Wilson is a professor of mathematics at the California Institute of Technology as well as a performer on and a collector of historical flutes. See www.oldflutes.com for some details on instruments in his collection and the history of the flute since 1500.

- Joe Wolfe is a professor of physics at the University of New South Wales, Sydney, Australia. His acoustics group researches musical instruments and maintains a helpful website at www.phys.unsw.edu.au/music/.

- Trevor Wye is a renowned flute player, teacher, and music editor and is the author of the *Practice Books for the Flute* series, which has received worldwide acclaim, and a musical biography of his teacher, Marcel Moyse. He was the founder of the International Summer School, the biggest flute summer camp in the world in the 1970s and '80s, and of the British Flute Society. Formerly a professor at the Guildhall School of Music, London, and the Royal Northern College of Music, Manchester, he performs a unique 50 Variations on the "Carnival of Venice" on 60 different flutes and teaches at his flute studio in Kent.

Others who helped less frequently, but whose contributions were nonetheless very important to the completion of the book, are Bob Afifi, Philippe Allain-Dupré, Anderson Silver Plating, Pierre-Yves Artaud, Allan Badley, William Bennett, Kathy Blocki, Amy Rice Blumenthal, Adrian Brett, Thomas Brögger, Casey Burns, Thomas Burns, Susan Cantrick, Lou Carlini, Clive Catterall, Michael E. Charness, M.D., Roberto De Franceschi, Dominy Clements, Elmer Cole, Barbara Conable, William Conable, Pablo Núñez Crespi, Virginie Desrante, Robert Dick, Adrian Duncan, Virginia Dunsby, Kyle Dzapo, Roberto Fabbriciani, Benoit Fabre, Bob Fink, Francis Firth, Neville Fletcher, Robert J. Ford, Raymond Foster, Brian Frederiksen, Kyle Gann, Patricia George, Antonio Giuliani, Colin Goldie, Harold Gomez, Richard Hahn, Hammy Hamilton, Jacob Head, Jelle Hogenhuis, Roger Holman, David Jadunath, Robin Jakeways, Scott Joray, Daniel Kirchner, Ton Kooiman, Anne La Berge, Andrew Lane, Christopher Lee, Ho-Fan Lee, John Levine, Gary Lewis, Mike MacMahon, Kyrill Magg, Jim McCabe, Mats Möller, Jeremy Montagu, J. Kenneth Moore, Alexander Murray, Susan Nelson, Nancy Nourse, Mary O'Brien, Shozo Ogura, Ulrich von Olnhausen, Stefan Otte, James Pellerite, Thomas Pinschof, Anne Pollack, Chris Potter, John Rayworth, Jackie Richardson, Sydney Rott, Aart van Saarloos, Joe Sallenger, Harold Seeley, David Shorey, Laurie Sokoloff, Jorge Solis, Mark Sparks, Eldred Spell, Patricia Spencer, Mimi Stillman, Michael C. Stoune, Nigel Street, David Symington, Toshio Takahashi, Atsuo Takanishi, Nikolaj Tarasov, Catherine Thompson, Phil Unger, Desrante Virginie, Carol L. Ward-Bamford, John Weeks, Charles Wells, Brooks de Wetter-Smith, Brad White, John Wion, and Matthias Ziegler.

To these I must add the flutemakers: Altus Flutes; Boaz Berney; Brannen Brothers Flutemakers, Inc.; Burkart-Phelan, Inc. (Jim Phelan); Daniel Deitch; Sanford Drelinger; Folkers & Powell (Ardal Powell); Mara Lee Goosman; Tom Green; Michael A. Greer; Matti Kähönen; Keefe Piccolos (Jim Keefe); Eva Kingma; Monty H. Levenson; John Lunn Flutes, Ltd.; Miyazawa Flutes; Jack Moore; J. L. Smith & Co.; Pearl Flutes; Simon Polak; Sankyo Flutes, U.S.A.; Jim Schmidt; David Straubinger; Sweetheart Flute Co. (Walt Sweet); Verne Q. Powell Flutes, Inc. (Steven A. Wasser, president); Wm. S. Haynes Flute Co. (Gerardo Discepolo, president); and David Wimberly.

Over the years of studying the flute, I have learned from many teachers, both privately (noted with an asterisk below) and/or in lectures or master classes. The following are some of those who made a lasting impression and hence have indirectly contributed to the substance of this book: Robert Aitken*, Aldo Baerten, Samuel Baron, Jamie Baum, Jeanne Baxtresser*, William Bennett, Robert Bigio, Helen Blackburn, Wissam

Boustany, Frans Brüggen, Camille Churchfield, Penelope Clarke, Tadeu Coelho, Francis Colpron, Immanuel Davis, Michel Debost, Robert Dick, Aralee Dorough, Mathieu Dufour, Martha Durkin, Doriet Dwyer, Paul Edmund-Davies, Angeleita Floyd, Brian Frederiksen, Sir James Galway, Patricia George, Geoffrey Gilbert*, Bernard Goldberg, Ornulf Gulbransen, Richard Hahn, Lois Herbine, Virginia Helmer, Tina Hess, Susan Hoeppner, Katherine Hoover, Harry Houdeshel*, Jan Kocman, Christopher Krueger, Christian Larde*, Amy Likar, Peter Lloyd, Lynne Krayer-Luke, Alain Marion, Peter Middleton, Virginia Markson, Michelle Miller, William Montgomery, Mike Mower, Louis Moyse*, Marcel Moyse, Lisa Nelson, Leslie Newman, Per Oien, Greg Pattillo, James Pellerite, Lea Pearson, Celine Pendergrast, Keith Pettway, Marina Piccinini, George Pope, Jean-Pierre Rampal, Laurel Ridd, Paula Robison, Nora Shulmann, Janet See, Clare Southworth, Patricia Spencer, Douglas Stewart*, Alexa Still, Albert Tipton*, Keith Underwood, Werner van Zweeden, Jim Walker, Jed Wentz, Trevor Wye, Marjorie Yates*, and Matthias Zieger

Thanks should also go to the following:

- the music retailer Topwind
- my editor at Scarecrow Press, Renée Camus, for her keen oversight in the production of the book
- my parents, without whose encouragement and financial assistance I could not have studied as often and with as many people as I did
- my mother, who introduced me to the flute when I did not even know what one was, and from whom I also learned how to be organized—a necessary quality for dictionary writing
- my husband, whose idea it was to write this book, without whose invaluable help this book would not have been written, and who put up with me on days when I thought the project could not be done (his oft-repeated quote from Lao Tzu, "A journey of a thousand miles begins with a single step," helped me to plod onward)
- my friends who put up with my difficult schedule and who are still my friends
- my daughter, Tess Vincent, for her help with illustrations
- my son, Trevor Vincent, for his help with filing and mathematical calculations

Common Abbreviations

abbr.	abbreviation		kg	kilogram
app.	appendix		kHz	kilohertz
b.	born		L	left hand (see also fingering diagrams in the introduction)
BFS	British Flute Society			
bib.	bibliography		L1, L2, etc.	first finger left hand, second finger left hand, etc.
C	Celsius			
ca.	circa		Lat.	Latin
cf.	compare		LT	left-hand thumb
cm	centimeter		m	meter
d.	died		mm	millimeter
DCM	Dayton C. Miller		NFA	National Flute Association
def.	definition		no(s).	number(s)
ed.	edition		OBE	Order of the British Empire
Eng.	English		obs.	obsolete
F	Fahrenheit		Op.	opus
fig(s).	figure(s)		pl.	plural
Fr.	French		R	right hand (see also fingering diagrams in the introduction)
ft.	feet			
g	grams		R1, R2, etc.	first finger right hand, second finger right hand, etc.
Ger.	German			
Hz	Hertz		rev.	revised
in.	inches		RT	right-hand thumb
instr.	instrument		syn.	synonym
It.	Italian		trans.	translator, translation
k	karat		v.	verb

Illustrations

Introduction

About This Dictionary

The modern flute is properly called the Boehm flute. It is widely used and differs in only minor ways from the instrument introduced by flutemaker Theobald Boehm in 1847. *A Dictionary for the Modern Flutist* is the first dictionary of flute terms. The entries include the most common flute-related words that a player of the modern flute may encounter. This book includes definitions from such areas as technique, parts, repair, acoustics, articulations, intonation, common ornaments, flutemaking, flute history, music books, and more. For more detailed information on the performing practice of various ornaments in different periods, consult books such as those listed in the bibliography under "Early Performance Practice" and "Historical Methods, Treatises, and Tutors," as a thorough discussion goes beyond the scope of this book.

Also included are definitions of other types of Boehm-system flutes (e.g., piccolo, alto flute, bass flute, contrabass flute), modified Boehm-system flutes (e.g., Rockstro Model flute, Murray flute, quarter-tone flute), predecessors of the modern flute (e.g., early flutes such as the Renaissance flute, Baroque flute, and simple-system flutes such as the eight-keyed flute and Meyer-system flutes), other non-Boehm-system flutes (e.g., Equisonant flute, Siccama Diatonic flute, Giorgi flute, Carte System flutes, Radcliff System flute, Reform flute), and flute classifications (e.g., side-blown flute, end-blown flute, duct flute). When the term *flute* is mentioned in the body of the dictionary, it refers to the Boehm flute unless otherwise noted.

There are short biographical entries for people who are directly related to the development of flute *terms*. These entries are not meant to be all-inclusive with respect to covering important flute personalities as this would be beyond the scope of this book.

The book is fully illustrated and has several appendixes presenting many of these illustrations and more information on certain topics, including a complete listing of modern Boehm-system flutes, and articles by Trevor Wye and David Shorey. There is also a selected bibliography at the end of the book.

My research is based on more than 45 years of studying the flute with world-renowned teachers, doing surveys, conducting interviews, and attending master classes, flute fairs, and flute conventions. I have also done extensive research in libraries, including the Dayton C. Miller Flute Collection in Washington, D.C., the Paris Conservatoire archives, my large personal flute library, and the Internet (including participation in 10 Internet flute discussion lists). Where necessary, I reached out to various experts in the flute community and elsewhere for more information. Makers of flute types, parts, or flute-related products defined in the dictionary were consulted and the definitions approved.

How Entry Terms Are Shown

The entry terms are listed in bold type in their most commonly used form. When a diagonal slash is used

Figure 01. **Boehm-system sterling silver flute in C. Made in 1969 by V. Q. Powell Flutes, Inc., and owned by the author.** *Photo courtesy Dwight Vincent.*

between two or more words of an entry term (e.g., "middle joint/piece"), it means that either of these words may be used by flutists to mean the same thing in the given context. When the slash is used between two note names, such as "G/A," it means *to*, as in "from the note G to A." Parentheses around one word in an entry—for example, "middle (note)"—signifies that that word is optional in the terminology and may or may not be used with the other word(s) of the entry.

Directly following the entry term, there may also be an alternate spelling, information about the etymology, the language from which an entry term is derived (if different than English) and its meaning in that language, the abbreviation for that term, or the plural form of the word. Following this, there may be one or more listings of the word in another language.

Words that are in bold within an entry have their own definitions in this book; other related entries may be listed at the end of the entry. Foreign words not in common usage in English are italicized, as are some other words for emphasis. Common abbreviations used throughout the book are defined in the list of abbreviations on page xv.

Entries are alphabetized letter by letter, and ♭ and ♯ are alphabetized as if spelled out as "flat" and "sharp," respectively. Thus, the entry for "B♭ Side Lever" appears after the entry for "Bevel" and before the one for "B Foot Joint."

Octave Designations

The term *octave designation* refers to the pitch name of a note according to which octave it is in. There are quite a few systems in use for designating the octave. Flutists mainly use two of these. The first, which is preferred by the scientific community, labels the piano's lowest C as "C_1" (C_0 is inaudible). The same note in higher octaves is designated C_2, C_3, and so on up to C_8. C_4 is the equivalent of "low C" on the flute or a piano's middle C.

As the flute is primarily a treble instrument, however, players sometimes find it more convenient to label its lowest C (piano middle C) as "C_1" in place of the scientific standard of C_4, and this is the convention used in this book. To accommodate the lower-pitched members of the flute family, the following system, which is based on the famous Helmholtz system, is used for C's in eight octaves from lowest to highest (with C_1 representing low C on the flute or piano middle C):

$$CCC \quad CC \quad C \quad c \quad C_1 \quad C_2 \quad C_3 \quad C_4$$

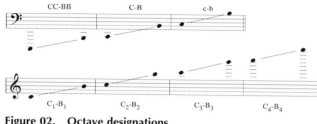

Figure 02.   Octave designations.

The note names for each octave designation are illustrated in figure 02. See also the entries for *high* (1), *higher note*, *low* (1), *lower note* (1), *first octave*, *second octave*, *third octave*, *fourth octave*, *range*, and *register* (1).

Fingering Diagrams

Fingerings for the Boehm flute will be shown using fingering diagrams such as:

T 1 2 3 - / 1 2 3 4C.

This particular fingering diagram is for the note C in the first octave of the flute (i.e., C_1 or low C). The diagram is to be read from left to right. The numbers and letters (except Tr1 and Tr2) represent the flute keys that need to be pressed and also the fingers that need to be used to press the keys (see figure 03). Dashes signify that a key is not being pressed. The diagonal line between the numbers separates the left and right hands.

Fingers or key touches operated by certain fingers may be named in definitions by *R* for "right hand" or *L* for "left hand" followed by a number representing the finger or key operated by that finger. For example, R1 refers to the first finger of the right hand (that is, the one next to the thumb) or to the F key which is operated by this finger; R2 refers to the second finger of the right hand or to the E key which is operated by this finger; and so on. T represents the thumb. The first finger is sometimes referred to as the index finger, forefinger, or pointer finger; the second finger as the middle finger; the third finger as ring finger; and the fourth or shortest finger as the baby finger, little finger, or pinkie. See also the entry for *home* (2).

Fingerings for keyless, one-keyed, simple-system, or other flutes with six finger holes are shown in this book using fingering diagrams such as:

1 2 3 /4 - - D♯.

This illustrated fingering assumes there is a D♯ key and shows that it is to be opened for the note F♯ in the

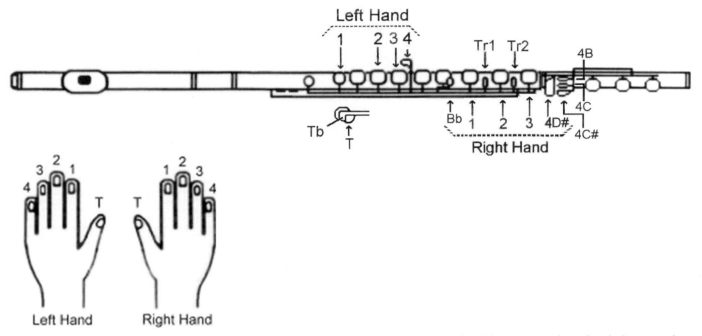

Figure 03.   **Labeled Boehm flute and hands for interpreting fingerings. Some keys on the foot joint are spread out for clarity.** *Drawings by Susan Maclagan; edited by Tess Vincent.*

first and second octave of these flutes. The numbers represent the finger holes that need to be covered by the fingers and also the fingers used (see figure 04). Letters are used to represent keys that should be pressed. Again, a dash signifies that a finger hole is not to be covered, and

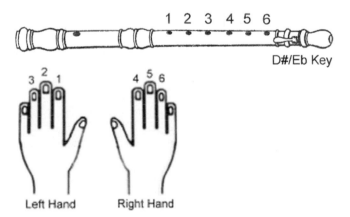

Figure 04.   **Labeled simple-system flute and hands for interpreting fingerings. (Flute reprinted by permission of Boosey & Hawkes, Inc., from *A Treatise on the Flute* by Richard Shepherd Rockstro, 223.)** *Hand drawings by Susan Maclagan; edited by Tess Vincent.*

the diagonal line between the numbers separates the left and right hands.

Flute and Part Names

Unless otherwise noted, modern flute-naming terminology will be used for designating flutes and parts. For further information, see the entries for *"flute in..."* (2) and *transposing instruments*. A list of the various types of Boehm-system flutes can be found in appendix 1.

Information regarding the key and tone-hole names of the modern concert flute, which can also be applied to most other members of the Boehm flute family, can be found in appendix 8. The tone-hole names of the one-keyed flute can be found in appendix 2, number 1. These names can also be applied to simple-system flutes. For other flute types, any key and tone-hole names mentioned in definitions will be found in the illustrations of these flutes.

All directional references (i.e., left, right, north, south, upper, lower, etc.) applied to flute parts are as if viewed from a player's perspective.

The Dictionary

A

A. May refer to the note A₁, which is commonly used to **tune** the instruments of the orchestra and other smaller **ensembles**. *See also* CONCERT FLUTE (5); CONCERT PITCH (1); DUPLICATE G♯ TONE HOLE; "FLUTE PITCHED AT A = . . ."; FREQUENCY; HIGH-PITCHED FLUTE; INTONATION; LOW-PITCHED FLUTE; MODERN SCALE; OCTAVE LENGTH; PITCH; PROFESSIONAL FLUTE; SCALE; SCALING; TRADITIONAL SCALE; TUNER; TUNING FORK; TUNING NOTE; TUNING UP (1). For **early flutes**, *see also* BAROQUE FLUTE (1); BAROQUE PITCH; CLASSICAL FLUTE; *CORPS DE RECHANGE*; PRATTEN'S PERFECTED; RENAISSANCE FLUTE.

ABDOMEN KICK. A movement of the abdomen that is used when a strong **attack** is desired. The abdomen kick is achieved by taking a breath in and using the abdominal muscles to kick at the airstream, rather like a dog barking. Repeated kicks are one method of beginning **vibrato**. *Syn.:* breath kick/push; also incorrectly referred to as a *diaphragm kick*, *diaphragm accent*, or *diaphragm thrust* (*see* DIAPHRAGM KICK for an explanation). *See also* ABDOMINAL VIBRATO.

ABDOMINAL BREATHING. A method of breathing where inhalation and exhalation are by use of the abdomen. The abdomen expands as the breath is taken in and contracts when breathing out. *See also* BREATH SUPPORT; CHEST BREATHING; CIRCULAR BREATHING; DIAPHRAGMATIC BREATHING; PRESSURE.

ABDOMINAL VIBRATO. A type of **vibrato** where the abdominal muscles are used to regularly vary the air pressure. Abdominal vibrato is usually used to initiate the musculature in the throat to generate a controllable vibrato used widely by **flutists**. When the abdomen causes motion in the throat in the area of the **larynx**, due to

the sympathetic vibrations of the **vocal folds** within the larynx, this type of vibrato does not cause any throat tension. May be called "thoraco-abdominal vibrato" by some people, since the thorax (i.e., the chest and the muscles between the ribs) as well as the abdominal muscles are used in its production. Also incorrectly referred to as "**diaphragm** vibrato"; the diaphragm is not involved in producing this type of vibrato. *See also* ABDOMEN KICK; BREATH VIBRATO; LARYNGEAL VIBRATO; NANNY-GOAT VIBRATO.

ABSOLUTE PITCH. The ability to identify or sing a particular **pitch** by ear, or to name the key of a composition without an external reference. Many think they have absolute pitch, when in fact, they have **relative pitch**. Absolute pitch is rare. Also called *perfect pitch*.

ACCIACCATURA. Also *accacciatura*, *accaciatura* (It. *acciaccare* to crush). **1.** An **ornament** used in keyboard music and often notated as a small nonharmonic note a tone or a semitone below a **principal note** or with a diagonal line across the stem of a chord. It is played simultaneously with the principal note or chord and then released immediately while the principal note or chord is held for any remaining time value. It was popular in the Baroque and pre-Classical periods. **2.** An ornament used in instrumental music and notated as a small note with a diagonal line through its stem.

Around the mid-19th century, this notation meant a short, on-beat *appoggiatura*:

At that time, a number of writers began to call the short appoggiatura an acciaccatura. This usage of the term *acciaccatura* was inaccurate, however, as it went against how the term was already being used in keyboard music (see def. 1), where it meant that the principal note was to be played simultaneously with the ornament. Today the term *acciaccatura* is still used by many musicians when they mean a short appoggiatura, although many interpret the small-note-slashed-stem notation, no matter what it is called, as a short, pre-beat ornament:

This pre-beat interpretation is inaccurate for most 19th-century music and some 20th-century music as well. *See also* GRACE NOTES.

ACOUSTICAL LENGTH. 1. In the **flute** world, the same as **sounding length. 2.** Acoustically speaking, slightly related to, but not the same as, the sounding length. If there are zero pressure **nodes** inside a **pipe**, as is the case for the **fundamental notes** on the flute (up to $C\#_2$), then the acoustical length is half a wavelength. If there is one pressure node in the pipe, as is the case for the **second register** (i.e., second **harmonic**) above each of the flute's fundamental notes, then the acoustical length is one wavelength, and so on.

ACOUSTIC IMPEDANCE. Acoustic impedance is the ratio of the acoustic **pressure** to the acoustic volume flow (in both cases, *acoustic* refers to the oscillating component and not to the steady pressure or flow). For example a small **finger hole** has higher impedance than a large hole because it takes more pressure to produce the same volume flow. The maximum in pressure does not generally occur at the same time as the maximum in flow—acousticians say they are "out of phase." Accordingly, the impedance has a *phase* to express that delay as well as an *amplitude*. The phase results from the contributions of the out-of-phase components, which are mass and compressibility. The impedance of such elements is called *reactance*, to distinguish it from the in-phase component, which is *resistance*. The first two components are responsible for the ability to oscillate—for example, a mass on the end of a spring will continue to bob up and down after compressing the spring and letting go. The resistance component (in this case, air friction) will remove energy, and the motion will eventually cease. Mathematically, the impedance is often expressed as a pair of quantities in order to encompass both its amplitude and phase. *See also* ACOUSTIC IMPEDANCE SPECTRUM.

ACOUSTIC IMPEDANCE SPECTRUM. If oscillating flow having a certain **frequency** (e.g., air) is introduced at any point in an acoustically responsive system (e.g., the **embouchure hole** of a **flute**), the oscillating pressure developed at this point will be a measure of the impedance for that frequency. Recording the amplitude of the impedance as a function of the frequency results in a graph of the impedance spectrum.

Much of the behavior of the flute for any given **fingering** may be deduced from the acoustic impedance spectrum measured at the embouchure hole. When the impedance is low, air flows in and out of the embouchure hole easily, and a strong vibration can be produced. Thus a flute plays notes at the frequencies of minima (i.e., valleys in the curve of the graph) in the acoustic impedance spectrum. This spectrum has the useful feature that it is measured without involving a player and so is a measure of properties of the flute alone. Examples of impedance spectra for various flutes are available at www.phys.unsw.edu.au/music/flute. *See also* ACOUSTIC IMPEDANCE; RESONANCE; RESPONSE; STOPPER; VIRTUAL FLUTE (2).

ACOUSTICS. 1. The science that deals with the study of sound. *See* ACOUSTICAL LENGTH; ACOUSTIC IMPEDANCE; ACOUSTIC IMPEDANCE SPECTRUM; AIR COLUMN; AIR JET; AIR REED; ANTINODE; ATTACK; BEATS; BELL; BREAK; BRIGHT TONE; CENT; CONCERT PITCH; CRACKING; CROSS-FINGERING; CUTOFF FREQUENCY; DARK TONE; DENSITY; DIFFERENCE TONE; EDGE TONE; END CORRECTION; EQUAL TEMPERAMENT; FLUTE; FREQUENCY; FULL TONE; FUNDAMENTAL; FUNDAMENTAL FINGERING; FUNDAMENTAL RESONANCE; HARMONIC; HARMONIC FINGERING; HARMONIC SERIES; HELMHOLTZ RESONATOR; HERTZ; HOLLOW TONE; INTENSITY; INTERNAL TUNING; JET; JUST INTONATION; MEANTONE TEMPERAMENT; NATURAL HARMONICS; NODE; OVERBLOWING; OVERCUTTING; OVERTONES; "PARABOLIC"; PARTIALS; PITCH; PRESSURE; PROJECTION; PURE TONES; REGISTER; REGISTER HOLE; RESISTANCE; RESONANCE; RESPONSE; SOUNDING HOLE; SOUNDING LENGTH; SOUND SPECTRUM; STANDING WAVE; STOPPER; TEMPERAMENT; TONE COLOR; UNDERCUTTING; VEILED TONE; VENT HOLE; VIBRATO; VIRTUAL FLUTE; WHISTLE TONE. **2.** The quality of the environment where music is produced.

ACTION. The movement of the **key mechanism**. *See also* MATIT CARBON-FIBER FLUTE; DORUS G♯ KEY; LOST MOTION; ROCKSTRO MODEL FLUTE; SPRING. For **early flutes**, *see also* FLAT SPRING (2).

ADJUSTMENT. The correction or regulation of the flute **key mechanism** to ensure that **pads seal** correctly, or that two or more linked key **cups** close simultaneously. This is done by adding or removing **cork, felt,** or **paper shims** from key **clutches**, or by turning an **adjustment screw** with a screwdriver. **Key rise,** the height a cup is allowed to rise above a **tone hole,** is adjusted by controlling the thickness of the **kicker** cushioning material. For example, in figure 1, when the plate (**lug** or **adjustment plate**) attached to the bottom of the C♯ **spatula** key is

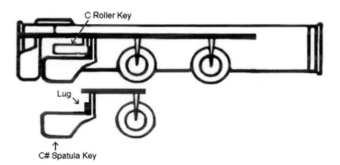

Figure 1. The parts involved in an adjustment of the link between the C♯ spatula key and the C roller key on the foot joint. *Drawing by Tess Vincent.*

pressed by the C **roller** key on the **foot joint**, it should go down simultaneously with the C♯ spatula key. If it does not, there needs to be a clutch adjustment of the link between these keys. This usually consists of cementing a thin piece of cork or similar material on top of the lug that is soldered to the bottom of the C♯ spatula key in the joint between the key and its **extension arm**.

The mechanism is said to be underadjusted when a key that is moved by activating another key closes its tone hole *after*, instead of simultaneously with, the activating key. It is said to be overadjusted when a key that is moved by activating another key closes its tone hole *before*, instead of simultaneously with, the activating key. Both of these situations are due to the incorrect thickness of material between the clutches regulating the alignment of two or more key cups, or to badly regulated adjustment screws. *See also* BRÖGGER MEKANIK; CARTE 1851 SYSTEM FLUTE; CLEAN-OIL-AND-ADJUST; FEELER GAUGE; FINISH (4); FINISHER; FLUTE SUIT; OVERHAUL; PISONI PADS; PIVOT SCREW; REPAD; RETUNING; SOFT MECHANISM; STRAUBINGER PAD.

ADJUSTMENT PAPER. *See* SHIM.

ADJUSTMENT PLATE. Same as **lug**. Also called **clutch** plate.

ADJUSTMENT SCREWS. Small screws mounted in the **key mechanism** of **student flutes** and on some **professional flutes**. Their purpose is to control the simultaneous closure between linked **keys**. If two or more keys do not work simultaneously, there will be a **leak** between the key **pad** and the **tone hole** chimney, and the sound may be weak on notes below this crucial point. Keys must be in perfect regulation for the flute to play properly. Using adjustment screws makes the job of regulating keywork fast and easy when compared to cutting and gluing **shims** between **clutch** plates.

The number and placement of adjustment screws varies. On student flutes, there are commonly four, which are usually placed in full view near the A, F, E, and D keys. They control the linkages between these keys and the F♯ and B♭ keys. The adjustment screws are also placed on the underside of the mechanism for cosmetic reasons or to discourage the inexperienced from adjusting them; adjustment screws of this type are said to be **underslung** or hidden from view. *Syn.:* regulating screws. *See also* ADJUSTMENT; BRÖGGER SYSTEM; CYLINDRICAL BOEHM FLUTE (1); FACTORY-MADE FLUTE; GLUE; HANDMADE FLUTE; KEY RISE; LOST MOTION.

ADJUSTMENT TAB. *See* ADJUSTMENT; LUG.

AEOLIAN SOUND. Also *eolian sound*. A sound that is produced as if by the wind. This effect is achieved by creating a **breathy sound** with or without tone. Depending on the composer's instructions, an aeolian sound can range from a breathy sound with little or no **pitch** to a pitched sound with only a little breathiness. It is easily produced by playing the **flute** with an unfocused sound. This may be accomplished by making the mouth **aperture** larger than usual. The larger the aperture, the more unfocused and breathy the tone. There is no standard notation for the aeolian sound. A breathy aeolian sound with no pitch might be notated as

and a breathy aeolian sound with pitch as:

Also called *air sound* or *breath sound*. *See also* EXTENDED TECHNIQUE; JET WHISTLE; RESIDUAL TONE.

AEROPHONE. 1. A class of musical instruments that use a body of vibrating air to produce the sound. For example, bagpipes, **recorders**, accordions, organs, and members of the **woodwind** and brass families are all aerophones. Aerophones are one of four instrument classes from the E. M. von Hornbostel and C. Sachs musical instrument classification system. They may be further classified according to whether the air is confined or unconfined by the instrument's **body** and how the vibration is generated. For example, **flutes** are classified as **wind instruments** that produce a sound when the air is directed at an edge. **2.** Any of the instruments within the aerophone class.

AFRICAN BLACKWOOD. Scientific name: *Dalbergia melanoxylon*. A heavy, exceptionally dense, highly durable, environmentally stable, fine and even textured, straight-grained, **polishable**, water-resistant, slightly oily hardwood. It varies in color from a charcoal gray to brown, but darkens to jet black or dark brown after **oiling**. It is found in the savannah regions of eastern Africa (mainly Tanzania and Mozambique). African blackwood is one of the most common woods used in flutemaking today. It is used to make various parts, such as the **tubes** of more expensive modern **flutes** and **piccolos** and some modern replicas of **early flutes**. Although African blackwood is not an endangered species, there are concerns that it is a declining resource. *Syn.:* blackwood, granadilla wood, babanus (local name in Sudan), grenadilla (Mozambique), mufunjo (Uganda), mpingo or mugembe (Tanzania), mukelete (Zimbabwe). Due to its resemblance to **ebony**, it is also called Mozambique ebony. *See also* DENSITY; FRUITWOOD (1); GREEN LINE.

AGE-HARDENING. A process that increases the hardness and strength of some metals and usually decreases ductility by restructuring the crystal growth of the metal **alloy**. Age-hardening may occur naturally as metal ages, or it may be artificially enforced by controlled heat treatments, the exact process depending on the material. The degree of hardness and strength achieved by age-hardening depends on the metal treated, as each has its own parameters to achieve an optimum of these qualities. Some believe that there is a positive effect on the tone of **flutes** whose **tubes** have been age-hardened, but there seem to be no controlled studies supporting this belief, and acoustic theory predicts that—as long as the **bore** is sufficiently smooth, rigid, and impermeable—the material should not affect the **tone quality** or **response**. Experiments to date support the acoustic theory. *Syn.:* aging, precipitation hardening.

AGRICOLA (SORE), MARTIN (b. Schwiebus, Lower Silesia [now Świebodzin, Poland], ca. 1486; d. Magdeburg, 1556). A German composer, music theorist, music teacher, choirmaster, and author of *Musica instrumentalis deudsch*, an important work about musical instruments (Wittenberg, 1529; rev. & enlarged 1545; Eng. trans. W. Hettrick [Cambridge, 1994]). *See also* BREATH VIBRATO.

AÎNÉ. Fr. elder, eldest, senior. May be stamped on **early flutes** after a flutemaker's name. The term is used to differentiate the maker from other younger members of his family when they have the same first name. *See also* JEUNE.

AIR COLUMN. 1. The air enclosed inside the **tubing** of **wind instruments**. When the air column vibrates, sounds are produced. *See also* DENSITY; FLUTE (1); FREQUENCY; MODE; SOUNDING LENGTH; WALKING-STICK FLUTE. **2.** The air enclosed inside the tubing of wind instruments

along with the airflow from the lungs to the lips and any air in cavities, such as the mouth cavity, which comes into contact with this airflow. *See also* BREATH SUPPORT; PNEUMO PRO.

AIR FLUTE. An invisible **flute** that a person pretends to play.

AIR JET. A stream of fast-moving air. **Flutists** use their lips to form an air jet when they play. *Syn.:* jet. *See also* AIR REED (1); CRACKING; EDGE TONE; FLUTE (1); HARMONIC (1, 2); OVERBLOWING.

AIR REED. 1. The airflow from the player's lips to the **blowing edge** of the **embouchure hole**. The **air jet** is also called "air reed" in an attempt to unify the description of the **flute** with that of single-reed instruments like the clarinet. Because the jet consists of air that mixes with the surrounding air and the reed is an elastic solid body, the oscillation of an air jet is fundamentally different from that of a reed. Therefore, trying to unify both is generally misleading when it comes to the understanding of either. **2.** A **platinum** (Platinum-Air-Reed®) or **gold** (Gold-Air-Reed®) insert that replaces around 70 percent of the length of the blowing edge (see app. 10, fig. 4). It begins at the same height as the blowing edge and extends very slightly below the thickness of the **lip plate** into the **riser** on **Sanford Drelinger**'s **silver** or gold lip plates. It is made from very hard gold or platinum **alloys**. To either side of the air reed is a microchannel that intersects the blowing surface, which is claimed to help facilitate a smoother **overtone** pattern throughout the octaves. The air reed was invented by head-joint maker Drelinger and patented in the United States in 1992 (patent #5,105,705). It is intended to eliminate the buzz sound and provide the quickest and cleanest **response** when playing a flute with a razor-sharp blowing edge.

ALBISI, ABELARDO (b. Cortemaggiore, Italy, 1872; d. Switzerland, 1938). The **principal flutist** of the Milan opera from 1898. He was also a professor, composer, author, and designer of the **Albisiphon**. *See also FLAUTINO* (4).

ALBISIPHON. Also incorrectly spelled *Albisiphone*. **1.** The Albisiphon in C (see fig. 2), which is the first type of **Boehm-system bass flute** (*see* BASS FLUTE [1]) that is worthy of note. It was invented in 1910 by **Abelardo Albisi** and made by **Luigi Vanotti** of Milan. The flute is held vertically to enable the player to reach the widely spaced **tone holes**. The **embouchure plate** is situated on a short horizontal tube at the end of a coiled tube and blown transversely like a regular **flute**. The coil is neces-

Figure 2.   An Albisiphon in C. *Photo courtesy Joseph Sallenger.*

FLUTE. **2.** *Obs.* A **contrabass flute**, this terminology arising when the **alto flute** (in G) was referred to as a bass flute (in G). This meaning is not used today. **3.** Rarely, the vertically held Albisiphon in F, which is similar to the Albisiphon in C, but its notes sound a perfect fifth below a concert flute.

ALCOHOL. A class of colorless, volatile, flammable liquids having the general formula C_xH_xOH (the -OH is referred to as an "alcohol group" by chemists). *Denatured alcohol* is used by flutemakers, repairers, and some **flutists** to clean various parts, such as the **pads**, **steel** rods, and **key tubing** of the **flute**. It is also used as fuel for alcohol lamps. Denatured alcohol is the same thing as *ethanol* or *ethyl alcohol*, with the formula C_2H_5OH (and which is used for alcoholic beverages), except that it also contains small amounts of poisonous chemicals, such as *methanol* or *isopropyl alcohol*, to prevent it from being used as a beverage. Isopropyl alcohol, with a chemical formula of $CH_3CH(OH)CH_3$, is most commonly used by people in the flute world in a diluted state (70 percent alcohol, 30 percent water—sold as *rubbing alcohol*) when they want to sterilize a metal **embouchure plate**. Ethanol can also be used for this purpose. Isopropyl alcohol is also called *isopropanol, IPA, propan-2-ol,* or *2-propanol*. *See also* LACQUER.

ALEXANDER, F. (FREDERICK) MATTHIAS (b. Tasmania, Australia, 1869; d. London, 1955). An Australian actor-reciter and teacher who developed the **Alexander technique**.

ALEXANDER TECHNIQUE. An educational method of improving neuromuscular coordination in order to help control tension, thereby aiding people to go about their daily activities with more ease. For **flute** players, studying the Alexander technique can result in improvements in all aspects of their playing, including the **embouchure**, breathing, finger **technique**, **articulation**, balancing the instrument, and so on. The Alexander technique was developed in the 1890s by **F. Matthias Alexander**, who discovered it while trying to find a cure for his problem with recurrent hoarseness during performances, which, if not solved, would have ruined his actor-reciter career. *See also* BODY MAPPING.

ALIGNMENT DOTS. *See* app. 3C, fig. 5; GUIDE LINES (1).

ALLOY. A metal that is composed of a combination of other metals or of a metal and a nonmetallic substance. For example, **coin silver**, **sterling silver**, and **Britannia silver** are some of the **silver** alloys used in flutemaking.

sary because the length of the Albisiphon is about 38.7 in. (98.2 cm). The lowest note of the Albisiphon was B, an octave below a modern **concert flute** with a **B foot joint** and had a **range** of about two and a half octaves. The instrument met with immediate success. Several composers of the period, including Puccini, Mascagni, and Albisi himself, wrote for the instrument. However, it was reported that some **flutists** felt that it was hard to play due to its wide **bore** (1.46 in./37.2 mm in the original model). *Syn.:* Albisiphon in C, baritone **flute in C**. *See also* FLUTE FAMILY (2); PINSCHOFON; VERTICAL

Nickel-silver, which is also used in flutemaking, is an alloy of copper, zinc, and **nickel,** having no silver at all. *See also* AGE-HARDENING; BASE METAL; BRASS; FIRE SCALE; GOLD; GOLD FLUTE; GS ALLOY; HEAT-TREATING; *MAILLECHORT;* PALLADIUM; PCM-SILVER ALLOY; PLATINUM; PLATINUM FLUTE; QUENCHING; SILVER BRAZING; SILVER FLUTE (1); SOFT MECHANISM; SOLDER; SOLID; SOLID GOLD; SOLID SILVER; STEEL (1); TARNISH.

ALTERNATE FINGERINGS. Special **fingerings** which are used instead of **basic fingerings** to facilitate the playing of certain notes. Some alternate fingerings can help to improve a note's **intonation, response,** and volume or to obtain a different **tone color.** Others make it easier to play an awkward combination of notes or play a **passage** quickly.

There are three different kinds of alternate fingerings:

1. fingerings that involve pressing an extra **key** and/or omitting a key that would normally be depressed for a note (resulting in an extra **tone hole** being covered or omitted for a particular note)
2. fingerings that use **half-holing**
3. fingerings that give **harmonics**

An example of an alternate fingering that can be used to play the notes $F\sharp_1$ or $F\sharp_2$ more quickly in a passage is:

$$T\ 1\ 2\ 3\ -\ /\ -\ 2\ -\ 4D\sharp.$$

This is the type of alternate fingering that involves pressing one extra key (i.e., the E key, or R2) and omitting a key (i.e., the D key, or R3) which a flutist would normally depress for this note.

There is controversy over when to use alternate fingerings. Some feel that they should be used sparingly, or with caution, because although they may improve one thing about a note, they may have a negative effect on something else, such as tone, intonation, or dynamics. For example, in using the $F\sharp$ fingering shown above, the flutist may be able to play more quickly in certain situations, but the intonation and **tone quality** will suffer. *Syn.*: altered fingerings, artistic fingerings, auxiliary fingerings, fake fingerings, irregular fingerings, shortcut fingerings, simplified fingerings, trick fingerings. *See also* CHARANGA FLUTE (1); CLOSED-KEY SYSTEM; FINGERING CHART; FLUTE FAMILY (2); FRENCH-MODEL FLUTE (1); G$\sharp$ KEY (1); KEY VIBRATO; QUARTER-TONE FLUTE; SHADING (1); TIMBRAL NOTE/TONE; TRILL FINGERING; TRILL KEYS; VIRTUAL FLUTE (2). For **early flutes,** *see* *also* AUGMENTED FINGERINGS; BAROQUE FLUTE (1); FACSIMILE; VEILED TONE (1).

ALTÈS, JOSEPH HENRI (b. Rouen, Seine-Maritime, France, 1826; d. Paris, 1895). A French **flutist, principal flutist** in several French orchestras, flute professor at the **Paris Conservatoire** from 1868 to 1893, composer, and author of the renowned *Célèbre méthode complète de flûte* (Paris, 1880), the first major **Boehm** flute method.

ALTFLÖTE. **1.** Ger. for **alto flute** (in G). **2.** Ger. for tenor **recorder** in the late Baroque.

ALTISSIMO. It. highest. **1.** The **highest notes** of a musical instrument. *See also* REGISTER (1). **2.** Those notes higher than the normal **range** of an instrument, which today would mean above D_4 on the **concert flute. Paul Taffanel** (1844–1908), father of the modern **French flute school,** considered the normal range to extend to B_3, so in this case, *altissimo* would mean above B_3. *See also* FALSET NOTES; FOURTH OCTAVE; SOPRANO FLUTE IN F.

ALTO FLUTE. It. *flauto contralto, flauto en sol;* Fr. *flûte alto, flûte contralto en sol, flûte en sol;* Ger. *Altflöte.* A common member of the **Boehm flute** family (*see* FLUTE FAMILY [2]), **pitched** in G, sounding a fourth lower than the **concert flute** in C. Like the concert flute, the alto flute is **side-blown;** it uses the same **fingering system** and, except for small playing changes, is played in a similar way. Its **range** is around three octaves, from the note sounding as g to G_3 (written C_1 to C_4; *see* TRANSPOSING INSTRUMENTS).

The length of the alto flute with a C **foot** and **straight head joint** is about 34.5 in. (88 cm). Traditionally, alto flutes have been made with straight head joints, but there are alto flutes being made with **curved head joints,** making them shorter in effective length and thus easier to hold for some. Appendix 6, figure 3, shows an alto flute with a straight head joint.

With relatively few changes, the modern alto flute is the achievement of **Theobald Boehm** around 1854 or 1855.

The alto flute is becoming more and more popular and is being used in **solo** playing, studio work, and **ensembles** of all sizes, though it is not a regular member of the band or symphony orchestra. Due to its increasing popularity, more music is being written for the instrument.

The alto flute, also called the alto **flute in G,** has been called a **bass flute** in G when the bass flute in C was uncommon; an example is in Gustav Holtz's (1874–1934) suite *The Planets.* It is sometimes also referred to incorrectly as a *flûte d'amour,* but that is a different instrument. *See also* app. 6; ALBISIPHON (2); CONCERT PITCH (2); *FLAUTONE;* FLUTE BAND; FLUTE CHOIR; FLUTE FLAG; FLUTE STAND; MEMBRANE HEAD JOINT; PRINCIPAL FLUTIST (3); QUARTER-TONE FLUTE; *SCHLEIFKLAPPE;* SQUAREONE FLUTE.

AMADIO, JOHN (b. Christchurch, New Zealand, 1884; d. Melbourne, Australia, 1964). An internationally renowned **flutist**, teacher, and recording artist. *See also* *FLÛTE D'AMOUR;* RADCLIFF SYSTEM FLUTE.

ANCHOR-TONGUE EMBOUCHURE. A type of **embouchure** in which the tongue pushes the lower lip forward to help support it when it is forming the embouchure. Many **flutists** feel that using this type of embouchure makes it difficult to **articulate** clearly, particularly in fast passages. This should not be confused with a tongue position used for articulation where, because a performer's tongue is particularly long, it is anchored below the inside of the lower teeth and the player then articulates using the center of the tongue.

ANDERSEN, JOACHIM (b. Copenhagen, 1847; d. Copenhagen, 1909). The founding **principal flutist** of the Berlin Philharmonic Orchestra in 1882, a conductor, and a composer of flute **studies** and **pieces** for flute and piano/orchestra.

ANGLED HEAD JOINT. A **head joint** that is bent in such a way that it enables the player to hold the **body** of the instrument in a lower position than usual. Angled head joints are available with various degrees of bend. Using one can make **flutes**, such as the **concert flute**, easier and more comfortable to play, since there is a shift in both the weight of the flute and the right arm to a lower position. It is particularly helpful to those people who may have neck, shoulder, and/or back pain while playing. On the other hand, due to the angle of the flute, **extended techniques** may be more difficult. An example of the angled head joint is the Swan Neck head joint by **Maarten Visser** (b. 1959, see app. 10, fig. 6).

The angled head joint is not as common as the **straight** or **curved head joint** and must be specially ordered. *See also* BOW; VERTICAL HEAD JOINT.

ANNEALING. A process used in flutemaking to **heat-treat** metal and then cool it at a prescribed rate in order to restore its malleability and prevent brittleness. *See also* COLD DRAWING; DRAWING; PATCHING; STRESS RELIEVING; STRETCHING.

ANTINODE. A point, line, or surface of a vibrating object that has the greatest oscillation. In a sound wave, there are two types of antinode: a *displacement* (or *velocity*) *antinode*, where the vibration of the air has greatest amplitude, and a *pressure antinode*, where there is maximum pressure variation. An example of a pressure antinode in the **fundamental** of a **flute** occurs at a point near halfway between the **embouchure hole** and the first open **tone hole** (i.e., a **sounding hole**) for any note in the **low register** (up to $C\#_2$); in this example, the velocity antinodes are near the two open ends (see fig. 43). *See also* NODE.

APERTURE. 1. The small opening in the mouth that shapes and directs the airstream against the **blowing wall**. The aperture is usually in the center of the lips, but may occasionally be off to one side in an **off-centered aperture**. It is very important for the aperture to be lined up centrally with the **embouchure hole**. If the aperture is too large, then a **breathy tone** will result. In order to change the **register**, loudness, **tone quality**, or **intonation** and to be expressive, **flutists** make regular adjustments to the size and shape of the aperture. *See also* AEOLIAN SOUND; OPEN EMBOUCHURE (2); OVERBLOWING; RESIDUAL TONE; TEARDROP EMBOUCHURE; TONE COLOR. **2.** Finger aperture; same as **finger hole**. *See also* TONE HOLE.

APPOGGIATURA. It. *appoggiare* to lean upon. The Italian term *appoggiatura* is used today for two different **ornaments**: the long appoggiatura and the short appoggiatura. It is notated as a small note close to and often **slurred** to a normal-size note, which is referred to as the **principal** or main note.

1. The *long appoggiatura* is an ornamental note that postpones the playing of the principal note following it by stealing time from it. Delaying the principal note may create a dissonance with the prevailing harmony. Long appoggiaturas are played on the beat and **leaned** on or accented. The principal note (or resolution) after it is played more softly.

In the Baroque and Classical periods, the long appoggiatura was notated as a small note of various time values a step above or below the principal note and was slurred to the principal note. Its notated time value did not necessarily correspond to its actual time value in performance. It was held for different lengths of time, depending on certain rules that pertained to the time value of the principal note and on how the music was being interpreted. For some examples of how a long appoggiatura might be played, see figure 3. The long appoggiatura may also be played longer or shorter than usual, depending on the context in which it is used. Around the beginning of the Romantic period (ca. 1820–1910), composers began writing out long appoggiaturas in full notation, as they generally do today.

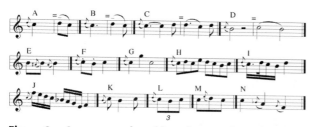

Figure 3. Some examples of how long (A through D) and short *appoggiaturas* (E through N) might be written and played.

Some examples of how a long appoggiatura might be written and played are shown in figure 3:

A. If the appoggiatura is before a principal note whose time value can be divided equally by two (e.g., a quarter note), then it is played for the length of one-half of the principal note and the principal note is played for the remaining time value.
B. If the appoggiatura is before a principal note whose time value can be divided equally by three (i.e., it is before a dotted note), then it is held for the length of two-thirds of the principal note and the principal note is held for the remaining time value.
C. If the appoggiatura is before a dotted principal note and tied to another note in 6/8 or 6/4 time, then the appoggiatura is played for the length of the dotted note and the principal note is played for the length of the second note in the tie.
D. If the appoggiatura is before a principal note that is followed by a rest, then the appoggiatura is played for the length of the principal note, and the principal note is played for the length of the rest. The rest then no longer exists.

2. The *short appoggiatura* is intended by the composer to be held for a short amount of time, *regardless* of the duration of the principal note. (This type of ornament is sometimes incorrectly referred to as an **acciaccatura**, which is actually a different type of ornament.) The short appoggiatura usually briefly postpones the playing of the principal note following it by stealing time from it. Short appoggiaturas do not vary much in length, although they may be played slightly longer in slower tempos to match the style of the music. They are usually unaccented or played more softly than the principal note. Whether or not to give the short appoggiatura an accent is generally left to the discretion of the performer.

Like the long appoggiatura, the short appoggiatura was notated in the Baroque and Classical periods as a small note of various time values (which did not necessarily correspond to its actual time value in performance) and was slurred to the principal note that followed it. Unlike the long appoggiatura, however, it might be notated more than a step above or below the principal note.

Since both types of appoggiaturas were notated as small notes in the Baroque and Classical periods, it was not always easy to tell them apart from the notation. However, there are some clues that can give the player some direction (see fig. 3). For instance, short appoggiaturas tended to be notated as a small note of short time value (e.g., an eighth or sixteenth note) in the 18th century, whereas around the start of the Romantic period, a diagonal slash was added to its stem to more clearly distinguish it from the long appoggiatura. Examples of when a short appoggiatura may be played instead of a long appoggiatura include:

E. when it is before two or more repeated notes
F. when it is before detached or short notes
G. when it is before a note that will leap to another note
H. when it is at the start of a phrase
I. when it is before a dotted note that is part of a beamed group of notes in a faster tempo
J. when it leaps to the principal note in faster tempos
K. when it appears with syncopations
L. when it is before a triplet, to avoid obscuring the rhythm
M. when the melody is such that a note rises the interval of a second and immediately returns to the same note, the short appoggiatura will occur just before the middle note
N. Between the notes of a descending third in French Baroque music, the appoggiatura is short and pre-beat and is called a passing appoggiatura.

Although most short appoggiaturas are played lively and on the beat, in French Baroque music and French-inspired Baroque music like that of **Johann Joachim Quantz** (1697–1773), many of the ornaments written as small notes were intended to be pre-beat ornaments and to be played in a more charming manner. When the appoggiatura "fills" a descending third in French Baroque music, it is short and pre-beat and is called a "passing appoggiatura" (see figure 3, section N). One may also come across short appoggiaturas played as pre-beat ornaments in the 19th century. In more recent times, they are played before the beat.

Other notations and names have been used for appoggiaturas. *Appoggiature, port-de-voix* (Fr. for an ascending appoggiatura), *portamento* (It.), and *Vorschlag* (Ger.) are some of the terms used. *See also* GRACE NOTES.

ARM. 1. Same as **key arm**. *See also* BEVELING; STRINGER. **2.** *See* BRIDGE. **3.** *See* EXTENSION ARM. **4.** *See* KICKER. **5.** *See* VAULTED CLUTCH.

ARTAUD, PIERRE-YVES (b. Paris, 1946). A French flute **soloist** who performs internationally, researcher, coauthor of *Present Day Flutes* (see bib. under "Contemporary Flute"), flute and chamber music professor at the **Paris Conservatoire** from 1991 (substituted for **Michel Debost** in 1989) to this day, promoter of contemporary flute music, and founder of the Arcadie flute quartet (1965) and the French Flute Orchestra (1985).

ARTICULATED KEY. A **key** that consists of sections held together by a joint. There are no articulated keys on a standard **flute**, but some might be found on a **simple-system flute** (or replica of it). For example, see the articulated **low C** and **C♯ keys** on the **foot joint** of a **nine-keyed flute**, ca. 1819, in figure 4. In this case, the keys are articulated because the **shank** consists of two pieces that are jointed together instead of one unjointed piece. Each piece is mounted on a separate axle. When a **flutist** pushes the **touch** of either the low C or low C♯ key down, the far end of that shank goes up; when that is raised, it raises the connecting shank, which has the effect of closing the **key flap** on the **tone hole**. Most **eight-keyed flutes** were made in this way; later ones adopted the modern Boehm **foot** arrangement. Another example of an articulated key is **Theobald Boehm's** (1794–1881) design for the closed G♯ key, but it did not become popular and is not used today. For other woodwind instruments, the definition can be extended to include, for example, the so-called articulated G♯ on the full Boehm-system clarinet. *See also* RING-KEY FLUTE.

ARTICULATION. 1. The means by which a performer produces music clearly with sound and silence.

Figure 4. Articulated keys on a foot joint. From a nine-key cocuswood flute by Monzani & Co., London, ca. 1819. *Photo courtesy Rick Wilson.*

This is accomplished by manipulating the start, duration, and release of notes. Articulation in music is similar to articulation in speech, but with notes instead of words. Articulations are indicated in the music by symbols, words, or abbreviations (see def. 2). Articulation is a component of **phrasing**. *See also* ALEXANDER TECHNIQUE; ANCHOR-TONGUE EMBOUCHURE; BELL TONE; B♭ FOOT JOINT; BROSSA F♯ LEVER; CHARANGA FLUTE (1); *DÉTACHÉ;* DIRECTION; EMBOUCHURE HOLE; FLUTE FAMILY (2); FRENCH FLUTE SCHOOL; FRENCH TONGUING; *LOURÉ; PORTATO;* SECOND FLUTIST; SECTION LEADER; SIMMONS F♯ KEY; SLUR; SPLIT F♯ MECHANISM; STACCATO; SUBCONTRABASS FLUTE IN C; SUBCONTR'ALTO FLUTE IN G; *TENUTO;* TONGUE PIZZICATO. For **early flutes**, *see also* BAROQUE FLUTE (1). **2.** Articulation marks, indicated in music by words, abbreviations, or symbols such as a dot, dash, or curve:

$$\textmusic{ ♩ \quad ♩ \quad ♩̣ \quad ♩ }$$

See also EDIT; FRENCH FLUTE SCHOOL; *LOURÉ; PORTATO;* SLUR; STACCATO; *TENUTO.* **3.** The act of **tonguing**.

ARTIFICIAL IVORY. A type of material, such as cast polyester or Micarta (both types of plastics), that looks, feels, and works to some extent like real **ivory**. It is used in flutemaking and repairs for flute parts such as the **mounts** and end **caps** on replicas of wooden **one-keyed, two-keyed,** and **simple-system flutes**. It is used as a replacement for real ivory, since the harvesting of real ivory is illegal under most circumstances and the material is therefore nearly unobtainable. *Syn.:* fake or alternative ivory.

ASSEMBLY. 1. *See* CORK ASSEMBLY. **2.** *See* SECTION (3). **3.** *See* LIP PLATE ASSEMBLY. **4.** *See* KEY ASSEMBLY. **5. Trill key** assembly. *See also* SECTION (2).

ASSISTANT FIRST/PRINCIPAL FLUTIST. *See* PRINCIPAL FLUTIST (3).

ASSOCIATE FIRST/PRINCIPAL FLUTIST. *See* PRINCIPAL FLUTIST (4).

ATTACK. The start of a note. Strictly, this refers to the part at the beginning of the note during which such things as amplitude, **pitch**, and **harmonic** content are changing rapidly. Such momentary changes are characteristic of the instrument producing the note, and the attack transient can be an important aspect of its **tone color**. Recordings of notes played by a French horn and a **flute** can be indistinguishable if the attack portion of the note is removed, but the identity of the instrument becomes obvious if it is included. The attack transient for a **tongued** note in the flute is faster for **high notes** than for **low notes** and lasts one-tenth of a second or less, during which time the amplitude rises from zero to that of the steady tone and some variation in harmonic content also occurs. *See also* ABDOMEN KICK; FRENCH TONGUING; ORCHESTRAL MODEL FLUTE; SUBCONTRA'ALTO FLUTE IN G; SUBCONTRABASS FLUTE IN C.

AUGMENTED FINGERING. A type of **alternate fingering** that is used to purposely change the **pitch** of a note so that it becomes up to one-third of a semitone **sharper** than the expected pitch for the note for expressive purposes. *See also* AUGMENTED NOTES.

AUGMENTED NOTES. Certain notes that are purposely chosen by **flutists** to be played slightly **out of tune** (**sharper**) in order to play them, and thus the music, more expressively. To achieve this **expressive intonation** effect, special **fingerings** called **augmented fingerings** may be used. For example, on the modern **Boehm flute**, an augmented fingering for $C\sharp_2$ of

$$T - 2\ 3 - / \ 1\ 2\ 3\ 4C\sharp$$

would produce a sharper $C\sharp_2$ than the **basic fingering**:

$$- - - - - / - - - 4D\sharp.$$

The use of an augmented fingering was once common in two contexts: (1) when the note appeared as a leading note (or **sensitive note**) in a major scale (e.g., $C\sharp_2$ in D major); and (2) when it appeared between, and a semitone lower than, two notes with the same letter name (e.g., $C\sharp_2$ when it appears between two D_2's), no matter what the key (this would include semitone **trills**, **turns**, and triplets).

Augmented notes seem to be unknown before the very late 18th century, but became commonly used by flutists in the first half of the 19th century, particularly in France and England. They are not commonly used by today's modern flutists, but are used by some of today's **early-flute** players when they play 19th-century music. *See also* INTONATION.

AULOPHOBIA. An anxiety disorder characterized by an intense fear of seeing, handling, or playing a **flute** or flute-like **wind instrument**.

AULOS. An ancient Greek double reed-pipe instrument. The word is often mistranslated as "**flute**" in modern sources. *See also* TIBIA (1).

AURUMITE®. A layered combination of **precious metals** used in flutemaking to make the **tubing** (including **drawn tone holes**) of more-expensive **flutes**. It consists of an inner layer of 14-**karat** rose gold **soldered** to an outer layer of **sterling silver**, or an inner layer of sterling silver soldered to an outer layer of 9k rose gold. The resulting **wall** thickness is .016 in. (0.4 mm) and is made up of 25 percent gold and 75 percent sterling silver. Unlike the gold used in **gold-plated** flutes, the gold in Aurumite will not wear off. Aurumite was invented in 1986 by **J. James Phelan** while he was an employee at V. Q. Powell Flutes, Inc., and was patented in 1990 (#4,962,007) as "Flute Tubing of Laminated Metal Including a Bonded Layer of Precious Metal Alloy." The assignee is V. Q. Powell Flutes. *See also* FILLER (3).

AUTOMATON. A mechanical device made to carry out the work generally done by a human being. The most famous historical **flute** automatons were two life-size androids built by **Jacques de Vaucanson** in 1738. One was a flute player that was able to play 12 different melodies on a German flute by blowing into the **blowhole**, moving its lips and tongue, and moving its fingers over the **tone holes**. The other was a **tabor pipe** player who played the **pipe** with one hand and a drum accompaniment with a stick in the other hand; it could play 20 different tunes. Figure 5 shows a vignette from ca. 1900 that illustrates the two flute automatons by Vaucanson.

More recently, an anthropomorphic **flutist** robot has been developed by a team of researchers at Waseda University since 1990 (see fig. 5). The robot emulates human flute playing by mechanically simulating the organs (lips, lungs, neck, arms, fingers, **tonguing**, and **vibrato**) required to play a conventional flute. The team's main research goals are clarifying human motor control, enabling communication with humans at an emotional level, and introducing novel teaching tools. The WF4-RII ("Waseda Flutist No. 4 Refined II") is the latest version of the flutist robot, capable of performing a musical score as well as interacting with a musical partner (e.g., performing a **duet** and teaching beginner flutists). The WF-4RII system is controlled by three computers: the first controls each of the mechanical parts, the second generates the accompaniment MIDI (musical instrument digital interface) data, and the third processes the visual information from the eyes of the robot (two charge-coupled device [CCD] cameras).

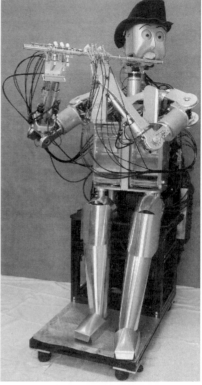

Figure 5. *Left:* A vignette from ca. 1900 illustrating the two flute automatons by Jacques de Vaucanson. *Vignette courtesy Philippe Rouillé, http://www.musicamecanica.org.*
Right: An anthropomorphic flutist robot: Waseda Flutist No. 4 Refined II (WF4-RII).
Photo courtesy Takanishi Laboratory at Waseda University in Tokyo, Japan.

AUXILIARY NOTE. *See* LOWER NOTE (2); UPPER NOTE (2).

AXE. Used frequently to mean guitar and infrequently to mean the **flute**, but can refer to any instrument. *Cf.* **horn**.

AXLE. 1. *See* **steel**. *See also* BEARING; PINNED MECHANISM. **2.** *See* **pin** (2). *See also* BEARING.

AXLE PIN. *See* **pin** (2).

AXLE TUBING. Same as **key tubing**.

ℬ

BACK-CONNECTOR. Any rectangular-shaped **clutch** that is on the side of the **flute** nearest the player (see app. 4, fig. 6; app. 7, fig. 13). Depending on the brand and model of flute, it usually consists of a rectangular base, on top of which are two or three tabs, each of which connects to the **key tubing** with an armlike extension.

The **standard flute** has a back-connector to the right of the closed **G♯ key cup**. Its purpose is to connect some of the right-hand keys with the left-hand keys (e.g., the **B♭ side lever** with the B♭ key, and the F key with the B♭ key) and also some right-hand keys with other right-hand keys (i.e., the D key with the F♯ key, and the D key with the E key).

Syn.: back-clutch, back-connection. Other names for the tab part of a back-connector are *back-connector tail, connection lug, adjustment bar, back-connector kicker* and **spade**. *See also* app. 4; BRÖGGER MEKANIK; BRÖGGER SYSTEM; CYLINDRICAL BOEHM FLUTE (1); GLUE; KEY MECHANISM; VAULTED CLUTCH.

BACK-FINGERING. Rarely used to mean the same as **cross-fingering**.

BACK WALL. The near side of the **embouchure wall**, opposite to where the **flutist** aims his air stream to produce a sound. *Cf.* **blowing wall**.

BADGER, ALFRED G. (b. Connecticut, 1814/15; d. Brooklyn, N.Y., 1892). An American **woodwind** maker, specializing in **flutes**, and an author. His business prospered in the Eastern United States from about 1838 to 1892. Badger was the first commercial manufacturer of **Boehm flutes** in the United States (1846) and the earliest musical instrument maker to use **ebonite** (1851). *See also* CYLINDRICAL BOEHM FLUTE.

BAECHI, KASPAR (b. Zollikon, Switzerland, 1964). A Swiss flutemaker, specializing in antique flute repair and custom modifications. *See also* ROBERT DICK GLISSANDO HEADJOINT.

BAINBRIDGE, WILLIAM (d. ca. 1831). An English **woodwind** maker and inventor whose business flourished in London from 1803 to 1831. He also performed on oboe, **flute**, and **flageolet** in two theaters and was a composer, teacher, and author of **tutors**.

BAKELITE™. Scientific name: polyoxybenzylmethylenglycolanhydride. A type of brown, hard, durable, brittle, insoluble, nonflammable, infusible, moldable, carvable, versatile, inexpensive plastic that is made from formaldehyde and phenol. It is formed by combining these substances under heat and pressure. It was the first completely synthetic plastic, invented by chemist Leo Hendrik Baekeland (1863–1944) and patented in 1907. It became very popular for making a multitude of products, including various **flute** parts, such as the **embouchure plate** and **rollers**. Depending on the **filler** material used, the color of the Bakelite could be slightly changed to mottled yellow-brown, green-brown, red-brown, or black.

BAMBOO FLUTE. Usually refers to any keyless **flute** made of bamboo (e.g., a **shakuhachi**). *See also* STOPPER.

BAND. 1. Same as RING (2); MOUNT (1). **2.** *See* EMBOUCHURE BAND. **3.** *See* FLUTE BAND. **4.** *See* BAND FLUTE. **5.** *See* RING BANDING.

BAND FLUTE. Usually refers to a 19th- or early 20th-century **transverse flute** that has a **conical bore**, consists of at least two sections, and has one or more **keys**. Band flutes are usually **pitched** in flat keys to make the music easier to read. They are named after their **six-fingered note** (e.g., a B♭ band flute sounds B♭ when its six-fingered note is played). Band flutes are mainly used for ceili playing and in wind bands (e.g., particularly patriotic marching **flute bands**).

BAROQUE FLUTE. 1. A modern term for the type of **transverse flute** with six **finger holes** and one **key** that was used in the latter part of the Baroque period (ca.

1670–1750) and into the Classical period, at least by amateurs. The dates of the Baroque period are usually given as 1600–1750, but the term "Baroque flute" is not used for the keyless flute prior to about 1670, that instrument being essentially the same as the **Renaissance flute**. The original Baroque flutes were most often made of wood, had a **conical bore**, and were in three or four pieces. The extra key not only improved the E♭/D♯ but also allowed for more **fingerings** to produce more pitches, which in turn allowed the instrument to play in more keys than a keyless six-hole **flute** or a Renaissance flute. For more information about its physical features, *see* **one-keyed flute** and appendix 2 (nos. 1 and 2).

The **range** of the standard-sized Baroque flute was around two to two and a half octaves up from the lowest **six-fingered note** D_1, although the preferred range, according to some sources, was D_1 to E_3. The flutes were very **low pitched** (ranging from a semitone to a tone lower than the standard modern **pitch** for the note **A**, which is 440 Hz).

The instrument was first popular in France, where the earliest French flutes tended to be ornately **turned**. The first **tutor** for the new flute was published in 1707 by **Jacques Martin Hotteterre** (see bib. under "Historical Methods, Treatises, and Tutors"). This and later books, notably the 1752 *Versuch*, a **treatise** by **Johann Joachim Quantz**, explain the **articulations** and **ornamentation** used at the time. They also advise that notes with flats are to be played at a slightly higher pitch than the enharmonic notes with sharps—for example, B♭ is higher than A♯—the difference to be made with either **alternate fingerings** or an adjustment of the breath. This is a property of all varieties of **Meantone** tuning.

Today, the Baroque flute is the most popularly played **early flute**. As a result, many modern Baroque flutes are now being made, based on early 18th-century originals.

See also BAROQUE PITCH; BREATH VIBRATO; BULBOUS HEAD JOINT; CLASSICAL FLUTE; *CORPS D'AMOUR*; CUT-OFF FREQUENCY; E♭ FLUTE; FINIAL; "FLUTE IN . . ." (1); FOURTH FLUTE (1); HIGH-PITCHED FLUTE (2); INTONATION; INVERTED CONICAL BORE; PERIOD INSTRUMENT; PICCOLO (1); QUANTZ FLUTE; QUINT FLUTE (1); RANGE (2); SECOND FLUTE (1); SIMPLE SYSTEM (1, 3); THIRD FLUTE (1); *TRAVERSO*; TUNING RINGS; TWO-KEYED FLUTE; VEILED TONE (1); VOICE FLUTE (1).

2. The term is sometimes used to refer to the type of one-key flute made significantly later than 1750, even though this term is inaccurate, as the Baroque period is said to end around 1750. These later instruments tend to have narrower **bores** and are higher pitched. They are **brighter** in **tone quality** and their **high notes** are more easily played. However, some early flutists feel that they often lack the **resonant** and mellow sound that is characteristic of the true Baroque flute (def. 1), especially in the lowest octave.

BAROQUE PITCH. A term used today by players of copies of **Baroque flutes** and other instruments to mean from a semitone to a tone **flatter** than **A** = 440 Hz (i.e., from 392 Hz to 415 Hz). The **pitch** A = 415 Hz is most often intended by this term, as many copies of Baroque flutes are made at this pitch. Though the term is quite common, some feel that it should be avoided, because there was no standard pitch in the Baroque era, as the term implies, and most flutes made at this time are actually somewhat below 415 Hz in pitch. *See also* MURRAY FLUTE.

BARREL. 1. The top part of the **middle joint** of a metal **flute** that serves as a **socket** into which the **head joint tenon** (near the head joint's open end) is inserted when the flute is put together. The top and bottom of the barrel are usually clearly defined with a metal **ring** (def. 2) surrounding the **tube** at these locations (see app. 7, fig. 3). Also called a *receiver*, *sleeve*, or *socket*. *See also* FLAUTINO (3); HANDMADE FLUTE; HEAD-JOINT REFITTING; HONING; SERIAL NUMBER. **2.** On some late 18th-, 19th-, and early 20th-century flutes, or replicas of them, the barrel is a separate lower part of the head joint (see app. 3 fig. A, nos. 1 and 2) that contains a socket for the **upper middle joint** tenon and functions as a **tuning slide**. Since the barrel is part of the head joint, it is not always considered an extra **joint**. Thus, clarification may be needed when discussing how many joints a flute has when there is a separate barrel. A head joint with such a barrel may be called a **tuning head**. *Syn.*: head joint barrel, barrel joint, tuning barrel. *See also* BULBOUS HEAD JOINT; HEAD-JOINT LINING. **3.** *See* EMBOUCHURE BARREL.

BARREL EMBOUCHURE PLATE. *See* EMBOUCHURE BARREL.

BARREL JOINT. *See* BARREL (2); TUNING HEAD.

BARREL TUBING. Same as **key tubing**.

BARRÈRE, GEORGES (b. Bordeaux, France, 1876; d. New York, 1944). A French flute **soloist** and orchestral player for 35 years. His orchestra career included playing in several French orchestras and the New York Symphony Orchestra (the latter from 1905). Barrère was also an author, chamber musician, and conductor. He played an important role in the development of chamber music and the chamber symphony, discovered flute composi-

tions, inspired composers to add to the flute **repertoire**, promoted the **silver flute**, and taught at the Institute of Musical Art (which became the Julliard School of Music in 1926) for 39 years. *See also* FLEURY, LOUIS FRANÇOIS; LORA, ARTHUR; PLATINUM FLUTE; SPOON FLUTE.

BASE METAL. 1. Any common, nonprecious metal. *Cf.* **precious metal**. **2.** The metal underneath **plating**. The base metal of plated **student flutes** is usually either **nickel-silver** or yellow **brass**. *See also* EMBOUCHURE RECUT; GOLD-PLATING; SILVER FLUTE (3); STRIKE PLATE. **3.** The most predominant metal in an **alloy**. *See also* FLUX.

BASIC FINGERINGS. Those **fingerings** that are used preferentially because they are said to give the best overall performance in terms of **tone quality**, **intonation**, dynamic balance, controllability, and digital simplicity. The better the flute's **scale**, the more this statement holds true. Basic fingerings are represented on a **fingering chart** found in most flute **method** books. To avoid confusion, basic fingerings are often learned before **alternate fingerings**. *Syn.*: normal fingerings, regular fingerings, standard fingerings. *See also* B♭ FINGERINGS; FUNDAMENTAL (2); FUNDAMENTAL FINGERING; FUNDAMENTAL NOTE; FUNDAMENTAL RESONANCE (1); HARMONIC (2); KEY VIBRATO; RESONANCE; TRILL FINGERINGS; TRILL KEYS; VEILED TONE (2). For **early flutes**, *see also* AUGMENTED FINGERINGS; CLOSED-KEY SYSTEM; ONE-KEYED FLUTE.

BASSE DE FLÛTE. Fr. for basset **recorder** in the late Baroque.

***BASSFLÖTE.* 1.** Ger. for **bass flute** (1). **2.** Ger. for basset **recorder** in the late Baroque.

BASS FLUTE. 1. It. *flauto basso*; Fr. *flûte basse*; Ger. *Bassflöte*. A common member of the **Boehm flute** family (*see* FLUTE FAMILY [2]), **pitched** in C, sounding an octave lower than the **concert flute** in C. Like the concert flute, the bass flute (see app. 6, fig. 4) is **side-blown**; it uses the same **fingering system** and, except for small playing changes, is played in a similar way. Its **range** is about three octaves, from the note sounding as c to C_3 (written C_1–C_4; *see* TRANSPOSING INSTRUMENTS).

The length of the bass flute is twice that of the concert flute, so it is necessary for the **head joint** to be doubled back upon itself (*see* CURVED HEAD JOINT) to make it easier to hold. Its full length with a C **foot** is about 51.6 in. (1.31 m). The effective length, from the open end to the top of the **bow** where the flute starts to double back, is about 37 in. (.94 m). For a bass flute with a B foot, the full length is 53.5 in. (1.36 m) and the effective length is about 39.4 in. (1 m).

The **Albisiphon** of 1910 was the first type of bass flute that had any lasting value. It was not until the 1930s that the bass flute was perfected by Rudall, Carte & Co. of London.

The bass flute is becoming more popular and is being used in recordings, studio work, and **ensembles** of all sizes, although it is not a regular member of the band or symphony orchestra. Due to its increasing popularity, more music is being written for the instrument.

Generally, when the term *bass flute* is used alone, as in the discussion above, it means the bass **flute in C**, which is the most common type of bass flute. Other less common types include the bass flute in A♭, the bass flute in D♭, the bass flute in E♭, and those mentioned in definitions 2–4 below. *See also* app. 6; CRUTCH; *FLAUTONE*; FLUTE BAND; FLUTE CHOIR; FLUTE STAND; MEMBRANE HEAD JOINT; PINSCHOFON; QUARTER-TONE FLUTE; RESISTANCE PLUG; SUBBASS FLUTE; VALGON RINGS.

2. The *big bore bass flute* is an uncommon type of bass flute (in C) that has a wider **bore** than the regular bass flute described above (i.e., 1.4 in./35 mm instead of 1.2 in./30 mm). The large bore helps the **low register** to **respond** more easily and with more volume. It has a **Cooper scale** and can be played vertically when using a T-shaped head or transversely when using a curved head. The height of the instrument with a T-head and a C foot is 41.5 in. (1.06 m). Its full length, including any bends, is 49.6 in. (1.26 m). It was introduced to the flute world in 2005 by Dutch flutemaker **Eva Kingma** (b. 1956). *Cf.* Albisiphon.

3. The *upright bass flute in C until G* is an uncommon type of bass flute that is vertically played and has a T-shaped head joint and a **foot joint** that extends the range to a G (below a regular bass flute's c). To accommodate the extra **keys** that are required for the additional notes, there is a different arrangement of the keys so that the flute can be more easily **fingered**. For example, there is a right-hand thumb key for **low A♭** and G, and there is a left-hand lever for low B♭. Some of the keys have **open holes**. The full length of the flute, including any bends, is about 67.7 in. (1.72 m). The height of the instrument, from the open end to the highest point, is approximately 53.5 in. (1.36 m). The flute was specially designed by flutemaker Kingma for flutist **Matthias Ziegler** for the contemporary flute **repertoire**. He finds that the flute has a wide tonal palette and an unusually large range (for a **low-pitched** instrument) of three and one-half octaves. Because of the long vacuum-like tubing, the flute is nicknamed the "Hoover" after the vacuum cleaner. *See also* SUBBASS FLUTE. *Cf.* Pinschofon.

4. The *bass flute in F* is an uncommon type of bass flute that sounds a perfect 12th below written pitch. It is basically the same as the vertically held **contr'alto flute**

in G except that the bass flute in F is pitched one whole step (a tone) lower. Renowned flutist **Robert Dick** (b. 1950) owns the prototype for the bass flute in F, which was made by the Kotato Flute Company. His flute is the only bass flute in F that is held transversely and looks similar to a traditional bass flute in C. Bass flutes in F (**six-fingered note** G) were made for the British Guards' Flute Bands and for the Belfast **flute bands** in the 1930s. *Syn.:* **contrabass flute** in F, subbass flute in F, contratenor flute.

5. *Obs.* In the past, when the bass flute (in C) was uncommon, the term *bass flute* sometimes referred to the **alto flute** (in G). For example, in Gustav Holst's *The Planets*, a part is scored for "bass flute in G," but alto flute in G is what is meant. This meaning for the bass flute is not used today. *See also* Albisiphon (2).

6. *See* RENAISSANCE FLUTE; TENOR FLUTE (1).

7. British term for the basset **recorder** in the late Baroque.

BATCH MARK. A Roman numeral that was carved into some parts such as the ends of **tenons**, or on **mounts** or on the underside of **keys** of some 18th-century **flutes** to help keep track of the parts during production. The number indicated that the parts belonged to a particular flute in a series.

B/C CONVERTIBLE FOOT JOINT. A type of **foot joint** that can be made into either a **C foot joint** or a **B foot joint** with the use of extensions that are attached to the **foot's body** just beyond the **low C♯ tone hole**. To make a C foot, a short extension is used; to make a B foot, a longer extension with an extra **key** and tone hole is used (see app. 9, fig. 9).

The convertible foot was invented in 1974 by flutist **Elmer Cole** and was first built onto flutemaker **Albert Cooper's** flute no. 149 at that time. In 1981, Cole had Brannen-Cooper flute no. 101 made to his specifications. As Cole envisaged, these **flutes** have no **socket** between the E and D♯ tone holes—unlike the convertible foot today, which does have a socket between these holes. Cole preferred the former configuration as he feels that it is lighter, vibrates better, and there is no **leakage** or loosening problem between the E and D♯ holes. *Syn.:* conversion foot joint. The extensions may also be called *extension sleeves. See also* BOEHM FLUTE (1).

B/C TRILL KEY/LEVER. Same as **B trill key/lever.**

B/C♯ TRILL KEY. An alternative name for the **C♯ trill key,** so called because one of the main purposes of the key is to facilitate the B/C♯ **trill** in the **first** and **second octaves.**

BEAD. 1. Used infrequently to mean the same thing as **tone-hole rim. 2.** May refer to the exposed **solder** that is visible around a soldered **joint. 3.** On **one-keyed** and **simple-system flutes**, may refer to the **knob** of a **block-mount**.

BEARING. Any machine part in or on which another part, such as an axle or a **pin**, revolves. For the **flute**, the ends of a **steel** (rod) form bearings in **posts**. The bearings on the flute are usually either cylindrical or conical (see app. 7, fig. 4). Flutemaker **Jonathon Landell Sr.** (b. 1946) uses a pair of small ball bearings to minimize friction on either side of the **king post**: one bearing services the **keys** of the right-hand **section**, the other the keys of the left-hand section.

BEATS. A periodic fluctuation of the **intensity** of a tone that is produced when two simultaneously played notes are close to, but not exactly at, the same **pitch** or **in tune** with each other. A similar phenomenon occurs when the **harmonics** of notes react to each other in the same way. Adjustment of the beats between harmonics of two different notes is the principal technique used in piano tuning.

The pitch of the beat tone lies between those of the two played notes. The number of beats or intensifications per second is equal to the difference in **frequency** between the two notes. The faster the beats are, the more **out of tune** the notes. When the beats disappear, the notes are in tune. Beats are usually noticed only in sustained notes. In particular, two **flutes** in the higher **registers** are ideal for listening to beats because of the **purity** of the tone, but beats are more difficult to hear when the two notes contain strong harmonics, as is the case in the **low register** of the flute. When the notes contain many harmonics, such as those on the oboe or violin, it is much harder still. *See also* DIFFERENCE TONE; EQUAL TEMPERAMENT; JUST INTONATION; MEANTONE TEMPERAMENT (1); PURE INTERVAL; TUNING UP; VOCALIZING/SINGING WHILE PLAYING.

BED. Same as **seat** (1).

BEGINNER FLUTE. Same as **student flute.** *See also* INTERMEDIATE FLUTE.

BELL. 1. A flaring out at the very end of the flute **tube**, farthest away from the **head joint** (see fig. 31). It can be seen on some older flutes. The addition of a bell increases the high **frequency** radiation (i.e., there is more radiation of high **harmonics**). **2.** *See* BELL TONE.

BELL TONE. A type of **articulation** where the **flutist** tongues a series of notes beginning the first with a full

sound and then tapering the sound off until there is almost nothing left (like a fast one-note diminuendo). The next note is played immediately in the same manner so as to avoid silence between the notes. The articulation gets its name from the bell-like sound of each note.

Since there is usually no standard type of articulation marking for the bell tone in **flute** music, although some flutists may play bell tones when they see the marking for mezzo-**staccato**:

),

it is commonly applied according to the performer's musical tastes. *See also* PORTAMENTO; PORTATO; TONGUING.

BE-MODE (MEMBRANE SOUND) HEAD JOINT. *See* MEMBRANE HEAD JOINT.

BENDING. Same as **note bending**.

BENNETT, WILLIAM (INGHAM BROOKE) (b. London, 1936). An international flute **soloist, flutist** in many leading English orchestras, flute professor, flute designer, music editor, and recording artist, awarded an OBE in 1995. *See* BENNETT SCALE; COLE SCALE; COOPER SCALE; OVERCUTTING; PATCHING; RETUNING; WIBB.

BENNETT SCALE. A flute **scale** developed by flutist **William Bennett** from the 1970s onward under the influence of flutist **Elmer Cole**. Although the **Cooper** and Bennett scales are worked from the same set of principles devised by Cole, Bennett has chosen a slightly longer **schema**—with a different diameter displacement graph, a greater stretch at the upper end of the scale, and a different **open-hole** allowance—to produce a scale that, most notably, put the G and B **tone holes** slightly higher and the C♯ **vent hole** slightly lower than **Albert Cooper**'s. Both of these scales, however, have been in a constant evolution, as no scale is definitive.

An early version of the Bennett scale was introduced to the United States by flutemaker **Jonathan Landell Sr.** in 1972, and an improved version of 1978, given to flutemaker **Jack Moore**, has proved very successful and has been used by many makers with only minimal further improvements.

Along with the Cooper scale, the Bennett scale is one of the most famous of the many new schemas for the position of the tone holes that enables the flutist to play more accurately at the given **pitch**. *See also* COLE SCALE.

BETA BLOCKERS. A class of prescription drugs that decrease performance anxiety by blocking the effects of adrenaline at beta-adrenergic receptors of the heart, muscle, salivary glands, and sweat glands. Beta blockers decrease sweaty palms, rapid heart beat, dry mouth, and tremor in performance situations. They do not block the excitement of performance, but rather reduce those effects of adrenaline that can degrade performance. Certain beta blockers (e.g., Inderal) are sometimes used by musicians to help control nervousness (and the unpleasant physical symptoms associated with it) in a performance situation. Certain medical conditions, such as a slow heart rate, heart failure, or asthma, preclude certain people from taking the medication, so it is very important that beta blockers be taken only under medical supervision.

BEVEL. A surface that meets another at an angle other than a right angle. For example, the **embouchure plate** joins the **blowing wall** at an angle that is not a right angle.

BEVELING. To cut something, such as the **blowing edge**, in such a way that an angle other than a right angle is formed. A **flute** with French-pointed **key arms** is sometimes said to have beveled keywork, since the point of the arms has been made by beveling each side. Beveling is necessary in order to produce the sharp center line of the arm. *See also* OVERCUTTING; UNDERCUTTING (1).

B♭ FINGERINGS. There are three basic B♭ **fingerings** used for the **first** and **second octaves** of the **flute**:

- the *one-and-one* (named after the fact that the first finger of each hand or the first **key** is used) or the *"long" B♭*: T1 - - - / 1 - - D♯
- the *thumb key* (named after the digit that depresses the **B♭ thumb key**) or Briccialdi B♭ lever: Tb 1 - - - / - - - D♯
- the *side lever* (named after the fact that this key is off to the side of the main set of keywork on the **middle joint**): T 1 - - -/ B♭ - - D♯

The **one-and-one B♭ fingering** (or **long B♭ fingering**) can be used in any situation, although it may not be the best fingering choice for speed and/or smoothness. Certain rules apply as to when the thumb key and the **side lever B♭ fingerings** can be used. For example, the **thumb key B♭ fingering** is best used in **passages** where the B♭ thumb key can remain depressed much or all of the time without influencing other notes. This includes passages where there is a B♭₁ (or B♭₂), but no C♭₁ (or C♭₂ or C♭₃) or G♭₃; or passages with an A♯₁ (or A♯₂) but no B₁ (or B₂ or B₃) or F♯₃. This fingering is also used in the playing of some **trills**.

The side lever B♭ fingering is used for **trill fingerings** and is also used where a smooth connection is needed between B and B♭ (or A♯) in the first or second

octaves, such as in a chromatic scale or a chromatic-like passage (e.g., A₁-B♭₁-B₁-C₂), or where smooth playing is required in moving from G to B♭ (or A♯) in the first or second octaves (e.g., G₁-B♭₁-B₁-B♭₁). In the former case, the B♭ side lever can be held down for A₁ and B♭₁. In the latter case, the B♭ side lever can be held down while G and of course B♭ are **fingered**.

Of interest is that on flutemaker **Theobald Boehm**'s original 1832 and 1847 model flutes, **flutists** could *only* use the one-and-one B♭ fingering. *See also* DUPLICATE KEYS; CYLINDRICAL BOEHM FLUTE; RING-KEY FLUTE.

B♭ FOOT JOINT. Abbr. B♭ foot. A rare type of **foot joint** that gets its name because the **lowest note** that can be produced is **low b♭**. This foot joint enables the **flutist** to play two notes lower than with a **C foot joint** (low b and low b♭). The B♭ foot joint is a little longer than a **B foot joint**, and there is an extra **tone hole** covered by a key **cup**, which is operated by a **roller touchpiece** or **left-hand lever** (see app. 5, fig. 1). Its extra length and **keys** make it even heavier than the B foot joint. **Articulation** can be more sluggish, too. Surprisingly, the extra length may make E₂ and F₂ easier to produce clearly, and with good **articulation**, than on some flutes with a B foot. To date, very little music has been written with a low b♭, thus making it unnecessary for most flutists to own one. *See also* BUZZ-TONE; GOLD FLUTE (1).

B♭ SHAKE KEY/LEVER. Same as **B♭ side lever**.

B♭ SIDE LEVER. A (usually) standard elevated **spatula-**like extension of the B♭ key **cup** which, when depressed, closes the B♭ **key**. Also called an *auxiliary key, B♭ lever, B♭ side key, B♭ shake key, B♭ trill key/lever, chromatic B♭, knuckle key, lean key, side key, side lever B♭ key, side B♭ lever, A♯ lever/key, A♯/B♭ chromatic key, side B♭,* or *trill-tab. See also* B♭ FINGERINGS; B♭ THUMB KEY; BOEHM FLUTE (1); B TRILL KEY; CASTING; CYLINDRICAL BOEHM FLUTE (1, 3); DUPLICATE KEYS; INTERMEDIATE FLUTE; PINLESS MECHANISM; PROFESSIONAL FLUTE; RING-KEY FLUTE; SIDE LEVER B♭ FINGERING; SECTION (2); SIDE KEY/LEVER; SPLIT F♯ MECHANISM; STUDENT FLUTE.

B♭ THUMB KEY/LEVER. 1. Usually, the **Briccialdi B♭ lever**. 2. The B♭ thumb key part of the **reversed thumb keys** (see app. 5, fig. 6). *See also* B♭ SIDE LEVER; BOEHM FLUTE; CYLINDRICAL BOEHM FLUTE; DUPLICATE KEYS; FLAT SPRING (1); KICKER; RING-KEY FLUTE; THUMB KEY B♭ FINGERING.

B FOOT JOINT. Abbr. B foot. A type of **foot joint** that gets its name because the **lowest note** that can be produced is **low b** (see app. 7, fig. 12; app. 9, fig. 3).

This foot joint enables the **flutist** to play one note lower than with a **C foot joint**. There are at least four reasons that many flutists prefer a **flute** with a B foot over one with a C foot: They find that a flute with a B foot (1) is useful to have if they are playing a lot of music that requires the note B (i.e., mainly modern flute music and orchestral music), though the number of **pieces** requiring a B foot is very small; (2) has a **darker tone color**; (3) has improved **intonation** on a few **third-octave** notes; and (4) enables them to achieve more special effects. There are, however, some disadvantages. The B foot often makes a clear tone and **articulation** of E$_2$ and F$_2$ more difficult; it is a more expensive type of foot, since it is longer than a C foot; and its extra weight may make it more difficult to manage for smaller students or students with shoulder or neck problems. *See also* B/C CONVERTIBLE FOOT JOINT; B♭ FOOT JOINT; BOEHM FLUTE; BRIDGE; D FOOT JOINT; FOOT-JOINT CLUSTER; GIZMO KEY; INTERMEDIATE FLUTE; LOW B KEY, LOW C KEY, LOW C♯KEY, ETC.; MODEL NUMBER; PROFESSIONAL FLUTE; ROLLER; SOUNDING LENGTH (3); STEP-UP FLUTE (1); STUDENT FLUTE. For **early flutes**, *see also* D FOOT JOINT, NINE-KEYED FLUTE; TEN-KEYED FLUTE.

BIGIO, ROBERT (b. Cairo, Egypt, 1951). A British/Canadian **flutist**, flute designer, maker of **Boehm flutes**, author, and editor of *Pan*, the journal of the BFS. *See also* BIGIO CROWN AND STOPPER.

BIGIO CROWN AND STOPPER. A popular modern replacement for the **cork assembly** (def. 1). It consists of a **crown** originally made out of **African blackwood** and a thin **stopper** (ca. 0.31 in./8 mm by 0.66 in./17 mm) at first made out of Delrin, a hard plastic (see app. 10, fig. 7). There is a small hole running through the middle of the crown. Both the crown and the stopper are held in place by a silicone ring, called an **O-ring**.

The device was invented by **Robert Bigio** in the late 20th century and is believed by many **flutists** to improve the **response** and make the sound bigger and more even throughout the flute's **range**. At the suggestion of **David Symington**, a keen amateur flute player from London, Bigio recently experimented with many different metals for stoppers and crowns before settling on zirconium, which he and many flutists feel produces excellent results. The Bigio crown and stopper must be specially ordered, as the inner diameter of the **tubing** at the crown location must be measured to insure a proper fit. *Cf.* O-Ring (2).

BILLET. A short thick piece of wood that is used in the making of the **tube**-like parts of wooden **flutes**. *See also* ROUGHING; SEASONING.

BILLY-GOAT VIBRATO. Same as **nanny-goat vibrato**.

BIND. To stick so as to be prevented from moving freely. For example, a dirty **key mechanism**, or a screw which is too tight, may cause flute **keys** to bind. *See also* G KEYS; HYGROMETER; PINLESS MECHANISM.

BISBIGLIANDO. It. whispering. A direction to vary the **tone color** of one note by performing **key** or **lip vibrato**. The **flutist** may be required to perform either type of **vibrato** at any particular speed or even change progressively in speed. Although slight **pitch** changes may occur when using either of these **techniques**, the emphasis should be on tonal variation.

Bisbigliando is shown in music by the word or the abbreviation *bisb.* A squiggly line indicating duration may follow the word, and any special **fingering** may be shown above a note. For example,

shows that a bisbigliando is to be performed on G♯$_1$, and

shows that a bisbigliando is to be performed on D$_2$, between the regularly played note and its **harmonic**. *See also* EXTENDED TECHNIQUE.

BLADDER SKIN. Another name for the material that is used for the outermost layer of most flute key **pads**, so called because it is made from the lining of a cow's intestine. **Double-skin** or *double bladder skin* refers to a pad with two layers of skin. *See also* FISHSKIN.

BLAVET, MICHEL (b. Besançon, France, c. 1700; d. Paris, 1768). A renowned French flute **soloist** and master of the bassoon, Blavet held positions in court and in French orchestras. He also taught and composed. *See also* LEFT-HANDED FLUTE.

BLIP NOTE. A term coined by the author to refer to an extra note that sounds unintentionally between two notes. It is usually caused when the fingers do not move as a unit when playing from one note to the next, but may also be caused by a **sticky pad** delaying the release of a **key**. For example, if a student does not move his fingers as a unit from F$_1$ to A$_1$, he may play the blip note G$_1$. Playing a blip note is a common beginner problem.

BLOCK. *See* BLOCK-MOUNT; PIN (2).

BLOCK-AND-PIN KEY-MOUNT. *See* BLOCK-MOUNT.

BLOCKFLÖTE. German name for the **recorder** since **Michael Praetorius** (1619). *See also* BLOCKFLUTE.

BLOCKFLUTE. Modern name for the **recorder** first used since at least F. J. Giesbert's recorder **tutor** (Mainz: Schott, 1936) as a translation of *Blockflöte* and used more recently by Dutch recorder players, who presumably derived it from *blokfluit* (the Dutch word for their instrument).

BLOCKI, HERBERT (b. Wisconsin, 1921). An American engineer and marbling design inventor. He invented the **Pneumo Pro** along with **Kathy Blocki**.

BLOCKI, KATHY (b. Pennsylvania, 1960). An American **flutist**, flute teacher, and author of the *Blocki Flute Method*. She invented the **Pneumo Pro** along with **Herbert Blocki**.

BLOCK-MOUNT. A method of mounting **keys** on **one-keyed flutes, two-keyed flutes, simple-system flutes,** and other **wind instruments** that was common in the 18th and 19th centuries (see app. 3, C, fig. 1). A block of wood or **ivory** was left during the **turning** of the **flute** and stood proud on the flute **body** (see app. 3, B, fig. 6). A narrow **channel** was cut through the block, parallel to the body, to accept the key **shank**. A hole was then drilled through the block and a **lug** in the key shank so that an axle **pin** could be inserted for the key to **pivot** on. A thin tongue-like piece of **brass** or **tempered steel** was used as a **spring** to keep the **key touch** elevated until the key was activated. The spring was attached to the flute body and to the key in various ways (*see* FLAT SPRING [2]). (A similar block, but without a perforation and pin, is often used to support the shank of a **long key** at some point between the pivot and the **pad**.) *Syn.:* block-and-pin **key-mount,** pin-in-block key-mount. *See also* BEAD (3); FLAP KEY; KNOB (2); LINING; POST-MOUNT; RING-MOUNT; SADDLE-MOUNT; SALT-SPOON KEY; THICKENING.

BLOWHOLE. Same as EMBOUCHURE HOLE. *See* BLOWING EDGE.

BLOWING EDGE. The part of the **flute** where the top of the **blowhole** and **blowing wall** meet. *Syn.:* **leading edge,** strike edge, voicing edge. *See also* EDGE TONE; EMBOUCHURE-HOLE BUSHING; FLUTE (1); MODERN HEAD JOINT; OVERBLOWING; TRADITIONAL HEAD JOINT.

BLOWING WALL. The side of the **embouchure wall** where the **flutist** aims his airstream to produce a sound (see fig. 6 and app. 7, fig. 11). The standard angle of the blowing wall is 7° from the plane of the **blowing edge**. Figure 6 shows the transverse section of a flute **embou-**

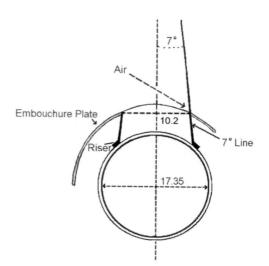

Figure 6.   Transverse section of a flute embouchure hole showing the standard 7° angle of the blowing wall when compared to the vertical direction. *Drawing by Tess Vincent.*

chure hole and the standard 7° angle of the blowing wall when compared to the vertical direction. The 0.68 in. (17.35 mm) measurement is the diameter of the head joint **bore** at the embouchure hole centerline location. The 0.40 in. (10.2 mm) measurement is the width of the embouchure hole from the **back wall** to the blowing wall. *Syn.:* strike wall, far wall, front wall, blow wall. *See also* APERTURE (1); BEVEL; BLOWING EDGE; CENTERING; FALL-OFF; *REFORMMUNDLOCH* (1); RISER; SWEET SPOT; TONE COLOR; UNDERCUTTING (3); VOICING

BODY. The resonating chamber (or sounding box) of a musical instrument. **1.** On **Boehm flutes,** usually refers to the **middle joint,** but sometimes to both the middle joint and **foot joint.** *See also* BODYMAKER; CYLINDRICAL BOEHM FLUTE (3); DIRECT-MOUNT; END CORRECTION; OIL (2); POST-MOUNT; RIB-MOUNT; THINNED (HEAD OR BODY) JOINTS; UNIBODY; WALL (1). **2.** On a three-joint **one-keyed** or **simple-system flute,** it may have the meaning stated in definition 1, but on a four-joint one-keyed or simple-system flute, it may refer to the upper and lower middle joints or to both the middle joints and foot joint. *See also* CONICAL BORE; OIL (2); RING BANDING; THICKENING; TONE-HOLE BUSHING; UNIBODY. **3.** When referring to the tone, body refers to the substance of the tone. A flute tone with more "body" would probably have a larger proportion of **fundamental.** *Cf.* **full tone.**

BODY JOINT. Usually refers only to the **middle joint.** *See also* BODY (1, 2).

BODY-LINE G♯ TONE HOLE. An alternate name for the G♯ **tone hole** under the lower **G key.** It is used to distinguish this G♯ tone hole from the G♯ tone hole under the closed **G♯ key**. *See also* DUPLICATE G♯ TONE HOLE; INDEPENDENT G♯ TONE HOLE.

BODYMAKER. The name of the craftsman in a flute-making company who specializes in preparing the flute **body** for the addition of the **key mechanism**. Depending on the company and the materials used, the bodymaker may do various things. For example, for a metal flute, the worker may **hard solder** the **posts** to the **ribs**, **solder** (or **draw**) any **tone holes** to the **body tube**, cut out the material within the soldered-on tone holes, mill out the cutouts in the ribs to make them fit up against the tone holes at the right angle and distance, drill out the posts to the right size for the **steels** (rods) to pass through, tap the posts that need threads, and do a preliminary **buffing**. *See also* FINISHER; HEAD-JOINT MAKER; STRINGER; TUBE/TUBING (1).

BODY MAPPING. The deliberate correcting and refining of one's body map (also called *body image, body schema, body model,* or *internal representation* by neurophysiologists who study it) to improve movement. The body map is one's body represented in the brain to control movement, so a correct, refined body map assures that a **flutist** plays naturally and efficiently and therefore avoids injury. Body Mapping was discovered and developed as an adjunct to the **Alexander Technique** by **William Conable** and **Barbara Conable** beginning around 1975. See www.bodymap.org for more information.

BODY TUBE/TUBING. Same as **middle joint** and/or **foot joint tube/tubing**. *See also* BODYMAKER; COLD DRAWING; DRAWING; FIFE (1); RETUNING; SERIAL NUMBER; WALL (1).

BOEHM (BÖHM), THEOBALD FRIEDRICH (b. Munich, 1794; d. Munich, 1881). A German flutemaker and inventor who thrived in Munich from 1828 to 1839 and from 1847 to 1861. His inventions include the modern **concert** or **Boehm flute** in 1847. Boehm was also a renowned **flutist** and **principal** of the Bavarian State Opera, as well as a goldsmith, engineer, composer, teacher, industrial metallurgist, and author of *The Flute and Flute-Playing in Acoustical, Technical, & Artistic Aspects* (see bib. under "Repair, Maintenance and Construction"). *See also* introduction; app. 4; app. 8; ALTO FLUTE; ARTICULATED KEY; B♭ FINGERINGS; BOEHM FLUTE; BOEHM SYSTEM; BRASS; BRICCIALDI B♭ LEVER; CAPELLER, JOHANN NEPOMUK; CARTE 1851 SYSTEM FLUTE; CLASSICAL FLUTE; COCHE, VICTOR JEAN BAPTISTE; COCUSWOOD; COLE SCALE; COOPER SCALE; CRUTCH; CYLINDRICAL BOEHM FLUTE; DORUS G♯ KEY; DUPLICATE G♯ TONE HOLE; EIGHT-KEYED

FLUTE (2); EMBOUCHURE HOLE; FRENCH-MODEL FLUTE; GERMAN FLUTE (3); G KEYS; GLASS FLUTE; GODFROY, VINCENT HYPOLITE; GREVE, RUDOLPH; G♯ KEY (1); MENDLER, CARL, SR.; MURRAY FLUTE; NICHOLSON, CHARLES, JR.; NICHOLSON'S IMPROVED FLUTE; NOLAN, FREDERICK; OPEN-KEY SYSTEM; "PARABOLIC"; PRATTEN'S PERFECTED FLUTE; REFORM FLUTE (1); RETUNING; REVERSED THUMB KEYS; RING KEY; RING-KEY FLUTE; RUDALL, GEORGE; SCALE (1); SCALING; SCHEMA; *SCHLEIFKLAPPE;* SILVER FLUTE; TRADITIONAL SCALE; VAULTED CLUTCH.

BOEHM FLUTE. Also *Böhm flute.* **1.** The common name for the **standard flute** in use today (see fig. 01). The Boehm flute is the most common member of the **flute family**. It has a **range** of a little over three octaves from the note sounding as **low C$_1$**, or low b if a **B foot joint** is used, to D$_4$. Although some can play up to F$_{\sharp 4}$, most prefer to stay within the low C$_1$ (or Low b) to D$_4$ range. The length of the flute with a **C foot joint** and **straight head joint** is about 26.4 in. (67 cm); with a B foot, it is around 28.3 in. (72 cm).

With relatively few changes, the Boehm flute today is the achievement of **Theobald Boehm** in 1847. Most modern flutes have the following features: a **B♭ side lever**, a **Briccialdi B♭ lever**, a closed **G♯ key**, a **C or B foot joint**, **drawn** or **soldered tone holes**, **drawn tubing**, a **head-joint cork**, in-line or offset **G keys**, needle **springs** (but **flat springs** for the thumb keys), **open-hole** or **closed-hole keys**, a **pinned** or **pinless mechanism**, and a **straight head joint**. This is the type of flute that can be found in most musical instrument stores in the industrialized world. It may have some of the following options: choice of material, **B/C convertible foot joint**, **C♯ roller**, **C♯ trill key**, **D foot joint**, **D♯ roller**, **G/A trill key**, **engraving**, **gizmo key**, **high G♯ mechanism**, **key extensions**, **left-hand lever**, **lower G insert**, open G♯ key, **split E mechanism**, or **split F♯ mechanism**.

Today, the Boehm flute is used in **solo** playing, studio work, and **ensembles** of all sizes and is a regular member of the band or symphony orchestra. Due to its popularity, much music is being written for the instrument.

The standard-size Boehm flute is also called the *concert flute* (def. 1) or *concert flute in C,* particularly when other flute types are also being mentioned. Other names are *orchestral flute* or *concert-pitch flute. See also* app. 1; COLE SCALE; COOPER, ALBERT; MURRAY FLUTE; SQUARE-ONE FLUTE.

2. The term may also refer to the original flutes invented by Boehm, such as the 1847 **cylindrical Boehm flute**. If the Boehm flute is other than the modern version described above, usually a date will modify the term (e.g., "1832 Boehm flute"). Alternatively, a **bore** description may be used to distinguish a particular Boehm flute from the modern Boehm flute (e.g., the conical Boehm flute; *see* RING-KEY FLUTE). *See also* BOEHM SYSTEM; DORUS, LOUIS; EQUISONANT FLUTE; GODFROY, VINCENT HYPOLITE; GUARDS' MODEL FLUTE; ORDINARY FLUTE; ROCKSTRO MODEL FLUTE; RUDALL, GEORGE; TULOU, JEAN-LOUIS.

BOEHM-GORDON CONTROVERSY. *See* COCHE, VICTOR JEAN BAPTISTE.

BOEHM SYSTEM. Also *Böhm-system.* An arrangement of **keys, key mechanism,** and **tone holes** for the **flute** that is based on the scientific placement of equal-sized holes for the notes of the **equal-tempered** chromatic scale, yet allows the **key touches** to be within reach of the player's fingers. Older methods of applying keys and holes favored the lay of the fingers of an average hand. The Boehm-system made the tone throughout the flute's range more even and strong and with improved **intonation.** It was invented and developed between 1830 and 1847 by **Theobald Boehm** and is, with some modifications, the **system** that is still in use today. Flutes that have this system are called **Boehm flutes.** The Boehm-system principle was later adapted by other **wind instrument** makers to the oboe, clarinet, saxophone, bassoon, and **flageolet.** *See also* app. 6; BORNE, FRANÇOIS; CARTE 1851 SYSTEM FLUTE; CARTE 1867 SYSTEM FLUTE; COLTMAN C♯; CYLINDRICAL BORE; EQUISONANT FLUTE; FLUTE BAND; FLUTE FAMILY (2); HEAD-JOINT LINING (1); IRISH FLUTE (1); MATIT CARBON-FIBER FLUTE; NEW SYSTEM; OPEN-KEY SYSTEM; QUARTER-TONE FLUTE; RANGE (2); SCHEMA; SIMPLE-SYSTEM FLUTE (1).

BONDING. The process of joining two or more materials mechanically or metallurgically by any of several different ways, including coextrusion, **cold drawing,** co-rolling, welding, diffusion bonding, casting, heavy chemical deposition, or heavy electroplating. *See also* CLADDING; CLAD METAL.

BONNEVILLE, AUGUSTE. A French maker of **Boehm flutes** whose flutemaking business flourished in Paris from 1876 to after 1950. *See also* MAILLECHORT; PLATING; RETUNING; SOLDERED TONE HOLES.

BOOT. A long, thin, metal adjustable support spike that is attached to the **foot joint** end (usually) of some large vertically held **flutes** of the **Boehm flute** family (*see* FLUTE FAMILY [2]), such as the **contrabass** and **contr'alto flutes,** to make it easier to adjust the instrument to a player's height. *Syn.:* end pin. *See also* WALKING-STICK FLUTE.

BO-PEP. One of three small, popular, modern plastic snap-on devices that assist some players in holding their **flutes** more easily. Two of these devices (one for small hands, the other for large hands) are designed to be attached to the flute **body** where L1 meets the flute. Another is designed to be attached to the flute body where the RT meets the flute (see app. 12, figs. 17 and 18). In all cases, the body of the flute is built out. **Flutists** who use the devices find that they help to balance the flute and reduce tension in the fingers and hands. These improvements can also help to improve **technique.** Many flutists add a protective material, such as Scotch tape, to the edges of the Bo-Pep devices to prevent them from superficially scratching the flute. Mineral **oil** may also be used. The Bo-Peps were invented by **Boleslaw Peplowski** (b. 1940). *See also* CRUTCH; THUMB REST; WART.

BORE. The hollow space inside the flute **tube,** or sometimes just the diameter of this space. The **flute** is said to have a **cylindrical bore,** although in actuality, only the bore of the **middle joint** and **foot joint** are cylindrical. The bore of the **head joint** gradually **tapers,** usually getting slightly smaller from the open end to the closed end (*see* "PARABOLIC"). *See also* AGE-HARDENING; ALBISIPHON (1); BASS FLUTE (2); BLOWING WALL; BULBOUS HEAD JOINT; CHAMBERING; CONICAL BORE; CUTOFF FREQUENCY; DENSITY; DORUS G♯ KEY; EDGE TONE; FAJARDO WEDGEHEAD; HEAD-JOINT CORK; HONING; INTERNAL TUNING; OIL (2); PICCOLO (1); REAM; RESISTANCE (1); RESONANCE (1); RETUNING (2); RIBS; STEP; TUNING RINGS; WALKING-STICK FLUTE. For **early flutes,** *see also* BAROQUE FLUTE; CHARANGA FLUTE (1); CLASSICAL FLUTE; EIGHT-KEYED FLUTE; INVERTED CONICAL BORE; LAPPING; ONE-KEYED FLUTE; RANGE (2); RENAISSANCE FLUTE; SIX-KEYED FLUTE; TWO-KEYED FLUTE.

BORNE, FRANÇOIS (1840–1920). A French **woodwind** maker, **flute** designer, **flutist,** flute professor at Toulouse Conservatory, composer, and author. Borne developed the Borne-Julliot System flutes (essentially modified **Boehm systems**) in 1889–1890 with **Djalma Julliot.**

BOTTOM NOTES. Usually refers to notes in the **first octave.** For **flutes** with a **B foot,** it also includes the note **low b** below the first octave. *See also* MIDDLE (NOTE); TOP NOTES.

BOTTOM OCTAVE. Same as **first octave.** *See also* MIDDLE OCTAVE; TOP OCTAVE.

BOTTOM REGISTER. Same as **first register.** *See also* REGISTER (1).

BOW. The curved **tubing** of some **wind instruments**. *Syn.:* **crook**, elbow.

BOX. A short telescoped tube section on the **foot joint** which slides over the lower end, or **tenon**, of the **middle joint** when the **flute** is assembled (see app. 7, fig. 12). Also called a *receiver*, *sleeve*, or *socket*. *See also* TIP (1).

BOXWOOD. Scientific name: *Buxus sempervirens*. A relatively lightweight, fine-grained, slightly porous, unstable, **polishable**, dense hardwood that is native to Europe, North Africa, and western Asia. Boxwood gradually changes in color from light yellow to a yellow-brown over a period of time. Boxwood **flutes** that are dark brown in color have probably been stained by use of a chemical such as nitric acid.

Boxwood is not good at retaining its shape, since it is porous, absorbs moisture readily, and often contains unstable "reaction wood," probably from not growing vertically. Due to these problems, it has a tendency to warp, crack, and bend with changes in humidity. This movement also makes it difficult for **keys** to stay regulated. Despite these drawbacks, boxwood was a popular material for making the **tubes** of **transverse flutes** and **recorders** in the Baroque and Classical periods. This is probably due to its availability, beauty, easy workability, and the reputed "sweet" sound produced from flutes made of this wood. It did, however, become increasingly unpopular with makers as the complexity of flute **key mechanisms** increased.

Boxwood is still used today for making replicas. Careful selection and preparation of the wood, thorough **seasoning** and **stress relieving** by the flute maker before starting to make the flute, and careful adherence to the maker's care instructions by the new owner makes the warping and cracking of boxwood less likely. *Syn.:* box. *See also* COCUSWOOD; DENSITY; FRUITWOOD (2); ONE-KEYED FLUTE.

BRANNEN, BICK W. (b. Boston, 1941). An American maker of **Boehm flutes**, a **flute** designer, and cofounder in 1974 and president of Brannen Brothers Flutemakers, Inc. *See also* QUARTER-TONE FLUTE; ROBERT DICK GLISSANDO HEADJOINT.

BRASS. A metallic **alloy** consisting mainly of copper and zinc in varying proportions and sometimes small amounts of other metals. Depending on the proportions of metals in the brass, the properties and color of the brass will vary. For example, **nickel-silver** is considered by some to be "white brass" with **nickel** added. **Theobald Boehm**'s first **cylindrical flute** in 1947 was made of brass and originally **gold-plated** (see fig. 11B). Since brass is a very affordable and machinable metal, it is used to make various parts, such as the **tubing** and **keys**, of **student flutes**. Brass **flutes** are usually **plated** with nickel or **silver**. *See also* BASE METAL (2); CYLINDRICAL BOEHM FLUTE (3); EMBOUCHURE RECUT; FACTORY-MADE FLUTE; FLAT SPRING; LACQUER; RETUNING; SILVER-PLATING; STEP-UP FLUTE (1). For **early flutes** and other non-**Boehm-system** flutes, *see also* BLOCK-MOUNT; KEY FLAP; LINING; ONE-KEYED FLUTE; PIN (2); POST-MOUNT; SADDLE-MOUNT.

BRAZING. 1. In metallurgy, the process of joining two or more close-fitting pieces of metal together with a nonferrous **filler** metal that has a melting point somewhat below that of the metals to be joined but is generally *above* about 840°F (449°C). The parts are usually heated together by gas flame and **fluxed** to prevent oxidation. The brazing metal in the form of wire or strip is fed in and, in its molten state, drawn into the joint to make a neat and strong bond. Such a bond is much stronger than a **soft soldered** joint. *See also* FIRE SCALE. **2.** In flutemaking, usually the same as **hard soldering**, **silver soldering**, or **silver brazing**. *See also* PATCHING; POST-MOUNT; RETUNING; RIB-MOUNT.

BREAK. 1. The point where one **register** changes ("breaks") into another. These points, for the **flute**, are from $C\#_2$ to D_2, $C\#_3$ to D_3, and $G\#_3$ to A_3. Some people regard $D\#_2$ to E_2 as the first break. *Syn.:* register break. **2.** The point in a note being played at which it jumps to a higher- or lower-pitched note (i.e., a **harmonic**). *Syn.:* crack. *See also* CRACKING.

BREAKING-IN (PERIOD). In general, refers to an initial period of time during which any working parts are activated and begin to function effectively.

With regard to wooden **flutes** or **head joints** that are new or have not been played for a long time, this usually refers to an initial period of time during which the moisture content is gradually built up in the wood, so as to avoid cracking. During this period, the instrument is played for short amounts of time—say, 10 minutes in the morning, afternoon, and evening—with a thorough swabbing after each playing session to remove moisture. The length of each playing session is gradually increased over several days or weeks. Since flutemakers may have certain regimens that they like to have followed for the instruments they make, it is best to check with the maker before breaking in a new flute.

With regard to metal flutes or head joints, breaking-in usually refers to an initial period of time during which the player learns how to get the best out of his instrument. For example, he will want to know the dynamic range that he can expect, the variety of **tone colors**, how well the instrument responds, and so on. This will take more time if the player has been used to playing another instrument, because what worked for him on the old instrument might not work on the new. *Syn.:* playing-in. *See also* SEASONING; WARM-UP.

BREATH BUILDER. A translucent plastic cylinder about 6 in. (15 cm) tall with a diameter of the enclosed Ping-Pong ball (see app. 12, fig. 7). It is used to practice control of inhalation and exhalation independently of the **flute**. One end of the cylinder is sealed, and the other has three holes that are used to vary the **resistance** to the air movement. Resistance is lowered by closing one or two holes with fingers. Two plastic straws, one narrow and one wide, come with the device. One straw is attached to a chimney surrounding the hole that the player plans to blow through. The narrower straw will have less airflow and greater air **pressure**, and the (preferred) wider straw will have the opposite—more airflow under less pressure. Various breathing exercises are practiced while the player is breathing in and out of the straw with minimal effort. To help avoid hyperventilation, breaks must be frequent (e.g., two to three minutes). Practicing breathing on the Breath Builder is beneficial, since the **flutist** can concentrate on only their breathing and not the flute—later reapplying what is learned when playing the flute. The device was developed by the late bassoonist Harold Hansen of Las Vegas, Nevada. *Cf.* **breathing bag**.

BREATHING BAG. A rubber bag, of around 5 or 6 liters (5.3–6.3 U.S. quarts) capacity and with a short tube attached, that is used to practice control of inhalation and exhalation independently of the **flute** (see app. 12, fig. 10). It is best if the bag is a little larger than the flutist's normal lung capacity so that there is room for improvement. The flutist practices various breathing exercises while breathing in and out of the bag through the tubing. Since the flutist is rebreathing air during the process, hyperventilation is avoided. Using a breathing bag to practice breathing is beneficial in that it helps the player to focus on improving her breathing without worrying about playing the flute. It is also useful in giving the player an idea of her lung capacity. *Cf.* **Breath Builder**.

BREATH KICK/PUSH. Same as **abdomen kick**.

BREATH SUPPORT. An enigmatic expression that means different activities to different players. Broadly, most would agree that it is the control and manipulation of air speed and/or that it is the control of the **pressure** behind the breath. Physically, it involves the use of the abdominal muscles (which some incorrectly refer to as "the **diaphragm**") to maintain pressure behind the **air column**. Some insist that it is also the use of the chest musculature in addition to the abdominal area to maintain this pressure (*see* CHEST BREATHING). Certainly, many students benefit from help in this field to accomplish some of the **technical** requirements of performance, including the study of tone production; speedy octave playing; the clean manipulation of larger intervals; the clarity and tone of the **third** and **fourth octaves**; and very quiet playing especially in the extremes of the compass, to mention but a few, and also including the study of **piccolo** playing. It is further recommended for undertaking the initial steps in the study of **vibrato**. There is a growing consensus, however, that the term "support" is overused or offered as a blanket remedy for any of the common performing problems; it has been referred to as the "Holy Word of Teaching." *Syn.:* support. *See also* ABDOMINAL BREATHING; PROJECTION.

BREATH VIBRATO. A type of **vibrato** that is produced with the breath. Today, breath vibrato is the type of vibrato most often used by **flutists**. Its employment depends on the music and the taste of the player. It can be used on a single note as an **ornament**, or continuously as a component of tone.

An early source that mentions breath vibrato is **Martin Agricola** (1529), who recommends that the **flute** be played with a "trembling breath," but breath vibrato is not mentioned again in historical sources until the second half of the 18th century. Throughout the 18th century, players of **Baroque** and **simple-system flutes** often preferred **finger vibrato** and did not use much, if any, breath vibrato. When vibrato of any sort was used, it was considered to be an ornament and was employed infrequently. **Anton Bernhard Fürstenau**, in *Die Kunst des Flötenspiels* (1844), for example, uses the term *Bebung* for breath vibrato and indicates its use in some of his compositions on about one note in every eight measures.

In general, modern flutists do not use the term "*breath* vibrato," but it is understood when the term *vibrato* is used. *See also* ABDOMINAL VIBRATO; LARYNGEAL VIBRATO; NANNY-GOAT VIBRATO.

BREATHY SOUND/TONE. 1. A tone that is characterized by superfluous breath noises. It can be caused by a number of factors such as incorrect alignment of the player's **embouchure** with the **embouchure plate** or **leaks** between the key **pad** and **tone-hole rim**. *Syn.:* airy, windy, fuzzy, unfocused (sound/tone). *See also* APERTURE (1); CENTERING; FOCUSING; PURE TONE (2); TONE COLOR. **2.** *See* AEOLIAN SOUND. **3.** *See* JET WHISTLE. **4.** *See* RESIDUAL TONE.

BRESSAN, PIERRE (PETER) JAILLARD (b. Bourg-en-Bresse, France, 1663; d. Tournai, Belgium, 1731). A French **woodwind** maker, renowned for his **recorders**, **transverse flutes**, and oboes and whose business thrived in London from 1688 to 1730. He was also a music publisher. *See also* REVERSE TENON.

BRICCIALDI, GIULIO (b. Terni, Italy, 1818; d. Florence, 1881). An Italian **woodwind** inventor who thrived in Florence. He was also a **flutist**, professor, **soloist** and orchestra player, and composer (see figure 11). *See also* BRICCIALDI B♭ LEVER; CYLINDRICAL BOEHM FLUTE.

BRICCIALDI B♭ (B FLAT) LEVER. A **key touch**, often shaped something like a teardrop, that overlaps the B key **cup** found on the **middle joint** (see app. 7, fig. 7). When depressed by the left thumb, it closes the B **key** and the B♭ key simultaneously. The Briccialdi B♭ lever was named by **Richard Shepherd Rockstro** (1890), who claimed Italian flutist **Giulio Briccialdi** first had this lever built by the firm Rudall & Rose onto a **flute** by the firm of **Godfroy** and **Lot** in London in 1849. Godfroy and Lot immediately started using it on most of their flutes, while **Boehm** and **Rudall & Rose** continued to seek other ways of playing B♭ with the thumb. Prior to 1890, and often afterwards, this key was simply referred to as the "French B♭" or "the thumb key like Lot of Paris makes," since Godfroy and Lot had so famously adopted it. This key has become commonplace and is found on almost all flutes made today. The Briccialdi B♭ lever is used to create an additional **fingering** for $B\flat_1$ and $B\flat_2$ and make some **passages** with these notes easier to play. *Syn.:* **B♭ thumb key/lever** (1), Briccialdi key, Briccialdi thumb key, Briccialdi's B♭ thumbplate. *See also* B♭ FINGERINGS; B♭ SIDE LEVER; BOEHM FLUTE (1); BRÖGGER SYSTEM; CYLINDRICAL BOEHM FLUTE (1); EXTENSION ARM; REVERSED THUMB KEYS; RING-KEY FLUTE; SPRING; THUMB KEY B♭ FINGERING.

BRIDGE. A piece of rod or **tubing** that juts out from, and is attached to, the **key tubing** and connects **keys** or parts of keys together. Some examples are the bridge that connects the C **roller** with the C key **cup** on the **C** or **B foot joints** (see app. 9, fig. 3) and the rod part of the **split E mechanism** that carries the motion from the E key around the back of the F and F♯ keys to the **extension arm** (see app. 9, fig. 4). The **Brögger Mekanik** and **Brögger System** make extensive use of bridges (see fig. 7). *See also* KEY ARM; PINLESS MECHANISM.

BRIGHT TONE. A tone in which the higher **harmonics** may be relatively strong. *See also* CYLINDRICAL BOEHM FLUTE (3); DARK TONE; *DÉTIMBRÉ*; FULL TONE; GIZMO KEY; HOLLOW TONE; *TIMBRÉ*; TONE COLOR; VIRTUAL FLUTE (2). For **early flutes**, *see also* BAROQUE FLUTE (2); CLASSICAL FLUTE.

BRILLE. Ger. spectacles. **1.** A **key** configuration that began to appear on some **simple-system flutes** in the mid-19th century (e.g., flutes made by **Siccama**, **Schwedler**, and others) and was intended to improve the **intonation** of $C\sharp_2$, which was usually **flat**. (This is unlike the modern **concert flute** where the $C\sharp_2$ has a tendency to be **sharp**.) The device consisted of an extra **padded** key over a smallish duplicate C **vent hole** that was bored between two **ring key**–covered **finger holes** for L1 and L2. All of these keys were mounted on a short axle and supported by **posts** (*see* POST-MOUNT). The end result was a contrivance that resembled eyeglasses, hence the name *Brille* (see app. 3, B, fig. 3). The extra hole brought the flat note $C\sharp_2$ up to **pitch** when this note was played with the regular **fingering** (i.e., all fingers up except for R4, which needs to press the D♯/E♭ key on the **foot joint**). For all other notes, depressing either of the ring keys for L1 or L2 closed the extra hole. Some fingering charts of the time recommended opening the C-key to raise the pitch of $C\sharp_2$. The Brille did the same thing, but automatically. Although not its original purpose, the Brille indirectly improved the **tuning** of C_2 as well as $C\sharp_2$, since by adding the Brille, the flutemaker could afford to make the hole operated by L1 a little smaller, thus **flattening** the pitch of an otherwise sharp C_2. *Syn.:* $C\sharp$ Brille. **2.** Sometimes refers to various key configurations that look similar to, but are not the same as, the $C\sharp$ Brille described above. This is not the usual intended meaning for the term. **3.** May mean the same thing as *ring key*.

BRITANNIA SILVER. A **silver alloy** that contains 95.83 percent silver and 4.17 copper and other hardening elements. It is used to make various **flute** parts. *Syn.:* **silver 958.** *Cf.* **coin silver, sterling silver.**

BRÖGGER, JOHAN (b. Copenhagen, 1936). A Danish maker of **Boehm flutes**, gold- and silversmith, inventor, luthier, and instrument restorer and repairer. *See also* BRÖGGER ACOUSTIC; BRÖGGER MEKANIK; BRÖGGER SYSTEM.

BRÖGGER ACOUSTIC. A term used by Brannen Brothers Flutemakers, Inc., to refer to Danish flutemaker **Johan Brögger**'s adaptation of the old concept of **undercutting tone holes** on wooden and metal **flutes**. The company claims that this will produce a more even **tone quality**, especially across the **register breaks**. According to Brannen Brothers, flute players who prefer this modification find that it creates less **resistance**. It is standard on their **gold** and **platinum flutes**.

BRÖGGER MEKANIK™. A major mechanical modification developed by Brannen Brothers Flutemakers, Inc., in collaboration with Danish flutemaker **Johan Brögger** around 1986 and trademarked by Brannen Brothers. The right- and left-hand **section keys** are linked using **bridges** and nonrotating shafts rather than **pins** (*see* PINLESS MECHANISM). Full-size **back-connectors** are used for **adjustments** between all **mainline** keys (see fig. 7, *top*). According to the manufacturers, the mechanism allows the flutemaker to regulate the **spring** tension of each key independently, thus allowing for a much more even feel for the performer. They claim that an equally important feature is the increased strength of the mechanism due to the special hardened **steel** screws used on the mainline and **foot joint** sections. The company asserts that the use of bridges and back-connectors to link keys results in a quieter **action** with less friction and wear between its moving parts, helps prevent **binding** between keys, reduces adjustment problems, and makes servicing easier than on a **pinned mechanism**. *Cf.* **Brögger System**.

The principle of this design was in use by Rudall, Carte & Co. early in the 20th century.

BRÖGGER SYSTEM™. A modification of the **Brögger Mekanik** that was designed by Danish flutemaker **Johan Brögger** (b. 1936), trademarked by Miyazawa, and put into production in 2005. A major difference between the two **key mechanisms** is the Brögger thumb **key** design (see fig. 7, *bottom*). Instead of the traditional **post-mount** (i.e., the **key tubing** being perpendicular to the main key tubing) and **flat springs**, the Brögger thumb key has a diagonal post-mount with longer key tubing and needle **springs**. According to the Miyazawa Company, the longer key tubing of the Brögger thumb configuration allows for a more stable thumb key and the needle springs permit a lighter **action**.

Both the Brögger Mekanik and Brögger System use hidden **bridges** and have **pinless** left- and right-hand **sections**. On the Brögger Mekanik, however, the B♭ key, thumb B♭ **kicker**, A/B♭ **clutch**, F/B♭ **back-connector**, and B♭ **side lever** are made separately and **soldered** onto the bridge. With the Brögger System, the bridge incorporates the thumb B♭ kicker, A/B♭ clutch, and F/B♭ back-connector as all one piece. The B♭ key and B♭ side lever are still soldered to this piece. Miyazawa claims that this translates into increased stability because the bridge and the kickers are drop-**forged** as one piece of metal.

There are similar differences just like this in the right-hand assembly also. On the Brögger System right-hand assembly, the bridge incorporates the F-F♯ clutch and the E-F♯ and D-F♯ clutch, with **adjusting screws** lo-

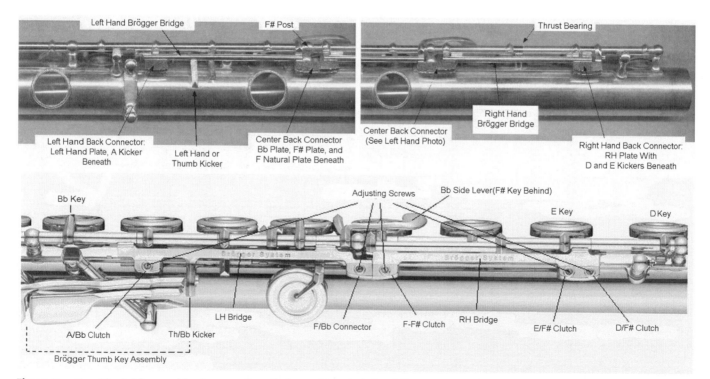

Figure 7. *Top:* **The bridges and back-connectors that are characteristic of the Brögger Mekanik key mechanism.** *Photo by Conrad A. Marvin and courtesy Brannen Brothers, Flutemakers, Inc.*

Bottom: **The bridges, curved back-connectors, and thumb key that are characteristic of the Brögger System key mechanism.** *Photo courtesy Miyazawa Flutes.*

cated on each connecting point. The right-hand bridge is soldered at two points: to the tubing of the F$_\sharp$ key and to a small piece of tubing between the E and D keys. Other differences include curved, instead of straight, back-connectors and adjusting screws located on each connecting point of the Brögger System. According to Miyazawa, the curved back-connectors are lighter than straight ones and the adjusting screws make it easier for technicians to regulate the left- and right-hand mechanisms.

BROSSA, JEAN FIRMIN (1839–1914). A **woodwind** maker, **flute** designer, **principal flutist** of the Halle Orchestra from 1870 to 1900, and flute professor of the Manchester College of Music. *See also* BROSSA F$_\sharp$ LEVER.

BROSSA F$_\sharp$ LEVER. A small, elevated, **spatula**-like **key** extension of the F$_\sharp$ key which is located above the D **key arm** (see app. 5, fig. 5), found on some older **Boehm flutes** such as those made by Rudall, Carte & Co. and very occasionally incorporated into modern-day **flutes** and **piccolos**. It is operated by R3 and allows the player to close the F$_\sharp$ key without closing the D or E key. This enables all the **tone holes** below the F$_\sharp$ key to remain open, thus ensuring better **venting** for F$_\sharp$ in the first three octaves and making them more acoustically correct than on the regular Boehm flute (*see* OPEN-KEY SYSTEM). The improved venting has several effects:

- For F$_{\sharp 3}$ on both flute and piccolo, it makes F$_{\sharp 3}$ slightly **sharper** and improves the **response** by making F$_{\sharp 3}$ clearer, less **resistant**, and easier to **articulate** than when using the D key.
- For F$_{\sharp 1}$ + F$_{\sharp 2}$ on the flute, it barely affects the **timbre** or **intonation**, if at all, compared with using the D key, but on the piccolo the effect is more noticeable.
- It corrects the narrow **tuning** produced by the standard **trill fingerings** for E$_1$-F$_{\sharp 1}$, E$_2$-F$_{\sharp 2}$, F$_1$-F$_{\sharp 1}$, and F$_2$-F$_{\sharp 2}$.
- It allows the player to avoid some **cross-fingerings** in the right hand (e.g., in the sequences G$_1$-F$_{\sharp 1}$-E$_1$-F$_{\sharp 1}$-G$_1$ and G$_2$-F$_{\sharp 2}$-E$_2$-F$_{\sharp 2}$-G$_2$). This is beneficial in an exposed legato passage where fingering from F$_\sharp$ to E and back to F$_\sharp$ needs to be as smooth as possible.

The Brossa F$_\sharp$ **lever** was invented by **Jean Firmin Brossa** in the mid-19th century. It has been more popular than the **Rockstro F$_\sharp$ lever** (which achieves the same purpose), but not popular enough to become standard on flutes today. The main reason for this is probably because, on an **open-hole flute**, a similar effect on individual F$_\sharp$'s can be partially achieved by depressing only the **rim** of

the D key. Another reason may be that many people are not aware of the key and its benefits and tend to follow the crowd when choosing flute options.

When the Brossa F$_\sharp$ lever is used in conjunction with **split A keys** on a **split F$_\sharp$ mechanism**, it completes the theoretically perfect F$_{\sharp 3}$ venting, with the consequent ease and stability of F$_{\sharp 3}$. *Syn.:* F$_\sharp$ lever.

B TRILL KEY/LEVER. A nonstandard elevated **spatula**-like extension of the B thumb **key** which is in the location where the **B♭ side lever** would otherwise go. When depressed with the side of R1 near the first knuckle, it closes the B thumb key farther up the flute. It can be used in **trill fingerings** such as B to C in the first two octaves and F$_{\sharp 3}$ to G$_3$. Since these **trills** are not difficult to execute with the LT, the B trill key is considered less versatile than the B♭ side lever. The B trill key is commonly seen on older German **Boehm flutes** in the 19th century (*see* CYLINDRICAL BOEHM FLUTE [1]). *Syn.:* B side lever, B natural trill key, B/C shake key, B/C trill key/lever.

BUFFARDIN, PIERRE-GABRIEL (b. Provence, France, ca. 1690; d. Paris, 1768). A French **woodwind** inventor who thrived in Dresden, Germany. He was also a flute virtuoso, an orchestra **flutist** in the Dresden Court orchestra from 1715 to 1749, a flute teacher, and a composer. *See also* FOOT REGISTER.

BUFFER. Same as **bumper**.

BUFFET, AUGUSTE, *JEUNE* (baptized La Couture, France, 1789; d. Anet, France, 1864). A French **woodwind** maker whose business thrived in Paris from 1830 to after 1885. Buffet was one of the first manufacturers of **Theobald Boehm**'s 1832 system **flutes** (*see* RING-KEY FLUTE) and an inventor of spade **clutches** (see app. 4), hollow tube rods (*see* KEY TUBING), the needle **spring**, the D$_\sharp$ trill hole (*see* TRILL KEYS [1]), and an improved clarinet. Despite having a son, he retained *"jeune"* after his name. *See also* DORUS G$_\sharp$ KEY; PINLESS MECHANISM; RETUNING.

BUFFING. A final process of **finishing** in which a piece of metal is **polished** by hand-rubbing it with a cloth covered with an abrasive compound (e.g., **rouge, tripoli**, etc.) or by holding it up to a quickly revolving wheel consisting of layers of cloth coated with an abrasive compound. Depending on the type of abrasive used, more or less of the metal will be cut away. Buffing is a process that is cost-effective and not time-consuming. It is used by **flute** repairers or makers when they want to polish and smoothen part of the flute, such as the **embouchure plate** or **tube**. A cleaning and degreasing procedure must follow buffing to remove the residual compound. *See also* BODYMAKER; BURNISHING; FINISH; FINISHER; RAGGING.

BULBOUS HEAD JOINT. A wooden **head joint** that swells out slightly near the open end. Today, it is often seen on **conical bore piccolos** (see fig. 30, *top*). Its purpose is to strengthen the wood at the **socket** and accommodate an extra **receiver** joint that is used for matching up the inner **tubing walls** when the head joint is put together with the **middle joint**. It can be found on **Baroque flutes** and the **barrels** of Continental **simple-system flutes**, but not so commonly on English-made simple-system flutes, which usually have a cylindrical barrel. It came back into style after 1847 in England, where it was used for **flutes** using Boehm's **bore**. **Thinned heads** made the swelling more obvious than it had been on nonthinned heads. *Syn.:* contoured head joint. *See also* HEAD JOINT LINING; THICKENINGS.

BUMPER. The **felt, cork,** or rubber attached to various parts of the **flute** (e.g., the underside of the D♯ **key** on the **foot joint** and the D and D♯ **trill keys** on the **middle joint**) to prevent the slight, but sharp, noise that would result if the keys were set in motion and a bumperless part hit the **tube**. Bumpers also contribute directly or indirectly to the distance a key can open above its associated **tone-hole rim** (i.e., the **key rise**) by either stopping the key's movement when it contacts the tubing (e.g., the bumper under the D♯ key) or being attached to a part of the **key mechanism** that stops the key's movement when it contacts the tubing (e.g., *see* KICKER). *Syn.:* buffer, stop, silencer. *See also* GLUE.

BURNISHING. The process of **finishing** in which the top layer of a piece of metal is **polished** by hand-rubbing it with a lubricated tool made of polished hard **steel**. Burnishing is nonabrasive, since the metal is compressed but not removed during the process. However, it is costly and time-consuming compared to **buffing**. Burnishing is generally used by flutemakers when they want to polish a part of the **flute**, particularly the **keywork**. This is the only polishing technique that brings out and enhances the sharp angular lines inherent in the keywork's geometric shapes. Flute repairers may burnish **tenons** to expand them. *See also* FINISH; HEAD JOINT REFITTING; RETUNING; SPINNING; STRETCHING.

BUSHED EMBOUCHURE. *See* EMBOUCHURE-HOLE BUSHING.

BUSHED FINGER/TONE HOLE. *See* TONE-HOLE BUSHING.

BUSHING. 1. A **lining**, often metal, that decreases the diameter of a hole, and in some cases, also reduces the friction of moving parts. For example, a bushing may be installed in the hole of a **post** to allow the end of a **steel** to fit more securely. *See also* EMBOUCHURE-HOLE BUSHING; TONE-HOLE BUSHING. **2.** A device that holds one thing to another. *See* FRENCH BUSHING.

BUTTERFLY HEADJOINT™. A patented **head joint** design that is characterized by the front part of the **embouchure plate**, beyond the **blowing edge**, being divided into two lobes with a channel in between (see app. 10, fig. 5). According to the late Canadian flutemaker **Jack P. Goosman** (1945–2002), who invented the head joint: "The airstream beyond the **blowhole** is changed in a particular way. As one plays a head joint, some air enters the blowhole and some air travels beyond the blowhole; in other words, the airstream is split by the edge of the blowhole. With a standard **lip plate**, the air that travels beyond the blowhole creates a **resistance**. This outside resistance inhibits the speed and amount of the air that enters the blowhole. The Butterfly channels some air down the groove past the blowhole and some air continues down the radius of the lip plate as on a standard lip plate. There are now two airstreams interacting with each other at an angle of approximately 45°. This interaction reduces the 'outside' resistance and allows air to enter the blowhole at a faster rate. By allowing the air to enter the blowhole at a faster rate, responsiveness is increased, dramatically, especially in the **low register** and the attack note."

The Butterfly Headjoint derives its name from the shape of the embouchure plate, which is reminiscent of a butterfly. However, Goosman said that the inspiration for the design came from watching the way blowing snow was being divided by the peak of a window during a snowstorm.

BUTTON. 1. Same as **cup. 2.** *See* FINGER BUTTON. **3.** Same as **crown. 4.** Same as **screw cap**.

BUZZ-HEAD. *See* MEMBRANE HEAD JOINT.

BUZZ-TONE. A French horn– or clarinet-like sound that is produced by blowing into the **embouchure hole** or into the upper end of the **middle joint** with compressed lips in such a way that they vibrate as if playing a brass instrument. Due to the fact that the embouchure hole is closed, the **flute** acts acoustically like a closed **tube**, and by varying lip tension and using special **fingerings**, **flutists** can buzz an unusually wide **range**, from AA to A♭₃, or more with a B♭ **foot**. Flutist **Robert B. Cantrick** (1917–2006) originated the **technique** and coined the term in

1962. In 1969, he completed a major **work** featuring the new sound: "Three Mimes," a theater piece for flute and baritone voice. Cantrick claims that while the buzz-tone can be tiring at first, with practice it can potentially enhance overall technical control via the development of the mouth and facial muscles. He suggests notating the sound as the abbreviation BZ written above the staff before the buzz notes, placing a small notehead above or below a regular notehead to indicate the fingering:

Today, the sound is often referred to as "trumpet-sound," and so is usually notated as

See also EXTENDED TECHNIQUE.

C

CANE FLUTE. Fr. *canne de flute.* A **recorder** in the shape of a cane or walking stick in the 18th century. *See also* WALKING-STICK FLUTE.

CANTRICK, ROBERT BIRDSALL (b. Monroe, Mich., 1917; d. Buffalo, N.Y., 2006). An American **flutist**, conductor, composer, author, and music professor who originated the **buzz-tone** in 1962.

CAP. 1. Same as **crown**, but usually used only when speaking of a similar part on **one-keyed** or **simple-system flutes** (see app. 3, A, fig. 3). *Syn.:* **button**, end cap. *See also* CORK ASSEMBLY (2); FINIAL; SCREW CAP; SCREW-CORK; SCREW-CORK INDICATOR; STOPPER; TURNING. **2. Tenon** caps. *See also* TENON PROTECTORS.

CAPELLER, JOHANN NEPOMUK (b. Ingolstadt, Germany, 1776; d. 1843). A German **woodwind** inventor who thrived in Munich. He was also a **flutist**, a composer, and a teacher of **Theobald Boehm**. *See also* TRILL KEYS.

CARBON FIBER. A very strong, lightweight, thin fiber made by heating carbon-containing synthetic fibers, such as rayon, until charred. It was originally developed for usage in the aerospace industry. It is used in flute-making to make the **tubing** of **flutes** invented by **Matti Kähönen**. *See also* MATIT CARBON-FIBER FLUTE.

CARBON-FIBER FLUTE. *See* MATIT CARBON-FIBER FLUTE.

CARD-BACKED PADS. Same as **traditional pads**. *See also* PAD; SALT-SPOON KEY.

CARTE, RICHARD (b. Silchester, England, 1808; d. Reigate, England, 1891). An English **woodwind** inventor who thrived in London. He was also a **principal flutist**, and author. Carte (originally Cart) joined the woodwind instrument–making firm of **Rudall** & **Rose** in 1850, which became Rudall, Rose & Carte with Carte as its proprietor in 1856. *See also* CARTE 1851 SYSTEM FLUTE; CARTE 1867 SYSTEM FLUTE; GOLD FLUTE; GUARDS' MODEL FLUTE.

CARTE 1851 SYSTEM FLUTE. A **flute** with the **cylindrical bore** and **tone hole** placement as used on **Boehm-system** flutes, but with a **fingering system** developed in 1850 by English flutemaker **Richard Carte**. This system combines the Boehm-system fingering with the **simple-system** fingering, but possibly more closely resembles the latter. Some Carte 1851 System flutes, especially the earliest ones, were wooden with **conical bores**, but the majority were metal flutes with **cylindrical bores**. They had an **open-key system** with complete **venting**. Figure 8 *(top)* shows a **silver** Rudall, Rose & Carte 1851 System flute.

The **key mechanism** patented by Carte was clever but intricate. It incorporated the open **G♯ key** introduced by **Theobald Boehm** in 1832 and restored the simple-system fingering in the right-hand

$$1\ 2\ 3\ /\ 4\ -\ -\ D_\sharp$$

for F♯ (i.e., R1 presses an F♯ key, not an F key as on Boehm-system flutes). There were three fingerings for F natural, which were the same as or similar to simple-system fingerings:

- 1 2 3 / 4 5 - D♯ with the short F key
- 1 2 3 / 4 - - D♯ with a new long F key
- the **fork fingering** 1 2 3 / 4 - 6 D♯

Of particular significance was the upper D tone hole, which was moved to a new location just to the left of the C♯ tone hole on the **middle joint** (see fig. 8, *bottom*). The new location for the upper D hole allowed for a new fingering, called "open D," for D_2 and D_3. The open D fingering is so called because all of the tone holes are opened for the fingering (i.e., all fingers are off the **keys**, save for the D♯ **touch**, which, when pressed, opens a tone hole). This is similar to the fingering for $C\sharp_2$ and $C\sharp_3$ on the Boehm **flute**. Having the newly located D hole also reduced the number of **cross-fingerings**.

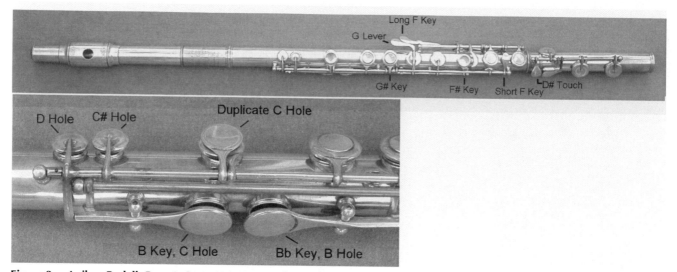

Figure 8. A silver Rudall, Rose & Carte 1851 System flute, London. Boehm's "Parabola," Carte's mechanism. MTM. (MTM is code for the serial number 161. The code is given by the letters of the words MUSIC TRADE, where M = 1, U = 2, S = 3, I = 4, C = 5, T = 6, R = 7, A = 8, D = 9, and E = 0.) *Photo courtesy Terry McGee.*

Even though Carte designed a key mechanism that was relatively complex, and so was more difficult to keep in **adjustment** than a Boehm flute, it was quite popular at the time. This is probably because it had some preferred fingerings, while at the same time maintaining, and sometimes even improving, the tone and better **intonation** that resulted from Boehm's 1847 equidistant tone holes and **open-key system**.

The Carte 1851 System flute was manufactured by the London flutemaking firm of **Rudall** & **Rose**, which Carte joined as a partner in 1851. Later the flute was made by Rudall, Carte & Co. Many such flutes were made in the second half of the 19th century, and the flute was available from the Rudall, Carte firm well into the 20th century. Although the Carte 1851 flute is well thought of today, it is not regularly played. *See also* CARTE 1867 SYSTEM FLUTE; OPEN NOTE; ORDINARY FLUTE (1); RADCLIFF SYSTEM FLUTE.

CARTE 1867 SYSTEM FLUTE. A modification of the **Carte 1851 System flute** whereby the **key mechanism** is altered, giving new **fingerings** for $F_{1/2}$, $F_{\#1/2}$, and $B\flat_{1/2}$. This modification consists of replacing the single **key touch** for R1 with two touches that are operated by R1: the upper touch gives $F_\#$, and the lower touch gives F-natural when LT, L1, L2, and L3 are also pressed on their respective **keys**. Figure 9 *(top)* shows a silver Carte 1867 System **flute** by **Rudall**, Carte & Co, made in 1891. The bottom picture shows the top and side views of F keys. A post that is attached to the F key touch presses the F key cup to sound F. The F-natural touch also closes the B♭ key. This enables a third fingering for $B\flat_{1/2}$, called the **one-and-one B♭ fingering** (the other

two B♭ fingerings are similar to those on the Carte 1851 System flute, but different from those on the modern **Boehm-system** flute).

Due to the F-key modification, there is no longer the need for the long F key or **forked** F fingerings present on the Carte 1851 System flute. The flute can be operated as a fully **open-key system** flute in the first two octaves. This is an improvement over the Boehm 1847 System (and modern) flutes, which have one necessary **cross-fingering** in the first two octaves, that for $F_\#$.

The Carte 1867 System flute was designed by **Richard Carte**, patented in 1866, and manufactured by the flutemaking company of Rudall, Carte & Co. in London. It was very popular in the British Empire until quite some time after World War II. Although very few people know about the system today, many of those who do consider it to be superior to the Boehm system.

Some Carte 1867 System flutes are stamped "Carte and Boehm Systems Combined," which is another name for the system. They are so called because most **right-hand fingerings** of the Boehm 1847 System (with open $G_\#$ key; *see* CYLINDRICAL BOEHM FLUTE) were incorporated (including F with R1, $F_\#$ with R3) while retaining the **simple-system** R1 $F_\#$ and the short F key. *See also* FLAT SPRING (1); GUARDS' MODEL FLUTE; ORDINARY FLUTE (1).

CASTING. 1. A process whereby molten metal is poured into a mold of the desired shape and allowed to cool. Certain parts of the **flute** are made in this way, especially those that are more complex or those that would be too costly if made by **forging**, which is another way of making metal parts. Although casting makes weaker parts than forging, the parts that are cast can be **heat**

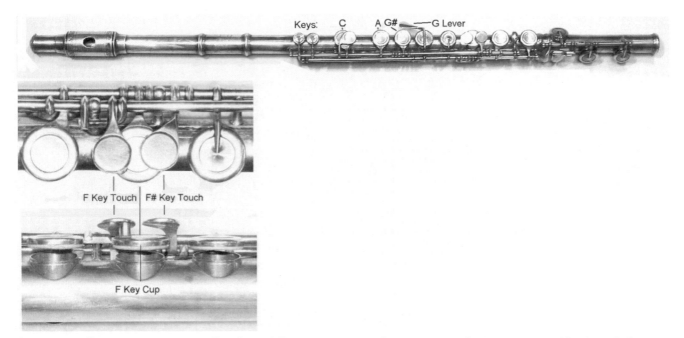

Keys: C   A G#   G Lever

F Key Touch | F# Key Touch

F Key Cup

Figure 9. A silver Carte 1867 System flute by Rudall, Carte & Co., London. Carte & Boehm's systems combined, made in 1891. *Photo courtesy Rick Wilson.*

treated to make them strong enough for flutemaking requirements. An example of a part that may be cast is the **B♭ side lever. 2.** A part made by casting (def. 1). *See also* DIE; HEAD-JOINT MAKER.

C/D TRILL KEY/LEVER. Same as D trill key and so called because one of its main uses is to facilitate the C/D **trill** in the **second octave**. *See also* TRILL KEYS.

CENT. A unit introduced by A. J. Ellis (1814–1890) for measuring small **pitch** intervals. There are 100 cents to the **equal temperament** semitone, the interval between two adjacent piano keys. Thus, a cent is equal to 1/100 of an equal-tempered semitone, or the 1,200th root of 2, which means a **frequency** difference of 0.06 percent. The octave contains 1,200 cents. Like its monetary homonym, it is a very small unit. An interval of one cent is too small to be heard by the human ear. *See also* JUST INTONATION; MEANTONE TEMPERAMENT.

CENTERING. Aiming the airstream at the **blowing wall** in such a way that no air is wasted and the sound is as clear as possible. This centering of the note is sometimes called "finding the core [or center] of the tone." *See also* FOCUSING; MOISTURE TRIANGLE; NOTE BENDING; OFF-CENTERED EMBOUCHURE; PROJECTION; SWEET SPOT.

CENTER JOINT/PIECE. Same as **middle joint**. On a four-joint **one-keyed** or **simple-system flute**, the

center joint is split into two pieces: the **upper middle joint/piece** and the **lower middle joint/piece**. *See also* CORPS DE RECHANGE.

C FOOT JOINT. Abbr. C foot. A **foot joint** (see app. 7, fig. 12) that gets its name because the **lowest note** that can be produced is C_1 (or **low C**). It competes in popularity with the **B foot joint**. There are at least five reasons that many **flutists** prefer a C foot over a B foot. They find that a flute with a C foot (1) has a more brilliant sound and ease of **response**; (2) is slightly easier to hold up (since it is slightly shorter and lighter); (3) is less expensive; (4) facilitates the playing of low C since it is easier to press the C **roller** key; and (5) the lower **middle register** notes, particularly E and F, speak more easily (though not always so—on a few flutes, these notes are better with a B foot; the reason is not known). *See also* B/C CONVERTIBLE FOOT JOINT; B♭ FOOT JOINT; BOEHM FLUTE (1); BRIDGE; D FOOT JOINT; FOOT JOINT; FOOT-JOINT CLUSTER; LOW B KEY, LOW C KEY, LOW C♯ KEY, ETC.; MODE; PROFESSIONAL FLUTE; SOUNDING LENGTH (3); TRANSPOSING INSTRUMENTS (1). For **early flutes**, *see also* app. 4; ARTICULATED KEYS; D FOOT JOINT, EXTENDED FOOT JOINT; FOOT REGISTER.

c/h. An abbreviation for "closed hole," which is short for **closed-hole key** or closed-hole cup. *Cf.* **o/h**.

CHAIR. A term used to describe the positional order of a musician in a particular section of an orchestra or band. It is usually used after an ordinal number (e.g., first chair, second chair, third chair, etc.) and often also before the name of a type of instrumentalist. For example, **first chair flutist** refers to the name for the **first flutist** in the **flute** section of an orchestra or band. Also called a *desk* or *seat*.

CHAMBERING. The process of slightly enlarging the **bore** of wooden **flutes** at certain places to improve the **intonation** and tone of defective notes. *See also* REAM; ROUGHING; STEP (1, 2); TURNING.

CHANNEL. The narrow passageway in the **block-mount, ring-mount,** or **saddle-mount** of **one-keyed** and many **simple-system flutes** (or replicas of them) that held the **shank** of the **key** (see app. 3, B, figs. 2 and 6). *Syn.:* keyway, key slot. *See also* FLAT SPRING (2); PIN (2).

CHARANGA FLUTE. 1. The wooden, six-holed **flute** used by players of *charanga*, a popular Cuban dance music played by an **ensemble** of flutes, violins, percussion, piano, bass, and vocals. This is most often a **five-** or **six-keyed**, short and relatively narrow, **conical-bored, simple-system** French-made flute from the 19th or early 20th century. Such flutes were common in Cuba due to the French charanga style being imported by a French-Haitian contingent who escaped from the Haitian War of Independence in 1789 and established themselves in Santiago de Cuba and became the main musical influence of these ensembles.

Charanga players prefer the **old system**, short, narrow-bored French flutes because it is easier to play the very **high notes** essential to this music on them. However, since the **Boehm flute** is easier to play and has more **fingering** possibilities, which allows for more ways to be expressive, it has become more commonly used, and the number of players on the old-style flute is diminishing.

Charanga music mainly makes use of the **third** and **fourth octaves**, where a very strong and short **articulation** is used. To help the highest notes speak, the **stopper** may be moved closer to the **embouchure hole**. Though this is detrimental to the tone and **intonation** of the little-used **first octave**, that is not considered a problem; when these **low notes** are required, players compensate by using special embouchure **techniques** or **alternate fingerings**. *See also* SOPRANO FLUTE IN F. **2.** The term may sometimes erroneously be used to refer to original 19th-century French five- and six-keyed flutes, probably because, for some people, the charanga flute is their first wooden flute experience.

CHASING. A centuries-old process whereby a specially handmade set of tools is used to make a design by com-

pressing metal. These tools sculpt a unique three-dimensional design on the surface of the metal. No metal is removed in the chasing process; when the metal is compressed, it hardens. Chasing on **flutes** is done to beautify the instrument. The usual parts that are chased are the **rims** of key **cups**, the **crown**, and the **rings** surrounding the flute **tube**. Some people feel that chasing reflects the light better than **engraving** and is thus more beautiful. It is more expensive, however, since it is more difficult to do. As an added advantage to beautifying the flute, chasing the keys may help prevent slippage due to perspiration.

CHERRIER, SOPHIE (b. Nancy, France, 1959). A French **flute soloist**, recording artist, flute professor of the **Paris Conservatoire** from 1998 to the present, and member of the **Ensemble** Intercontemporain, founded by Pierre Boulez.

CHEST BREATHING. A type of shallow breathing where the chest provides the effort involved in inhaling and exhaling. The chest expands on the breath in and contracts on the breath out. *See also* ABDOMINAL BREATHING; BREATH SUPPORT; CIRCULAR BREATHING.

CHEVROTEMENT. Fr. quivering. When referring to **flute**-playing or to **vibrato**, it means billy-goat or **nanny-goat vibrato**.

CHIMNEY. 1. The **riser** or **embouchure wall** of a metal **flute** with an **embouchure plate**, or the surrounding **walls** of an **embouchure hole** in a wooden or **ivory** flute. **2.** The *tone hole chimney*: the cylindrical **ring** part protruding up from around a **tone hole**. *Syn.:* bed, **pad seat, saddle, seat,** tone hole wall. *See also* DRAWN TONE HOLES; G♯ KEY (1); PATCHING; RETUNING; SOLDERED TONE HOLES; TONE-HOLE RIM; UNDERCUTTING (2); UP TONE-HOLE. **3.** The cylindrical ring part that extends down from the middle of an **open-hole cup**. *See* FRENCH BUSHING.

CHOPS. 1. Used infrequently to mean the same thing as **embouchure** (1). **2. Technical** ability. For example, someone might say: "Wow, great chops!" or "That piece took a lot of chops!"

CHRISTENSEN, JAMES (1935–). A prolific and popular composer/arranger and music director for Disneyland and Walt Disney World for 12 years. He has been a conductor of various ensembles, including the Community Band of America (Band at Sea) since 1994, and a trombone-clinician for UMI-Conn. *See also* FLUTE CHOIR.

CHUNKING. A practice **technique** in which the instrumentalist plays one inch of music notation (a "chunk") and then inserts a rest before repeating the process. **Patricia George** (b. 1942) coined the term in 1985 for use in practicing by musical instruments that involves only one staff. She bases the technique on research by John A. Sloboda (*The Musical Mind: The Cognitive Psychology of Music* [Oxford: Clarendon Press, 1985]) that shows that at normal viewing distance, the fovea (spot at the center of the retina) will take in an area of about one inch. In one-quarter of a second, this information is placed in short-term memory. Chunking three times a day at six-hour intervals for three to five days will place the information in long-term memory.

CIRCULAR BREATHING. A breathing **technique** used by **wind instrument** players to allow them to refresh the air in their lungs without stopping the sound. It is a technique used by glassblowers since ancient times. It is achieved by using the muscles of the cheeks and tongue to push out the air that has been stored in the cheeks, while inhaling through the nose. It is alternated with regular exhalation in such a way that the airflow is continuous. This procedure is repeated as long as an uninterrupted sound is required. The technique is useful for playing extended **passages** where a break to breathe would spoil the musical line. Circular breathing may be notated as an incomplete circle with an arrowhead at one end.

For specific instructions on how to circular-breathe, consult *Circular Breathing for the Flutist* by **Robert Dick** (New York: Multiple Breath Music Co., 1987). *See also* ABDOMINAL BREATHING; CHEST BREATHING.

CLADDING. 1. The process of **bonding** a thin metal to a thicker metal, producing a **clad metal**. The thickness of the bonded metal can vary, but is usually of a heavier thickness than **plating**. *See also* FUSING. **2.** The layer of metal that is bonded as described above.

CLAD METAL. A composite metal that consists of two or more layers of **bonded** metals. *See also* CLADDING.

CLASSICAL FLUTE. A modern term that refers to the **transverse one-keyed** and **simple-system flutes** used in the Classical period (ca. 1750–1820). **Flutes** during this time had six **finger holes**, from one to eight or more **keys**, and a narrow **conical bore** and were most often made of wood and in four pieces (see app. 2, figs. 6 and 10). Like the **Baroque flute**, the **range** of the standard-size Classical flute was about two and a half octaves from the lowest **six-fingered note** D_1, but the **high notes** (including F_3 and up to A_3) tended to be easier to play and **brighter** in tone due to the narrower **bore**.

The addition of keys allowed the notes outside of the **natural scale** of the instrument (i.e., the D-major scale for the standard-size Classical flute) to be sounded without **cross-fingerings**. This resulted in a stronger and more uniform tone and easier **intonation** throughout the range than could be achieved on Baroque flutes, which required cross-fingerings for some notes.

Classical flutes were generally higher in **pitch** than Baroque flutes, ranging from a semitone lower than the standard modern pitch of A = 440 Hz to sometimes slightly above. Modern replicas of late 18th-century flutes are often provided at A = 430 Hz.

Not all players and makers had the same ideas about **tuning**. Some, such as **Johann George Tromlitz** (1725–1805), still advocated a **tuning system** where flats were above sharps (e.g., B♭ higher than A♯) as in all varieties of **Meantone** tuning, while others no longer emphasized enharmonic differences.

Many books were written for the Classical flute. Worthy of mention are the **methods** by **John Gunn** (1793), **François Devienne** (1794), and **Antoine Hugot** and **Jean-Georges Wunderlich** (1804) and the **treatise** by Tromlitz (1791). See bibliography under "Historical Methods, Treatises, and Tutors."

The one-keyed flute remained common throughout the Classical period, though many virtuosi and professionals would have been using **keyed flutes** by 1800. Even **Theobald Boehm** (1794–1881) played on a one-keyed flute in his youth. Flutes with more keys first became popular in England. The earliest surviving keyed flutes and **fingering charts** for them show six keys. The Classical flute has recently undergone a revival. *See also* CORPS D'AMOUR; EIGHT-KEYED FLUTE; FIVE-KEYED FLUTE; FOUR-KEYED FLUTE; RENAISSANCE FLUTE; SIX-KEYED FLUTE.

CLEANING ROD. A long, thin rod used, along with a handkerchief or similar material, for drying the inside of the **flute** and as an aid in checking the position of the **stopper**. At one end there is an opening or "eye" for threading a cloth through for drying purposes. At the other is a groove that is meant to be 0.70 in. (17.3 mm) from the end (but is not always), used as an indicator for periodic control of the stopper position (*see* HEAD-JOINT CORK). It looks somewhat like a large sewing needle and is usually made of metal, wood, or plastic (see app. 12, fig. 1; app. 7, fig. 2). Sometimes referred to as a *swab stick*, *cleaning stick*, or *tuning rod*. *See also* **Flute Flag**.

CLEAN-OIL-AND-ADJUST. Abbr. C.O.A. **Flute** player jargon for a general checkup of the flute that should be undertaken at least once a year by a professional flute repairer. The flute is cleaned and **oiled** and any necessary **adjustments** are made. The frequency of C.O.A.'s depends on the climatic conditions, the acidity and oiliness of the **flutist**'s skin, the type of flute, the amount it is played, and how well it is taken care of. *Syn.:* general adjustment, tune-up. *See also* REPAD; OVERHAUL.

CLINTON, JOHN (b. Dublin, Ireland, 1809; d. London, 1864). An Irish **woodwind** inventor whose business prospered in London from 1854 until after his death. He was also a flute manufacturer, **principal** orchestral **flutist**, pianist, composer, flute and piano professor, and author. His written works include two major **treatises** on flute design and construction (1850, 1855), an essay on the **Boehm flute** as manufactured by **Rudall & Rose**, and **methods** for the 1832 Boehm flute (**ring-key flute**) and **Equisonant flute**.

CLOSED CUP. *See* CLOSED KEY.

CLOSED G♯ (G SHARP) KEY. *Syn.:* shut G♯ key, side G♯ key, **independent G♯ key.** *See* G♯ KEY (1).

CLOSED HOLE. Short for **closed-hole key**.

CLOSED-HOLE CUP. *See* CLOSED-HOLE KEY/CUP/ KEY CUP.

CLOSED-HOLE FLUTE. A **flute** with no perforations in any key **cups** and most commonly with offset **G keys.** Beginners usually start on a closed-hole flute and then proceed to an **open-hole flute** when they are more accomplished. A closed-hole flute has some advantages over an open-hole flute. For example, the player will never cause a **leak** due to **gardener's fingers** or to misplacing a finger on an **open-hole key**; will have a wide range of hand and finger positions since the fingers do not need to be as carefully placed as on an open-hole flute (this can be helpful to players who have physical problems with their hands or fingers, such as smallness or repetitive strain); and can slide the fingers on the **closed-hole keys** while moving through certain awkward fingerings, or press two keys closed with one finger, if desired, as there is no open hole that needs to be **sealed**. Also, some feel that closed-hole key **pads** are easier to repair. *Syn.:* plateau-model flute, covered-hole flute. *See also* app. 11; FRENCH-MODEL FLUTE; GERMAN FLUTE (3); GLISSANDO; KEY (1); OPEN-HOLE FLUTE; ORCHESTRAL MODEL FLUTE; PLUG (1); SCHEMA.

CLOSED-HOLE KEY/CUP/KEY CUP. A circular-shaped **key** with no hole or **chimney** in its center. *Syn.:* covered hole/key, plateau key/cup/key cup, solid key/ cup/key cup. A *dish* or *plain cup* is a closed-hole cup that

lacks any decorative features, such as a French-pointed **key arm** or a nipple in the center of the top surface. *See also* BOEHM FLUTE (1); C/H; CLOSED-HOLE FLUTE; CLOSED KEY; CUP; CYLINDRICAL BOEHM FLUTE (1, 3); FRENCH-MODEL FLUTE; INTERMEDIATE FLUTE; O/H; OPEN-HOLE KEY; ORCHESTRAL MODEL FLUTE; PAD; PAD WASHER; PROFESSIONAL FLUTE; SPUD; STUDENT FLUTE.

CLOSED KEY. A **key** that, when at rest, is normally kept closed over its associated **tone hole** by a **spring**. It opens when a player presses an attached **lever**. *Syn.:* closed-standing key. *See also* CLOSED-HOLE KEY; INTERNAL TUNING; OPEN KEY; PURSE PAD. For **early flutes**, *see also* CLOSED-KEY SYSTEM; CROSS KEY.

CLOSED-KEY SYSTEM. A flute **key system**, such as that of **simple-system flutes**, whereby for a particular **basic fingering**, **keys** on the **body** that are immediately below the **sounding hole**, and are closed when in their inactivated state, are left closed. For example, for the note A_1 on a simple-system flute, the sounding hole is A (**finger hole** 3). The note A_1 is **fingered** by covering finger holes 1 and 2; leaving finger holes 3, 4, 5, and 6 open; and leaving any normally **closed keys** below the sounding hole A closed. An exception to this is that, for some basic fingerings, it was recommended that one or more of the closed keys be opened to improve the **venting** and/or **intonation**. For example, for the notes $F_{\#1}$ and $F_{\#2}$, venting and intonation were improved by opening the short F key (see app. 2, fig. 4, for the location of this key).

A disadvantage with the closed-key system is that the various notes are unequally vented. For example, the notes $G_{1/2}$ are well vented by the large F♯ tone hole (R5) only a semitone away, whereas the note A is vented by a smaller G tone hole (R4) two semitones away. This leads to tonal and **response** unevenness. The main advantage is that any open finger holes can be used for such things as **alternate fingerings**, **finger vibrato**, and **glides** and for adjusting the intonation. *Syn.:* shut-key system. *See also* OPEN-KEY SYSTEM.

CLOSED-STANDING KEY. Same as **closed key**. *See also* app. 4, 8; CLOSED-KEY SYSTEM; CUP; KEY (1); DORUS G♯ KEY; EIGHT-KEYED FLUTE; FIVE-KEYED FLUTE; FOUR-KEYED FLUTE; G♯ KEY (2); PRATTEN'S PERFECTED; SIMPLE-SYSTEM FLUTE(1); SIX-KEYED FLUTE.

CLOSE TOUCH GIZMO. *See* **gizmo key**.

CLUTCH. 1. Any device that allows motion to be transmitted between two mechanism parts while maintaining the independence of one of them. Clutches consist generally of two **plates**, one of which may carry an **adjust-**

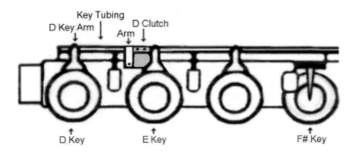

Figure 10. A clutch. *Drawing courtesy Tess Vincent.*

ment screw and/or a **pad** of cushioning material such as **cork** or **felt**, whose thickness is used to adjust the clutch. One plate may be a projection or **lug** attached to **key tubing** or, in some cases, to the underside of a **key** close to the key tubing.

When a clutch is activated by a player pressing a particular **flute** key, leverage is transferred from that key to another key (or keys) that is not directly pressed. For example, projecting from the key tubing near the E key on a **standard flute** with a **pinned mechanism** is the D clutch (see fig. 10), which is pinned to the right-hand **steel** within the key tubing. When the D key is pressed down, the motion is transferred through the D **key arm** and along the steel to a short arm above the D clutch, which presses the D clutch down. Since the F♯ key is pinned to the same steel as the D clutch, it also goes down.

Accurate clutch **adjustment** is required to time the closure of dependent keys. Depending on the clutch, this may be done by turning an adjustment screw present on the clutch plate, regulating the thickness of a **shim** (usually a piece of paper or cork that is placed between the clutch plate and a key arm or **kicker**), or bending the clutch plate.

A component of a clutch may be referred to as an *adjustment plate*, an *adjustment tab*, a *stop plate*, or a *lug*. *See also* BACK-CONNECTOR; BUFFET, AUGUSTE, *JEUNE*; DORUS G♯ KEY; G/A TRILL KEY (3); KEY MECHANISM; ROCKSTRO MODEL FLUTE; SPADE; VAULTED CLUTCH. Historian **David Shorey** (b. 1953) discusses the history and various types of clutches in appendix 8.

2. The mechanism part, such as a **lever**, that activates the device described above.

3. A **split E mechanism** clutch. *See also* PROFESSIONAL FLUTE.

4. *See* SPLIT F♯ MECHANISM.

C.O.A. An abbreviation for **clean-oil-and-adjust**.

COCHE, VICTOR JEAN BAPTISTE (b. Arras, France, 1806; d. Paris, 1881). A French **woodwind** inventor who thrived in Paris and was also a flute player,

teacher, and author. Coche instigated the infamous "Boehm-Gordon controversy" of 1838 in which **Theobald Boehm** was incorrectly accused of taking the credit for inventing the new **ring-key flute** away from Capt. **James Gordon**. Although the claim was supported in 1890 by **Richard Shepherd Rockstro**, it was later refuted by **Christopher Welch** in 1896. *See also* TRILL KEYS.

COCOA. In older **flute** literature, another name for **cocuswood**.

COCUSWOOD. Scientific name: *Brya ebenus*. A very hard, dense, resinous, nonabsorbent hardwood found in the West Indies and South America. It gradually changes in color from yellow-brown to medium brown over a period of time. Cocuswood **flutes** that are dark brown in color have probably been stained with a chemical such as nitric acid.

Along with **ebony** and **boxwood**, cocuswood was a choice material for certain flute parts, such as flute **bodies** and **head joints**, in the 19th century. Cocuswood flutes were probably popular because they not only were beautiful to look at but also had a beautiful, brilliant, and powerful tone. Of interest is the fact that famous flutist **Charles Nicholson Jr.** (1795–1837) preferred his flutes to be made of cocuswood as he felt the tone to be more **resonant**. It was his powerful playing that greatly influenced **Theobald Boehm** (1794–1881) to make improvements to the **simple-system flute** of the time. The end result of Boehm's work was his invention of the modern flute in 1847 (*see* BOEHM FLUTE).

Cocuswood is also good at retaining its shape, since it is nonabsorbent, but unfortunately, due to its resulting lack of elasticity, it is prone to **cracking**. The stable quality allows for any **keys** on cocuswood flutes to stay regulated for a longer period of time than on flutes made of some other woods such as boxwood. Many people are allergic to cocuswood, which necessitates the usage of an **embouchure plate** made from a different material, such as **ebonite**, **silver**, or **gold**, if the **flutist** is allergic to the wood.

Cocuswood is still occasionally used to make modern replicas of **early flutes** but is not regularly used due to the fact that it is now rare, expensive, and, as mentioned previously, prone to cracking. *Syn.:* Jamaican ebony, grenadilla wood, granadillo, green-, brown-, or West Indian ebony; sometimes referred to as cocoa wood in older flute catalogues. *See also* ONE-KEYED FLUTE; ROSEWOOD.

COIN SILVER. A variable **silver alloy**, the composition theoretically depending on the currency being used in a particular country. For example, in the United States,

American coin silver or **silver 900** (90 percent silver, 10 percent copper) is commonly used to make **flutes**. Coin silver **tarnishes** more readily than other types of silver used in flutemaking (e.g., **Britannia silver** or **sterling silver**) because of the higher copper content. *See also* GERMAN SILVER.

COLD DRAWING. A process used to draw unheated metal through a **die** to reduce the cross-section. It is used particularly when there is a need to obtain accurate reduction with no waste. Various **flute** parts, such as **springs, body tubes,** and **rings,** may be cold-drawn through a die plate. More complex shapes such as **tapered head joints** and **tone holes** can be drawn using special **mandrels.** Since they become harder during the process, the parts must be regularly **annealed** before any further **drawing** is done. *Syn.:* hard drawing. *See also* BONDING.

COLD WORKING. Any process (e.g., rolling, hammering, **forging, drawing, burnishing,** etc.) that is carried out by a flutemaker to metal at a low enough temperature (usually room temperature) to harden it.

COLE, ELMER (b. Walmer, Kent, England, 1938). A British chamber music, **solo,** and session **flutist;** an orchestra player, which included playing **principal** in the English National Opera from 1968 to 2002; and a flute designer of the **Cole scale** and the **B/C convertible foot joint.** *See also* BENNETT SCALE; COOPER SCALE; MODERN SCALE.

COLE SCALE. A flute **scale** developed by **Elmer Cole.** In the late 1950s, London-based **flutist** Cole felt that the scales in use at the time needed urgent revision. **William Bennett** was already **retuning** his own **Lot** flute by ear, using Plasticine or by removing and re-**soldering** the **saddles** in different positions (*see* PATCHING).

Cole's approach was to study the theory as set out by **Theobald Boehm** that resulted in the **Boehm flute** in 1847. He coined the term *8ve length* (now spelled *octave length* and also called *scale length*) to give a desired scale for the **pitch** (i.e., **A** = 440 Hz) from the measurement between the centers of the equal-sized **tone holes** for C_1 and C_2. Having established which octave length would give a usable result for a given pitch of **concert flute,** octave lengths for **alto, treble,** or other **flute** of any pitch can be calculated by extending the measurements outward as Boehm indicated. The mathematical series for this is the same as is used to position the frets on a guitar, except that in the case of the flute, some modifications are needed to allow for different sizes of tone holes. Boehm's **Schema** was a chart based on this mathematical series, and the figures for it can be found in his writings.

How Boehm himself made adjustments for different hole sizes is unknown, so Cole devised an allowance graph (now known as a displacement graph). This gives a small displacement to be added to the theoretical scale so that, toward the **head,** as the holes reduce in size, they will be placed higher up the flute **tube.** Assuming that the sizes chosen are fairly similar to a **Louis Lot,** Cole decided that the only holes that would remain unchanged from their theoretical positions would be the **foot** holes (though the **low D** hole would need to be placed in a **flatter** position, farther down the tube, due to the **sharpening** influence on D_2 of the $C_\sharp$ **vent hole**).

Cole's method of calculating the scale was adopted by flutemaker **Albert Cooper** for the **Cooper scale** and later by Bennett for the **Bennett scale.** Cole states that other corrections have been estimated for the effect on the pitch by open-key perforations (*see* OPEN-HOLE KEYS), normally considered a sharpening one, though there is a noticeable cumulative flattening effect when the **keys** are closed, caused by the extra cavities under five of the **flutist'**s fingers. Bennett and Cooper arrived at different scales because of the adjustments needed to account for all of the acoustical aberrations.

Cole believes that, despite these considerable adjustments, the basic mathematical series that Boehm chose for his Schema must be right, as it relates precisely to the vibration numbers for **equal temperament,** which no other series does. (For more scale information, see Coltman under "Repair, Maintenance, and Construction" in the bibliography.)

COLLECTION. A group of **pieces** by one or more composers contained in one music book. The pieces are usually selected by one person—the compiler (or selector)—who may also have **edited** the music. Buying pieces in a collection is often more economical than buying the pieces separately. *See also* PERFORMER'S EDITION; SHEET MUSIC.

COLOR TRILL. *See* KEY VIBRATO.

COLTMAN, JOHN W. (b. Cleveland, Ohio, 1915). An American physicist, **flutist,** flute collector, and acoustician who contributed significantly to present-day knowledge of the behavior of flutes and organ pipes. *See also* acknowledgments; COLTMAN $C_\sharp$; GREEN, TOM; MURRAY FLUTE.

COLTMAN $C_\sharp$. A modification to the **standard flute** that is designed to improve the tone and **intonation** of $C_{\sharp 2}$ and $C_{\sharp 3}$ and correct the intonation of some notes in the **upper register.** The modification consists of a new **tone hole** that is added to the flute between the $C_\sharp$ **vent**

hole and the C (thumb) hole (see app. 5, fig. 9). This new tone hole is used in combination with the C♯ vent hole to produce an improved C♯₂ and C♯₃. Because the new tone hole is automatically closed for the notes D₂, E♭₂, D₃, G♯₃, A₃, and B♭₃, the C♯ is used alone as a **vent** for these notes. This is unlike the regular **Boehm-system** flute, where the C♯ vent hole is used not only for these notes but also for C♯₂ and C♯₃. Having now two holes to deal with notes that are usually helped by only one hole (i.e., the C♯ vent hole) enables the holes to be resized and put in their proper acoustical locations. The Coltman C♯ does not require the **flutist** to learn any new **fingerings**. It was invented by physicist **John Coltman** in 1976. *See also* MURRAY FLUTE.

COMBINATION/COMBO CASE. A **flute** case that, unlike a **single case**, has space for the flute and another instrument or instrument part (e.g., a **piccolo** or an extra **head joint**). *Syn.:* combo case, double case. *See also* GLUE.

COMMON FLUTE. One of the names used in the 18th century for the **recorder** (also known as **English flute**) to distinguish it from the **transverse flute**, then known as the **German flute**. *See* TREBLE FLUTE.

COMPOUND TONGUING. Same as **multiple tonguing**.

CONABLE, BARBARA (b. Canton, Ill., 1940). American president of Andover Educators and Andover Press. She discovered and developed **body mapping** with **William Conable** around 1975.

CONABLE, WILLIAM (b. Buffalo, N.Y., 1942). An American cello professor. He discovered and developed **body mapping** with **Barbara Conable** around 1975.

CONCERT A, CONCERT B, ETC. *See* CONCERT PITCH (3).

CONCERT FLUTE. 1. In the Western world, a common, standard-size, **side-blown flute** in C. Today most **flutists** understand the term *concert flute* to mean a modern **Boehm flute** in C (see fig. 01; app. 6, fig. 2). It is often used to distinguish this type of flute from the other sizes in the Boehm **flute family** such as **bass flutes, alto flutes,** and **contrabass flutes** (see app. 6). *Syn.:* Boehm flute, orchestral flute, concert-pitch flute. *See also* CYLINDRICAL BOEHM FLUTE; *FLAUTO (2)*; *FLÛTE (3)*; "FLUTE IN . . ." (2); GERMAN FLUTE (1); *GRANDE FLÛTE*; *GROSSE FLÖTE*; HIGH NOTE; LOW NOTE; OPEN-KEY SYSTEM; ORDINARY FLUTE (2); RANGE (2); STANDARD FLUTE (1); TRANSPOSING INSTRUMENTS.

2. Historically, often a plain, **one-keyed, two-keyed,** or **simple-system flute** of the standard size (i.e., **six-finger note** D₁—*see* "FLUTE IN . . ." [1]). The term was used to distinguish this size of flute from other sizes such as **third flutes,** *flûtes d'amour,* **octave flutes,** and so on. **Rudall, Carte** catalogues from the 1930s use the term to describe eight- and ten-keyed simple-system flutes in C. *Syn.:* concert-pitch flute. *See also* ORDINARY FLUTE (1).

3. An English term used in the 18th century for the alto **recorder** or for a **transverse flute** of professional quality.

4. Some folk musicians use the term to distinguish the Boehm flute in C with the **tin whistle**.

5. A term applied to any size of some types of ethnic flutes (e.g., North Indian *bansuri* and Native American flutes) to indicate a model of instrument that is of high quality, including good **intonation**, so that it can be played in concert with other (modern) instruments. This means the **pitch** would be close to **A** = 440 Hz and the **tuning** close to **equal temperament**, rather than any traditional tuning.

CONCERT PITCH. 1. The standard reference **pitch** for Western music where, by international agreement in 1939, A₁ was fixed at a **frequency** of 440 **Hertz** (Hz) and all other notes adjusted accordingly. A reference pitch is needed so that all instruments can be **tuned** the same way when playing together. In fact, however, there is often a deviation from this standard, generally erring on the higher side, with some countries in western Europe playing as high as A = 446 Hz.

There has not always been a standard reference pitch for Western music. Prior to the 19th century, there was no pitch standard. Pitch would vary from town to town, within a town, and even within a church, if an organ's frayed pipes were trimmed, thus raising the organ's pitch. These pitch differences could make playing **in tune** very difficult indeed for any musician, particularly for a traveling musician.

A complete list of the pitches that were used goes beyond the scope of this book. Some historical pitches regularly mentioned by **flutists**, and thus worthy of note, are:

- Diapason normal, diapason pitch, French diapason pitch: A₁ = 435 Hz
- High pitch, old philharmonic pitch, band pitch: A₁ = 452–455 Hz
- Modern pitch, new philharmonic pitch: A₁ = 439–440 Hz
- Philosophical pitch: c₁ = 256 Hz (therefore A₁ = 430.5 Hz)
- Society of Arts pitch: A₁ = 445 Hz

To add to the confusion, pitch names tend to change depending on who is talking about them and when. For a substantial listing of pitches that have been used, consult the book *On the Sensations of Tone* by Hermann Helmholtz (New York: Dover, 1954), which contains charts of historical pitches in its appendixes.

The need to standardize pitch levels at least within a city or country gradually rose. France was the first country to attempt to standardize **tuning** in 1859 when the government set A_1 at 435 Hz. This was known as *diapason normal* and became popular not only in France but in other countries as well. The most widely used standard, however, became $A_1 = 440$ Hz. It was first proposed at a Stuttgart conference in 1838, but was not established until 1938 in Britain and in 1939 by the International Organization for Standardization (ISO). *See also* FREQUENCY; HIGH-PITCHED FLUTE (2); TRADITIONAL SCALE; TUNING FORK; TUNING NOTE; TUNING UP.

2. The actual pitch that is sounded by an instrument, irrespective of how the music is notated for that instrument. For example, "concert g" is the pitch that emits from the **alto flute** when a written C_1 is played. *See* TRANSPOSING INSTRUMENTS (1).

3. When an instrument, such as the **concert flute**, is pitched in the key of C, the instrument is said to be in "concert pitch." *See also* TRANSPOSING INSTRUMENTS (2).

CONE FLUTE. Same as **conical flute**.

CONICAL-BOEHM FLUTE. Also *conical Böhm flute*. Same as **ring-key flute**. *See also* FRENCH-MODEL FLUTE; GODFROY, VINCENT HYPOLITE.

CONICAL BORE. A **bore** with a diameter that decreases or increases over the length of the bore. Although most **one-keyed** and **simple-system flutes** from the late 17th century to the middle of the 19th century (and any replicas) are said to have had a conical bore, in reality only the **body** was conical (i.e., the bore got slightly smaller from the top of the body [next to the **head joint**] toward the end of the **foot joint**). Flutes with a **D foot joint** sometimes flared out slightly in the opposite direction. The bore of the head joint was **cylindrical**. Modern **piccolos** are available with a cylindrical or a conical bore. *See also* BAND FLUTE; BAROQUE FLUTE (1); BULBOUS HEAD JOINT; CARTE 1851 SYSTEM FLUTE; CLASSICAL FLUTE; CONICAL FLUTE; *CORPS DE RECHANGE;* EIGHT-KEYED FLUTE; FIFE (1, 3); FIVE-KEYED FLUTE; FOUR-KEYED FLUTE; HIGH G♯ MECHANISM; INVERTED CONICAL BORE; IRISH FLUTE; MEYER-SYSTEM FLUTE; MIDDLE JOINT (2); NINE-KEYED FLUTE; SIX-KEYED FLUTE; TEN-KEYED FLUTES; TWO-KEYED FLUTE.

CONICAL FLUTE. A **flute** with a **conical bore.** *Syn.:* cone flute. *See also* CHARANGA FLUTE; CYLINDRICAL BOEHM FLUTE (3); FLUTE FLAG. For **early flutes** and other non-**Boehm-system** flutes, *see also* CARTE 1851 SYSTEM FLUTE; CYLINDRICAL FLUTE; EIGHT-KEYED FLUTE; EQUISONANT FLUTE; FIVE-KEYED FLUTE; FOUR-KEYED FLUTE; INVERTED CONICAL BORE; IRISH FLUTE; NICHOLSON'S IMPROVED FLUTE; NINE-KEYED FLUTE; ONE-KEYED FLUTE; PRATTEN'S PERFECTED; QUANTZ FLUTE; REFORM FLUTE; RING-KEY FLUTE; SCREW-CORK (1); SICCAMA'S DIATONIC FLUTE; SIMPLE-SYSTEM FLUTE (1, 3); SIX-KEYED FLUTE; TEN-KEYED FLUTES; TULOU *FLÛTE PERFECTIONÉE;* TUNING SLIDE (2); TWO-KEYED FLUTE.

CONSERVATOIRE DE PARIS. *See* PARIS CONSERVATOIRE.

CONSORT FLUTE. British term for the alto **recorder** around 1700.

CONTRABASS FLUTE. It. *flauto contrabasso;* Fr. *flûte contrebasse;* Ger. *Kontrabassflöte.* **1.** An uncommon member of the **Boehm flute** family (*see* FLUTE FAMILY [2]), **pitched** in C, sounding an octave lower than the **bass flute** in C and two octaves lower than the **concert flute** in C. The contrabass flute is held almost vertically, with a horizontal **head joint** (see app. 6, fig. 6). It uses the same **fingering system** as the concert flute and, except for small changes, is played in a similar way. Its **range** is around three octaves from the note sounding as C to C_2 (written C_1 to C_4; *see* TRANSPOSING INSTRUMENTS).

The contrabass flute is approximately double the length of the bass flute, so it is necessary not only for the flute to be held vertically but also for the tubing at the **head** end to be bent into a large numeral-4 shape to make the instrument easier to play. The total length of the contrabass flute with a **B foot joint** is about 111 in. (2.82 m). The height of the instrument, from the open end to the highest point, is about 71 in. (1.80 m). It is usually supported by a long metal adjustable spike, or **boot**, under the **foot joint**, to make it easier to adapt the instrument to the player's height.

The contrabass flute was developed in the latter part of the 20th century. It is not yet commonly played, but due to a surge of interest in the **low-pitched flutes** in recent years, the amount of music that is written for it and its use are bound to increase. It has been used in **solo** playing, recordings, studio work, and **ensembles** such as **flute choirs** but is not a regular member of a band or an orchestra.

Generally, when the term *contrabass flute* is used alone, it means the contrabass **flute in C**. *Syn.:* octocontrabass flute in C, octobass flute. *See also* app. 1; *FLAU-*

TONE; FLUTE BAND; MEMBRANE HEAD JOINT; QUARTER-TONE FLUTE; RESISTANCE PLUG; SUBBASS FLUTE; UTILITY FLUTIST; VERTICAL FLUTE.

    2. An **Albisiphon** (2).

CONTR'ALTO FLUTE IN G. Also *contra-alto, contra alto, contralto.* An uncommon member of the **Boehm flute** family (see FLUTE FAMILY [2]), **pitched** in G, sounding an octave lower than the **alto flute** in G and an octave and a half lower than the **concert flute** in C. Unlike the concert flute, the contr'alto flute is held almost vertically, but it uses the same **fingering system** and, except for small changes, is played in a similar way. Its **range** is around three octaves from the note sounding as G to G_2 (written C_1 to C_4; *see* TRANSPOSING INSTRUMENTS).

    The contr'alto flute is approximately double the length of the alto flute, so it is necessary not only for the flute to be held vertically but also for the top part of the instrument to be bent into a shape like a figure 4 to make the instrument easier to use (see app. 6, fig. 5). It is usually supported by a long metal adjustable spike under the **foot joint** called a **boot**, to make it easier to adapt the instrument to the player's height. The full length of the contr'alto flute with a **B foot joint** is about 72 in. (1.83 m), and its height, from the open end to the highest point, is about 45.7 in. (1.16 m).

    The contr'alto flute was developed in the latter part of the 20th century. It is not yet commonly played, but due to the increased popularity of **low-pitched flutes** in recent years, the amount of music written for it is bound to increase. It has been used in **solo** playing, recordings, and **ensembles** such as **flute choirs**, but it is not a regular member of bands and orchestras. *Syn.:* **contrabass flute in G**, **subbass flute** in G. *See also* app. 6; BASS FLUTE (4); *FLAUTONE;* "FLUTE IN . . ."; QUARTER-TONE FLUTE; VERTICAL FLUTE.

CONTRATENOR FLUTE. Same as **bass flute** in F (def. 4).

COOPER, ALBERT (b. Hull, England, 1924). A renowned British maker of **Boehm flutes**, flute designer, author (see bib. under "Repair, Maintenance, and Construction"), and inventor of the **Cooper scale**. *See also* B/C CONVERTIBLE FOOT JOINT; COLE SCALE; EMBOUCHURE HOLE; MODERN SCALE; MURRAY FLUTE; ORCHESTRAL MODEL FLUTE; "PARABOLIC"; SPLIT F♯ MECHANISM; TRADITIONAL SCALE.

COOPER SCALE. 1. The **scale** devised by **Albert Cooper** with figures supplied by **Elmer Cole** in the 1960s. Both Cooper and Cole were dissatisfied with the **intonation** of the existing **flutes** and decided to recalculate **Theobald Boehm**'s **Schema**. They believed the Schema to refer to **tone hole** sizes of about 0.63 in. (16 mm), but for practical purposes, the hole sizes need to be graduated, becoming smaller toward the **head** end since some holes have a dual purpose, such as the C hole, which serves both for C and for G_3. Cole calculated a correction graph necessary to adjust the position of tone holes according to their size. Ideally, a flute should have ten or more different sizes, but for practical purposes, flutemakers chose to make five or six graduated sizes, which serve the purpose well enough.

    Cooper, after using the Schema for a time, felt that it needed further adjustment and compromised on two halves of two scales: for the scale from the A tone hole up to the **trill keys**, he used a **flatter-pitched** scale (the tone holes farther apart); from the A tone hole down, he used a **sharper** scale (with the **lowest notes** a little sharper). The resulting scale underwent small adjustments over the years in the light of criticism from London players, such as **William Bennett** and others, and became widely known as "Cooper's scale."

    V. Q. Powell Flutes, Inc., was the first to use the Cooper scale in 1974; Brannen Brothers Flutemakers, Inc., followed. Along with the **Bennett scale**, the Cooper scale is the most popular of the modern flute scales. *See also* BASS FLUTE (2); COLE SCALE; MODERN SCALE.

    2. Any modern flute scale that is essentially a modified Cooper scale. Once accepted by the flute community, any of these modified Cooper scales may take on a new name, usually that of the scale designer. A famous example of one of these modified Cooper scales is the Bennett scale, which was designed by William Bennett.

CO-PRINCIPAL FLUTIST. *See* PRINCIPAL FLUTIST (2).

CORE BAR. *See* ONE-PIECE CORE BAR.

CORK. 1. A light, thick, elastic, outer bark of the cork oak tree used to make various parts, such as the **plug** found in most **head joints** (see def. 2 below) and **bumpers** found on the undersides of some **keys** or key parts. *See also* ADJUSTMENT; CLUTCH (1); FELT; GLUE; KEY RISE; NEOPRENE; OVERHAUL; REPAD; RESISTANCE PLUG; SHIM (1). For **early flutes**, *see also* LAPPING. **2.** A **stopper** that is made of cork. *See* app. 11, note 3; CORK ASSEMBLY (1); CROWN; HEAD-JOINT CORK; O-RING (2); TUNING HEAD. For early flutes, *see also* CORK ASSEMBLY (2); *CORPS DE RECHANGE;* SCREW CAP; SCREW-CORK.

CORK ASSEMBLY. 1. The inside part of the traditional **head joint**, which usually includes the **head-joint cork**, two metal discs (**cork plates**) at both ends of the

cork, the **crown**, and a long metal screw to join the cork and crown together (see app. 7, fig. 2). This screw mechanism enables the cork to be moved by twisting and/or pushing the crown in specific ways. *Syn.:* crown assembly, head cork assembly, head crown assembly, head-joint cork assembly, head-joint **plug** assembly, head cork screw assembly, **stopper** assembly. *See also* BIGIO CROWN AND STOPPER; FAJARDO WEDGEHEAD; O-RING (2); STOPPER. **2.** The inside part of many 18th-, 19th-, and early 20th-century head joints (or replicas), which includes the cork stopper, a long threaded rod (**pin** or **screw-cork indicator**) of wood or **ivory** rigidly attached to the stopper, and the **cap** through which the threaded rod projects (see app. 3, A, fig. 5). It has a similar purpose to the cork assembly on **Boehm flutes** (see def. 1 above). *Syn.:* screw-cork assembly. *See also* SCREW-CORK.

CORK FACING. *See* CORK PLATE.

CORK PLATE. A metal disc that is usually found both sides of the traditional **head-joint cork** (see app. 7, fig. 2). Sometimes the cork plate on the east side of the **cork** is concave, with the inner part of the curve facing east. When there is only one **plate**, on the **embouchure** end, it may be called a *cork facing* or *cork face*, as in "The cork is faced with silver." *Syn.:* end plates, **end snappers**, holding plates, plates, **stopper** plates, washers. *See also* O-RING (2).

CORK PLUG. 1. A **stopper** that is made of **cork**. **2.** *See* PLUG (1).

CORK SCREW. The screw that attaches the **stopper** to the **cap** or **crown** and adjusts the stopper position. *See also* HEAD-JOINT CORK; SCREW-CORK.

CORPS D'AMOUR. Fr. body of love. An extra-long *corps de rechange* (**upper middle joint**) that was sometimes provided with a standard four-**joint** Baroque or early **Classical flute** to allow it to play as a *flûte d'amour* (see app. 3, B, fig. 1). It was **pitched** as much as a minor third below the highest (or one of the highest) -pitched upper middle joints. **Flutes** using a corps d'amour joint are said by some to have poor **intonation** and sonority for the **lowest notes** as compared to a regular flûte d'amour, since the pitch change was too great to be accommodated only with a larger joint. *Syn.:* (Eng.) *d'amour* joint.

CORPS DE RECHANGE. Fr. replacement body. The set of interchangeable upper middle parts of a four-piece **conical-bore transverse flute** that was introduced around 1720 to accommodate the varying **pitch** standards in various cities and provinces of the time (see

concert pitch 1). These upper middle parts had three **finger holes** and varied in length depending on the pitch desired (see app. 3, B, fig. 1). When intended for **simple-system flutes** later in the 18th century and early in the 19th century, these upper middle parts would have two or three **keys** each.

Up to seven corps de rechange might come with a **flute** to accommodate a number of different pitches within a range of about a semitone. Replacing the regular **upper middle joint** with a longer corps would lower the overall pitch of the flute, and a shorter corps would raise it. Having several corps de rechange avoided the impracticality of having to own several different transverse flutes of varying lengths to deal with the pitch changes from place to place. However, even with the corps de rechange, the **tuning** was not quite right. Using a different corps required that the **flutist** also adjust the position of a **cork** in the **head joint** to correct octave **intonation**—drawing it out (farther away from the **embouchure hole**) for a shorter corps, and pressing it in (closer to the embouchure hole) for a longer corps.

Unfortunately, this was still not enough of an intonation improvement. Since the **tone holes** on the **lower middle joint** were not respaced to accommodate the change in length from the corps, the flute was still **out of tune**. As a result, **foot registers** were introduced shortly after the corps de rechange to partially compensate for the change in length and lack of tone-hole respacing brought about by the corps de rechange.

Johann Joachim Quantz, in his **treatise**, *Versuch* of 1752, also recommended the use of the corps in music that was very loud or soft. A shorter corps could be used to **sharpen** the pitch when the music, such as in an adagio, required gentler blowing—which would otherwise **flatten** the pitch of the notes. A longer corps could be used to flatten the pitch when the music, such as in an allegro movement of a concerto where the accompaniment was strong, required more forceful blowing, which would otherwise sharpen the pitch of the notes.

By the early part of the 19th century, the **tuning slide** (def. 2) began to replace the corps de rechange. *See also* CORPS D'AMOUR; ONE-KEYED FLUTE; SCREW-CORK (1); TUNING RINGS; TWO-KEYED FLUTE.

CORROSION. The breaking down of essential properties in a material due to reactions with its surroundings. The most common example is rust, the reaction of iron and oxygen. With regard to the most common metals used in flute manufacture, corrosion occurs in **silver**, **nickel-silver**, and **steel** and to a lesser degree in stainless steel, **gold**, **platinum**, and **titanium**. Keeping the flute clean and dry will help to prevent corrosion. *See also* HEAD-JOINT LINING (1); NICKEL-PLATING; GOLD-

PLATING; PITTING; PLATING; PRECIOUS METAL; RHO-
DIUM-PLATING; SILVER-PLATING; STEEL (1); TARNISH.

CORTET, ROGER LOUIS EMILE (b. Nevers, Nièvre, France, 1904; d. 1950). An original member of the Wind **Quintet** of Paris, formed in 1929, and also a conductor and recording artist. *See also* CRUNELLE, GAS-TON GABRIELLE.

COUNTERBORE. 1. A flat-bottomed, cylindrically shaped enlargement of the top part of a smaller hole resulting in a stepped hole. The lower, narrower section may or may not be threaded. **Rollers** and certain key **posts**, such as those holding in place the **trill key** assembly (*see* SECTION [2]) on the **flute**, usually have holes with this design. **2.** The drill bit used to make a counterbore. **3.** *v.* To enlarge a hole with a counterbore. *Cf.* **countersink**.

COUNTERSINK. 1. An angular-shaped enlargement (usually 60°, but sometimes 90°) of the top part of a smaller hole resulting in a stepped hole. The lower, narrower section may or may not be threaded. The **rib** screws on wooden flutes usually have holes with this design in order to get them flush. **2.** A sharp-edged cutting tool that is used to make a countersink (def. 1). It is used in flutemaking or repair to do such things as sinking a screw **head** for a more stable fit. **3.** *v.* To widen the rim of a hole so that something, such as the head of a screw, can be made to fit flush or below the surface. In the case of a screw with a head, countersinking can enable the **flute** technician to screw the screw deeper into the hole, thus ensuring a tighter fit and less **play** than a headless screw. *See also* WALKING-STICK FLUTE. *Cf.* **counterbore**.

COVER. 1. A measure of how well a **key** pad is **seated** (i.e., sits) on the **tone hole**. If a **pad** covers well, then it fits on the tone hole in such a way that there are no **leaks**. **2.** How the lower lip is positioned on the **embouchure hole**, as in "You're covering too much."

COVERED-HOLE FLUTE. Same as **closed-hole flute**.

COVERED HOLE/KEY. Same as **closed-hole key**. *See also* CLOSED-HOLE FLUTE.

CRACK. 1. Same as **cracking**. **2.** A fracture in a solid material. Regarding cracks in metal **flutes**, *see* STRESS RELIEVING; in wooden flutes, *see* BOXWOOD; COCUSWOOD; CRACK PINNING; EBONITE; FILLER (2); GLUE; HEAD-JOINT LINING (1); LAPPING; OIL (2); RING BANDING.

CRACKING (A NOTE). Accidentally jumping to or partially playing a high- or low-pitched unintended note, which may result in a **multiphonic**. When the **air jet** speed, angle, or length is inappropriate, it can excite more than one **resonance**, or the resonance associated with an unintended note and **leaks** in certain locations or sloppy finger work can cause notes to jump up to another note. May be referred to as *breaking* or *splitting* (a note). *See also* RESISTANCE RINGS.

CRACK PINNING. A technique for closing cracks in wooden **woodwind instruments** in general, including wooden **flutes**. The crack is clamped closed and a very small hole is drilled through the wood, passing through the crack at something near a right angle. Crack wire—a thin wire with a fine screw thread—is then screwed through the hole and cut off at each end. A long crack requires a number of these pins to keep it closed—approximately every 0.6 in. (15 mm). Some repairers attempt to disguise the ends of the crack pins with suitably colored **glue**. The method is generally successful where the crack is not under stress. *Cf.* **ring banding**.

CRESCENT KEY. An obsolete type of **key** with a thin (padless), crescent-shaped metal **touchpiece** that hovered above the edge of a small **finger hole** on some 19th-century **flutes**. Like the **ring key**, when the finger closed the hole, the crescent key was also depressed and at the same time activated a **key mechanism** to close or partially close at least one **tone hole** at another location on the flute. **Heinrich Pottgiesser**, a **woodwind** inventor, used the crescent key in combination with a padded ring key on his 1824 flute (see app. 3, B, fig. 8). When the crescent key over finger hole 2 (B hole) was pressed down with L2, the ring key partially closed finger hole 1 (C$_\sharp$ hole), bringing **forked** C$_2$ down to **pitch**. When the crescent key was released, the pitch of C$_{\sharp 2}$ went up. Capt. **James Gordon**, a flute designer, used crescent keys on his flutes around 1826, but none of his flutes have survived. His crescent keys implemented a useful way of opening or closing a hole underneath a finger, while, at the same time, fully opening or closing a distant hole with a padded cup. **Benedikt Pentenrieder** made extensive use of crescent keys around 1840, before switching to ring keys. *Syn.:* crescent touchpiece.

CRITICAL EDITION. Essentially an enhanced **scholarly edition**. Generally, all available sources are consulted and an exhaustive critical report is appended, listing all discrepancies in and between sources. Where textual information is missing in a source or sources, the editor will not usually seek to provide a solution, as the editor of a scholarly edition does, which can leave the work unperformable. *See also* EDIT; FACSIMILE; PERFORMER'S EDITION; *URTEXT*.

CROOK. Prior to the invention of valves, around 1815, a detachable piece of coiled **tubing** was fitted into horns or trumpets to alter the tubing length and thus change the **tuning**. Other instrumentalists have since adopted the term to mean a bent piece of tubing, such as that on a flute's **curved head joint**. Bends in tubing are also called *bows* or *elbows*.

CROSS-BLOWN FLUTE. Same as **transverse flute**. *Syn.:* cross flute.

CROSS-FINGERING. 1. A **fingering** in which some **tone holes** are covered out of sequence, leaving others uncovered or **vented**. For example, cross-fingering may be used to:

- produce a new note (e.g., F, G$\sharp$, B$\flat$, and C in the **first** and **second octaves** of the **one-keyed flute**)
- improve the **response, intonation,** and **tone quality** (particularly clearness and strength) of an existing note (e.g., on the modern **concert flute**, C$\sharp_2$ and C$\sharp_3$ with either or both R2 and R3 closed)
- produce an unusual **tone color** or **shaded** note, as is required in **extended techniques**
- create a **register hole** by making a **low note** unplayable and so favor the playing of a **high note** (e.g., the standard fingering for F$_2$ becomes that for F$_3$ when L2 vents about three-quarters of the way along the flute **tube**)

Also called *back-fingering*, *split fingering*, or *fork fingering*, though the latter term usually refers only to a specific type of cross-fingering. *See also* BROSSA F$\sharp$ LEVER; CUTOFF FREQUENCY. For **early flutes** or other non-**Boehm-system** flutes, *see also* CARTE 1851 SYSTEM FLUTE; CLASSICAL FLUTE; FOUR-KEYED FLUTE; GIORGI FLUTE; G$\sharp$ KEY (2); SIMPLE-SYSTEM FLUTE (1); VEILED TONE (1).

2. Occasionally used to refer to a type of out-of-sequence fingering that improves the finger placement of an existing note with little noticeable difference in its response, intonation, or tone quality (e.g., on a modern concert flute, B$\flat_1$ or $_2$ using the **one-and-one B$\flat$ fingering** and F$\sharp_1$ or $_2$). Some do not consider these fingerings cross-fingerings because their primary function is mechanical and not acoustical. *See also* CARTE 1867 SYSTEM FLUTE; REGISTER (1).

3. Occasionally used to refer to a consecutive pair of fingerings in which one or more fingers are raised at the same time as one or more fingers are put down. This

double action can be difficult for some people and hinder **technique**. For example, when playing from C$_2$ to D$_2$ on the modern concert flute, two fingers go up and six go down at the same time. Many do not consider these fingerings cross-fingerings because their primary function has to do with finger movement and not acoustics.

CROSS FLUTE. Same as **transverse flute**. *Syn.:* cross-blown flute.

CROSS KEY. A small **closed key** on **simple-system flutes** that lies across the **body** between two **finger holes**. The cross or short F key is an example of a cross key (see app. 3, C, fig. 3). *See also* EIGHT-KEYED FLUTE; FIVE-KEYED FLUTE; FOUR-KEYED FLUTE; G$\sharp$ KEY (2); LONG KEY; NINE-KEYED FLUTE; SHORT KEY; SIX-KEYED FLUTE; TEN-KEYED FLUTE.

CROWN. A **cap** at the closed end of the **head joint** (see app. 7, figs. 2 and 10). There are many crown styles. A crown may be hollow or solid or have a hole through its center. Sometimes they are decorated with precious gems. Some **flutists** use a heavier or lighter crown, or a specific crown style, because they feel that it has a positive effect on their flute tone. Nagahara Flutes makes a locking crown to avoid the problem of the crown becoming loose and/or buzzing.

On most modern **Boehm flute** head joints, the crown is attached by a screw mechanism to a **cork** inside the head joint, called the **head-joint cork** (see app. 7, fig. 2). Turning the crown moves the cork, for which there is a preferred position. Deviating from this will affect the notes from D$_3$ upward, and if moved excessively, both the tone and the lower-**pitched** notes will be affected as well. *Syn.:* button, cap, crown piece, end cap, head cap, head crown, head-joint cap, **knob, screw cap,** tuning cap, tuning knob. *See also* BIGIO CROWN AND STOPPER; CHASING; CORK ASSEMBLY (1); CORK SCREW; ENGRAVING; SHEET METAL; STOPPER.

CRUNELLE, GASTON GABRIELLE (b. Douai, Nord, France, 1898; d. France, 1990). A French **flutist** who was the **principal flutist** in L'Opéra Comique from 1932 to 1963, a flute professor at the **Paris Conservatoire** from 1941 to 1969 (with **Marcel Moyse** 1946–1948 and **Roger Cortet**, deputy, 1949–1950), and a recording artist.

CRUTCH. A T-shaped supporting device that can be attached to the underside of older flute **bodies** to the left of the thumb keys (see app. 5, figs. 6 and 11). It was claimed to steady and support the flute's weight and thus free up the fingers, especially L1. It rests between the thumb and L1. The distance of the crutch from the flute body can often be changed by adjusting a screw.

The crutch is said to have been invented by **Theobald Boehm** and is referred to as "Boehm's crutch." Some find that the crutch hinders the movement of the left-hand fingers and the thumb. It is seldom seen on **concert flutes** today, but it can be found on some modern **bass flutes**, where it helps to support the heavier weight.

Another supporting device, called the **wart**, is often seen on metal flutes that also have a crutch. (Other devices that are used by flutists to help them support their flute include the **Bo-Pep** and **thumb rest**.) *See also* CYLINDRICAL BOEHM FLUTE (1).

CRYOGENICS. A branch of physics that studies what happens at very low temperatures. Although not scientifically proven, a small number of **flute** manufacturers claim that controlled deep-freezing and then warming of metal flutes using liquid nitrogen can improve the **response, resonance,** and loudness of the instrument. They also feel that it makes the **tubing** and **keys** stronger. The reasoning behind this claim is that this process could readjust the metal structure in such a way that it would relieve the stress in the metal that was caused during manufacturing (e.g., through **soldering**, bending, hammering, and so on).

During the relatively inexpensive cryogenics process, each flute **joint** (with or without all its parts) is wrapped for protection and then placed in a freezer. Here the temperature of the parts is gradually lowered to −184°C (−300°F), at the rate of about one degree a minute. After remaining at this temperature for many hours, the temperature of the parts is gradually raised to room temperature. The whole process can take a few days. *Syn.:* cryogeny, low-temperature physics. *See also* STRESS RELIEVING.

CRYSTAL. With regard to **flutes**, usually refers to very clear, high-quality glass. *See also* GLASS FLUTE.

C♯ BRILLE. *See* $br\,il\,l\,e$.

C♯/D♯ TRILL KEY/LEVER. Same as D trill key and so called since one of its main uses is to facilitate the C♯/D♯ trill in the **second** and **third** octaves. *See also* TRILL KEYS.

C♯ TRILL KEY. A nonstandard **spatula**-like **key** that is usually above and to the left of the **B♭ side lever**. It opens an extra **tone hole** to the left of the thumb keys when depressed (see app. 9, fig. 7). It was patented in France in 1909 by **Cornélie Villedieu Laubé**.

The C♯ trill key is one of the most versatile of all the optional keys offered to the **flutist**. It facilitates extra **trills**:

- B/C♯ trill and C/C♯ trill in the **first** and **second octaves**
- $F_{\sharp_3}/G_{\sharp_3}$ trill
- $G_3/A_{\flat_3}$ trill
- G_3/A_3 trill
- $A_{\flat_3}/B_{\flat_3}$ trill: finger

and some **tremolos**:

- to $C_{\sharp_2}$ from G_1, $A_{\flat_1}$, A_1, $B_{\flat_1}$, B_1, or C_2
- to $C_{\sharp_3}$ from A_2, $B_{\flat_2}$, B_2, or C_3
- to D_2 from G_1, $A_{\flat_1}$, A_1, $B_{\flat_1}$, or B_1
- to $D_{\sharp_2}$ from G_1, $A_{\flat_1}$, A_1, $B_{\flat_1}$, or B_1

It also assists in the production of some notes: $A_{\flat_3}$ is easier to play softly and **in-tune**, and $C_{\sharp_2}$ is easier to play with more color and stability without losing the **pitch**. Through experimentation, a flutist will find even more uses for the C♯ trill key.

Sometimes the C♯ trill key is referred to as the *G/A trill key* or the *B/C♯ trill key* since one of its best purposes is in facilitating the G_3/A_3 trill, the $B_1/C_{\sharp_2}$ trill, and the $B_2/C_{\sharp_3}$ trill. However, the "G/A trill key" naming is unfortunate since there is actually a key called the **G/A trill key**. In addition, it is rarely referred to as the *Laubé C♯*. *See also* B/C♯ TRILL KEY; BOEHM FLUTE (1); C♯ VENT HOLE; MODEL NUMBER; PROFESSIONAL FLUTE; QUARTER-TONE FLUTE.

C♯ VENT HOLE. Another name for the upper C♯ **tone hole** on the **middle joint**. It is so called because it not only serves to produce the notes $C_{\sharp_2}$ and $C_{\sharp_3}$ but also is made smaller and placed in a compromised position higher up on the flute **tube** than it should be for $C_{\sharp_2}$ so that it may also serve as a **vent** or **register hole** for D_2, $D_{\sharp_2}$, D_3, $G_{\sharp_3}$, and A_3. Unfortunately, since the hole size and position are not the best for $C_{\sharp_2}$, it may have **intonation** or tone problems, depending on the **flute** model and player. The **C♯ trill key** or **Coltman C♯** can make it easier to play a good $C_{\sharp_2}$. *See also* BENNETT SCALE; COLE SCALE; RING-KEY FLUTE; VEILED TONE (2).

CUE. 1. A short **passage** taken from one **ensemble** part and written in smaller notes in another part as a prompt. Usually written as a guide to making an entry or to give guidance to the player of important **solos** in the other **parts**, but it may actually be played if strengthening of another part is needed or if the instrumentalist who plays the cue is away. **2.** A signal given by an instrumentalist or conductor to a player to take some form of action. A signal to start a note, passage, or phrase is called a *cue-in*, and a signal to end a note, passage, or phrase is called a *cutoff*.

CUP. The name for the **key** that is cup-like in shape and contains a **pad** (see app. 7, figs. 8 and 9). This type of key "cups" a pad by curving around it in such a way that it covers one side of the pad and most of the pad edge. There are two main kinds: **closed-hole (key) cups** and **open-hole (key) cups,** and they may be **closed-** or **open-standing.** *Syn.:* button, cupped key, key cup, pad cup. *See also* app. 11; ADJUSTMENT; CHASING; DAP; DISH; DUPLICATE KEYS; ENGRAVING; FINGER BUTTON; FINISHER; FLOATING; FRENCH CUP; FRENCH-POINTED KEY; HANDMADE FLUTE; KEY ARMS; KEY RISE; LEVELING (1); MEMBRANE HEAD JOINT; OPEN-HOLE FLUTE; OPEN KEY; PAD; PISONI PADS; PLUG (1); QUARTER-TONE FLUTE; RING (1); SHEET METAL; SHIM (1); SPUD; STAMPING; STRINGER; TOUCHPIECE. For **early flutes,** *see also* app. 3B, fig. 7; SALT-SPOON KEY.

CURVED HEAD JOINT. A commonly used **head joint** that curves around on itself. It reduces the distance from the **embouchure** to the hands and is therefore shorter and easier for smaller **flutists** to play, as compared to the **standard flute.** The traditional **bass flute** comes only with a curved head because of the otherwise impossible stretch (see app. 6, fig. 4). The curved head joint is often used on a standard flute **body** (sometimes without the standard **D** and **D♯ trill keys** and the **low C♯** and C keys to lessen the weight) for small beginners, who would find the standard flute, with a **straight head joint,** difficult to handle. Another usage is for crowded marching bands, because the curved head makes the total length shorter and more compact. *Syn.:* U-shaped head joint, J-curve head joint, recurved head joint. *See also* ALTO FLUTE; ANGLED HEAD JOINT; CROOK; STUDENT FLUTE; VERTICAL HEAD JOINT.

CUSHION. The softest part of a **pad.** In the case of **traditional pads,** this is the part that is made of **felt.** Also called a *filler*.

CUSP. Same as **wing** (see figs. 35 and 36). *See also* REFORM FLUTE (1, 3); *REFORMMUNDLOCH* (1).

CUSPED EMBOUCHURE PLATE. Same as **winged embouchure plate**.

CUT. The collective characteristics of the **embouchure plate** and **riser** that distinguish one **head joint** from another. These collective characteristics have a great influence on the overall tone and **response** of the **flute.** *Syn.:* embouchure cut. *See also* EMBOUCHURE RECUT.

CUTOFF. *See* CUE (2).

CUTOFF FREQUENCY. In musical instruments, the **frequency** beyond which a lattice or succession of open holes ceases to reflect and begins to transmit energy down the **bore.** For the **flute,** the first open **tone hole,** together with any open tone holes farther downstream, has a low **impedance** at low frequencies and acts to terminate the **resonant** column. As the frequency increases, the hole impedance increases, creating more **pressure** down the **tube,** so that the next hole takes more of the flow. With further increases in frequency, more and more holes are involved, and at the cutoff frequency, the wave will propagate down the tube. For waves with frequencies substantially lower than the cutoff frequency, the first open tone hole is nearly a pressure **node,** and so the distance from this tone hole to the **embouchure hole** approximately determines the possible wavelengths and thus the notes that may be played in this frequency range.

Loosely speaking, the flute behaves at low frequencies as though it ended somewhere near the first open tone hole (*see* END CORRECTION). Consequently, for frequencies well below the cutoff, **cross-fingering** (closing one or more tone holes below one or more open tone holes) has only a modest effect on **pitch,** the effect increasing as one approaches the cutoff. At frequencies substantially higher than the cutoff frequency, waves propagate past open tone holes relatively easily, making it complicated to work out the possible notes that could be played. The frequency of the cutoff depends on the size of the tone holes (and on their spacing, as well as the bore diameter) and increases as the tone hole diameter increases. Thus, for the modern **Boehm flute,** where most of the tone holes are large, the cutoff frequency is around 2 kHz (ca. B_3), but for the **Baroque flute,** where the tone holes are rather smaller and more widely spaced, the cutoff frequency is lower, at around 1.1 kHz (ca. D_3).

Consequently, for the modern flute, cross-fingering has only a modest effect on the pitch of notes in the **first register,** and an increasing effect in the higher **registers.** Cross-fingering has a noticeable effect on the **timbre,** particularly of loud notes, because for loud notes (which have a greater number of higher **harmonics** sounding than do soft notes), even low-pitched notes have harmonics above the cutoff frequency. Cross-fingering on a Baroque flute, in contrast, is effective over a wide frequency range and, as a result, is the normal **technique** for achieving notes that do not fall in the scale of D major. Due to the fact that the first register is farther from the cutoff frequency than is the second, different cross-fingerings are usually required in the different registers.

For simple **fingerings** (i.e., those without cross-fingering), the cutoff frequency limits the number of **resonances** that a **flutist** can play (flutists usually call these "harmonics"). Well below the cutoff, the flute behaves approximately as a simple **pipe** with a length slightly exceeding that between the embouchure and the first open tone hole, and so one can play several notes (i.e., harmonics) in the **harmonic series** by **overblowing**, because the flute has resonances at frequencies close to the harmonic series. Near to and above the cutoff, the frequencies of the resonances are no longer close to those of the harmonic series, and so the overblown notes, if possible, are no longer close to the harmonic series. Consequently, one can overblow fewer notes in the harmonic series on a Baroque flute than on a modern instrument. *See also* SOUNDING HOLE.

CYLINDRICAL BOEHM FLUTE. Also *cylindrical Böhm flute*. **1.** Usually refers to modified versions of **Theobald Boehm**'s original 1847 **cylindrical flute**, which first came about as the **Boehm flute** gained in popularity during the 19th century. Some common modified versions included the German model (from flutemakers such as Boehm and **Carl Mendler**) and the **French-model flute** (from flutemakers such as **Vincent Godfroy** and **Louis Lot**).

Features of the German model usually included an open **G**♯ **key**, **reversed thumb keys**, a **side lever** for B that can be used for the B/C **trill** (see B TRILL KEY), padded **plateau key cups**, offset **G keys**, a **crutch**, and sometimes a *Schleifklappe* and were most often made of wood.

Features of the French-model flute, which is the flute most often used today, included a closed **G**♯ key (at first, this was a **Dorus G**♯ **key**, later an **independent G**♯ **key**), a **Briccialdi B**♭ **key** assembly, a side lever for B♭/A♯

that can be used for the the A♯/B trill, padded **open-hole key** cups, French **key arms** on closed-hole keys, and in-line **G keys** and were most often made of metal. Also present on the French-model flute then and most flutes now are a **pinned mechanism**, a **back connector**, **adjustment screws**, **pivot screws**, needle **springs**, **key tubing**, and **steels**.

The 19th-century English and American Boehm flutes were varied, often including features from both the French and German models. The most important 19th-century English flutemaker of Boehm flutes was **Rudall, Carte & Co.** (earlier Rudall & Rose, then Rudall, Rose, Carte & Co.), and the most important 19th-century American flutemaker was **Alfred G. Badger**.

2. The modern **concert flute** (1).

3. May also refer to the 1847 cylindrical flute in C designed by Boehm, which is almost identical to the flutes we play today (see fig. 11, *bottom*). It is made of **brass** and, except for the addition of a D♯ **trill key**, has a **key mechanism** similar to his 1832 **conical flute** (see the **ring-key flute** in fig. 11). Eventually Boehm replaced the **ring keys** with **padded closed-hole keys** and also made flutes from wood, or later, sometimes with a metal **head**.

As with the 1832 conical flute, **tuning** adjustments could be made to the cylindrical flute's **scale** by extending the head-joint **tenon** from the middle joint **socket**, adjusting the **head-joint cork**, or changing the playing in some way.

With the introduction of the 1847 model, Boehm improved aspects of his 1832 conical flute, which included making the **body** cylindrical and the head-joint "**parabolic**," the latter to enable correct octaves tuning. The cylindrical body allowed for the **tone holes** to be further enlarged, which increased the volume and **brightness** of the tone, particularly in the **low register**. On his original 1847 model, as on his original 1832 model, there

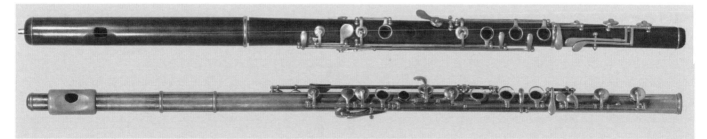

Figure 11. *(Top)* **Theobald Boehm's 1832 ring-key flute in C:** 1832 system, conical, open G♯, modern style key cups, post-mount, D trill, double-holed thumb key, and alternate R3 B-lever. Three sections, partial tuning slide. Cocuswood, nickel-silver keys, ring keys, ferrules. Boxwood crutch. *(Bottom)* **Theobald Boehm's first cylindrical C flute:** 1847 system, cylindrical. Post-mount, open G♯. Right-hand trill key for B♭/C (thumb). Unibody. Brass flute tube and cap, originally gold-plated. Boxwood embouchure barrel, nickel-silver keys and posts. Ebony crutch. Presented to Briccialdi. *Photos from the Dayton C. Miller Collection, Music Division, Library of Congress, DCM 0974, DCM 0652.*

was no **B♭ thumb key** or **B♭ side lever**, possibly because Boehm did not consider these essential.

See also BOEHM SYSTEM; CARTE 1867 SYSTEM FLUTE; FRENCH FLUTE SCHOOL; NICHOLSON'S IMPROVED FLUTE; OPEN-KEY SYSTEM; PARIS CONSERVATOIRE; ROCKSTRO MODEL FLUTE (1); SCHEMA; STANDARD FLUTE (1).

CYLINDRICAL BORE. A **bore** with a diameter that remains the same for the entire **tube** length. Although all Western **flutes** from the Renaissance period up to the late 17th century, and a continuously growing number of flutes since the middle of the 19th century, are said to have cylindrical bores, in reality, only the **Renaissance flute** had a true cylindrical bore. In practice, on the flute of today (and most **Boehm** and modified **Boehm-system flutes** since 1847), only the bore of the **middle joint** and **foot joint** are cylindrical. The bore of the **head joint** tapers, getting smaller from the open to usually the closed end (see "**parabolic**"). Modern **piccolos** are available with a cylindrical or a **conical bore**. Many ethnic flutes have a cylindrical bore. See also CYLINDRICAL FLUTE; FAJARDO WEDGEHEAD; HEAD JOINT LINING. For **early flutes** and other non-Boehm-system flutes, see also CARTE 1851 SYSTEM FLUTE; FIFE (1); HEAD-JOINT LINING; PRATTEN'S PERFECTED.

CYLINDRICAL FLUTE. A flute with a **cylindrical bore**. See also CYLINDRICAL BOEHM FLUTE; MURRAY FLUTE; ROCKSTRO MODEL FLUTE; THINNED (HEAD OR BODY) JOINTS. For **early flutes** and other non-**Boehm-system** flutes, see CARTE 1851 SYSTEM FLUTE; CARTE 1867 SYSTEM FLUTE; GIORGI FLUTE; OLD SYSTEM (2); PRATTEN'S PERFECTED; RADCLIFF SYSTEM FLUTE; RENAISSANCE FLUTE.

𝒟

DAMPIT®. The brand name of a popular **humidifier** for wooden instruments. It is a thin, flexible, perforated plastic tube with a sponge wick (see app. 12, fig. 15). The Dampit, after being submerged in water and having any excess water removed by wiping the tube and squeezing its end, is placed inside of a wooden instrument (when not in use) or in its case. It is said to help prevent the instrument from warping, cracking, or un-gluing. It does this by slowly releasing moisture into the air. See also HYGROMETER.

DAP. 1. The middle part of a key **cup** or **finger button** (see app. 7, fig. 8). An *ornamental dap* has decorative features such as a nipple-shaped point in the middle top part

of a key cup, while a *plain dap* is devoid of such features. See also CUP; DISH; RING (1). **2.** *v.* To produce forms, such as key cups, by the use of special **dies** and punches.

DARK TONE. A tone in which the lower **harmonics** may be relatively strong. See also B FOOT JOINT; BRIGHT TONE; DENSITY; *DÉTIMBRÉ*; D FOOT JOINT; *FLÛTE D'AMOUR*; FULL TONE; HOLLOW TONE; *TIMBRÉ*; TONE COLOR.

DAYTON C. MILLER SYNDROME. Also *DCM Syndrome*. An uncontrolled interest in the developmental history of the **flute**. The patient becomes preoccupied both with physical objects and with systems of categorization. As the collection increases in size, the conceptual categories change, and the sufferer is compelled to acquire more items. This eponymous condition is named after Prof. **Dayton C. Miller** (1866–1941), an experimental physicist and systematic collector of musical instruments and related paraphernalia. The term was coined by psychiatrist **John Braverman Levine** in 1998. Dr. Miller's collection at the time of his death numbered around 1,426 instruments, most of them flutes. The Dayton C. Miller Collection is now part of the Music Division of the Library of Congress in Washington, D.C. See also DCM.

DCM. Abbr. for **Dayton Clarence Miller**, a renowned collector of musical instruments and related paraphernalia. The abbreviation DCM is used, along with a number, to identify various items, such as musical instruments, in the collection. The collection to date consists of around 1,700 musical instruments (primarily **flutes**), statuary, iconography, books, music, tutors, patents, and other materials that mostly have to do with the flute. The entire collection is housed in the Music Division of the Library of Congress in Washington, D.C. The collection of musical instruments can be viewed online at http://memory.loc.gov/ammem/dcmhtml/dmhome.html. See also DAYTON C. MILLER SYNDROME; "FLUTE IN . . ." (2).

DEBOST, MICHEL (b. Paris, 1934). A French flute **soloist** and recording artist who was the **principal flutist** of the Société des Concerts/Orchestre de Paris from 1959 to 1989. Debost was also a **flute** professor at the **Paris Conservatoire** from 1981 to 1990 (on leave 1989–1990) and has been a flute professor at the Oberlin Conservatory of Music since 1989. He is author of *The Simple Flute from A to Z* (Oxford: OUP, 2002) and a columnist for *Flute Talk*. See also ARTAUD, PIERRE-YVES.

DECIMETTE. An **ensemble** of, or a **piece** for, 10 musicians. *Syn.:* dectet, dextet.

DECORATION. Same as **ornament**.

DEEP WALL. *See* **riser**.

DE LA SONORITÉ. Fr. Part of the title to a famous **flute** tone exercise book *De la Sonorité: Art et technique* (*Of the Sonorousness: Art and Technique*), by flutist **Marcel Moyse** (1889–1984). A translation of the title that is probably closer to what Moyse had in mind is *The Art and Technique of Tone Production*.

DELICATE MECHANISM. Same as **soft mechanism**.

DENSITY. The density of a material is the mass per unit volume. The standard unit of density in the *système internationale* is the kilogram per cubic meter; grams per cubic centimeter are also often used. The density of a material depends on the mass of molecules and on their average separation. It also depends on the temperature and **pressure**, especially for gases.

In air, molecules are widely spaced, so the density at room temperature is typically only 0.0012–0.0013 g/cm^3 (1.2–1.3 kg/m^3). Water molecules are less massive than most other atmospheric air molecules, so humid air is less dense than dry air. In addition, air expands when heated, so warm air is less dense than cold air. For both of these reasons, the speed of sound is faster in warm, humid air than it is in cold, dry air, and this makes **flutes** play **sharper** when they are "warmed up" (*see* WARM-UP [2]). Carbon dioxide in the breath has a small contrary effect, slightly **flattening** the **pitch**.

Liquid water has a density of 1 g/cm^3 (1,000 kg/m^3). Most woods used for flutemaking have densities similar to that of water, but metals are considerably denser. For example, pure **silver** has a density about 10 times that of water. Many players of metal flutes feel that, all other things being equal, the denser the material, the **darker** the sound. However, acoustic theory predicts that, as long as the **bore** is sufficiently smooth, rigid, and impermeable, the material should not affect the **tone quality** or **response**, and experiments to date support this theory.

In wooden flutes, denser timbers are usually firmer, finer in grain (smoother), and less porous, making a more efficient vessel for the vibrating **air column**. As a result, wooden flutemakers over history have always gravitated toward the finest and densest timbers available to them.

The densities of some other common metals used in modern flute manufacture are, in g/cm^3, 8.6 for **nickel-silver**, 10.5 for pure silver, 10.2–10.3 for **sterling silver**, 12.9–14.6 for 14-**karat gold** (compared to 19.3 for pure gold), and 21.5 for pure **platinum** (multiply these values by 1,000 for kg/m^3). *See also* PALLADIUM; PLATINUM FLUTE; TITANIUM; WALL (1).

DESCANT. Also *discant*. In the 17th century, the highest-pitched member of a family of musical instruments, for example, the descant **flute** or descant **recorder**. *See also* FLAUTINO (2); RENAISSANCE FLUTE.

DESK. 1. The part of a music stand that holds the music. 2. A music stand in an **ensemble**. The "first **flute** desk" is the music stand that is used by the **first flutist** in an ensemble. 3. Same as **chair**.

DESSUS DE FLÛTE. Fr. for the sopranino **recorder** in the late Baroque.

DÉTACHÉ. Fr. detached. An **articulation** that directs the player to perform a series of notes slightly separated or detached from each other. Also called **staccato**.

DÉTIMBRÉ. Fr. discolored, faded. A sound with fewer **overtones** than usual. Some **flutists** may describe this sound as "**hollow**." The opposite of *timbré*.

DEVIENNE, FRANÇOIS (b. Joinville, Haute-Marne, France, 1759; d. Paris, 1803). A French **flute** and bassoon **soloist**, bassoonist at the Orchestre de l'Opéra in 1779 and other French **ensembles**, sergeant of administration at the Musique de la Garde Nationale (forerunner of the **Paris Conservatoire**) in 1793, prolific composer, author of a famous *Méthode* (1794; see bib. under "Historical Methods, Treatises, and Tutors") for the **one-keyed flute**, and a flute professor at the Paris Conservatoire from 1795 to 1803, where he taught the first flute class. *See also* CLASSICAL FLUTE.

D FOOT JOINT. Abbr. D foot. A **foot joint** that gets its name because the lowest note that can be produced is D_1. It consists of a short piece of **tubing** with a $D\sharp$ **key** and a $D\sharp$ **tone hole** (see app. 7, fig. 12, far right).

The D foot joint was common on 18th- and early 19th-century **flutes** (*see* ONE-KEYED FLUTE), but in more recent times, only a few have been made for modern flutes. It may be used on occasion, instead of a regular **C** or **B foot joint**, because:

- it is good for extended practicing since it is shorter and lighter;
- it **responds** more easily and evenly in the **low register**, particularly **low D_1** and $E\flat_1$, making it useful for some music, such as Baroque music, in which the low register is commonly featured.

Some **flutists** feel that the tone of the modern **concert flute** with a D foot joint tends to be less **dark**, **projecting**, and **full** than the flute with either a C or B foot joint. Some also feel that it is too **sharp** in the **third register** and that its shortness changes the balance of the flute because there is less weight at the end. The change in balance may be a problem for some people. *See also* B/C CONVERTIBLE FOOT JOINT; B♭ FOOT JOINT; BOEHM FLUTE; SOUNDING LENGTH (3). For **early flutes** and other non-**Boehm-system** flutes, *see also* CONICAL BORE; EXTENDED FOOT JOINT; FOOT REGISTER; IRISH FLUTE (1); SIX-KEYED FLUTE.

DIAPHRAGM. A dome-shaped (rather like an upturned salad bowl) involuntary muscle separating the chest and abdominal cavities. The diaphragm helps us to inhale. By contracting downward and flattening, it allows the lungs to expand, and air is drawn in. Upon exhalation, the diaphragm relaxes and moves upward, resuming its dome-like shape. It is not used when exhaling, despite many assertions to the contrary in **flute** literature. *See also* ABDOMINAL VIBRATO; BREATH SUPPORT; DIAPHRAGMATIC BREATHING; DIAPHRAGM KICK.

DIAPHRAGMATIC BREATHING. A term erroneously used to mean **abdominal breathing**. The **diaphragm** is an involuntary muscle that assists only in inhaling, not in blowing air out.

DIAPHRAGM KICK. Same as **abdomen kick**. This usage is erroneous, however, since the **diaphragm** is not used for blowing (or "kicking") air out. *Syn.:* diaphragm accent, diaphragm thrust.

DIAPHRAGM VIBRATO. *See* ABDOMINAL VIBRATO.

DICK, ROBERT (b. New York City, 1950). A renowned American **flute** player, teacher, composer, flute designer, recording artist, and author in the contemporary music field. *See also* BASS FLUTE (4); CIRCULAR BREATHING; GHOST TONE; MULTIPHONIC; RESIDUAL TONE; ROAR FLUTTER; ROBERT DICK GLISSANDO HEADJOINT; THROAT TUNING.

DIE. Pl. *dies.* **1.** A tool for cutting out, shaping, or **stamping** raw material. There are various types of dies used in flutemaking, depending on the shape desired. A *forming* or **casting** *die* may be used to make keywork. It consists of a **steel** mold in two parts, each shaped to the profile required. They are brought together, and liquid metal is forced under **pressure** into the cavity. Once set, the two halves are opened to reveal a cast component. A *stamping die* may also be used to make keywork. It con-

sists of a die plate with one side formed to a particular shape. Metal is placed on the die and a huge press, often with the opposite side of the die pattern on the ramming part of the press, slams down on the metal, forcing it into the shape of the die. A *drawing die* is used to make flute **tubing** and **rings**. A *screw-cutting die* is used to make flute screws. It consists of a circular piece of hardened steel with an internal threaded hole. Cutting edges are produced by boring three other holes arranged around the central one and overlapping it. The tool is held in a special holder, usually on a **lathe**, and fed onto the end of a plain circular bar or rod. As the bar revolves, it draws the die onto itself, which then cuts the thread. *See also* COLD DRAWING; DAP (2); EXTRUDING; EXTRUSION; FORGING. **2.** *v.* To cut, form, or stamp with a die.

DIFFERENCE TONE. A faint note resulting from sounding two notes of very different **pitch** simultaneously. This phenomenon is more obvious if the notes are of a **pure tone**, that is, without **harmonics**. The **frequency** of the difference tone is the arithmetical difference in frequency between these two notes (or their multiples). It will sound more like a buzzing than a note, and softer and usually lower in pitch than the lower of the two notes. For example, if two **flutists** play notes with a frequency of 1,319 Hz (i.e., E_3) and 1,047 Hz (C_3), the major third will be heard together with a third note with a frequency of 272 Hz (1,319 Hz minus 1,047 Hz equals 272 Hz, a note that lies between C_1 and $C_{\#1}$). When the two notes are very close together, the pitch of the difference tone is too low to be heard as a note, and a **beating** effect is experienced instead.

Some **flutists** use this acoustical phenomenon to help them with their **tuning**. To do this, flutists listen to the difference tone in relation to the two notes being played. In the example above, the frequencies for the interval are those of an **equal-tempered** third. This, to some, is an unpleasant interval in a sustained chord and the difference tone needs to be **tuned** by adjusting the interval. This is done by changing the pitch of one of the two notes, usually by **flattening** E_3, to make a just third (*see* JUST INTONATION), an interval with a frequency ratio of 5:4, so that the frequency and therefore the pitch of the difference tone is lowered and sounds as C_1 (262 Hz).

The phenomenon is observable in Georg Philipp Telemann's **recorder** duets, where a three-part chord can be heard when the upper two notes, the third and fifth, are played; the **fundamental** can also be heard loudly due to the purity of the recorder's tone. **Trevor Wye** wrote several trios for two flutes in his book *A Practice Book for the Flute*, vol. 4, *Intonation* (Borough Green, Sevenoaks, Kent, 1983), exploiting this curiosity.

Due to the absence of upper harmonics in the **second octave**, two flutes are ideal for demonstrating difference tones. *Syn.:* differential tone, beat note, Tartini's tone (after Italian violinist Giuseppe Tartini, who is said to have reported them ca. 1714), resultant tone. *See also* VOCALIZING/SINGING WHILE PLAYING.

DIRECTION. A **phrasing** concept in which the music should sound as though it is moving toward a goal, such as a particular note or chord. The **flutist** uses various **techniques** to make the music flow, including varying the dynamics, **vibrato**, **articulation**, **tone color**, time, and rhythm. *See also* GROUPING.

DIRECT-MOUNT. A **key mechanism** that is mounted on **posts** that are directly attached to the flute **body** instead of being attached to **ribs** or **straps**. On metal flutes, the posts are soldered directly to the flute's body. On wooden flutes, the post ends are threaded and then screwed directly into tapped holes in the body. Direct-mounting is less common and less preferable to **rib-mounting** (see RIBS for reasons why). *See also* KEY-MOUNT; POST-MOUNT.

DISCANT. Same as **descant**.

DISCANTFLÖTE. Ger. for alto **recorder** in G in the Renaissance and alto recorder in F in the late Baroque.

DISH. A term used by flutemakers and repairers to describe the concave shape of some **flute** parts, such as the middle part of a key **cup** (i.e., the **dap**).

DOLZFLÖTE. Ger. for transverse **recorder** around 1600.

DONUT. *See* LOWER G INSERT.

DORUS, LOUIS (b. Vincent-Joseph Van Steenkiste in Valenciennes, Nord, France, 1813; d. Etrétat, France, 1896). A renowned French **flutist** who was the **principal flutist** in various French orchestras, a flute professor at the **Paris Conservatoire** from 1860 to 1868, a designer of the **Dorus G♯ key**, a composer, and an author of a **method** for **Boehm** 1832 **flute**. *See also* RING-KEY FLUTE.

DORUS G♯ KEY. A two-key configuration that was designed, but unpatented, by **flutist Louis Dorus** and used by Parisian flutemakers **Vincent Godfroy**, **Louis Lot**, and **Auguste Buffet** *jeune* from 1838 as an alternative to the open G♯ key of **Boehm**'s 1832 **flute** (see RING-KEY FLUTE). It was introduced in an attempt to maintain **Theobald Boehm**'s concept of **open-standing keys**, while at the same time giving older players the same G♯ **action** they had been used to on **simple-system flutes**.

The Dorus G♯ key assembly consists of two open-standing **keys**: a **ring key** named G over the A **tone hole**, which is operated by L3, and a padded key **cup** named G♯ over the G♯ tone hole, with a rigidly attached **lever** that is activated by L4 (see fig 12, *left*). Both keys rotate on the same **shaft**, but each has its own needle **spring** of differing strengths, a stronger spring for the ring key and a weaker one for the key cup. The ring key is linked to the key cup by means of a **clutch**. When only the ring key is depressed (see fig. 12, *right*), both keys, united by the clutch, close to produce the note G. When both the ring key and lever are depressed (see fig. 12, *middle*), the G♯ cup remains open and G♯ sounds. This retains the preferred traditional function the lever had as a **closed-standing key** on the older simple-system flutes (the

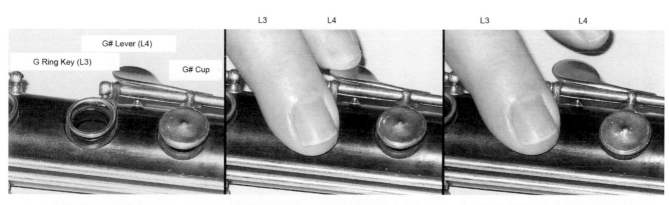

| G# Lever (L4) | | L3   L4 | L3   L4 |

G Ring Key (L3)   G# Cup

G Ring Key and G# Cup Open | When both the Ring Key (L3) and the G# Lever (L4) are depressed, the G# Cup remains open and G# Sounds | When only the Ring Key (L3) is depressed both the Ring Key and G# KeyCup close producing G.

Figure 12. **The Dorus G♯ key from a cocuswood conical Boehm flute made by Claire Godfroy aîné, Paris, ca. 1845.** *Photo courtesy Rick Wilson.*

commonly used closed G♯ key on modern flutes has exactly the same function). But unlike the simple-system flutes and the modern flute, the lever does nothing when the ring key is *not* depressed, and L4 may be allowed to rest on it for notes above G♯, thus stabilizing the flute.

One aspect of the Dorus G♯ key as compared to the modern closed G♯ key is that it did not require a **duplicate G♯ tone hole**. Some players felt that any extra tone hole harmed the tone because the **bore** was not as smooth. Another aspect is that the axle was on the opposite side of the flute from the player, unlike the modern **key mechanism** where the main axles are on the player's side.

The Dorus G♯ key had some disadvantages because it relied on two opposing springs of differing strengths. They were difficult to adjust to the correct tension and, even when properly adjusted, resulted in a feel for the player that was not uniform and possibly bothersome to some. The more powerful spring also made the G♯/A **trill** more difficult.

Overall, the Dorus G♯ key was a success because it retained the old G♯ **fingering**, and thus it was commonly used until the 1860s introduction of the side or **independent G♯** key commonly used today. Lot, for example, first mentions the side G♯ on flute no. 479, made July 31, 1860 (*see* G♯ key #1).

Despite the fact that the Dorus G♯ contrivance is really comprised of two open-standing keys, it is sometimes confusingly referred to as a *closed G♯ key* because it functions like a traditional closed G♯ key when the ring key is depressed. *See also* CLOSED KEY; CYLINDRICAL BOEHM FLUTE (1); OPEN KEY.

DOUBLE ACTION. Same as **lost motion**.

DOUBLE BASS FLUTE. British term for the bass **recorder** in the late Baroque.

DOUBLE CASE. Same as **combination case**. *Cf.* **single case**.

DOUBLE CONTRABASS FLUTE. Same as **subcontrabass flute in C**.

DOUBLE CONTR'ALTO FLUTE IN G. Same as **subcontr'alto flute in G**.

DOUBLE-SKIN. Refers to key **pads** that are covered by a double layer of **fishskin**. Pads are normally made with two **skins**, the extra layer providing a backup if the outer skin gets damaged, allowing the **flute** to continue to be played until the pad is replaced. *Syn.:* double bladder-skin

DOUBLE STOP. Two notes sounded together. *Syn.:* two-note **multiphonic**. *Cf.* **triple stop**.

DOUBLE TONGUING. A type of **multiple tonguing** where two syllables, such as "tu ku," "thu ku," or "du ku," are used to facilitate the **tonguing** of notes in fast passages where **single tonguing** is not possible (sixteenth notes, etc.). In these situations, double tonguing can ease fatigue and tension of the tongue. This applies whenever notes are grouped in two or multiples of two.

For double tonguing, two parts of the tongue are used alternately to silently pronounce the syllables, one for each note. In each group of two using the pattern *tu-ku*, the first note is played with *tu* and the second with *ku*, as in:

The position and stroke of the tongue for *tu* is the same as for single tonguing. For the *ku* syllable, the middle part touches the hard **palate** (see app. 13, fig. 3). The syllables are repeated rapidly for the length of the passage.

Note that in certain cases, such as where a rest, a tie, or a **slur** interrupts the normal multiple-of-two grouping, some **flutists** find it easier to repeat the syllable *tu* to articulate both the first and following note, as in:

Historically, a large variety of syllables has been used to suggest two different movements of the tongue. **Johann Joachim Quantz**, for example, in his famous 1752 **treatise** *Versuch*, suggests using "did'll" for the fastest notes, as they can be somewhat smoother, though perhaps less distinct, than the modern *tu-ku*. In addition to this double tonguing, flutists in the Baroque era often used a pair of syllables, such as *tu-ru* or *ti-ri*, in passages of moderate quickness. In this case, it was expected that the syllables would produce an uneven rhythm; the *ru* or *ri* syllable was longer and on the beat, and the *tu* or *ti* before the beat. *See also* TREMOLO (2); TRIPLE TONGUING.

DOUBLING. Within the context of an **ensemble**, either of the following: **1.** Playing two or more different instruments in the same performance. For example, a **flutist** may double on the **piccolo**, saxophone, or clarinet, among others. *See also* SECOND FLUTIST; THIRD FLUTIST. **2.** Playing the same part in unison with (or an octave higher than) another instrumentalist. For example, a piccoloist may play the same part in unison with (or an octave higher than) a flutist, thus doubling the flutist or it could be said that the flutist is doubling the piccoloist.

DRAWING. A process used in metalworking to shape or elongate material. **Flute** parts with a constant cross-section (e.g., wire or **body tubing**) are usually drawn, in factories that may also make such components for other industries such as jewelry making. **Annealed** metal is pulled through a hole in a **die** or a draw-plate (a **steel** plate with one or more holes). The material reduces in size and takes on the shape of the hole. The process is repeated with dies that have progressively smaller holes, until the part reaches the desired diameter and shape.

Most **head joints** are drawn to the desired **taper** by flutemakers from factory-made cylindrical tubing. The tubing is placed over a steel **mandrel** that has the shape of the finished **head**. The tube, along with the mandrel, is then forced through a flexible donut-shaped draw-plate to impart the shape. *See also* BODYMAKER; COLD DRAWING; COLD WORKING; DRAWN TONE HOLES; DRAWN TUBING; TUBE/TUBING (1).

DRAWN TONE HOLES. Tone holes surrounded by short cylindrical tubes that are "drawn" continuously out from the flute **tube** by a special hole-making machine (all holes at once) or by hand (one hole at a time) with a special pulling tool operated by a craftsman. The earliest drawn tone holes had straight **chimneys**, with no rolled edges. Today, the top edges of the drawn tone hole chimneys are rounded outward or "rolled" (see app. 7, fig. 16, *right*). Drawn tone holes are usually seen on flutes with thicker tubing since, if the tubing is too thin, the **drawing** process will crack the tone hole.

Drawn tone holes were invented by flutemaker **George W. Haynes** in 1898. He was the first to make a flute with drawn tone holes (**DCM** 0118), but it was **William S. Haynes**, his brother and the more business-like of the two, who filed the patent in 1914.

There is controversy in the flute community as to whether the flute sound is improved by drawn tone holes or **soldered tone holes**. Two things that are not disputed, however, are that both drawn and soldered tone holes affect the **intonation** in terms of the placement, diameter, and height of the chimney and that the labor costs are higher for soldered tone holes, because they take longer to make. *Syn.:* extruded tone holes, integral tone holes. *See also* AURUMITE; BODYMAKER; BOEHM FLUTE (1); EXTRUSION (2); FACTORY-MADE FLUTE; HANDMADE FLUTE; INTERMEDIATE FLUTE; PROFESSIONAL FLUTE; ROLLED TONE HOLES; SADDLE (1); STUDENT FLUTE; UNDERCUTTING (2); WALL (1).

DRAWN TUBING. Tubing made by using a **drawing** process. The first drawn flute tubes were made by **George W. Haynes** and **William S. Haynes** in 1898.

Most metal flutes today are made with drawn tubing. *Syn.:* seamless tubing. *See also* BOEHM FLUTE (1); GOLD FLUTE (1); SEAMED TUBING; WALL (1).

DRELINGER, SANFORD (b. New York, 1943). An American Boehm **head joint** designer and maker, author of *Drelinger Headjoint Company Questions and Answers*, **flutist**, and engineer. *See also* AIR REED (2); UPRITE HEADJOINT; VERTICAL FLUTE; VERTICAL HEAD JOINT.

D♯ TRILL KEY/LEVER. *See* TRILL KEYS. *See also* ROCK-STRO F♯ LEVER.

D TRILL KEY/LEVER. *See* TRILL KEYS. *See also* MURRAY FLUTE.

DUCT FLUTE. Any of a family of **flutes** that use a whistle-type **mouthpiece** (see fig. 13) to produce the sound, including the **recorder**, **tin whistle**, **tabor pipe**, and **flageolet** (see app. 1, figs. 1–5 for examples of duct flutes). **Finger holes**, or some other means for producing different pitches, differentiate the duct flute from a simple **whistle** (def. 1). The sound is produced when air is blown through a slit-shaped channel (the *duct* or *flue*) in the mouthpiece at the top end and directed against the sharp edge (*lip*) at the base of a large hole (*mouth* or *window*) cut in the **body** just below the mouthpiece. The duct may be internal (most common), external (e.g., Javanese suling), or both (e.g., pre-Columbian Mexican and Apache flutes). Even the player's tongue can act as a duct by protruding into the otherwise open end. The geometry of the duct and mouth are critical for tone and **response**, but both vary widely because people have different ideas of what constitutes an ideal sound (e.g., Baroque recorders versus modern versions). Duct flutes are made of many materials such as clay, wood, cane, plastic, or metal. *Syn.:* whistle flute. *See also* FIPPLE FLUTE; *FISTULA* (1); *FLÛTE* (1); FLUTE FAMILY (1); PANPIPES. For information about other flute classifications, *see* END-BLOWN FLUTE; GLOBULAR FLUTE; MULTIPLE FLUTE; NOSE FLUTE; NOTCHED FLUTE; OVERTONE FLUTE; SIDE-BLOWN FLUTE; VERTICAL FLUTE; VESSEL FLUTE.

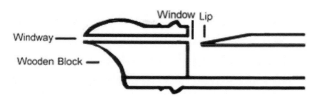

Figure 13. The whistle-type mouthpiece of a recorder. *Drawing by Tess Vincent.*

DUET/DUO. 1. An **ensemble** of two musicians. Popular pairings include a **flute** duo, flute and guitar, flute and harp, and flute and violin. **2.** A **piece** for two musicians.

DUPLICATE G♯ TONE HOLE. 1. On the **flute** with a closed **G♯ key**, the **tone hole** under the lower **G key**. The purpose of this tone hole is to correct the **venting** problem for $A_{1/2}$ by being open when either of these two notes is played. This follows the principle of **Theobald Boehm**'s **open-key system**, which did not allow any closed tone holes immediately below the one from which the tone is being emitted (i.e., below the **sounding hole**). If there was no duplicate G♯ tone hole, $A_{1/2}$ would sound muffled and **flat**. Boehm himself violated his own principle, however, by producing a closed G♯ flute with no duplicate hole. The A was muffled and the design was never copied. *Syn.:* in-line G♯ tone hole, bodyline G♯ tone hole, mainline G♯ tone hole, alternate G♯ tone hole. *See also* DORUS G♯ KEY; DUPLICATE TONE HOLES; LOWER G INSERT; RF MODIFICATION; SPLIT E MECHANISM. **2.** The term may also incorrectly refer to the tone hole under the closed G♯ key **cup**. This naming has probably been used because Boehm's original flute had the G♯ tone hole on top of the flute (under the G key cup; see fig. 20, *top*), and when the **independent G♯ tone hole** was introduced by **Louis Lot** about 1860, it became, historically, the new or "duplicate" hole. In reality, however, the most functional G♯ hole shifted from the top to the side when the new hole was added.

DUPLICATE KEYS. Either duplicate **touches/levers** or duplicate **plates/cups** with the same letter name. Duplicate **keys** serve various purposes. They may be used to make difficult **passages** easier to play, to allow for improved **venting**, or to enable automatic control of another key.

On the modern **Boehm flute**, there are very few duplicate keys. On Boehm flutes with a closed **G♯ key**, two **G key** cups allow for the **flutist** to use the traditional **fingering** for $G♯_{1/2}$ (i.e., the fingering used on the **simple-system flute**), while at the same time allowing for the proper venting of A_1 or A_2. On many Boehm flutes, there are duplicate B♭ key touches: the B♭ **thumb key** touch, and the B♭ **side lever** key touch. When either of these key touches is activated, it causes the connecting B♭ key cup to cover the same B **tone hole**. If both of these key touches are present on a **flute**, they offer the flutist different fingering choices for $B♭_{1/2}$, which can ease finger **technique** (see B♭ FINGERINGS). Some Boehm flutes have **left-hand levers** that allow, in certain situations, for the flutist to operate the **foot joint** keys more easily with the left hand instead of the right hand (see app. 6, fig. 1).

See also HIGH G♯ MECHANISM; MURRAY FLUTE; QUARTER-TONE FLUTE; SIMMONS F♯ KEY; SPLIT A KEY (2).

On the simple-system flute, duplicate keys for the notes outside the **natural scale** are sometimes provided. The most common (on the **flute in D**, so called after its lowest **six-fingered note**) are keys for the notes F and B♭, in both the **first** and **second octaves**, but duplicate keys for the notes G♯, E♭, and C may also be present. The reason for these five duplicate keys is to facilitate passages (especially those that are **slurred**) that would otherwise be difficult or impossible if the normal keys were used. *See also* DUPLICATE TONE HOLES; SIX-KEYED FLUTE.

DUPLICATE TONE HOLES. Two **tone holes** with the same letter name. They serve two purposes: to ensure correct **venting**, and to make difficult **passages** easier to play—although the latter applies only when the holes are provided with **duplicate keys**. On the standard modern **Boehm flute** with a closed **G♯ key**, there is only one duplicate tone hole: the **duplicate G♯ tone hole** under the lower **G key**. It serves to prevent a venting problem for $A_{1/2}$ that would occur if there were only one G♯ tone hole.

On the **simple-system flute**, the duplicate holes are normally associated with duplicate keys. They may control the same tone hole or duplicate tone holes, depending on the maker's preference. The most frequently seen duplicate keys for the simple-system flute are those for the note F in both the **first** and **second octaves**. Often these keys controlled duplicate tone holes, one under the short or cross-F key and the other under the long F key (see app. 6, C, fig. 3). In this and most other simple-system duplicate-hole cases, it is really the duplicate keys that simplify passages, not the duplicate holes.

See also COLTMAN C♯; C♯ TRILL KEY; HIGH G♯ MECHANISM; ROCKSTRO MODEL FLUTE; SIMMONS F♯ KEY. For **early flutes** and other non-**Boehm-system** flutes, *see also* *BRILLE* (1); REFORM FLUTE (1).

DUVERGER, NICHOLAS. A flute professor at the **Paris Conservatoire** from 1795 to 1802.

ℰ

EARLY FLUTE. An ambiguous term, but one which usually refers to historical pre-**Boehm flutes** of the medieval, **Renaissance, Baroque,** and **Classical** periods and sometimes the Romantic period. *See also* AFRICAN BLACKWOOD; *AÎNÉ;* ARTICULATED KEY; AUGMENTED NOTES; COCUSWOOD; FOOT JOINT; FRUITWOOD (1); *JEUNE;* LEATHERS; *NACH;* PAD IMPRESSION; RANGE (2); SIMPLE-

SYSTEM FLUTE (1, 3); STANDARD FLUTE (1); TONE HOLES (1); TUNING RINGS; VEILED TONE (1).

EAR TRAINING. Exercises used to train musicians to listen more acutely so that they will become more musically aware. There are many different ear-training exercises. In general, they involve trying to hear and identify one aspect of a musical composition in isolation. This might be the **pitches** of individual notes, the intervals, the chords, the rhythmic patterns, the melodies, or other elements. Ear training is an integral part of the requirements in many practical instrumental exams. *See also* RELATIVE PITCH.

EBONITE. A hard, black, nonresilient, strong, durable, shiny (when polished) rubber that has been vulcanized with sulfur. It was first used in flutemaking around 1851 to make various parts, such as the **tubing, embouchure plates**, and **rollers. Alfred G. Badger** was the earliest musical instrument maker to use ebonite.

Ebonite became quite popular in flutemaking, particularly because it was such a stable material. For example, it did not have the moisture-absorbing problem of wood, which could cause warpage or cracking, and it was not affected by temperature changes as was **silver**, which caused the overall **pitch** of the instrument to change. In fact, flute designer **Richard Shepherd Rockstro** (treatise, 1890) thought it to be the best material ever used for flute tubing. There was, however, one drawback: Ebonite turned an ugly greenish-brown with extended exposure to strong ultraviolet light.

Ebonite is still made, but at the moment it is not a popular flutemaking material. *Syn.:* hard rubber, vulcanite. *See also* COCUSWOOD; REFORM FLUTE (1).

EBONY. 1. A black, satiny (when polished), hard, heavy, and durable type of tropical hardwood that is a member of the genus *Diospyros* and grows in Asia and Africa. It was used in flutemaking during the **Baroque** and **Classical** periods to make various parts, such as **bodies** and **head joints**, and is used for the making of replicas today. Flutemaker **Johann Joachim Quantz** preferred to use ebony for his flutes. **2.** Any of several tropical, dense, dark-colored woods similar to true ebony, such as "Mozambique ebony" (**African blackwood**). *See also* COCUSWOOD; ONE-KEYED FLUTE.

EDGE TONE. A sound that is produced, in the absence of a nearby resonator, when a moving stream of air directed at an edge—such as at the edge of a tautly held piece of paper—divides in such a way that it moves continuously from one side of the edge to the other. In the case of paper, the sound produced is a feeble, high-pitched, airy whistle. The initial sound that a **flute** produces when a **flutist** blows at the **blowing edge** is an edge tone, but in this case, the pure edge tone is not usually sustained, because the **resonances** of the **bore** influence the **air jet**. Instead, the jet is "captured" and amplified by a resonance in the **tubing** that has a similar **frequency**.

EDIT. To prepare a **work** for publication or performance. The basic tasks of the editor of musical works are to find the surviving sources of the work and establish a text based on those sources, including correcting errors. Editors may also suggest performance markings (e.g., **articulations**, dynamics, breathing marks, etc.). In certain kinds of edition (see CRITICAL EDITION; SCHOLARLY EDITION; *URTEXT*), the editorial decisions are clearly differentiated from what is found in the sources. In the kind of **performer's edition** popular in the 19th and earlier 20th centuries, now going out of fashion, there was no such differentiation. Editions of the same work by different editors can vary, to a smaller or larger extent, depending on the nature and quality of the editorial research. *See also* COLLECTION; FACSIMILE.

E♭ FLUTE. An uncommon member of the **Boehm flute** family (see FLUTE FAMILY [2]), **pitched** in E♭, sounding a minor third above the **concert flute** in C. The E♭ flute is **side-blown** like the concert flute, uses the same **fingering system**, and, except for small playing changes, is played in a similar way. Its **range** is around three octaves from the note sounding as $E♭_1$ to $E♭_4$ (written C_1 to C_4; *see* TRANSPOSING INSTRUMENTS), and it is about 22.5 in. (57 cm) long.

It is not certain when the first E♭ flute was made, but it is clear from the number of extant flutes that its development generally followed that of the concert flute and that it was more popular in earlier times than it is today.

Simple-system five- or **six-keyed conical** E♭ flutes can still be found in the **flute bands** of Ireland and Scotland today and are usually named *E♭ sopranos, E♭ flutes,* or *piccolos*—and not after their **six-fingered note**, F, as might be expected. In the bands that use them, there is usually only one player, who plays the "top" or "piccolo" **part**, which is referred to as "soprano" in the music. One-keyed E♭ flutes are still being made for some beginners of the **Baroque flute** who find it too difficult to reach the **finger holes** on a full-size Baroque **flute in D**.

Very little music has been specifically written for the E♭ flute, and it is not commonly played. It may be heard in some **flute choirs** or in small **ensembles** such as flute **quartets**. Its employment can enrich the overall **tone quality** of the flutes and the piccolos in a band. It can also be used as a substitute for the E♭ clarinet in large ensembles when this type of clarinet is unavailable. It is not, however, a regular member of the band or symphony orchestra. Students who are too small to hold the concert flute will find the E♭ flute a suitable beginning instrument.

Today the E♭ flute is sometimes referred to as an *E♭ soprano flute, flute in E♭,* **flute in the key of E♭, flute pitched in E♭,** *soprano flute in E♭, treble flute in E♭,* or *Terzflöte* (*terz* is German for "third"). *See* app. 1.

EGG, LES (1944–). Maker of **Boehm flutes**, flute repairer, and author who introduced the **O-ring** (a **stopper**).

EIGHT-KEYED FLUTE. 1. A **simple-system** (or **keyed**) **transverse flute** that evolved from, and was similar to, the earlier wooden or **ivory conical-bored one-keyed flute** in D except that it had eight keys (see app. 2, figs. 8 and 9). It was common in all of Europe in the 19th century and into the 20th and was the most common type of simple-system flute in England. It has been revived in modern times, and some people play originals (or replicas) of the instrument for Classical or Romantic-period music.

The most common type of eight-keyed flute had six **closed-standing keys** (namely, the B♭, G♯, C, short and long F keys), a closed D♯ key, and two **open-standing keys** (i.e., the C and C♯ keys) on an **extended foot joint**. (Of interest is that almost all simple-system flutes with more than eight keys include these eight keys.) *See also* app. 4; ARTICULATED KEY; EQUISONANT FLUTE; FIVE-KEYED FLUTE; FOUR-KEYED FLUTE; GLASS FLUTE; GUILLOU, JOSEPH; IRISH FLUTE; KEYED FLUTE; NINE-KEYED FLUTE; OLD SYSTEM (2); PRATTEN'S PERFECTED; RUDALL; SICCAMA DIATONIC FLUTE; SIX-KEYED FLUTE; TEN-KEYED FLUTE; TULOU *FLÛTE PERFECTIONÉE*; TWO-KEYED FLUTE.

2. An eight-keyed flute with an extra B♭ **lever** that controls a single B♭ **tone hole** with another B♭ lever. One is a full key with **shank, flap,** and **touch,** and the other is just a lever. For example, **Theobald Boehm's** (1794–1881) and **Rudolph Greve's** (1806–1862) simple-system flutes often have an extra B♭ lever. *See also* nine-keyed flute.

3. Generically, any 19th-century simple-system flute. This usage should be avoided, however, because these instruments can have anywhere from 4 to 20 keys.

ELASTIC BALLS/PLUGS. Same as **purse pads**.

ELBOW. Same as **bow** or **crook**.

EMBELLISHMENT. Same as **ornament**.

EMBOUCHURE. Fr. mouthpiece. **1.** The form that the lips and surrounding muscles take when a **wind instrument** is played. This may include their position in relation to the **flute**. Although there are certain aspects about the embouchure that are common amongst **flutists**, the shape varies from person to person depending on the characteristics of the lips. Also called *"lip"* or *"chops."* The expression "set [or form] your embouchure" means that the flutist should get the lips and surrounding muscles set up in the correct way for playing the flute. *See also* ALEXANDER TECHNIQUE; ANCHOR-TONGUE EMBOUCHURE; APERTURE; BREATHY SOUND/TONE; CHARANGA FLUTE (1); FLUTE (1); FLUTE FAMILY (2); OVERBLOWING; SIDE EMBOUCHURE; SMILE EMBOUCHURE; SOUNDING LENGTH (2); TEARDROP EMBOUCHURE; TECHNIQUE; TEMPERAMENT; TONE COLOR; TUNING SLIDE (1); TUNING UP (1); VERTICAL FLUTE; WINGED-LIP PLATE. For **early flutes**, *see also* NICHOLSON'S IMPROVED FLUTE; ONE-KEYED FLUTE; VEILED TONE (1). **2.** May refer to the **embouchure plate**, the **embouchure hole**, the area immediately surrounding the embouchure hole, or any combination of these parts, and sometimes also the **riser**. *See also REFORMMUNDLOCH;* STOPPER.

EMBOUCHURE BAND. Same as **lip plate ferrule**.

EMBOUCHURE BARREL. A type of cylindrical or barrel-shaped metal **embouchure plate** that surrounded the **tubing** of the **head joint** at the **embouchure hole** location on some **flutes** in the later part of the 19th century (see app. 5, fig. 3). The main purpose of the embouchure barrel was to add some thickness at the embouchure hole location so that the maker can shape the embouchure (e.g., by undercutting) and so preserve the flute's acoustical properties.

In its earlier form, the embouchure barrel was made of wood or **ivory**. Later, it was covered with a metal veneer that was usually made of the same metal as the tubing. Sometimes the material under the veneer was omitted, leaving an airspace. In this case, the embouchure hole and **embouchure wall** were formed by **soldering** a small tapered tube of suitable dimensions to the embouchure plate and head-joint tubing at the embouchure hole location.

The embouchure barrel type of embouchure plate did not become popular. One reason for this is probably because it added excessive weight to the head joint. *Syn.:* barrel embouchure plate, barrel mouthpiece. *Cf.* **lip plate ferrule**.

EMBOUCHURE BUSHING. Same as **embouchure-hole bushing**.

EMBOUCHURE HOLE. The hole in the **head joint** into or across which the **flutist** blows to produce a sound (see app. 7, fig. 11). Flutemakers use the size and shape of the embouchure hole, as well as the height and angle of the **walls** or **riser**, to define the tone, **response**, and **articulation** of their **flutes**.

The shape of the embouchure hole has changed throughout flute history. Early 18th-century *traversos* were generally cut with round holes of various sizes and tapers into the **bore** (see fig. 14, *left*). Late 18th-century and most 19th-century wooden flutes were generally cut with oval holes (see fig. 14, *middle*), reflecting the need for more air as more was asked of the flutes. It is a difficult task to make the hole big enough for sound but not *too* big, lest the **pitch**, response, and tone become wayward. The configuration of the embouchure hole also has to agree with the other dimensions of the flute.

The **Theobald Boehm**–style rounded rectangle (see fig. 14, *right*) was first introduced on his wooden 1832 System flutes (*see* RING-KEY FLUTE), and continued to be used on Boehm's wooden and later his **silver flutes**. Boehm recommended a hole size of 10 × 12 mm (0.39 × 0.47 in.), with the riser walls angled at 7°, but most of his flutes have holes slightly larger and walls much steeper.

French makers, such as **Louis Lot** and **Vincent Godfroy**, used Boehm's recommended rounded-rectangular shape and 7° walls on their silver flutes from the 1850s on. The Lot flute, and this **embouchure**, became the standard **professional flute** in the 20th century and is the basis of the "**French-model**" **flute** today. In the late 1920s, **William S. Haynes** and **Verne Q. Powell** used the Lot model for their **handmade flutes**, after having made wooden and silver flutes based on Boehm and **Carl Mendler**'s design, copying Boehm's rounded-rectangular hole and steeper (ca. 5°) sides, for many years.

Modern changes to Lot's Boehm-inspired embouchure have included the famous modifications of **Albert Cooper**, now retired, in which the embouchure hole is enlarged and the top east and west sides of the riser, and often the bottom part of these sides, are cut back and slightly rounded (see UNDERCUTTING [1]; OVERCUTTING). Many flutists agree that these modifications eliminate some of the **resistance** and have the effect of bypassing the work of creating strength in the quiet notes, for the benefit of ease in creating loud notes. Scholars differ over whether this has an overall salutary effect on the audience, but it does make it easier for the flutist to play loudly.

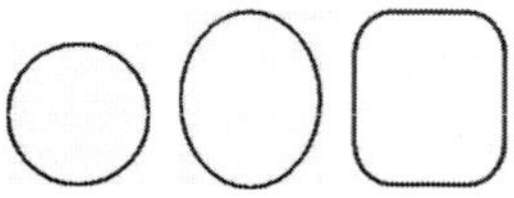

Figure 14. Embouchure hole shapes. *Drawing by Tess Vincent.*

Modern silver flute makers eschew the oval hole; it is too intimate for the force they seek. Wooden flute makers, especially those building on the English traditions (see IRISH FLUTES), continue to employ oval holes to great effect. *Syn.:* embouchure, blowhole, mouth hole, mouth tone hole, tone hole. *See also* ACOUSTIC IMPEDANCE SPECTRUM; AIR REED; BLOWING EDGE; BLOWING WALL; CHIMNEY (1); COVER (2); CUTOFF FREQUENCY; EMBOUCHURE PLATE; EMBOUCHURE RECUT; END CORRECTION; HELMHOLTZ RESONATOR; INLAYING (1); INTERNAL TUNING; INTONATION; KEY SLAP; LEADING EDGE; LINING; MODERN HEAD JOINT; NODE; OPEN EMBOUCHURE (1); OVERBLOWING; ROLL-IN; SOUNDING HOLE; STANDING WAVE; STOP (1); STOPPER; TRADITIONAL HEAD JOINT; VENTING (1); WING (1). For **early flutes**, *see also* EMBOUCHURE-HOLE BUSHING; NICHOLSON'S IMPROVED FLUTE.

EMBOUCHURE-HOLE BUSHING. A ring-shaped piece of metal, wood, or **ivory** that has been integrated into the part of a wooden **flute** surrounding the **embouchure hole** (see app. 3, A, fig. 7). It was most common in the 19th century. The renowned flutist **Charles Nicholson Jr.** (1795–1837) was a strong advocate of an **ivory bushing** (*see* NICHOLSON'S IMPROVED FLUTE). A **bushing** was added to prevent wear or damage, repair a worn or damaged embouchure hole, preserve the sharp **blowing edge**, or achieve a decorative effect. Some may have thought that a bushing of a different material than the **tube** helped to achieve an alternative tonal effect. *Syn.:* bushed embouchure, embouchure bushing, embouchure ring, insert. *See also* TONE-HOLE BUSHING.

EMBOUCHURE PLATE. An oval-shaped curved metal plate attached to the **head joint** upon which the **flutist** rests his lower lip when playing (see app. 7, figs. 10 and 11). The embouchure plate, in combination with the **riser**, in effect takes the place of the thick **wall** of the wooden flute **head** in the **blowhole** location. Since the walls of metal heads are much thinner, it is necessary to have a raised platform to recreate an **embouchure wall** or riser.

The curvature of the plate varies from maker to maker. Both the north part facing the audience and the south part nearest the player affect the tone of the **flute** and the shape of the south part can also affect how comfortable the embouchure plate will be on the mouth and chin. The shape of the sides of the embouchure plate on the edge of the blowhole can also influence the ease with which the player **focuses** the airstream.

Every maker offers its own style of embouchure plate that is said to improve the tone or to facilitate playing. Some embouchure plate shapes are so individual that they have been given names, one of these being the

"Reform embouchure" associated with **Otto Mönnig**'s flutes and *Reformmundloch* of the early 20th century, re-introduced more recently as the **winged lip plate**, which has a slightly raised area on both sides of the **embouchure hole**.

Syn.: **lip**, lip plate, **embouchure**, mouthpiece, mouth plate. *See also* AIR REED (2); ALCOHOL; BEVEL; BUFFING; BUTTERFLY HEADJOINT; COCUSWOOD; CUT; EBONITE; EMBOUCHURE BARREL; EMBOUCHURE RECUT; ENGRAVING; FALL-OFF; FLANGE; HEAD-JOINT MAKER; INLAYING (2); LIP PLATE FERRULE; MOISTURE TRIANGLE; MODERN HEAD JOINT; OVERCUTTING; PITTING; PROFESSIONAL FLUTE; RAISED EMBOUCHURE PLATE; REFORM FLUTE (1); RISER; ROLL-IN; SHEET METAL; SILVER FLUTE (1, 3); THINNED (HEAD OR BODY) JOINTS; VOICING.

EMBOUCHURE RECUT. A method intended to improve the tone, **response**, and dynamic capability of a **flute** by reshaping the **riser** that includes the areas where it meets the **embouchure plate** and the flute **tube**, and often the embouchure plate. This is achieved by taking material away from the **embouchure wall** with special tools. It should only be hand-done by an expert flute technician, as the **head joint** can be easily ruined by an unskilled worker.

Not all head joints are good candidates for recutting. For example, head joints with large **embouchure holes** are not a good choice because there is a limit as to how much material can be cut away, and as a result, there is less room for improvement. Inexpensive lower-quality head joints, usually found on **student flutes**, are not good contenders, either, since embouchure recutting is expensive and labor-intensive. Also, since most student flutes are made from **nickel-silver** or yellow **brass** which is plated, this operation could spoil the appearance of the **plating**, expose the **base metal**, and require replating.

Overall, embouchure recutting, if successful, could allow an improvement to take place in the playing abilities of a **flutist**, since the embouchure wall, including the area where it meets the embouchure plate, can be finely tuned to individual ideals of how a flutist would like to sound when playing. *See also* CUT; INLAYING (1); OVERCUTTING; UNDERCUTTING (1); VOICING.

EMBOUCHURE WALL. May refer to the **riser**, or to one of the four riser walls, but usually includes the width of the **embouchure plate** and the **tubing** to which the riser is attached. Sometimes referred to as simply a **wall** (2). *See also* BLOWING WALL; INTONATION; RESISTANCE (1); UNDERCUTTING (1, 3); VOICING.

E MECHANISM. Abbr. E mech. *See* SPLIT E MECHANISM.

END-BLOWN FLUTE. 1. Any of a family of **flutes** that produce a sound when air is blown against the sharp edge at the top open end of a **tube**. Some examples include the **shakuhachi** and **kena**. These flutes have a notch at the top end that acts as the blowing or voicing edge, so are also called *notched flutes*. End-blown flutes without a notch (e.g., North African and Middle Eastern *nay*) are also called *rim flutes* because the rim at the top end acts as the blowing edge. **Panpipes** are a set of end-blown flutes. The **Boehm-system** Wesley End-Blown Flute and **Giorgi flute** may also be called end-blown flutes. *See also* FLUTE FAMILY (1). For information about other flute classifications, *see* DUCT FLUTE; GLOBULAR FLUTE; MULTIPLE FLUTE; NOSE FLUTE; OVERTONE FLUTE; SIDE-BLOWN FLUTE; VESSEL FLUTE; VERTICAL FLUTE; WHISTLE. **2.** The term may refer to *any* flute that is held vertically downwards from the mouth, but scholars prefer the meaning to be restricted to definition 1.

END CAP. Same as **cap**.

END CORRECTION. The half-wavelength of the first **resonance** of a **pipe** open at both ends is slightly longer than the length of the pipe. The end correction is therefore a small extra length that must be added to the length of a **tube** at one end to make a correction for the way sound waves are radiated and reflected from the pipe (the "end effect") and thus to enable simple calculation of the resonant **frequencies** of the air in the tube. (This calculation is half-wavelength = effective length = real length + end effect at each end.)

Covering the **embouchure hole** with the lips affects the end correction. This can be demonstrated by comparing the sound the flute makes when a flutist plays an unblown key slap while his lower lip is over the embouchure hole in the usual playing position with his lower lip off the embouchure hole.

For a cylindrical tube, like that of the flute **body**, the end correction is about 0.6 times the radius of the tube. For an open hole, the situation is much more complicated and, in general, the end correction is greater than for a simple end. At frequencies approaching or exceeding the **cutoff frequency**, the concepts of effective length and end effect are not useful. *See also* SOUNDING LENGTH (2).

END EFFECT. *See* **end correction**.

END SNAPPERS. An old term used by the Haynes Company to refer to the two metal discs that are to either side of the **head joint cork**. *See also* CORK PLATES.

ENGLISH FLUTE. In the 18th century, one of the names for the **recorder**, used to distinguish it from the (**transverse**) **flute**, which was generally called the **German flute**. Also found in the form *common English flute* (*see* COMMON FLUTE).

ENGRAVING. A process whereby a tool is used to carve a design into the **flute** by metal removal. Engraving is used to imprint the maker's name and other information; embellish certain parts such as the **crown**, the **embouchure plate**, the **rings** (def. 2) surrounding the **tubing**, and the **rims** of key **cups** (see app. 10, figs. 2 and 4); or create a nonslip area on the embouchure plate where the mouth comes into contact. *See also* BOEHM FLUTE (1); CHASING; SERIAL NUMBER.

ENHARMONIC KEYS. *See* **two-keyed flute**.

ENSEMBLE. Fr. together, togetherness. **1.** A group of musicians of any size that plays music together. Most **flute** music is written to be played in an ensemble. *See also* A; CHAIR; CHARANGA FLUTE; CUE; DECIMETTE; DESK (2, 3); DOUBLING; DUET/DUO; EQUAL TEMPERAMENT; FIRST CHAIR FLUTIST; FIRST FLUTIST; FLUTE BAND; FLUTE CHOIR; INTERNAL TUNING; LEAD (1, 2); LYRE; MASTER CLASS; NONET; OCTET; PART; PITCH (2); PRINCIPAL FLUTIST; QUARTET; QUINTET; SECOND FLUTIST; SEPTET; SESSION; SEXTET; THIRD FLUTIST; TRIO; TUNING NOTE; TUNING UP; WIND QUINTET. For **early flute**s, *see also* FOOT REGISTER; RENAISSANCE FLUTE. **2.** The quality of togetherness in the performance of an ensemble.

EQUAL TEMPERAMENT. Abbr. ET. A **tuning system** in which all 12 semitones in an octave are set equal to each other. In this system, notes like B♭ and A♯ are *enharmonic;* in other words, they have the same **pitch**. As a pure octave has a frequency ratio of 2:1 (the **higher note** having twice the **frequency** of the lower), the frequency ratio of the ET semitone (let us call it r) must be such that r multiplied by itself 12 times equals 2—that is, r is the 12th root of 2, or 1.0595. Thus, in ET, a semitone rise increases the frequency by approximately 6 percent. For comparison, the semitone between the third and fourth or seventh and eighth notes of a major scale derived by **Just Intonation** has the ratio 16:15, which means a difference in frequency of approximately 6.7 percent, while other semitones have a variety of different ratios.

Apart from the octave, there are no Just intervals in ET. However, the fifths and fourths are very close. The thirds are clearly different: a Just major third is $5/4 = 1.250$ (386 cents), while an ET major third is r to the fourth power, or 1.260 (400 cents by definition). Although the ET third has moderately fast **beats**, especially when played on two flutes, listeners can get accustomed to the ET intervals and accept them as

correct **intonation**, particularly in melodic rather than harmonic context.

ET is especially practical for fixed-pitch instruments, such as the piano, since it allows instruments with 12 notes to the octave to modulate freely and to sound similar in all keys. Because the three strings struck by a single hammer in the piano are **tuned** to slightly different frequencies, the interference caused by thirds is well disguised. However, tuning problems arise when two or more strings or **winds** play in an **ensemble** with piano.

The flute **tone holes** are calculated and placed so that the intonation, without a player's compensation, is closer to ET than to Just Intonation (*see* SCALE). However, for various reasons, including unavoidable design compromises, the uncompensated intonation is never exactly ET. Fortunately, it is easy for a **flutist** to compensate and change the intonation with a combination of **air jet** speed and **embouchure hole** coverage. Consequently, a sensitive musician can play in agreement with the **sharp** major thirds of a piano, when required, and also play Just thirds to make a pleasant chord with another flutist. Experienced players often do this unconsciously.

Historically, ET was described in the West as early as the 16th century and became common in the 19th century. *See also* app. 3; BOEHM SYSTEM; COLE SCALE; DIFFERENCE TONE; EXPRESSIVE INTONATION (1); MEAN-TONE TEMPERAMENT; RING-KEY FLUTE; ROCKSTRO MODEL FLUTE; TEMPERAMENT; TUNER; TUNING (2); WELL-TEMPERAMENT.

EQUISONANT FLUTE. A development of the **eight-keyed conical flute** having no long F key, but with a **trill key** for D/C and D/C♯ **trills** and a right-hand **key mechanism** that retained the old F♯ fingering

$$1\ 2\ 3\ /\ 4\ -\ -\ \text{D}♯$$

and restored the old **forked** F fingering (but with the D♯ key) as

$$1\ 2\ 3\ /\ 4\ -\ 6\ \text{D}♯.$$

Possibly the most characteristic feature, however, is the thumb key, which when depressed can play either B♭ or C, depending on whether one or two left-hand holes are covered.

Flutist **John Clinton** (1810–1864) made these changes in an attempt to improve on the weaknesses of the **Boehm-system** flute (i.e., difficulties with: performing **passages** that included F♯ and/or B♭ in the **first** and **second octaves**; the **cross-fingerings**; and the **sharp** and thin **tone quality** in the **third octave** of the conical **Boehm flute**), while at the same time retaining the

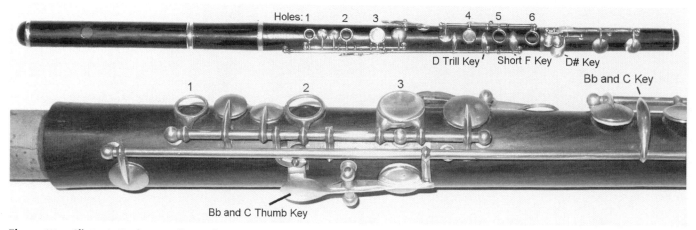

Holes: 1   2   3   4   5   6

D Trill Key   Short F Key   D# Key

Bb and C Key

1   2   3

Bb and C Thumb Key

Figure 15.   Clinton's Equisonant flute. *Photo courtesy Rick Wilson.*

preferred **simple-system** fingering. Clinton presented a new flute design to the Great Exhibition in 1851 (see fig. 15). It was manufactured for him by Henry Potter and continued to be made and sold by Potter. The name "Equisonant" was not applied to Clinton's flutes until they were being manufactured by Clinton and Co., set up in 1855. The term *Equisonant*, meaning "of the same or like sound," was applied to the flute in order to direct attention to its capability of producing all the notes of the flute with a uniform tone and **intonation**. The flute met with limited success. *See also* ORDINARY FLUTE (1).

ESSAY. *See* VERSUCH.

ET. 1. An abbreviation for **extended technique**. **2.** An abbreviation for **equal temperament**.

ÉTUDE. Fr. **study**.

EUTERPE. In ancient Greek mythology, one of the nine muses or goddesses, daughters of Mnemosyne and Zeus, who presided over music or lyric poetry. Euterpe is represented with a **flute**.

EXCERPTS. Passages selected from standard **works**, such as orchestra or opera works, because of their prominence or difficulty. At an audition, candidates are expected to know these passages very well and perhaps play them from memory. Collections of excerpts have been published for practice purposes, and individual **flute** parts can also be purchased from specialist flute music shops. The most commonly chosen excerpts from orchestra and opera audition lists around the world are listed in appendix 14. *See also* SOLO (3).

EXPRESSIVE INTONATION. 1. Adjusting the **pitch** of a note away from **equal temperament**, according to the position of the note in a chord and the prin-

ciple of **Just Intonation**, in order to improve the harmony. *See also* INTONATION. **2.** Purposely adjusting the pitch of a note, perhaps defying harmonic principles, in order to be expressive—for example, "blue notes" and raised leading notes. *See also* AUGMENTED FINGERINGS; AUGMENTED NOTES.

EXTENDED FOOT JOINT. 1. A **foot joint** that is longer than normal. The term is usually used only when speaking of a foot joint on some **two-keyed** and **simple-system flutes** in D (named after the **six-fingered note**) that enables the production of notes below D_1 (usually only **low C_1** and low $C_{\#1}$; e.g., *see* EIGHT-KEYED FLUTE; SIX-KEYED FLUTE). The term probably came about to distinguish such foot joints from the most commonly used foot joint of the time, the **D foot joint**, which enabled the production of notes only as low as D_1. *Syn.:* long foot. **2.** *See* B/C CONVERTIBLE FOOT JOINT. **3.** *See* FOOT REGISTER. **4.** *See* FOSTER EXTENSION. **5.** *See* IRISH FLUTE (1).

EXTENDED TECHNIQUE. Abbr. ET. A special effect arising from producing a sound on the **flute** by a means other than the traditional way of playing. Examples of extended techniques are the sounds obtained by **vocalizing/singing while playing**, when a key **cup** is slapped down (i.e., a **key slap**), or when two or more notes are played at the same time (*see* MULTIPHONIC). Other types of sounds that have been referred to as extended techniques include **Aeolian sound,** *bisbigliando,* **buzz-tone** (or trumpet sound), **flutter-tonguing, ghost tone, glissando, jet whistle, key vibrato, lip glissando, lip vibrato, microtone, note bending, percussive sound, roar-flutter, residual tone,** *smorzato,* **tongue click, tongue pizzicato, tongue ram, tongue slap, tongue stop, tongue thrust,** and **whistle tones.** There is a movement to ban the use of the term *extended technique* since many of these have become part of a **flutist's** basic **technique**

and are thus no more special than traditional techniques such as **double tonguing**, legato, or **staccato**. *See also* ANGLED HEAD JOINT; B FOOT JOINT; CROSS-FINGERING (1); HALF-HOLING; HARMONIC (3); OPEN-HOLE FLUTE; QUARTER-TONE FLUTE; ROLL-IN; STOP (1).

EXTENSION ARM. A thin piece of metal that connects one **key** or key part with another so that they may work together. For example, the **Briccialdi B♭ lever** has an extension arm that connects it to the **kicker** of the B♭ key (see app. 7, fig. 7) and the **split E mechanism** lever arches and pulls down the lower **G key** (see app. 9, fig. 4). *See also* ADJUSTMENT; BRIDGE; FLAT SPRING (1); KEY ARM; ROLLER.

EXTENSION SLEEVE. *See* B/C CONVERTIBLE FOOT JOINT; FOOT REGISTER; FOSTER EXTENSION.

EXTRUDED TONE HOLES. Same as **drawn tone holes**.

EXTRUDING. A process that flutemakers use to shape a material (usually metal) by forcing it through a **die**. *Syn.:* **extrusion**.

EXTRUSION. 1. The process of **extruding**, or forcing a material (usually metal) out of its regular position. The material is squeezed through a **die** by using a mechanical or hydraulic press. Extrusion of **flute** parts is usually done with cold parts, but may be done to parts at other temperatures not higher than approximately 50 to 75 percent of the metal's melting point. **2.** A flute part, such as a **drawn tone hole**, that a flutemaker has formed by extruding. *See also* **rolled tone holes**.

F

FABBRICIANI, ROBERTO (b. Arezzo, Italy, 1949). An international Italian **flute soloist**, flute professor,

composer, conductor, and designer of the **hyperbass flute**.

FACILITATOR. 1. High E facilitator (*see* LOWER G INSERT, SPLIT E MECHANISM). **2.** High C facilitator (*see* GIZMO KEY). **3.** High G♯ facilitator (*see* HIGH G♯ MECHANISM).

FACING. 1. Turning the ends of cylindrical components, such as **key tubing**, true and square. **2.** *See* CORK PLATE.

FACSIMILE. Lat. *fac simile* make similar. An exact copy or reproduction of a **piece** of music made by photographing or photocopying the original text. Generally, a facsimile has no **editorial** additions or alterations, but some publishers introduce corrections, surreptitious or otherwise. Because of the earlier styles of music notation, modern performers may have difficulty reading facsimiles.

Figure 16 shows a facsimile from No. 3 (p. 25) of *Nicholson's Preceptive Lessons for the Flute* (1821). The title translates as "All through the Night." The o's and x's stand for specific **alternate fingerings**. For example, "o" means to **finger** the C♯₂ as

- 2 3/4 5 6 C♯ on the **simple-system flute**

- - 2 3 - /1 2 3 4 C♯ on the **Boehm flute**.

The sign means to apply a vibration (**finger vibrato**) to the note under the sign; "2dL.H" and "D♯" signify the fingers to be used for the vibration. The ⌒ sign means to perform a **glide** (a type of **glissando**) for the notes under the sign. *See also* CRITICAL EDITION; PERFORMER'S EDITION; SCHOLARLY EDITION; *URTEXT*.

FACTORY-MADE FLUTE. An ambiguous term for a **flute** that is not custom-made and has less precision handwork than a **handmade flute**. Quality varies greatly. As it is likely to be made from an inexpensive

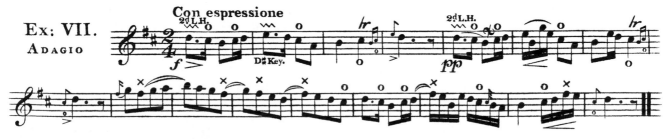

Figure 16. A facsimile from No. 3 of *Nicholson's Preceptive Lessons for the Flute* (London: Clementi & Co., 1821) 25. The title translates as *All through the Night.*

metal, such as **brass** or **nickel-silver,** and **plated** with **nickel** or more often **silver,** it is relatively cheap. It will usually have **drawn** rather than **soldered tone holes** and Y-**arms** rather than French-pointed arms (*see* KEY ARMS). Factory-made flutes ordinarily have **adjustment screws.** If a **flutist** is unsure whether a flute is factory-made, she can quote the **serial** or **model number**—usually found on the barrel of the middle joint or **rib**—to a reputable flute retailer, who will advise her. *Syn.:* production-line flute. *See also* STUDENT FLUTE.

FAJARDO, RAOUL J. (b. Santiago, Cuba, 1919). A physics professor, **flute** player, flute teacher, composer, author, and designer of the **Fajardo Wedgehead.**

FAJARDO WEDGEHEAD™. A **cylindrical bore head joint** for the **flute** with an adjustable long, slender acoustical wedge that extends along the **bore** and gradually tapers inward from an attached **stopper**—which replaces the traditional **head joint cork**—to the **tenon** (see app. 5, fig. 4). The purpose of the wedge is to allow the player the option of altering the **tone color, response,** and **intonation** of the instrument by adjusting the wedge rotationally or laterally in relation to the **embouchure hole.** The Fajardo Wedgehead was invented by **Raoul J. Fajardo,** was patented in the United States in November 1977, and is now made by **David Wimberley** (b.1951). *Syn.:* double adjustable head joint, Wedgehead, Fajardo double adjustable flute wedge head joint.

FAKE BOOK. A collection of usually well-known tunes with accompanying chord symbols that represent the harmony. It is so called because when using such a book the player doesn't need to "fake it" when requested to play an unfamiliar popular piece of music. Fake books are commonly used by jazz and popular musicians. Many fake books are illegal due to copyright royalties not being paid.

FALL-OFF. The angle that the north part of the **lip plate** makes with the **blowing wall.**

FALSE NOTES. Infrequently used term for notes that are **out of tune.**

FALSET NOTES. An older term which refers to notes that are outside of the normal, easily obtainable **range** of a **wind instrument.** For example, **flutist** Jacques Martin Hotteterre, in his 1707 **tutor** *Principles of the Flute, Recorder and Oboe,* regarded notes above E_3 to be "falset" notes on the **one-keyed flute** of his time. *Cf. altissimo.*

FAR WALL. Same as **blowing wall.**

FEELER GAUGE. A thin piece of paper, such as cigarette paper or cassette tape, which is used to check how evenly a key **pad** is covering a **tone hole** or how well one **key** is adjusted to another that is mechanically linked to it (*see* ADJUSTMENT). This is done by putting the paper at various spots between a pad and the **tone-hole rim,** closing the key, and then very gently pulling the paper out. If a pad is not covering evenly, it will be easier to pull out the paper in some spots than others. If one key is not adjusted to another linked key, the paper will come out more easily from one key than the other. This is a highly skilled process best left to professional repairers.

FEET. Plural of *foot* when it stands for **foot joint.** Seldom used.

FELT. 1. A cloth made of pressed wool or other fibers (e.g., fur or hair). It is used in flutemaking to make various parts, such as the parts of key **pads** (see app. 7, fig. 6) and **bumpers** found on the undersides of **keys** or key parts. **2.** A material similar to the felt described above, but made from other fibers and used in the same way. **3.** Any object made from felt.

    See also ADJUSTMENT; CLUTCH (1); CORK; CUSHION; FELT PADS; GLUE; KEY RISE; NEOPRENE; OVERHAUL; PAD; PISONI PADS; REPAD; SHIM; STRAUBINGER PAD; SYNTHETIC PAD.

FELT PADS. Another name for traditional key **pads,** so called because the main component is felt.

FERRULE. 1. Similar to **ring** (2) or **mount** (1), but generally only used when referring to wooden flutes. **2.** *See* LIP-PLATE FERRULE.

FIFARA/FIFARO. It. for **flute** in the 16th and 17th centuries.

FIFE. From Ger. *Pfeife* pipe. Pl. *fifes.* **1.** Usually, a small, **high-pitched, side-blown flute,** made in one piece (sometimes two), with six **finger holes,** a narrow **cylindrical bore** throughout, and rarely any **keys** (see app. 1, fig. 9). It may be made of wood, metal, or, in modern times, plastic. Fifes appeared by the late Medieval period. By the late 18th century, wooden fifes often had **ferrules** of metal or other material at both ends and an exterior that tapered toward the top and bottom of the instrument.

    The fife's **range** is two and a half to three octaves. The high notes are shrill and can be easily heard over drums or other instruments, but the weaker lowest octave is not generally used with instruments such as drums, which could drown out the fife's sound. Since the **low** notes are rarely used, some **fingering charts** give the fife's range as an octave and a half to two octaves, omitting the lowest octave.

The most common fifes are in B♭ and C (named after the **six-fingered notes**; *see* "FLUTE IN . . ." [1]). When comparing the six-fingered notes of these fifes with the same **fingered** note on a **Boehm flute** in C, the B♭ fife sounds a minor sixth above and the C fife sounds a minor seventh above. Some fingering charts show that the B♭ fife sounds a minor sixth above the written **pitch** in fife music, and the C fife a minor seventh; others show that the instruments sound an octave plus a minor sixth and an octave plus a minor seventh, respectively.

Since the 1950s, some fife manufacturers have experimented with two-piece tunable fifes, more **tone holes,** and different **bore** shapes (e.g., a cylindrical head and conical **body** or a cylindrical body with a "**parabolic**" **head joint**). The aim of the changes was to more closely match **equal temperament** and to extend the total range to as much as three chromatic octaves without **half-holing** or **cross-fingering** and to achieve a stronger bottom octave.

Some think of the fife as a **piccolo,** but the piccolo, since its appearance in the early 18th century, has always had a taper in part of its bore (and at least one **key**), while the traditional fife has always had a **cylindrical bore**. Both instruments specialize in **high notes,** but the fife was originally used by the military for marching with drums, signaling, accompanying heralds and emissaries, and so on, while the piccolo first found a home in the orchestra. The fife could therefore remain sturdy and simple, while the piccolo acquired more keys so as to be more chromatic and better able to play increasingly complex music. When, in the 19th century, some fifes acquired keys or changed bores, there was less difference between those fifes and piccolos. In more recent times, however, the piccolo has taken over the fife's role in most bands. *See also* FLAGEOLET (1); *FLÛTE* (1); NATURAL SCALE; SIMPLE SYSTEM (4).

2. A **high-pitched flute** in fife corps or **flute bands.** For example, the highest-voiced B♭ flute (named after the six-fingered note and sounding a minor sixth above the six-fingered note, or D_1, on the Boehm flute in C) in British flute bands has often been called a fife.

3. A plastic student-model instrument made by Yamaha that, although called a fife, is quite different from the true fife described in definition 1. It has a **conical bore,** eight finger holes (one in the back for the thumb), and a **fingering system** that mimics the Boehm piccolo to some extent. Also like the piccolo, it is pitched in C and sounds an octave higher than the written pitch, but has a smaller range of a little over two octaves from the note sounding as C_2 to E_4 (written as C_1 to E_3; *see*

TRANSPOSING INSTRUMENTS). This is unlike the traditional fife, which sounds almost two octaves above the written pitch. Some Boehm flute teachers like to start beginners on this instrument before proceeding on to the Boehm flute.

FIFTH FLUTE. An 18th-century name for the modern soprano **recorder** in C (named after the seven-fingered note), a fifth above the modern alto (British treble) recorder in F. *Cf.* **third flute** (2), **fourth flute** (4), **octave flute** (2), **quint flute** (2), **sixth flute**.

FILLER. 1. Same as **cushion. 2.** A **crack**-filling compound for damaged wooden instruments. **3.** An intermediate layer of dissimilar metal between two other layers of metal used to help adhesion. For example, in the case of **Aurumite,** the filler metal is **silver solder.** *See also* BRAZING (1); FUSING; SOLDERING. **4.** *See* BAKELITE.

FINGER (A NOTE). *v.* To place the fingers in the correct **fingering** position for a particular note, without necessarily playing the note. *See also* FINGERING THROUGH; FUNDAMENTAL (2); HARMONIC (2, 3); SLUR; TRANSPOSING INSTRUMENTS; WHISTLE TONE.

FINGER BUTTON. The padless **cup**-like **key** that is attached to, and operates, the **upper C key.** *See also* DAP (1).

FINGER HOLES. Tone holes that are directly covered by the fingers. *Syn.:* finger tone holes, note holes. *See also* ACOUSTIC IMPEDANCE; *CORPS DE RECHANGE;* CRESCENT KEY; FINGERING DIAGRAMS; FINGER VIBRATO; FLUTE (1); FLUTE FAMILY (1); GLIDE; HALF-HOLING; MODE; NATURAL SCALE; O (2); ONE-KEYED FLUTE; OPEN NOTE; PRINCIPAL RANK; RENAISSANCE FLUTE; SHADING (2); SICCAMA DIATONIC FLUTE; SIMPLE-SYSTEM FLUTE; STANDING WAVE; TONE-HOLE BUSHING; X.

FINGERING. The arrangement of fingers on the **keys** or **finger holes** used to play a certain note. Fingerings are usually shown in **fingering diagrams** on a **fingering chart,** but may also be individually shown in flute **method** books. *See also* ACOUSTIC IMPEDANCE SPECTRUM; ALTERNATE FINGERINGS; BASIC FINGERINGS; B♭ FINGERINGS; *BISBIGLIANDO;* BRICCIALDI B♭ LEVER; BUZZ TONE; CHARANGA FLUTE; CROSS-FINGERING; CUTOFF FREQUENCY; DUPLICATE KEYS; FINGER; FINGERING SYSTEM; FINGERING THROUGH; FLUTE FAMILY (2); FORK FINGERING; G♯ KEY (1); HALF-HOLING; HARMONIC (2, 3); HOME BASE; JET WHISTLE; KEY SLAP; KEY VIBRATO; LEFT-HAND FINGERING; LEFT-HAND LEVER; LONG B♭ FINGERING; MICROTONES; MULTIPHONIC; O (2); OPEN FINGERING; OPEN-HOLE FLUTE; OPEN-KEY SYSTEM; OVERBLOWING;

PERFORMER'S EDITION; PROJECTION; QUARTER-TONE FLUTE; REGISTER (1); RESONANCE (1); RESPONSE; RIGHT-HAND FINGERING; RING-KEY FLUTE; SIDE-LEVER B♭ FINGERING; SPLIT E MECHANISM; SPLIT F♯ MECHANISM; STANDING WAVE; THUMB-KEY B♭ FINGERING; TRANSPOSING INSTRUMENTS; *TREMOLO* (1); TRILL FINGERING; VIRTUAL FLUTE (2); WARM-UP (1); WHISTLE TONES; X. For **early flutes** and other non-**Boehm-system** flutes, *see also* AUGMENTED FINGERING; AUGMENTED NOTES; BAROQUE FLUTE (1); *BRILLE* (1); CARTE 1851 SYSTEM FLUTE; CARTE 1867 SYSTEM FLUTE; FOUR-KEYED FLUTE; GIORGI FLUTE; GUARDS' MODEL FLUTE; MEYER-SYSTEM FLUTE (1); O (2); PRATTEN'S PERFECTED; X.

FINGERING CHART. A chart showing **fingerings** for the different notes of the **flute**. The fingerings are indicated in **fingering diagrams**. There are various types of fingering charts, such as the basic, trill, and alternate fingering charts. The *basic fingering chart* shows the standard or **basic fingerings** for the different notes. It is the fingering chart found in most flute **method** books. Any unlabeled flute fingering chart is probably a basic fingering chart, and the words "fingering chart" are often synonymous with the basic chart. The *trill fingering chart* shows how to play **trill fingerings** and can often be found alongside a basic fingering chart. An *alternate fingering chart* shows **alternate fingerings** for the different notes and is not common. Good alternate fingerings can be found by asking experienced players or going to **master classes**, where they are discussed in the context of the music. **Flutists** may even experiment to find their own alternate fingerings should the need arise. The meanings for any signs used in the charts are usually indicated. *See also* G♯ KEY (1). For **early flutes**, *see also* CLASSICAL FLUTE; ONE-KEYED FLUTE; RANGE (2).

FINGERING DIAGRAMS. Diagrams that indicate the arrangement of fingers on the **keys** or **finger holes** used to play the notes on **woodwind** instruments. These may be shown individually in **method** books or as a group in a **fingering chart**. For instructions on how to read the fingering diagrams in this book, see the section "Fingering Diagrams" in the introduction. In other books, there may be different ways of indicating fingering information. *See also* BISBIGLIANDO; HARMONIC (3); KEY SLAP; MULTIPHONIC; O (2); X.

FINGERING SYSTEM. A collection of independent but interrelated **fingerings** that are organized so as to accomplish the playing of a particular **range** of musical notes. With the exception of the **high register**, for which many fingerings are possible, a maker must decide on a fingering system before (or perhaps during) construction.

Usually the flutemaker will choose a system that is a compromise between ease of playing, comfort, and ease of construction, while at the same time meeting the **tuning** requirements. *See also* BOEHM SYSTEM. For **early flutes** and other non-**Boehm-system** flutes, *see also* CARTE 1851 SYSTEM FLUTE; IRISH FLUTE (1); OLD SYSTEM (2); RADCLIFF SYSTEM FLUTE; SCHMIDT, JIM.

FINGERING THROUGH. The procedure of **fingering** each note in a group of notes without actually playing each one. *See also* FINGER.

FINGER PLATE. Any type of **key** activated by the finger. *See also* PERFORATED PLATES; PLATE (2).

FINGER VIBRATO. An older type of **vibrato** that was produced by tapping a finger directly on, or on the edge of, a **finger hole** at more or less regular intervals. It could be done in two ways, the ear being the judge as to which to use: either by repeatedly partially covering and uncovering the **sounding hole** with the appropriate finger or by repeatedly partially or completely covering and uncovering an open hole beyond the sounding hole with the appropriate finger. When either method was used, the **pitch** of the note **flattened** and then returned to the correct pitch. To stop the vibrato, the **flutist** raised the moving finger. A flutist desiring to produce vibrato on very **low notes**, where no uncovered finger hole was available, did so by shaking the **flute** gently with the right hand.

Finger vibrato was best done on a flute with finger holes, but could also work to some extent on a flute with **ring keys** or **open-hole keys**. For example, on a flute without any **keys** covering the fifth and sixth holes, a flutist might produce vibrato by partially or completely covering and uncovering either of these holes with R2 or R3, respectively, when playing a G_1 or A_1. The finger vibrato was not always notated, but when it was, it was sometimes shown as a wavy line above a note 〰 (see also fig. 16).

Finger vibrato was an expressive **technique** that was used in the 18th and 19th centuries and was meant to be used very sparingly, more like an **ornament**, in such places as on longer notes. It was particularly popular in France in the earlier part of the 18th century, where it was referred to as *flattement*. There is evidence of this in the first Baroque flute **tutor** (1707) by **Jacques Martin Hotteterre** which includes fingerings for flattement on every note. Finger vibrato was also popular with such early 19th-century English flutists as **Charles Nicholson Jr.**, who referred to it as "vibration." **Johann Joachim Quantz**, in his renowned *Versuch* (1752) recommended its use with *messa di voce* (making a progressive crescendo and diminuendo on a sustained note). **Anton Bernhard Fürstenau**, in his tutor (1844), briefly discusses both finger vibrato *(Klopfen)* and **breath vibrato** *(Bebung)*. His examples show vibrato being used on about one note in every eight bars.

Finger vibrato is also called *tremblement minuer* (French); *vibrato* (19th-century English); *close shake*, *lesser shake*, *softening*, or *sweetening* (17th- and 18th-century English); *Bebung* (German); and *tremolo* (Italian). Today, it is most often referred to by the French name *flattement*. *See also* BREATH VIBRATO; CLOSED-KEY SYSTEM; NICHOLSON'S IMPROVED FLUTE.

FINIAL. An ornament, such as a floral sculpture, that is on top of something. When applied to **flutes**, it usually means an ornately **turned end cap** as may be seen on early French **Baroque flutes** (see app. 3, A, fig. 6).

FINISH. Something that completes the outer boundary of something. In flutemaking, **flute** repair, and flute maintenance, the term *finish* may refer to the following. **1.** The final treatment or coating of a flute part such as applying **polish** to metal flute **tubing** or **oil** to the **body** of a wooden flute. *See also* BUFFING; BURNISHING; PLATING; RAGGING; TITANIUM (the latter regarding anodizing). **2.** The resulting surface texture produced by the treatment described above. It may be rough, grainy, smooth, and so on. A *high* finish is one that is very shiny; a *low* finish is not as shiny. *See also* FRUITWOOD. **3.** A material used to surface or finish something. *See* PLATING; ROUGE (1); TRIPOLI; SILVER-PLATING. **4.** The process of making final **adjustments** to the flute by doing such things as **padding**, polishing, and so on to get the flute looking and performing to its maximum. *See* FINISHER.

FINISHER. The craftsman in a flutemaking company who specializes in the final **polishing** and **padding** of a new **flute**. Depending on the company and the materials used, the finisher may do various things. For example, for a metal flute, the worker may:

- check the **pad cups** for flatness, as this may have been distorted by the heat of **soldering** or by the **stringer** not fitting the cup correctly to the flute
- check the **tone holes** for flatness, in case the **bodymaker** missed something
- fine-tune the fit of the keywork to the flute, including such things as installing the **springs** and adjusting their tension, which affects how a **key** operates, and adjusting the fit of the rods or **steels**, which affects the flute's ability to stay in **adjustment**
- do the final **buffing**
- put the pads in the cups so they are **level** with the tone holes, which may include **shimming** to

make any parts on the pad that are hitting the tone hole too lightly hit in the same way as the rest of the pad
- put in the adjustment between linked keys
- get the **head joint** assigned to that flute and make sure the **fit** is just right
- do more buffing, if necessitated by any minor scratches or scuffs
- reassemble the keywork
- **oil** the flute in the appropriate places
- make any last-minute fine-tuning of adjustments
- fine-tune the way the flute fits into the case

See also HEAD JOINT MAKER.

FINISHING. The process of completing the outer boundary of something, such as completing the surface of metal **flute tubing** by **buffing**, **burnishing**, or **polishing**. *See also* PICKLE; RAGGING.

FIPPLE FLUTE. Usually, a **duct flute** (e.g., **recorder**, **tin whistle**, **flageolet**). The term *fipple* has also been used to refer to some part of the duct flute, but authorities cannot agree on which part, so some scholars think it best to avoid the terms *fipple* and *fipple flute* and use *duct flute* instead.

FIRE SCALE. Also *firescale*. A thin, flaky, whitish film that can form on a metal surface, caused by spontaneous oxidation from high heat, such as from **brazing**. On **silver**, the fire scale is usually purplish; on **gold**, different shades of yellow may be seen. The **precious metal** in the **alloy** is not what turns this color; rather, it is, in the case of silver and gold alloys, the copper in the mix that does.

Various **fluxes** can help to reduce the amount of scale that forms on metal when heating it. Should fire scale occur, however, it can penetrate more deeply into metal than **tarnish** and is therefore harder to remove. Flutemakers may file, scrape, or sand the metal to remove any fire scale that has formed on a **flute** part. Unfortunately, these methods for removing fire scale can be time-consuming and difficult to do without harming the definition of the flute part that is being made. As a result, less time-consuming and destructive processes, such as **pickling**, may be used to remove fire scale. *Syn.:* fire stain.

FIRST CHAIR FLUTIST. The first or **principal flutist** of the **flute** section in a professional orchestra or band who plays the first flute **part**. *See also* CHAIR; FIRST FLUTIST; LEAD; SECTION LEADER.

FIRST FLUTIST. In an **ensemble** having two or more **flutists**, the flutist who plays the first flute **part** (usually the main flute part containing more **high notes** and melodies than any other flute parts). In certain situations, there can be more than one first flutist. *See also* CHAIR; DESK (2); FIRST CHAIR FLUTIST; JUST INTONATION; LEAD; PRINCIPAL FLUTIST; SECOND FLUTIST; SECTION LEADER; THIRD FLUTIST; TUNING UP (1).

FIRST OCTAVE. The notes contained in the lowest-**pitched** octave of a musical instrument. On the **flute** with a **C foot joint**, these notes are from C_1 to B_1. Flutes with a **B foot joint** have one extra note below the first octave: the note b. *Syn.:* **low notes**, low octave, **low register**, **first register**, bottom notes, bottom octave, bottom register. *See also* "Octave Designation" in the introduction; app. 8; CHARANGA FLUTE (1); FOURTH OCTAVE; LOW (1); LOW B, LOW C, LOW C♯, ETC.; RANGE (1); REGISTER (1); SECOND OCTAVE; THIRD OCTAVE. For **early flutes**, *see also* BAROQUE FLUTE (2); RANGE (2); RENAISSANCE FLUTE; TWO-KEYED FLUTE.

FIRST REGISTER. Usually refers to the **first octave**. Same as **low**/bottom/**fundamental register**. *See also* BASS FLUTE (2); CUTOFF FREQUENCY; CYLINDRICAL BOEHM FLUTE (3); FUNDAMENTAL (2); REGISTER (1); RISER; SECOND REGISTER; STANDING WAVE; THIRD REGISTER.

FIRST TRILL KEY. Same as D **trill key**.

FISHSKIN. A thin, strong, airtight skin that is taken from the lining of a cow's intestine and used to cover the key **pads** of **flutes** (see app. 7, fig. 6). It may have gotten its name because it can have the glossy look and feel of the skin of a fish. The purpose of the fishskin is to hold the pad materials together and to create an airtight **seal** between the pad and the **tone-hole rim**. *Syn.:* **bladder skin**, **goldbeater's skin**, skin. *See also* DOUBLE-SKIN; SINGLE-SKIN; STRAUBINGER PADS.

FISTULA. Lat. tube or pipe. **1.** In ancient Rome, a shepherd's **pipe** (**duct flute** or reed pipe). **2.** In the Middle Ages (12th–15th centuries), various members of the **flute family** (duct flutes, **panpipes**).

FIT. 1. A repair job undertaken by a flutemaker or repairer to make any flute **tenon** the proper size and shape for the **socket** with which it connects. *See also* FINISHER; HEAD-JOINT MAKER; HEAD-JOINT REFITTING; LAPPING. **2.** *See* INTERFERENCE FIT. **3.** *See* SLIP FIT.

FITTINGS. Any detachable parts of the **flute**, including **keys** and **mounts**. This term is usually used only when talking about older flutes. *See* SICCAMA DIATONIC FLUTE; TUBE/TUBING.

FIVE-KEYED FLUTE. A **simple-system** (or **keyed**) **transverse flute** (or replica of it) that evolved from, and was similar to, the earlier wooden (or **ivory**), **conical-bored**, **one-keyed flute** in D except that it had five **closed-standing keys** (i.e., the by now standard **key** for D♯ and, most often, the additional keys for B♭, G♯, F, and C) (see app. 2, fig. 5).

The C key in the form called the "long C key" or "C **shake** key" was first added to the **flute** in the early 19th century, possibly by the flutemaker **Tebaldo Monzani**, who mentioned it in his 1806 patent. This C key was operated by R1. It controlled the C hole between the C♯ hole and the B hole, and when opened, it produced the note C_2 or C_3.

With the addition of the new C key, there was one key for each note outside of the D-major scale—D♯, F, G♯, B♭, and C—and each note had its own **tone hole** for the first time (i.e., those of the one-keyed flute: the six **finger holes** [C♯, B, A, G, F♯, E]; the D♯ tone hole under the D♯ key; the open **foot joint** end, which was essentially the "tone hole" for the note D; the new tone holes introduced on the **four-keyed flute** [those for the notes B♭, G♯, and F]; and the new tone hole of the five-keyed flute for the note C). However, even though the new C key produced a perfectly good note, it was little used (except for a **trill** with B, or when C was the **highest note** in a phrase) because the right hand needed to make an awkward movement from covering a finger hole to operating the C **touch** when using the key.

The five-keyed flute was played throughout the 19th century and was particularly popular in France. It has been revived in modern times, and some people play originals or replicas of the instrument for Classical-period or Charanga music. *See also* CHARANGA FLUTE; EIGHT-KEYED FLUTE; MULTIKEYED FLUTE; NINE-KEYED FLUTE; SIX-KEYED FLUTE; TEN-KEYED FLUTE; TULOU *FLÛTE PERFECTIONÉE*; TWO-KEYED FLUTE.

FLAGEOLET. From Old French *flageol*, in turn derived from the Latin verb *flare*, to breathe.

1. Any of a variety of historical **duct flutes** that were usually played vertically and had a narrow tapering **bore**. Early flageolets had a beaked **mouthpiece** like the **recorder** (see app. 1, fig. 4), but in the 18th century this was replaced by a slim nozzle of bone or **ivory** that was connected to a pear-shaped, sponge-filled chamber or **barrel** (see app. 1, fig. 5). The sponge was meant to absorb the moisture from the breath so that it would not block the narrow windway. Early flageolets had a **range** of no more than two octaves, but some of the

tutors in the 19th century show a range of more than two octaves.

Flageolets were popular in England, France, and Germany from the 17th to 19th centuries, although the scarcity of music in the second half of the 18th century suggests that there may have been a drop in popularity at this time. There are two types of flageolets: French and English.

Early *French flageolets* had four **finger holes** in the front and two thumb holes in the back; later on, several **keys** were added to allow for semitones and to improve octaving. A standard model was called the *quadrille flageolet* and was equipped with five keys. Some flageolets had similar keywork to the Boehm 1832 System **flute** (*see* RING-KEY FLUTE).

Until 1800, French flageolets were made in a variety of keys, the most common being in D, F, G, and A (named after the **six-fingered notes** D_2, F_2, G_2, and A_2, respectively). In the course of the 19th century, the flageolet in A became the standard **pitch**. Even though flageolets in A with a **Boehm system** have an additional extension of two semitones down to G, the instrument is still considered to be in A since this pitch sounds when all principal finger holes are closed. Notes are produced by using sequential **fingerings, cross-fingerings, half-holing**, and **overblowing**. Standard instruments in A with a nozzle mouthpiece are about 15 in. (37–39 cm) in total length. Another type of flageolet was the *bird flageolet* used to teach pet birds to sing. They were usually pitched in D, a fourth above the regular French flageolet, and were very short (e.g., 4 in./11 cm and pitched in A, with six-fingered note of A_3).

English flageolets retained the shape of the French flageolet, but came in different sizes. The standard English *octave flageolet* measures about 16 in. (41 cm) in total length, including the barrel and mouthpiece. It has seven finger holes on the top side of the instrument and a thumb hole in the back. At first, the thumb hole functioned as a **register hole**, but around 1800 this function was transferred to the uppermost hole on the top side of the instrument and the thumb hole became a regular tone hole. To effect this change, the uppermost hole was partially plugged with a special wooden device. This allowed the instrument to produce a C instead of a C♯ when all of the finger holes were uncovered and reduced some of the cross-fingerings. Ivory studs were often present between the finger holes to guide the fingers. Like French flageolets, English flageolets came in a variety of sizes, but the most popular were **pitched** in D, a perfect fifth below standard French flageolets. Notes are produced in the same way as on the French flageolet, that is, by using sequential fingerings, cross-fingerings, half-holing, and overblowing.

Other varieties of the English flageolet have the beak projecting out of the side of the barrel so that they can be played similarly to a **transverse flute**. These are usually the same length as the **concert flute** and are in unison with it, but an octave lower than the standard English flageolet. Often the **head joint** of these instruments can be removed and a normal flute head joint used, making a real flute. Very occasionally these "flute-flageolets" were also double instruments. At the end of the 19th century, some flageolets had the **body** of a **piccolo** or **fife** and interchangeable flageolet and piccolo or fife **heads**.

Around 1805, **William Bainbridge** produced multiple flageolets with the help of performer and composer John Parry (1776–1851). They differed from regular flageolets in that they had two, or sometimes even three, flageolet bodies joined together in parallel and inserted into the bottom of a chamber containing the sponge (*see* MULTIPLE FLUTE). Each flageolet shared a common mouthpiece or nozzle, but the voicing edges were in the chamber and had a lever-operated shutter so that one of the flageolets could be prevented from sounding if the player did not wish to play in harmony. A longer third body was also sometimes fitted, played by the thumbs to give a bass to the harmonies played on the other two bodies with the fingers. *See also* FLAUTINO (1); *FLAUTO PICCOLO* (1).

2. A **tin whistle** or other duct flute. *See also* FIPPLE FLUTE.

3. A *flageolet sound/tone*. Same as **whistle tone**.

4. A synonym for **harmonic**, for example, on flutes and other instruments.

FLAGEOLET FINGERING. *See* HARMONIC (3).

FLANGE. A protruding rim, **rib**, collar, or similar component that is used to strengthen part of the **flute**, hold part of the flute in place, or attach one part of the flute to another. An example of a flange is the **rim** at the bottom of the **riser**, which is used to attach the riser and **embouchure plate** to the **head joint** (see fig. 6). *See also* FRENCH BUSHING.

FLAP KEY. A flute **key** that consisted of a **silver** or **brass key flap** (**plate** or cover) faced with leather, a **shank**, and a **touchpiece** (see app. 3, B, fig. 2; app. 3, C, fig. 4). Flap keys were used on most 18th- and early 19th-century **flutes** and are now also used on replicas. A metal **flat spring** was attached to the flap key at some point on its underside. There was a more or less semicircular **lug** with a hole near the middle of the flap key's shank. The lug's hole was used to accept a **pin** on which the key was suspended in a wooden or **ivory block-mount**; later in some countries, such as Germany, it was occasionally used to accept a screw on which the key was suspended in a metal **saddle**. *Syn.:* flat key. *See also* PEWTER PLUGS; SALT-SPOON KEYS.

FLASH PLATE. A general term for a thin coat of **plating**. It can be any dimension, but is usually 0.0001 in. (ca. 0.0025 mm).

FLAT. Lower than the correct **pitch** for a given note. When an instrument or voice is said to be flat, most of its notes are sounding below their correct pitches. *Cf.* **sharp**. *See also* COOPER SCALE; DENSITY; DUPLICATE G♯ TONE HOLE (1); FLUTTER-TONGUING; HALF-HOLING; INTERNAL TUNING; INTONATION; LIP GLISSANDO; LOW (2); LOWER G INSERT; LOWERING A NOTE; LOWER NOTE (1); ORCHESTRAL MODEL FLUTE; OUT-OF-TUNE; PLUG (1); PYTHAGOREAN TUNING; RETUNING; ROLL-IN; SHORTENED HEAD JOINT; STOPPER; TRADITIONAL SCALE; TUNING SLIDE (1). For **early flutes and other non-Boehm-system flutes,** *see also* BRILLE (1); *CORPS DE RECHANGE; FINGER VIBRATO;* FOOT REGISTER; RETUNING (2) TUNING SLIDE (2); TWO-KEYED FLUTE.

FLAT KEY. Same as **flap key.**

FLAT SPRING. A tongue-like hammered piece of **brass** or **tempered steel**, the purpose of which is to keep the **touch** of the **key** elevated until it is put into use. Flat (key) springs are attached to the **flute** in a variety of ways.

1. On the standard modern **Boehm flute**, there is one flat spring under the B thumb key extension, and sometimes there is another under the B♭ **thumb key** extension. Each flat spring is attached with a screw near the end of the **extension arm** with the free end near or under a **touch** and pushing downward against the flute's **body**.

The rest of the **springs** on the modern flute are needle springs. This type became the most commonly used on **Boehm-system** flutes and other more complex systems (e.g., the **Carte 1867**, some **Reform flutes**, etc.). *See also* BRÖGGER SYSTEM; RING-KEY FLUTE; SHEET METAL.

2. On **one-keyed, two-keyed,** and **simple-system flutes,** the flat springs were usually situated in such a way that one end was under the touch or **shank** of the key and the other end was almost directly under the axle **pin** or screw in the **channel** of the **key-mount** (very occasionally the same arrangement mentioned in definition 1 above was used) (see app. 3, B, figs. 2, 6, and 7). The spring was most commonly attached with a rivet (and sometimes a screw) to the touch, **lever,** or shank part of the key, with the free end pushing downward against the bottom part of the particular key-mount's channel. It could also be

attached by wedging it (and later screwing it) to the body of the flute in the channel area of a key-mount instead of to the touch, with the free end pushing upward against the underside of the **touchpiece**.

In some cases, and for a slightly smoother **action,** two flat springs (called *double springs*) of different materials were used. One configuration has the end of one of the springs riveted to the touch of the key, and the end of the other spring screwed into the wood directly below it. The free ends of the double springs pressed against each other. In doing so, the working length of the spring was essentially doubled while keeping it in the same space.

The flat spring, used in these ways, is the oldest type of spring used in the making of flutes. It was used on one-keyed, two-keyed, and simple-system flutes from the late 17th century into the 20th century. It is also used on replicas. Not only is it easy to make, but by judicious selection of material thickness, width, and proximity of the tip to the hinge point, the maker can achieve a snappiness of action not achievable by any other spring type.

Overall, makers try to reduce the "winding-up" feel of all springs by making them long and thin rather than short and stubby. The force needed to open or close a key should be as constant as possible within the key travel. If it is necessary to use a particularly short spring due to space limitations, it is sometimes possible to arrange for its action point to move slightly during the key travel, giving it gradually less leverage. This gives the player the impression of moving a longer, thinner spring. This is particularly easy to do with flat springs. *Syn.:* leaf springs. *See also* BLOCK-MOUNT; FLAP KEY; POST-MOUNT; SALT-SPOON KEY.

FLATTEMENT. Fr. **finger vibrato.**

FLATTEN. *v.* To make a note lower (more **flat**) in pitch. *Cf.* **sharpen.**

FLATTER. Lower (more **flat**) than another note (i.e., more **out of tune**). *Cf.* **sharper.**

FLATTERZUNGE. Ger. **flutter-tonguing.**

FLAUTINO. It. little **flute. 1.** A general Italian name for any small flute such as a **recorder** or a **flageolet.** The exact type of instrument depends on the time and place that the word is used. *Cf.* **flautone. 2.** In early 17th-century Italy, sometimes used to mean the **descant recorder** in G (based on the seven-fingered note). **3.** Used throughout the 18th century to mean a small recorder. **4.** The name marked on the **barrel** of some higher-pitched **Boehm flutes** by **Abelardo Albisi** (1872–1938). One of these flutes was made especially for Albisi's opera *La Parisina* (1913). This flute is also called *flauto usignuolo* (nightingale flute) because the music it plays represents a nightingale. It is **pitched** in G, sounding a fifth higher than the **concert flute** in C (**DCM** 1345).

FLAUTIST. A **flute** player. The word is first documented in 1860. It probably comes from the Italian word *flautista*, derived from *flauto*. The word *flautist* has the same meaning as *flutist*, but to some people, "flautist" sounds more sophisticated.

FLAUTO. It. **flute**; pl. *flauti*. Abbr. fl. **1.** From the late 15th century to about the middle of the 18th century, the standard Italian name for the **recorder**, used to distinguish it from the *flauto traverso* (**transverse flute**). **2.** In modern usage, the orchestral or **concert flute** in C. **3.** *See also* FLAUTIST.

FLAUTO A BECCO. It. beaked **flute**. Italian term for a **recorder**.

FLAUTO BASSO. It. **bass flute**. Italian and British term for the basset **recorder** in the late Baroque.

FLAUTO CONTRALTO. It. alto flute. Abbr. f. c'alto. **1.** An **alto flute**. **2.** Italian term for the alto **recorder** in the late Baroque.

FLAUTO D'ALLEMAGNA. It. **German flute**.

FLAUTO D'AMORE. It. **flute** of love. *See flûte d'amour.*

FLAUTO DIRITTO. Italian term for a **recorder**.

FLAUTO DOLCE. Italian term for a **recorder**.

FLAUTO EN SOL. Italian term for an **alto flute**.

FLAUTO GRANDE. It. big flute. Abbr. fl. gr. Italian term for the (**concert**) **flute**, used to distinguish it from the **piccolo**, which is sometimes calledor *flauto piccolo* (small flute).

FLAUTONE. It. Abbr. fltne. A general name for any large **flute** (or **recorder**) such as an **alto flute** or a **bass flute**. The exact type of instrument meant depends on the time and place the word is used. *Cf. flautino.*

FLAUTO PICCOLO. It. small flute. **1.** In the 18th century, a small **recorder** or **flageolet**. **2.** At the beginning of the 19th century, a **piccolo**. **3.** Today, a less common Italian term for piccolo. The exact type of instrument depends on the time and place the word is used. *See also* OTTAVINO.

FLAUTO SOPRANO. Italian term for soprano **recorder** in the late Baroque.

FLAUTO TAILLO. German term for tenor **recorder** in the late Baroque.

FLAUTO TENORO. Italian term for tenor **recorder** in the late Baroque.

FLAUTO TRAVERSO. It. **transverse flute**. *See also* FLAUTO (1); TRAVERSO.

FLAUTO USIGNUOLO. It. nightingale flute. *See FLAUTINO* (3).

FLEURY, LOUIS FRANÇOIS (b. Lyons, France, 1878; d. Paris, 1926). A renowned French flute **soloist**, chamber and orchestral musician, and from 1902, member of the Société Moderne des Instruments à Vent, which he directed from 1905 to his death, replacing **Georges Barrère**. Fleury also founded the Société des Concerts d'Autrefois, commissioned more than a hundred pieces of chamber music, and was an **editor** of 18th-century flute music and an author. *See also* TAFFANEL, CLAUDE-PAUL; T. & G.

FLOATING. A procedure used by flutemakers and repairers for **seating** small key **pads** whereby the pad is moved or "floated" on heated **glue** into position in a key **cup**. During the procedure, no part of the pad makes contact with the pad cup. On the modern **concert flute**, the **trill key** pads and the **upper C key** pad are floated into position.

FLÖTE. Ger. **flute**; pl. *Flöten*. Abbr. F. **1.** The standard German name for the **recorder** from the 16th century to the mid-18th century. **2.** A modern German term for the **flute**, which occasionally also embraces recorder. *See also* GRÖSSE FLUTE.

FLUSH BANDING. *See* RING BANDING.

FLUTE. From Middle English *flowte* or *floyte*, from Anglo-French *flaüte*, from Old French *flaüste*, from Lat. *flare*. It. *flauto*; Fr. *flûte*; Ger. *Flöte*. **1.** A member of a large family of **wind instruments** in which the sound is produced by directing a narrow stream of air, called an **air jet**, against a sharp edge, either directly or by means of a duct. The airstream causes an acoustic perturbation at the edge of the **blowhole** (see fig. 17 for an example

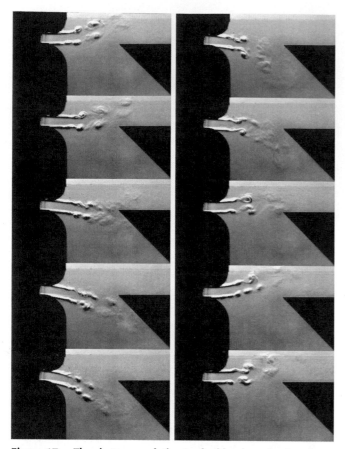

Figure 17. **The airstream relative to the blowing edge in a flute-like geometry.** *Photo courtesy Benoit Fabre, Paris 6 University, France, and Avraham Hirschberg, Technical University Eindhoven, The Netherlands.*

Figure 18. *Top:* **The oldest playable flute, made about 33,000 years ago.** *Photo courtesy Institute of Cultural Relics and Archaeology of Henan Province, Zhengzhou, China.* Bottom: **Representation of possibly the oldest flute fragment, 43,000 years old.** *Drawing courtesy Bob Fink.*

of how this is done on the modern **concert flute**). This perturbation starts the **air column** in the flute vibrating, and this coupling between air column and jet forces the air jet oscillation to synchronize to one of the **resonances** of the air column, creating a feedback loop.

Figure 17 shows the airstream relative to the **blowing edge** in a flute-like geometry. The photos show the blowing area: rounded lips *(left)*, air jet *(middle)*, and blowing edge *(right)*. During the steady part of a note played on a flute, the jet issuing from the lips of the player oscillates around the blowing edge. The picture shows 10 steps of one cycle of the jet oscillation or one sound period. Although the jet is blown using a wind tunnel and aluminum lips, the jet oscillation is similar to that observed in real flute-playing conditions.

For the concert flute, in order to change the **pitch**, **finger holes** are opened and closed directly by the fingers or by **keys** and/or the air speed is increased or decreased together with the adjustment of the lip position by manipulating the **embouchure**.

It is not known when the first flute was invented, although it seems probable that it dates back to prehis-

toric humans. The Latin word for flute is **tibia**, which is also the word for the shinbone. This suggests that one of the first flutes could have been made out of animal, bird, or human bones. Perhaps ancient man blew into a hollow animal bone by accident and produced a sound. These facts are supported by various archaeological findings in different parts of the world. For example, what is thought to be the oldest fragment of a flute was found in a Slovenian cave by Ivan Turk in 1995. It is said to have been made by Neanderthals about 43,000 years ago from the femur bone of a cave bear (see fig. 18, *bottom*). Two holes are complete and two are partial. The partial holes are at the end of the bone.

The oldest confirmed flute was made about 33,000 years ago from the wing bone of a large vulture and was discovered in France. The oldest flute that is still playable was made about 9,000 years ago from the wing bone of a red-crowned crane and was discovered in China (see fig. 18, *top*). It is in one piece, about 8 in. (20.3 cm) long, and has seven main holes with a tiny additional hole near the seventh; this additional hole may have been used to correct the intonation of the original seventh hole. This flute would have been held vertically downward and played by blowing against a sharp edge at the top open end of a **tube**.

Today we call flutes like the playable one above **end-blown flutes**, and there are many varieties of them. Another type of flute that came into use was held horizontally from the player's mouth and played by blowing against the sharp edge of a hole in the side of a tube. Today we call such flutes **side-blown flutes**. One variety of the side-blown flute, and the one that is the most commonly played flute today, is the modern orchestral or concert flute. For information about other flute classifications, *see* AEROPHONE; DUCT FLUTE; FLUTE FAMILY; GLOBULAR FLUTE; MULTIPLE FLUTE; NOSE FLUTE; NOTCHED FLUTE; OVERTONE FLUTE; VERTICAL FLUTE; VESSEL FLUTE; WHISTLE.

2. In Europe from the late 15th to the mid-18th century, *flute* (in various languages) was used to mean the recorder as a means to distinguish it from the **transverse flute**, the predecessor of the modern orchestral or concert flute of today. In England, the term *flute* meant the transverse flute until the 1670s, when it changed its meaning to recorder, before taking on its modern meaning (def. 3) about the mid-18th century.

3. Since the second half of the 18th century, after the transverse flute overtook the recorder in popularity, *flute* has usually meant the side-blown orchestral flute. It is the most common type of flute and a member of the flute family (def. 2). It is also the flute that most people think of when they think of the flute today, and the one that this book is mostly about. *See also* BOEHM FLUTE; CONCERT FLUTE (1–3).

4. A long rounded concave groove or channel, many of which are sometimes carved lengthwise and side-by-side along the outside of wooden or **glass flute tubing**. They not only act as a decorative feature but also help to lighten the overall weight of the flute. In appendix 2, figure 8, "flutes" may be seen in a glass flute of **Claude Laurent** (?–1848). *See also* FLUTING (2); SPUD.

FLÛTE. Fr. **flute. 1.** In the Middle Ages, spelled *fla-hute, flaüte, fleüte,* the term apparently referred to any **duct flute**. By the 15th century, it could also mean a **recorder, transverse flute,** or **fife. 2.** In the 16th through early 18th centuries, one of the standard names for the recorder in France. Other names used included *flûte à neuf trous, flûte d'Angleterre, flûte douce,* and *flûte à bec.* **3.** In modern usage, the orchestral or **concert flute**. *See also GRANDE FLÛTE.*

FLÛTE À BEC. Fr. beaked **flute. 1.** One of the standard names for the **recorder** in France in the 18th century, the others being *flûte* and *flûte douce. See also FLÛTE D'ANGLETERRE.* **2.** The standard modern French name for the recorder.

FLÛTE ALLEMANDE. Fr. German flute. Also *flûte d'Allemagne.* The standard French name for the **flute** in the 16th and 17th centuries, and one of the two standard names (along with *flûte traversière*) in the 18th century. *Cf. flûte d'Angleterre.*

FLÛTE ALTO. Fr. **alto flute.**

FLÛTE À NEUF TROUS. Fr. **flute** with nine holes. One of the standard names for the **recorder** in France in the 16th and early 17th centuries, the other being simply *flûte.* It was so called because makers duplicated the lowest hole, to accommodate the needs of both right- and left-handed players. The unused hole was **stopped** with wax, leaving the usual eight holes for playing. In modern recorders and Baroque copies, it is not necessary to have an extra hole for this purpose, because the foot joint can

be moved to accommodate both right- and left-handed players. (For more information about double recorder holes, *see* RECORDER.) *See also FLÛTE D'ANGLETERRE.*

FLUTE BAND. A type of band consisting only of **flutes** and percussion (e.g., bass drum, snare drum, cymbals, bells). The bands were often military or patriotic in origin, but many were formed by large commercial companies (e.g., shipbuilders, mines, or foundries) to improve morale. Many bands today are community based.

The flutes used are of various sizes and **pitches**. Older bands used wooden **simple-system flutes**. For example, an older band might consist of:

- 1 E♭ **piccolo**
- 6 or more B♭ flutes playing in three parts and pitched a sixth above the **ordinary flute** in D
- 3 F-flutes playing in three parts and pitched a third higher
- 3 E♭ flutes pitched a minor second higher
- 3 B♭ **bass flutes** pitched a major third below
- 2 F bass flutes pitched a major sixth below
- 1 E♭ bass flute pitched a major seventh below

(These flutes were usually named after their **six-fingered note**.)

Today's flute bands use various types of flutes depending on the type of band (e.g., melody band, part-band, etc.), its goals, and the availability and cost of flutes. For example, *part-bands*—bands that play music in multiple **parts**—usually use an array of **Boehm-system** flutes. A band today might consist of:

- 1 piccolo in C
- **solo**, first, and second **treble flute in G**, one player per part
- unlimited numbers on **concert flutes** in C, but usually only one solo, and more on the first, second, and third
- 4–6 **alto flutes** in G, often in two parts
- 4–6 basses in C

There might also be one or two **contrabass flutes** in C, if the band can afford to buy them. (Boehm-system flutes are usually named after the note that sounds when C is **fingered**.) These bands most often play transcriptions of Classical masterworks and arrangements of popular tunes, many from the 1940s and '50s.

Melody bands are bands that play traditional tunes, marches, and popular tunes in unison. They may use simple-system flutes or Boehm-system flutes.

Flute bands have been around for more than 150 years (e.g., the Churchill Flute Band of Londonderry was formed in 1835). They have been most popular in Northern Ireland, but can be found elsewhere, particularly in Scotland where Irish people have emigrated. They are usually very much a part of community life and can be found in numerous villages and towns playing in concerts, parades, rallies, contests, weddings, church services, and so on. It is not uncommon to see all ages of players in these bands, and some even have a training band that feeds into the main band when the students are ready. Women have been included in flute bands since the middle 1980s, partly to offset declining membership. While the bands often claim to be nonsectarian, they mostly admit Protestants to membership.

Sir James Galway (b.1939) made his start as a flutist in the Onward Flute Band in Belfast, which consisted of 16 flutes, a bass drum, side drums, triangles, and a cymbal. *See also* BAND FLUTE; E♭ FLUTE; FIFE (2); FLUTE CHOIR; "FLUTE IN . . ." (2).

FLÛTE BASSE. Fr. **bass flute**.

FLUTE CHOIR. A modern term that refers to an **ensemble** consisting of **flutists** on various members of the **Boehm flute** family—usually **piccolo** in C, **concert flute** in C, **alto flute** in G, **bass flute** in C, and sometimes **contrabass flute** in C (*see* FLUTE FAMILY [2] and app. 6 for examples of other possible members). The number and kind of **flutes** varies from one flute choir to another, but there are usually five or more. To date, the largest flute choir in the world is the one that plays at the National Flute Convention in the United States every August. Consisting of 1,500 or more audience members, the choir plays a 1973 arrangement of the J. S. Bach Air from the Suite No. 3 in D by **James Christensen** to signal the close of the convention.

Although there have always been groups of flutists who enjoyed playing together, ensembles called "flute choirs" did not surface until the 1960s when the popularity of the flute started to soar. This was mainly due to the popularity of **Jean-Pierre Rampal**, who made many recordings and toured the world playing in concerts on his flute. As a result of his fame, bands and orchestras met their quota of flute players, and flutists needed another outlet in which to play their flutes. Flute choirs sprung up to meet their needs.

At first, they consisted mostly of concert flutes in C, often also including piccolos and E♭ **flutes**. As there was little or no appropriate music at the time, flute **quartets** and **trios** were used, doubling the **parts** as necessary. To meet the growing demand for music, flutists and composers started arranging and composing music. Because **low-pitched flutes** were rare or nonexistent, it was difficult to give a true rendition of the original music upon which

their arrangements were based, so flutists employed players of string bass, cello, bassoon, bass clarinet, piano, or tuba to fill in the missing voices. Over the years, however, as flute choirs became more popular, lower-pitched flutes such as alto flutes, bass flutes, and contrabass flutes gradually supplemented or replaced these other instruments, and more music was composed or arranged to meet the demand. Flute choirs are now popular in many countries around the world. *Cf.* **flute band**.

FLÛTE CONTRALTO EN SOL. French term for **alto flute in G**. *Syn.: flûte en sol.*

FLÛTE D'ALLEMAGNE. Fr., German flute. The standard French term for the **flute** in the 16th and 17th centuries, and one of the standard terms in the 18th century, the other being *flûte traversière.* Variant of *Flûte allemande. Cf. flûte d'Angleterre.*

FLÛTE D'AMOUR. Fr. flute of love. It. *flauto d'amore;* Ger. *Liebesflöte.* **1.** There are two kinds of modern *flûtes d'amour* with **Boehm systems**, though neither is common: a flûte d'amour in A, which sounds a minor third below the **concert flute** in C, and one in B♭, which sounds a major second below the concert flute. Both flûtes d'amour have the same **fingering system** and are played in a similar way to the concert flute. The flûte in A, with a **B foot joint**, has a length of about 32 in. (82 cm); the one in B♭, with a **C foot joint**, has a length of almost 29.5 in. (75 cm). The **range** of both flutes is about three octaves.

Australasian virtuoso **John Amadio** (1884–1964) used a **Radcliff System** flûte d'amour in B♭ as a **solo** instrument and for accompanying singers in the 1930s. The flûte d'amour was revived in the 1970s in Europe and the United States, but to date, there has been little composed for it, the players normally using transposed popular flute **repertoire**. It is used in solo playing, studio work, and **ensembles**, though is not a regular member of the band or symphony orchestra.

The B♭ d'amour has been referred to as a **tenor flute**—a name many flutists think should be reserved for a flute type with a **pitch** between a **bass** and an **alto flute**. *See also* FLUTE CHOIR; FLUTE FAMILY (2).

2. Three kinds of flûte d'amour were popular in the 18th and early 19th centuries:

- One in B (named after the **six-fingered note** and a minor third below the standard **Baroque flute in D**)
- One in B♭ (a major third below the D flute); these were called "tenor flutes" in England, and there

are some extant instruments made by **Stanesby Jr.** and Schuchart.

- One in C (a major second below the D flute); some flutes in D had a *corps d'amour* enabling them to be played as a flûte d'amour in C.

The flûte d'amour ("flute of love") could have been named after its own beautiful **dark**, rich, mellow quality of tone, which may have evoked thoughts of love. Nevertheless, despite its beautiful tone, it did not remain popular and nearly went extinct. In fact, when Giuseppe Verdi scored three flûtes d'amour in the "Sacred Egyptian Dance" in the act 1 finale of his opera *Aida* (1871), the flutes had to be specially made because there were none in existence. The instruments' popularity peaked in Germany around the 1740s and the 1790s, and in Vienna in the first half of the 19th century.

Strangely, even though the flûte d'amour was popular for some time, very little original music for the instrument has survived. There are around 30 compositions by Christoph Graupner, a concerto by Johann M. Molter, and one by Johann A. Hasse. A large body of **works**, mostly all-flute **pieces** (e.g., **trios** and **quartets**), was written by Viennese composers in the first half of the 19th century. As **Johann Joachim Quantz** mentions in his famous **treatise** *Versuch* (1752), the flûte d'amour could transpose normal flute music. *See also* VOICE FLUTE (2).

3. *See* ALTO FLUTE (2).

FLÛTE D'ANGLETERRE. Fr. flute of England. A 17th-century French term for **recorder** or **English flute**. *Syn.: flûte douce, flûte. Cf. flûte allemande.*

FLÛTE DE VOIX. Fr. for **voice flute** in the late Baroque.

FLÛTE DOUCE. Fr. sweet (or soft) flute. One of the standard names for the **recorder** in France in the 17th and 18th centuries, the others being *flûte* and *flûte d'Angleterre* in the 17th century and *flûte* and *flûte à bec* in the 18th.

FLÛTE EN SOL. French term for **alto flute** in G. *Syn.: flûte contralto en sol.*

FLUTE FAMILY. 1. Any of the family of edge-blown **wind instruments** (where the player directs a stream of air at an edge to produce a tone), including all types of **flutes** and flute-like instruments. Flutes in this category are known to have existed since prehistoric times, and today, number well over a thousand. They may be classified according to how they are blown (e.g., **side-blown** or **end-blown flutes**), by their shape (e.g., tubular or

vessel flutes), or by their sound-producing mechanism (e.g., **duct flutes**). Sometimes flutes are joined together to make **multiple flutes**. All the above may have **finger holes** and/or **keys** and an open or closed lower end. *See* FISTULA (2), FRUITWOOD (1), and app. 1 for examples of each type. For information about other flute classifications, *see* GLOBULAR FLUTE; NOSE FLUTE; NOTCHED FLUTE; OVERTONE FLUTE; VERTICAL FLUTE; WHISTLE.

2. Any of the family of edge-blown flutes (see above) using the **Boehm system** are collectively called the **Boehm flute** family. Today, the most common members, in order from lowest to highest **pitch**, are the **contrabass flute** in C, the **bass flute** in C, the **alto flute** in G, the **concert flute** in C, and the **piccolo** in C. For other members, see appendix 6.

Boehm flutes are named after the sound that is produced when C is **fingered** (*see* "FLUTE IN . . ." [2]), and most have a **range** of around three octaves. They have been made from a variety of materials, the most common today being **silver**, **gold**, **silver-plated nickel-silver**, or **wood**.

Changing from one flute type to another is relatively easy, because the **fingerings** remain the same (*see* TRANSPOSING INSTRUMENTS), although many **flutists** prefer to use **alternate fingerings** to improve **intonation** and **response**. The player, however, will need to get accustomed to the slightly new **embouchure**, a different air speed and **articulation**, and a new playing position. *See also* app. 1; AEROPHONE; BOOT; FLUTE BAND; FLUTE CHOIR; G♯ KEY (1); MEMBRANE HEAD JOINT; RESISTANCE RINGS; STRAIGHT HEAD JOINT; UTILITY FLUTIST.

FLUTE FLAG. A popular cleaning device that enables all moisture to be **swabbed** from the **flute tubing**, including the hard-to-reach area above the **embouchure hole**. It consists of an acetyl plastic rod, 28 in. (71 cm) or 14 in. (36 cm) in length, with a rectangular piece of soft and absorbent man-made fabric about 9 in. by 1.3 in. (23 cm by 3 cm) attached like a flag to one end (see app. 12, fig. 4). The longer rod is useful for players who want to clean their flute without taking it apart, enabling them to leave their **head joint** setup in the location that was established when **tuning up**. It can be divided into two pieces to make it easy for traveling or to clean a disassembled flute. The shorter rod is for those who prefer disassembling their flutes for cleaning. The Flute Flag was invented by Roger Holman (1945–), an amateur flutist, in 2001 in San Diego and is also available for **piccolos** (Piccolo Flags), **alto flutes**, and **conical flutes**. *Cf.* **cleaning rod**.

"FLUTE IN . . ." The expression "flute in" followed by a letter name—for example, "flute in G"—is a way of naming a **flute** and usually has one of three meanings.

(For simplicity in defining the expression, the letter X is used below to stand for any note name [letter] used in the naming of flutes.) Sometimes, the terminology "X-flute" is used instead of "flute in X." This may have the same meaning as in either definition 1 or 2 below, although some scholars use "X-flute" to mean the older method of naming (def. 1) and "flute in X" to mean the modern method (def. 2). For example, by this convention, a Baroque flute would be both a D-flute and a flute in C.

1. In the older system of naming flutes, "flute in X" refers to a flute whose **six-fingered note** is X. By around 1900, this way of naming flutes was out of fashion for all orchestral flutes, especially members of the **Boehm flute** family. Today this way of naming flutes is usually reserved for **Baroque flutes, simple-system flutes,** and folk flutes (e.g., **fifes, Irish flutes, tin whistles**).

2. In the modern system of naming flutes, "flute in X" refers to a flute that sounds an X note when a written and **fingered** C is played. (The six-fingered note in this case would be one whole tone above the note represented by X.) This system of naming flutes is always used today for modern Boehm- (or modified Boehm-) system flutes such as the modern **concert flute,** but it also became common in the early 20th century for **one-keyed flutes** and simple-system flutes, as well as all other **wind** and brass instruments.

The scholarly trend is to use the modern system for all wind and brass instruments (e.g., the flutes in the **Dayton C. Miller** collection are named in this way; *see* DCM). Since this trend is not universal, the older flutes and folk instruments discussed in this book are named and defined in the way current players of these instruments do and/or as they are called in historical sources.

Sometimes the older and modern systems of naming are used together, with the name of one system in parentheses, as in "flute in G (or A)." In this example, the flute in G is the modern way of naming, and the letter name in brackets (note A, one whole tone above the note G) refers to the old way of naming. For other ways of naming flutes, *see* "FLUTE IN THE KEY OF . . ."; "FLUTE PITCHED IN . . ."; FOURTH FLUTE (1); HIGH-END FLUTE; HIGH-PITCHED FLUTE; INTERMEDIATE FLUTE; LOW-END FLUTE; LOW-PITCHED FLUTE; NATURAL SCALE; OCTAVE FLUTE; PROFESSIONAL FLUTE; SECOND FLUTE (1); STEP-UP FLUTE; STUDENT FLUTE; THIRD FLUTE (1); TRANSPOSING INSTRUMENTS.

3. Occasionally flutes will be named after their lowest note, which is not necessarily the six-fingered note nor the note that sounds when C is fingered. For example, the **recorder** is named after the seven-fingered note. The modern concert flute with a **B foot joint** may be referred to erroneously as a flute in B. This naming system is rarely used.

"FLUTE IN A," "FLUTE IN B," ETC. *See* "FLUTE IN . . ."

"FLUTE IN THE KEY OF . . ." This expression (or **"flute pitched in . . ."**), followed by a letter name, as in "flute in the key of G," is a way of naming a **flute.** It may either have the same meaning as **"flute in . . ."** or refer only to the **natural scale** upon which an instrument is built.

FLUTENIST. *Obs.* A **flutist, flautist,** or **flute** player. Apparently derived from the German *Flötenist.*

FLUTE PEG. Same as **flute stand.**

"FLUTE PITCHED AT A = . . ." This expression, followed by a number—as in "flute pitched at A = 440"—refers to a **flute** with a **scale** designed to play **in tune** when its A_1 is **tuned** to a particular **frequency** (in **Hertz**). *See also* "FLUTE PITCHED IN . . ."; HIGH-PITCHED FLUTE; LOW-PITCHED FLUTE.

"FLUTE PITCHED IN . . ." Same as **"flute in the key of . . ."** Also "flute pitched in the key of . . ." *See also* "FLUTE IN . . ."; "FLUTE PITCHED AT A = . . ."

FLUTER. Also *flouter, flowter.* From Fr. *flaûteur.* Archaic term for **flute** player, used until the end of the 19th century. *Flutist* and *flautist* have replaced this term.

FLUTE SECTION. *See* CHAIR; FIRST CHAIR FLUTIST; FIRST FLUTIST; PRINCIPAL FLUTIST; SECOND FLUTIST; SECTION (1); SECTIONAL; THIRD FLUTIST; UTILITY FLUTIST.

FLUTE STAND. A device used to hold a **flute** vertically when it is not being played (see app. 12, fig. 14). It consists of a vertical peg attached centrally to a horizontal base. The vertical position helps to prevent moisture from collecting on the key **pads** and provides a way of resting a flute in a small space. The flute stand may be combined with similar stands for one or more other instruments such as the **alto flute,** the **bass flute,** and/or the **piccolo.** *Syn.:* flute peg, flute spike.

FLUTE SUIT™. A device that is placed around the flute's **body** in a coat-like fashion and is intended to stabilize the **pads** and help avoid **leaks** when traveling, during changing environmental conditions, and whenever the flute pads need extra support, such as when storing a second flute. The Flute Suit consists of numerous small elastic/velvet strips that are clasped close with Velcro fasteners (see app. 12, fig. 6). When placed around specific **keys** on the flute's body, the strips depress the keys, thus forcing the pads into contact with the **tone holes** and reinforcing the **pad impressions**. According to flute repairer **Anne H. Pollack** (b.1958), the designer of the device in 1994, the end result is that the flute pads and **adjustments** are stabilized and will **seal** better.

FLÛTE TRAVERSIÈRE. Fr. **transverse flute. 1.** One of the two standard names for the **flute** (along with *flûte allemande*) in the 18th century (similar to the terms *flaüste traversienne* and *flahute traversaine* found in the 13th and 14th centuries). **2.** A term used today to distinguish the flute from the **recorder**.

FLUTING. Same etymology as for *flute.* **1.** *v.* Archaic for "playing the flute." **2.** *v.* Making concave grooves or flutes (def. 4) in an object such as a wooden or glass **head joint** (see app. 2, fig. 8).

FLUTIST. Fr. *flûtiste.* A **flute** player. The word *flutist* is first documented in 1603 and means the same as *flautist. See also* FIRST CHAIR FLUTIST; FIRST FLUTIST; *FLAUTISTA*; FLUTENIST; FLUTER; PRINCIPAL FLUTIST; SECOND FLUTIST; THIRD FLUTIST.

FLUTTER-TONGUING. It. *frullato;* Ger. *Flatterzunge.* Abbr. flatter, flat. A purring sound produced by allowing the airflow to rapidly flutter (or roll) the tip of the tongue or the **uvula** while playing a note. Neither type of flutter-tonguing is really "**tonguing**" in the usual sense of the word. Tonguing involves the releasing of the airstream using the tongue as the valve; the tongue actively controls the airflow. Flutter-tonguing is just the opposite: The airflow, in a way, is controlling the tongue.

Flutter-tonguing is shown in many different ways; some examples include:

The choice of which flutter-tonguing method to employ depends on the ability of the player, since there is no indication in music about which to use. *See also* EXTENDED TECHNIQUE; ROAR-FLUTTER; *TREMOLO* (2).

FLUX. A substance used to promote fusion during the **soldering** process. Flux serves to keep the soldered joint free from oxidation, which in turn helps the solder to flow and adhere to the **base metal**. There are different types of flux depending on the type of soldering. Flutemakers and repairers use acid- or rosin-based liquid fluxes (many also contain zinc chloride) for low-temperature **soft soldering**. For high-temperature **hard soldering**, they use paste fluxes that usually contain fluorides and potassium salts. *See also* BRAZING (1); FIRE SCALE.

FMG. An abbreviation for Flutemakers Guild, Ltd., which was founded in 1961 by seven Rudall, Carte craftsmen who decided that a move to the Boosey & Hawkes (which owned Rudall, Carte at the time) factory in Edgware, Middlesex, England, would be too far. The founding members of the guild were Ewan McDougall, David Keen, John Wicks, Roger Harris, David Tebbutt, Bob Wells, and Harry Seeley. C. S. Padgett was the director of the guild from its inception. Wicks and Wells eventually went back to Rudall, Carte. Three trainees were taken on during the life of the guild: Howel Roberts, Martin Gordon, and Chris Bouckley, with the last eventually leaving to go into the computing world. Of the original makers, all are now retired except for McDougall, who passed away in 1999. Seeley was the last to retire, in 1998. The guild struggled on for a while, but eventually had to fold.

The guild members made a wide range of **flutes** that included the most common members of the **flute family** (i.e., **piccolo, concert flute, alto flute, bass flute**) and an uncommon thinned wood flute (*see* THINNED [HEAD OR BODY] JOINTS). Of the options offered, the most unusual was the one that allowed **flutists** to design their own flute **scale**.

FOCUSING. Shaping and sizing the airstream efficiently so that no air is wasted and the sound is clear. This process of producing a note is sometimes called "focusing the tone" of that note. *See also* AEOLIAN SOUND; CENTERING; EMBOUCHURE PLATE; MOISTURE TRIANGLE; PROJECTION; RESIDUAL TONE; SWEET SPOT; WINGED LIP PLATE.

FOOT. 1. Same as **foot joint. 2.** Same as **kicker. 3.** *See also* LUG.

FOOT JOINT. Abbr. FJ, fj, **foot**. Pl. *feet*. The end section of the **flute** and the shortest of the three sections (see app. 7, fig. 1). Foot **joints** are named after the lowest obtainable note that they produce on the standard instrument in use. On the modern flute, the foot joint is cylindrical in shape like the **middle joint**. The foot joint of **early flutes** from the **Baroque** period onward usually tapered to its end, the final length being cylindrical or flared slightly outward.

There are two main types of foot joints on the modern flute—a **C foot joint** and a **B foot joint** (see app. 7, fig. 12)—and three less common ones: the **D foot joint** (see app. 7, fig. 12), **B/C convertible foot joint** (see app. 9, fig. 9), and **B♭ foot joint** (see app. 5, fig. 1). **Simple-system flutes** in the Viennese style were sometimes made, as early as 1820, with foot joints that extended as low as the note a and even g!

Also called a *tail* or, when attached to the middle joint, a *foot end* (*see* UNIBODY). *See also* app. 4; app. 11; BODY (1, 2); BOOT; BORE; BOX; COLE SCALE; "FLUTE IN . . ." (3); FOOT-JOINT CLUSTER; FOOT-JOINT NOTES; FOSTER EXTENSION; GUIDELINES (1); HEAD JOINT; INTONATION; KEYS (1); KEY TUBING; LEFT-HAND FLUTE; LEFT-HAND LEVERS; PICCOLO (1); RESISTANCE PLUG; RESISTANCE RINGS; RIBS; RING (2); ROCKSTRO MODEL FLUTE; ROLLER; SHORTENED HEAD JOINT; SOUNDING HOLE; SQUAREONE FLUTE; TENON JOINT; TIP (1); TRANSPOSING INSTRUMENTS (1); TUNING UP (2). For **early flutes**, *see also* ARTICULATED KEY; CONICAL BORE; EXTENDED FOOT JOINT; FOOT REGISTER; ONE-KEYED FLUTE; SIX-KEYED FLUTE; TIP (3); TWO-KEYED FLUTE.

FOOT-JOINT CLUSTER. The group of **touchpieces** on the **foot joint** that are within close proximity of each other. This includes the D♯ key, the **low C♯ key**, and the low C key on a **C foot joint** and the low b key and usually the **gizmo key** on a **B foot joint**. *Syn.:* foot-joint table.

FOOT-JOINT NOTES. Notes that can be produced only with the aid of a **foot joint**. These notes will be different depending on the type of foot joint used. For the **C foot joint**, they are C_1, $C_{\sharp 1}$, and $D_{\sharp 1}$. *See also* app. 11; RETUNING (2); ROCKSTRO MODEL FLUTE (1); TRADITIONAL SCALE.

FOOT-JOINT TABLE. Same as **foot-joint cluster**.

FOOT REGISTER. On some four-jointed **simple-system flutes**, a short end piece and **tenon** combination that could be slid into or out of the **foot joint** (up to about 0.5 in./1.3 cm) in a similar manner to a telescope (see app. 3, C, fig. 4). The foot register is said to have been invented by **Pierre-Gabriel Buffardin** shortly after the invention of the *corps de rechange* (said to be ca. 1720) to enable the **flutist** to play more **in tune** when changing from one corps de rechange to another. This tuning problem arose because of the change in length from one corps to another and the lack of **tone hole** respacing on the lower **joints** for each different corps.

A longer corps required the end piece to be pulled out to make the foot joint longer; a shorter one required the end piece to be pushed in to make the foot joint shorter. Adjustment of the foot register primarily affected the **low** and **middle** D, **flattening** them when extracted, but it had an effect on some **third octave** notes as well.

Just how much the foot register needed to be adjusted depended on the players and how they liked to play their D's. To aid the player with how much of the register to pull out for the corps, there were often incised lines about 0.1 in. (2.5 mm) apart and sometimes also numbers between the lines. For example, if the player chose to push the register all the way in with the shortest corps (which was often the case), the register would then be pulled out the width of one ring (or the ring labeled 1, in the case where numbers are present) with the second shortest corps.

Even though the original purpose of the foot register was to help improve the **tuning** of flutes with corps de rechange, they were sometimes seen on flutes without these parts. In this case, the register helped with fine tuning. When the **head joint** (or head joint proper of a **tuning head**) was pulled out a small amount for tuning purposes, the register could be slightly extracted as well. Large changes were not required as with a corps.

The foot register met with mixed success. It was rejected by **Johann Joachim Quantz** in his treatise (1752) (1697–1773) as having so little effect as to be useless. Registers were rarely seen after the early 1800s—probably because the **C foot joint** was becoming more common (registers had only been used on D foot flutes) and the **pitch** of **ensembles** in various locations was becoming less variable, so fewer tuning adjustments were needed. The foot register is often referred to as *register* and sometimes as *index foot* or *tuning register*. *See also* ONE-KEYED FLUTE.

FORCE FIT. Same as **interference fit** or *press fit*. *Cf.* **slip fit**.

FORGING. A process whereby metal is forced to adopt a particular shape by hammering it, usually between two **dies**, which together form the desired shape. One die remains stationary, while the other is attached to the underside of a drop-hammer machine or press. Forging is done by flutemakers to make various **flute** parts. The process can also be carried out manually using hammers and an anvil. Since the act of hammering makes the metal harder and stronger, forging makes for stronger parts than **casting**, which is another way of making metal parts. However, forging is generally done only when many identical flute parts are to be made, since the dies used in the forging process are expensive. An example of a part that may be forged is a **key arm**. *Syn.:* drop forging. *See also* HAYNES, GEORGE WINFIELD.

FORK FINGERING. Abbr. forked. Usually the same as **cross-fingering**. Sometimes, however, this term may refer to a specific type of cross-fingering where, for part of the **fingering**, only the first and third fingers of either hand are used. For example, F_3 is a fork fingering:

$$T\ 1 - 3 - /\ 1 - - 4D_\sharp$$

Syn.: forked fingering, split fingering. For **early flutes** and other non-**Boehm-system** flutes, *see also* CARTE 1851 SYSTEM FLUTE; CARTE 1867 SYSTEM FLUTE; CRESCENT KEY; FOUR-KEYED FLUTE; RADCLIFF SYSTEM FLUTE.

FORWARD TONGUING. *See* FRENCH TONGUING.

FOSTER, RAYMOND (b. Connecticut, 1939). A Westinghouse engineer, recording engineer, and acoustician who invented the **Foster extension**.

FOSTER EXTENSION. A metal **tube** about 2.5 in. (6.4 cm) long (including the 0.5 in./1.3 cm **tenon**) that fits into the end of the **foot joint** (see app. 12, fig. 12). Right below the tenon are two large holes directly opposite each other and around 0.75 in. (1.9 cm) in diameter. The purpose of the holes is to terminate the **air column** and thus prevent the **flute** from dropping in **pitch**. The extensions come in **sterling silver** or 14-**karat gold** and are quite expensive. One or more may be used at a time. Depending on a particular flute's diameter, the tenon may need to be resized. It is claimed that some players experience an increase in depth of tone and an improvement in dynamic control and **projection** when using the extensions. The extension was invented by **Raymond Foster** (patent pending as of 2007). Available exclusively through the Carolyn Nussbaum Music Co.

FOUR-KEYED FLUTE. A **simple-system** (or **keyed**) **transverse flute** (or replica of it) that evolved from, and was similar to, the earlier wooden (or **ivory**), **conical-bored**, **one-keyed flute** in D except that it had four **closed-standing keys** (i.e., the by now standard **key** for D♯ and, most often, the additional keys for B♭, G♯, and F) (see app. 2, fig. 4).

The new B♭, G♯, and F keys were first added to the flute in the 1750s by flutemakers in London. The B♭ key was operated by the LT and controlled a **tone hole** (the B♭ hole) between the B hole and the A hole. When opened, it produced the note B♭ (or A♯) in the **first** or **second octave**. The key for the note G♯ (or A♭), like the "closed **G♯ key**" on the modern flute, was operated by L4. It controlled a tone hole (the G♯ tone hole) between the A hole and G hole, and when opened, it produced the note G♯ (or A♭) in the first or second octave. The key for F was operated by R3. It controlled a tone hole (the F tone hole) between the E and F♯ **finger holes**; when opened, it produced the note F in the first or second octave. Since this form of the F key lay across the flute **body**, it was later called the "**cross** [or short] F **key**." Unfortunately, since the finger used for the F key was also used to cover the E hole, it now had double

duties, which required it to be raised or lowered while shifting sideways. This made **slurring** from D or E♭ to F, and vice versa, very difficult to do because there was a problem of accidentally sounding the extra note E when moving between these notes.

With the addition of these new keys, each note, except for C (i.e., C₂ and C₃), had its own tone hole for the first time (i.e., those of the one-keyed flute: the six finger holes [C♯, B, A, G, F♯, E]; the D♯ tone hole under the D♯ key; the open **foot joint** end, which was essentially the "tone hole" for the note D; and the new tone holes of the four-keyed flute [those for the notes B♭, G♯, and F]). This more complete system of tone holes and keys enabled the **flutist**, if so desired, to use new **fingerings** for the notes F, G♯, and B. These new fingerings increased the volume of these three notes and allowed for improved **intonation** over the **fork fingerings** that were previously used for these notes on the one-keyed flute. Overall, the improvements eliminated most **veiled notes** and thus allowed for all of the notes of the flute to be more equal in tone and volume than they had been before on the one-keyed flute.

However, despite these improvements, many performers around 1800 did not readily accept the new key changes. Some players used the new keys for trills as well as for sustained notes, but used the old fingerings of the one-keyed flute for much of the **passage**-work. Also, despite the new keys, lip and breath adjustments were still needed to play **in tune**. By the 1830s, the four-keyed flute had become very popular, but by then was no longer state-of-the-art. It has been revived in modern times, and some people play originals or replicas of the instrument for Classical-period or Irish music. *See also* CLASSICAL FLUTE; EIGHT-KEYED FLUTE; FIVE-KEYED FLUTE; G♯ KEY (2); NINE-KEYED FLUTE; SIX-KEYED FLUTE; TEN-KEYED FLUTE; TWO-KEYED FLUTE.

FOURTH FLUTE. 1. The name for a **flute** that is **pitched** a perfect fourth above the **standard flute** in use. Therefore, since the standard flute today is the "**concert flute** in C," the term *fourth flute* would refer to a "flute in F." (In an older terminology used for **Baroque** and **simple-system flutes**, the standard-size flute was considered to be "in D," so a fourth flute would be said to be "in G.") This way of naming is rarely used today. (For other ways of naming flutes, *see* "FLUTE IN . . . ," "FLUTE IN THE KEY OF . . . ," and TRANSPOSING INSTRUMENTS.) *Cf.* **second flute** (1), **third flute** (1). **2.** The fourth flute part. **3.** Fourth **flutist**. *See* THIRD FLUTIST. **4.** An 18th-century name for a soprano **recorder** in B♭ (named after the seven-fingered note), a fourth above the modern alto (British: treble) recorder in F. *Cf.* third flute (2), **fifth flute, sixth flute, octave flute** (2), **quart flute**.

FOURTH OCTAVE. The notes contained in the octave that is three octaves above the lowest-pitched octave of a musical instrument. On the **flute**, these notes are from C$_4$ to F$_{\sharp 4}$ and are the instrument's highest notes, although most **flutists** prefer to play no higher than D$_4$. This octave is sometimes referred to by names usually reserved for the **third octave**—upper octave/notes/**register; high notes**/register; **top** octave/**notes**/register—but is more often referred to as the *altissimo* register. *See also* "Octave Designation" in the introduction; BREATH SUPPORT; CHARANGA FLUTE (1); GIZMO KEY; HIGH (1); HIGH REGISTER; RANGE; REGISTER (1); WHISTLE TONES. For **early flutes**, *see also* FALSET NOTES.

FOURTH REGISTER. Usually refers to the **fourth octave**. *See also* ALTISSIMO; REGISTER (1).

FRACTIONAL TONE. Same as **microtone**.

FRAIZING. Same as **undercutting** (2), but generally only refers to **tone holes**.

FREDERICK THE GREAT (FRIEDRICH II, KING OF PRUSSIA) (b. Berlin, 1712; d. Potsdam, 1786). German sovereign (reigned 1740–1786), **flutist**, patron of music, librettist, and composer whose output included **flute** sonatas and concertos. At the beginning of his reign, he established a court orchestra and opera in a newly built opera house. This required that he hire many musicians. These included **Johann Joachim Quantz**, who had previously taught Frederick the flute. Quantz was hired in 1741 to play flute, direct instrumental soirées, and compose. Frederick was a major influence on the composers who worked for him.

FREE-BLOWING. Describes a **flute** that **responds** very easily. Some **flutists** would say such a flute had little **resistance**, while others might say it had the correct resistance to get a good tone easily.

FRENCH. An ambiguous term, but which usually means the same thing as **open-hole key** or **French cup**. *See also* FRENCH-MODEL FLUTE.

FRENCH ARM. *See* KEY ARM.

FRENCH ARTICULATION. *See* FRENCH TONGUING.

FRENCH B♭. *See* BRICCIALDI B♭ LEVER.

FRENCH BUSHING. A small **ring** of metal or plastic (e.g., Delrin) between 0.08 and 0.12 in. (2–3 mm) high that has one end turned slightly outward to form a lip or **flange** (see app. 7, fig. 15). It is placed over the short metal cylindrical part, or **chimney**, that extends down from the middle of an **open-hole key cup**. The purpose of the French bushing is to hold the **pad** of an open-hole key in place. It usually does this by forming an **interference fit** with the chimney of the cup. *Syn.:* French grommet, grommet, pad retaining ring. *See also* BUSHING (2); GOLD PAD; LEAK; SHEET METAL; SPUD.

FRENCH CUP. Same as **open-hole (key) cup**.

FRENCH FLUTE SCHOOL. Although the renowned **Paris Conservatoire**, and thus a French school of **flute** playing, has existed since 1795, the term "French Flute School" usually applies only to a French-influenced style of flute teaching and playing that emanated in the early 20th century from the work of **flutist Paul Taffanel** (1844–1908) at this institution (now the Conservatoire National Supérieur de Musique et de Danse de Paris) and is the one most influential in modern consciousness. This style spread throughout Europe and America as graduates of the Paris Conservatoire, starting with those of Taffanel, took up orchestral and teaching positions and made recordings. It was originally noted for its use of the **French-model silver flute** with **open holes** (see CYLINDRICAL BOEHM FLUTE [1]) and a methodical study of tone, **technique**, and **articulation**, though curiously not of **intonation**. Standard **repertoire** (*see* MORCEAU DE CONCOURS) and specific teaching materials such as the Taffanel-**Gaubert method** and the tone exercises of legendary flutist **Marcel Moyse** were studied. As the French style spread throughout the developed world, it continued to evolve. Aspects of flute playing such as tone, repertoire, pedagogy, and the instrument continued to change. This makes the term less easily definable in a modern sense. *See also* ALTISSIMO (2).

FRENCH GROMMET. Same as **French bushing**.

FRENCH KEY/CUP/KEY CUP. Same as **open-hole key**.

FRENCH-MODEL FLUTE. A modified version of **Theobald Boehm**'s 1847 cylindrical flute, which today is referred to as an **open-hole flute** and most commonly has in-line **G keys** (see CYLINDRICAL BOEHM FLUTE [1]). It is so called because two French flutemakers, **Vincent Godfroy** and **Louis Lot**, introduced the five **open-hole keys** (named A, G, F, E, and D) to the **middle joint** of this **flute** around 1849, probably to increase the number of **alternate fingerings** that had previously been so popular. These **keys** had been **ring keys** on the conical **Boehm flute** of 1832 (see RING-KEY FLUTE), but had been replaced by **closed-hole keys** on the cylindrical Boehm flute of 1847. *See also* CLOSED-HOLE FLUTE; EMBOUCHURE HOLE; FRENCH FLUTE SCHOOL; ORCHESTRAL MODEL FLUTE.

FRENCH-POINTED ARM. *See* KEY ARM.

FRENCH-POINTED KEY/CUP/KEY CUP. A **key cup** that is attached to **key tubing** by a French-pointed arm. *Syn.:* French-pointed key arm. *See also* BEVELING; KEY ARM.

FRENCH-STYLE CASE. A **flute** carrier that comes with more expensive flutes. The carrier is a velvet-lined wooden case with rounded corners. It is covered with a thin layer of leather that has been stretched over the wood and forms a natural hinge. The carrier is usually made with sliding locks, which are located on the opposite side of the leather hinge. This type of case has no handle and usually comes with a cover. *See also* GLUE.

FRENCH-TONGUING. The use of the tongue in a forward position, as opposed to **tonguing** against the roof of the mouth. French-trained players since **Paul Taffanel** (1844–1908) have modified or adapted this approach to suit their individual teaching methods, but broadly it is taught by beginning notes with the tip of the tongue between the lips. As the speed of the notes increases, and as this form of **attack** becomes impracticable, the tongue is withdrawn until it is behind or between the teeth. The exact position of the tip of the tongue for faster tonguing depends on both the player and the clarity of the **articulation**. To many French-influenced players, there is no other way to articulate. In the 1990s, Dr. **Jochen Gärtner** of Germany filmed and recorded three French players and three German players thought to be typical of their flutistic schooling. He asked each to play a series of exercises in different parts of the compass while an X-ray camera observed the position of their respective tongues: the clarity of attack of the three French players (**Alain Marion**, **Raymond Guiot**, and **Aurèle Nicolet**) was clearly heard to be superior to the three German players, a point every professor at the **Paris Conservatoire** has been making since the days of Taffanel. *Syn.:* forward tonguing, French articulation, tongue out.

FREQUENCY. The number of vibrations per second of an object—for example, a violin string, the tines of a **tuning fork**, or the **air column** in a **flute**. Frequency is measured in cycles per second, which is given the special name of **Hertz** (abbr. Hz). The **pitch** of a musical note is determined by the frequency of its sound wave. The higher the frequency of the sound wave, the higher the pitch of the emitted sound; the lower the frequency of the sound wave, the lower the pitch of the emitted sound. A frequency of about 440 Hz is called **A** by musicians, although historically the frequency of A has varied a good deal (*see* CONCERT PITCH).

Musical intervals are determined by frequency ratios. For example, a frequency of 880 Hz (2:1 times 440 Hz) is also an A, but is an octave higher. A frequency of 660 Hz (3:2 times 440) is a fifth higher—an E—and 587 Hz (4:3 times 440) is a fourth higher—a D. To convert pitch to frequency and back, see www.phys.unsw.edu.au/jw/notes.html (note that the scientific method for designating the octave is used at this site; *see* "Octave Designation" in the introduction). *See also* ACOUSTIC IMPEDANCE SPECTRUM; BEATS; BELL (1); CENT; CONCERT PITCH (1); CUTOFF FREQUENCY; DIFFERENCE TONE; EDGE TONE; END CORRECTION; EQUAL TEMPERAMENT; FUNDAMENTAL; FUNDAMENTAL RESONANCE; HARMONIC; HARMONIC SERIES; HELMHOLTZ RESONATOR; JUST INTONATION; MEANTONE TEMPERAMENT (1); MODE; OVERTONES; PARTIAL; PITCH; REGISTER (1); REGISTER HOLE; RESONANCE (1); RESPONSE; SOUNDING HOLE; SOUND SPECTRUM; STOPPER; VEILED TONE (2); VIBRATO; VIRTUAL FLUTE (2).

FRONT WALL. Same as **blowing wall**.

FRUITWOOD. 1. Any type of wood that is from a fruit tree. Several different types of fruitwood have been used for flutemaking. These include pearwood (genus *Pyrus*), cherrywood (genus *Prunus*), and plumwood (genus *Prunus*). These three woods have many characteristics in common. Compared to the now very popular and more commonly used **African blackwood**, they usually have a fine and uniform grain and are durable and lightweight. However, they are more inclined to warp than African blackwood. Cherry, plum, and pear compare in hardness with other North American hardwoods, which are softer than the tropical hardwoods such as African blackwood. As a result, they **turn** easily when using very sharp tools. They also take a nice **finish**.

Cherrywood has sapwood that is whitish and heartwood that varies in color from light to darkish red, with further darkening upon exposure to light. Pearwood ranges in color from flesh tones to pink, with shades of red. Plumwood has sapwood that is dark yellow in color, while the heartwood is streaked a reddish-tan to warm brown. Their light weight makes them a good choice for making larger members of the **flute family** (e.g., tenor and bass **recorders**).

Fruitwood was used in flutemaking during the **Renaissance** period to make flute **tubes**. Today, it is used for the making of some replicas of **early flutes**, but is not popular for the making of flutes from the modern **Boehm** flute family. The most popular fruitwoods are those that can be stained a beautiful color, work up a nice finish, and sound well.

2. The term *fruitwood* has been applied to any wood, other than **boxwood**, that is light in color (e.g., apple, blonde, or stained maple). It has also been applied to material that is lightweight or apparently inferior.

FRULLATO. It. flutter-tonguing.

F♯ LEVER. *See* BROSSA F♯ LEVER; MURRAY FLUTE; ROCKSTRO F♯ LEVER; ROCKSTRO MODEL FLUTE; SPLIT F♯ MECHANISM; SIMMONS F♯ KEY.

FULL TONE. 1. A tone having a good balance of higher and lower **partials**, among other attributes, throughout the entire **range**. In the beginning stages of playing, the **flutist** usually strives for the louder full tone, because it is the easiest to achieve. *See also* BODY (3); BRIGHT TONE; DARK TONE; *DÉTIMBRÉ*; HOLLOW TONE; TIMBRÉ; TONE COLOR. 2. Tones that are loud. *See also* RESONANCE (2); VEILED TONE.

FUNDAMENTAL. 1. A **frequency** component: in a complex sustained sound of definite **pitch**, the fundamental is usually the component of lowest frequency. Sounds with definite pitch are usually periodic—they repeat after a period T. The fundamental frequency is $f = 1/T$. A periodic sound also has frequency components in the **harmonic series** (i.e., frequencies f, $2f$, $3f$, etc.; *see* HARMONIC [1]). The fundamental is the frequency component with frequency f. *Syn.:* first harmonic, first **partial**, lowest partial. *See also* BODY (3); DIFFERENCE TONE; OVERTONES; PITCH (1); PURE TONE (1); RESONANCE (1). 2. The lowest, or fundamental, note that can be produced using a **basic fingering** in the **first register** of the **flute** (i.e., notes up to $C_{\#2}$). For these **fingerings**, the flute stores energy in vibrations (called **resonances**) at one or more particular frequencies in the harmonic series. This means that a **flutist** can **finger** any **fundamental note** up to $C_{\#2}$ and **overblow** and/or shorten the **air jet** to produce up to seven or more notes almost exactly in the harmonic series. *See also* ANTINODE; HARMONIC (2, 3); NODE; OVERTONE FLUTE; PANPIPES; REGISTER HOLE.

FUNDAMENTAL FINGERING. Any **basic fingerings** for notes up to $C_{\#2}$. Most other basic fingerings in the flute's **range** are derived from these notes. *See also* FUNDAMENTAL (2).

FUNDAMENTAL NOTE. Any notes up to $C_{\#2}$ that are produced using **basic fingerings**. *See also* ACOUSTI-

CAL LENGTH (2); FUNDAMENTAL (2); HARMONIC (2, 3); HYPERBASS FLUTE; REGISTER (1).

FUNDAMENTAL REGISTER. Same as **low register**. *See also* REGISTER (1).

FUNDAMENTAL RESONANCE. The first **resonance** (called a "**harmonic**" by **flutists**), or the resonance having the lowest **frequency**. Usually used only in connection with the **basic fingerings** up to $C_{\#2}$. *See also* SOUNDING HOLE.

FÜRSTENAU, ANTON BERNHARD (b. Münster, Germany, 1792; d. Dresden, Germany, 1852). A German flute **soloist** who traveled throughout Europe at an early age performing on a traditional German **keyed flute**. He also played in various orchestras such as the Dresden Orchestra, where he was **principal flutist** from 1820 to 1852. Fürstenau was a prolific flute composer and the author of flute **tutors** in 1826 and ca. 1844 (see bib. under "Historical Methods, Treatises, and Tutors"). *See also* BREATH VIBRATO; FINGER VIBRATO.

FUSING. The process of attaching two pieces of metal at high temperature without the use of a **filler** metal. Two examples are "marriage of metals" and "friction welding." *Cf.* **bonding, cladding, plating.**

G

GALWAY, SIR JAMES (b. Belfast, Ireland, 1939). A world-renowned **flutist**, **flute** teacher, recording artist, conductor, editor, arts promoter, president of *Flutewise* and the BFS, and author of *The Flute* (London: Macdonald, 1982) and *James Galway* (London: Chappell & Co./Elm Tree Books, 1978). Galway received the OBE in 1977 and was knighted in 2001. He was formerly the **principal** orchestra player in various orchestras, including the Berlin Philharmonic from 1969 to 1975. *See also* FLUTE BAND; TIN WHISTLE.

GARDENER'S FINGERS. A term coined by renowned flutist **Trevor Wye** (b.1935) to represent one or more scratched fingertips—possibly as the result of rose pruning or other gardening work—that cause small but detectable **leaks** in the **seal** of **open-hole keys** and may cause the **flutist** to suspect a leak in the **flute**. This problem has been measured using a pneumatic leak testing machine, with which players were tested with and without cling film on their fingers. Flutists should avoid

scratching their fingertips if playing an **open-hole flute**. *See also* CLOSED-HOLE FLUTE.

GÄRTNER, JOCHEN. A **flutist**, teacher, and author (see bib. under "Pedagogy"). He studied medicine and investigated specific body functions in relation to **flute** playing. *See also* FRENCH TONGUING.

G/A TRILL KEY. 1. A small nonstandard **key** found on some flute **middle joints** to the left of the **D trill key** lever (see app. 9, fig. 6). The G/A trill key facilitates the G$_3$ to A$_3$ **trill**, since the player moves both this key and the D trill key with one finger (R1) when trilling. Note that another, more versatile nonstandard key—the **C$_\sharp$ trill key**—also facilitates the G$_3$ to A$_3$ trill, but the **intonation** and **response** are not as good.

The addition of the G/A trill key to the **flute** necessitates two extra small **tone holes** be made in the **tube**: one to the right of the **thumb keys** and the other to the left of the thumb keys. These tone holes are covered by extra **padded** key cups mounted on a single rod, thus adding a little extra weight to the flute. The G/A trill key is usually found on a flute with a **split E mechanism**, since this mechanism makes the G$_3$ to A$_3$ trill difficult. *See also* BOEHM FLUTE (1); PROFESSIONAL FLUTE.

2. Sometimes, confusingly, an alternative name for the C$_\sharp$ trill key, since one of the main purposes of the C$_\sharp$ trill key is to facilitate the G$_3$ to A$_3$ trill.

3. An uncommon elevated **spatula**-like extension of the upper **G key** cup (L3) on closed G$_\sharp$ key flutes. It is placed over the F$_\sharp$ key cup and, when depressed by R1, closes the upper G cup. It facilitates the G/A trill in the first two octaves. There is a similar extension on some open G$_\sharp$ key flutes that facilitates the same trill. It is an extra open-standing **touch** for the G **lever** (normally controlled by L4) that also, by means of a **clutch**, closes the G$_\sharp$ hole, if not already closed by L3.

4. A form of the G/A trill key that appears on some **simple-system** and **Reform flutes** after 1885.

GAUBERT, PHILIPPE (b. Cahors, France, 1879; d. Paris, 1941). A renowned French **flutist**, a **principal flutist** in some French orchestras, a conductor, a prolific composer, a **flute** professor at the **Paris Conservatoire** from 1919 to 1939, and the coauthor (with **Paul Taffanel**) of a famous flute **method** (see bib. under "Pedagogy"). *See also* MORDENT (2); T. & G.

G DISC. *See* LOWER G INSERT.

G DONUT (RING). *See* LOWER G INSERT.

GEORGE, PATRICIA DENGLER (b. Lubbock, Texas, 1942). **Solo** and orchestral **flutist**, Flute Spa **master class** teacher, contributing editor to *Flute Talk* magazine, and monthly columnist in *The Teacher's Studio*. *See also* CHUNKING.

GERMAN FLUTE. It. *flauto d'allemagna;* Fr. *flûte allemande, flûte d'Allemagne.* **1.** During the 18th century, the most common name in English for the predecessor of the (**concert**) **flute** as we know it today. It was used to distinguish the **standard flute** of the time from the **recorder**, which was sometimes called the **English flute**. The term faded from use after around 1800. *See also* MONZANI, TEBALDO; TRANSVERSE FLUTE (1). **2.** Any **flute** made in Germany. **3.** The **offset G, closed-hole flute**, developed first by **Theobald Boehm** in 1847. *See also* CYLINDRICAL BOEHM FLUTE (1).

GERMAN SILVER. Same as **nickel-silver**. Not to be confused with German **coin silver**. *See also* MAILLECHORT; TIN FLUTE (1).

GHOST TONE. A term coined by **Robert Dick** around 1975 to refer to a very soft diffuse whistle sound he produced on the **flute** that sounded "ghostly" to his ears. It can be produced by raising the back of the tongue close to the roof of the mouth and blowing across the **embouchure hole** in such a way as to make a soft, rather unfocused whistle. The whistled note will be amplified by the flute. The particular whistled note produced depends on the **pitch** to which the mouth is **tuned** by the tongue position, but will usually be the **fundamental** or a tritone above a **fundamental fingering**. A ghost-tone **glissando** will sound when the tongue is moved around in the mouth.

A ghost tone is notated by writing the term *ghost tone* or *ghost* above the ghost tone gesture, which may be notated with precise pitch and **fingering** or graphically represented with a line or lines in the shape of the musical gesture (a line going up for an ascending ghost tone, one going down for a descending ghost tone, a wavy line for an oscillating ghost tone, and so forth). Ghost tones may be combined **multiphonically** with **whistle tones**. *See also* EXTENDED TECHNIQUE.

GIG. *Slang.* A music-playing job booking for musicians, as in "The **flutist** was hired to play a gig in a restaurant."

G INSERT. *See* LOWER G INSERT.

GIORGI, CARLO TOMMASO (b. 1856; d. Viareggio, Italy, 1953). An Italian **woodwind** inventor who

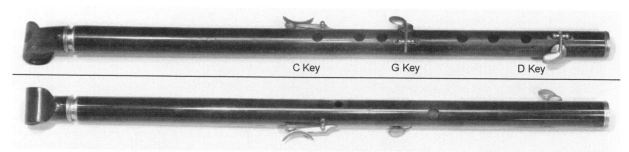

Figure 19.   A Giorgi flute, top and bottom views. *Photo courtesy Rick Wilson.*

designed the **Giorgi flute**. His business thrived in Florence. Giorgi was also an acoustician, **flutist, flute** professor, and author. *See also* END-BLOWN FLUTE.

GIORGI FLUTE. A vertically played **cylindrical flute** manufactured from the late 1880s on. It had 11 **tone holes** (12 if the hole at the open end of the **body** is included) and an **embouchure plate** at the end of a short piece of **tubing** that fits into a long one-piece body via a **tuning slide** (see fig. 19 for a top and bottom view). There is one tone hole for each semitone, from $D\sharp_1$ to $C\sharp_2$, which is placed in its acoustically correct position. The hole at the open end of the body enables the **flutist** to play the notes D_1 and D_2. The 11 tone holes require that the flutist use all eight fingertips, the third phalanx of the left-hand index finger, and both thumbs.

The Giorgi system of tone holes allows the player to play a complete chromatic scale up to $G\sharp_3$ by simply opening each hole independently. No troublesome **cross-fingering** is necessary for these notes. Because of the ease of **fingering** and playing position, the light weight, and the low cost, the Giorgi flute was advertised as, or said to be, an ideal instrument for students.

The Giorgi flute was designed by **Carlo Giorgi** (1856–1953) and first patented in Italy in 1888. From the patent, it can be seen that Giorgi preferred his flute to have no **keys**, but that keys could be added. There is evidence of keys on extant Giorgi flutes, which most commonly have three **open-standing keys** added to help players (particularly those with small hands) reach the tone holes. *See also* END-BLOWN FLUTE (1); OPEN-KEY SYSTEM; ORDINARY FLUTE (1).

GIZMO KEY. Also *gizmo*. An elevated **spatula**-like extension of the **low b key** found on many **B foot joints** (see app. 9, fig. 3). Since the gizmo key is isolated, it can be **fingered** to depress the low b key without accidentally depressing other **keys**.

The gizmo key was developed by renowned flute-maker **Verne Q. Powell** in the 1930s after being given the idea by flutist **Arthur Lora**. The location of the gizmo key can vary, but is traditionally to the right of the

C and B **rollers**. A gizmo that is positioned closer to the hand, to the upper left of the $D\sharp$ key, has been coined a "close **touch** gizmo" by the author.

An alternative name for the gizmo key is the *high C facilitator*, a name it acquired because it makes C_4 easier to play. Some flutists find that the gizmo key also facilitates some other **fourth octave** notes and the $B\flat_3$ to C_4 **trill** when it is pressed at the same time as the $D\sharp$ key with R4.

The gizmo key can alternatively be made to depress all three **foot joint** keys instead: $C\sharp$, C, and B. When configured in this way, it has the same advantages as the traditional gizmo and the extra advantage that it makes C_4 slightly **flatter** and less **bright**. *See also* BOEHM FLUTE (1); FOOT-JOINT CLUSTER; INTERMEDIATE FLUTE; PROFESSIONAL FLUTE; STUDENT FLUTE.

G KEYS. Two key **cups** on the **middle joint** of a closed $G\sharp$ **key** flute, which are mechanically linked and may be offset or in-line. *Offset* key cups are independently mounted and do not line up with the remainder of the left-hand **keys**, whereas *in-line* G keys are carried on the same rod or **steel** as the A and $B\flat$ keys and do line up (see the shaded keys in app. 9, fig. 1). Offset G keys were invented by **Theobald Boehm** and **Carl Mendler** about 1854.

Players who have shorter fingers, smaller hands, shorter arms, or wrist or tendon problems may find the offset G key flute easier to play. Although the offset G keys are generally considered to be mechanically superior to the in-line G keys, in that they do not have **binding** problems, there is no acoustical difference between flutes made with either type of key configuration, so the choice is often a matter of personal comfort.

Less common are *half offset G keys* or *half in-line G keys*. These terms refer to an arrangement of the G keys when they are positioned halfway between a fully offset and a fully in-line arrangement. The balance of the flute is the same in each case.

Syn.: (for G key to the left of the $G\sharp$ lever) upper G key, (for G key to the right of the $G\sharp$ lever) lower G key. *See also* BOEHM FLUTE (1); CLOSED-HOLE FLUTE; CYLIN-

DRICAL BOEHM FLUTE (1); DUPLICATE G♯ TONE HOLE (1); DUPLICATE KEYS; DUPLICATE TONE HOLE; EXTENSION ARM; FRENCH-MODEL FLUTE; G/A TRILL KEY (3); GERMAN FLUTE (3); INTERMEDIATE FLUTE; LOWER G INSERT; MAINLINE; MODEL NUMBER; OPEN-HOLE FLUTE; PINLESS MECHANISM; PROFESSIONAL FLUTE; RF MODIFICATION; SECTION (2); SPLIT E MECHANISM; SPLIT G KEYS; STUDENT FLUTE.

GLASS FLUTE. A **flute** in which the **tube** is made from glass. Parts other than the tube are made from a different material such as **silver**.

Claude Laurent (?–1848) was the famous maker of **crystal** glass-**bodied** flutes and **piccolos** from 1806 to 1848. His use of glass necessitated mechanical improvements in the flute that are still applied to **woodwind** instruments today. These improvements, listed in his French patent of 1806, included silver **tenons** and **sockets** for the **joints**; extra-long **springs**, resulting in increased resilience; and **keys** mounted in short silver **posts** that were attached either to silver sockets on the flute tube or to silver metal **plates** that were then screwed to the flute tube. Most of Laurent's flutes had no more than eight keys (*see* EIGHT-KEYED FLUTE), and only one was built to **Theobald Boehm**'s 1832 System (*see* RING-KEY FLUTE).

Both to beautify and lessen the weight of the thick glass tubing, Laurent cut the tubes on the outside with either **flutes** (def. 4) or diamond-shaped facets, avoiding vulnerable parts, such as **joints**, keys, and **tone holes**, so as not to weaken them. Unlike other materials used at this time, such as wood or **ivory**, glass resists the problems caused by humidity and temperature, and as a result, these flutes had the advantage of remaining dimensionally stable.

Laurent's crystal flutes were considered luxury items and were owned only by the wealthy or privileged. Among their owners were Napoleon I and his brothers, Louis Napoleon, the king of Holland, and Joseph Bonaparte, king of Spain.

Glass flutes as elaborate as Laurent's are no longer made, although handcrafted keyless Pyrex glass flutes, decorated with kiln-fired glass enamels and 22-**karat gold**, are made by Hall Crystal Flutes, Inc. *See also* app. 2, fig. 8; INLAYING (1); POST-MOUNT.

GLIDE. An expressive 18th- and 19th-century **technique** that involved sliding a finger or fingers gradually off (or occasionally onto) any flute **finger hole** or holes to achieve a continuous **pitch** change from one note to another. It is notated by two curved lines in the shape of a crescent between the two notes:

(see also fig. 16). The glide was popular among English **flutists**, including the famous flutist **Charles Nicholson Jr.** (1795–1837). For a better glide effect, Nicholson liked to crescendo during the glide and play the second note **sharper** than normal because of its tendency to sound **flat**. To make the gliding easier, he liked to have the wood flattened near the R4 and R5 finger holes of his flute. Today the glide is most often played by early flutists on **simple-system flutes**, Irish flutists on **Irish flutes**, and ethnic flutists on instruments such as the *bansuri*. *Syn.:* smear. *See also* CLOSED-KEY SYSTEM; GLISSANDO; HALF-HOLING; NICHOLSON'S IMPROVED FLUTE; OPEN-HOLE FLUTE; *PORTAMENTO*; POTTER, WILLIAM HENRY.

GLISSANDO. From Fr. *glisser* to slide. Pl. *glissandi*. A special effect in music where the player connects two notes by either using a fast chromatic scale or, more commonly, sliding the fingers off **keys** with or without **pitch bending**. On the piano, the player uses one finger to slide along the keyboard to the arrival note. Glissandi on the **flute** can be done in three ways:

- The **flutist** can gradually uncover the holes of a keyless flute one at a time. On an **open-holed flute**, the player gradually uncovers the open holes and then releases the key. Using this method, an almost continuous glissando can be produced up to A♯₃ (see Robert Dick, *The Other Flute* [in bib. under "Contemporary Flute"], 76–82, for more specific instructions). This type of glissando may be notated as

  ♩ or ♩ or ♩

  with or without the word *gliss.* above the line connecting the notes.
- The flutist can play all the regular notes between two given notes on an open or **closed-hole flute**. This type of glissando is called a *chromatic glissando* and may be notated with the words *chrom. gliss.* written next to a straight line connecting two notes.
- The flutist can play a **lip glissando**.

See also EXTENDED TECHNIQUE; GHOST TONE; HALF-HOLING; *PORTAMENTO*; QUARTER-TONE FLUTE; ROBERT DICK GLISSANDO HEADJOINT. For **early flutes**, *see also* GLIDE.

GLISSANDO HEADJOINT. *See* ROBERT DICK GLISSANDO HEADJOINT.

GLOBULAR FLUTE. A type of **vessel flute** that is spherical in shape. The **ocarina** is an example of a globular flute (see app. 1, fig. 15). The term sometimes means any vessel flute. For information about other flute classi-fications, *see* DUCT FLUTE; END-BLOWN FLUTE; MULTIPLE FLUTE; NOSE FLUTE; NOTCHED FLUTE; OVERTONE FLUTE; SIDE-BLOWN FLUTE; VERTICAL FLUTE; WHISTLE.

GLOTTAL STOP. A very short sound that is pro-duced by the rapid closing and opening of the glottis (the space between the **vocal folds**) while air continues to flow from the lungs. It is used extensively in many types of English pronunciation, especially at the ends of words (e.g., by many English speakers for the *t* sounds in words like *what, it,* or "that **flute**"). It sounds a little like the start of a cough. Its function is like that of the tongue: to stop the air and then allow the slightly pressurized air to sound the note, but it is not generally used in modern flute playing. Some **flutists** make this sound by mistake when the throat is too tense, when **tonguing**, blowing out, or when doing preparatory **vibrato** exercises. *See also* NANNY-GOAT VIBRATO; THROAT TUNING; VOCALIZING/ SINGING WHILE PLAYING.

GLUE. Any of a wide variety of adhesive substances. Flutemakers and repair technicians use various glues, depending on what is required for the job. Some of these include:

- *Shellac:* Made from the droppings and shells of the lac bug, shellac may be used for such things as gluing in **shims, pads, corks,** and **felts.** Even though shellac is brittle and runs when over-heated, it has been the most popular **flute** glue for the last hundred or more years. It is slowly being replaced by modern synthetic glues such as hot melt adhesive. *See also* LACQUER.
- *Contact cement/glue:* An adhesive cement that bonds on contact. It may be water or solvent based and is used to attach cork, felt, and the like to **bumpers, kickers, back-connectors,** and **tenons** or for fixing case linings. A thin coat is ap-plied to each piece, the glue is allowed to partially dry, and then the parts are pressed together.
- *Cyanoacrylate:* A generic name for a range of very strong adhesive substances with similar chemis-try including an acrylate base. They set almost instantly and are waterproof. They are usually sold under names like Superglue and Krazy Glue. Uses include attaching cork or felt to bumpers on kickers, keeping screws in place, or repairing thin **cracks** in wooden flutes that are not under exces-sive stress. Cured cyanoacrylate can be softened with acetone (an ingredient in some nail polish removers), made brittle if cold, or weakened if frozen or heated.

- *Hot melt (adhesive):* A type of solvent-free adhe-sive which is often derived from a mixture of a thermoplastic polymer base with additives that provide the required adhesive and structural prop-erties. It is applied after being heated to a molten state and sets rapidly upon cooling to form a solid bond between two layers. It is moisture resistant and can be reused when heated about 180°F (80°C). Hot melt is a modern substitute for shel-lac and may be used to glue in certain pads or flute case parts. *Syn.:* hot glue.
- *Loctite®:* A range of anaerobic adhesive-type sub-stances used for locking metal **key** parts to **steels** and keeping screws tight. Although liquid in the bottle, they cure in the absence of oxygen when trapped between close fitting metal parts. A va-riety of shear strengths are obtainable according to product number and conditions of use. The liquids also vary in viscosity to suit different joint gaps. Joints can be broken with heat.
- *Mucilage:* A thick, sticky substance used as an adhesive for pad making, **adjustments,** or other repairs. It is often made by dissolving gum in water, but ingredients may vary, depending on the usage.

See also INLAYING (1); PIVOT SCREWS.

GODFROY (GODEFROY, GODEFROID), VIN-CENT HYPOLITE (b. Paris, 1806; d. Paris, 1868). A French **woodwind** maker whose business thrived in Paris from 1836 to 1868 (from 1836 to 1855, he was in partnership with his brother-in-law **Louis Lot** under the name Société Godfroy fils et Lot). The firm made the first **conical** 1832 **Boehm flute** (*see* RING-KEY FLUTE) outside of **Theobald Boehm**'s workshop in 1837. *See also* app. 4; BRICCIALDI B♭ LEVER; CYLINDRICAL BOEHM FLUTE; DORUS G♯ KEY; EMBOUCHURE HOLE; FRENCH-MODEL FLUTE; VAULTED CLUTCH.

GOLD. A metallic element and one of the **precious met-als.** For flutemaking, it is **alloyed** with other metals, mainly copper, zinc, and **silver** in varying amounts. These metals alloyed with gold alter the hardness, corrosion resistance, ductility, and maleability and give it color variety—known as rose, **white,** and **yellow** gold. Gold is also used for **plat-ing** silver for protection against allergies, for aesthetic rea-sons, or for its resistance to **corrosion** (*see* GOLD-PLATING).

Gold content is standardized by the **karat** (*carat* in Europe) system, which is a measure of the number of parts of gold in 24 parts of the alloy. Thus, 24k means the metal is pure gold, while something of 14k gold would consist of 14 parts of gold and 10 parts of one or more other metals. **Gold flutes** are usually made from 9k, 14k, and 18k gold. *See also* AURUMITE; COCUSWOOD; DENSITY; FIRE SCALE; FLUTE FAMILY (2); GOLDBEATER'S SKIN; GOLD PADS; GS ALLOY; HALLMARK; HANDMADE FLUTE; PCM-SILVER ALLOY; PROFESSIONAL FLUTE; RED; RETUNING; SEAMED TUBING; SILVER FLUTE (1); SOLID GOLD; SPRING; STRESS RELIEVING; TARNISH.

GOLDBEATER'S SKIN. Same as **fishskin**, but so called because it is used by goldbeaters to separate the leaves of **gold** which they make by hammering. *See also* **pad**.

GOLD FLUTE. 1. A **flute** of which at least the **tube** is made from an **alloy** containing **gold**. Gold was only occasionally used for flutemaking in the 19th century. The first gold flutes were made by **Rudall, Rose & Carte** in London; one of these was displayed at the Second London International Exhibition of Industry and Art in 1862. **Louis Lot** of Paris made one gold flute, no. 1,375, in 1869 that was subsequently owned and made famous by the late **Jean-Pierre Rampal**. **Emil Rittershausen** of Berlin made a gold flute in 1896 that was owned by **Emil Prill**. **John C. Haynes** & Co. in Boston (whose flutemakers were **William S.** and **George W. Haynes**) also made an 18-**karat** gold flute in 1896; this was the first 18k gold flute made in America and the first flute known to have been made with a **drawn tube**. **Dayton C. Miller** made a 22k gold flute (DCM 0010) with 18k gold **keys** and **ribs** at the beginning of the 20th century. It was made of one continuously drawn tube, including the **tapered** head, and had a B♭ **foot joint** with an open G♯ **key** and an unadjustable D. C. Miller **scale**.

Today, gold flutes have become quite popular and all of the major high-end flutemakers offer them. The most popular alloy is 14k rose gold due to the color of the material and tradition. The choice of 14k is probably due to the fact that this is a common alloy readily available at jewelers' supply houses where some flute manufacturers buy their gold.

Gold flutes are, after **silver**, the second most popular flutes played by professionals. Parts other than the tube on gold flutes, such as the keys and **rings** (def. 2) are commonly made from silver. Small parts of the **key mechanism** are usually made from other metals (e.g., the **pins**, **pivot screws**, and the **steels** are usually made from stainless **steel** or carbon tool steel). *Syn.:* **solid-gold** flute. *See also* HALLMARK; NICKEL-SILVER FLUTE; PLATINUM FLUTE; SEAMED TUBING; SILVER FLUTE; SPLIT E MECHANISM; SPRING; TARNISH; WALL (1).

2. Misleadingly, a flute of which the **body** tube is of some metal other than gold, but which has been **gold plated**. Parts other than the tube and **plating** are as described above.

GOLD PADS. An increasingly popular **pad** invented and patented by flutemaker **Jim Schmidt** as an alternative to the **traditional pad**. It was introduced to the **flute** world around 1999 (gold pads are also available for saxophones). According to the maker, it is designed specifically for high-quality, **handmade flutes** and consists of a thin layer of fine **gold** powder embedded into the surface of a specialized durable film. The gold powder is embedded so that the particles of gold will be mechanically bonded into the film and exposed at the surface. Making the pad in this way allows it to remain soft so that it will close quietly on a **tone hole**. The film is attached to a moisture-resistant Ultrasuede cushion by a special bonding process that makes it very flat and smooth. The **cushion** rests on a plastic backing and is surrounded by a thin outer plastic lipped collar that serves to retain and hold the surface film in position. There is also an inner plastic collar that prevents the **pad retainer washer** or **French bushing** from being buried too deeply into the cushion, thus avoiding wrinkles. **Shims** are placed between the plastic backing and the key **cup** to bring the pad to its correct height and level in the same way that traditional pads are installed.

According to the maker, gold pads have several advantages over traditional animal-skin pads: They are more durable in that they do not tear or wear as easily as **bladder skin**, nor do they absorb moisture and warp. These beneficial qualities allow for a more consistent **seal** of the pad. Many **flutists** report that the reflective quality of the gold metal makes for a fuller, more **resonant** and **responsive** sound. To achieve the best results from gold pads, a flute must be in excellent mechanical **adjustment** and installed by an expert repairer. *Syn.:* gold powder pads, JS pads, Jim Schmidt pads, Schmidt pads.

Prior to making the gold powder pads, Schmidt was making **gold-plated** (or gold-foil) pads, which were made in a similar way except that, instead of using a thin layer of gold powder, a thin layer of pure gold was plated onto the specialized durable film on the pad-sealing surface. These earlier pads have been replaced by the gold powder pads.

GOLD-PLATING. A thin coating of **gold** used to cover the **body** and/or keywork of a metal **flute** for protection from **corrosion** or to protect the player from a **base metal** to which he is allergic. Gold is chemically inactive, so gold-plating is more durable than **silver-plating** because it does not **tarnish**. However, it is softer than silver and abrades or rubs through more quickly. Even though gold-plating on band instruments is 10 to 20 times thicker than typical jewelry, gold-plating is still not thick enough to give long-term protection to the base metal. Therefore, gold-plating shops put a full thickness of silver plate on the base metal before the gold-plate. Gold-plating is one of the least frequently used types of **plating**, probably due to its expense. *See also* AURUMITE®; BRASS; GOLD FLUTE (2); GOLD PADS; NICKEL-PLATING; PLATING; RHODIUM-PLATING; SILVER-PLATING; SOLID GOLD.

GOMEZ, HAROLD (b. Vancouver, B.C., 1946). An orchestral clarinetist, author of clarinet books, teacher, conductor, and music examiner who invented various items for the clarinet, the patented Gomez Music Stand Trays, and the **Valgon Rings** for the **flute, piccolo, bass flute,** and clarinet.

GOOSMAN, JACK P. (1945–2002). A Canadian maker of **Boehm flutes**, flute designer, and **flutist**. *See also* BUTTERFLY HEADJOINT.

GORDON, JAMES (CAREL GERHARD). (b. Cape of Good Hope, 1791; d. Lausanne, Switzerland, 1838). A Scottish and Cape Dutch **woodwind** inventor whose business thrived in Lausanne. He was also an amateur flutemaker and player, a French-Swiss army captain, and an author. *See also* COCHE, VICTOR JEAN BAPTISTE; CRESCENT KEY.

GRACE NOTES. The extra notes or **ornaments** that are added to the **principal note** to grace, decorate, or embellish it. Grace notes can enhance the harmony, emphasize a high point in a phrase, or make a rhythm more incisive. They are shown as one or more small notes written before or after a normal-size principal note (see the diagrams under *ACCIACCATURA, APPOGGIATURA,* TRILL, and TURN). Depending on the context in which they are found, they subtract their time value from either the preceding or following principal note. Large groups of grace notes are an exception in that they may take up the time value of an entire note to which they are attached and may be played with rhythmic freedom.

GRANDE BASSE DE FLÛTE. French term for bass **recorder** in the late Baroque.

GRANDE FLÛTE. Fr. large **flute**. Abbr. gde. fl. A French term that refers to the **concert flute**, used to distinguish it from the **piccolo**, which is often called *petite flûte* (small flute). *See also* FLÛTE (2).

GREASE GUARDS. Same as **tenon protectors**.

GREEN, TOM (b. Elkhart, Ind., 1941). An American maker of **Boehm flutes**, using **Bennett, Coltman,** and Laszewski **scales**. *See also* MURRAY FLUTE.

GREEN LINE. Describes instruments made out of a combination of **African blackwood** (grenadilla wood) powder, polycarbonate fibers, and a bonding polymer—a new material developed to make use of the scraps of grenadilla wood left over in regular musical instrument manufacture. Green-line instruments are said to have the same acoustic properties as natural wood instruments. However, unlike natural wood, they are not affected by changes of temperature and humidity, and they do not crack. To date, very few **flutes** have been made from this material, but it is quite likely that its usage will increase in the future as grenadilla wood becomes scarcer.

GRENADILLA WOOD. Same as **African blackwood**.

GREVE (GREVÉ), RUDOLPH (b. Mannheim, Germany, 1806; d. Munich, 1862). A **woodwind** maker who worked for **Theobald Boehm** from 1829 to 1839, before taking over the business in 1839 and using the name "Boehm & Greve." From 1846, he was no longer allowed to use Boehm's name, so he worked independently. His business thrived in Munich, Germany, until 1862. Along with Boehm, Greve invented the **vaulted clutch** in 1832. *See also* app. 4; EIGHT-KEYED FLUTE (2).

GROMMET. Same as **French bushing**.

GROSSE FLÖTE. Ger. large flute. Abbr. gr. Fl. Pl. *Flöten.* A German term that refers to the **concert flute**, used to distinguish it from the **piccolo**, which is sometimes called *kleine Flöte* (small flute).

GROSSE TAILLE DE FLÛTE. An 18th-century French term for **voice flute**.

GROUPING. A **phrasing technique** where the musician visualizes notes to be grouped in a way that gives flow or **direction** to the music. Grouping can also help the player to tackle difficult **passages** and play more evenly. As a visual aid, brackets are penciled in over the notes that are to be grouped together. The legendary **flute** pedagogue **William Kincaid** (1895–1967) is known for his idiosyncratic grouping method (see John Krell, *Kincaidiana* [Malibu, Calif.: Trio Associates, 1973; rev. 1977] for more information).

GS ALLOY. A gold-silver **alloy**, used in flutemaking by the Miyazawa Flutes Co. to make **head joints, barrels, tubing,** and **tone holes**. It consists of 10 percent **gold**, along with 89.5 percent **silver** and semiprecious metals that have been mixed together. The end result, according to Miyazawa, is an alloy that has an expanded **harmonic** range when compared to **sterling silver** and results in more **tone color** possibilities at the **flutist**'s disposal. The

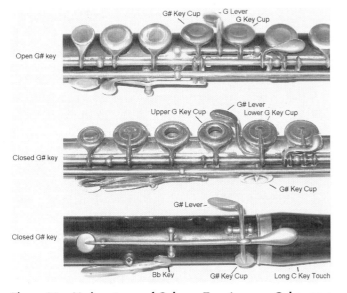

Figure 20. Various types of $G_\sharp$ keys. *Top:* An open $G_\sharp$ key on a silver-plated cylindrical Boehm-system flute by Ate Bonneville, Paris, ca. 1912. *Middle:* A closed $G_\sharp$ key on a grenadilla Boehm-system flute by W. R. Meinell, New York, ca. 1890. *Bottom:* A closed $G_\sharp$ key on a simple-system five-key cocuswood flute by Tulou, Paris, ca. 1835. *Photos courtesy Rick Wilson.*

alloy also has the benefit of being resistant to **tarnish**. The standard tubing is 0.015 in. (0.38 mm) thick, but heavy-**wall** tubing is available by special order.

$G_\sharp$ **KEY. 1. A key** on the **middle joint**. The $G_\sharp$ key may be open- or closed-standing. Most **flutists** play a **flute** with a closed $G_\sharp$ key, which consists of two parts: a key **cup** in the center of the underside of the flute, and a **touchpiece** in the form of a lever on top of the flute (see fig. 20, *middle*). The closed $G_\sharp$ key gets its name because when at rest it is kept closed over a **tone hole** by a **spring**. It can be opened by pressing the $G_\sharp$ lever with L4. On flutes with a closed $G_\sharp$ key, the **G keys** are linked and will close together when L3 presses the upper G key. This key linkage has a negative effect on some notes, especially E_3 (*see* SPLIT E MECHANISM).

Some flutists prefer an open $G_\sharp$ key, which is in the center of the topside of the flute (see fig. 20, *top*). At rest, this key is normally kept open over a tone hole by a spring, hence its name. It is closed when pressed by L3.

On flutes with an open $G_\sharp$ key, the key cups just above and below the lever for L4 are not linked. This lever, called the G lever, is attached to and closes the G key cup just below it (toward the **foot joint**) when it is depressed.

Today the open $G_\sharp$ key is unusual and needs to be specially ordered. It was, however, part of **Theobald Boehm**'s flute of 1847 (*see* CYLINDRICAL BOEHM FLUTE [3]), the predecessor of our modern flute, and for many reasons was much preferred by Boehm over any type of closed $G_\sharp$ key. For example, the flute with an open $G_\sharp$ key:

- is said to be better acoustically in the production of E_3 because this note is correctly **vented**. This is because there is only one tone hole open (i.e., A) between closed tone holes when playing E_3, instead of two (i.e., A and $G_\sharp$) as there is on the closed $G_\sharp$ key system.
- may be easier to balance for some flutists, since the little finger can be left down on the G lever for all notes except for A_1, A_2, $G_{\sharp3}$, and $D_{\sharp3}$. With the little finger down most of the time, the flute is more stable. It then becomes easier to play certain **passages** more smoothly or legato.
- allows for new **alternate fingerings**, some of which improve certain notes such as A_3 in specific situations.
- eliminates contrary motion in the left hand, which will facilitate **technique** when playing chromatic passages that include G and $G_\sharp/A_\flat$.
- has a simpler **key mechanism** as it has one less tone hole and key cup, so the flute is more easily maintained.
- is a little lighter since there is one less key and **pad**.

Although open $G_\sharp$ key flutes are available, some flutists choose to have their own closed $G_\sharp$ key flutes converted to the open $G_\sharp$ key system. This inexpensive procedure needs to be done by a competent repairer and involves having the hole under the closed $G_\sharp$ key cup covered with a patch (see **patching**) and the $G_\sharp$ lever disconnected from the closed $G_\sharp$ key cup and connected to the lower G key cup. The tone hole **chimney** under the now defunct closed $G_\sharp$ key cup may be removed. Some, however, prefer to leave it in situ in case they decide to convert back to the closed $G_\sharp$ system later on, perhaps making it easier to resell the instrument.

Even though Boehm's open $G_\sharp$ key has advantages, it necessitated a drastic change from the **fingering** of the **simple-system flutes**. To lessen the difficulty of switching to the **new system** and attract players of the old flutes, flutemakers in France introduced various forms of closed $G_\sharp$ keys in the mid-19th century (e.g., the **Dorus $G_\sharp$ key**). Although the open $G_\sharp$ key remained in use in Germany in the 19th century, the closed $G_\sharp$ key eventually became predominant everywhere along with the French-style instrument.

Reasons, including the one above, that some flutists today may prefer flutes with a closed $G_\sharp$ key are:

- When their flute is in for repairs, they will be able to easily rent or borrow a flute with a closed $G_\sharp$ key.
- It will be easy for them to buy or play on other members of the Boehm **flute family**, since most

of these instruments will have the same **key system.**

- Their flute teacher may be familiar with only the closed G♯ key system.
- Few, if any, beginner flutes are being made with open G♯ keys.
- Modern **fingering charts** and flute **methods** are usually for flutes with a closed G♯ key.
- There will be more flutes to compare and choose from when they decide to upgrade.
- Holding down L4 on the G lever of an open G♯ key system restricts the movement of L3 on the G♯ key.

Since overall there has been little demand for the flutes with an open G♯ key, flutemakers continue to make most flutes with a closed G♯ key. This makes it harder to get open G♯ key flutes. It does appear, however, that more advanced players see the advantages of the open G♯ key flute and are switching to a flute with this key configuration. It is clear, though, that unless there is a greater demand for a flute with an open G♯ key, the closed G♯ key flute will continue to predominate.

The closed G♯ key cup on the closed G♯ key flute may be referred to as an *independent G♯ key*, a *side G♯ key*, or a *shut G♯ key*, and the attached G♯ lever as a G♯ **spatula.** The G lever on the open G♯ key flute may be referred to as a G touchpiece, or a G spatula. When the term *G♯ key* is not described as being "open" or "closed," it usually refers to a closed G♯ key.

See also BOEHM FLUTE (1); INLAYING (1); LEFT-HAND LEVER; LOWER G INSERT; MURRAY FLUTE; PROFESSIONAL FLUTE; SPLIT MECHANISM.

For the closed G♯ key, *see also* ARTICULATED KEY; BACK-CONNECTOR; BODY-LINE G♯ TONE HOLE; CYLINDRICAL BOEHM FLUTE (1); DUPLICATE G♯ TONE HOLE; DUPLICATE KEYS; DUPLICATE TONE HOLES; FOUR-KEYED FLUTE; G KEYS; GUARDS' MODEL FLUTE; HIGH G♯ MECHANISM/FACILITATOR; INDEPENDENT G♯ TONE HOLE; INTERMEDIATE FLUTE; KEY EXTENSIONS; LEFT-HAND FLUTE; LEVER; LOWER G INSERT; QUARTER-TONE FLUTE; RADCLIFF SYSTEM FLUTE; RF MODIFICATION; SPLIT G KEYS; STUDENT FLUTE; WATERLINE KEYS.

For the open G♯ key, *see also* CARTE 1851 SYSTEM FLUTE; CARTE 1867 SYSTEM FLUTE; CYLINDRICAL BOEHM FLUTE (2, 3); DORUS G♯ KEY; G/A TRILL KEY (3); GOLD FLUTE (1); HIGH G♯ MECHANISM/FACILITATOR; REFORM FLUTE (1); REVERSED THUMB KEYS; RING-KEY FLUTE; ROCKSTRO MODEL FLUTE (1); SPLIT F♯ MECHANISM.

2. On simple-system flutes, a closed-standing key on the middle joint of a three-piece flute and on the upper or lower joint of a four-piece flute (see fig. 20, *bottom*). This closed G♯ key was among the small group of keys added to the 18th-century **one-keyed flute** to create the Classical **four-** and **six-keyed flutes.**

It was first applied to the flute (along with the **cross F key,** and the B♭ key) by English instrument makers in the 1750s. It was originally invented to provide an alternative, cleaner, more **resonant,** louder, and clearer **tone quality** for the note G♯₁, which until this time could only be **cross-fingered** and, as a result, had a **veiled tone.** It improved the tone of G♯₂ in the same way. It was also helpful, along with the B♭ key, in improving the tone quality and **intonation** of the hitherto difficult F₃ on the one-keyed flute. In the beginning, the key was slow to gain acceptance. Many players did not bother using it, and others did not like it because they thought keys harmed the tone. *See also* ARTICULATED KEY; DORUS G♯ KEY; DUPLICATE KEYS; EIGHT-KEYED FLUTE; FIVE-KEYED FLUTE; LOWER G INSERT; NINE-KEYED FLUTE; RING-KEY FLUTE; ROCKSTRO MODEL FLUTE; TEN-KEYED FLUTE; TWO-KEYED FLUTE.

G SOPRANO/TREBLE FLUTE. *See* **treble flute in G.**

GUARDS' MODEL FLUTE. A modification of the **Carte 1867 System flute** to make its **fingering** closer to that of the **Boehm flute** and the **simple-system flute.** The open **G♯ key** of the 1867 System was replaced with a **closed G♯ key,** and the note sounded with all fingers off save for the D♯ key was changed from the "open D" (D₂) of the 1867 System to "open C♯" (C♯₂). The Guards' Model Flute was manufactured by the flutemaking company of **Rudall, Carte** & Co. in London.

GUIDELINES. 1. Short lines engraved on the **head joint, middle joint,** and **foot joint** of some metal **flutes** (see app. 7, figs. 3 and 10). They can be used as reference marks to help line up the **joints** properly when the flute is assembled. On some wooden flutes, small metal alignment dots pressed into the wood are used for the same purpose (see app. 3, C, fig. 5; *see also* NICHOLSON'S IMPROVED FLUTE). **2.** *See* SCREW-CORK. **3.** *See* FOOT REGISTER.

GUILLOU, JOSEPH (b. Paris, 1787; d. Saint-Pétersbourg, France, 1853). A French **flutist** of **eight-keyed flutes,** orchestra player in various French orchestras, composer, and **flute** professor at the **Paris Conservatoire,** 1816–1829. Guillou created *L'Artiste Russe,* a French magazine about Russian musicians.

GUIOT, RAYMOND (b. Roubaix, France, 1930). A French **flutist,** pianist, teacher (including assisting **Alain Marion** at the **Paris Conservatoire),** orchestra player in various French orchestras, recording artist, and composer. *See also* FRENCH TONGUING.

GUNN, JOHN (b. Edinburgh, Scotland, ca. 1765; d. Edinburgh, 1824). Scholar, cellist, **flautist**, cello and **flute** teacher, and author of several **treatises** for various instruments, including two for the flute: *The Art of Playing the German-Flute on New Principles* (London, 1793) and *The School of the German-Flute* (London, ca. 1795). *See also* CLASSICAL FLUTE.

H

HALF-HOLING. The placement of a finger in such a way as to partially cover a **finger hole** or a hole in a **key** (i.e., the hole in an **open-hole key cup**) or to depress an open-hole key cup without covering the central opening. Half-holing is used to modify a **fingering** so as to create new (**alternate**) **fingerings** in order to facilitate the playing of certain **trills**, the changing of the **tone color** of notes for more expressiveness or for improving the **intonation** of notes, the making of special effects such as the **glissando** or **glide**, some **microtones** and **multiphonics**, or some combination of the above. Two examples of alternate fingerings that use half-holing to alter the intonation are: (1) For a **flatter** F_3, finger F_3 or

$$T\ 1\ -\ 3\ -\ /\ 1\ -\ -\ 4D\sharp$$

and press the **rim** of the E key down without covering the hole in the key; and (2) for a **sharper** A_2, finger B_2 or

$$T\ 1\ -\ -\ -\ /\ -\ -\ -\ 4D\sharp$$

and cover half of the hole in the A key. *Syn.:* half-stopping, half-venting, **shading** (def. 2). *See also* OPEN-HOLE FLUTE. For **early flutes**, *see also* SIMPLE-SYSTEM FLUTE (1).

HALF-OFFSET G KEYS. *Syn.:* semi-offset G keys. *See* G KEYS.

HALF-STOPPING. Same as **half-holing**.

HALF-TRILL. *See* PRALLTRILLER.

HALF-VENTING. Same as **half-holing**.

HALLMARK. A quality control mark that may be found on some **flute** parts made of **precious metal**, such as **silver**, **gold**, or **platinum**, to certify its purity. It is usually a fraction of an inch (or a few millimeters) across

Figure 21. A hallmark used in the United Kingdom for sterling silver flute parts. *Illustration courtesy Sheffield Assay Office, United Kingdom.*

and is applied after the part has been quality tested at an assay office that is independent from the flutemaker. Figure 21 shows a hallmark used in the United Kingdom for **sterling silver** flute parts. The symbols, from left to right, mean:

- SAO = Sheffield Assay Office (sponsor's mark)
- 925 = 925 parts per thousand silver, i.e., sterling silver (standard mark)
- Rose = Town mark, to show the item was assayed and hallmarked at Sheffield
- Lion denotes Sterling silver (pictorial standard mark)
- e = date-letter (for 2004)

Since January 1, 1999, the first three marks are compulsory and together constitute a U.K. hallmark. The last two marks are now voluntary. In certain countries, including Britain, it is illegal to describe a flute as being made from a precious metal unless certain parts have been hallmarked. *See also* RED; SILVER FLUTE (2); SOLID; WHITE; YELLOW.

HANDCUT EMBOUCHURE HOLE. *See* BEVELING; EMBOUCHURE RECUT; OVERCUTTING; PROFESSIONAL FLUTE; UNDERCUTTING; VOICING.

HANDMADE FLUTE. An ambiguous term that often signifies a **flute**, whether production-line or custom-made, that has more precision handwork than a **factory-made flute**. Due to this, and the fact that it is usually made from a valuable metal such as **silver**, **gold**, or **platinum** (although wooden flutes are making a comeback), it will be more expensive than a factory-made flute. Handmade flutes have optional French-pointed arms on solid key **cups**, rather than Y-arms, and do not often have **adjustment screws**. Until recently, handmade flutes usually had **soldered tone holes** rather than **drawn tone holes**, but the latter are now being seen more often. The owner can check with the manufacturer whether a flute is handmade by quoting the **serial number** found on the **barrel**, **rib**, or elsewhere. *See also* EMBOUCHURE HOLE; GOLD PADS; PIVOT SCREWS; PROFESSIONAL FLUTE.

HARD DRAWING. Same as **cold drawing**. *See also* DRAWING.

HARD SOLDER. Same as high-temperature **solder** or **silver solder**. *See also* BODYMAKER; BRAZING; FLUX; INLAYING (1); PATCHING; POST-MOUNT; RETUNING; RIB-MOUNT.

HARMONIC. A member of a series of **frequency** components, called the *harmonic series*, whose frequency is an integral multiple of the lowest frequency in the series, the *fundamental*. The second and higher harmonics in the harmonic series are sometimes called *overtones*. For the **flutist**, the term *harmonic* may refer to one of the following three things (*see also* NATURAL HARMONICS).

1. A frequency component of a note of definite **pitch**. A sound of definite pitch, such as that produced on a **flute**, consists of a vibration that is periodic (i.e., the vibration repeats after a period, T) and is considered as being composed of a sum of harmonics. If the frequency of the fundamental is $f = 1/T$, then the frequencies of the other harmonics are nf, where n is an integer—that is, the frequencies of the harmonics in the harmonic series are f, $2f$, $3f$, $4f$, and so on.

If a flutist plays a steady note with no **vibrato** and no pitch change, then the vibration cycle of the **air jet** repeats exactly over a cycle and contains several harmonics of various strengths. These will appear in the **sound spectrum** of the note. Their relative sizes are one of the things that contribute to the **timbre** of the sound. Each note of the flute has at least a few harmonics, whose number and strength depend on whether the note is played loudly or softly and on some other details of playing. *See also* ACOUSTICAL LENGTH (2); ATTACK; BEATS; BELL (1); BRIGHT TONE; CUTOFF FREQUENCY; DARK TONE; DIFFERENCE TONE; FULL TONE; HOLLOW TONE; MODE; PARTIALS; PROJECTION; PURE INTERVAL; PURE TONE (1); RESONANCE (1); TONE COLOR; VEILED TONE (1, 2).

2. A **higher note** produced from the **basic fingering**. For most basic fingerings in the low **range** of the flute, the flute stores energy in vibrations (called *resonances*) at one or more particular frequencies. Two or more of these resonances occur at frequencies almost exactly in the harmonic ratios (1:2:3, etc.). This means that a flutist can **finger** any **fundamental note** up to $C\sharp_2$ and **overblow** and/or shorten the air jet to produce up to eight or more notes almost exactly in the harmonic series. For example, the **fingering** for **low C** can be used to produce C_2, G_2, C_3, E_3, G_3, and so forth. The faster the air speed, or the shorter the length of the air jet, the higher the pitch of the harmonic.

For fingerings in the top half of the range, fewer harmonics (in this sense of the term) are obtainable, due to the filtering effect of one or more open **tone holes** (*see* CUTOFF FREQUENCY). Playing higher harmonic resonances is normal for the **second register** of the flute (i.e., from D_2 to $C\sharp_3$). E_2, for example, is played using the second resonance of the fingering for E_1, and the harmonics of the higher note are just the even harmonics of the lower. You can also play other harmonics with this fingering, and when doing so, they have a slightly different timbre (i.e., a different blend of harmonics or overtones) from that of the basic fingered note (see def. 3). *See also* ALTERNATE FINGERINGS; BREAK (2); CUT-OFF FREQUENCY; FUNDAMENTAL (2); FUNDAMENTAL RESONANCE; HYPERBASS FLUTE; JUST INTONATION; REGISTER (1); REGISTER HOLE; RESONANCE #1; RESPONSE; TUNING UP (2).

3. A small circle above a note

A composer may require the flutist to play a note with a different timbre than usual. To indicate this, a circle ° is placed above or below a notehead. This indicates that the flutist must use a fingering that produces a harmonic for the note indicated. (This fingering is sometimes called a *harmonic* or *flageolet fingering* and the note produced may be called a *flageolet* instead of a *harmonic*.) Sometimes there are two different notes: a regular-shaped note and a diamond-shaped note:

The regular-shaped note signifies the harmonic that is to be sounded when the diamond-shaped note is fingered and overblown. Since it is sometimes possible to use different fingerings for a given harmonic, and as composers do not always write down which fingering to use, it is helpful to become familiar with the harmonic series for the fundamental notes so that the best fingering for a given **tone color** can be chosen. *See also* BISBIGLIANDO; EXTENDED TECHNIQUE; KEY SLAP.

HARMONIC FINGERING. *See* HARMONIC (2, 3).

HARMONIC SERIES. An ordered series of **frequencies** with ratios that are integer multiples of a **fundamental** (i.e., f, $2f$, $3f$, $4f$, etc., where f is the frequency of the fundamental). **Wind instruments** produce sounds that consist of repeated vibrations and are made up of component frequencies in **harmonic** ratios. Thus, a note with a fundamental frequency f also contains the frequencies $2f$, $3f$, and so on, although the **pitch** is determined by the frequency f. The relative strengths of these harmonics, or **sound spectrum**, are one aspect that gives an instrument its characteristic sound quality. For the **flute**, the following are the harmonic series for the stated notes:

- b: b, B_1, $F\sharp_2$, B_2, $D\sharp_3$, $F\sharp_3$, very flat A_3, B_3, $C\sharp_4$, $D\sharp_4$
- C_1: C_1, C_2, G_2, C_3, E_3, G_3, very flat $A\sharp_3$, C_4, D_4, E_4

- $C_{\sharp 1}$: $C_{\sharp 1}$, $C_{\sharp 2}$, $G_{\sharp 2}$, $C_{\sharp 3}$, $E_{\sharp 3}$, $G_{\sharp 3}$, very flat B_3, $C_{\sharp 4}$, $D_{\sharp 4}$
- D_1: D_1, D_2, A_2, D_3, $F_{\sharp 3}$, A_3, very flat C_4, D_4
- $E_{\flat 1}$: $E_{\flat 1}$, $E_{\flat 2}$, $B_{\flat 2}$, $E_{\flat 3}$, G_3, $B_{\flat 3}$, very flat $C_{\sharp 4}$, $E_{\flat 4}$
- E_1: E_1, E_2, B_2, E_3, $G_{\sharp 3}$, B_3, very flat D_4
- F_1: F_1, F_2, C_3, F_3, A_3, C_4, very flat $D_{\sharp 4}$
- $F_{\sharp 1}$: $F_{\sharp 1}$, $F_{\sharp 2}$, $C_{\sharp 2}$, $F_{\sharp 3}$, $A_{\sharp 3}$, $C_{\sharp 4}$
- G_1: G_1, G_2, D_3, G_3, B_3, D_4
- $A_{\flat 1}$: $A_{\flat 1}$, $A_{\flat 2}$, $E_{\flat 3}$, $A_{\flat 3}$, C_4
- A_1: A_1, A_2, E_3, A_3, $C_{\sharp 3}$
- $B_{\flat 1}$: $B_{\flat 1}$, $B_{\flat 2}$, F_3, $B_{\flat 3}$, D_4
- B_1: B_1, B_2, $F_{\sharp 3}$, B_3
- C_2: C_2, C_3, G_3, C_4
- $C_{\sharp 2}$: $C_{\sharp 2}$, $C_{\sharp 3}$, $G_{\sharp 3}$, $C_{\sharp 4}$

Each series continues indefinitely but here is arbitrarily terminated at around D_4.

The lowest frequency or note in the series is usually called the *fundamental, first harmonic,* or *first **partial**.* In the spectrum of a given note, any of the harmonics above the first may also be called an *upper partial.* Alternatively, the second harmonic may be called the *second partial*; the third harmonic, the *third partial*; and so on. (Sometimes a different naming system is used in which the term **overtone** is used for any of the harmonics above the fundamental.)

When a flute tone is played softly, the upper partials are weaker in sound than the fundamental, but when a flute note is played loudly, some of them may be stronger than the fundamental. One of the special features that helps identify a flute from other **wind instruments** is the relatively strong fundamental. *Syn.:* overtone series. *See also* CUTOFF FREQUENCY; JUST INTONATION; RESONANCE (1).

HAUTE CONTRE DE FLÛTE. French term for soprano **recorder** in the late Baroque.

HAYNES, GEORGE WINFIELD (b. East Providence, R.I., 1866; d. Los Angeles, 1947). An American **woodwind** maker specializing in flutemaking. He was also a jeweler, a toolmaker, and a noted woodwind repairman. In 1898, he invented one-piece drop-**forged keys** and **drawn tone holes**. George W. Haynes and **William S. Haynes** founded the William S. Haynes Co. of Boston in 1900, starting with flute no. 507. The business thrived until 1936. *See also* DRAWN TUBING; GOLD FLUTE; HAYNES, JOHN C.; PLATINUM FLUTE; RETUNING; SEAMED TUBING; SOLDERED TONE HOLES.

HAYNES, JOHN C. (b. Brighton, Mass., 1830; d. 1907). A **woodwind** maker whose business flourished in Boston from 1861 to 1900. He was also a flute importer

and a publisher. His relationship to **George W. Haynes** and **William S. Haynes** is unknown, although the latter was superintendent of flutemaking at the business from 1894 to 1900. *See also* GOLD FLUTE.

HAYNES, WILLIAM SHERMAN (b. East Providence, R.I., 1864; d. Winter Park, Fla., 1939). An American **woodwind** maker specializing in flutemaking. He was also an author, a silversmith, and the inventor about 1914 of an aluminum **tube** for **wind instruments**. William S. Haynes and **George W. Haynes** founded the William S. Haynes Co. of Boston in 1900 and it prospered until 1936. *See also* DRAWN TONE HOLES; DRAWN TUBING; EMBOUCHURE HOLE; GOLD FLUTE; HAYNES, JOHN C.; RETUNING; SPOON FLUTE.

HEAD. 1. An alternative name for **head joint**. **2.** The top of a screw or **pin**. *See also* PIVOT SCREW.

HEAD CORK. A **stopper** that is made of **cork**. *See also* HEAD JOINT CORK; SCREW-CORK.

HEAD JOINT. Also headjoint, head-joint. Abbr. head, Hj/hj. The part of the **flute** that the **flutist** blows into. Along with the **foot joint** and **middle joint**, it is one of the three major parts of a flute (see app. 7, fig. 1). The head joint is slightly **tapered**, usually getting smaller from the open end to the closed end. For this reason, the shape is sometimes referred to as "**parabolic**." It is the only part of the flute that is normally without **keys** (*see* MEMBRANE HEAD JOINT). It has the most influence on the flute's tone, because this is where the sound originates. The head joint has many different parts (see app. 7; figs. 2, 10, and 11). *Syn.:* head piece.

See also ANGLED HEAD JOINT; BARREL (1); BLOWING WALL; BORE; BREAKING-IN (PERIOD); BULBOUS HEAD JOINT; BUTTERFLY HEADJOINT; COLD DRAWING; COMBINATION CASE; CONICAL BORE; CORK ASSEMBLY (1); CROWN; CURVED HEAD JOINT; CUT; CYLINDRICAL BOEHM FLUTE (3); DRAWING; EBONITE; EMBOUCHURE HOLE; EMBOUCHURE PLATE; EMBOUCHURE RECUT; EMBOUCHURE WALL; FAJARDO WEDGEHEAD; FINISHER; FLUTE FLAG; FLUTING; GUIDELINES (1); HEAD-JOINT CORK; HEAD-JOINT LINING; HEAD-JOINT MAKER; HEAD-JOINT NOTES; HEAD-JOINT REFITTING; HOME (1); INTERMEDIATE FLUTE; INTERNAL TUNING; INTONATION; JOINT; MODERN HEAD JOINT; MULTIPHONIC; MURRAY FLUTE; OIL (2); OLNHAUSEN RING; O-RING (2); PLATING; PLATING-UP; PNEUMO PRO; PROFESSIONAL FLUTE; RESISTANCE RINGS; RESPONSE; RISER; ROBERT DICK GLISSANDO HEADJOINT; SEAL; SEAMED TUBING; SHAKULUTE; SHORTENED HEAD JOINT; SILVER FLUTE (3); SLIP FIT; SOUNDING LENGTH (3); SPINNING; STEEL (1); STOPPER; STRAIGHT

HEAD JOINT; TENON; TENON JOINT; THINNED (BODY AND HEAD) JOINTS; TIP (1); TRADITIONAL HEAD JOINT; TUNING SLIDE (1); TUNING UP; UPPER CHAMBER; UPRITE HEADJOINT; VERTICAL HEAD JOINT; VOICING; WALL (1); WING-LIP HEAD JOINT.

For **early flutes** or other non-**Boehm-system** flutes, *see also* BARREL (2); CORK ASSEMBLY (2); *CORPS DE RECHANGE*; FOOT REGISTER; INVERTED CONICAL BORE; IVORY; ONE-KEYED FLUTE; REVERSE TENON; SCREW-CORK (1); SCREW-CORK ASSEMBLY; TIP (3) TUNING HEAD; TUNING RINGS; TUNING SLIDE (2); TWO-KEYED FLUTE.

HEAD-JOINT CORK. Abbr. cork. A carefully fitted **cork plug** inside most **head joints** near the **crown** and hidden from view (see app. 7, fig. 2). Its purpose is to **seal** off the end of the **flute** and create a cavity of air adjacent to the **embouchure hole** (*see* HELMHOLTZ RESONATOR; STOPPER). On modern flutes, there are metal **plates** attached to each end (*see* CORK PLATE). A screw joins the cork and crown together. This screw mechanism enables the cork to be moved by turning, or by turning and pushing, the crown in specific ways.

The placement of the cork is set by the flutemaker and is intended not to be altered (unless by advanced players for their individual **tuning** requirements) because it will affect the tuning (particularly the **third octave**), **response**, and tone of the instrument. However, sometimes the cork becomes loose and moves out of place due to drying out, shrinking, or warping or because the **flutist** has unintentionally moved the cork by twisting the crown. In these cases, the flutist will have to adjust the cork, allowing the player to optimize the third-octave response to suit personal preference.

To adjust the cork, the flutist inserts the **cleaning rod**'s grooved end into the head joint as far as it will go. The distance of the groove from the end of the cleaning rod should be the same distance as the **bore** diameter at the center of the embouchure hole and is most often 0.68 in. (17.3 mm). When the cork is properly adjusted, the groove, when viewed through the embouchure hole, should line up with the center of the hole (see app. 7, fig. 2).

The flutist can adjust the cork by tightening the crown, or by unscrewing it and pushing the assembly back into the head joint with the palm of the hand, until the correct position of the groove on the cleaning rod is obtained. To insure that the cork remains in the correct location, the flutist needs to check its placement occasionally, particularly if there is a tuning problem with the third octave.

Syn.: cork plug, cork stopper, end cork, end plug, head cork, head stopper, **plug**, stopper. Most corks are made to be adjustable and may be called *screw-corks* or *tuning corks*, although the term *screw-cork* is generally reserved for a type of head-joint cork assembly found on 18th- and 19th-century flutes or replicas. *See also* BOEHM FLUTE; CORK ASSEMBLY (1); CYLINDRICAL BOEHM FLUTE (3); FAJARDO WEDGEHEAD; HEAD-JOINT MAKER; OLNHAUSEN RING; OVERHAUL; "PARABOLIC"; PROFESSIONAL FLUTE; STUDENT FLUTE; TUNING SLIDE (1).

HEAD-JOINT CORK ASSEMBLY. Same as **cork assembly** (1).

HEAD-JOINT LINING. A thin metal **tube** that fit into some late 18th-, 19th-, and early 20th-century wooden or **ivory** head joints. These **head joints** were either fully or partially lined.

1. A full metal lining was common in English and German **one-keyed flutes** and **simple-system flutes** with two-piece head joints (or **tuning heads**) by the middle of the 19th century, but was rare in France. The tuning head, which was patented by flutemaker **Richard Potter** in 1785, consisted of a lined "head joint proper" and a lined **barrel** joint (or tuning barrel; *see* BARREL [2]). *See* TUNING HEAD for more detailed information on its construction.

Full linings are also found in the "**parabolic**" head joints of many English and German wooden **cylindrical Boehm-system** flutes, such as **Rudall-Carte** and **Boehm-Mendler** flutes, and other systems with a **cylindrical bore**, such as the Rudall-Carte **Radcliff System flutes**. The lining in the head joints of these flutes was **tapered** to fit the supposedly parabolic shape of the head joint. It extended fully or partially into the airspace of the **socket** and was separated from the socket wall, which was also lined, by a small annular region of airspace so that the **tenon** part of the flute's **body** could fit into this space when the flute was assembled.

One purpose of the full head-joint lining, and perhaps its original purpose, was to prevent the head joint from cracking by keeping moisture away from the wood. Unfortunately, although any linings initially prevented the head joint from cracking, the head joints had a tendency to eventually crack with age, as the wood or ivory dried and shrank, or if moisture got between the liner and the head joint parts and caused **corrosion**.

Some people claimed that another purpose of the full head-joint lining was to strengthen or otherwise improve the tone of the flute. Others insisted that it was detrimental to the tone, as it made the tone harsh. Thus, whether or not to have a lining in a head joint became a matter of argument and/or of taste.

2. Partial linings were sometimes used in the lower part of a one-piece head joint and also in the lower part of the head joint proper of a tuning head. They were constructed in the same way as for full liners except that the lining extended only a few inches (several centimeters) up from the open end of the head joint instead of for its entire length. This obviates objections to the effect of the lining on the flute tone. Today, the trend is for modern wooden flutes to use as little lining as will hold a metal tenon in a one-piece wooden head joint. *See also* THINNED (HEAD OR BODY) JOINTS.

HEAD-JOINT MAKER. The craftsman in a flute-making company who specializes in making the **head joint** for new **flutes**. Depending on the company and the materials used, the head-joint maker may do various things. For example, for a metal flute, the worker may:

- draw a straight (cylindrical) **tube** to the desired **taper** on a **mandrel**
- **stress-relieve** the tube by means of **heat treatment**
- cut the tube to the final length
- prepare the **lip plate** by hammering, filing, sanding, and so forth (depending on the company, he may or may not have been the one to **stamp** or **cast** the lip plate)
- clean up the **riser** (usually a **casting**) and **solder** it to the lip plate
- cut a rough hole through the lip plate
- solder the riser and lip plate to the tube
- cut a rough hole in the tube that now becomes part of the overall height of the riser
- smoothen any rough cutting by filing, scraping, or using various tools, such as rotary hand tools
- **undercut** or **overcut** the riser
- **polish** all parts of the head joint, both inside and out
- fit a **stopper**, usually a **head joint cork**

Once finished, the head-joint maker would either put the head joint aside or, if it was going on a specific flute, **fit** it to that flute. *See also* BODYMAKER; FINISHER; STRINGER.

HEAD-JOINT NOTES. Notes that can only be sounded on the **head joint** alone. These notes are approximately: $A\flat_2$, $A\flat_3$, A_1, E_3, and $C\sharp_4$. To produce A_1, the hole at the end of the head joint is covered with the palm of the hand; for $A\flat_2$, the hole is left open; and for $A\flat_3$, E_3, and $C\sharp_3$, the flutist **overblows**.

HEAD-JOINT REFITTING. The process of making the **head-joint** tenon from one brand or model of flute **fit** the **barrel** or **socket** of another that is either too big or too small for it. This can be done in several ways, de-

pending on size of the **tenon**, how much of a change is needed, and whether a permanent change is desired.

To fit a tenon that is too big, its outside diameter needs to be reduced by sanding, filing, **spinning**, **swaging**, **turning**, or **honing**. To fit a tenon that is too small, its outside diameter needs to be made larger by **burnishing**, **plating-up**, or **soldering** extra metal or a metal **sleeve** onto the tenon. Very small changes, including making a tenon round again and removing dents, can be done with a special tool available from instrument makers' suppliers. Burnishing is good for smaller alterations, plating-up for larger, and a sleeve for the largest change. These jobs are best done by a qualified technician. Alternatively, for a less permanent change, "magic" tape, or teflon tape, can be added to the outside of a tenon. Flutemakers can also make a new barrel or socket to fit the tenon, but this is not commonly done. *Syn.:* head-joint resizing, head-joint sizing. *See also* PLATING; SEAMED TUBING; STRETCHING; WALL (1).

HEAD-JOINT RESIZING/SIZING. Same as **head-joint refitting**.

HEAD PIECE. Same as **head joint**.

HEAD STOPPER. Same as **stopper**.

HEARTPIECE. Same as **lower (middle) joint/piece**.

HEAT-TREATING. A controlled heating and cooling process used in flutemaking as a way to change the properties of a metal or its **alloy**. This process usually affects properties such as strength, hardness, ductility, and malleability of both pure metals and their alloys. *See also* ANNEALING; CASTING (1); HEAD-JOINT MAKER; QUENCHING; SPRING; STRESS RELIEVING; TEMPER (1, 3).

HELMHOLTZ RESONATOR. A container of gas with an opening. For example, an empty bottle is a Helmholtz resonator. Acoustically there are two parts: the air in the largest part of the bottle acts like a **spring**, in that the pressure rises when it is compressed. The air in the neck is a mass that can vibrate on this spring. Like a mass on a spring, it can vibrate at a particular **frequency** when supplied with energy from an outside source—for instance, by blowing over the top of the bottle. For a **flute**, the most important Helmholtz resonator is formed by the air in the **embouchure hole** (the mass in this case) and the air between the embouchure hole and the **stopper** (the spring). Its purpose is to improve the **tuning** of octaves. Its effect depends only on the volume of the air between the embouchure hole and the stopper, not the shape of the cavity. *Syn.:* Helmholtz oscillator. *See also* HEAD JOINT CORK; "PARABOLIC."

HENNEBAINS, ADOLPHE (b. Saint Omer, Pas-de-Calais, France, 1862; d. Paris, 1914). A French **solo flutist** who played in a wind band, was **principal flutist** in various French orchestras, and served as a **flute** professor at the **Paris Conservatoire** from 1909 to 1914.

HERTZ. Abbr. Hz. A unit of **frequency** that is equal to one cycle per second. The term is named after a famous German physicist, Heinrich Rudolf Hertz (1857–1894). *See also* CONCERT PITCH (1); SOUND SPECTRUM.

HIGH. 1. A designation for a particular note in the **third octave** (or sometimes in the **fourth octave**) of the **flute**. For example, a **flutist** might say: "Play a high E," which would usually mean to play E_3. **2.** With respect to **intonation**, a note is said to be high when it is **sharp** in **pitch**. For example, a flutist might say: "Your $C_\sharp$ is high."

HIGH C FACILITATOR. Same as **gizmo key**.

HIGH E FACILITATOR. *See* LOWER G INSERT; SPLIT E MECHANISM.

HIGH-END FLUTE. A **professional**-model **flute**. *Cf.* **low-end flute**. *See also* GOLD FLUTE (1).

HIGHER NOTE. In general, a note that is **sharper** than another note, that is, **high** in **pitch** relative to another note. *See also* INTONATION; LOWER NOTE (1); RAISING A NOTE; TUNING SLIDE (2).

HIGH G$_\sharp$ MECHANISM/FACILITATOR. A linkage connecting the **G$_\sharp$ key** with the B-natural thumb key, found mostly on **piccolos** and occasionally on **flutes**. The purpose of the high G$_\sharp$ mechanism is to improve G$_{\sharp 3}$. While favored by some players, it is not accepted by many others because it decreases the **response** of C_4. The G$_\sharp$ mechanism works automatically when using the normal **fingering** for G$_{\sharp 3}$. On both the piccolo and the flute, the **key mechanism** partially closes the B-natural thumb key when the G$_\sharp$ lever is depressed. The G$_{\sharp 3}$ is thereby made easier to play and is more **in tune**.

It is important that this mechanism be properly adjusted, because the **venting height** of the thumb key will affect the amount of improvement of the G$_{\sharp 3}$ and the possible reduction of response of C_4.

On the conical piccolo, many players find that the G$_\sharp$ mechanism obviates the need to add R2 and R3 when playing G$_{\sharp 3}$. (This is a standard fingering on the conical piccolo.) **Conical bore** piccolos typically have two **tone holes** that are controlled by the B-natural thumb key, and there are two types of high G$_\sharp$ mechanisms available for conical piccolos with the double-thumb tone-hole design. With the first type, the G$_\sharp$ mechanism partially closes the B-natural thumb key and **shades** both tone holes. With the second type, the B-natural thumb key is split into two keys and the G$_\sharp$ mechanism closes only the **key** over the tone hole farther from the **head joint**. *See also* BOEHM FLUTE (1); ORCHESTRAL MODEL FLUTE; PROFESSIONAL FLUTE; SPLIT MECHANISM; SPLIT E MECHANISM.

HIGH NOTE. Any of the highest-sounding notes of a musical instrument: for the **concert flute**, any note above and including C_3. *See also* ALTISSIMO; ATTACK; CHARANGA FLUTE (1); CROSS-FINGERING (1); FIRST FLUTIST; FOURTH OCTAVE; HARMONIC (2); HIGH (1); LOW B, LOW C, LOW C$_\sharp$, ETC.; LOW NOTE; MIDDLE (NOTE); OVERBLOWING; RETUNING; RING-KEY FLUTE; TOP NOTES; TREBLE FLUTE IN G. For **early flutes**, *see also* BAROQUE FLUTE; CLASSICAL FLUTE; SCREW-CORK (1).

HIGH-PITCHED FLUTE. 1. A **flute** that sounds higher than another flute by a certain interval. For example, a **piccolo** sounds higher than a **concert flute**, and a **flute "in E$_\flat$,"** or "in D$_\flat$" is higher pitched than a flute "in C," even though all may be **tuned** to A = 440 Hz.

2. A flute that has been made to a higher (or highest) **pitch** for A than any one of a number of other pitches in general use at a given time or for a certain type of flute. There was no universally accepted pitch standard until A_1 was set at 440 Hz by convention in 1939, and despite this agreed-upon **concert pitch**, there are still different pitches in use at this time.

Today, some players might feel that a modern **Boehm flute** pitched at A_1 = 446 Hz is high pitched but one pitched at A_1 = 440 Hz is low pitched, and that a modern copy of a **Baroque flute** at A_1 = 440 Hz is high pitched while one pitched at A_1 = 415 Hz is low pitched.

In the late 19th and early 20th centuries, one could find significantly different pitches being used in the same location. For example, in London, flutes at pitches of both A = 439 Hz (New Philharmonic pitch) and A = 452 Hz (Old Philharmonic pitch) were furnished by **Rudall, Carte**, and these were called "low pitch" and "high pitch" for short. Many **German flutes** from this period have the initials HP (high pitch) or LP (low pitch) stamped on them. In this case, LP usually denotes a pitch in the range A_1 = 435 Hz (diapason normal) to roughly 440 Hz, while a flute stamped HP would be tuned at A_1 = 444 Hz to 450 Hz or above. *See also* CLASSICAL FLUTE; "FLUTE PITCHED AT A = . . ."; "FLUTE PITCHED IN . . ."; LOW-PITCHED FLUTE; MODERN SCALE; PRATTEN'S PERFECTED; SOUNDING LENGTH (3).

HIGH REGISTER. Usually, the **third octave**, but may also refer to the **fourth octave**. *Syn.:* top register, upper register. *See also* BEATS; FINGERING SYSTEM; LOW REGISTER; MIDDLE REGISTER; REGISTER (1); RISER; UNDERCUTTING (1).

HIGH-TEMPERATURE SOLDER. Same as hard or silver **solder**. *See also* FLUX; INLAYING (1).

HIGH WALL. *See* RISER.

HINGE-ROD. 1. Same as **steels. 2.** Sometimes incorrectly used to refer to **key tubing**.

HINGE TUBING. Same as **key tubing**.

HIP. Short for "historically informed performance," which is a musical performance where any performing members try to present the music in a manner inspired by what they can discover about performance from the time and place in which the music was composed. This may include playing on instruments suited to the time and studying period flute **methods** and other contemporary documents and sources.

HOLLOW TONE. A tone with weaker **overtones**. Sometimes referred to as an *aquarium tone, yellow tone, natural tone,* or **pure tone** (def. 2). *See also* BRIGHT TONE; DARK TONE; *DÉTIMBRÉ;* FULL TONE; *TIMBRÉ;* TONE COLOR.

HOME. 1. The position of a **joint** when it is fully connected with another joint. For example, a **flutist** might say that the **head joint** is "fully home." **2.** *See* **home base**.

HOME BASE. A term coined by the author to refer to a helpful position for the **flutist**'s fingers to rest before starting to play or to return to before using another **fingering**. It helps the flutist to get her bearings and makes the **flute** easier to balance. The location of the fingers in home base is just above or on the **keys** used to finger $E\flat_3$. This position can be represented by the fingering

T 1 2 3 4 / 1 2 3 4D♯.

The right-hand thumb does not depress a key, but is in place more or less under the right-hand F key, depending on the player.

The proper position of the fingers in home base is critical for **technique** and because some of the fingers will have to operate more than one key. While certain aspects about this position are common among flutists,

it will vary from person to person, depending on the physical characteristics of the person's hands, wrists, and arms. Overall, the most desirable position of the fingers and hands is best worked on with an experienced flute teacher. Some may refer to it as the *get-ready* or *home* position. *See also* SIX-FINGERED NOTE.

HOMOGENEOUS TONE. A tone where there is a blending of **tone color** of adjacent notes. This means that notes are produced in such a way that they flow smoothly from one tone color to the next. For example, if a scale is played on the piano from bottom to top, there is a gradual change in the tone color, but it is almost imperceptible between adjacent notes. It is not possible to achieve a uniform tone throughout all the notes of the **flute** due to its construction. As a part of basic **technique**, **flutists** strive to have the flute tone change almost unnoticeably in tone color throughout its **range** in the same way as the piano.

HONING. Sharpening or smoothening something with a whetstone. For example, the outside diameter of a flute's **head joint tenon** may be *honed* to fit the **barrel** of the **middle joint** (*see* HEAD JOINT REFITTING). A honing machine may be used to make a **bore** perfectly **cylindrical**.

"HOOVER" BASS FLUTE (IN C). *See* BASS FLUTE (3).

HORN. Used infrequently to mean the **flute**, but can refer to any **wind instrument**. *Cf.* **axe**.

HOTTETERRE "LE ROMAIN" (HAULTE-TERRE, HAUTERRE, HAUTETERRE, HOTETERRE, HOTERRE, OBTERRE, ETC.), JACQUES MARTIN (b. Paris, 1673; d. Paris, 1763). A French **flutist**, musette player, **flute** teacher, composer, and author of the earliest **transverse flute tutor** in 1707 (with **recorder**, oboe; see bib. under "Historical Methods, Treatises, and Tutors"). *See also* BAROQUE FLUTE (1); FALSET NOTES; FINGER VIBRATO; ONE-KEYED FLUTE; RANGE.

H.P. Also HP, H. Abbr. for "**high pitch**." *See also* HIGH-PITCHED FLUTE (2); L.P.

HUDSON, JOHN (n.d). A **woodwind** maker whose business thrived in London from 1853 to 1857. *See also* PRATTEN'S PERFECTED.

HUGOT, ANTOINE *(LE JEUNE)* (b. Paris, 1761; d. Paris, 1803). A French **flutist**, composer, **principal**

flutist in various French orchestras, **flute** professor at the **Paris Conservatoire** from 1795 to 1803, and author of *Méthode de flûte* in 1801 (see bib. under "Historical Methods, Treatises, and Tutors"), which was edited by **Johann Wunderlich** in 1804 and used at the Paris Conservatoire from 1804 until about 1845. *See also* CLASSICAL FLUTE.

HUMIDIFIER. A device used for humidifying the inside of wooden instrument cases, said to help prevent the instruments from cracking. *See* DAMPIT; HYGROMETER.

HUMORING. A **technique** where the **flutist** makes a slight adjustment to the **pitch** of a note to play more **in tune**. The flutist does this by altering his playing in some way, such as by changing his lips. *Cf.* **note bending, lipping, shading**.

HW PAD-SAVER®. A cylindrical brush formed by twisting together two wire rods that support short pieces of a soft microfiber projecting outward from the rods (see app. 12, fig. 5). According to **George Koregelos**, inventor of the Pad-Saver in 1975, it was designed to be left inside the **body** of the **flute** when not in use, where it is claimed that the fiber wicks corrosive moisture from the **pads**, **tone holes**, and **bore**. It can be used alone or, for maximum performance, in conjunction with a traditional cleaning cloth.

HYGROMETER. A device often kept in wooden musical instrument cases to monitor the humidity. Having an instrument dry out too much could lead to loose **joints, binding keys, rings** coming loose, and cracking. If overhumidified, it could lead to the development of sticking joints and mold. *See also* HUMIDIFIER.

HYPERBASS FLUTE. Also *hyper-bass flute*. The largest and **lowest-pitched flute** in the world. It is **pitched** in C. Its full length is about 40.4 ft. (12.3 m) and its height about 13.8 ft. (4.2 m). The lowest note is 16.35 Hz, four octaves below the **concert flute**'s C_1, or one octave below the piano's lowest C. The flute does not have a complete **range**, but can play six **fundamental notes** (CCC, GG, D, A, e, C_1) and the **harmonics** based on these notes. To change from one harmonic series to another, a **register** plug is removed from one of the flute's six **joints**. When this is done, the flute will sound the harmonics for that particular **tube** length.

The hyperbass flute was designed by flutist **Roberto Fabbriciani** in 1976 and built by flutemaker **Francesco Romei** in 2001. To date, it has been used only in **solo** concerts and recordings.

I

IMPEDANCE. *See* ACOUSTIC IMPEDANCE; ACOUSTIC IMPEDANCE SPECTRUM; CUTOFF FREQUENCY; STOPPER.

INDEPENDENT G♯ KEY. Another name for the closed **G♯ key**. Renowned flutemaker **Louis Lot** may have coined the term when he used it in his record book on November 28, 1860, for flute no. 479. *Syn.:* side G♯ key. *See also* CYLINDRICAL BOEHM FLUTE (1); DORUS G♯ KEY; INDEPENDENT G♯ TONE HOLE.

INDEPENDENT G♯ TONE HOLE. On a **flute** with a closed **G♯ key**, the **tone hole** under this **key**. *See* DUPLICATE G♯ TONE HOLE (2).

INDICATOR (ROD). *See* SCREW-CORK INDICATOR.

INLAYING. 1. The process of insetting a patch into an unwanted hole in a flute **tube**. In the case of metal flutes, the patch is placed inside and **hard-soldered** into the tube. This process may be disadvantageous, because it involves softening the tube, which may, in turn, alter the tonal properties of the flute. However, the process also has advantages since there is no overlapping of metal. On a wooden flute, the technique involves making a matching wooden **plug** and cutting it to exactly fit inside and on top of the **saddle seat** of an unwanted **tone hole** and **gluing** it into place. The new tone hole can then be cut in its new position. In these processes, the inner and outer dimensions of the flute tube can be maintained and any inlaying work can be made almost undetectable.

Inlaying may be used when **retuning** a flute, converting a closed **G♯ key** flute to an open **G♯ key** flute, or repairing a badly damaged flute. On wooden flutes, it may also be done to fill in and recut the **embouchure hole** if it has been worn or damaged. *Cf.* **patching, stretching**.

2. The process of setting various materials into the surface of certain flute parts, such as the **keys** or **embouchure plate**. The inlaying of flute parts is done for various reasons. For example, British flutemaker **Stephen Wessel** (b.1945) inlays his stainless **steel** flute keys with hard polished black plastic to make the flute lighter and more **responsive** (see fig. 22, showing Wessel's inlayed thumb-key assembly). *See also* AIR REED (2); EMBOUCHURE-HOLE BUSHING; TONE-HOLE BUSHING.

IN-LINE G KEYS. *See* G KEYS.

INSERT. 1. *See* BUSHING (1). **2.** *See* INLAYING (2). **3.** *See* LOWER G INSERT. **4.** *See* PLUG (1). **5.** *See* AIR REED (2).

Figure 22. Stainless steel thumb keys inlaid with black plastic, made by Stephen Wessel. *Photo courtesy Stephen Wessel.*

INTEGRAL TONE HOLE. Same as **drawn tone hole**. *Syn.:* integral **saddles**.

INTENSITY. The rate of energy flow through a unit area. A term used to characterize sound, light, heat, etc. As used by acousticians, intensity is simply related to sound level in decibels. The term is used by **flutists** to mean a range of different things, which seem to differ widely among the people using the term—sometimes relating to the sound, sometimes to the means of producing it, and sometimes to the performance, but often without a clearly defined meaning. One definition from a highly respected book, *Kincaidiana* by **John Krell** (Malibu, Calif.: Trio Associates, 1973: 9), refers to *intensity* as the "supported **pressure** of focused air." *See also* BEATS; PITCH (1).

INTERFERENCE FIT. The mating of two parts under pressure, such that the inner diameter of one is smaller than the outer diameter of the other, or vice versa. An example of an interference fit is the common threadless type of **French bushing** that fits snugly in the open hole of an **open-hole key**. *Syn.:* force fit, press fit. *Cf.* **slip fit**.

INTERMEDIATE FLUTE. A **flute** with a higher-quality **key mechanism** and **head joint** than a **beginner flute** or **step-up flute** that will allow the player to develop to a more advanced level. There is an improvement in materials used to make various parts of the flute. For example, it may have a **silver riser** and **lip plate**, a silver **head**, or a silver head and **body**. It has either **open-hole** or **closed-hole keys**, in-line or offset **G keys**, a closed **G♯ key**, a **B♭ side lever**, Y-arms or French-pointed arms for closed-hole **keys** (*see* KEY ARMS), **drawn tone holes**, and a **C** or **B foot joint**, the latter having a **gizmo key**. Options that are usually seen only on **professional flutes**, such as **white gold springs** or silver keys, may also be available. Also called a *midrange, preprofessional,* or *advanced* flute. *See also* STUDENT FLUTE.

INTERNAL TUNING. Setting those variables that influence the **pitches** desired by the **flutist**. The pitches of the notes produced by the **flute** are determined by the following factors:

- length of the instrument
- size and placement of the **tone holes** and their **key** covers (*see* SCALE)
- **bore**, including variations in the diameter such as the **taper** in the **head joint** (*see also* "PARABOLIC")
- perforations in the keys (*see* OPEN-HOLE KEYS)
- cavities under **closed keys**
- amount of withdrawal of the head joint (*see* TUNING UP)
- setting of the **stopper**
- **resonance** effects in the player's mouth and throat
- coverage of the **embouchure hole** by the lips
- manner of blowing by the flutist (*see* OVERBLOWING)
- temperature, humidity, and composition of the air in the **tube**

The first five are fixed by the designer of the flute; the remainder are at least partially under the control of the flutist. The last factors—the temperature, humidity, and composition of the air in the tube—are all affected by the player's breath. Apart from the humidity, the chief variables in composition are the carbon dioxide and oxygen content. It is therefore desirable to breathe silently into the flute just before playing, if it has not been played for a time, such as a long silent interval in an **ensemble** number.

While the **pitch** of any particular note can be adjusted as desired by varying these quantities, other notes will also be affected, not necessarily advantageously. Withdrawing the head joint, for example, **flattens** C_2 twice as much as it does **low C**. Pushing the stopper in will **sharpen** notes in the **third register** more and more as the scale in this **register** is ascended. Effects of mouth and throat resonance are small. Blowing with more **pressure** will sharpen any note—an effect that can be compensated for by increasing lip coverage of the **embouchure hole** either by rolling the flute in (*see* ROLL-IN) or extending the lips. *See also* SHORTENED HEAD JOINT.

INTONATION. Originally, a short phrase of plainsong often sung by the precentor to give the church choir a sense of an appropriate **pitch**. Nowadays, *intonation* refers now to how "**in tune**" a musician is as we listen to the oboe or a piano playing an **A** or check with a **tuning** machine (*see* TUNER). If a musician has good intonation—is in tune—then she is generally playing all the notes at an appropriate pitch. If she has poor intonation, or is "**out of tune**," then she is playing her notes **higher** (i.e., **sharper**) or **lower** (**flatter**) than an appropriate pitch—or even more likely, a mixture of both!

Whether the pitch of a note is appropriate or not depends on the **tuning system** being used and the context of the note in the music being played. Ideally, modern **flutists** attempt to use a flexible (**Just**) **intonation** system that creates pure or **beatless** intervals with a bass note or attempts to create pure, beatless intervals with the (other) notes in a chord. Practically, however, the best they can do is to try to fit into an accompanying less-than-pure chord as best they can. In some cases, their efforts will lean towards **equal temperament** (e.g., when playing a chromatic scale), and at other times, they will make melodic deviations from equal temperament such as raising the thirds in minor chords and **flattening** them in major chords so as to get closer to a Just tuning. Some call the latter way of playing "**expressive intonation**." On occasion, flutists may even violate both equal temperament and Just tuning for purposes of playing more expressively, such as when the **flute**'s note is not in a chord (e.g., raised leading notes; *see* AUGMENTED NOTES); to some, this is "expressive intonation."

The tuning of the flute by the flutemaker has varied over the centuries so that the flutist could more easily play in tune with the tuning system being used at the time. For example, the tuning of the **Baroque flute** was influenced by the varieties of **Meantone** and **Well temperaments** in use in the 18th century. Modern flutes are **tuned** close to equal temperament, but with a stretched **scale**, especially in the **upper register**.

Today, most flutists purchase flutes with a good **modern scale** that will make it easier for them to play in tune. Since flutes are made to suit the fashionable pitch of each country, they should buy a flute that has been built to the pitch required by their own region.

Before playing, the flute is warmed up to room temperature. (The warmer the flute, the sharper it will play; the colder, the flatter.) As a one-time procedure, the **octave length** of the flute is checked by following the procedure outlined in TUNING UP (def. 2). Then the **head joint** is placed in the best position to play at the pitch required (*see* TUNING UP [1]).

Much has to be done by the player even if his flute has been well made. Some flutemakers have their own deviations from what is an ideal scale—such as a sharp C♯ or a **foot joint** that is too short for **middle** D and E♭, among other problems—which will necessitate more corrective work by the performer. The quality of the result will vary depending on the skill of the player. To adjust the intonation, a player may:

- increase the air speed to play sharper (or reduce it to play flatter)
- blow higher on the **embouchure wall** to play sharper (lower to play flatter)
- make the **aperture** smaller to play sharper (larger to play flatter), which has the effect of increasing (decreasing) the air speed
- cover less of the **embouchure hole** with the lower lip to play sharper (cover more to play flatter)
- use an **alternate fingering** to play sharper or flatter

See also BASIC FINGERINGS; B FOOT JOINT; BOEHM SYSTEM; BROSSA F♯ LEVER; CARTE 1851 SYSTEM FLUTE; CHARANGA FLUTE (1); COLTMAN C♯; COOPER SCALE; C♯ VENT HOLE; CROSS-FINGERING (1); DRAWN TONE HOLES; FAJARDO WEDGEHEAD; FLUTE FAMILY (2); FRENCH FLUTE SCHOOL; G/A TRILL KEY (1); HALF-HOLING; HIGH (2); INTERNAL TUNING; KEY (3); KEY RISE; LEAK; LOW (2); LOWER G INSERT; NOTE BENDING; OPEN-HOLE FLUTE; ORCHESTRAL MODEL FLUTE; O-RING (2); PICCOLO (1); REAL-TIME-TUNING-ANALYSIS; REAM; RETUNING; ROCKSTRO MODEL FLUTE (1); ROLL-OUT; *SCHLEIFKLAPPE*; SECOND FLUTIST; STEP; TEMPERAMENT; THROAT TUNING; VENT HOLE (1); VIRTUAL FLUTE. For **early flutes** and other non-Boehm-system flutes, *see also* BRILLE (1); CHAMBERING; CLASSICAL FLUTE; CLOSED-KEY SYSTEM; CONCERT FLUTE (5); *CORPS D'AMOUR; CORPS DE RECHANGE;* FOUR-KEYED FLUTE; G♯ KEY (2); PRATTEN'S PERFECTED; SCREW-CORK; SICCAMA DIATONIC FLUTE; TUNING HEAD; TUNING SLIDE (2); TWO-KEYED FLUTE.

IN TUNE. A state where the notes being played are at an appropriate **pitch**. *See also* BEATS; CONCERT PITCH (1); C♯ TRILL KEY; "FLUTE PITCHED AT A = . . ."; HIGH G♯ MECHANISM/FACILITATOR; HUMORING; INTONATION; LIPPING; METRONOME; MODERN SCALE; MURRAY FLUTE; OUT OF TUNE; "PARABOLIC"; SHADING; SOUNDING LENGTH (3); STOPPER; TRADITIONAL SCALE; TUNER; TUNING FORK; TUNING NOTE; TUNING SLIDE (1); TUNING UP; VOCALIZING/SINGING WHILE PLAYING. For **early flutes** or other non-**Boehm-system** flutes, *see also* FOOT REGISTER; FOUR-KEYED FLUTE; RENAISSANCE FLUTE; SCREW-CORK (1); TWO-KEYED FLUTE; WELL-TEMPERAMENT.

INVERTED CONICAL BORE. The **bore** of a **conical flute** for which the **head joint** end is larger than the **foot joint** end. The bodies of **Baroque flutes** and Baroque and modern **recorders** have an inverted conical bore. *Syn.:* inverse conical bore. *See also* CONICAL BORE.

IRISH FLUTE. 1. A modern (ca. 1970s) development of the 19th-century English **eight-keyed, simple-system flute** that is used for playing traditional Irish music (see fig. 23). It has a **conical bore** and six large **finger holes**, but may be fully keyed (essentially making it a replica of

Figure 23. Examples of Irish flutes made by Australian maker Terry McGee in African blackwood and sterling silver. *Photos courtesy Terry McGee.*

the original English eight-keyed simple-system **flutes**) or more commonly have up to six **keys** with no **low C** or C♯ keys. Six-keyed Irish flutes are more common because the low C and C♯ keys of the eight-keyed simple-system flute are not often needed for Irish music; flutes with these keys are also expensive to make and difficult to keep regulated. Figure 23 *(bottom)* shows a six-key Irish flute with long **D foot joint** and traditional elliptical **embouchure**. The two holes on the foot are where the C and C♯ keys were fitted on the 19th-century eight-key original.

Keyless Irish flutes are also frequently used and seem to have developed around the 1970s in several countries by makers with no knowledge of each other's doings. Figure 23 *(top)* shows a keyless Irish flute with integral foot and modern-style "rounded rectangle" embouchure. Both flutes in figure 23 were made by Australian maker **Terry McGee** (b. 1948) in **African blackwood** and **sterling silver** and have their heads slightly extended to show the location of the **tuning slide**.

The Irish flute is most frequently in the key of D, which in this case means that the **six-fingered note** (almost always the lowest note) is D (*see* "FLUTE IN . . ." for more information about flute naming). It is most suitable for playing tunes in the keys of D and G major and E, A, and B minor. These are the most commonly used keys in the playing of traditional Irish music.

Some people prefer to play Irish music on modern **Boehm-system** (or modified Boehm-system) **concert flutes**. However, these types of flutes are less popular for playing traditional Irish music due to the complex **fingering system** and the lack of finger holes that could be used for the expressive **technique** of sliding from one note to another. There is also the potential problem of key noise on these highly mechanized flutes. Noise of this sort is not appropriate for the rapidly moving Irish dance music, particularly when it is played with the appropriate **ornamentation**. *See also* EMBOUCHURE HOLE; GLIDE; KEYED FLUTE (2); PRATTEN'S PERFECTED (2); SESSION.

2. The term is sometimes used to refer to original 19th-century English eight-keyed flutes. This is probably because for many players, their first contact with these instruments is through Irish music. Many feel that this is incorrect usage, however, since these instruments were not originally called "Irish flutes" by their makers.

IVORY. The hard, porous, creamy-white substance that is composed primarily of dentin and forms the tusks of the elephant. Many people believe that the ivory from elephant's tusks is the only "true" ivory, but others also consider the tusks of certain other mammals (e.g., the walrus, hippopotamus, narwhal, and mammoth) to be ivory.

Ivory from elephant's tusks was used in early flute-making, primarily from the 18th to early 20th centuries, to make various parts, such as **bodies**, **head joints**, end **caps**, and **mounts**. Earlier in this time period, entire **flutes** were sometimes made of ivory. However, because ivory was costly, it was usually used only for more expensive instruments. Later, probably due to the expense, it became more common (especially in Germany) to see only head joints made from ivory on a wooden body, and these head joints were usually metal-lined (*see* HEAD-JOINT LINING). In England, however, these types of flutes were never popular. Instead, ivory **embouchure-hole bushings** may sometimes be found. In fact, the renowned English flutist **Charles Nicholson Jr.** (1795–1837) recommended a wooden flute with an ivory embouchure bushing over a completely wooden flute.

Ivory is similar to wood in that it is not stable and will shrink or expand depending on humidity and temperature changes caused by usage or the environment. These changes may cause the instrument to crack. Also, like wood, ivory is a porous material and can stain easily when coming into contact with such things as lipstick or ink.

Today, since it is generally illegal to harvest real ivory, imitation or **artificial ivory** is usually used whenever new flutes (including replicas) or flute parts are made. *See also* FIVE-KEYED FLUTE; FOUR-KEYED FLUTE; GLASS FLUTE; LAPPING; MOUNTS (1); NICHOLSON'S IMPROVED FLUTE; ONE-KEYED FLUTE; TEN-KEYED FLUTE; THICKENING; TIP (3).

JET. Short for **air jet**. *See also* FLUTE (1); OVERBLOWING; PRESSURE; RESONANCE (1); WHISTLE TONE.

JET WHISTLE. A breathy **flute** sound that varies from a short, violent "shriek" to a very soft, sustained sound. A jet whistle is produced when the player places the mouth over the **embouchure hole** and blows a stream of air into the flute. The **pitch, tone quality**, volume, and duration of the jet whistle are affected by the choice of **fingering**, breath pressure, vowel shape of the mouth, and angle of the embouchure hole relative to the lips. A jet whistle may be notated as

Syn.: air rush, jet blow. *See also* AEOLIAN SOUND; AIR REED (1); EXTENDED TECHNIQUE; KEY SLAP; RESIDUAL TONE; STOP (1).

JEUNE. Fr. young, youngest, junior. Abbr. JNE. A term used to differentiate an individual from other older members of his family when they have the same first name. It may be stamped in its full or abbreviated form on **early flutes** after a flutemaker's name, as in the case of **A. Buffet** *jeune*. Cf. *aîné*.

JOINT. Any part of the **flute** that joins together with another part. *Syn.:* **piece**, section, part. *See also* BOX; BULBOUS HEAD JOINT; FOOT JOINT; GUIDELINES (1); HEAD JOINT; HOME (1); HYGROMETER; LEAK; MIDDLE JOINT; OUT OF ROUND; SOCKET; TENON JOINT; TENON PROTECTORS; THINNED (HEAD OR BODY) JOINTS; TIP (1); TURNING; UNIBODY. For **early flutes** and other non-**Boehm-system** flutes *see* BARREL (2); *CORPS D'AMOUR; CORPS DE RECHANGE;* FOOT REGISTER; HEARTPIECE; LAPPING; LOWER (MIDDLE) JOINT/PIECE; RENAISSANCE FLUTE; RETUNING (2); REVERSE TENON; TIP (1, 3); TURNING; UPPER (MIDDLE) JOINT/PIECE; WALKING-STICK FLUTE.

JOINT CAP/COVER/PROTECTOR. Same as **tenon protector**.

JULLIOT, DJALMA (n.d.). A French **woodwind** maker and inventor whose business thrived in France from 1890 until at least 1925. Julliot developed the Borne-Julliot System flutes (which were essentially various modified **Boehm-system** flutes), with **François Borne**, from 1889 to 1901. Julliot made a **bass flute** in 1910 and was an author (see bib. under "Repair, Maintenance, and Construction"). *See also* SPLIT E MECHANISM.

JUST INTONATION. A method of playing music where **harmonic** intervals are **tuned** so as to eliminate **beats** between some of the most important combinations of notes. The distances between these notes are based on the **harmonic series**. Just Intonation can be used by players of instruments such as the **flute** and string instruments where the **pitch** of notes is not mechanically fixed. Players continually adjust the pitch of their instruments as they play to blend well with other instruments.

When harmonic intervals are beatless, they are said to be "**pure**" or Just. Pure intervals are those whose **frequencies** have ratios that can be expressed in terms of small whole numbers, like 5 and 4. For example, pitches of 550 Hz and 440 Hz have the frequency ratio of 5:4. This ratio is called a pure major third since the interval is beatless. One Just diatonic scale has notes whose frequencies are in the ratios (to the tonic): 1:1 (unison), 9:8 (major tone), 5:4 (Just major third), 4:3 (perfect fourth), 3:2 (perfect fifth), 5:3 (Just major sixth), 15:8 (Just major seventh, played as a Just major third above the fifth), and 2:1 (octave). Note that there are two whole tones in the Just scale: 9:8 (the major tone) is the interval between the first and second notes, the fourth and fifth notes, and the sixth and seventh notes in an ascending scale. 10:9 (the minor tone) falls between the second and third and between the fifth and sixth notes in an ascending scale. The Just semitone is 16:15. This scale has beatless major triads, but the minor triad on the supertonic (second, fourth, and sixth notes of the scale) is far from harmonious since the relationship of the perfect fifth 5:3 to 9:8 in the minor triad is 40:27 rather than the more consonant relationship of the perfect fifth 3:2 to 1:1 in the major triad. This is an example of one of the complications that arise in Just Intonation (and in most **temperaments**): the player will use a different pitch according to context.

The **cent** is a unit used for measuring small pitch differences. In **equal temperament** (ET)—a **tuning system** that is widely used today for instruments where the pitch of notes is mechanically fixed, such as pianos and many organs—the semitone consists of 100 cents by definition, and thus the major third is 400 cents, while the pure major third (frequency ratio 5:4) is 386 cents. The intervals in ET are not pure or beatless.

The **flutist** can play in Just Intonation when required or desired. Modern flutes, played without consciously adjusting the pitch, usually play intervals closer to ET than Just Intonation. To alter an ET interval so that it sounds in Just Intonation, or beatless, the interval must be narrowed or widened. For example, if A_2 is 880 Hz, then $C\sharp_3$ is 1,109 Hz in ET. If one flutist is playing A_2 at 880 Hz and another is playing $C\sharp_3$ at 1,109 Hz, to play in Just Intonation or make this interval beatless, the second flutist could lower the $C\sharp_3$ significantly (29 Hz or 14 cents down from the $C\sharp_3$ of ET) or the first flutist could raise the A by the same amount (29 Hz or 14 cents up from the $C\sharp_3$ of ET).

The deviations from ET for the intervals important in harmony are listed below:

- A pure minor third with the frequency ratio 6:5 (316 cents) must be widened by 16 cents, as it is 16 cents higher than three ET semitones.
- A pure major third with the frequency ratio of 5:4 (386 cents) must be narrowed by 14 cents, as it is 14 cents narrower than four ET semitones.
- A pure perfect fourth with the frequency ratio of 4:3 (498 cents) should, in principle, be narrowed by 2 cents, as it is 2 cents narrower than five ET semitones.
- A pure perfect fifth, with the frequency ratio of 3:2 (702 cents) must be widened by 2 cents, as it is 2 cents wider than seven ET semitones.
- A pure minor sixth, with the frequency ratio of 8:5 (814 cents) must be widened by 14 cents, as it is 14 cents wider than eight ET semitones.
- A pure major sixth, with the frequency ratio of 5:3 (884 cents) must be narrowed by 16 cents, as it is 16 cents narrower than nine ET semitones.

A unison (with the frequency ratio of 1:1) and a perfect octave (with the frequency ratio of 2:1) remain unaltered.

Few, if any, ears can detect a difference of five cents or less, so musicians pay more attention to correcting their **tuning** for those intervals where there is a higher cent difference. Seconds, sevenths, and tritones are not listed, since it is rare or impossible to play these dissonant intervals beatless, and their pitch in performance is a matter of taste. Other intervals are not listed because it is mathematically impossible for all important intervals between pairs of notes in a single 12-note chromatic scale to be pure. In particular, it is impossible to tune a traditional keyboard so that all important intervals are pure, and this is why the need for temperaments, such as ET, arose.

Unlike ET, Just Intonation requires players to use a different tuning in different keys, since a difference in pitch must be shown between enharmonic notes (e.g., A♯ and B♭). While this is no problem for violins, flutes, and the like, it is not possible for traditional keyboards. Many electronic keyboards, however (e.g., the once ubiquitous Yamaha DX7), allow the player to choose from a range of temperaments in different keys. Harpsichords are rarely tuned in ET, and many pipe organs are also tuned in other temperaments.

Just Intonation is sometimes referred to as *pure intonation* or a **natural scale**. *See also* DIFFERENCE TONE; INTONATION; PYTHAGOREAN TUNING.

k. 1. Abbr. for **karat**. **2.** Abbr. for **key** (on a musical instrument).

KÄHÖNEN, MATTI (b. Karjalohja, Finland, 1952). A Finnish amateur **flutist**, industrial designer, maker of **Boehm flutes**, and designer of the **Matit carbon-fiber flute** around 1993.

KARAT. Abbr. k. Variation of *carat*. A measure of **gold** quality. *See also* **tarnish**.

KENA. Also *qena, quena*. A type of ancient South American tubular **end-blown flute** (see app. 1, fig. 11) with a notch cut into the **tube** at the upper end and usually seven **finger holes** (six in front, and a thumb hole at the back). The sound is produced by placing the mouth at the top of the tube and blowing a quick, narrow airstream against the edge at the bottom of the notch. Today, kena flutes are made from various materials, such as cane, wood, plastic, and copper, but in ancient times, they were often made from **gold**, **silver**, ceramic, bone, and cane. *See also* AEROPHONE; NOTCHED FLUTE.

KEY. 1. Abbr. k. A single part of the **flute** mechanism that controls the covering of a **tone hole** which cannot be covered by a finger because it is too large or out of reach. On the modern **Boehm flute**, it can consist of either a **padded cup** to close the tone hole or an easily reached **lever** that is attached directly or indirectly to the padded cup. Depending on the shape of the lever or how it works, it may alternatively be called a *spatula, roller, touchpiece*, or *touch*. Key **cups** requiring pressing to close them are called *open cups/keys* or *open-standing cups/keys*; cups already closed and requiring action to open them are called *closed cups/keys* or *closed-standing cups/keys*. Key cups that have holes in the middle of them are called *open-hole keys/cups/key cups* and make the flute an **open-hole flute**; key cups with no perforations are called *closed-hole keys/ cups/key cups* and the flute, a *closed-hole flute*. All of the keys on the flute have note names (see app. 8, figs. 1 and 2). Keys may sometimes be referred to as *plates*.

See also ADJUSTMENT; ADJUSTMENT SCREWS; ALTERNATE FINGERINGS; ARTICULATED KEY; BASS FLUTE (3); BIND; BLIP NOTE; BOEHM SYSTEM; BOXWOOD; BRASS; BRIDGE; BUMPER; CHASING; CLUTCH (1); COCUSWOOD; CORK (1); CRYOGENICS; DAP; DUPLICATE KEYS; ENGRAVING; EXTENDED TECHNIQUES; EXTENSION ARM; FEELER GAUGE; FINGERING DIAGRAMS; FINGER PLATE; FINISHER; FITTINGS; FLAT SPRINGS; FLUTE FAMILY (1); GLUE; GOLD

FLUTE (1); HAYNES, GEORGE WINFIELD; HOME BASE; HY-GROMETER; INLAYING (2); INTERMEDIATE FLUTE; INTERNAL TUNING; KEY ARMS; KEY ASSEMBLY; KEYED FLUTE (2); KEY EXTENSIONS; KEY MECHANISM; KEY-MOUNT; KEY RISE; KEY SLAP; KEY TUBING; LEFT-HAND FLUTE; LOST MOTION; MATIT CARBON-FIBER FLUTE; MEMBRANE HEAD JOINT; MURRAY FLUTE; NATURAL SCALE; O (2); OPEN-KEY SYSTEM; OVERHAUL; PAD; PAPER WASHER; PICCOLO (1); PIN (1); PINCHOFON; PINLESS MECHANISM; PLATINUM FLUTE; PLAY CONDITION; POINTED CUP/KEY; POST-MOUNT; PROFESSIONAL FLUTE; QUARTER-TONE FLUTE; REPAD; RIBS; RING (1); RING KEY; ROCKSTRO MODEL FLUTE; SHIM (1); SILVER FLUTE (1); SILVER-PLATING; SOFT MECHANISM; SOUNDING HOLE; SPINNING; SPRING; SQUAREONE FLUTE; STAMPING; STEEL (1); STEP-UP FLUTE (2); STRINGER; STUDENT FLUTE; SWAGING; THICKENING; TONE HOLES; TRANSPOSING INSTRUMENT (1); TURNING; VAULTED CLUTCH; VENT KEY; VIRTUAL FLUTE (2); WALKING-STICK FLUTE; WATERLINE KEYS; X.

For **foot joint** keys, *see also* FOOT-JOINT CLUSTER; GIZMO KEY; LOW B KEY, LOW C KEY, LOW C♯ KEY, ETC.; ROLLER; SIMPLE-SYSTEM FLUTE (1).

For **middle joint** keys, *see also* BEARING; B♭ FINGERINGS; B♭ SIDE LEVER; B♭ THUMB KEY; BRICCIALDI B♭ LEVER; BROSSA F♯ LEVER; B TRILL KEY; COLE SCALE; C♯ TRILL KEY; FINGER BUTTON; FRENCH-MODEL FLUTE; G/A TRILL KEY; G KEYS; G♯ KEY (1); HIGH G♯ MECHANISM/FACILITATOR; LEFT-HAND LEVERS; LONG B♭ FINGERING; LOWER G INSERT; MAINLINE; PLUG (1); REVERSED THUMB KEYS; RF MODIFICATION; ROCKSTRO F♯ LEVER; SECTION (2); SHORT B♭ FINGERING; SIDE KEY/LEVER; SIMPLE-SYSTEM FLUTE (1); SPLIT E MECHANISM; SPLIT F♯ MECHANISM; TRILL KEYS; UPPER C KEY; UPPER C♯ KEY.

For **early flutes** or other non-Boehm-system flutes, *see also* ARTICULATED KEYS, BAROQUE FLUTE (1); BATCH MARK; BLOCK-MOUNT; BOXWOOD, *BRILLE*; CARTE 1851 SYSTEM FLUTE; CARTE 1867 SYSTEM FLUTE; CHANNEL; CLASSICAL FLUTE; CLOSED-KEY SYSTEM; CRESCENT KEY; CROSS KEY; DUPLICATE KEYS, EIGHT-KEYED FLUTE; FIVE-KEYED FLUTE; FLAP KEY; FOUR-KEYED FLUTE; G♯ KEY (2); KEYED FLUTE (1); KEY FLAP; LONG KEY; MULTIKEYED FLUTE; NINE-KEYED FLUTE; OLD SYSTEM (2); ONE-KEYED FLUTE; PEWTER PLUG; PIN (2); POST-MOUNT, REFORM FLUTE (1); RING #1, RING KEY #1, SADDLE-MOUNT; SALT-SPOON KEY; SHORT KEY; SIX-FINGERED NOTE; SIX-KEYED FLUTE; TEN-KEYED FLUTE; TWO-KEYED FLUTE.

2. *See* "FLUTE IN THE KEY OF . . ."

3. The expression to play "off key" means to play either in the wrong key or not at the correct **pitch**.

KEY ARMS. The part that connects key **cups** to the **key tubing**. There are two main shapes: the Y-arm, which is Y-shaped, and the less common French-pointed arm, which is icicle-shaped (see app. 7, fig. 8). The Y-arm is most often used to connect **closed-hole keys**, but may be used to connect **open-hole keys**.

Many players find French-pointed arms more aesthetically pleasing than the usual Y-arms, but since French-pointed arms extend across to the center of a **key**, they can only be used to connect keys that are not pressed by fingers, as they would otherwise be uncomfortable. The French-pointed arm is also called a *French arm*, *French point*, or *pointed arm*. The key cup with such an arm is also called a *French key/cup/key cup*, *French pointed key/cup/key cup*, or *styled key*.

Some flutemakers believe that keys with French-pointed arms are stronger front-to-back and keys with Y-arms are stronger side-to-side. The French-pointed arms may have been devised to make certain keys more stable. Many **flutists** find the French-pointed arm more aesthetically pleasing than the Y-arm. Syn. arms, cup arms, tone arms. *See also* BEVELING; BRIDGE; CLUTCH (1); CYLINDRICAL BOEHM FLUTE (1); EXTENSION ARM; FACTORY-MADE FLUTE; FORGING; HANDMADE FLUTE; INTERMEDIATE FLUTE; KEY MECHANISM; PROFESSIONAL FLUTE; RETUNING; SHANK; STRINGER.

KEY ASSEMBLY. Collections of **keys** and **key mechanisms** that are joined together. For example, left-hand **section** (def. 2), right-hand section, trill section.

KEY CLICK. *See* KEY SLAP.

KEY CUP. Same as **cup**.

KEYED FLUTE. A term used in various circles to refer to the type of **flute** with several **keys**. **1.** In the second half of the 18th and early 19th centuries, the flute with usually four or more keys that developed from the **one-keyed flute**. *See also* app. 4; CLASSICAL FLUTE; EIGHT-KEYED FLUTE; FIVE-KEYED FLUTE; FOUR-KEYED FLUTE; MULTI-KEYED FLUTE; NATURAL SCALE; NINE-KEYED FLUTE; SIMPLE-SYSTEM FLUTE (1); SIX-KEYED FLUTE; TEN-KEYED FLUTE. **2.** As used by traditional **Irish flute** players and makers, an "Irish flute" with one or more keys (but often four to eight), as opposed to the keyless Irish flute.

KEY EXTENSIONS. Removable pieces of metal, plastic, or other material that extend the length of a **key** (see app. 9, fig. 10). The purpose of key extensions is to help ease hand position problems, such as muscle strain, that some **flutists** encounter when playing. Common places where the key extensions might be used are the **G♯ lever**, the **upper C key**, or any of the **open-hole keys**. Key extensions are a cheaper alternative than having special keys custom-made. *See also* BOEHM FLUTE; PROFESSIONAL FLUTE.

KEY FLAP. The flat (or very slightly curved), usually square or round, **silver** or **brass** part (**plate** or **cover**) of most 18th- and early 19th-century **flute keys** and many modern replicas. It was faced with a piece of soft material, such as leather, to ensure that it **sealed** the **tone hole** underneath when it was in the closed-standing position (see app. 3, B, fig. 2). A suitably shaped flat (or slightly curved) surface was made around the tone hole for the leather flap to close against. *Syn.:* flaps, flat key flaps. Square key flaps or round key flaps may be referred to as *square flaps* or *round flaps*, respectively. *See also* FLAP KEY.

KEY FOOT. 1. Same as **kicker**. **2.** *See* LUG.

KEY HEIGHT. Same as **key rise**.

KEYLESS FLUTES. *See* BAMBOO FLUTE; BAROQUE FLUTE (1); FIFE; FLAGEOLET; "FLUTE IN . . ." (1); GLASS FLUTE; GLISSANDO; IRISH FLUTE; KEYED FLUTE (2); LEFT-HANDED FLUTE; NATURAL SCALE; OVERTONE FLUTE; PANPIPES; RECORDER; RENAISSANCE FLUTE; SHAKUHACHI; SIMPLE-SYSTEM FLUTE (4); TABOR PIPE; TIN WHISTLE; WHISTLE (1).

KEY MECHANISM. Also *mechanism*. All those parts of the **flute** that support the operation of the **keys**. For example, **adjustment screws**, **back-connectors**, **clutches**, **key arms**, **key tubing**, **lugs**, **kickers**, **pivot screws**, **posts**, **steels**, and any **pins** or **ribs** are all parts of the key mechanism. *Syn.:* keywork. *See also* app. 4; ACTION; ADJUSTMENT; BIND; BODYMAKER; BOEHM SYSTEM; BURNISH; CYLINDRICAL BOEHM FLUTE (3); DIE; DIRECT-MOUNT; DORUS G♯ KEY; FINISHER; GOLD FLUTE (1); G♯ KEY (1); HIGH G♯ MECHANISM/FACILITATOR; INTERMEDIATE FLUTE; JULLIOT, DJALMA; KEY ASSEMBLY; KEY SYSTEM; MAINLINE; MODEL NUMBER; MURRAY FLUTE; NICKEL-SILVER FLUTE; OIL (1); ONE-PIECE CORE BAR; OVERHAUL; PINLESS MECHANISM; PINNED MECHANISM; PLATINUM FLUTE; POST-MOUNT; REPAD; QUARTER-TONE FLUTE; RETUNING (1); RIB-MOUNT; RING KEY (1); RING-KEY FLUTE; ROCKSTRO POSITION/GRIP; SECTION (2); SILVER FLUTE (1); SOFT MECHANISM; SPLIT MECHANISM; SPLIT E MECHANISM; SPLIT F♯ MECHANISM; STRINGER; SWAGING; TOUCHPIECE; UNDERSLUNG. For **early flutes** and other non-Boehm-system flutes, *see also* BOXWOOD; CARTE 1851 SYSTEM FLUTE; CARTE 1867 SYSTEM FLUTE; CRESCENT KEY; LONG KEY; POTTER, WILLIAM HENRY; RING-KEY (1).

KEY-MOUNT. A device that affixes the **keys** to the **flute body**. *See also* DIRECT-MOUNT; POST-MOUNT; RIB-MOUNT. For **early flutes** and other non-**Boehm-system** flutes, *see also* BLOCK-MOUNT; FLAT SPRING (2); POST-MOUNT; RING-MOUNT; SADDLE-MOUNT.

KEY-ON-KEY. *See* QUARTER-TONE FLUTE.

KEY PAD. Same as **pad**.

KEY PERCUSSION. *See* KEY SLAP.

KEY RISE. The distance between a key **pad** and its associated **tone-hole rim** when the key is open. The key rise is measured at the front of the **key** where the distance from the **tone hole** is the greatest. Too great a rise will have a detrimental effect on how fast the **flutist** can play, while too little will adversely affect the tone. A change in key rise can affect the flute's **scale** and thus its **intonation**.

The key rise is regulated by the **pad** placement in the key **cup**, by **kickers**, and by **adjustment screws** or thin pieces of paper (*see* SHIM), **cork**, or **felt** glued to certain parts of the **flute**. *Syn.:* key height, venting height. *See also* app. 3, B; fig. 8; ADJUSTMENT; BUMPER; HIGH G♯ MECHANISM.

KEY SLAP. A **percussive sound** used in contemporary **flute** music and achieved by slapping one or more **keys** down in such a way that a percussive sound and note arises. The player may blow at the same time or not, depending on the effect required by the composition. The exact **pitch** produced depends on the **fingering** and how much of the **embouchure hole** is covered. The embouchure hole can be left completely open or covered by varying amounts with the lower lip, the tongue, or the curved part of the chin. The more the embouchure hole is covered, the lower the pitch.

The common notation for a key slap is a plus sign + above or below the note to be played:

Sometimes a **fingering diagram** is provided to let the **flutist** know which key to slap. Often a key above the last **closed key** for a particular fingering is the preferred choice. The X-shaped notehead in the notation

shows the note to be fingered while doing a key slap. The bracketed plus sign in the notation

shows that the embouchure hole is **stopped** (def. 1); the diamond-shaped notehead shows the note to be fingered, and the regular notehead, the pitch sounded.

The key slap can be used along with other special effects such as **harmonics, multiphonics, whistle tones, jet whistles, tongue clicks,** and **tongue pizzicatos.** It was first used by Edgard Varèse in his 1936 piece "Density 21.5." *Syn.:* key click, pop tone. *See also* END CORRECTION; EXTENDED TECHNIQUE; RESONANCE (1).

KEY SLOT. Same as **channel**.

KEY SYSTEM. The system of keywork peculiar to a particular **flute**. *See also* CLOSED-KEY SYSTEM; G♯ KEY (1); KEY MECHANISM; OPEN-KEY SYSTEM.

KEY TOUCH. Same as **touchpiece** or **touch** (1). *See also* LEVER.

KEY TUBING. The hollow metal rods on the **middle joint** and **foot joint** that hold **steels** and suspend most of the **keys** above the **flute** so that they may move up and down (see app. 7, figs. 3, 5, 8, and 12). Key tubing was invented by **Auguste Buffet** *jeune* in 1838. *Syn.:* **axle tubing, barrel tubing, hinge tubing, mechanism tubing.** May also be referred to as *sleeves*. *See also* app. 4; ALCOHOL; BRIDGE; BRÖGGER SYSTEM; CYLINDRICAL BOEHM FLUTE (1); EXTENSION ARM; FACING; HINGE-ROD (2); KEY ARMS; KEY MECHANISM; MATIT CARBON-FIBER FLUTE; MURRAY FLUTE; PIN (1); PINLESS MECHANISM; PINNED MECHANISM; PIVOT SCREWS; PLAY; POST-MOUNT; RAGGING; REAM; RETUNING; SPINNING; STRINGER; SWAGING; TELESCOPING (1); TURNING.

KEY VIBRATO. A type of **vibrato** produced by alternating between a **basic fingering** and an **alternate fingering** for a particular note. These **fingering** changes may be done at any speed or even change progressively in speed. When the fingering changes are performed rapidly in a **trill**-like manner, the **technique** may be referred to as a *timbral trill, color trill, tone color trill,* or *microtonal trill*. Slight **pitch** changes may occur, but the emphasis should be on tonal variation. Key vibrato may be notated as KV↑ or KV↓, with the arrow referring to the desired pitch direction. *See also* BISBIGLIANDO; EXTENDED TECHNIQUE.

KEYWAY. Same as **channel**.

KEYWORK. Same as **key mechanism**.

KICKER. A metal arm that extends down toward the flute **body** from the **key tubing** and is attached directly or indirectly to one or more **keys** on the opposite (or near-opposite) side of the flute. It regulates how far any affected key can open by stopping the key's movement when it contacts the flute body (see app. 7, fig. 5). The kicker provides the extra function of closing the B♭ key when the B♭ **thumb key** is depressed. *Syn.:* foot, key foot, **stop**, key tail, tail. *See also* ADJUSTMENT; BACK-CONNECTOR; BUMPER; CLUTCH (1); EXTENSION ARM; GLUE; KEY MECHANISM; KEY RISE; PIN (1); PINLESS MECHANISM; PINNED MECHANISM; SECTION (2); STRINGER.

KINCAID, WILLIAM (b. Minneapolis, Minn., 1895; d. Philadelphia, 1967). A renowned American **flutist** and chamber and orchestra player. His orchestral career included playing as **solo flutist** in the Philadelphia Orchestra from 1921 to 1960. Kincaid was also a **flute** teacher at the Curtis Institute from 1924 to 1967, a recording artist, and the author of a flute **method**. *See also* GROUPING; PLATINUM FLUTE; SHAFFER, ELAINE.

KINGMA, EVA (b. Kortenhoef, The Netherlands, 1956). A Dutch flutemaker of low-pitched **Boehm-** & Kingma-**system flutes**, flute designer, and **flutist**. *See also* app. 6; BASS FLUTE (2, 3); LEFT-HANDED FLUTE; MURRAY FLUTE; QUARTER-TONE FLUTE; ROBERT DICK GLISSANDO HEADJOINT.

KINGMA-SYSTEM FLUTE. *See* QUARTER-TONE FLUTE.

KING POST. A **post** which is located between the F♯ key and the lower **G key** (see app. 7, fig. 3). It is an important post on the **flute**, supporting both the left- and right-hand **sections** (def. 2) and often (but not always) the G♯ lever that **pivots** on it. *Syn.:* main post, F♯ post, **mainline** post. *See also* BEARING; ONE-PIECE CORE BAR.

KIRST, FRIEDRICH GABRIEL AUGUST (b. Dresden, Germany, ca. 1750; d. Berlin, 1806). A German **woodwind** maker whose business thrived in Potsdam from 1772 to 1804. *See also* TWO-KEYED FLUTE.

KLEINE QUARTFLÖTE. Ger. little fourth flute. An 18th-century name for a **flute** that is **pitched** a perfect fourth higher than the **standard flute** in use. At that time, the standard-size flute was considered to be a **simple-system flute** "in D" (using the **six-fingered note** name), so a high fourth flute would be said to be in G. (For other ways of naming flutes, *see* "FLUTE IN . . . ," "FLUTE IN THE KEY OF . . . ," and TRANSPOSING INSTRUMENTS.)

KLEIN FLÖTE. German for "small flute" or "piccolo."

KNOB. Also *nob*. **1.** *See* THICKENING. **2.** A term used in the 19th century to refer to one of the two raised portions of wood that comprises a **block-mount**. *Syn.:* **bead**. *See also* PIN (2). **3.** Same as **crown**. **4.** *See* WART.

KOKOPELLI. An ancient deity of the Hopi Indian tribe of the Southwestern United States who is said to have represented fertility. It was believed that Kokopelli would bring good fortune to the Hopi tribe, guaranteeing success in hunting, growing food, and human conception no matter where the tribe went. Kokopelli is usually depicted as a dancing, humpbacked **flute** player and can be found in Hopi rock art that is between 500 and 1,300 years old. One legend has it that his hump is a bag of seeds that he scattered from village to village. His magic flute playing warmed the earth and brought the rain to sprout the seeds.

KOOIMAN, TON (b. Bloemendaal, The Netherlands, 1954). A Dutch **woodwind** maker and developer of accessories, such as the PRIMA **Thumb Rest** in 2003 (see app. 12, fig. 16), to improve woodwind ergonomics.

KOREGELOS, GEORGE (b. Mt. Vernon, N.Y., 1927). An American maker of Koregelos **flutes**, inventor of the **HW Pad-Saver** in 1975, and owner of House of Woodwinds, a repair shop, for 45 years.

KRELL, JOHN C. (b. Saginaw, Mich., 1915; d. Philadelphia, 1999). An American **flutist, flute** and solo **piccolo** player with the Philadelphia Orchestra for 30 years, flute teacher, composer, and author of *Kincaidiana: A Flute Player's Notebook* (Malibu, Calif.: Trio Associates, 1973; rev. 1977). *See also* GROUPING; INTENSITY.

KRISHNA. One of the most popular deities in Hinduism. He is the eighth avatar or reincarnation of the god Vishnu, preserver of humankind. Krishna is always blue in color and is often depicted playing the **flute**.

KRUSPE, CARL, JR. (b. Erfurt, Germany, 1865; d. 1929). A German **woodwind** maker whose business thrived in Leipzig from 1893 to 1929. From 1895, he worked with **Maximilian Schwedler** on the **Reform flute**.

L

LACQUER. A resinous, glossy varnish consisting of shellac (*see* GLUE) dissolved in **alcohol** and often colored with various pigments. It is occasionally used in flutemaking as a decorative colored coating on such things as the **brass flute tubing** of less expensive **flutes**.

LAFLEURANCE, LÉOPOLD JEAN BAPTISTE (b. Bordeaux, France, 1865; d. Paris, 1951). A French orchestra **flutist** and acting **flute** professor at the **Paris Conservatoire** from 1914 to 1920.

LANDELL, JONATHON, SR. (b. Philadelphia, 1946). An American maker of **Boehm flutes**, flute de-

signer, flutemaking and repair teacher, **flutist**, and author of *The Landell Flute Tune-up Manual* (Vergennes: Vermont Guild of Flute Making, 1983). *See also* acknowledgments; BEARING; BENNETT SCALE; TITANIUM.

LAPPING. Waxed thread or a thin **cork** sheet that is wrapped around the **tenons** of wooden or **ivory** flutes so that they **fit** tightly to their corresponding **sockets** (see app. 3, A, figs. 1 and 3). The lapping is greased regularly so that the tenon will fit easily into its socket. Thread lapping was usually the only type used on **wind instruments** until the middle of the 19th century. After that time, cork lapping became more common. Both types can be found on replicas today.

Both ways of lapping the tenons have advantages and disadvantages. Cork wrapping is considered advantageous due to its greater compressibility; it does not hinder the natural contraction and expansion of the tenon caused by breath and humidity in the air that could cause cracking or a need for **adjustment**. Waxed thread may put **pressure** on the tenon if there is too much or if it has swollen from moisture, forcing the **bore** to slightly contract and possibly affect the flute's **tuning**; on the other hand, it is advantageous in that small amounts can be added or removed to ensure an airtight fit.

Regardless of what is wrapped around the tenon, there is still a danger of the socket cracking should changes in heat or humidity cause more tenon swelling or socket shrinking than permitted by the lapping. *See also* TUNING SLIDE (2); TURNING.

LARYNGEAL VIBRATO. A type of desirable **vibrato** where the muscles on either side of the **vocal folds** are caused to move, which in turn fluctuates the air **pressure**. The commonly used speed of vibrato used by musicians, as measured by Carl Seashore, a prominent American psychologist, is from four to seven pulses per second. *See also* ABDOMINAL VIBRATO; BREATH VIBRATO; LARYNX; NANNY-GOAT VIBRATO.

LARYNX. The part of the throat containing the **vocal folds** (sometimes called *vocal cords*). The larynx forms part of the passageway for air moving from the top of the throat to the lungs (see app. 13, figs. 12 and 13). The most visually prominent part of the larynx, especially in adult males, is the bulge in the front part of the neck called the *Adam's apple*. The position of the larynx and the amount of space between the vocal folds can influence the "openness" of the throat and the flute tone (*see* OPEN THROAT). Popularly called the *voice box. See also* ABDOMINAL VIBRATO; LARYNGEAL VIBRATO; NANNY-GOAT VIBRATO; RESONANCE (2); VIBRATO.

LATHE. A machine which is used in flutemaking or repair for shaping a piece of wood, metal, or other material by rotating it against a stationary cutting tool. *See also* DIE; SPINNING; THICKENING; THINNED (HEAD OR BODY) JOINTS; TURNING (1).

LAUBÉ, CORNÉLIE VILLEDIEU (b. France). A **woodwind** inventor who thrived in France. She patented the **C♯ trill key** (the Laubé C♯) in France in 1909.

LAUBÉ C♯. Same as **C♯ trill key**.

LAURENT, CLAUDE (b. Langres, France, ?; d. Paris, 1848). A French flutemaker whose business thrived in Paris from 1805 to 1848. Laurent invented the **glass flute** manufacturing process in 1806 and developed the use of metal-lined **sockets** and **posts** mounted on **plates** screwed to the flute **body** (*see* POST-MOUNT). *See also* FLUTE (4).

LEAD. 1. The main **part** in any **section** of an **ensemble**. **2.** The person who plays the main part as defined above. *See also* FIRST CHAIR FLUTIST; FIRST FLUTIST; PRINCIPAL FLUTIST; SECTION LEADER. **3.** *See* LEAD SOLDER; SOFT SOLDER; SOLDER.

LEADING EDGE. 1. The edge of the **embouchure hole** toward which the **flutist** aims the airstream. Usually called the *blowing edge*. **2.** The edge of a **tone hole** that first encounters the air being blown by the flutist.

LEAD SOLDER. A type of soft or low-temperature **solder** consisting of lead and tin that was used in the past. *See also* SOFT SOLDER.

LEAF SPRING. Same as **flat spring**.

LEAK. An unwanted seepage of air from any part of the **flute** that can affect the **tone quality**, playability, and **intonation**. The most common place for leaks to occur is between a key **pad** and the **tone-hole rim**. Leaks can also occur where the tone hole **chimney** and the **tubing** meet, where the **joints** are attached, between a **French bushing** and the chimney that holds it, in the **seal** between the **stopper** and the **head joint** tubing, or between a finger with rough skin and an open hole (*see* GARDENER'S FINGERS). More rarely, they can occur on older flutes where the **socket** is **soldered** to the tube. Any leak on the flute affects all notes below it. *See also* ADJUSTMENT SCREWS; B/C CONVERTIBLE FOOT JOINT; BREATHY TONE (1); CLOSED-HOLE FLUTE; CRACKING (A NOTE); COVER (1); O-RING (2); PAD IMPRESSION; ROCKSTRO MODEL FLUTE; ROLLED TONE HOLE; UP TONE-HOLE; VEILED TONE (3); VENTING (1). For **early flutes,** *see also* PEWTER PLUGS.

LEAN. *v.* To play a note with a little more dynamic stress than it would normally be played. For example, a teacher might tell a student to "lean on a note." *Appoggiaturas* are usually played in this manner. *See also* TENUTO (2).

LEAP. Any interval that is the distance of a third or larger (i.e., the notes do not move stepwise). For example, a leap of a fifth is the distance of five note letter names (e.g., from C to G). *Syn.:* jump, skip.

LEATHER. *See* FRENCH-STYLE CASE. For **early flutes,** *see also* FLAP KEY; KEY FLAP; LEATHERS; PURSE PAD; SALT-SPOON KEY.

LEATHERS. Flat key **pads** that are made from leather or a synthetic alternative. They can be found attached to the underside of the **flap keys** on many **simple-system flutes** (see app. 3, B, fig. 2). *See also* KEY FLAP.

LEBRET, LOUIS LÉON JOSEPH (1862–post 1928). A **woodwind** maker specializing in metal **Boehm flutes** whose business thrived in Paris from 1888 to about 1932. He was also an ex-employee of **Louis Lot**. *See also* MAILLECHORT; RETUNING.

LEE, HO-FAN (b. Taipei, China, 1963). A **flutist**, flute designer, **editor**, author, and inventor of the Thumbport **thumb rest** in 2005 (see app. 12, fig. 19).

LEFT-HANDED FLUTE. A **transverse flute** that is played on the left-hand side of the body instead of the right.

It is possible to play a **flute** on either side of the body provided the **blowing edge** is sharp and the flute is keyless, has only one **key** that is movable to either side of the flute, or has a **key mechanism** that has been built for it to be played that way. On the **one-keyed flute**, the **foot joint** can be turned toward the player to the proper position for the finger to operate the key; this key was sometimes made in the shape of a fishtail to make this easier. It is commonly believed that **Michel Blavet**, a famous flutist, played the one-keyed flute on the left-hand side. When more keys were gradually introduced to the transverse flute, it was no longer possible to play on the left-hand side of the body unless the flute was custom made.

Right-handed **Boehm-system** flutes are the norm today and in the past, but occasionally a left-handed Boehm-system **flute in C** may be seen. One by **Rudall**,

Figure 24. A left-handed Boehm-system flute in C, made from cocuswood with silver-plated keys and ferrules by Rudall, Carte & Co., London, 1892. Closed G♯ key, added open D♯ key. Head joint lining extends to within the socket where it functions as a tuning slide. *From the Dayton C. Miller Collection, Music Division, Library of Congress, DCM 0833.*

Carte & Co. in London in 1892 can be seen in figure 24. It is constructed of **cocuswood** with **silver-plated** keys and **ferrules**, has a closed **G♯ key** and an added open **D♯ key**. The **head joint** is **lined** and extends to within the **socket** where it functions as a **tuning slide**. Dutch flute-maker **Eva Kingma** (b. 1956) has made two left-handed Boehm-system flutes for people with physical disabilities. *See also* RENAISSANCE FLUTE.

LEFT-HAND FINGERINGS. The **fingerings** for **left-hand notes**. Usually, this means the fingerings from G_1 to $C♯_2$, but it may also refer to the fingerings from G_2 to $C♯_3$. *Cf.* **right-hand fingerings**.

LEFT-HAND LEVER. Any elevated nonstandard **spatula**-like extension of any **foot joint key** that is occasionally found on some **middle joints** near the G♯ lever on closed **G♯ key** flutes and operated by L4 (see app. 5, fig. 1). The purpose of the left-hand **lever** is to facilitate or make possible some difficult or impossible right-hand movements of the little finger. The lever can either open the D♯ key or close the **low C♯ key** or low b key; in any of these cases, it renders some **trills** and difficult **fingerings** with the left hand more amenable and can smooth out chromatic scales. The extra mechanism adds a little weight to the **flute**. Since the lever in question is operated by L4, it cannot be built onto flutes with an open G♯ key.

The terminology "left-hand lever" is not generally used when referring to the G♯ lever on a flute with a closed **G♯ key** (or the G lever on a flute with an open G♯ key) even though this key is a lever operated by the left hand. *See also* B♭ FOOT JOINT; BOEHM FLUTE; DUPLICATE KEYS.

LEFT-HAND NOTES. Usually, the notes on the flute from G_1 to $C♯_2$, although the term may also refer to the notes from G_2 to $C♯_3$. *See also* RIGHT-HAND NOTES; SHORTENED HEAD JOINT; TRADITIONAL SCALE; TUNING SLIDE (1).

LEFT-HAND SECTION. *See* SECTION (2). *See also* BEARING; ONE-PIECE CORE BAR; PINLESS MECHANISM.

LEVELING. Matching the surface of a key **pad** with its corresponding **tone hole rim** in order to achieve a hermetic **seal** between the pad and the rim. It is done by a **flute** repairer or flutemaker in two ways: flattening the top edge of the tone-hole rim to make it flat in relation to the key **cup**, thus allowing a technician to more easily **seat pads** and/or placing **shims** of different sizes and thicknesses under a pad to level it and make the pad face match the tone-hole rim profile. It is crucial that pads match up with the tone-hole rim in order to achieve a hermetic **seal** between the pad and the rim, because how well a pad seals has a big influence on how well the flute will **respond** and sound when it is played. *Syn.* for the second method: **seating**, shimming. *See also* FINISHER; PAPER WASHER, ROLLED TONE HOLES.

LEVENSON, MONTY H. (b. Brooklyn, N.Y., 1946). An American maker of traditional Japanese **shakuhachi** flutes since 1970 and innovator of the Precision Cast Bore Technology and **Shakulute**, a shakuhachi **head joint** for the **silver flute**.

LEVER. A key touch which, when pressed, activates a **tone hole** cover at a distance. Levers come in various shapes and sizes (e.g., the closed **G♯ key**/lever and the D and D♯ trill keys/levers). More broad-shaped levers are usually called *spatulas;* levers that are shaped like a cylinder and can be rolled by a finger are usually called *rollers*. Simple levers are classified as first-order, second-order, and third-order which characterizes them according to the relative positions of the "effort," "fulcrum" (or axle), and "load." Often quoted examples are the see-saw (first order: fulcrum in the middle, e.g., D♯ key), wheel-barrow (second order: load in the middle, e.g., G lever on open G♯ key flute) and tweezers (third order: effort in the middle, e.g., B thumb key). *Syn.:* **touchpiece**, touch. *See also* BROSSA F♯ LEVER; CLOSED KEY; CLUTCH (2); DUPLICATE KEYS; LEFT-HAND LEVER; ROCKSTRO F♯ LEVER; ROCKSTRO MODEL FLUTE; STRINGER.

LEVINE, JOHN BRAVERMAN (b. Lowell, Mass., 1947). An American amateur **flutist**, formerly member of the NFA Performance Health Care Committee 2000–2005, physician, and clinical instructor in psychiatry at Harvard Medical School. *See also* DAYTON C. MILLER SYNDROME.

LINING. Historically, certain parts of wooden **flutes** were often lined with metal, such as **brass** or **silver**. This includes **barrels, block-mounts, embouchure holes, head joints**, the **sockets** of **joints**, and **tone holes**. *See also* BUSHING (1); EMBOUCHURE-HOLE BUSHING; HEAD-JOINT LINING; LEFT-HANDED FLUTE; PEWTER PLUGS; TONE-HOLE BUSHING; TUNING HEAD; TUNING SLIDE (2).

LIP. 1. Same as **embouchure** (1). **2.** Same as **embouchure plate**. **3.** *See* LIPPING. **4.** *See* DUCT FLUTE. **5.** *See* FRENCH BUSHING.

LIP GLISSANDO. A type of **glissando** where the **pitch** of a note is raised or lowered with the lips. To play **sharper**, the lips are moved as though playing a **high note** (*see* OVERBLOWING), but not as much as they would be to actually produce the high note. To play **flatter**, the lips are moved as though playing a **low note**, but again not as much as they would be to actually produce the low note. To extend the range of the lip glissando, or for a more dramatic effect at any point during the glissando, the pitch may be further altered by:

- rolling the **flute** in with the wrists to **flatten** (or out to **sharpen)**
- bending the head downward to flatten (upward to sharpen)
- lessening the breath **pressure** to flatten (increasing it to sharpen)

The lip glissando may be notated by using the notation for a **note bend** (i.e., a line pointing upward or downward from a note in the direction of the pitch change, along with the words *lip gliss*). If the words *lip gliss* are not present with the straight or curved line, the **flutist** can decide which of the **techniques** for bending the pitch of the note to use. *Syn.:* lip bend (*see* NOTE BENDING). *See also* EXTENDED TECHNIQUE.

LIPPING. A **technique** where the **flutist** makes a slight adjustment to the **pitch** of a note with the lips to play more **in tune**. *Syn.:* **lip**. *Cf.* **note bending, humoring, shading**.

LIP PIZZICATO. *See* TONGUE PIZZICATO (1).

LIP PLATE. *See* EMBOUCHURE PLATE.

LIP-PLATE ASSEMBLY. The **embouchure plate** and the **riser**.

LIP-PLATE FERRULE. A type of cylinder-shaped metal **embouchure plate** that surrounded, and was usu-

ally flush with, the outer surface of the wooden **tube** of the **head joint** at the **embouchure hole** location on some **flutes** in the 19th and early 20th centuries (see app. 5, fig. 8). Sometimes referred to as an *embouchure band*. *Cf.* **embouchure barrel**.

LIP VIBRATO. A type of **vibrato** that is produced by modifying the lip **pressure** at the center and/or sides of the mouth. Slight **pitch** changes may occur, but the emphasis should be on tonal variation. Lip vibrato may be notated as L.V. or the abbreviation *vib.* followed by a picture of the lips. *See also* BISBIGLIANDO; EXTENDED TECHNIQUE; *SMORZATO*.

LONG B♭ FINGERING. Same as **one-and-one B♭ fingering**. It is probably so called because it is reminiscent of the "**long B♭ key**" on the **simple-system flute**, which was controlled by R1 (see app. 2, fig. 10). *Cf.* **short B♭ fingering**.

LONG KEY. Any **key** on a **simple-system flute** that has keywork or **shanks** that are extra long or distant from the **tone hole** they control (see app. 2 and app. 3, C, fig. 3, for a long F key). *See also* CROSS KEY; LONG B♭ FINGERING; SHORT KEY. For **early flutes** and other non-**Boehm-system** flutes, *see also* BLOCK-MOUNT; CARTE 1851 SYSTEM FLUTE; DUPLICATE TONE HOLES; EIGHT-KEYED FLUTE; EQUISONANT FLUTE; FIVE-KEYED FLUTE; NICHOLSON'S IMPROVED FLUTE; NINE-KEYED FLUTE; SIX-KEYED FLUTE; TEN-KEYED FLUTE.

LONG TONE. A note that is held as long as possible. **Flutists** play long tones as a tone **warm-up** exercise. The practice of sustaining notes strengthens the lip muscles and helps with breathing, which in turn improves the tone and builds endurance.

LOPATIN, LEONARD (b. Brooklyn, N.Y., 1954). An American **flutist**, orchestra player, recording artist, maker of **Boehm flutes**. He was the creator of the Lopatin **scale** and designer of the **SquareONE flute family** (**concert flute**, 1989; **alto flute**, 2005; **piccolo**, 2008/9). *See also* acknowledgments; STEEL; TUNING RINGS.

LORA, ARTHUR (b. Vicenza, Italy, 1903; d. 1992). A **flutist, principal** orchestra player, and **flute** teacher. His teaching career included being a flute professor at Julliard from 1925 to 1978 and being assistant to **Georges Barrère** from 1925 to 1944. *See also* GIZMO KEY.

LOST MOTION. Excess **play** in any **key** that is linked to another key, such that one of the linked keys moves before activating the key it is linked to. Lost motion is commonly associated with changes in **pad seating** during repair. A **flute** should be carefully regulated by adding or removing paper **shims** or by changing the **adjustment screws** only after the pads have been properly adjusted to **seal** perfectly. Lost motion makes for imprecise key **action**, which can hinder finger **technique**. *Syn.:* **double action**. *See also* ADJUSTMENT; CLUTCH; PIN (1).

LOT, LOUIS ESPRIT (b. La Couture, France, 1807; d. Chatou, France, 1896). A **woodwind** maker and **flute** designer whose business thrived in Paris from 1855 to 1876. In 1860, Lot became the official **Boehm flute** supplier to the **Paris Conservatoire**. Lot was considered by many to be the "Stradivarius" of flutemakers. *See also* app. 4; BRICCIALDI B♭ LEVER; COLE SCALE; CYLINDRICAL BOEHM FLUTE; DORUS G♯ KEY; EMBOUCHURE HOLE; FRENCH-MODEL FLUTE; GODFROY, VINCENT HYPOLITE; GOLD FLUTE (1); INDEPENDENT G♯ KEY; LEBRET, LOUIS LÉON JOSEPH; *MAILLECHORT;* PLATING; RETUNING; RING-KEY FLUTE; SOLDERED TONE HOLES; VAULTED CLUTCH; VILLETTE, H. D..

LOURÉ. Fr., from *loure*, an old stately dance. Same as *portato* (1) or *mezzo-***staccato**.

LOW. 1. A designation for a particular note in the **first octave** of the **flute** and when there is a **B foot joint**, also **low b.** For example, a **flutist** might say: "Play a low C," meaning to play C_1. *See also* LOWER NOTE (1). **2.** With respect to **intonation**, a note is said to be low when it is **flat** in **pitch**. For example, a flutist might say: "Your C is low."

LOW b, LOW C, LOW C♯, ETC. A particular note in the **first octave** of the **concert flute** and **also low b,** when there is a **B foot joint**. For example, if a **flutist** says, "Play a low C," this means that the note C in the first octave—that is, C_1—should be played. The term is used to distinguish a particular **low note** from **high notes** with the same letter name in the flute **range**. *See also* B/C CONVERTIBLE FOOT JOINT; B♭ FOOT JOINT; COLE SCALE; INTERNAL TUNING; LOW NOTE; MODE; MURRAY FLUTE; REGISTER (1); TRANSPOSING INSTRUMENTS (1); TREBLE FLUTE IN G. For **early flutes,** *see also* EXTENDED FOOT JOINT (1); FOOT REGISTER.

LOW b KEY, LOW C KEY, LOW C♯ KEY, ETC. The definitive (usually **foot joint**) **key** that needs to be pressed to produce a particular **low note**. The term *low* is probably added to the key names to distinguish them from other keys of the same name. *See also* ARTICULATED KEY; B/C CONVERTIBLE FOOT JOINT; B FOOT JOINT; CURVED HEAD JOINT; FOOT-JOINT CLUSTER; GIZMO KEY; LEFT-HAND LEVER; MURRAY FLUTE; RING-KEY FLUTE; ROLLER; STUDENT FLUTE; TRANSPOSING INSTRUMENT (1); UPPER C KEY. For **early flutes,** *see also* SIX-KEYED FLUTE; TEN-KEYED FLUTE.

LOW-END FLUTE. A **student**-model **flute**. *Cf.* **high-end flute**.

LOWER BODY/CENTER JOINT. *See* LOWER (MIDDLE) JOINT/PIECE.

LOWER G INSERT. A removable, nonstandard, flat, donut-shaped ring or half-moon-shaped disc that can be inserted at anytime by a flutemaker or a repairer into the **duplicate G♯ tone hole** (under the **lower G key**) on the **middle joint** of a **flute** with a closed **G♯ key,** thus filling up part of the **tone hole,** in order to improve the **response** and **intonation** of E_3 (see app. 9, fig. 11). Using a lower G insert is a more economical way of improving these things than the **split E mechanism,** but it does not do as good a job as this mechanism since the tone hole under the lower **G key** needs to be completely closed for the best improvement in E_3. Conversely, it **flattens** A_1 and A_2. Another key configuration used today that can improve E_3 is the open G♯ key. *See also* RF (RAYMOND FABRIZIO) MODIFICATION. *Syn.:* E assist, G insert, high E facilitator. The lower G insert with a half-moon shape is also called a *G disc/disk.* The lower G insert with a flat donut shape is also called a *G donut ring, G donut,* or *donut. See also* BOEHM FLUTE; PROFESSIONAL FLUTE.

LOWER G KEY. *See* G KEYS.

LOWERING A NOTE. *v.* Making a note **lower** or **flatter** in **pitch** by changing the playing in some way. For example, if a musician lowers the note A_1 a semitone, the result is $A♭_1$. *See also* RAISING A NOTE; TUNING.

LOWER (MIDDLE) JOINT/PIECE. The lower middle part of a four-piece **simple-system flute**. *Syn.:* **heartpiece,** lower center, lower body/center joint, lower joint/piece. *See also* CORPS DE RECHANGE; FOOT REGISTER; MIDDLE JOINT (2).

LOWER NOTE. 1. In general, a note that is **flatter** than another note, that is, **low** in **pitch** relative to another note. *See also* HIGHER NOTE; INTONATION; TUNING SLIDE (2). **2.** An ornamental note that is lower in pitch by a semitone or whole tone from a proceeding or a following **principal note** in **ornaments**. For example, *see* MORDENT (1); TURN. *Syn.:* lower auxiliary note, lower subsidiary note, lower neighbor. *Cf.* **upper note** (2).

LOWER TRILL KEY/LEVER. Same as **D♯ trill key/ lever.** *See* TRILL KEYS.

LOW NOTE. Any of the lowest-sounding notes of a musical instrument: for the **concert flute,** any note below and including B₁. *See also* ATTACK; CHARANGA FLUTE; CROWN; CROSS-FINGERING (1); FIRST OCTAVE; HIGH NOTE; LOW B, LOW C, LOW C♯, ETC.; MIDDLE C; MIDDLE (NOTE); OVERCUTTING. For **early flutes** and other non-**Boehm-system** flutes, *see also* FIFE (1); FINGER VIBRATO; RANGE (2); RENAISSANCE FLUTE; SCREW-CORK (1); TUNING SLIDE (2).

LOW OCTAVE. Same as **first octave.**

LOW-PITCHED FLUTE. 1. A **flute** that sounds lower than another flute by a certain interval. For example, a **bass flute** sounds lower than a **concert flute,** and a **flute "in C"** is lower pitched than a flute "in E♭," even though all may be **tuned to A** = 440 Hz. *See also* FLUTE CHOIR; HYPERBASS FLUTE. **2.** A flute that has been made to a lower (or lowest) **pitch** for A than any one of a number of other pitches in general use at a given time or for a certain type of flute. *See* HIGH-PITCHED FLUTE for examples. Some late 19th- and early 20th-century flutes are stamped L.P. or LP, abbreviations for "low pitch." *See also* BAROQUE FLUTE (1); "FLUTE PITCHED AT A = . . ."; "FLUTE PITCHED IN . . . ."

LOW REGISTER. Usually, the **first octave.** *See also* ANTINODE; BASS FLUTE (2); BEATS; CYLINDRICAL BOEHM FLUTE (3); D FOOT JOINT; HIGH REGISTER; MIDDLE REGISTER; NODE; REGISTER (1); RESONANCE (1); RISER; STOPPER; UNDERCUTTING.

LOW-TEMPERATURE SOLDER. Same as **soft solder.** *See also* LEAD SOLDER; FLUX; SOLDER.

LOW WALL. *See* RISER.

L.P. Also LP. Abbr. for "**low pitch.**" *See also* H.P.; LOW-PITCHED FLUTE (2).

LUG. A projection from the **flute** by which another part is held or supported (see fig. 1; app. 3, B. fig. 7; app. 7, fig. 13). For example, a *lug catch* is another name for a **spring catch** (see app. 7, fig. 5); it holds the end of a needle **spring.** An adjustment tab is a lug that holds material used in adjustments. A **key foot** or foot is a lug that forms part of the **back-connector** (see app. 7, fig. 13). *See also* ADJUSTMENT; CLUTCH (1); KEY MECHANISM; PINNED MECHANISM; SECTION (2); SOLDER. For **early flutes,** *see also* BLOCK-MOUNT; FLAP KEY; SALT-SPOON KEY.

LYRE. A small music stand, so called because they often resemble the ancient Greek U-shaped harp-like instrument of the same name. Some are made to be clamped onto the **flute** and others to be attached to the wrist (see app. 12, fig. 13). They are most often used in marching bands.

ℳ

MAGNETIC RETAINER. *See* SPUD.

MAILLECHORT. French term for **German silver** or **nickel-silver.** An **alloy** which, when used in industry, often consists of 18 percent **nickel** with varying amounts of copper and zinc. In more general terms, any nickel-silver alloy. It was used in flutemaking in France. Many of the finest old French **flutes** by flutemakers such as **Auguste Bonneville, Louis Lot, Claude Rive,** and **Louis Léon Joseph Lebret** are said to be made from maillechort, but analysis has shown that the materials used have a much lower nickel content, usually 6.7 percent, and in some cases as low as 4 percent. Also called *tin* in England (*see* TIN FLUTE [1]), although there is no tin in the metal. *See also* NICKEL-SILVER FLUTE.

MAINLINE. The group of eight **tone holes,** their corresponding **keys,** and the support mechanism between the D key and the B♭ key on the **middle joint,** but excluding any offset **G keys.** The term derives from the facts that this group forms the heart of the **key mechanism** and the keys and tone holes are in line with each other. It is important to note that the mainline keys, unlike the other keys on the middle joint, are not independent of each other. As a result, the distance of the mainline keys from the tone holes must be precise so that any linked keys may work exactly together. *See also* BRÖGGER ME-KANIK; SECTION (2).

MAIN NOTE. Same as **principal note.**

MANDREL. A tight-fitting shaft that is inserted into the flute **tube** to hold it securely while it is being worked on by a flutemaker or a repairer. *See also* COLD DRAWING; DRAWING; HEAD-JOINT MAKER; SEAMED TUBING.

MARION, ALAIN (b. Marseille, France, 1938; d. Seoul, Korea, 1998). An international French flute **solo-ist,** founding member of L'Orchestre de Paris in 1967, recording artist, and **flute** professor at the **Paris Conservatoire** from 1977 to 1998 (where he was **Jean-Pierre**

Rampal's assistant from 1974). *See also* FRENCH TONGU-ING; GUIOT, RAYMOND.

MARSYAS. In ancient Greek mythology, a satyr who is said to have found the **flute** that the Greek goddess Athena invented but threw away because it made her look ugly when she played it. Marsyas became so good at the flute that he decided to challenge Apollo (a Greek god who played the lyre) to a music contest. Apollo agreed to compete as long as the winner could do what he wanted with the loser. The contest, judged by the Muses, was awarded to Apollo. Apollo flayed Marsyas for being so presumptuous, thinking that he could outplay a god. The river Marsyas was created from the blood of Marsyas or from the tears of the mourners.

MASTER CLASS. A lesson (usually advanced) given by an experienced teacher to a group of students. Ordinarily one student plays at a time (this person may be part of a small **ensemble**) and is judged critically by the teacher, while other students observe. The student playing is the *performer*, and the students observing are *auditors*. Another category attending master classes is the *participant*, who is not usually taught individually in front of the other students, but who may be taught privately by the teacher's assistant or in a group with other participants and performers. When the performers and participants are not being taught, they audit the class. A master class can last for a few hours on just one day to two or three hours twice a day for one week or more. *See also* FINGER-ING CHART; REPERTOIRE (2).

MATIT CARBON-FIBER FLUTE. A modern, innovative, but rare **Boehm-system** flute that uses **carbon fibers** bound together with epoxy plastic for the **tubing**, magnets instead of metal **springs**, and silicon rings instead of key **pads** (see fig. 25). The **embouchure plate** is usually made from **silver** or **titanium**, but the keywork may be made from titanium, silver, or **silver-plated brass** and have **open-** or **closed-hole keys** and a **C** or **B foot joint**. The open-hole keys in the left hand are off-center and can be rotated to suit the player's hand position. The flute is easy to hold, as the instrument is very lightweight (more so if titanium is used for the keywork) and the balance of the flute has been improved by moving the **key**

tubing of the right-hand key **section** from the player's side to the audience side.

The carbon-fiber flute was designed by **Matti Kähönen** in Karjalohja, Finland, and was introduced to the flute world at the NFA convention in Boston in 1993. It is produced by ACROBAATTI OY/Matti Kähönen in Helsinki with the trademark "Matit." The carbon-fiber **body** construction and magnetic key **action** were patented in Europe and the United States by Kähönen for all **wind instruments**. The original design of the flute is covered by the international copyright legislation. *Syn.:* carbon flute, Matit flute, Matit carbon-fiber flute.

MATUSIFLUTE. *See* MEMBRANE HEAD JOINT.

McGEE, TERRY (WILLIAM TERENCE). (b. Croyden, England, 1948). A flutemaker, researcher, repairer, and restorer in Australia since 1974. McGee is one of possibly several independent initial developers of the "**Irish flute**." He has introduced numerous innovations, including the "New Improved **Tuning Slide**," which was devised to prevent cracking of wooden flutes due to seasonal movement. For catalog and research results, see www.mcgee-flutes.com.

See also REAL-TIME-TUNING-ANALYSIS.

MEANTONE TEMPERAMENT. Also Mean-tone Temperament. **1.** Commonly refers to *1/4-comma Meantone*, a historical **temperament**, or **tuning** of a **scale**, in which the fifths are made smaller than pure (*see* PURE INTERVAL) so as to allow for pure major thirds, those which have no interference **beats**. In this system, the fifth has a **frequency** ratio slightly less than a pure fifth (i.e., 697 instead of 702 **cents**), and the pure major thirds are 386 cents. The amount of **out-of-tuneness** of the fifth is said to be a ¼ of a syntonic comma of approximately 22 cents, hence the name *1/4-comma Meantone*.

1/4-comma Meantone was first described in 1523 by Pietro Aron, an Italian theorist, though it may have been in use prior to that date. It dominated European music until it was gradually replaced by other varieties of Meantone (see def. 2 below), and any of the various 18th-century temperaments for keyboard, collectively called **Well-temperaments**, which could be used to play in all keys. These, in turn, were gradually replaced

Figure 25.   The Matit carbon-fiber flute. *Photo courtesy Matti Kähönen.*

by **equal temperament**, a **tuning system** in which all intervals except the octave are slightly mistuned so that music can be played equally well in any key. Meantone temperament, on the other hand, allows for some perfectly **tuned** intervals, but when it is truncated to 12 notes so as to be applied to a keyboard, it works well only in keys with no more than two sharps or flats. Beyond these keys, the out-of-tuneness becomes gradually more apparent.

The natural tuning of the **Renaissance flute** has some similarities with ¼-comma Meantone tuning because, for example, major semitones such as C♯-D are about 50 percent larger than minor semitones like B♭-B and F-F♯. One-quarter-comma Meantone may be referred to as *regular Meantone*.

2. A variety of Meantone in which the major third is slightly smaller or, more commonly, larger than pure. The closer the third is to pure, the more harmonious the triad. How much the interval deviated from pure depended on the tuner, as each one had his own idea about how the intervals should sound. For example, in the 18th century, organ builder Gottfried Silbermann used ⅙-comma Meantone for tuning his organs, where the fifth was about 698 cents. The size of the intervals used in ⅙-comma Meantone are between those of equal temperament and true ¼-comma Meantone (e.g., in equal temperament, the major third is 400 cents, and in ¼-comma Meantone, it is 386 cents; in ⅙-comma Meantone, it is about 393 cents, halfway between 400 and 386).

One-sixth-comma Meantone matches almost exactly the variety of regular Meantone, with 55 commas to the octave (five in a major semitone and four in a minor semitone) alluded to in the 18th-century **treatises** by **Johann Joachim Quantz** (1752), Leopold Mozart (1756), and **Johann George Tromlitz** (1791). The **Baroque flute** can match this easily. Unlike a keyboard with only 12 notes to the octave, the flute and violin were expected to follow an extended Meantone (i.e., with more than 12 notes to the octave) and distinguish enharmonic notes such as G♯ and A♭, with the A♭ sharper than the G♯. (The actual **intonation** of the flute or violin in concert with other instruments would, of course, depend on the musical context.)

A characteristic of all varieties of Meantone is that the diatonic semitone is larger than the chromatic semitone (e.g., G♯ to A will be wider than A♭ to A). This results in the leading tone being further from the tonic than in equal temperament. A thorough discussion of the varieties of Meantone goes beyond the scope of this book. *See also* CLASSICAL FLUTE; TUNER; TWO-KEYED FLUTE.

MECHANICAL FLUTE. *See* AUTOMATON.

MECHANISM. *See* KEY MECHANISM.

MECHANISM RODS. Same as **steels** (2).

MECHANISM TUBING. Same as **key tubing**.

MEMBRANE HEAD JOINT. A term coined by flutist **Trevor Wye** and the author to refer to a **head joint** with two extra holes on the **tube**, each covered by a plastic membrane and a damping key **cup**. The **flute** plays normally with the key cups down, but when they are raised, the membranes vibrate, giving a buzzing and reedy quality to the sound. The action is identical to that of the familiar kazoo. The tone emulates the *dizi*, a Chinese membrane flute, sometimes called a *mirliton* in Europe. The placement and size of the membrane-covered holes is critical. The buzzing would disappear for those notes where it is near a pressure **node**, and for this reason placement on the **body** of the flute is avoided.

Since the idea of this specialized head joint is to emulate the higher-pitched dizi flute, it is best used on flutes with a higher pitch, such as the **concert flute** in C and the **soprano flute in F**. Some **flutists**, however, enjoy the buzzy sound that they can achieve on other members of the **flute family**. Contemporary flutist **Matthias Ziegler**, for example, has a single hole with an adjustable membrane on the **heads** of all his flutes: concert, **alto**, **bass**, and **contrabass**. The membrane sound can be switched on or off during playing by moving a cord attached to the right-hand thumb. Ziegler refers to the heads as *Matusiflutes*.

The flutemaking company Kotato makes a soprano flute in F with a membrane head. They call the sound produced when the membranes vibrate, "*Be-mode*" (membrane sound), and when not vibrating, "regular mode." *Syn.*: **buzz-head**.

MENDLER, CARL, SR. (b. Munich, Germany, 1833; d. Munich, 1914). A German watchmaker who worked for **Theobald Boehm** from 1854. In 1862, he was established in business as Boehm & Mendler. *See also* CYLINDRICAL BOEHM FLUTE; EMBOUCHURE HOLE; G KEYS.

METHOD. 1. A music instruction book that contains music and/or exercises for a student to work on while learning the basics of playing a musical instrument. The organization of the method is such that the music and exercises are usually in progressive order from easy to difficult. Methods often contain some instructions on how to play an instrument and a brief discussion of music **theory**. Some famous **flute** methods are **Joseph Henri Altès**'s *Célèbre méthode complète de flûte* and **Paul Taffanel** and **Philippe Gaubert**'s *Méthode complète de flûte. See also* BASIC FINGERINGS; FINGERING CHART; FIN-

GERING DIAGRAMS; FRENCH FLUTE SCHOOL; G♯ KEY (1); MORDENT (2); *PRALLTRILLER;* T. & G; TREATISE; TUTOR. For **early flutes** and other non-**Boehm-system** flutes, *see also* CLASSICAL FLUTE; HIP; PERFORMANCE PRACTICE (1). A bibliography of flute methods can be found at http://flutehistory.com/Resources/Lists/Flute.methods.php3. **2.** Loosely, all methods (def. 1), tutors, and treatises. **3.** *See* SUZUKI METHOD.

METRONOME. A device, first patented by Johannes N. Maelzel in 1816, that emits an audible or visible signal to mark regular intervals of time. Metronomes indicate the number of beats per minute and also the speed at which music should be played.

The speed on older mechanical metronomes is shown by a swinging pendulum and is changed by moving a weight higher or lower on a rod—the higher the weight, the slower the speed. The pendulum is made to operate by winding a key. The numbers marked on the face of the metronome represent the number of beats per minute. The rate for mechanical metronomes can be varied from about 40 to 208 beats per minute.

More recent metronomes are electronic and indicate speed by audible beats, a flashing light, or both. The speed range for electronic metronomes varies and can be from around 20 to 432 beats per minute. Added features can include an adjustable volume control, a chime to highlight certain beats more than others, the capability of adding additional beats to represent various groupings of notes, and the ability to generate one or more notes that can be used to help judge whether specific notes are **in tune**.

Electronic metronomes are usually preferred over mechanical metronomes since they tend to be more accurate and have more features.

MEYER, HEINRICH FRIEDRICH (b. 1814; d. Hanover, Germany, 1897). A **woodwind** maker who founded an eponymous firm that prospered in Hanover from 1848 into the early 20th century, specializing in **simple-system flutes**, known as **Meyer-system flutes**.

MEYER-SYSTEM FLUTE. 1. A **conical-bore, simple-system flute** of usually eight or more **keys** modeled after instruments made in the **Heinrich Friedrich Meyer** factory in Hanover, Germany (see app. 2, fig. 13). The factory prospered from 1848 until the early 20th century, and the high-quality Meyer flutes (Ger. *Meyerflöten*) were so popular that many inexpensive and sometimes poor copies were made. These copies were called *Meyer-system* flutes and were sometimes stamped "*nach Meyer*" or "*nach/H.F. Meyer/Hannover,*" labeling the instrument explicitly as an imitation of Meyer's work (*nach* means

"after" and is used here in the sense of "in the style of" or "in imitation of"). Though the term "Meyer system" was common, it was the details of his design that were admired, rather than any special "system" of keys or **fingering**. *See also* REFORM FLUTE (1). **2.** Since, at one time, the Meyer-system flutes were so popular, the term was sometimes incorrectly used as a generic term to refer to almost any German simple-system flute.

MICROINTERVAL. Same as **microtone**.

MICROTONAL TRILL. *See* KEY VIBRATO.

MICROTONE. An interval smaller than a semitone (a semitone being the smallest interval in traditional Western music). For example, any note between the notes C_1 and $C_{\sharp 1}$ would be a microtone. One common kind of microtone is a *quarter-tone*, which is half of a semitone. Some microtones are as small as a 32nd of a tone! To play a note a microtone away from another note, **note bending** and/or specialized **fingerings** are used. For example, the fingering

$$- 1\ 2\ 3 - / 1 - 3 -$$

can be used to play a quarter-tone between B_1 and C_2 and

$$T - - - - / 1 - - 4D_\sharp$$

can be used to play a quarter-tone between C_2 and $C_{\sharp 2}$.

Special accidental symbols are used to notate microtonal **pitches**. For example, any of the symbols ♮ ♭ ⅃ ↓ may be used to represent a quarter-tone flat, and any of the symbols ♮ ♯ ↑ ↑ may be used to represent a quarter-tone sharp. *Syn.:* fractional tone, microinterval. *See also* EXTENDED TECHNIQUE; HALF-HOLING; OPEN-HOLE FLUTE; QUARTER-TONE FLUTE; VIRTUAL FLUTE.

MIDDLE (NOTE). Any note in the **second octave** of the **flute**. For example, "middle D" means D_2. *See also* HIGH NOTE; INTONATION; LOW NOTE; MIDDLE C.

MIDDLE C. The note C in the middle or **second octave** of the **flute**. In this book, also called C_2 (where 2 designates the second octave). This is not to be confused with the middle C note which is nearest to the middle of the piano keyboard or to the middle of the Grand Staff. *See also* MIDDLE (NOTE).

MIDDLE JOINT/PIECE. 1. The middle and longest of the three **flute** parts. Its **bore** is **cylindrical** in shape (see app. 7, fig. 1). *Syn.:* **body**, body **tube/tubing, center**

joint/piece. *See also* BARREL (1); BOX; BUZZ TONE; FOOT JOINT; FRENCH-MODEL FLUTE; GUIDELINES (1); HEAD JOINT; JOINT; KEYS (1); KEY TUBING; RESISTANCE RINGS; REVERSED THUMB KEYS; RIBS; RING (2); SECTION (2); TENON; TENON JOINT; TIP (1); UNIBODY; WART. **2.** On a three-joint **simple-system flute**, the middle and longest of the three major parts (see app. 2, fig. 1). Its bore is **conical** in shape. *Syn.:* body, body tube, center joint. On a four-joint simple-system flute, the middle two conical pieces (see app. 2, fig. 2). *See also* CORPS DE RECHANGE; HEARTPIECE; JOINT; LOWER (MIDDLE) JOINT/PIECE; SCREW-CORK (1); TIP (3); UPPER (MIDDLE) JOINT/PIECE.

MIDDLE OCTAVE. Same as **second octave**. *Cf.* **top octave, bottom octave**.

MIDDLE REGISTER. Same as **second register**. *See also* REGISTER (1).

MILLER, DAYTON CLARENCE (b. Strongville, Ohio, 1866; d. Cleveland, Ohio, 1941). An American **woodwind** maker whose business thrived in Cleveland from 1901 to 1905. Miller was also a distinguished scientist, acoustician, physics professor, amateur **flutist**, author (see bib. under "Flute Family," "Reference," and "Repair, Maintenance, and Construction"), and renowned collector of musical instruments, particularly **flutes**, and related paraphernalia which are housed at the Library of Congress in Washington, D.C. (see http://memory.loc.gov/ammem/dcmhtml/dmhome.html). In 1909, Miller developed the *phonodeik*, a device that analyzes the waveforms of various instruments. *See also* DAYTON C. MILLER SYNDROME; DCM; "FLUTE IN . . ." (2); GOLD FLUTE.

MODE. A manner of vibrating. A mode having a single **resonance** frequency is called a *normal mode*. The term *mode* is used mainly in describing geometrically the possible ways in which a system can vibrate. For example, a **flute** with all the **finger holes** closed has normal modes that are quite simple: They all consist of **standing waves** having one or more half-waves in the **air column** between the **embouchure hole** and the open end of the flute. When the **flutist** sounds this note (e.g., **low C** on a **C foot joint** flute) several of these normal modes are excited simultaneously, so that the mode of vibration is made up of the sum of various normal modes. The flutist's manner of blowing will determine which normal modes are present and their relative amplitudes, thus determining the **harmonic** content of the emitted sound. More complicated modes occur for example in the vibration of bells, string instrument bodies, drum heads, and room reverberation. Singing in the bathroom and listening for those notes that reverberate loudly can help to identify the frequencies of the bathroom's modes. *See also* REGISTER HOLE; RESONANCE (1); VEILED TONE (1).

MODEL NUMBER. A code consisting of numbers and letters representing a description or "recipe" of a particular **flute**'s features. It is common on flutes that were made as a series. Take, for example, a Jupiter flute with a model number of 611RBSO. As is common with other companies, these models are defined by **silver** content in progression; a lower number means that there is less silver than a higher number. In Jupiter flutes, *611* means that the flute has a silver **head** and that the **body** is **plated**; *711* means that the flute is all silver. The *R* in this particular model number stands for **ribbed**, *B* means **B foot joint**, *S* means **silver-plated** (keywork and body that are not already designated as being made of silver by some other part of the code), and the *O* stands for offset **G keys**. There may also be other letters in model numbers to designate other options on any particular flute. For example, an *E* usually means that there is a **split E mechanism** on the flute, and a *C♯* may mean that there is a **C♯ trill key**. Model numbers are not always on the flute, but if they are, they can be placed almost anywhere.

Once the model number is known, a listing of its features can be found on published information sheets from the manufacturer or on the Internet. If there is no model number, the **flutist** will have to rely on an experienced flutemaker or repairer for help if the features are not obvious to the eye.

Though the model number is common to a series of flutes, it relays more information about the construction of the flute than does the **serial number**. For example, it can convey detailed information about how the flute was made to a new owner or help the police to identify a lost or stolen flute. *See also* **factory-made flute**.

MODERN HEAD JOINT. A **head joint** which, in general, has a larger, more rectangular **embouchure hole** than a **traditional head joint**; a sharp **blowing edge**; top sides (east and west) of the **riser** that are **overcut**; and bottom sides that are more **undercut**. Also, the **lip plate** may have a second radius that causes the north side of the lip plate to drop off more quickly.

MODERN SCALE. A type of flute **scale** where the **tone hole**s are located in their acoustically correct position to suit the modern **higher-pitched flutes** (e.g., **A** = 442, 444, or 446 Hz). The modern scale has a shorter scale, or **octave length**, than a **traditional-scale** flute built to the same **pitch** (e.g., A_1 = 440 Hz), which makes the flute easier to play **in tune** than a traditional-scale flute.

Although all modern scales are based on the same principle, flutemakers have slightly different versions with different name designations. Some just call it the modern scale or **new scale**, and others modify it and give it their own name. The most widely renowned champion of the modern scale was flutemaker **Albert Cooper**, who designed the **Cooper scale** based on flutist **Elmer Cole's Schema** in the 1960s. Though Cooper's scale was available for flutemakers to use or to copy, many were slow to change, though in the 1990s, players increasingly forced the change on them. For reasons stated above, the Cooper scale may sometimes be referred to as a *short scale*. *See also* BENNETT SCALE; COLE SCALE; INTONATION; MURRAY FLUTE.

MOISTURE TRIANGLE. A term coined by the author in 1974 to refer to a triangular-shaped piece of condensation originating from the **flutist's** breath and appearing on the north side of the **embouchure plate** when the temperature of the **flute** is lower than the air being blown into it. The best time to look for the moisture triangle is at the beginning of the practice session before the flute has **warmed up**.

The moisture triangle can be used as an indicator of how well a flutist's airstream is **centered** and **focused**. When it is directed efficiently, the triangle will be small (*how* small depends on the note) and centered with the **embouchure hole**. As the flutist ascends in **pitch**, the moisture triangle will become even smaller, but still remain centered with the embouchure hole. *See also* SWEET SPOT.

MOLDINGS. Also mouldings. Same as **ring** (2), **tip** (1, 3).

MÖNNIG, MORITZ-MAX (b. Leipzig, Germany, 1875; d. 1949). A German **woodwind** maker and flute designer whose business flourished in Leipzig from 1904 until after 1950. Around 1921, he started to produce **Reform flutes**.

MÖNNIG, OTTO (b. Markneukirchen, Germany, 1862; d. Leipzig, Germany, 1943). A German **woodwind** maker and flute designer whose business thrived in Germany from 1887 to 1943. Mönnig introduced the *Reformmundloch* in 1904. *See also* EMBOUCHURE PLATE; WINGED LIP PLATE.

MONZANI, TEBALDO (THEOBALD) (b. Verona, Italy, 1762; d. Margate, Kent, England, 1839). An Italian **woodwind** maker whose business thrived in London from around 1807 to 1829. He was also a **solo** and **principal** orchestra **flutist**, composer, music publisher,

oboist, and author of a flute **tutor**, *Instructions for the German Flute* (1st ed., 1801). *See also* FIVE-KEYED FLUTE; REVERSE TENON; WINGED LIP PLATE.

MOORE, JACK (b. Elkhart, Ind., 1929). An American maker of **Boehm flutes** (using the **Bennett scale**) and keywork designer for the **Murray flute**.

MORCEAU DE CONCOURS. Fr. piece for competition. The **pieces** set for the annual competition in France—the *Concours* (changed to *examen de fin d'études*, 1989–90)—which is held, instead of an exam, at the famous Conservatoire National Supérieur de Musique et de Danse de Paris (CNSMDP, formerly the *Conservatoire de Paris*), the principal music school in France. All candidates prepare the same piece or pieces for the competition and are given only a few weeks to practice them.

Since the beginning of the Conservatoire, many of these pieces have been commissioned and have become **flute** literature standards. Some of these are: "Sicilienne and Burlesque" by A. Casella, "Concertino" by C. Chaminade, the Concerto no. 7 in E minor by **François Devienne**, "Sonatina" by Dutilleux, "Concertino" by A. Duvernoy, "Cantabile and Presto" by G. Enesco, "Fantaisie" by G. Faure, "Andante and Scherzo" by L. Ganne, "Fantaisie" and "Nocturne and Allegro Scherzando" by Ph. Gaubert, "Chant de Linos" by A. Jolivet, "Fantaisie" by G. Hue, "Concerto" by J. Ibert, *"Le Merle Noir"* by O. Messiaen, "Ballade" in G Minor by A. Perilhou, "Sonatina" by P. Sancan, "Andante Pastoral and Scherzettino" by P. Taffanel, and *"Pour Flûte et un Instrument"* and "Nine Pieces" by Marius Constant. *See also* FRENCH FLUTE SCHOOL; PARIS CONSERVATOIRE.

MORDENT. Also *mordant*. From Lat. *mordere* to bite. The English term *mordent* is used today for two different **ornaments: 1.** The *lower mordent* is a musical ornament in which there is a rapid and unmeasured alternation between the **principal note**, the note below, and back again to the principal note. This form of mordent is common in Baroque music and is indicated with the symbol ⬳ above the principal note. The note below (also called the *lower note*) is not explicitly shown in the notation. It is a whole tone or a semitone lower than the principal note, depending on the prevailing key and any accidental below the lower mordent symbol. See figure 26 for some examples of how mordent symbols might be written and played.

The lower mordent as used in Baroque music is expected to be performed in a quick, biting manner so as to emphasize the note. A mordent on a longer note may have several alternations. Some composers used the sign ⬳ to indicate when they wanted one more alternation.

Figure 26. Examples of how mordent symbols might be written and played.

Other notations and names were used for this ornament in the 18th century (e.g., beat, *pincé, pincement, battement*).

2. The *upper mordent* is a musical ornament in which there is a rapid and unmeasured alternation between the principal note, the note *above* (called the *upper note*), and back again to the principal note. The mordent in this form is indicated by ᷻. The upper note is not explicitly shown in the notation. It is a whole tone or a semitone higher than the principal note, depending on the prevailing key and any accidental above the upper mordent symbol. This type of mordent is essentially a short **trill** and is sometimes called a *passing trill, half-trill, transient trill* (or *shake*), or *Schneller* in German (see fig. 26).

So as not to confuse the (upper) mordent with the Baroque (lower) mordent, it may be preferable to use the term *passing trill* for this ornament, even though important sources, such as the renowned **Taffanel** and **Gaubert** flute **method** (1923), use the term *mordent*.

From about the middle of the Baroque period up to about the end of the Classical period, the ᷻ sign appearing on the lower note of two notes descending by step meant that a *Pralltriller*, or short trill with an upper note start, should be played when time permitted, and not an upper mordent. In this case, the note with the ᷻ sign was often tied to the preceding note.

MOUNTS. 1. An older term that usually refers to the **rings** (def. 2) that surround the flute **tubing** at various locations on many wooden and some **ivory** flutes to reinforce, decorate, or protect the tube. Mounts on these flutes were often made of ivory, **silver**, **nickel-silver**, or sometimes horn. On modern replicas, **artificial ivory** or plastic is often used. Also called *ferrules, bands,* or *tips*. *See also* BATCH MARK; FITTINGS. **2.** Same as **key-mounts**.

MOUTH HOLE. 1. *See* APERTURE (1). **2.** Same as **embouchure hole**.

MOUTHPIECE. The part of a **wind instrument** that goes in or on the mouth. For example, on modern metal **Boehm-system** flutes, it is the **embouchure plate**.

MOUTH PLATE. Same as **embouchure plate**.

MOUTH TONE HOLE. Infrequently used to mean **embouchure hole**.

MOYSE, MARCEL (b. Saint-Amour, Jura, France, 1889; d. Brattleboro, Vt., 1984). A legendary French flute **soloist** and **principal flutist** in various French orchestras. He was also a **flute** professor at the **Paris Conservatoire** from 1932 to 1950, a recording artist, and an author/composer/**editor** of many flute exercise and **study** books. *See also* CRUNELLE, GASTON GABRIELLE; *DE LA SONORITÉ*; FRENCH FLUTE SCHOOL; MULTIPLE TONGUING; TAKAHASHI, TOSHIO.

MOZAMBIQUE EBONY. Same as **African blackwood**.

MULTIKEYED FLUTE. Usually refers to a **simple-system flute** with **keys** for other semitones than D♯ or E♭. *See also* CLASSICAL FLUTE; *CORPS DE RECHANGE*; KEYED FLUTE (1); MEYER-SYSTEM FLUTE; SIMPLE-SYSTEM FLUTE (1).

MULTIPHONIC. The sound arising when two or more notes are produced simultaneously from one **fingering** on a **woodwind** instrument. The **flute** is capable of producing up to five notes at one time depending on the fingering, the **embouchure technique**, and the quality of the flute, particularly the **head joint**. For any flute fingering, the **flutist** can get at least one multiphonic note combination; for some fingerings, there can be a choice of four to six distinct multiphonic note combinations to play.

Three different embouchure techniques are used to produce multiphonics. Which one to use depends on the size of the multiphonic being played. Common to all three are the placement of the jaw (positioned for the lowest note) and **throat tuning** on the weaker (or weakest) **pitch** (i.e., holding the throat in the position it would be if singing the weaker or weakest pitch). Producing small-interval multiphonics (notes generally a whole step or less apart) also requires the flutist to blow a steady airstream and find the angle of the flute that best suits both notes. Medium-interval multiphonics (notes about a minor third to a major 10th apart) further require the flutist to broaden the airstream vertically in such a way that the proper blowing angle and air speed is found for all the notes simultaneously. In addition, large-interval multiphonics (notes larger than a major 10th apart) require the flutist to use a single-pitch airstream aimed at the lowest note and to increase the air speed until the upper note(s) sound along with the lowest note.

Multiphonics are primarily found in music dating from 1958 to the present. They are shown as several notes vertically aligned. Special notations inform the player about which fingering is required. For example, a multiphonic might be illustrated as

or

The regular noteheads show the pitches sounding; the diamond-shaped notehead and the **fingering diagram** show which fingering to use.

A multiphonic is sometimes referred to as a *multiple sonority*, a term coined by **Robert Dick** (b.1950). It is also called a *split tone*, but since this term is inaccurate as to the means by which multiphonics are produced, some think it should be avoided. Multiphonics may also be called by a different name depending on how many notes it contains (e.g., *double-stop* for a two-note multiphonic, *triple-stop* for a three-note multiphonic). *See also* CRACKING; EXTENDED TECHNIQUE; GHOST TONE; HALF-HOLING; KEY SLAP; OPEN-HOLE FLUTE; PARTIALS; QUARTER-TONE FLUTE; RESIDUAL TONE; RESONANCE (1); RESPONSE; VIRTUAL FLUTE (2).

MULTIPLE FLUTE. Any from a family of **duct flutes** in which two or more of these instruments are joined to make one instrument and are blown simultaneously (see app. 1, figs. 12 and 13). These **flutes** come in various configurations. For example, they may be identical; one or more may be shorter than any of the others; one or more might have a series of **finger holes** and one may have no finger holes and act as a drone; one or more may have differently placed finger holes; they may have separate blowholes or share a blowhole; one mouth (large hole just below the mouthpiece) might be lower than the other; and so on. Some people may simply play two flutes together! *See also* FLAGEOLET (1b); FLUTE FAMILY (1). For information about other flute classifications, *see* END-BLOWN FLUTE; GLOBULAR FLUTE; NOSE FLUTE; NOTCHED FLUTE; OVERTONE FLUTE; SIDE-BLOWN FLUTE; VERTICAL FLUTE; VESSEL FLUTE; WHISTLE.

MULTIPLE TONGUING. A type of **tonguing** where more than one syllable is used to facilitate the tonguing of the notes in a **passage**. The tongue is moved in the same way as if the **flutist** was saying syllables such as "tu ku," "tu ku tu," or "thu ku." One syllable is used for each note. Multiple tonguing is used as a substitute for **single tonguing** in situations where faster speeds are required or where the flutist must tongue for an extended amount of time. In these cases, fatigue, tongue tension, and unevenness may set in if the passage were single tongued. There are two kinds of multiple tonguing: **double tonguing** and **triple tonguing**. Some players such as the legendary flute player and teacher **Marcel Moyse** (1889–1984) used combinations of single and double tonguing such as *tu-ku-tu-tu*. He advocated this for medium-speed pieces like the Mozart concertos. *Syn.:* compound tonguing.

MURRAY, ALEXANDER (b. South Shields, U.K., 1929). A British **flutist**, **flute** designer, flute professor, recording artist, and **principal flutist** of some British orchestras. He has also been an **Alexander technique** instructor since 1955 and an author on the flute and the Alexander technique. *See also* MURRAY FLUTE; SPLIT F$\sharp$ MECHANISM.

MURRAY FLUTE. A modification of the cylindrical 1847 **Boehm flute** that went through over 40 years of experimentation and development, starting in 1959. It was flutist **Alexander Murray**'s aim to make the flute that **Theobald Boehm** had dreamed of making: one that is better **in tune**, easier to play, simple in design, mechanically reliable, and based on the principle that the **keys** should be open when at rest. Standard features and claims of the Murray mechanism include:

a. a **Coltman C$\sharp$**
b. a small D **vent hole** that aids $D_{2/3/4}$, $D\sharp_2$, A_3, and $B\flat_3$
c. **reversed thumb-keys**
d. an open **G$\sharp$ key**
e. an additional D **trill** with a larger-diameter hole placed farther down the column. This was originally provided to obtain a more accurate interval for the C$\sharp$/D trill, typically too **sharp** on the conventional Boehm flute. When used together with the normal **D trill key**, it enables a better-**tuned** C$\sharp$/D$\sharp$ trill. It also provides a high G/A trill.
f. a double key for **low D**, making it possible to close the D$\sharp$ and D keys simultaneously with R3. This is necessary for facilitating the C/D and C$\sharp$/D trill in the **first octave**. When this key is not employed, the C/E$\flat$ *tremolo* in the first octave is easy, as is the C$\sharp$/D$\sharp$ trill.
g. a special F$\sharp$ lever that is fingered with L4 (*see* SPLIT F$\sharp$ MECHANISM)

h. an open D♯ key that frees R4 for fingering F♯ using the F♯ lever

i. **foot-joint key tubing** that has been moved to the near side of the body, which is said to allow for an improved mechanical advantage as the leverage increases with each additional key

j. a redesigned **head-joint taper** to improve the **tuning** of the **partials** of C_2 and $C\sharp_2$ resulting in an improved **response** and legato when playing octaves

Figure 27 shows a silver-plated Murray-system flute, no. 7, by Armstrong, 1972, with all the above features except for (a), (e), and (j).

The latest development of the Murray flute features a Laszewski **Scale**™ and head joint, and a quarter-tone **key mechanism** (e.g., *see* QUARTER-TONE FLUTE), but it can play as a regular Murray flute with the Murray altered trill keys, Coltman C♯, special F♯ lever, open G♯, and reversed thumb keys. The Laszewski Scale was developed by Ron Laszewski, a mathematician/physicist who developed the scale by using his special computer program called Traverso. The quarter-tone mechanism was inspired by flutemaker **Eva Kingma**'s system sometime after 1987 on a flute by Brannen Brothers Flutemakers, Inc. The flute was built in two pieces: a head joint and

a **unibody**, which simplified both the mechanism and **fingering**. It was designed for a **pitch** of A_1 = 392 Hz. Murray wanted to build a flute at his favorite **Baroque pitch**, and he was curious to hear what a lower pitch would be like on a modern flute since he prefers the tone of the lower Baroque instruments. Essentially, it is a **flute in B♭** and can be played with other modern instruments today simply by transposing up one whole tone (*see* TRANSPOSING INSTRUMENTS).

Despite the improvements, the Murray flute has not taken over the well-established closed G♯ key Boehm flute as the **standard flute** today. This could be because flutists are used to the regular Boehm flute and fear that a change to a new system would be too difficult.

The Murray flute was designed by Murray and made in the 1960s by **Albert Cooper** and, later on, also **Jack Moore**. Today they can be specially ordered from Moore, **David Wimberly**, and **Tom Green**.

𝒩

NACH. A German word that may be seen stamped on some **early flutes** before a flutemaker's name. When seen on a **flute**, it means "after" and is used in the sense

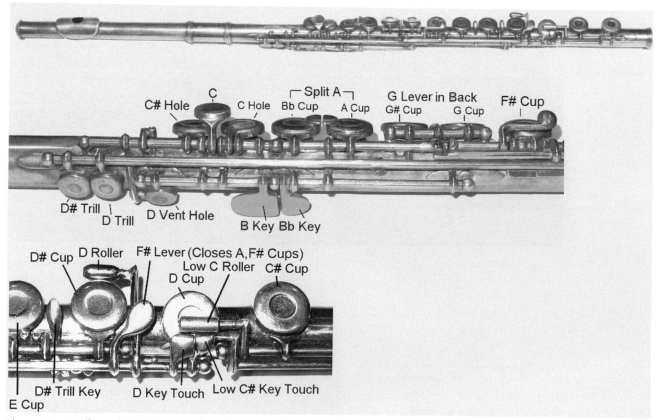

Figure 27.   A silver-plated Murray-system flute, no. 7, by Armstrong, 1972. *Photo courtesy Rick Wilson.*

of "in the style of" or "in imitation of." *See also* MEYER-SYSTEM FLUTES.

NANNY-GOAT VIBRATO. A generally undesirable fast **vibrato** which may sound to some like the bleating of a nanny goat, hence the name. The fluctuations in **pitch** are too fast and angular to be musically tasteful. It is thought to be caused by throat tension, which can also result in a smaller tone and cause vocal noises (*see* GLOTTAL STOP). *Syn.:* billy-goat vibrato, **chevrotement** (French for "quivering" or "quavering"; *chevre* is French for goat). Since, like the **laryngeal vibrato**, this sound is also sometimes referred to as *throat vibrato*, it can be confused with the larynx vibrato in discussions. *See also* ABDOMINAL VIBRATO; BREATH VIBRATO.

NASAL CAVITIES. Also *nasal cavity*. Two large spaces behind the nostrils (see app. 13, fig. 1) and extending backwards to the area above the soft **palate**. Sounds like [m] and [n], as in "mum" and "none," involve air flowing through the nasal cavities to the nostrils and beyond. The soft palate (*syn.* velum) controls the flow of air into and out of the nasal cavities. When the soft palate is raised and touches the back wall of the throat (*pharynx*), no air can get between the nasal cavities and the mouth; when the soft palate is lowered, the air moves freely between the two areas. (**Flutists** who breathe in through the nose will automatically have the soft palate in the lowered position.)

Some flutists feel that the nasal cavities play a role in improving the **resonance** of the **flute** when they play. If a flutist lowers the soft palate even slightly when playing, some air will flow into the nasal cavities and possibly resonate there. If the soft palate remains up, resonance is still possible, but only as a result of the air in the mouth transmitting vibrations through the top of the mouth into the nasal cavities.

NATURAL HARMONICS. In acoustics, generally only the **harmonics** that are played on an open string. The harmonics that are played on a stopped string (i.e., stopping a string with one finger while another finger touches the string at a particular **node**) are called *artificial harmonics*. Unlike the strings, **flutists** do not make a clear distinction in terminology between the types of harmonics that they produce. Thus they use the term *natural harmonic* for the same purposes as *harmonic*, a practice that some feel should be discouraged.

NATURAL SCALE. An ambiguous term that is occasionally applied today to **wind instruments** with **finger holes** and refers to the easiest "scale" that results when the fingers are raised one at a time, from the bottom to the top of the instrument. On some instruments, there is a minor deviation from the idea of lifting fingers one by one, but some still use the term *natural scale* for these instruments. For example, the **recorder** scale from the seven-finger note is fingered:

```
1 2 3 / 4 5 6 7
1 2 3 / 4 5 6 -
1 2 3 / 4 5 - -
1 2 3 / 4 - 6 7
1 2 3 / - - - -
1 2 - / - - - -
1 - - / - - - -
- 2 - / - - - -
```

(with the thumb hole closed for all notes). Similarly, the natural **Renaissance flute** scale is not obtained by lifting fingers one by one, nor is the Native American flute.

The scale is often, but need not be, a diatonic major scale. The term is most useful for simple instruments with no **keys** or the early keyed forms of Western instruments, when it is most obvious to players what the basic and easiest scale is. It may start with the **six-fingered note** or seven-fingered note, depending on the instrument. The notion of natural scale is less applicable to the more complex modern keyed instruments, which can play all scales easily. The standard-size **simple-system flute** has a natural scale of D, no matter how many keys. Wind instruments such as **penny whistles**, **fifes**, and six-hole **flutes** are often named after their natural scale. A penny whistle in D will have **low note** D and natural scale of D major. *See also* CLASSICAL FLUTE; DUPLICATE KEYS; FLUTE IN THE KEY OF . . ."; PICCOLO.

NEOPRENE. A synthetic rubber that is sometimes used as a substitute for **cork** to make various **flute** parts. It is very resistant to **oil**, heat, light, and oxidation. *See also* ADJUSTMENT; BUMPER; FELT; O-RING (2); SHIM (1).

NEW SCALE. Usually refers to a **modern scale**. *Cf.* **old scale.**

NEW SYSTEM. Usually refers to the **Boehm system**. *See also* G♯ KEY; OLD SYSTEM; OPEN-KEY SYSTEM.

NICHOLSON, CHARLES, JR. (b. Liverpool, England, 1795; d. London, 1837). An English **woodwind** inventor who thrived in London. He was also a renowned **flutist**, **principal flutist** in some British orchestras, teacher, composer, and author of flute **methods** (see bib. under "Historical Methods, Treatises, and Tutors"). Nicholson's impressive playing greatly influenced **Theobald Boehm** to make improvements to the **simple-**

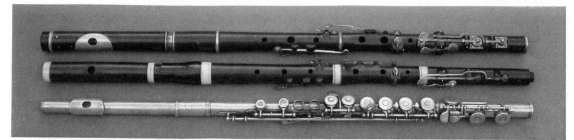

Figure 28.   A comparison of tone hole sizes. *Top:* A Nicholson's Improved flute made of stained cocuswood with silver fittings by Thomas Prowse, London, ca. 1830. *Middle:* A William Henry Potter flute made of ebony, ivory mounts, silver keys, London, first quarter 19th century. *Bottom:* An Armstrong-model flute with silver head, probably silver-plated keys and body, ca. 1970s. *Photo courtesy Terry McGee.*

system flute of the time. *See also* COCUSWOOD; EMBOU-CHURE-HOLE BUSHING; FINGER VIBRATO; GLIDE; IVORY; NICHOLSON'S IMPROVED FLUTE; RUDALL (1).

NICHOLSON, CHARLES, SR. (n.d.). British **flutist** and flute designer. Around 1820 Nicholson enlarged the **tone holes,** and these were widely copied by other makers. *See* NICHOLSON'S IMPROVED FLUTE; RUDALL (1).

NICHOLSON'S IMPROVED FLUTE. A seven- or **eight-keyed, simple-system flute** with large **tone holes** and **embouchure hole** that was popularized by **Charles Nicholson Jr.** in the early 19th century. Due to the large holes, the **flute**'s tone was powerful, though the flute was still capable of being played with the delicate sound of flutes with smaller holes. The large holes also made **glides** (a type of **glissando**) more effective and the vibration (**finger vibrato**) clearer in sound. Nicholson's flutes require a strong **embouchure** to produce the reedy tone that Nicholson advocated.

The Nicholson's Improved flute developed from **Charles Nicholson Sr.**'s experimentation with large holes. It was promoted by the younger Nicholson and first made in London by Messrs. Clementi & Co. (1802–1831) and later by **Thomas Prowse** (1816–1868), both of whom stamped these flutes "Nicholson's Improved."

For his personal flutes, however, Charles Nicholson Jr. preferred not only large tone holes but also a sharkskin-lined indentation in the wood for L1 for comfort, flattened areas around the **right-hand fingering** holes for easier glides, a thinning of wood in the embouchure hole area, an **ivory embouchure-hole bushing,** alignment dots carved into each side of every **joint** for easier joint alignment (*see* app. 3, C; GUIDELINES [1]), and no long F **key.**

Due to Nicholson's impressive playing, flutes of the type he used became quite popular in England and were used by many public performers. It was his powerful tone on a large-holed flute in 1831 in London that so influenced **Theobald Boehm,** who decided to undertake to remodel the flute of the time. The culmination of his work is his invention of the **cylindrical Boehm flute** in 1847 upon which our modern **concert flute** is based.

Figure 28 shows a comparison of tone holes sizes on a Nicholson's Improved flute made around 1830 *(top)* and a **William Henry Potter** flute made in the first quarter of the 19th century *(middle).* The bottom photo shows an Armstrong Model flute from the 1970s with key sizes just large enough to cover the tone holes. Nicholson preferred to play on the Potter flute prior to the development of Nicholson's Improved Flute. *See also* PRATTEN'S PERFECTED; RUDALL.

NICKEL. A **tarnish**-resistant metallic element used in flutemaking as an **alloying** metal in "**nickel-silver**" and as a **plating** metal in its pure form. Nickel can cause an allergic reaction in some people when it comes into contact with the skin and is slightly carcinogenic. *See also* BRASS; FACTORY-MADE FLUTE; *MAILLECHORT;* NICKEL-PLATING; NICKEL-SILVER FLUTE; STEEL (1); TARNISH.

NICKEL-PLATING. A coating of **nickel** that is used on some less expensive **flutes** for protection against **corrosion.** Nickel is a harder type of **plating,** which makes it more mechanically durable for **student flutes,** but nickel is attacked by body acids and coastal atmospheres more than **silver.** *See also* GOLD-PLATING; RHODIUM-PLATING; SILVER-PLATING; STEP-UP FLUTE (1).

NICKEL-SILVER. An **alloy** that consists of varying amounts of copper, zinc, and **nickel.** The higher the copper content, the more ductile and resistant the nickel-silver is to **corrosion;** the higher the nickel content, the less ductile and corrosion resistant, but the stronger and harder the metal. Despite its name and the fact that it looks a little like **silver,** it does not contain any of that **precious** metal. Since it is a fairly hard, durable, and affordable metal that resists **tarnish,** nickel-silver is commonly used in the manufacture of **student flutes**, where it is **plated** with silver or occasionally with **nickel** (*see* NICKEL-SILVER FLUTE). *Syn.:* **German silver**. *See also* BASE METAL (2); BRASS; DENSITY; EMBOUCHURE RECUT; FACTORY-MADE FLUTE; FLUTE FAMILY (2); *MAIL-LECHORT*; MOUNTS (1); SILVER-PLATING; STEP-UP FLUTE (1); STRETCHING; TIN FLUTE (1).

NICKEL-SILVER FLUTE. A **flute** of which at least the **tubing** is made from **nickel-silver**. It is usually **plated** with **nickel** or **silver**. Parts other than the tubing on a nickel-silver flute, such as the **embouchure plate**, are sometimes made from a different metal, such as silver. Small parts of the **key mechanism**, such as the **pivot screws**, the rods (**steels**), and any **pins**, are made from other metals, such as stainless **steel** or carbon tool steel. Modern nickel-silver is often made up of 18 percent nickel with varying amounts of copper and zinc. Mid-19th-century flutes were said to be made of *maillechort*, a type of nickel-silver that was commonly 6.7 percent nickel with copper and zinc. *See also* GOLD FLUTE; PLATINUM FLUTE; SILVER FLUTE; SPRING; STRIKE PLATE; TIN FLUTE (1).

NICOLET, AURÈLE (b. Neuchâtel, Switzerland, 1926). A Swiss **flutist, soloist**, teacher, recording artist, and orchestra player, including as **principal flute** of the Berlin Philharmonic from 1950 to 1959. *See* FRENCH TONGUING.

NINE-KEYED FLUTE. A **simple-system** (or **keyed**) **transverse flute** (or replica of it) that evolved from, and was similar to, the earlier wooden (or **ivory**) **conical-bored**, **eight-keyed flute** in D except that it had nine **keys** (see app. 2, figs. 10 and 11). Both of the two most popular types included the eight keys of the eight-keyed flute. The ninth key was either an additional key or **lever** for B♭, or a **long key** for controlling a hole on a longer **B foot joint** for **low b**. Sometimes both keys were present, for a total of 10 keys. An eight-keyed flute with an extra B♭ lever, rather than a separate hole and key, is still called an eight-keyed flute by some.

Nine-keyed flutes appeared in Europe shortly after 1800, although flutes with the B foot joint for low b were more common in Germany and Austria than in England and France. In modern times, some replicas of nine-keyed flutes are being made. *See also* ARTICULATED KEY; EIGHT-KEYED FLUTE; FIVE-KEYED FLUTE; FOUR-KEYED FLUTE; ONE-KEYED FLUTE; SIX-KEYED FLUTE; TEN-KEYED FLUTE; TWO-KEYED FLUTE.

NOB. 1. Same as **knob. 2.** Certain types of **wings** (see fig. 36). *See also* REFORM FLUTE.

NODE. A point, line, or surface of a vibrating object that has the least amount of oscillation. In a sound wave, there are two types of node: a *displacement* (or *velocity*) *node*, at which there is no vibration of the air, and a *pressure node*, where the sound **pressure** is at a minimum. An example of a pressure node in the **fundamental** of a **flute** occurs near the **embouchure hole** or near the first open **tone hole** (i.e., a **sounding hole**) for any note in the **low register** (up to C$_\sharp$). In this example, the velocity node is midway between the two ends (see fig. 43). *See also* ACOUSTICAL LENGTH (2); ANTINODE; CUTOFF FREQUENCY; MEMBRANE HEAD JOINT; NATURAL HARMONICS; STOPPER.

NOLAN, FREDERICK (n.d.). A **woodwind** inventor who prospered in Stratford, England. Nolan introduced the **ring key** in 1808. It was developed later by **Theobald Boehm** (1794–1881).

NONET. An **ensemble** of, or a **piece** for, nine musicians.

NONON, JACQUES (b. Metz, France, 1802; d. post 1867). A French **woodwind** maker whose business thrived in Paris from 1853 to 1867. *See* TULOU *FLÛTE PERFECTIONÉE*.

NOODLING. Improvising on a musical instrument without much thought as to what one is playing. For example, this is commonly done before large student **ensemble** rehearsals.

NOSE FLUTE. Any of a family of **flutes** in which the flute is sounded by nasal breath rather than by mouth breath (see app. 1, fig. 14). They may be **end-blown** or **side-blown**. The player plugs one nostril with tobacco or a rag, or presses it closed with a finger, and blows out of the other nostril. Nose flutes are common in the Pacific Islands (particularly Polynesia) and Southeast Asia. Since the nasal breath is thought by some primitive cultures to have special powers, the instrument may have originated from an attempt by the people of these cultures to include nasal breathing in the musical part of their religious ceremonies. For information about other flute classifications, *see* DUCT FLUTE; GLOBULAR FLUTE; MULTIPLE FLUTE; NOTCHED FLUTE; OVERTONE FLUTE; VERTICAL FLUTE; VESSEL FLUTE; WHISTLE.

NOTCHED FLUTE. Any of a family of **end-blown flutes** in which part of the upper rim of a (usually) cylindrical **pipe** has a U- or a V-shaped notch (e.g., a **kena** or **shakuhachi**). The sound is produced when the player rests the unnotched side of the notched end against his chin or lower lip, purses his lips or draws them tightly back over his teeth, and directs a concentrated stream of air against the sharp edge of the notch. More notes can be produced by **overblowing** or by using the **finger holes**, of which there are often only two or three. Notched flutes are usually made from bone, horn, wood, bamboo, and occasionally metal. They are common in Africa, the Far East, the Pacific Islands, and Central and South America. *See also* WHISTLE (1). For information about other flute classifications, *see* DUCT FLUTE; GLOBULAR FLUTE; MULTIPLE FLUTE; NOSE FLUTE; OVERTONE FLUTE; SIDE-BLOWN FLUTE; VESSEL FLUTE; VERTICAL FLUTE; WHISTLE.

NOTE BENDING. A **technique** used for altering the **pitch** of a note by using any or all of the following: jaw, lips, head, and alteration of the air speed. It can also be achieved by moving the **embouchure hole** in or out with the arms to cover and uncover it (*see* ROLL-IN; ROLL-OUT). A **flutist** may use note bending to find the **center** or core of the tone in tone exercises, work on lip flexibility, examine the possibilities for altering the **intonation,** or alter the pitch of a note at any time for special effect (i.e., **ornamental** or **expressive** purposes). It may be indicated in music by a straight or curved line above a notehead, pointing upward or downward to indicate the direction of the bend:

The technique is common in jazz and modern music. *Syn.:* pitch bend, bending. *See also* EXTENDED TECHNIQUE; GLISSANDO; HUMORING; LIP GLISSANDO; LIPPING; MICROTONES; SHADING.

NOTE HOLES. Same as **tone holes.**

NOTE SENSIBLE. Fr. **sensitive note.** *See also* AUGMENTED NOTES.

O

o. 1. A small "o," when placed over a note, indicates that that note should be played as a **harmonic** (def. 3). **2.** In a **fingering diagram,** an open **finger hole** or **key,** as in xxx ooo, where **x** means a closed finger hole or key. **3.** *See* MODEL NUMBER.

OCARINA. It. little goose. A special form of **vessel flute** invented by Giuseppe Luigi Donati (1836–1925) around 1853 in Italy. It is often similar in shape to a sweet potato, hence its nickname—"sweet potato" (see

app. 1, fig. 15). Ocarinas are popular with amateur musicians because of their simplicity and low cost. *See also* GLOBULAR FLUTE.

OCTAVE FLUTE. 1. A term for the **piccolo** during the late 18th and 19th centuries, because the instrument was **pitched** an octave above the **standard flute** in use (i.e., each note of the octave flute sounded an octave higher than the corresponding note on the standard flute). Therefore, if the term were used in reference to the standard flute today (i.e., the "**concert flute** in C"), it would refer to a "piccolo in C." This way of naming is now rarely used. (For other ways of naming flutes, which can also be applied to naming piccolos, *see* "FLUTE IN . . ."; "FLUTE IN THE KEY OF . . ."; TRANSPOSING INSTRUMENTS.) For *octave piccolo, see* PICCOLO. **2.** In the Baroque period, a sopranino **recorder** in F (named after the seven-fingered note), an octave above the modern alto (British: treble) recorder in F, the standard size of recorder in the late Baroque period. *Cf.* **third flute** (2), **fourth flute** (4), **fifth flute, sixth flute.**

OCTAVE KEY. *See* SCHLEIFKLAPPE.

OCTAVE LENGTH. The measured length of a **tube** or fingerboard on an instrument, which determines the division of that length into 12 equal parts or semitones. On a **concert flute**, the octave length is the distance between the center of the C_2 **tone hole** (under the **B♭ thumb key**) and the **low** C_1 tone hole (under the **low b key** on a flute with a **B foot joint**). If the flute has a **C foot joint**, the measurement is still made from C_2 to C_1, but the **scale** is measured with a theoretical low C_1 tone hole, as if the flute had a B foot.

The octave or **scale length** is determined by the flute manufacturer and is the fundamental measurement from which the rest of the flute scale is developed. Perhaps strangely, the flute's octave length can vary from manufacturer to manufacturer. This is not the case on some other instruments, such as the guitar, where the method of determining fret placement, and thus the semitones, for a given scale length is standard for each instrument. Flute scales, on the other hand, show a diversity of opinion about the division of the octave, since makers do not agree on what compromises need to be made in order to get all three **registers in tune**.

The lower the **pitch** of a flute (e.g., $A_1 = 440$ Hz as compared to $A_1 = 444$ Hz), the longer the octave length becomes. The position of the tone holes within that octave length are moved proportionally outward from a fixed A tone hole to suit that particular octave length. As the pitch of a flute rises, the octave length becomes shorter, and the position of the tone holes within that octave length must also be moved proportionally inward toward a fixed A tone hole to suit that particular octave length. In the recent past, some flutemakers erroneously changed the pitch for the note A_1 (e.g., when shortening a **head joint**—*see* SHORTENED HEAD JOINT) without changing the octave length or the position of the tone holes to suit the new pitch. This results in a flute that is **out of tune** with itself except for one note: A_1.

The term *octave length* was first coined by **Elmer Cole** (b. 1938), but originally spelled *8ve length*. *See also* COLE SCALE; INTONATION; MODERN SCALE; SCALING; SOUNDING LENGTH; TUNING SLIDE (1); TUNING UP (2).

OCTET. An **ensemble** of, or a **piece** for, eight musicians. A common type of octet is the double quartet: usually a **wind** quartet plus a string quartet.

OCTOBASS FLUTE. Same as **contrabass flute** in C.

OCTOCONTRALTO FLUTE IN G. Same as **subcontr'alto flute in G**.

OCTOCONTRABASS FLUTE IN G. Same as **subcontr'alto flute in G**.

OFF-CENTERED APERTURE. An **aperture** that does not form in the center of the mouth but is off to one side. Having an off-centered aperture is due to an asymmetrical natural formation of the lips and teeth, or sometimes to the playing position. This means that the **flutist** will need to modify the instructions in books about lip and tongue placement and relate all references to the standard centered aperture and tongue to the location of his own off-centered aperture and tongue. It is generally thought to be just as effective as a centered **embouchure**, and many players are not exactly lined up centrally anyway. *Syn.:* offset embouchure, side embouchure. Some people have two off-centered apertures; this is usually called a **teardrop embouchure**.

OFFSET G KEYS. *See* G KEYS. *See also* MODEL NUMBER.

o/h. An abbreviation for "open-hole," which is short for **open-hole key** or open-hole cup. *Cf.* **c/h**.

OIL. Any of a wide variety of generally slippery, combustible, and viscous substances that are of animal, mineral, vegetable, or synthetic origin. They are also liquid or liquefiable at room temperatures (or by warming), soluble in various organic solvents such as ether (but not in water), and leave a greasy stain on paper or cloth. Oil that is used in the **flute** world has various purposes, depending on what it is used for and whether it is used on metal or wood.

1. *Lubricating oils* for metal are usually a petroleum product (e.g., motor oil, sewing machine oil, watchmaker oil) or a synthetic oil. Each flute technician has a favorite oil for use in lubricating the **key mechanism**. Depending on the quality and age of the flute, a technician will use a different viscosity of oil for different applications. In general, the best metal lubricants will be long lasting and help to prevent both **corrosion** and direct metal-to-metal contact, which causes wear. *See also* FINISHER; PEWTER PLUG; QUENCHING.

2. *Preserving oils* for wood are usually a vegetable oil (e.g., linseed oil, almond oil) or a synthetic oil. Wood oils may be classed as drying or nondrying. *Drying* oils, such as linseed and tung oils, are often favored because they are easily controlled and cure by slow oxidation both inside and on the surface of the wood, forming a moisture-resistant film. The main disadvantage of a drying oil is that any excess, if not wiped away, will form gummy deposits in the **bore** and around **tone holes** and cause small changes in the bore's geometry. *Nondrying* oils, such as almond, peanut, and olive oils, stay in liquid form and will not harden. These oils penetrate the surface to some extent, but require much rubbing to avoid stickiness. They are probably equally as effective as drying oils for moisture resistance and can be reapplied often without the danger of creating semihard deposits.

As with the oils used on metals, each technician may have a favorite oil for treating the various wooden parts of the flute, such as the **body** and **head joint**, so as to help prevent moisture from penetrating the wood. Moisture soaking into the wood from the atmosphere or playing causes it to swell. When the wood dries out in a drier atmosphere or in storage, it shrinks. The stresses caused by this cycle of swelling and shrinking can be enough to crack the wood. In general, the best flute wood oils have less of a tendency to go rancid over time, have the ability to soak well and quickly into the wood, and are not sticky. *See also* **African blackwood**.

3. *v.* To lubricate or treat by doing such things as supplying, covering, or **polishing** with oil.

See also CLEAN-OIL-AND-ADJUST; FINISH; NEOPRENE; OVERHAUL; QUENCHING; REPAD.

OLD SCALE. Usually refers to a **traditional scale**. *Cf.* **new scale**.

OLD SYSTEM. 1. Same as *simple system* (*see* SIMPLE-SYSTEM FLUTE [1]). *See also* NEW SYSTEM; RING-KEY FLUTE. **2.** As used in **Rudall, Carte** catalogs and by others, mechanized **cylindrical flutes** with large **tone holes**

and, insofar as possible, the same **keys** and **fingering system** as the simple-system **eight-key flute**.

OLNHAUSEN, ULRICH VON (b. Frauenzimmern, Germany, 1946). A German mechanical design engineer, **flute** teacher, and designer of musical instruments. *See also* OLNHAUSEN RING.

OLNHAUSEN RING. A removable **silver** ring with a thin outer **cork** layer that is placed in the **head joint** at a specific location below the **embouchure hole** with a specially designed stick (see app. 10, fig. 8). It is said to enhance the tone by reducing any hiss and providing a stronger core or **center** to the tone, which is more **focused** throughout the **range** of the flute. **Intonation** in the **third octave** is also said to be improved, and **articulation** is more secure. Since the cork layer is compressible, one ring size can fit all standard **concert flute** head joints. The protective cork layer protects the head-joint **wall** from gouging. It was developed by **Ulrich von Olnhausen** and **Peter Vermeiden** over a number of years and was finally ready for use in the mid-1990s. It was at first called the "Vermeiden Ring" and later changed to the current name. It is also available for the **piccolo**. The Olnhausen Ring is used along with a **stopper**, such as the traditional **head-joint cork**. *See also* RESISTANCE RINGS.

ONE-AND-ONE B♮ FINGERING. One of the basic B♮ **fingerings** in the **first** and **second octaves** of the **flute**. The name is commonly used to distinguish it from two other **basic fingerings** and probably arose because the **fingering** requires that the **flutist** depress the "first" **key** and "first" finger of both hands (i.e., L1 and R1, along with LT and R4). *Syn.:* **cross-fingering** B♮, **fork** B♮ fingering, **long B♮ fingering**, 1 + 1 B♮ fingering, RH (right-hand) B♮ fingering. *See also* CARTE 1867 SYSTEM FLUTE; REGISTER (1); SIDE LEVER B♮ FINGERING; THUMB KEY B♮ FINGERING.

ONE-KEYED FLUTE. A **transverse flute** with a single **key** for D♯ or E♭ and a **conical bore**, which evolved between about 1660 and 1680 and continued to be played well into the 19th century (see app. 5, figs. 1 and 2). In modern times, this **flute** has been revived, performers using originals or replicas.

Originally, it was divided into three sections or **joints**: the **head joint**, with a small **embouchure hole**; the **middle joint**, with six small **finger holes** for the first three fingers of each hand; and the **foot joint**, with a single hole covered by the lone key. The addition of the key not only improved the E♭/D♯ but also allowed for more **fingerings** to produce more pitches, which in turn allowed the instrument to play in more keys than

a keyless six-hole flute or a **Renaissance flute**. In the 1720s, the middle joint was further divided into **upper** and **lower joint**s, which eased both manufacture and maintenance. Many flutes were also equipped with interchangeable upper joints, known as *corps de rechange*, which allowed the player to perform at the many pitches found when traveling (*see* CONCERT PITCH [1]). Shortly after the division of the middle joint, a **foot register**, and in some cases a **tuning slide** in the head joint, were also added to help with **tuning**.

The head joint was **stopped** at one end by a cork **stopper** and end **cap**. The stopper served to **seal** off the end of the flute and was adjusted to give the best balance between the sonority of the lowest notes and the tuning of the highest notes. In the beginning, the end cap was not connected to the stopper, only satisfying visual requirements, and was moved by pushing it in with the hand and out with a dowel. Later on, the stopper was attached to a screw that threaded through the end cap and allowed the stopper to be adjusted by turning the end cap (see SCREW-CORK [1]).

Although the flute was said to have a conical bore, the head joint remained cylindrical. The middle joint tapered, more or less regularly, from the part nearest the head joint to the foot joint. Most of the time, the taper continued to the end of the foot joint. Sometimes, however, the foot joint was cylindrical or flared slightly outward.

One-keyed flutes were most often made of **boxwood, ebony, cocuswood,** or **ivory**; the key, of **brass** or **silver**; and the **ferrules** and cap, of ivory, bone, or silver. **Thickenings** were usually left in the wood or ivory to strengthen the **sockets** or to act as a **block-mount** for the key.

The standard-size one-keyed flute was known as a **flute in D** (def. 1) since it was based on the D-major scale with D_1 as its lowest note (i.e., when the six finger holes on the middle joints were opened, one at a time in sequence, a D-major scale resulted). In order to play this basic scale **in tune**, however, the player was required to make **embouchure** and/or breathing adjustments. To produce other notes, **cross-fingerings** were used, some of which were difficult to **tune**, produced a different **timbre** from the other **basic fingerings**, and were sometimes awkward to **finger**. The cross-fingered F_3 tended to be **sharp** and was so difficult to sound that **Jacques Martin Hotteterre**, author of the first **tutor** for the instrument in 1707, left it off his **fingering chart**! Later on in the century, with improvements in flutemaking, the note F_3 was commonly written in music for the one-keyed flute and played. To produce the note $D_{\sharp 1}$ or $E_{\flat 1}$, the flutist covered all the open holes with the fingers and opened the key by pressing on it with R4.

The usable **range** of the early one-keyed flute was a little more than two octaves, from D_1 to E_3, but later in the 18th century, with improvements in flutemaking, a full two and a half octaves, from D_1 to A_3, was expected, the easiest keys being those with one or two sharps.

Today, the 17th- and 18th-century (but not usually the 19th-century) one-keyed flute is often referred to as a *traverso*. Those made in the second half of the Baroque period (ca. 1660–1750), or modern copies of these, are often called *Baroque flutes;* one-keyed flutes later than this should not be called Baroque flutes. *See also* BEAD (3); CENTER JOINT/PIECE; CLASSICAL FLUTE; CONCERT FLUTE (2); DEVIENNE, FRANÇOIS; D FOOT JOINT; EIGHT-KEYED FLUTE; FALSET NOTES; FIVE-KEYED FLUTE; FLAT SPRING (2); FOUR-KEYED FLUTE; G♯ KEY (2); HEAD JOINT LINING; LEFT-HANDED FLUTE; NINE-KEYED FLUTE; PERIOD INSTRUMENT; PEWTER PLUG; REVERSE TENON; SIMPLE-SYSTEM FLUTE (1, 3); SIX-KEYED FLUTE; TEN-KEYED FLUTE; TUNING HEAD; TUNING SLIDE (2); TWO-KEYED FLUTE; VEILED TONE (1).

ONE-PIECE CORE BAR. A unique type of **pinless** stationary **steel** that extends from the **upper C key** post on the **middle joint**, through the **key tubing** of the left-hand **section keys**, and threads into a tapped **king post** next to the $F♯$ key on all Pearl **flutes** (see app. 7, fig. 3, for **post** locations). Beyond the threaded part of the core bar, there is a slightly conical **pilot tip** that extends out the far side of the king post and serves to lock in and support the right-hand section steel between the king post and the D post.

The one-piece core bar replaces the two steels of the traditional left-hand **pinned mechanism** on the standard flute. This two-steel set-up can result in a problem with **key-mechanism** wear and play at the king post location due to the movement of the steel ends in the king post when the flute is being played. According to Pearl, this problem is overcome with the one-piece core bar, resulting in a key mechanism that is more stable and easier to keep in **adjustment**.

OPEN C♯. Another name for $C♯_2$ or $C♯_3$, so called because no **tone-holes** are covered by fingers pressing on **keys** for either of these notes. *Cf.* "open D" (see CARTE 1851 SYSTEM FLUTE).

OPEN CUP/KEY. Same as open-standing key; *see* OPEN KEY. *See also* CUP; KEY (1).

OPEN D. *See* CARTE 1851 SYSTEM FLUTE. *Cf.* **open C♯.**

OPEN D♯ KEY. *See* MURRAY FLUTE. *See also* LEFT-HANDED FLUTE.

OPEN EMBOUCHURE. 1. A more open than average **embouchure hole. 2.** A more open than average mouth **aperture** and/or mouth cavity.

OPEN FINGERING. The **fingering** used to produce an **open note.**

OPEN G♯ KEY. *See* G♯ KEY.

OPEN-HOLE. Short for **open-hole key.**

OPEN-HOLE CUP. Same as **open-hole key.** *See also* CHIMNEY (3); CUP.

OPEN-HOLE FLUTE. A **flute** with five perforated key **cups**—the A, upper G, F, E, and D cups—over the **tone holes** that produce B♭, A, F♯, F, and E, respectively. It often has in-line **G keys**, though the demand now for offset G keys seems to be changing this concept (see app. 9, fig. 1, *bottom*).

An open-hole flute has some advantages over a **closed-hole flute.** Through a **technique** called **half-holing** (i.e., depressing a specific **open-hole key,** but leaving the hole in the **key** either partially or fully open), the open-hole flute can be used to create new **fingerings** that allow for the playing of certain **trills;** the changing of the **tone color** of notes for more expressiveness, or for altering the **intonation** of certain **third octave** notes; the making of special effects such as **glissandi** and **glides,** some **microtones,** and some **multiphonics;** or combinations of the above. Another benefit of the open holes is that they encourage accurate finger placement—an important aid to secure technique.

Due to these advantages, most professional **flutists** play on an open-hole flute. Some amateur flutists start on an open-hole flute, as well, but this is not usual. Since the open-hole flute can be difficult to play due to the initial difficulty in learning how to cover the holes correctly while pressing keys down, flutists get specially designed **plugs** (def. 1) to put in the open-hole keys until they are more accomplished. The use of plugs, however, alters the intonation detrimentally. For this reason and the fact that the **scale,** or tone hole placement, is different for closed- and open-hole flutes (because the perforations in the cups have a **sharpening** effect on the note produced by the tone hole beneath it), the plugs should be used only temporarily. *Syn.:* **French-model flute.** *See also* app. 11; BROSSA F♯ LEVER; CLOSED-HOLE FLUTE; CYLINDRICAL BOEHM FLUTE (1); GARDENER'S FINGERS; ORCHESTRAL MODEL FLUTE; ROCKSTRO F♯ LEVER; SCHEMA; SIMMONS F♯ KEY.

OPEN-HOLE KEY/CUP/KEY CUP. A circular-shaped **key** with a hole or **chimney** in its center. The chimney forms the elongated hole through the key **cup**. *Syn.:* French key/cup/key cup, French-style key, French-style pad cup, perforated key/plate, open cup, **ring key** (2). *See also* app. 11; BOEHM FLUTE (1); CLOSED-HOLE FLUTE; CLOSED-HOLE KEY/CUP/KEY CUP; COLE SCALE; CYLINDRICAL BOEHM FLUTE (1); FINGER VIBRATO; FRENCH; FRENCH BUSHING; FRENCH FLUTE SCHOOL; FRENCH-MODEL FLUTE; GARDENER'S FINGERS; HALF-HOLING; INTERFERENCE FIT; INTERMEDIATE FLUTE; INTERNAL TUNING; KEY ARMS; KEY EXTENSIONS; O/H; OPEN-HOLE FLUTE; OPEN KEY; ORCHESTRAL MODEL FLUTE; PAD; *PORTAMENTO*; PROFESSIONAL FLUTE; QUARTER-TONE FLUTE; SHADING (2); SPLIT F♯ MECHANISM; STEP-UP (1); STUDENT FLUTE.

OPEN KEY. A key **cup** that, when at rest, is kept open over its associated **tone hole** by a **spring** but can be closed by a finger. *Syn.:* open-standing key. *See also* CLOSED KEY; KEY (1); OPEN-HOLE KEY; OPEN-KEY SYSTEM.

OPEN-KEY SYSTEM. A **key system**, such as that of the modern **concert flute**, where for a particular **fingering**, all or at least most of the **tone holes** below the **sounding hole** (i.e., below the tone hole from which the tone is being emitted) are left open to act as **vents**. Full **venting** permits the notes to sound more brightly and clearly.

Theobald Boehm, father of the modern concert **flute**, invented the **Boehm system** in 1832 (*see* RING-KEY FLUTE), which was the first practical implementation of a virtually fully open-key system, one-and-one B♭ and F♯ being the only notes in the low octaves that do not have full venting. Indeed, comparing the two F♯ variants:

$$T\ 1\ 2\ 3 - / - - 3\ 4D\sharp \text{ and } T\ 1\ 2\ 3 - / - 2 - 4D\sharp$$

with the fully vented G:

$$T\ 1\ 2\ 3 - / - - - 4D\sharp$$

demonstrates the increased clarity of the fully vented note.

The **Carte 1851** and **1867 System flutes**, the **Radcliff System flute**, and the **Giorgi flute** are some examples of other types of flutes that have open-key systems. *See also* BROSSA F♯ LEVER; CLOSED-KEY SYSTEM; DUPLICATE G♯ TONE HOLE (1).

OPEN NOTE. The note that is produced when no **tone holes** are covered by fingers pressing on **keys** or **finger holes**. For the **standard flute**, this note is C♯$_2$ or C♯$_3$. Which of these two notes will sound depends on the

flutist's lip and blowing **techniques** (*see* OVERBLOWING). For information about "open D," *see* CARTE 1851 SYSTEM FLUTE. *See also* OPEN FINGERING.

OPEN-STANDING KEY. Same as **open key**. *See also* app. 8; CUP; DORUS G♯ KEY; EIGHT-KEYED FLUTE; G♯ KEY (1); KEY (1); OPEN-KEY SYSTEM. For early flutes or other non-Boehm system flutes, *see also* GIORGI FLUTE, REFORM FLUTE; SIMPLE-SYSTEM FLUTE (1); SIX-KEYED FLUTE.

OPEN THROAT. A traditional expression that refers to what many **flutists** feel is the optimum position of the throat for the purposes of aiding breathing and tone (especially **resonance**). Others believe that a variation in the throat is better (e.g., *see* THROAT TUNING), but all agree that the throat's position influences the sound of the **flute**. The position of the throat at the beginning of a yawn is what is referred to as an "open throat" and allows for the unrestricted passage of air through the throat and mouth. Different parts of the head and neck influence how "open" the throat is at any given time. For the most open position, the ideal arrangement is to have the back of the tongue down—as though a doctor were holding a tongue depressor there—and the mouth positioned as if making an "ah" sound. The tilt of the head is slight, the soft **palate** and **uvula** are as high up as possible so no air can escape through the nose, and the **larynx** is in a lowered position.

ORCHESTRAL MODEL FLUTE. A **flute** designed by **Albert Cooper** (b. 1924) to improve the **intonation** and **response** of the **third register** that some players find a challenge on **French-model flutes**. In particular, the Orchestral Model, to varying degrees, **sharpens** A$_3$ and A♯$_3$, **flattens** G♯$_3$ and C$_4$, and improves the **attack** of E$_3$, F♯$_3$, and G♯$_3$. To correct these notes, the Orchestral Model utilizes **closed-hole keys** in the left-hand **section**, **open-hole keys** in the right-hand section, an adjustment in size and placement of some left-hand **tone holes**, and a thumb mechanism that makes the thumb key close halfway when the G♯ **lever** is depressed. Cooper recommends that a **split E mechanism** be added to his flute model. As of this date, the Orchestral Model flute is being offered exclusively by Brannen Brothers Flutemakers, Inc. *Cf.* **closed-hole flute**, **open-hole flute**.

ORDINARY FLUTE. 1. A **simple-system flute**. This term is commonly used to distinguish this type of **flute** from the **Boehm flute** and other later-model flutes that were created as a reaction to the Boehm flute (the **Carte 1851** and **1867 System flutes**, **Equisonant flute**, **Radcliff System flute**, **Giorgi flute**, **Reform flute**, and others) **2.** The **standard flute** in use. Today, this flute is the Boehm or **concert flute** in C.

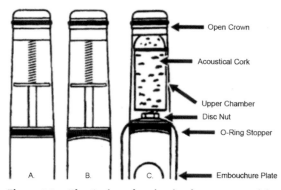

Open Crown

Acoustical Cork

Upper Chamber

Disc Nut

O-Ring Stopper

Embouchure Plate

A. B. C.

Figure 29. The O-ring, showing its three stages of development. *Drawing courtesy James J. Pellerite; minor editing by Tess Vincent.*

O-RING. 1. A gasket consisting of a ring of rubber or plastic used to **seal** the meeting-place between two surfaces and prevent the escape of air. *See also* BIGIO CROWN AND STOPPER.

2. A modern type of **stopper** used as an alternative to the traditional **cork assembly**. In its earliest stages, the O-ring stopper consisted of a disc made from **neoprene**, a synthetic rubber, which was sandwiched between the two metal **plates** (see fig. 29, *part A*). This stopper was attached to the **crown** by a screw, and unlike the traditional **cork**, the O-ring took up little space. This reportedly allowed for the space in the top of the **head joint** to act as a **resonating** chamber. The O-ring was claimed to improve legato playing, **response**, **articulation**, and evenness of **tone quality**. An added benefit was that, unlike the traditional cork, it was not prone to change in shape or size, made for a tighter seal, and avoided periodic replacement. Any looseness can cause air **leakage**, which in turn can cause faulty **intonation** and lack of response.

The O-ring stopper was said to have been introduced by **Leslie Eggs** in England in the 1970s. He later made the O-rings for **James J. Pellerite** in the United States, who eventually produced his own version that was similar to Eggs's except that new hardware was used and the stoppers were custom-fit. He further improved the design, making one side of the O-ring concave in shape (see fig. 29, *part B*). A later version, patented in 1980 as JP/Zalo O-Ring, added a suspended cork on the screw stem, which was set by the manufacturer and said to control the turbulence in the top part of the **upper chamber** of the head joint (see fig. 29, *part C*). *Cf.* Bigio crown and stopper, cork assembly.

ORNAMENTS. "Extra" notes added by composers or performers when appropriate or according to certain traditions. Ornaments decorate or embellish a melody and can enhance the harmony, make the rhythm more incisive, and add color. If the ornaments were omitted,

the music would still make sense, but their inclusion creates more interest for the listener.

The most common types of ornaments are the **trill**, the **mordent**, the *appoggiatura*, and the **turn**. These ornaments may be written out in full or in the form of small notes or shown by an abbreviation in the form of symbols. In an abbreviated form, more flexibility is implied.

The ornamental signs and their meanings have changed throughout history, and an in-depth study of these needs to be done in order to play them appropriately. *Syn.:* embellishments, decorations. *See also* ACCIACCATURA; BAROQUE FLUTE (1); BREATH VIBRATO; GRACE NOTES; LOWER NOTE (2); PERFORMANCE PRACTICE; PERFORMER'S EDITION; PRINCIPAL NOTE; *PRALLTRILLER;* UPPER NOTE (2).

OTTAVINO. Abbr. Ott. A common Italian word for **piccolo**. *See also* FLAUTO PICCOLO (2, 3).

OUT OF ROUND. Not round. In flutemaking and repair, this usually applies to **tenons** or **sockets** that have been damaged in such a way that they are no longer round.

OUT OF TUNE. A state where the note (or notes) being played is not at an appropriate **pitch**. *See also* BEATS; FALSE NOTES; FLAT; INTONATION; IN TUNE; SHARP; SHORTENED HEAD JOINT. For **early flutes**, *see* AUGMENTED NOTES; *CORPS DE RECHANGE.*

OVERADJUSTMENT. *See* ADJUSTMENT.

OVERBLOWING. A method of producing the **higher notes** on a **wind instrument**. For the **flute**, physicists believe that this is done by combining two effects: increasing the blowing **pressure** in the mouth of the player, together with moving the lips closer to the **blowing edge**. **Flutists** accomplish this by increasing the breath pressure, moving their lower lip closer to the blowing edge, rolling the **embouchure hole** toward the lips (*see* ROLL-IN), making the **aperture** smaller, or some combination of the above. The increased blowing pressure in the mouth causes the **air jet** velocity to increase. When the traveling time of the jet between the lips and the blowing edge becomes too small compared to the sound period, the flute switches to one of the higher **resonances** (often a **harmonic**) of that **fingering**. *See also* CUTOFF FREQUENCY; FUNDAMENTAL (2); INTERNAL TUNING; LIP GLISSANDO; OVERTONE FLUTE; PNEUMO PRO; REGISTER (1); SIMPLE-SYSTEM FLUTE (1); WHISTLE TONE.

OVERCUTTING. The process whereby the **headjoint maker** rounds and smoothes the edges where the

riser meets the **embouchure plate** (see fig. 49). This is usually done to only the east and west edges of the hole. It is claimed to make the sound clearer and improve the **response**, particularly for the **lowest notes**. Overcutting was popularized by renowned flutists **William Bennett** and **Trevor Wye** in the 1980s. It has since been adopted by almost all makers.

Sometimes overcutting is also done to the part of the riser that touches the lower lip. An overcut edge is sometimes referred to as being *beveled*. *Syn.:* round shouldering. *See also* EMBOUCHURE HOLE; EMBOUCHURE RECUT; MODERN HEAD JOINT; TRADITIONAL HEAD JOINT; VOICING; UNDERCUTTING.

OVERHAUL. The most complete repair job undertaken infrequently by a professional **flute** repairer. The flute is made to sound and look like new. During an overhaul, the flute is completely disassembled and the following things are done:

- all **corks**, **felts**, and **pads** in the **key mechanism** are replaced
- dents that affect the sound are removed
- anything that is wrong mechanically is fixed
- any bent **keys** are fixed
- the flute is thoroughly cleaned to remove dirt, body acids, **tarnish**, and so on
- the flute is **polished** and **oiled**
- the **head joint cork** is replaced

The flute is played to check the quality of the repairs and may be left for a week or so for the **adjustments** to settle in and then checked again.

The frequency at which overhauls are done depends on the condition of the flute. As many as five or six years may go by before a flute needs an overhaul. The general rule of thumb is that whenever several pads have become torn or frayed or have otherwise deteriorated, a flute needs an overhaul. Taking good care of the flute by doing such things as keeping it clean and taking it in for a regular **clean-oil-and-adjust** can postpone the need for an overhaul. *See also* PLAY CONDITION; REPAD; RETUNING.

OVERTONE FLUTE. A **flute** that consists of a simple **tube** with no **finger holes** and only produces **overtones**. Some are **end-blown** (like the Romanian *tirula*), some **duct**-blown (Slovakian *koncovka*), and some **side-blown** (Norwegian *selje-floyte*). By closing the open end with a finger, the player can produce one **fundamental** and, by **overblowing**, its overtones; by removing the finger from the open end, another fundamental can be produced and, by overblowing, its overtones. *Syn.:* harmonic flute. *See also* HYPERBASS FLUTE. For information about other flute classifications, *see* DUCT FLUTE; GLOBULAR FLUTE; MULTIPLE FLUTE; NOSE FLUTE; NOTCHED FLUTE; VERTICAL FLUTE; VESSEL FLUTE; WHISTLE.

OVERTONES. Frequency components that are above the lowest frequency (i.e., the **fundamental**) in a complex sound of definite **pitch**. In the **sound spectrum** of a given note, where the fundamental is also referred to as the *first harmonic*, the second harmonic may be called the *first overtone;* the third harmonic, the *second overtone;* and so on. This is the naming scheme preferred by acousticians. Confusingly, some equate overtones and harmonics and refer erroneously to the first overtone as the first harmonic, the second overtone as the second harmonic, and so on. Owing to the inconsistency between this and generally accepted usage, the term *overtone* is usually avoided by acousticians since *harmonics* and **partials** cover all the cases, and *overtones* simply adds confusion. *See also* DÉTIMBRÉ; HARMONIC SERIES; HOLLOW TONE; OVERTONE FLUTE; *TIMBRÉ.*

𝒫

PAD. A soft part fitted to the underside of a flute **key** that covers the **tone hole** when the key is depressed. On modern **Boehm flutes**, small pads are held in the **cup** with adhesive and larger pads with either **French bushings** for **open-hole keys** or a screw, **washer**, and **spud** or magnetic retainers for **closed-hole keys**. The most common type of pad, the *traditional pad*, is made of three layers: a cardboard base, woven wool **felt**, and a covering made from the lining of a cow's intestine (called *fishskin*, *goldbeater's skin*, or *bladder skin* in flute terminology). The pad covering may be either of one layer, called *single-skin*, or two layers, called *double-skin*, the extra layer helping the pads to last longer. Some pad coverings are white, and some are dyed yellow. The color of the covering has no effect on the quality (see app. 7, figs. 6 and 9).

It is vital that a pad **seal** the tone hole instantly, quietly, and with the lightest of **touch**. It is a highly skilled task to get traditional pads to fit efficiently. Even after they are fitted, traditional pads are very delicate and sensitive to changes in the weather, expanding or shrinking and changing their **seating** on the tone hole **chimney** and possibly causing **leaks**, although this is less common with a flute that has been well padded by an expert. The flute is particularly sensitive to leaks, and its **response** will be impaired if there are problems in this area. If the leak is very bad, squeezing a leaky key will not work and the pad will need to be reseated or replaced.

In an effort to improve upon traditional pads, an increasing number of flutemakers are using new pad materials, such as plastic instead of cardboard and synthetic felt instead of woven woolen felt, and are constructing the pads slightly differently in order that **adjustments** can be maintained despite changes in humidity and temperature. *Syn.*: key pad.

See also ADJUSTMENT SCREWS; ALCOHOL; BREATHY TONE (1); CARD-BACKED PADS; COVER (1); CUSHION; CYLINDRICAL BOEHM FLUTE (2, 3); FEELER GAUGE; FELT PADS; FINISH (4); FINISHER; FLOATING; FLUTE STAND; FLUTE SUIT; GLUE; GOLD PADS; HW PAD-SAVER; KEY RISE; LEVELING (2); LOST MOTION; MATIT CARBON-FIBER FLUTE; OVERHAUL; PAD CUP; PAD IMPRESSION; PAD RETAINER; PAD RETAINING RING; PAD SEAT; PAD WASHER; PAPER WASHER; PATCHING; PISONI, LUCIANO; PISONI PADS; PLAYING CONDITION; POLISH (1); REPAD; RING KEY; ROLLED TONE HOLE; SEAT (1); SHIM (1); STICKY PADS; STRAUBINGER PAD; SYNTHETIC PAD; TONE-HOLE RIM; VEILED TONE (3); WATERLINE KEYS. For information about the pads or pad substitutes used in **one-keyed**, **two-keyed**, and **simple-system flutes** (1, 3), *see* KEY FLAP; LEATHERS; PEWTER PLUG; PURSE PAD. For these flutes, *see also* TONE-HOLE BUSHING.

PAD CUP. Same as **cup**.

PAD IMPRESSION. The ring-shaped indentation on a **key** pad's surface which is caused when a **pad** contacts the **tone-hole rim**. Deep impressions are not commonly seen in high-quality flute padding, because the connection between notes is said to be clearer and crisper without an impression. **Student flute** pads have a deeper impression because the manufacturer uses heat and moisture while forcing the pad to **seal** with key clamps rather than spending the time with paper **shims** to eliminate air **leakage**. (For an illustration of a pad impression on an **early flute** pad, see app. 3, B, fig. 2.) *See also* FLUTE SUIT.

PAD RETAINER. A device used to hold a key **pad** in place. *See also* FRENCH BUSHING; PAD WASHER; SPUD.

PAD RETAINING RING. Same as **French bushing**.

PAD SEAT. Same as **chimney** (2). *See also* PISONI PADS; ROLLED TONE HOLES.

PAD WASHER. A small, flat or dome-shaped metal disc with a hole in the middle that is used to give tightness between the screw and the key **pad** of a large **closed-hole key cup** (see app. 7, fig. 9). Domed pad washers are said to improve the tone and **projection** over those **flutes** with flat pad washers and screws. *See also* SHEET METAL.

PALATAL PIZZICATO. *See* TONGUE PIZZICATO (2).

PALATE. The roof of the mouth. The palate consists of two parts: the hard palate (bone) and soft palate (muscle). The *hard palate* (see app. 13, fig. 3) is the front part of the roof of the mouth, behind the front teeth and extending backward about 2 to 3 inches (5 to 8 cm). All the teeth are set into the sides of the hard palate. When tonguing a [t] or a [d], a **flutist** touches the front part of the hard palate or upper teeth. The *soft palate* (syn.: velum) is the movable part of the roof of the mouth, attached to the rear edge of the hard palate (see app. 13, fig. 5). The muscle fibers of the soft palate meet in the **uvula**. When **double-tonguing**, the back of the tongue touches the soft palate for the [k] or [g]. The soft palate can be raised or lowered to close or open the passageway to the **nasal cavities**. Some believe that the raised position is the more **resonant** for **flute** playing. *See also* OPEN THROAT; PALATAL PIZZICATO.

PALLADIUM. A rare, **tarnish**-resistant metallic element with a **density** of about 0.43 lbs/in.^{3} (12 g/cm^3). It is used in flutemaking, where it is **alloyed** with other materials to make various parts, such as the **riser** and **tubing** of some expensive **flutes**. *See also* PCM-SILVER ALLOY.

PAN. In Greek mythology, the god of shepherds, fields, forests, wild animals, and flocks. He is usually depicted as half human and half goat. One legend has it that he pursued the nymph **Syrinx**, but she did not want anything to do with his aggressive advances and fled. She came to a river, where she was changed into reeds by river nymphs upon hearing her prayers. Since there was nothing left of Syrinx except for the reeds and the sound which the air produced in them, Pan bound the reeds of different sizes together, so that he could be close to her. He thus "invented" a musical instrument and named it *syrinx* in her memory. *See also* PANPIPES.

PAN FLUTE. Same as **panpipes**.

PANPIPES. One of the oldest and most widespread of **wind instruments**, having two or more vertical **pipes**, usually **stopped** (closed) at one end and graduating in size. The shorter the pipe, the higher the **fundamental** sound; the longer the pipe, the lower. The pipes are bound or glued together side by side (see app. 1, figs. 6 and 7), or in some areas circularly in a bundle. Sometimes there are two rows of pipes, in which case the row farther from the player may be open. Panpipes have no **finger holes** and are made from wood, cane, metal, pottery, and even stone. They are vertically played, the sound being produced by blowing across the open end so that a narrow airstream is directed against the sharp outer edge.

There are different kinds of panpipes. For example, Romanian panpipes (called *nai*)—a type made well known by **Gheorghe Zamfir** (b.1941)—consist of pipes joined together in a flat or curved row and are most commonly duct blown (*see* DUCT FLUTE). Those from South America have the pipes joined together in a straight single or double row. The South American variety often has narrow pipes that vary little in diameter in order to give a windy quality, whereas the Romanian style has pipes that vary from a wide to a narrow diameter in order to produce the best uniform **tone quality**.

There are various sizes of panpipes. The standard-size Romanian nai consists of 22 pipes and has a **range** of three octaves, starting from the G above the piano's middle C. Each pipe of the Romanian variety is **tuned** to a **pitch** in a major scale. The sharps and flats on these instruments are produced by changing the blowing angle of a pipe on the mouth. This can be achieved by moving either the panpipe or the jaw. The fundamental tuning of a pipe can be adjusted by using these methods or by moving any existing **cork** or wax **plug** in the end of each pipe or by dropping wax or any other pellets into each tube.

Panpipes are named after **Pan** (hence their English name), the patron god of the Greek herdsmen who played the pipes. *Syn.:* Pandean pipes, Pan flute, syrinx, quills. The term *panpipes* is both singular and plural. *See also* END-BLOWN FLUTE (1); *FISTULA* (2).

PAPER SHIM. *See* ADJUSTMENT; PAPER WASHER.

PAPER WASHER. A small, thin, circular piece of paper of varying diameter and thickness with a hole in the middle, often called a *shim*, *paper shim*, or *full shim*. Parts of paper washers are often called *partial shims*. A full shim or one or more partial shims may be installed underneath a large **key** pad, when needed, to **level** out the **pad** and/or raise it to its correct height. Full shims may also be used to act as a base on which to **glue** other partial shims, which collectively have the same function as the full shim. Pads are leveled out and/or raised so that they will **seal** better with the **tone-hole rim**.

"PARABOLIC" (HEAD JOINT). An inaccurate term used to describe the shape of most modern **head joints**. The nearest true definition of a flute **head** shape could be a "truncated parabolic conoid." **Theobald Boehm**, inventor of the modern **concert flute** in 1847, referred to a parabolic head, but there does not seem to be any evidence that he or anyone else made one. The flute head does **taper**, getting gradually smaller from the open end (where the inside diameter is usually 0.75 in./19 mm) to-

ward the **head joint cork**, and this taper is usually curved. For some head joints, this taper continues to the closed end of the head joint, where it is about 0.67 in. (17.1 mm). For others, the taper does not continue, and the **tube** becomes cylindrical, so that the head joint cork may more easily slide in and out of the head joint. Renowned flutemaker **Albert Cooper** (b. 1924), among others, has made head joints that have no curve and are conically tapered; **Trevor Wye** (b. 1935) reports that players seem just as content with them as with those that have some sort of tapered curve.

The amount of taper affects the overall **response** of the flute. The taper of the head joint, along with a **Helmholtz resonator** formed by the air in the **riser** and the air between it and the head joint cork, keep the upper **resonances** of the flute in **harmonic** relation to the lower ones and so help to make the **registers** more **in tune**.

See also BORE; CYLINDRICAL BOEHM FLUTE (3); FOOT JOINT; HEAD JOINT LINING (1); INTERNAL TUNING; MIDDLE JOINT. For **early flutes** and other non-**Boehm-system** flutes, *see also* FIFE (1); PRATTEN'S PERFECTED; RADCLIFF SYSTEM FLUTE.

PARIS CONSERVATOIRE. A commonly used colloquial name for a famous music school that was founded in 1795 in Paris by Bernard Sarrette (1756–1858) and now called the Conservatoire National Supérieur de Musique et de Danse de Paris (CNSMDP)—not to be confused with several other *conservatoires* in Paris. It dominated music education in France and had a big influence on music education in many other developed countries around the world from about 1860 to at least 1950 (*see* FRENCH FLUTE SCHOOL).

Free entrance to the Conservatoire was granted by competitive audition every October. Students, once accepted, were taught the **flute** in a class setting, rather than in private lessons. Until 1945, there was only one flute class running at any one time, with usually only around 12 students. The number of students accepted depended on the number of vacancies in any particular class; often there were only two or three.

In order to graduate, the students had to perform in public examinations, called *concours* (competitions), which were held each July. Sometimes there were preliminary examinations held in June to eliminate any students who were not yet ready to take the final examination. These examinations included an assigned **piece** and accompanied **sight-reading**. The students were awarded grades depending on how well they performed individually against a set standard, rather than in comparison with other candidates. These grades were called First Prize *(Premier Prix)*, Second Prize, and First or Second Certificate of Merit *(Accessit)*. Since the students were competing against a set standard and not against each other, more than one student could receive any of the awards. A student could graduate with any of these grades, but obtaining the most prestigious of the grades, a First Prize, almost guaranteed a successful musical career. The concours became the *examen de fin d'études* (exam of end of studies) in the 1989–90 school year and were run in much the same way. This trend has continued.

In 1860, the famous **silver cylindrical Boehm flute** player **Louis Dorus** was appointed professor because the directors at the Conservatoire had decided to adopt the French-modified cylindrical Boehm flute (def. 3). **Louis Lot**, a flutemaker, was the Conservatoire's official supplier of these flutes. Today, many of his flutes are prized the world over.

The CNSMDP had its beginnings on January 3, 1783, when the École Royale de Chant et de Déclamation was founded to provide singers for the Paris Opera. In 1792, the École de Musique Municipale de Paris was founded in order to provide instrumentalists for the Musique de la Garde Nationale, which had been founded in 1790. On August 3, 1795, the two schools were united to become the Conservatoire de Musique. On March 3, 1806, the Conservatoire de Musique became the Conservatoire de Musique et de Déclamation. The school closed briefly in 1816. When it was reopened, it was renamed the École Royale de Musique et de Déclamation, but on April 20, 1822, the name reverted back to Conservatoire de Musique. In 1946, music and theater were separated, and the Conservatoire National d'Art Dramatique was founded. The Conservatoire de Musique is now the CNSMDP.

See also FRENCH TONGUING; *MORCEAU DE CONCOURS*. For information about the flute professors of the Conservatoire and their years of employment, *see* ALTÈS, JOSEPH HENRI; ARTAUD, PIERRE-YVES; CHERRIER, SOPHIE; CRUNELLE, GASTON GABRIELLE; DEBOST, MICHEL; DEVIENNE, FRANÇOIS; DORUS, LOUIS; DUVERGER, NICHOLAS; GAUBERT, PHILIPPE; GUILLOU, JOSEPH; HENNEBAINS, ADOLPHE; HUGOT, ANTOINE; LAFLEURANCE, LÉOPOLD JEAN BAPTISTE; MARION, ALAIN; MOYSE, MARCEL; RAMPAL, JEAN-PIERRE LOUIS; SCHNIETZHOEFFER, JACQUES; TAFFANEL, CLAUDE-PAUL; TULOU, JEAN-LOUIS; WUNDERLICH, JEAN-GEORGES.

PART. The specific music for a particular instrument (or group of instruments)—for example, **flute** part, piano part, and so on—or voice (or voices) in an **ensemble**, as opposed to a *score*, which contains all of the music for all of the instruments and any voices. The music may be in a separate booklet or on one or more specialized lines in a score. *See also* CUE (1); E♭ FLUTE; EXCERPTS; FIRST CHAIR FLUTIST; FIRST FLUTIST; FLUTE BAND; FLUTE CHOIR; LEAD; PRINCIPAL FLUTIST; REED BOOK; SECOND FLUTIST; THIRD FLUTIST; TREBLE FLUTE IN G; UTILITY FLUTIST.

PARTIALS. Frequency components of a complex sound. In the case of most sustained notes with definite **pitch**, the partials are in **harmonic** ratio and, in this particular case, they are called *harmonics*. In the case of sounds without definite pitch, as well as some pitched sounds (e.g., some **tuned** percussion), the partials are not harmonic. Because the frequency components of most **flute** sounds (**multiphonics** excepted) are harmonic, the term *partial* is not often needed. *See also* FULL TONE (1); FUNDAMENTAL (1); HARMONIC SERIES; OVERTONES.

PASSAGE. Any short part of a composition. *See also* ALTERNATE FINGERINGS; B♭ FINGERINGS; BRICCIALDI B♭ LEVER; CIRCULAR BREATHING; CUE (1); DUPLICATE KEYS; DUPLICATE TONE HOLES; EXCERPTS; GROUPING; G♯ KEY (1); MULTIPLE TONGUING; *PRALLTRILLER*; RUN; SINGLE TONGUING; SOLO (3); TRILL KEYS; TRIPLE TONGUING; VIRTUAL FLUTE.

PATCHING. The process of covering holes in a flute **tube** by applying metal patches. This can be done in two ways: either by **soft-soldering** a patch over a hole on the outside of the tube or, in the case of **retuning** the flute, by **hard-soldering** (or **brazing**) the tone-hole **chimney** to a piece of metal tube. In the latter instance, the **tone-hole** chimney and its surrounding metal patch are then cut to fit the flute and soft-soldered onto the tube in the new location. The metal inside the tone-hole chimney is then cut away, and the top of the tone-hole chimney is carefully flattened to ensure a good **seat** for the **pad**.

There is an overlapping of metal when patching. This has the disadvantage that the inner dimensions of the tube will not be maintained, though no adverse effect has been noted by players on the tone of the flute. It is also visually detectable. There is an advantage to patching, however, in that it is done with low-temperature **solder**, which will not soften (or **anneal**) the tube, and thus the tube maintains its original hardness—a factor that possibly may affect the tonal properties of the flute.

Patching, though possible on wooden flutes, would be hardly practical. In this case, the hole would need to be filled with matching wood and a new hole cut.

The **silver-soldered** patch procedure was invented in the late 1950s by flutist **William Bennett**. Patching is also used when repairing damaged flutes or when converting a closed **G♯ key** flute to an open G♯ key flute, where the unwanted closed G♯ sharp tone hole is covered with a patch. *See also* COLE SCALE; INLAYING (1); STRETCHING.

PCM-SILVER ALLOY. A silver **alloy**, used by Miyazawa Flutes, Ltd., to make **body tubing**. It consists of 65 percent **silver**, 25 percent copper, and 10 percent **gold** or **palladium**, mixed together and **plated** with silver. It has a **wall** thickness of 0.015 in. (0.038 mm). According to Miyazawa, the end result before plating is an alloy that is similar to rose gold in appearance. The company also claims that the alloy has a greater hardness, and thus **response** when the **flute** is played, than **sterling silver**, as well as a greater **density**, and thus more **tone color** possibilities when the flute is played, than **nickel-silver**.

PEDAL FLUTE. British term for the bass **recorder** ca. 1700.

PELLERITE, JAMES J. (b. Clearfield, Pa., 1926). A renowned American **Boehm flutist**, **principal flutist** in various orchestras, **flute** professor, flute designer, and publisher, who is now pursuing contemporary music on Native American flute. *See also* O-RING.

PENNY WHISTLE. Same as **tin whistle**. It may have gotten this name because traveling street musicians received pennies when playing to passersby. *See also* NATURAL SCALE.

PENTENRIEDER, BENEDIKT (b. Hesselfurt, Grafing, Germany, 1809; d. Au, Munich, Germany, 1849). A **woodwind** maker whose business thrived in Munich around 1836–1854. *See also* CRESCENT KEY.

PEPLOWSKI, BOLESLAW (b. Connecticut, 1940). An American clarinettist, saxophonist, sculptor, artist in pen and oil, and inventor of the **Bo-Pep**. *See also* THUMB REST.

PERCUSSIVE SOUND. The sound that results when one thing strikes another. The most common percussive sound used in **flute** playing is the **key slap**. *See also* EXTENDED TECHNIQUE; TONGUE CLICK; TONGUE PIZZICATO; TONGUE STOP.

PERCUSSIVE TONGUING. *See* TONGUE CLICK; TONGUE PIZZICATO; TONGUE STOP.

PERFECT PITCH. Same as **absolute pitch**.

PERFORATED KEY/PLATE. Same as **open-hole key**. *See also* FINGER PLATE; PLATE (2).

PERFORMANCE PRACTICE. 1. The aggregate of **techniques**, styles, **ornaments**, and so forth used in a particular historical period, geographical location, or subculture. Some musicians make a point of studying the performance practices of the period or region where the music they are playing was written. This can be quite different from the common modern style, and much of it is not visible in the written music but can only be discerned from various sources such as **method** books, recordings, or live concerts. **2.** How the music of a particular period, location, or subculture should be performed today.

PERFORMER'S EDITION. An edition of a musical composition or **collection** of compositions that includes additional performing directions or annotations intended either to facilitate its execution or shape an interpretation. These annotations may include such practical items as written-out **ornaments** and **fingerings**. The editors do not necessarily distinguish between the composer's text and what the editor added. *Syn.:* practical edition. *See also* CRITICAL EDITION; EDIT; FACSIMILE; SCHOLARLY EDITION; *URTEXT*.

PERIOD INSTRUMENT. An instrument from, or modeled after instruments from, the historical period when the music was written or first performed. The type of instrument will depend on the interval of time, or "period," under consideration. For example, a **one-keyed flute** might be used to play **Baroque** music and a **four-keyed flute** to play **Classical** music.

PETIT DESSUS DE FLÛTE. French term for soprano **recorder** in the late Baroque.

PETITE BASSE DE FLÛTE. French term for the basset **recorder** in the late Baroque.

PETITE FLÛTE. Fr. small flute. Abbr. *pte. fl.* French term for soprano **recorder** in the late Baroque, soon transferred to the **piccolo**.

PEWTER PLUG. A cone-shaped valve, usually made of pewter, that was loosely riveted to the end of a **key shank** and **stopped** the often metal-lined **tone holes** in some **one-keyed flutes** and many late 18th- and 19th-century wooden **simple-system flutes** (see app. 3, B, fig. 4). The pewter plugs were very durable and helped prevent **leaks**. However, they were costly to repair and it was necessary for the player to keep them **oiled** to help cut down any noise and to ensure that the plug **sealed**. Flutes with pewter plug **keys** became popular in Britain almost immediately after London flutemaker **Richard Potter** took out a patent in 1785 that included a listing of these keys. *Syn.:* plug keys. *See also* TONE-HOLE BUSHING. (For information about other materials that

stopped tone holes in simple-system flutes, *see* LEATH-ERS; PURSE PADS.)

PHELAN, J. JAMES (b. Bridgeport, Conn., 1951). An American engineer, musician, flutemaker, acoustician, author (see bib. under "Repair, Maintenance, and Construction"), and co-owner of Burkart-Phelan, Inc. *See also* AURUMITE.

PHRASING. The manner in which a musical phrase is interpreted and played, using time, rhythm, dynamics, stress, **articulation**, **tone color**, and so on to group the notes of a melody into **expressive** units and thus give meaning and purpose to music. *Syn.:* shaping. *See also* DIRECTION; GROUPING.

PICCOLO. Abbr. picc. It. *flauto piccolo, ottavino;* Fr. *petite flûte;* Ger. *kleine Flöte, Pickelflöte, Pikkoloflöte, Oktavflöte.* **1.** A common, highest-**pitched** member of the **Boehm flute** family (*see* FLUTE FAMILY [2]) that is pitched in C, sounding an octave higher than the **concert flute** in C, which enables it to be heard above all the other instruments in a band or symphony orchestra. Like the concert flute, the piccolo is **side-blown** and uses the same **fingering system**. Except for small changes, it is played in a similar way. Its **range** is around three octaves from the note sounding as D_2 to C_5 (written as D_1 to C_4; *see* TRANSPOSING INSTRUMENTS), although some piccolos are now occasionally being made that can play as low as B_1.

The piccolo is the smallest member of the flute family (see app. 6, fig. 1). It is slightly less than half of the concert flute's length, about 12.5 in. (32 cm). Unlike the concert flute, the piccolo lacks a **foot joint** and comes in two basic **bore** shapes: **conical** and **cylindrical** (see fig. 30). The conical piccolo has a bore with mainly a conical shape, like the **Baroque flute** (i.e., the bore gets slightly smaller from the top of the **body** toward the bottom, where it slightly flares out). The **head joint** bore is cylindrical. The cylindrical piccolo has a bore of cylindrical shape like the concert flute. The head joint bore, however, is conical, with the narrower part at the closed end.

The conical piccolo is more popular with professional players than the cylindrical piccolo because of its better **tone quality** and **intonation**. However, it tends to be difficult to play above A_3 or $B\flat_3$. The cylindrical piccolo is more popular with amateur players than the conical piccolo because it is easier to play, especially in the **third octave**. However, it tends to have a thin sound and fewer **tone colors**.

Next to the concert flute, the piccolo is the next most popular member of today's flute family. A lot of music has been written specifically for it. It is commonly used in **solo** playing, studio work, and **ensembles** of all sizes. This includes bands, orchestras, and **flute choirs**, where it is a regular member. The piccolo is also useful as a beginning instrument for students who are too small to hold the concert flute.

Generally, when the word *piccolo* is used alone, as in the discussion above, it means the piccolo in C (*see* "FLUTE IN . . ."). This is the most common piccolo played today, but there is also a less frequently played piccolo in D♭ (a semitone higher than the piccolo in C) that is sometimes used. Higher-pitched piccolos, such as the piccoletto in E♭ (a minor third higher than the piccolo in C) and even a one-of-a-kind **simple-system** octave piccolo (an octave higher than the piccolo in C) exist.

It is not certain when the first piccolo was made, but it is clear from the number of extant piccolos that it was quite popular in earlier times. It is often stated that the first appearance of the piccolo in a symphony was in 1805 in Beethoven's Fifth Symphony. While this appears to be true, it obscures the reality that small transverse octave flutes were being used in French opera at least 70 years prior to this. In the Renaissance, small **transverse flutes** in A formed part of consorts.

Whereas the development of the piccolo generally follows that of the concert flute, its acquisition of **keys** was generally slower than that of its larger counterpart. For example, in the first two decades or so of the 20th century, there were flutists who played the Boehm flute but still used a six-keyed simple-system piccolo in the **natural scale** of D major. It was the difficulty of performing on these latter piccolos in the predominantly **flat** keys of military bands that necessitated **flutists** use transposing D♭ piccolos. These piccolos were pitched one semitone higher than the standard piccolo, so their natural scale sounded in E♭, a frequently used tonality for band music, making the music technically easier. As the practice of having a matched Boehm fingering system for both the flute and piccolo became universal, much of the band music in use for piccolo was transposed in D♭, which is likely why old **Boehm-system** D♭ piccolos were built.

See also app. 6; AFRICAN BLACKWOOD; BREATH SUPPORT; BROSSA F♯ LEVER; BULBOUS HEAD JOINT; COMBINATION CASE; CONICAL BORE; DOUBLING; FIFE (1, 3); FLAGEOLET (1b); *FLAUTO GRANDE; FLAUTO PICCOLO* (2, 3);

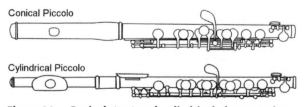

Figure 30. Conical *(top)* and cylindrical *(bottom)* piccolos. *Drawing courtesy J. L. Smith & Co.*

FLUTE BAND; FLUTE FLAG; FLUTE STAND; GLASS FLUTE; *GRANDE FLÛTE; GROSSE FLÖTE;* HIGH G♯ MECHANISM; HIGH-PITCHED FLUTE (1); OCTAVE FLUTE (1); OLNHAUSEN RING; *OTTAVINO;* PISONI PADS; PRINCIPAL FLUTIST (3); SECOND FLUTIST; SPLIT MECHANISM; SQUAREONE FLUTE; STRAUBINGER PAD; THIRD FLUTIST; TREBLE FLUTE IN G; UNIBODY; UTILITY FLUTIST; VALGON RINGS; WART. **2.** *See* E♭ FLUTE.

PICKELFLÖTE. An older German name for **piccolo**, the modern name being *klein Flöte*.

PICKLE. 1. An acid solution or bath that is used in flutemaking or repair to clean off scale (*see* FIRE SCALE) and oxides from metal. This needs to be done before any **plating** or **finishing**. Different recipes are used, depending on the metal and what needs to be removed. **2.** *v.* To treat with a pickle solution or bath.

PIECE. 1. A musical composition that is primarily meant to be played and listened to for pleasure. It may have secondary value as an instructional aid. A large piece may be referred to as a *work. See also* B FOOT JOINT; COLLECTION; DECIMETTE; DUET/DUO; EXCERPTS; FACSIMILE; METHOD; *MORCEAU DE CONCOURS;* NONET; OCTET; PARIS CONSERVATOIRE; PLATINUM FLUTE; QUARTET; QUINTET; REPERTOIRE; SCHOLARLY EDITION; SEPTET; SEXTET; SHEET MUSIC; SOLO (1, 3); STUDY; TRIO; TUTOR; *URTEXT;* WIND QUINTET. For **early flutes**, *see also* RANGE (2). **2.** *See* JOINT.

PIED PIPER OF HAMELIN. A legendary 13th-century musician who was hired by the town of Hamelin in Germany to get rid of its rat problem. He did this by charming the rats away with his **flute** playing to a river where they drowned. Despite his success, the town refused to pay him. In revenge, the Pied Piper then charmed all of Hamelin's children out of the town in the same way as the rats, and all were lost.

PILLAR. Same as **post**. *See also* PLATE (5).

PILOT TIP. A cylindrical end of a screw or **steel**.

PIN. 1. On **Boehm flutes** with **post-mounts** and **pinned mechanisms**, a tiny, short, tapered **steel** pin that rigidly connects some **keys**, and parts that need to be connected to them (e.g., **kickers** and **clutch** plates), to rotating **steels** inside the **key tubing** (see app. 7, fig. 8). Their purpose is to lock separated keys and parts together while allowing other keys and parts between them to remain independent. Pins are often made from sewing needles. *Syn.:* pinning needles. *See also* BRÖGGER MEKANIK; GOLD

FLUTE (1); KEY MECHANISM; NICKEL-SILVER FLUTE; PINLESS MECHANISM; PLATINUM FLUTE; SECTION (2); SILVER FLUTE (1); STRINGER. **2.** On **one-keyed, two-keyed,** and **simple-system flutes** with **block-mounts**, a thin, short, nontapered length of **brass** or other metal that suspends a key between the two **knobs** on either side of a carved-out **channel** in a wooden or **ivory** block or ring on flute **bodies** to act as a fulcrum for that key. The **head** of the pin is often bent in an L, O, or U shape (see app. 3, B, figs. 2, 6, and 7). Simple-system flutes with post-mounts have pins that are similar in function to those used for block-mounts. *Syn.:* axle, axle pin. *See also* BEARING; FLAP KEY; SADDLE-MOUNT; SALT-SPOON KEY. **3.** An older term for **tenon**. **4.** An alternative name for the **screw-cork indicator**. *See also* SCREW-CORK (1). **5.** *See* CRACK PINNING. **6.** Pin **spring**. **7.** End pin; same as **boot**. *See also* WALKING-STICK FLUTE.

PIN-IN-BLOCK KEY MOUNT. Same as **block-mount**.

PINLESS MECHANISM. A generic term for any type of **key mechanism** that connects **keys** without the use of **pins** (def. 1). There are various types of pinless mechanisms used on modern **flutes**. The pinless mechanism may be a type of mechanism that either uses **bridges** between keys to connect them, instead of pinning keys directly to a rotating **steel** axle (for examples, *see* BRÖGGER MEKANIK; BRÖGGER SYSTEM) or uses miniature screws instead of pins to link keys by attaching them to a rotating steel, as on the **pinned mechanism** of a traditional flute (both Pearl and **Wessel** flutes use this type of mechanism). **Auguste Buffet** *jeune* (1789–1864) made use of sections of square **key tubing** and square axles instead of pins or screws, but this mechanism was of limited application because these sections could be applied only at the outer ends of groups of keys. *See also* ONE-PIECE CORE BAR.

Some companies prefer to use a pinless mechanism only for the left-hand **section**. For example, until recently, V. Q. Powell Flutes, Inc., offered only a left-hand pinless mechanism. Powell's left-hand pinless mechanism has the B♭ **side lever** connected to the B♭ key by an additional bridge rod. This eliminates the need to secure either the B♭ **kicker** or the B♭ key to the steel with pins and allows the steel to turn freely within the **key tubing**.

Any type of pinless mechanism is preferred to a pinned mechanism if a **split E mechanism** option with in-line **G keys** is chosen. This is because a flute with at least a pinless left-hand mechanism helps to avoid a **binding** B♭ key (open or closed), which can be a problem if a split E mechanism is used on in-line G key flutes.

The pinless mechanism was also used by earlier flutemakers such as **Rudall, Carte** & Co. and **H. D.**

Villette. *See also* app. 4; BOEHM FLUTE; PINNED MECHANISM; PROFESSIONAL FLUTE.

PINNED MECHANISM. A **key mechanism** using small tapered **steel pins** to rigidly connect some **keys** and parts (e.g., **kickers** and **lugs**) to rotating **steel** axles inside the **key tubing**. Their purpose is to lock separated keys and parts together, while allowing other keys and parts between them to remain independent. Most modern **flutes** rely on a pinned mechanism. *See also* BOEHM FLUTE; CLUTCH (1); CYLINDRICAL BOEHM FLUTE (1); ONE-PIECE CORE BAR; PINLESS MECHANISM; POST-MOUNT; PROFESSIONAL FLUTE; SECTION (2); STEELS; STRINGER; STUDENT FLUTE.

PINNING NEEDLE. Same as **pin** (1).

PINSCHOF, THOMAS (b. Vienna, 1948). An Austrian **flutist**, **flute** teacher, flute designer, recording artist, author, conductor, and composer who designed the **Pinschofon** in the early 1970s.

PINSCHOFON. An uncommon type of **bass flute** (def. 1) with an extended **range** down to the G (or F with an optional **bell** attachment) below the **lowest note** of the standard modern bass flute in C. Unlike most modern bass flutes, the **body** of the Pinschofon is held vertically to enable the player to handle the extra length and weight required for the extended **low register**. Due to the extra length, the **head joint** is doubled back upon itself, and the instrument supported by an adjustable double spike on the **foot joint** (see fig. 31). The flaring at the end of the bell attachment slightly improves the **projection**. The instrument's full length, including the doubled-back part but excluding the spike, is about 86 in. (219 cm). With the bell, the length is extended to 88.6 in. (223 cm). The effective height from the top of the **embouchure plate** to the end of the foot joint, but excluding any bell attachment or spike, is about 50.4 in. (128 cm).

The Pinschofon's range is around three and a half octaves from the note sounding as F to at least a C$\sharp_3$ (written as f to C$\sharp_4$; *see* TRANSPOSING INSTRUMENTS). In addition to the standard **low b key**, the instrument has two extra **keys** for the low B♭ and A, and these are operated by L4. The keys for the extra low notes A♭, G, F♯, and F are operated by the RT.

The Pinschofon was one of the earliest of the **subbass flutes**. It was designed by Austrian **Thomas Pinschof** in the early 1970s and was first made for him by Werner Wetzel in Berlin and further improved by Wetzel's students and successors. It is not a commonly played flute, but due to a surge of interest in low-pitched

Figure 31. A Pinschofon. *Photo courtesy Thomas Pinschof.*

flutes such as the **alto**, bass, and **contrabass flute**s in recent years, its use may increase. It has been used in **solo** playing, recordings, studio work, and **ensembles** such as **flute choirs** where it shares the cello function with the contrabass flute. Although concertos have been written for it, it is not a regular member of a band or an orchestra. *See also* app. 6; ALBISIPHON (1); *FLAUTONE*; FLUTE FAMILY (2); "FLUTE IN . . ."; UPRIGHT BASSFLUTE IN C UNTIL G (BASS FLUTE [3]); VERTICAL FLUTE.

PIPE. 1. A general name for any hollow cylinder or cone in which air vibrates and produces a sound. All **wind instruments** and the organ fit into this category. *See* ACOUSTICAL LENGTH (2); CUTOFF FREQUENCY; END CORRECTION; *FISTULA* (1); NOTCHED FLUTE; STANDING WAVE. **2.** *See* AUTOMATON; TABOR PIPE. **3.** *See* PANPIPES.

PIPE AND TABOR. *See* AUTOMATON; TABOR PIPE.

PISONI, LUCIANO (b. Gardolo, Trento, Italy, 1947). An Italian inventor of a unique *CNC (Computer Numerical Control)* **pad**-making machinery and pads for many instruments. Pisoni started the company Music Center SpA in 1974. It is the largest manufacturer of **wind instrument** pads in the world and is now located in Gardolo, Italy. *See also* PISONI PADS.

PISONI PADS. A generic name that refers to the large variety of key **pads** offered by Music Center SpA in Gardolo, Italy, the largest manufacturer of pads for **wind instruments** in the world. The company was started by **Luciano Pisoni** in 1974 and produces a wide selection of traditional and nontraditional **flute** pads, all designed by Pisoni himself. The pads range in quality and cost to suit the design of any model of flute and are used by many flutemaking companies around the world. Technicians select pads and a method to install them based on the condition and grade of flute.

Some of the most popular traditional flute pads are the standard quality FL-40 and the medium quality DFL-40 that are used for **student flutes** and the high-quality DFL-140J, DFL-40T, and DFL-40HT that are used for **professional flutes**. The main difference between these pads is the type of **felt** used. The lower-quality pads use a softer felt that can easily adapt to any imperfections in the key **cups** and **tone-hole rims** since they can form a deeper **pad seat**. As a result, the flute does not need to be in perfect **adjustment** for the pad to perform well. A harder felt must be perfectly **seated** through **shimming** since it will not take as deep a pad seat to account for the uneven surface of some **tone holes**. Traditional resonators, such as metal rivets, can be centrally mounted on traditional flute pads.

Examples of nontraditional pads are the high-quality Sound, Star LP, and LP Gore pads. There are three different lines of Sound pads: Red Sound (medium consistency), Gold Sound (medium-soft consistency), and Blue Sound (medium-hard consistency). They were created in 1999 and consist of double **bladder skin**, pressed or woven felt, and a unique disc of synthetic material and cardboard.

Star LP pads were introduced in 1997. The larger pads consist of bladder skin, specially treated pressed felt for dimensional stability, a unique star-shaped **cushion** made from noise-reducing synthetic material, and an exclusive metal cup-like shell or flat disc to prevent distortion when the pad is fixed to the key cup. A cardboard disc glued under the shell fixes the bladder skin to the pad. The smaller pads feature a unique metal tube centrally located in the metal shell, and under the bladder skin, which acts as a resonator; the felt and noise-reduction material are cut in rings. The smaller Star LP pads are also available for professional **piccolos**.

The LP Gore pads, introduced in 2003 especially for wooden flutes, feature an exclusive water-resistant white Gore membrane to cover the pad parts. Under this material are a felt ring and a ring made of cardboard, foam, or other materials.

PITCH. 1. A measure of whether a note or a combination of notes is "**high**" or "**low**." Usually a low-pitched sound is a note that has slowly vibrating (i.e., low-**frequency**) air, and a high-pitched sound is one that has fast-vibrating (i.e., high-frequency) air. If a particular note is played lower than the desired pitch, then it is **flat**; if it is played higher, it is **sharp**.

Frequency is a physical variable: it can be measured by a machine. It is proportional to the logarithm of the frequency. (This means that for pitch to go up the same amount, the frequency must be multiplied by the same factor. For example, pitch goes up one octave every time the frequency is doubled, and it goes up one semitone every time the frequency is multiplied by approximately 1.06.) Pitch, on the other hand, is a psychological variable: it depends upon human perception and may differ from the simple logarithmic relationship. For example, the (perceived) pitch of a **pure tone** may go flat as the volume increases at a constant frequency. A combination of frequencies consisting only of several **harmonics** of an absent **fundamental** will be identified by a listener as having the pitch of the missing fundamental. When two notes an octave apart are presented one after the other, many people find that the physical octave (an exact doubling of frequency) is slightly too flat. The amount of *stretch* (the amount by which the frequency ratio exceeds 2:1) necessary to produce an apparent octave varies with the part of the scale being played, the **tone color** or harmonic content of the notes played, the **intensity** of the notes, the listener, and especially whether the notes are presented simultaneously or sequentially. Most **flutists** tend to play **sharper** as they ascend the scale. Their "stretching of the scale" may be greater than that called for by the perception of the average listener. In particular, when two instruments play in octaves, any stretching at all is disagreeable.

Some people have **absolute pitch** (also called *perfect pitch*), which enables them to identify or sing a note or to name the key of a composition without any reference, but most persons can employ only **relative pitch** with precision, in which only pitch *intervals* are identified or produced. The intervals depend on the ratios of the frequencies, not their differences. For example, two notes with a ratio of say 3:2 (e.g., $A_1 = 440$ Hz to $E_2 = 660$ Hz, or $C_1 = 262$ Hz to $G_1 = 393$ Hz) will be identified as perfect fifths because the ratios, not the differences, are equal, in spite of the fact that the frequency differences are not at all equal.

    See also app. 11; AIR REED (1); AUGMENTED FINGERINGS; BEATS; *BISBIGLIANDO;* CENT; CUTOFF FREQUENCY; DENSITY; DIFFERENCE TONE; EAR TRAINING; EMBOUCHURE HOLE; EXPRESSIVE INTONATION; FLUTE (1); FREQUENCY; GLISSANDO; HARMONIC (1); HARMONIC SERIES; HIGHER NOTE; HUMORING; INTONATION; IN TUNE; JUST INTONATION; KEY (3); KEY VIBRATO; LIPPING; LIP GLISSANDO; LIP VIBRATO; LOWERING A NOTE; LOWER NOTE (1); MICROTONE; MOISTURE TRIANGLE; NANNY-GOAT VIBRATO; NOTE BENDING; OUT OF TUNE; OVERTONES; PARTIALS; RAISING A NOTE; RESISTANCE (1); RESONANCE (1); ROBERT DICK GLISSANDO HEADJOINT; ROLL-IN; SECOND FLUTIST; SHADING; STOP (1); SWEET SPOT; TEMPER (4); THROAT TUNING; TRANSPOSING INSTRUMENTS; TUNER; TUNING NOTE; TUNING RINGS; TUNING SLIDE (1); VIBRATO; VOCALIZING/SINGING WHILE PLAYING. For **early flutes,** *see also BRILLE* (1); FINGER VIBRATO; GLIDE; TUNING SLIDE (2); TWO-KEYED FLUTE.

    2. A set pitch for musical instruments' **scale** that enables them to be made to a common standard. The international standard pitch at this time is A = 440 Hz. In the past, the pitch used for A_1 has varied over a wide range, and even now, usage of A = 442 Hz or higher is common (*see* CONCERT PITCH). The "pitch of the flute" refers to the pitch that the manufacturer has chosen for the entire flute, but is generally defined by the pitch of A_1. This pitch is determined by the distance from the center of the embouchure hole to the center of the A **tone hole** and some other variables, including tone hole and **bore** sizes and playing style.

    Once this pitch has been chosen, the manufacturer must size and position the tone holes so that the other notes are in tune with respect to A_1. Most flutes are now produced at $A_1 = 442$ Hz, but some **professional flutes** can be obtained with different pitches, usually with the note A_1 lying in the range of 440 to 446 Hz. The pitch that a **flutist** chooses will depend on such factors as what pitch the flutist plays at with a particular flute scale, the pitch at which his **ensemble** normally plays, and the temperature of the places in which he plays.

    Note that although manufacturers choose a pitch for the note A_1, a flutist can play the A_1 (and all the other notes for that matter) higher or lower in pitch by

changing her playing in certain ways (e.g., by using **embouchure** movement) or by adjusting the **head joint**. For example, if a flutist buys an $A_1 = 442$ Hz flute, she can easily play A_1 at 444 Hz or 440 Hz.

    See also COLE SCALE; COOPER SCALE; "FLUTE PITCHED AT A = . . ."; "FLUTE PITCHED IN . . ."; FOSTER EXTENSION; HIGH-PITCHED FLUTE; H.P.; INTERNAL TUNING; LOW-PITCHED FLUTE; L.P.; MODERN SCALE; MURRAY FLUTE; OCTAVE LENGTH; PROFESSIONAL FLUTE; RETUNING; SCALING; SCHEMA; SERIAL NUMBER; SHORTENED HEAD JOINT; SOUNDING HOLE; SOUNDING LENGTH (3); TEMPER (4); TRADITIONAL SCALE; TUNING UP. For **early flutes,** *see also* BAROQUE FLUTE (1); BAROQUE PITCH; CLASSICAL FLUTE; *CORPS D'AMOUR; CORPS DE RECHANGE;* FOOT REGISTER; SICCAMA DIATONIC FLUTE; TUNING RINGS.

PITCH BENDING. Same as **note bending**. *See also* GLIDE; GLISSANDO.

PITCHED. 1. *See* "FLUTE PITCHED IN . . ."; TRANSPOSING INSTRUMENTS (2). **2.** *See* HIGH-PITCHED FLUTE; LOW-PITCHED FLUTE.

PITTING. A type of **corrosion** seen on some **plated** flutes that is characterized by many small pin-size holes over the surface of the metal. Flutes with a pitting problem may be replated. To prevent pitting, clear nail polish sealer, adhesive tape, or a postage stamp can be applied to susceptible parts of the instrument (e.g., the chin side of the **embouchure plate**). *See also* SPRING.

PIVOT. 1. A short fixed shaft, rod, or screw ending in a **pivot point** on which another related part rotates. For example, the pivot point of a **flute**'s tapered **pivot screw** is a pivot on which a **steel rod** rotates. **2.** The act of turning on, or as if on, a pivot. For example, a flute steel turns or performs a pivot on its corresponding pivot screw. *See also* KING POST.

PIVOT POINT. The ends of **pivot screws** or the pointed ends of some **steel** rods (**steels**). *See also* PIVOT.

PIVOT SCREWS. Small screws that are inserted through **post** heads and into the ends of **steel** rods (commonly called *steels* or *rods*). Their purpose is to hold the steels in place inside **key tubing** in such a way that the steels can rotate on the tips of the screws (see app. 7, fig. 14). On a standard **concert flute**, there are three pivot screws: one in the post nearest the D key **cup** and one in each of the two posts that support the **trill keys**' steel.

    There are three types of pivot screws: headed conical, nonheaded conical, and (headed) cylindrical pivot screws. The best of the three is the *headed conical pivot screw*, since it mechanically locks in place (due to the shoulder), gives the least amount of friction between the screw end and the steel, and allows for not only a precision fit but also subsequent **adjustment** to take up wear. It has a cone-shaped tip that fits into a cone-shaped cavity in the end of a steel. It is usually seen on more expensive **flutes**.

The *headless conical pivot screw* is not as stable as the headed conical version because, without a **head**, it cannot mechanically lock in place. To help keep the screw in place, a sealer or adhesive (e.g., nail polish or **glue**) may be used. Alternatively, pivot screws with a slot in one side of the screw, for nyloc or other material, may be used as a brace to hold the screw in place. Unfortunately, the benefits of any material in the slot will be short-lived, as it will eventually wear out. Even when the material is new, it can cause the pivot screw to move off-center, as it is situated on only one side of the screw threads.

The *(headed) cylindrical pivot screw* is usually seen on less expensive flutes. It has a cylindrical-shaped tip that fits into a similarly shaped hole in the end of the steel. Since this type of pivot screw has a head, it can mechanically lock in place, which is good. However, even though the screw has cylindrically shaped sides, which makes it wear more slowly than the conical type, any wear cannot be taken up by advancing the screw as you would the conical type. Because of this, the screw has no provision for being precision fitted and simply acts as a mount for the steel with no lateral thrust, the pilot end simply being a cylindrical extension into the tube for purposes of mounting.

Overall, the relative advantages of all three types of screws depend on the design and workmanship. Some makers, for example, believe that to work well, the screws and corresponding **sockets** on a good **handmade flute** should have **polished** surfaces and be hardened.

Pivot screws may be made out of mild, carbon, or stainless steel. Stainless steel is preferable to other types of steel because it is resistant to rust. *Syn.:* **point screw, pivot;** for conical pivot screws: tapered pivot screw, pointed pivot screw; for cylindrical pivot screw: pilot pivot screw, cylindrical pivot screw, straight pivot screw. *See also* CYLINDRICAL BOEHM FLUTE (1); GOLD FLUTE (1); KEY MECHANISM; NICKEL-SILVER FLUTE; PIVOT POINT; PLATINUM FLUTE; POST-MOUNT; PROFESSIONAL FLUTE; STOP (3).

PIZZICATO. *See* TONGUE PIZZICATO.

PLAIN CUP/KEY/KEY CUP. *See* CLOSED-HOLE KEY/CUP/KEY CUP.

PLATE. 1. *See* PLATING. **2.** An older term for **key**. *See* FINGER PLATE; PERFORATED KEY/PLATE. **3.** *See* STOP PLATE. **4.** *See* EMBOUCHURE PLATE. **5.** Small, thin, flat metal pieces of various shapes, often oval, that are attached with small screws to the surface of the **body** and **foot joint** of 19th- and early 20th-century flutes or replicas of them (see app. 3, C, fig. 3). The **pillars** (or **posts**) that hold the **key mechanism** are **soldered** to these plates. This method of mounting **keys** was patented by **Claude Laurent** in 1806 as a way to attach keys to his **glass flutes**, but they quickly became common on wooden flutes, as well, especially in France. (Later, many makers would omit the plates and screw the posts directly into the wood.) *See also* RIB-MOUNT; SADDLE-MOUNT. (For information about what is used as a base for pillars on metal flutes, *see* RIBS; POST-MOUNT.) **6.** A clutch plate: same as **lug, adjustment** plate. *See also* ADJUSTMENT SCREWS; CLUTCH (1). **7.** *See* CORK PLATE.

PLATEAU KEY/CUP/KEY CUP. Same as **closed-hole key/cup/key cup.** *See also* CYLINDRICAL BOEHM FLUTE (1).

PLATEAU-MODEL FLUTE. A **closed-hole flute.**

PLATING. A thin metal coating, such as **silver**, applied to a **base metal**. The plating improves the **finish** (*see* SILVER-PLATING) and the wearing quality and helps to resist **corrosion**. It is sometimes used to add thickness during a **head joint refitting** or for protecting the skin from another metal to prevent allergic reactions. The quality and longevity of plated layers can vary tremendously, depending on the care with which they are applied and their thickness. They can also wear off by handling or from skin acidity. If it becomes necessary, plating can be reapplied, although that can be costly. The most common types of plating used in flutemaking are **nickel**, silver, and **gold. Student flutes** come in a variety of metals and are plated with silver or nickel and occasionally gold.

Modern plating is usually applied using an electrochemical process called *electrodeposition*. The **flute** is immersed in a solution of silver cyanide and an electrical charge is applied to force the silver from the solution to deposit onto the flute. Old plating, such as that used on old French flutes (e.g., **Louis Lots, Bonnevilles**), was applied using a chemical process called *fire or mercury gilding*. During this process, silver was dissolved in mercury and the flute was immersed in the resulting solution, which fused with the surface of the base metal. Then the flute was heated to dispel the mercury, leaving a very thick and dense silver deposit. This process is now extinct, probably for health reasons, as mercury and mercury vapor are toxic. Some **flutists** feel that the old mercury-based plating method gives a rich texture to the tone of flutes. This was especially effective on the flutes of Auguste Bonneville, whose plated instruments have historically been very popular. *See also* BASE METAL (2); BONDING; CLADDING; EMBOUCHURE RECUT; FACTORY-MADE FLUTE; FLASH PLATE; FUSING; GOLD FLUTE (2); GOLD-PLATING; NICKEL-PLATING; NICKEL-SILVER; NICKEL-SILVER FLUTE; PICKLE; PITTING; PLATING-UP; PLATINUM; POLISH (1); RHODIUM-PLATING; SILVER FLUTE (2); STRIKE PLATE; WALL (1).

PLATING-UP. Adding **plating** to an existing metal object, such as to the outside of a metal **head joint tenon**, by an electrical process. *See also* **head joint refitting**.

PLATINUM. A metallic element and one of the **precious metals**. It is occasionally used in flutemaking, where it is **alloyed** with other metals (mainly iridium), in varying amounts (*see* PLATINUM FLUTE). Platinum is also used for **plating** metal parts. Platinum is the densest of the precious metals, having a **density** of about 0.75 lbs./in.^{3} (21 g/cm^3) for pure platinum. Like **gold**, it is highly resistant to **corrosion** and **tarnish**. The main disadvantages of platinum are its cost and weight. *See also* HALLMARK; HANDMADE FLUTE; PROFESSIONAL FLUTE; RHODIUM-PLATING; SEAMED TUBING.

PLATINUM FLUTE. A **flute** where at least the **tubing** is made from **platinum**. Parts other than the tubing are often made from a different metal (e.g., the **keys** may be made of **silver** to make the flute more lightweight). Small parts of the **key mechanism** (e.g., the **pivot screws**, the **steels**, and any **pins**) are usually made from nonprecious metals such as stainless **steel** or carbon tool steel. Although platinum flutes are used by some professional **flutists**, they are not as popular as **silver flutes** and **gold flutes** due to their weight and high cost.

The famous **solo** flute **piece** "Density 21.5" by Edgard Varèse was composed in 1936 (rev. 1946) specifically for **Georges Barrère**'s new platinum Haynes flute, which, in July 1935, was the first all-platinum **alloy** flute. The title of the piece is based on the **density** of platinum (21.45g/cm^3), although it is interesting to note that Barrère's flute actually had a density of 21.6 g/cm^3.

The first platinum flute was made around 1932 or 1933 by **Rudall, Carte** & Co. One of the most famous flutes in the world is Powell no. 365, which was made in platinum by flutemaker **Verne Q. Powell** for the 1939 New York World's Fair and bought by flutist **William Kincaid**. It has a 0.01 in. (0.25 mm) platinum **body** with **sterling silver** mechanism, French-pointed arms (*see* KEY ARMS), in-line **G keys**, a **B foot joint**, and a **pitch** of A_1 = 440 Hz. It is **engraved** with the trylon and perisphere, symbolizing the 1939 World's Fair in New York. **Elaine Shaffer**, a pupil of Kincaid, inherited the flute from him. It was sold after her demise by her husband, conductor Efrem Kurtz, at Christie's Auction House in New York in 1987 for $187,000 to Stuart Pivar, a private collector, but is currently on display at the Metropolitan Museum of Art in New York City. *See also* HALLMARK; NICKEL-SILVER FLUTE; SEAMED TUBING; SPRING; TARNISH.

PLAY. Too much looseness in the moving parts of the **flute**. There are two types: end play and lateral. *End play* occurs when the **key tubing** or a **roller** moves too much from end to end along the **steel**. The cause of end play is usually either wear at the key tubing (or roller) ends or a bent **post**. *Lateral play*, also called *side play* or *radial play*, occurs when the key tubing or roller moves too much from side to side across the steel. The main cause of lateral play is the key tubing **bore** being too large for the steel, again due to wear. *Syn.:* slop. *See also* COUNTERSINK (3); LOST MOTION; SWAGING; TELESCOPING (1).

PLAYING CONDITION. Generally, the condition of a **flute** when it has had the minimum of repair work done in order to get it playing well. This may include re-**seating** or changing **pads** where needed, straightening a bent **key**, removing key noise, replacing broken **springs**, and so on. The amount and type of work required is an assessment opinion and will vary among repairers. The job of getting a flute into playing condition is not as complete a repair job as an **overhaul**, where certain things are done, whether necessary or not, in order to take the flute to "like new" condition. *Syn.:* working order.

PLAYING-IN. Same as **breaking-in**.

PLAY-TEST. Playing a musical instrument to see how well it performs. A repairer or **flutist** will play-test a **flute** after a repair to check the quality of the repair and to see if anything else needs to be done. A flutist will play-test many flutes to see which is the best before purchasing one. A performer will play-test a newly made flute in a flutemaking business and assess if anything else needs to be done before putting the flute up for sale.

PLUG. 1. A widely available, usually **cork** or plastic insert that fits into the holes in the A, upper G, F, E, and D key **cups** of **open-hole flutes** (see app. 9, fig. 2). The five open holes are E, F, F♯, A, and B♭. The inserts are used where difficulty is encountered in covering these holes. It should be noted that closed- and open-hole flutes require different **tone hole** positions, and the use of plugs **flattens** the notes under the open holes. If the use of plugs is found necessary, it should be resorted to purely as a temporary measure. The plugs may be removed one at a time over a period of a week or two. *Syn.:* inserts, finger plug inserts. **2.** The plug in the **head joint**. *See* BIGIO CROWN AND STOPPER; HEAD JOINT CORK; O-RING (2); SCREW-CORK; STOPPER. **3.** *See* RESISTANCE PLUG. **4. Register** plug. *See* HYPERBASS FLUTE. **5.** Plug **keys**. *See* PEWTER PLUG. **6.** Elastic balls/plugs. *See* PURSE PAD.

PNEUMO PRO. From the Greek *pneuma*, wind or breath. A tool to help players direct the air correctly (see app. 12, fig. 3). It is designed like a flute **head joint**, but has handles and an **embouchure** area that is cut all the way through, so that when the player blows into it, a series of propellers are set spinning to show the spread, direction, and speed of the **air column**. The flat surfaces of the handles are held parallel to the ground to insure that the correct angle of the air is not being achieved through rolling the Pneumo Pro flute in or out. The device was invented by **Kathy Blocki** and **Herbert Blocki** in 1999 and has a U.S. patent secured in 2002.

POINTED ARM/KEY ARM. Same as French-pointed arm. *See* KEY ARM.

POINTED CUP/KEY. A **key** with a French-pointed arm. *See* KEY ARM.

POINT SCREW. A screw with a pointed end, such as a tapered **pivot screw**.

POLISH. 1. *v.* To make something smooth and shiny, usually by friction. Flutemakers and repairers use various products and methods for polishing metal **flutes**, depending on the part being polished and the type of **finish** desired. They may hand-polish with a **rouge** cloth, **burnish** with a lubricated tool, or **buff** with **Tripoli**, rouge, or polishing compounds such as Tarnish-shield by 3M. Flute players sometimes use treated polishing cloths to polish the exterior of their flutes.

It is important to note that all products and methods that are used to polish metal are abrasive. Just *how* abrasive depends on the product and the method of polishing used. Extra care needs to be taken with plated instruments, as regular polishing can wear off the **plating**.

Depending on the type of polishing that is done, the flute may need to be disassembled before any work is done on it. Otherwise the **pads** could get damaged. *See also* FINISHER; HEAD-JOINT MAKER; OIL (3); OVERHAUL; PIVOT SCREW; RAGGING; STRINGER; TARNISH.

2. Anything that is used to make something smooth and shiny, such as rouge or Tripoli.

3. The state of being smooth and shiny. *See also* STEEL (1).

POLLACK, ANNE H. (b. Philadelphia, 1958). An American **flutist**, **flute** repair technician, and dealer in New York City. *See also* FLUTE SUIT.

PORTAMENTO. It. carrying. A carrying or sliding of the sound from one note to another in such a way that the intervening notes, although sounded, are indistinguishable. This type of articulation can be achieved on instruments such as the voice, bowed strings, and trombones. True portamento is possible only between some intervals on the standard **flute** and only when **open-hole keys** are available (*see* GLISSANDO). Sometimes **flutists** try to approximate the portamento effect by playing a note as a **bell tone**. *See also* GLIDE; *PORTATO* (2); ROBERT DICK GLISSANDO HEADJOINT.

PORTATO. It. carried. **1.** A type of **articulation** that usually means the same thing as *mezzo-**staccato***. *Syn.:* *louré*. *Cf.* **bell tone**. **2.** Sometimes erroneously used to mean the same thing as *portamento*.

POST-MOUNT. A method of mounting and supporting **keys** on the flute's **body** using two or more **posts**. The posts are mounted in various ways according to the material used for the body.

- On metal flutes, the posts are either **soft-soldered** directly to the body (called *direct-mount*) or, more commonly, **hard-soldered** or **brazed** onto thin, long, metal strips called *ribs* or *straps* (or *plates*, if they are short), which are then soft-soldered to the body (called *rib-mount*; see app. 7, figs. 4 and 5).
- On wooden flutes, the posts are either screwed directly into the wood or hard-soldered to ribs (straps or plates), which are then screwed to the body (see app. 3, C, fig. 2 and 5).

On flutes with less-complicated **key mechanisms**, including many **simple-system flutes**, and most modern thumb keys, the posts are attached to the flute about a thumb-width apart and support only one key between them. The head of each post is drilled to receive a **pin**, or a **steel** screw, that passes through a short piece of **tubing** and through a hole in the key **shank**. A thin strip of **brass** or tempered steel is used as a **spring** to keep the key **touch** elevated until the key is activated. It is attached to the flute or the key in a variety of ways (*see* FLAT SPRING [2]).

On flutes with more complex mechanisms, several posts are attached in line on the body when they need to support more than one key. Each post head is drilled to receive a **steel** or a **pivot screw** supporting a steel. The steel is encased by **key tubing** of various lengths. On traditional **pinned mechanisms**, small tapered pins connect some keys with the key tubing and steels so that when these keys are activated by fingers, they will move in synchrony with other connected keys. For each key, there is a needle spring that is fixed to a post with its free end pressing the back of the key to return it to its position.

Post-mounting was included in flutemaker **Claude Laurent**'s 1806 patent for **glass flutes**. He may have been the first to use it, since he needed a new method of mounting keys on glass. With the advent of complex keying systems in the mid-19th century, this method of mounting keys replaced the earlier **block-mount** method, which is now used only for some simple-system flutes. *Syn.* (for **early flutes**): post-and-rod; *see also* TULOU FLÛTE PERFECTIONÉE. *Cf.* **ring-mount, saddle-mount**.

POSTS. 1. Short pillars that support the **key mechanism**. They may be attached to the **ribs** or directly to the **body** of the **flute** (see app. 7, figs. 4 and 5). *Syn.:* key posts, pillars. *See also* BODYMAKER; BUSHING (1); COUNTERBORE (1); DIRECT-MOUNT; GLASS FLUTE; KING POST; PIVOT SCREWS; PLAY; RIB-MOUNT; SOLDER; SPRING; STEELS (2); STRINGER. **2.** *See* LAURENT, CLAUDE; POST-MOUNT; PLATE (5).

POTTER, HENRY (b. London, 1810; d. 1876). **Woodwind** and brass instrument maker whose business prospered in London from 1841 to after 1950. *See also* EQUISONANT FLUTE.

POTTER, RICHARD (b. Mitcham, Surrey, England, ca. 1726; buried London, 1806). A **woodwind** maker and inventor whose business thrived London from about 1745 to 1823. *See also* HEAD-JOINT LINING; PEWTER PLUG; TUNING HEAD; TUNING SLIDE.

POTTER, WILLIAM HENRY (b. London, 1760; d. Bromley, England, 1848). **Woodwind** maker who thrived in London from 1806 to 1837. He apprenticed under his father, **Richard Potter,** from 1774 and then joined his father's firm, which became Potter & Son about 1801. After his father's death around 1806, he continued the business. In 1808, Potter patented a flute **key mechanism** with a sideways sliding motion that enabled **flutists** to produce a **glide** by mechanical means. *See also* NICHOLSON'S IMPROVED FLUTE.

POTTGIESSER, HEINRICH WILHELM THEODOR (b. Voerde, Schwelm, Germany, 1766; d. Elberfeld, Germany, 1829). A German **woodwind** inventor who thrived in Elberfeld. He was also a physician, surgeon, amateur **flutist,** and author of articles on flute design. *See also* CRESCENT KEY.

POWELL, VERNE Q. (b. Danville, Ind., 1879; d. Boston, 1968). A renowned American **Boehm flute** and **piccolo** maker who thrived in Boston from 1926 to 1966. He was also a **flutist,** jeweler, and engraver. Powell developed the **gizmo key** in the 1930s. *See also* EMBOUCHURE HOLE; PLATINUM FLUTE; RETUNING; SPOON FLUTE.

PRAETORIUS (SCHULTHEISS, SCHULTZE), MICHAEL (b. Creuzburg an der Werra, Germany, ca. 1571; d. Wolfenbüttel, Germany, 1621). A prolific German composer, theorist, organist, musical director, and author of the encyclopedic *Syntagma musicum,* a renowned source for music history. *See also* BLOCKFLÖTE.

PRALLTRILLER. From Ger. *Prallen* to rebound or bounce. **1.** In the 18th century, a short rapid **trill** consisting of four notes: an accented **upper note** on the beat, followed by the **principal note** and the upper note again, and ending on the principal note. When time allows, the first upper note is slightly prolonged. There is a pause on the last sounding of the principal note that is long enough for the note to be distinctly heard. The Pralltriller occurs most often in **passages** that descend by step. In these cases, the first sounding of the upper note is often tied to the preceding note (a step above). In English sources, terms like *passing shake, half-trill, passing trill, transitory trill,* or *sudden shake* were used. The **ornament** was indicated with a ⌁, +, or *tr;* for example:

The + and *tr* were also used for ordinary trills (i.e., not half-trills). The + symbol went out of fashion sometime in the 18th century.

2. In 19th-century German sources, a very fast trill that consists of three notes: an accented principal note on the beat, followed by the upper note, and ending on the principal note. It is often illustrated in **methods** as being used on the first of every pair of **slurred** eighth or sixteenth notes in a descending scale. It was indicated with a ⌁ or *tr;* for example:

Sometime after the middle of the 19th century, French and English sources started using the term *mordent* (def. 2) for this ornament. This has led to confusion,

Figure 32. A Pratten's Perfected flute, ca. 1869. *Photo courtesy Terry McGee.*

because the term *mordent* had a different meaning in the 18th century.

PRATTEN, ROBERT SIDNEY (b. Bristol, England, 1824; d. Ramsgate, England, 1868). A British **woodwind** inventor whose business flourished in the United Kingdom, **principal flutist** in some British orchestras, **flute** designer, composer, and author of scale and exercise books for his **Pratten's Perfected** Flute.

PRATTEN'S PERFECTED. 1. A description applied to any of the **flutes** designed by **Robert Sidney Pratten** from 1852 on. At first, his efforts were directed at improving the **scale** of the English conical **eight-keyed flute** with six large open **finger holes** (*see* NICHOLSON'S IMPROVED FLUTE). The finger holes were set apart at a distance which favored the **pitches** in use earlier in the 19th century (e.g., A_1 = 433 Hz was in use in 1820 at the Philharmonic Concerts in London), but the flutes were difficult to play at the new professional standard of around A_1 = 452 Hz (*see* HIGH-PITCHED FLUTE [2]). To meet the higher standard, the new Pratten's Perfected had a dramatically shortened scale, which allowed for improved tone and **intonation**, while at the same time keeping the preferred **simple-system fingering** (except for the **third octave**, where some minor changes were necessary because of the larger **tone holes**).

In the beginning, Pratten's flutes appear to have relied on **Abel Siccama**'s **bore** (not surprisingly, as Pratten had been a Siccama player before developing his own model). Later on, Pratten attempted to transfer the **key mechanism** and **fingerings** of the eight-key flute to the **cylindrical bore** and "parabolic" **head joint** popularized by **Theobald Boehm** on his flute of 1847. His increasingly complex versions, furnished with either **conical** or cylindrical bores, involved up to 17 **keys**, many of which were open-standing, but included the six closed-standing keys of the old eight-key flute. Various Pratten models continued to be available into the 20th century.

Pratten's Perfected flute was introduced by Pratten in London in 1852 and made by **John Hudson**, first in his own workshop on Rathbone Street and from 1856 at Messrs. Boosey & Co. Figure 32 shows a Pratten's Perfected flute made of stained **cocuswood** with **nickel-silver fittings**, ca. 1869.

2. An expression (often abbreviated to Pratten, Pratten's, or Pratten's-style) used by some modern **Irish flute** makers and players to refer to **conical flutes** with at most eight keys, based on or very similar to Pratten's Perfected simple-system flutes. *See also* **Rudall** (1).

PRECIOUS METAL. A rare and costly metal such as **silver**, **gold**, **platinum**, **palladium**, or rhodium. These are also referred to as *noble* metals because they are resistant to **corrosion** or oxidation. *See also* AURUMITE; BASE METAL; FIRE SCALE; HALLMARK; NICKEL-SILVER; PROFESSIONAL FLUTE; RHODIUM-PLATING; SOLDER; STEEL (1).

PRESS FIT. Same as **interference fit** or force fit.

PRESSURE. The force per unit area exerted by a gas or fluid. Common units are pounds per square inch (English) or pascals (metric). The pascal is a very small unit; atmospheric pressure is about 15 lbs./in.^{2} (100,000 pascals or 100 kilopascals). For example, the air inside a balloon is at higher pressure than the air outside, so it pushes the balloon outward, but with equal force on each square inch of the balloon. (This is resisted by the tension in the balloon.) When your abdominal (and chest) muscles apply appropriate force, the pressure rises in the air in your lungs. When playing, the pressure in the mouth exceeds that in the atmosphere, so there is a net force acting on air between the slightly open lips. This net force accelerates this air, which then becomes the **air jet**. This is an example of a static or slowly varying pressure. Pressures are often stated numerically as the amount above or below atmospheric—a tire gauge reads the amount above atmospheric, for instance, not the absolute pressure. When sound is present, the pressure varies above and below atmospheric pressure, usually by a very tiny fraction. This varying component is called the *sound pressure*.

The **intensity** of a sound is proportional to the square of its sound pressure. The human ear is capable of hearing sound pressures over an enormous range. The sound pressure 100 m (328 ft.) from a jet airplane taking off might be 8.7 thousandths of a lb./in.^{2} (60 pascals) and a soft whisper 2.9 millionths of a lb./in.^{2} (0.02 pascals). The sound pressure inside a flute may be as much as 14.5 thousandths of a lb./in.^{2} (100 pascals). *See also* ACOUSTIC

IMPEDANCE; BREATH BUILDER; BREATH SUPPORT; CUT-OFF FREQUENCY; DENSITY; INTERNAL TUNING; STANDING WAVE; VIBRATO.

PRILL, EMIL (b. Stettin, Poland, 1867; d. 1940). A German **flute** teacher at Königslicher Hochschule für Music in Berlin (1903–1934) and elsewhere. He was also **principal flutist** in various German orchestras. *See also* GOLD FLUTE.

PRINCIPAL FLUTIST. 1. Abbr. principal. The **flutist** with the highest rank in the **flute** section of a professional orchestra or band, who plays the first flute **part** containing most of the **solos** and receives the highest salary. *Syn.:* **first chair flutist, first flutist, solo flutist, soloist.** *See also* LEAD; UTILITY FLUTIST. For a historical listing of principal flutists throughout the world, see http://homepage.mac.com/johnwion/orchestra.html. For a current listing, see www.larrykrantz.com/sections.htm.

2. *Co-principal flutist:* The flutist in some professional orchestras and bands whose duties involve two separate possibilities, although how the role is specifically defined varies from one **ensemble** to another:

  a. Two people in the **section** may be called co-principals, in which case they usually alternate playing the principal parts without regard to **repertoire**. The system may involve dividing up concerts (e.g., first half/second half, alternating which player plays which half) or alternating weeks. In either case, each player will also play nonprincipal parts if the entire flute section is needed.
  b. One person is designated the principal and another the co-principal. In this case, the co-principal has more or less the same role as the associate principal flutist (see def. 4 below), although the title co-principal has more prestige and suggests that the flutist with this title is more capable of handling the principal's job, should this be required because the principal does not want to play a particular **piece** or is ill, away, or delayed.

The co-principal flutist usually has a higher salary than any untitled players of the orchestra (i.e., **second flutist, third flutist,** and so on). This title often earns the player "overscale"—an arbitrary amount of money paid weekly above the standard base salary called for in the master contract of the ensemble.

3. *Assistant principal flutist:* An ambiguous term that generally refers to the flutist in some professional orchestras and bands whose duties mainly include sharing the role of principal flutist. How this role is specifically defined varies, depending on the ensemble. For example, the assistant principal flutist may play the first flute part in one or more of the **pieces** in a concert that the principal flutist is not willing to play. This can ease the workload of the principal flutist. In some cases, the assistant principal flutist may take over the responsibility of the principal flutist when he or she is ill, away, or delayed. At certain times, the assistant principal flutist may be called upon to double another section member's part for purposes of reinforcing that part (*see* DOUBLING). The assistant principal may also be called upon to play another flute part altogether (e.g., third flute, **piccolo, alto flute**) if one is required by the music and there is no one else to play these parts. The assistant principal flutist usually earns the player overscale, which often amounts to a lower salary than the principal flutist, but a higher salary than any untitled players of the orchestra. *Syn.:* assistant first flutist.

4. *Associate principal flutist:* An ambiguous term that generally refers to the flutist in some professional orchestras and bands who has the same duties as the assistant principal flutist (i.e., sharing the role of principal flutist), except that his title implies that he is more capable of handling the principal's job, should this be required. The associate principal flutist may also be more likely to negotiate, or be awarded, solo appearances with the orchestra, whereas the assistant principal flutist is rarely given that opportunity. As with the assistant principal flutist, how the role of the associate principal flutist is specifically defined can differ depending on the group. The title "associate principal flutist" usually earns the player overscale, which places her salary lower than the principal flutist's, but higher than any untitled players of the orchestra. *Syn.:* associate first flutist.

PRINCIPAL HOLES. *See* PRINCIPAL RANK.

PRINCIPAL NOTE. The note that is embellished or decorated by an **ornament**. When a sign representing an ornament is used, the principal note is shown as a normal-size note under or next to the ornament sign. For example, the following notes are principal notes for a **trill**, a lower **mordent**, an *appoggiatura*, and a **turn**:

Syn.: main note. *See also* ACCIACCATURA; GRACE NOTE; LOWER NOTE (2); *PRALLTRILLER*; UPPER NOTE (2).

PRINCIPAL RANK. The six main **finger holes** or any **key**-covered **tone holes** on **one-keyed, two-keyed,** or **simple-system flutes** that are covered by the first three fingers of each hand (see app. 2, fig. 1, for an illustration showing the general location of the finger holes). *Syn.:* principal holes. *See also* SIX-FINGERED NOTE.

PROFESSIONAL FLUTE. An ambiguous term that usually refers to a custom-designed, **handmade,** or production-line **hand-finished concert flute** for advanced players. These **flutes** are most often made from a **precious metal** (e.g., **silver, gold,** or **platinum**) or wood and usually feature a **handcut embouchure hole;** French-pointed arms (*see* KEY ARMS); tapered **pivot screws,** when present; a B♭ **side lever; springs** made of a superior metal such as **white** gold or stainless **steel;** a **pinned** or **pinless mechanism; soldered tone holes** or **drawn tone holes;** and no **adjustment screws.** Options include **open-hole keys** (sometimes **closed-hole keys**); in-line, offset, or half-offset **G keys;** a closed or open **G♯ key;** variations in **pitch** (e.g., A = 440 Hz to 446 Hz) and **wall** thickness; a **C** or **B foot joint** (the latter **foot joint** usually coming with a **gizmo key**); a special type of **embouchure plate** such as a **winged lip plate;** a **head-joint cork** or specialized alternative, and the following **key mechanism** parts: a **split E mechanism** with or without a **clutch,** a **lower G insert,** a **C♯ trill key,** a **G/A trill key,** a **D♯ roller** key, a **C♯ roller** key, a **high G♯ mechanism,** and a **split F♯ mechanism** with or without a clutch. Special requests, such as built-in **key extensions** for short fingers, are often accepted.

Many professional players choose to have a different metal for various parts such as the **head joint,** embouchure plate, **riser, rings,** or **keys** either to make the flute cheaper (e.g., silver keys and rings on a **gold flute**) or to enhance the tonal properties of the flute (e.g., a gold riser on a **silver flute**). The professional flute offers the best performance capabilities of all the different grades of concert flutes. *Syn.:* artist flute, **high-end flute.** *See also* EMBOUCHURE HOLE; INTERMEDIATE FLUTE; PLATINUM FLUTE; RETUNING; STEP-UP FLUTE; STUDENT FLUTE.

PROJECTION. Actions by a performer intended to intensify the sound heard by a listener at distant parts of the performance space. What a player may do to achieve this is arguable. Acousticians point out that when an instrument is accompanied, a note is easier to distinguish when it is played with **vibrato,** more high **harmonics,** slightly earlier than the accompaniment, or synchronized with a visible body movement than it would be without such features. Many **flutists** believe certain factors that can help projection include **focusing, centering,** and **supporting** the flute tone; optimal posture; the use of best **fingering** for a particular note; and even merely thinking of directing the flute tone to the back of the audience. The effectiveness of such actions may lie largely in the imagination of the performer. *See also* PINSCHOFON; RESISTANCE (1); SUBCONTRABASS FLUTE IN C; SUBCONTR'ALTO FLUTE IN G.

PROWSE, THOMAS. A **woodwind** maker whose business thrived in London from 1816 to 1868, a music retailer, and a publisher. According to **Richard Shepherd Rockstro,** Prowse worked for Clementi & Co. Prowse's son, Thomas Jr., succeeded him. *See also* NICHOLSON'S IMPROVED FLUTE.

PURE INTERVAL. A **harmonic** interval that is **beatless.** *See also* JUST INTONATION; MEANTONE TEMPERAMENT; PYTHAGOREAN TUNING.

PURE TONE. 1. *Scientific definition:* A sound with only one **harmonic,** the **fundamental;** a sine (or cosine) wave. A **tuning fork** produces a pure tone shortly after being struck. Many instruments, including **flutes,** when played softly, produce sounds that are close to a pure tone (i.e., have weak higher harmonics). Relatively stronger higher harmonics, and so a less sinusoidal waveform, are produced when played more loudly. *See also* BEATS; DIFFERENCE TONE; PITCH (1); WHISTLE TONE.

2. Flutists use "pure tone" less formally in various contexts. For example, they may think of a pure tone as:

- a flute sound that is without any extraneous noise, such as breath noise (*see* BREATHY TONE);
- an ideal flute sound (this meaning for the term is ambiguous, since what constitutes an ideal flute sound for one flutist might not be for another); or
- a sound with few harmonics.

See also DÉTIMBRÉ; HOLLOW TONE.

PURSE PAD. A flute key **pad** that appeared in England in the early part of the 19th century. It got its name from its resemblance to a drawstring purse. It consisted of a small, thin, circular piece of kid leather, which was drawn up with a thread, like a drawstring bag, around a ball of fine wool. The purse pads were used only in **salt-spoon keys.** Since there was no cardboard backing to help the pad keep its shape (as there is on modern **traditional pads**) and because they were normally used in **closed keys** where the pressure on the pad would be continuous, the pads, in time, often took on the shape of the top part of the **tone holes** and would even get stuck in them. *Syn.:* stuffed pad, elastic ball, elastic plug. (For information about other materials which **stopped** tone holes in **simple-system flutes,** *see* LEATHERS; PEWTER PLUG.)

PYTHAGOREAN TUNING. A historical **temperament,** or **tuning** of a scale, in which all fifths, except for one (the "wolf fifth"), are made pure (*see* PURE INTERval). The Pythagorean scale is derived from a series of perfect fifths. To build the scale, one starts with a note and **tunes** it to a perfect fifth (702 **cents** with a **frequency** ratio of 3:2) above. The fifth is then used as a new starting note and a perfect fifth is tuned or calculated above it. This process is repeated 11 times so as to end up with all the notes of a scale. The Pythagorean diatonic scale (the white keys on the piano) has frequency intervals in ratios of 9:8 (major second), 9:8, 256:243 (minor second), 9:8, 9:8, 9:8, and 256:243. Thus all the whole tones are alike, in contrast to the Just scale (*see* JUST INTONATION), which has two different sizes of whole tones, 9:8 (major tone) and 10:9 (minor tone). An important difference between these two scales lies in the thirds: the Pythagorean third is **sharp** (408 cents), while the Just third is **flat** (386 cents) compared to the **equal-tempered** scale. Although the Pythagorean scale is not often referred to in discussions of tuning, it turns out that string musicians and choral groups sometimes perform closer to a Pythagorean than a Just scale, in particular preferring the sharper third rather than the flatter one.

Theoretical and practical use of Pythagorean tuning in China goes back several thousand years. It is named after the ancient Greek mathematician and philosopher Pythagoras (fl. ca. 550 B.C.), who first demonstrated, using a monochord, that stretched strings whose lengths were proportional to small whole numbers produced harmonious chords when sounded together (e.g., in dividing the string in two, the same note sounded; in dividing it so the ratio of lengths was 3 to 2, a musical fifth sounded). The entire scale was devised in the Middle Ages and was the first scale to have a mathematical description. It was used in the Medieval and Renaissance periods, where perfect fifths and fourths were prevalent in the music.

Q

QUANTZ FLUTE. A **transverse, two-keyed, conical flute** made and promoted by **Johann Joachim Quantz**.

QUANTZ, JOHANN JOACHIM (b. Oberscheden, Hanover, Germany, 1697; d. Potsdam, Germany, 1773). A German **woodwind** maker and **flute** inventor whose business thrived in Berlin from 1739 to 1773. Quantz was also a famous **flutist**, performer, composer, flute teacher (including of **Frederick the Great** of Prussia), oboist, and author of an influential **treatise** in 1752, the *Versuch*. *See also* APPOGGIATURA; BAROQUE FLUTE (1); *CORPS DE RECHANGE*; DOUBLE TONGUING; EBONY; FINGER VIBRATO; *FLÛTE D'AMOUR* (2); FOOT REGISTER; MEANTONE TEMPERAMENT (2); QUANTZ FLUTE; SCREW-CORK; TUNING HEAD; TUNING SLIDE (2); TWO-KEYED FLUTE.

QUARTER-TONE FLUTE. A standard **Boehm-system concert flute** in C with offset **G keys**, **open-hole keys**, a **B foot joint** with **gizmo key**, a nonstandard **C♯ trill key**, and six other nonstandard additional **keys** (called *up keys*). Five of the up keys are on top of the following key **cups**, forming "double cups" or "key on keys": B♭, B thumb, F♯, closed **G♯**, and C♯ trill. The sixth up key is on the **foot joint**, just below the C♯ **spatula** key and over its own **tone hole**, and does not rest on top of any key cup. Each up key that forms a double cup is operated by pressing a **lever** and is smaller than the key cup, but large enough to cover a hole in the key cup that it rests on. Figure 33 shows the **key mechanism** of the quarter-tone **flute**.

The quarter-tone flute allows the **flutist** to play the traditional flute **repertoire** with the usual **fingerings**, as well as all contemporary special effects, including some

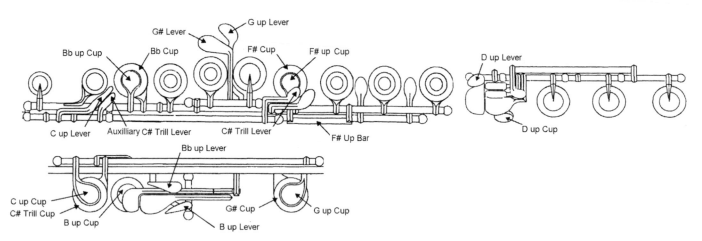

Figure 33.   The key mechanism of the quarter-tone flute. *Drawing courtesy Brannen Brothers Flutemakers, Inc.*

effects not previously possible on a standard open-hole concert flute, such as a complete quarter-tone scale, a smooth **glissando** with no gaps from C_1 to C_4, and chromatic progressions of **multiphonics**. Since it is possible to half-**vent** more key cups on the quarter-tone flute than on the standard flute, more **alternate fingerings, microtones**, and multiphonics are possible.

The quarter-tone flute was invented by **Eva Kingma** (b. 1956) in collaboration with **Bickford W. Brannen** (b. 1941) sometime after Kingma's invention of the quarter-tone **bass flute** in 1987. It was created for flutists who play contemporary music employing **extended techniques**, but can also be used for playing non-Western music and jazz. A quarter-tone flute based on Kingma's key mechanism may also be called a Kingma System flute. Brannen Brothers Flutemakers, Inc., and Sankyo Flutes make quarter-tone concert flutes. Apart from the quarter-tone bass flute, Kingma also makes quarter-tone **alto flutes in G, contr'alto flutes in G, contrabass flutes in C**, and **subcontr'alto flutes in G**. *See also* MURRAY FLUTE.

QUARTER-TONE TRILL. A type of timbral or microtonal **trill** where the notes are a quarter-tone (or less) apart.

QUARTET. 1. An **ensemble** of four musicians. A **flute** quartet may consist of four **flutists**, or a flutist plus a string trio (i.e., a violinist, a violist, and a cellist). A **woodwind** quartet is composed only of woodwinds and most often consists of a flutist, an oboist, a clarinettist, and a bassoonist. A **wind** quartet is composed of a mix of woodwind and brass instruments. *See also* E♭ FLUTE; FLUTE CHOIR; *FLÛTE D'AMOUR* (2); OCTET. **2.** A **piece** for four musicians.

QUART FLUTE. From Lat. *quartus* fourth. Fourth flute. This designation was used in Dutch, French, German, and Latin in the 17th and 18th centuries (as *Quartfluit, flûte de quart, Quartflöte, Quartfleute, Quartflette*) for a **recorder** in C (either soprano or tenor), calculating a fourth up from the G-alto or a fourth down from the F-alto. *Cf.* **fourth flute**.

QUENCHING. A part of the **heat-treating** process used by flutemakers and repairers whereby metals or **alloys** (such as the **steel** used for some **flute** tools) are cooled quickly in order to achieve desired properties. Quenching is most often attained by immersing the metal in **oil** or water. Quenching has no effect on most copper-based alloys, other than to speed up the cooling process.

QUERFLÖTE. Ger. for **transverse flute**.

QUERPFEIFE. One of the two main German terms for the **transverse Renaissance flute** from the 16th to early 17th centuries, the other being *Zwerchpfeife*.

QUINTE DE FLÛTE. Fr. for tenor **recorder** in the late Baroque.

QUINTET. 1. An **ensemble** of five musicians. For example, a **wind quintet** commonly consists of a **flutist**, an oboist, a clarinettist, a bassoonist, and a French hornist. *See also* WOODWIND QUINTET. **2.** A **piece** for five musicians.

QUINT FLUTE. From Lat. *quintus* fifth. Fifth flute. **1.** The name for a **flute** that is pitched a perfect fifth above the **standard flute** in use. Therefore, since the standard flute today is the **concert flute** in C, the term *fifth flute* presently refers to a **flute in G**. (In an older terminology used for **Baroque** and **simple-system flutes**, the standard-size flute was considered to be "in D," so a fifth flute would be said to be "in A.") However, this way of naming is rarely used today. (For other ways of naming flutes, *see* "FLUTE IN THE KEY OF . . ." and TRANSPOSING INSTRUMENTS.) *Cf.* **fourth flute** (1), **second flute** (1), **third flute** (1). **2.** A term used occasionally in Dutch and German in the 17th and 18th centuries to refer to various **recorders** (basset, tenor, soprano, soprano in D_2) a fifth away from a standard instrument—for example, an alto in F or G. *Cf.* **fifth flute**.

ℛ

RADCLIFF, JOHN R. (b. Liverpool, England, 1842; d. 1917). A British **woodwind** inventor in the United Kingdom. He was also a **principal flutist** in an orchestra and designer of the **Radcliff System flute**. *See also* FLÛTE D'AMOUR.

RADCLIFF SYSTEM FLUTE. A **flute** with the cylindrical **body**, "**parabolic**" **head joint**, large **tone holes**, and the tone hole placement used on the 1847 **Boehm flutes** (and so with a similar sound), but with a **fingering system** that was a modification of the combined Boehm and simple-system **fingering** on the **Carte 1851 System flute**. Unlike the Carte 1851 System, the Radcliff System had a closed **G♯ key** and an open C♯ (where all fingers off [except for the D♯ key] sounds $C♯_2$, as on the Boehm flute). Like the Carte 1851 System, the Radcliff System fingering for F♯ was

TT♭ 1 2 3 - / 1 - - 4D♯

(with the thumb keys closed), and there were three fingerings for F-natural, similar to fingerings for F on **simple-system flutes**. Like the Carte 1851 flute, the Radcliff could be played as a fully **open-keyed system** in the first two octaves, without any **fork fingerings**, which is a theoretical improvement over the Boehm 1847 (and modern) systems, where there are *only* fork fingerings for F♯.

Despite the closed G♯ key, the E_3 is correctly **vented**, with only the A tone hole open, since the F♯ key closes the G♯ hole as well as the G hole. This is unlike the E_3 on the Boehm flute (with a closed G♯ key), which, without a **split E mechanism**, is overvented with both the A and the G♯ tone holes open.

The Radcliff System flute was designed by **John R. Radcliff** in 1870 and manufactured in London by the flutemaking company of **Rudall, Rose & Carte** and later by Rudall, Carte & Co. Figure 34 shows a Radcliff System flute made from **cocuswood** with a **thinned** head by Rudall, Carte & Co. in 1927.

Radcliff's aim with the new flute was to simplify the Carte 1851 System for players of the simple-system flute by restoring versions of the closed G♯ key and the fingering for C♯. The Radcliff System flute became quite popular in New Zealand and Australia, probably due to the fact that a world acclaimed soloist, **John Amadio** (1884–1964), played that system. *Syn.:* Radcliff Model. *See also FLÛTE D'AMOUR* (1); HEAD-JOINT LINING (1); ORDINARY FLUTE (1).

RADIUSING. Same as **undercutting**.

RAGGING. A method of using a rag to **polish**, **finish**, or sand round surfaces on instruments (e.g., the **key tubing** on **flutes**) that are difficult to get at with a **buffing** wheel. The rag is saturated with an abrasive, such as **oil** and pumice stone, and either moved in a back-and-forth shoe-shining motion across the instrument part that needs to be worked on or held tautly between one hand and a vice while the instrument part is moved up and down against the rag.

RAISED EMBOUCHURE PLATE. May refer to a part of the **embouchure plate** being raised (e.g., *see* REFORM FLUTE; *REFORMMUNDLOCH*; WINGED LIP PLATE) or to the entire embouchure plate being raised above the **tubing** as seen on all modern metal flutes.

RAISING A NOTE. Making a note **higher** or **sharpening** it in **pitch** by changing the playing in some way. For example, if a musician raises the note G_1 a semitone, $G_{\sharp 1}$ will sound. *See also* INTONATION; LOWERING A NOTE.

RAMPAL, JEAN-PIERRE LOUIS (b. Marseilles, France, 1922; d. Paris, 2000). A French flute **soloist** who helped to restore the **flute** to the international popularity it had in the 18th century as a **solo** instrument. Rampal was also an orchestra player, chamber musician, prolific recording artist, conductor, music **editor**, and flute professor at the **Paris Conservatoire** from 1969 to 1983. Rampal's autobiography was entitled *Music, My Love* (New York: Random House, 1989). *See also* FLUTE CHOIR; GOLD FLUTE (1); MARION, ALAIN.

RANGE. All the available notes of a particular instrument. **1.** The range of the **flute** with a **C foot joint** is just over three octaves from the note sounding as **low** C_1 (or low b, if a **B foot joint** is used) to D_4. There is an extended and less predictable range up to $F_{\sharp 4}$, but as the notes up to D_4 are the most easily accessible and the most frequently played, they are referred to as the basic range in this book. Notes above $F_{\sharp 4}$ to C_5 can be produced as **whistle tones**. *See also ALTISSIMO*; BUZZ TONE; FINGERING SYSTEM; FIRST OCTAVE; FLUTE FAMILY (2); FOURTH OCTAVE; FUNDAMENTAL FINGERING; HARMONIC (2); HOMOGENEOUS TONE; LOW B, LOW C, LOW C♯, ETC.; REGISTER (1); SECOND OCTAVE; SOUNDING HOLE; THIRD OCTAVE.

2. The effective ranges of various **earlier flutes** (and replicas) were more limited than that of the modern **concert flute** (see above), although some of the early **fingering charts** may suggest otherwise. The range of the **Renaissance flute** was from D_1 to A_3, with the **lowest notes** being weak and some of the **highest notes** (above D_3, and F_3 and A_3 in particular) being difficult, depending on the flute.

The **bore** change of the **Baroque flute** improved the strength and sonority of the low notes. Its common range was from D_1 to E_3, though late Baroque sources give the range as D_1 to A_3, the same as the Renaissance flute. The highest notes may be found in some **pieces**, but **Jacques Martin Hotteterre**, author of the first **tutor** for the **one-keyed transverse flute** in 1707, reported that F_3 could rarely be played and omits this and notes above G_3 in the book's fingering chart.

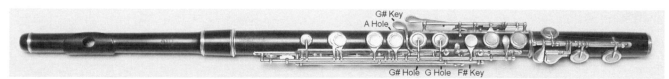

Figure 34.   A Radcliff System flute by Rudall, Carte & Co., London, 1927. *Photo courtesy Rick Wilson.*

The **Classical flute** had the same range as the Renaissance and Baroque flutes (i.e., from D_1 to A_3), but by the time of this type of flute, most of the notes in this range were being utilized. However, the note A_3 was difficult to sound and was avoided by most composers until the late 18th and early 19th centuries. By the end of the 18th century, **flutists** were expected to play up to A_3, despite the difficulties of that note.

By the early 1800s, probably due to the demands of both composers and virtuoso flutists, the flute range was extended in both directions. The note $B\flat_3$ was available for **simple-system flutes**, but appeared infrequently in compositions because it was difficult to sound. By the midcentury, however, the notes $B\flat_3$, B_3, and C_4 were being used on simple-system flutes, **Boehm-system**, and modified Boehm-system flutes. Also at this time, low b (and the B foot) had become popular with players of German and Viennese simple-system flutes, but not with the players of Boehm-system flutes because the latter flutes were not yet popular in areas where the low b had become popular. Some Viennese-style simple-system flutes were capable of playing low b♭, low a, and even low g! *See also* FALSET NOTES; FOOT JOINT.

REAL TIME TUNING ANALYSIS. Free computer software for measuring the **intonation** of **flutes** while playing at normal speed and thus avoiding the danger of the player inadvertently correcting notes when playing into a **tuner.** Conceived by Australian flutemaker and researcher **Terry McGee** (b. 1948) and realized by New Zealand flute player and computer scientist **Graeme Roxburgh** in 2008. *See* www.mcgee-flutes.com/RTTA.htm.

REAM. To shape, taper, enlarge, or smooth the inner surface of a hole with a reamer tool. For example, the internal **bore** of metal **key tubing** might need to be reamed out to remove dents or to make it larger so that it can hold a larger **steel.** The internal bore of a wooden flute **tube** might need to be reamed out to take a distorted bore back to its original state. It most likely became distorted because of the wet-and-dry cycles caused by playing and storing the instrument. The distortion has an effect on the tone and **intonation** and must be corrected for the flute to play at its best. *See also* CHAMBERING; RETUNING (2); ROUGHING; STEP; STRINGER; TURN (2); TURNING.

RECEIVER. Same as **box** or **socket.** *See also* BARREL (1); BULBOUS HEAD JOINT.

RECORDER. It. *flauto dolce, flauto diritto, flauto a becco;* Fr. *flûte à bec, flûte douce;* Ger. *Blockflöte, Schnabelflöte.* A common type of **duct flute,** normally vertically held, usually made of wood or plastic, with a whistle-type **mouthpiece** and a **bore** that varies from a **cylindrical bore** for some Renaissance recorders to a wide **tapering** bore (with the widest part being at the mouthpiece; *see* INVERTED CONICAL BORE) for Baroque and most modern recorders (see app. 1, fig. 1, for an example of one of the most common types of recorders today). There are usually seven **finger holes** in front, labeled 1 through 7, and a thumb hole at the back for the thumb of the left hand. Sometimes the lowest holes are covered with **keys,** and sometimes there are double holes where a single hole would normally be. Any double holes on modern recorders provide easier playing of some nondiatonic notes and easier control of the **tuning** of other **high notes** (double holes on the *flûte à neuf trous* had a different purpose). A few surviving 18th-century recorders have double holes (on holes 3, 6, and 7), although this appears to have been a rare modification. Today, double holes are almost universally applied to Baroque-style instruments, while Renaissance-style recorders continue to have only single holes.

The sound is produced by blowing through the whistle-type mouthpiece at one end (see fig. 13). Different notes can be produced by covering the holes in various combinations, with higher notes also being produced by a slight increase in breath pressure and a partial opening of the thumb hole for **register** changes. Recorders are made in various sizes, the most popular today being the soprano or **descant** in C (named after the seven-fingered note). The recorder was popular from the 14th to 18th centuries, but for various reasons, took a back seat to the **transverse flute** in the late 18th century and all of the 19th century and was revived in the 20th. Today, it is most commonly used for teaching music to young children in school, but has attracted a large body of amateurs and many professionals.

From the 1670s and well into the 18th century, the recorder was referred to in England as a "**flute,**" while the predecessor of the flute as we know it today was called the "**German flute.**" The recorder is also called *common flute* and *English flute. See also* AEROPHONE; *ALTFLÖTE* (2); BAROQUE FLUTE (1); *BASSE DE FLÛTE; BASSFLÖTE* (2); BASS FLUTE (7); *BLOCKFLUTE;* BOXWOOD; BRESSAN, PIERRE (PETER) JAILLARD; CANE FLUTE; CONCERT FLUTE (3); CONSORT FLUTE; *DESSUS DE FLÛTE;* DIFFERENCE TONES; *DISCANTFLÖTE; DOLZFLÖTE;* DOUBLE BASS FLUTE; FIFTH FLUTE; FIPPLE FLUTE; FLAGEOLET (1); *FLAUTINO* (1–3); *FLAUTO* (1); *FLAUTO BASSO; FLAUTO CONTRALTO* (2); *FLAUTONE; FLAUTO PICCOLO* (1); *FLAUTO SOPRANO; FLAUTO TAILLO; FLAUTO TENORO; FLÖTE; FLÛTE* (1, 2); *FLÛTE D'ANGLETERRE; FLÛTE DE VOIX;* "FLUTE IN . . ." (3); *FLÛTE TRAVERSIÈRE* (2); FOURTH FLUTE (4); FRUITWOOD (1); *GRANDE BASSE DE FLÛTE; HAUTE CONTRE DE FLÛTE;* HOTTETERRE, JACQUES MARTIN; NATURAL SCALE; OCTAVE FLUTE (2); PEDAL

FLUTE; *PETIT DESSUS DE FLÛTE; PETITE BASSE DE FLÛTE; PETITE FLÛTE;* QUART FLUTE; QUINT FLUTE (2); *QUINTE DE FLÛTE;* SIXTH FLUTE; SMALL FLUTE; SUZUKI METHOD; *TAILLE; TAILLE DE FLÛTE; TENORFLÖTE;* THIRD FLUTE (2); TREBLE FLUTE; VOICE FLUTE (1).

RECUT EMBOUCHURE. *See* EMBOUCHURE RECUT.

RED. When referring to a metal, *rose gold.* Rose gold **flutes** must be referred to as "red" flutes in the United Kingdom unless they have passed quality tests at an assay office and subsequently been **hallmarked.** *Cf.* **white, yellow.**

REED BOOK. A book that contains various **woodwind parts** for one musician to play in a musical production.

REFITTING HEAD JOINT. *See* **head-joint refitting.**

REFORM EMBOUCHURE. 1. *See REFORMMUNDLOCH.* **2.** *See* EMBOUCHURE PLATE. **3.** *See* WINGED LIP PLATE.

REFORM FLUTE. 1. A modification, announced in 1898, of earlier Schwedler-Kruspe **flutes,** themselves elaborations of the standard German **simple-system flute** (e.g., Meyer flute—see **Meyer-system flute** [1]). It is characterized by:

- three **sections,** including a metal cylindrical **head joint** and a wooden conical **body** with a **foot joint** similar to **Theobald Boehm**'s (1794–1881);
- an improved **bore** that allows for a more penetrating sound, particularly in the **low register;**
- an **ebonite embouchure plate** and Schwedler **embouchure** (Schwedler-Mundloch) with raised **cusps** on the east and west sides of the **embouchure hole;**
- at least five of the six **finger holes** of the simple-system flute (i.e., those for E, F$\sharp$, G, A, B, C$\sharp$) mostly or completely controlled by **ring keys** or **open-standing keys;**
- an improved **key mechanism** consisting mainly of axles and needle **springs;** and
- two new **trill keys:** one that was mainly used for the G_3-A_3 **trill** (with the **touch** between the fourth and fifth finger holes) and another that was mainly used for the D_3-E_3 trill with the touch below the fourth hole.

The main feature, or "reform," that distinguishes it from earlier German-made flutes, including earlier Schwedler 1885 and 1895 model flutes, is an F$\sharp$-mechanism. This mechanism was added to relieve the player from the task of having to keep a (long or short) F key open as often as possible (players were advised to do this for most notes on simple-system flutes with four or more **keys**) and especially for the F$\sharp$, which otherwise tended to be **flat.** The F$\sharp$-mechanism consists of a duplicate F hole that was open-standing at rest, but was closed by **ring** or **covered keys** for R2 or R3. This improves the **venting** in all three octaves and greatly eases **technique.** Now the F key was needed only for two notes: the F's in the first two octaves. The importance of this automatic venting was thought sufficient by its inventors to justify the name "reform."

Many later Reform flutes also have:

- a D-mechanism (or D-E$\flat$ mechanism), which opens a small extra D hole just east of the regular D hole (to sharpen the D_1 and D_2) whenever R3 is on its key (introduced 1904); and
- an F-mechanism (called an "F-F$\sharp$-mechanism" by Schwedler), which allows both F$\sharp$ and F-natural in the first three octaves to be **fingered** with R1, thus improving technique and tone, as there was no longer a need for any short F or long F key to sound F (introduced in 1912).

Figure 35, top and bottom left and right, shows a Reform flute of grenadilla and nickel-silver with a close-up of the embouchure plate and the D-mechanism by Schwedler & Kruspe in Leipzig around 1915. The left middle part shows a close-up of the F-mechanism from a Reform flute made by **Moritz-Max Mönnig** in Leipzig about 1930.

Maximilian Schwedler's (1853–1940) aim with the Reform flute was to improve on the simple-system flute, as he had done with his earlier models, while at the same time maintaining the tonal characteristics of the simple-system flute that he so liked. Around 1921, Mönnig's Leipzig flutemaking firm took over production of the Reform flutes from **Carl Kruspe Jr.**

The Reform flute was quite common in German orchestras for a time, but its popularity dwindled around the 1920s. This is possibly due to the fact that the highest notes (i.e., those around C_4) were harder to play than on the **Boehm flute.** It could also be due to the complexity of the key mechanism which, in 1912, had to be made to operate 21 **tone holes,** as compared to the 14 tone holes of the **Boehm-system** flute with an open **G$\sharp$ key** and **B foot joint.**

Although the Reform flute per se is not in use today, an embouchure plate with cusps is a feature that is frequently seen on modern head joints (*see* WINGED LIP PLATE), but this is not the Schwedler embouchure and has nothing to do with Reform flutes.

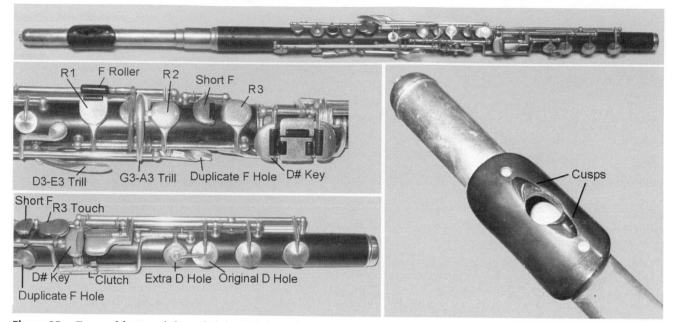

Figure 35. *Top and bottom left, and right:* A Reform flute with a close-up of the embouchure plate and the D-mechanism by Schwedler & Kruspe, Leipzig, ca. 1915. *Left, middle:* A close-up of the F-mechanism from a Reform flute by Moritz Max Möennig, Leipzig, ca. 1930. *Photo courtesy Rick Wilson.*

The Reform flute is also called the *"Reformfloete System Schwedler-Kruspe"* or *"Modell* 1898 System Schwedler-Kruspe.*" See also* FLAT SPRING (1); ORDINARY FLUTE (1).

2. Sometimes a reference to the Schwedler flute models of 1885 and 1895, although these flutes did not have the "reform" (i.e., the F♯-mechanism), so it is inaccurate to call them Reform flutes.

3. Sometimes a reference to a **conical flute** by any maker that has a metal, wood, or **ivory** head joint with the Schwedler embouchure (i.e., with his distinctive cusps on either side of the embouchure hole). It is inaccurate to call these flutes Reform flutes unless they have the "reform" mentioned in definition 1. *See also* RAISED EMBOUCHURE PLATE; *REFORMMUNDLOCH* (1).

REFORMMUNDLOCH. Ger. Reform mouth hole. **1.** A modification of the area around the **embouchure hole** that was introduced by **Otto Mönnig** in 1904 primarily for **Boehm flutes.** It features a raised **blowing wall** and **wings** or **cusps** to either side of the embouchure hole (see fig. 36) and is similar to the modern **winged lip plate.** *See also* EMBOUCHURE PLATE; RAISED EMBOUCHURE PLATE. **2.** Sometimes, inaccurately, a reference to an earlier modification introduced by **Maximilian Schwedler** and **Carl Kruspe Jr.** on the **Reform flute** (see fig. 35) that has raised bumps to the left and right of the mouth hole, but no raised blowing wall, nor a winged appearance. **3.** *See* WINGED LIP PLATE.

REGISTER. 1. A limited **range** of notes that has a distinct **tone quality** or is produced in a similar manner. Definition of the exact division of the **concert flute**'s range into registers varies among **flutists,** but it usually has the same meaning as the term *octave.* In this case, the **first register** is the same as the **first octave;** the **second register** is the same as the **second octave;** the **third register** is the same as the **third octave;** and the fourth register is the same as the **fourth octave.**

Sometimes the term *register* refers to ranges of notes that are produced on the flute in a similar way.

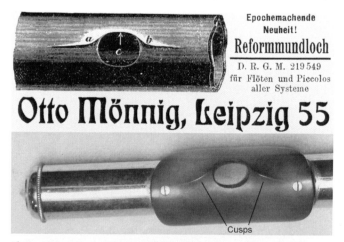

Figure 36. *Top: Reformmundloch* from an Otto Mönnig, ca. 1906. *Bottom:* The embouchure plate from a grenadilla flute stamped "Edelton," origin unknown, early 20th century. *Photo and drawing courtesy Rick Wilson.*

In this case, most flutists agree that the first register is from **low C$_1$** (or low b, if the flutist has a **B foot joint**) to at least C$_{\sharp 2}$. These notes may also be called *fundamental notes* or *first harmonics* (acoustically, this means that they are played using the **resonance** with the lowest **frequency** available for that **fingering**). Most of these notes are played by uncovering more **tone holes** in succession as higher-pitched notes are played (F$_{\sharp 1}$ and the **one-and-one B$_{\flat 1}$** require special fingerings; *see* CROSS-FINGERING [2]).

Flutists also agree that the notes from E$_2$ to C$_{\sharp 3}$ are from the second register. These notes, which may also be called *second harmonics* (i.e., they use the second resonance), are **overblown** from first-octave fingerings. They need a little more air speed or shorter lip-to-edge distance or a combination of both than the notes in the first register in order to be produced.

Flutists often disagree about what register the other notes in the range belong, because they cannot agree from which harmonic a particular note is based. For example, some flutists (particularly those whose instruments do not have a **split E mechanism**) think that the note E$_3$ is based on the third resonance (i.e., the "third harmonic") of A$_1$, and others (especially those with the split E mechanism) believe that it is based on the fourth resonance/harmonic of E$_1$.

Syn.: (first register) bottom register, fundamental register, **low register**; (second register) middle register; (third register) high register, top register, upper register; (fourth register) *altissimo* register. The fourth register may also confusingly be occasionally referred to with the same alternate names as the third register. *See also* APERTURE (1); BEATS; BREAK (1); CUTOFF FREQUENCY; FINGERING SYSTEM; FUNDAMENTAL (2); INTERNAL TUNING; INTONATION; OCTAVE LENGTH; "PARABOLIC"; REGISTER CHANGE; RISER.

2. *See* FOOT REGISTER.

REGISTER BREAK. *See* BREAK (1).

REGISTER CHANGE. The act of playing from one **register** to another. In some cases, this means playing from one octave to another. For example, a **flutist** playing from G$_1$ to G$_2$ is making a register change.

REGISTER HOLE. On reed instruments, one or more additional small holes in the upper part of the column, fitted with normally closed register **keys**. Opening a register hole weakens or shifts the **frequencies** of lower **modes** (i.e., **resonances** or, in **flutists'** terms, "**harmonics**") to discourage their sounding and thus to assure the sounding of an **upper register** note. On the **flute**, the upper C$_\sharp$ hole acts as a register hole for D$_2$, E$_{\flat 2}$, and D$_3$, but is usually not known by that name; instead it is often referred to as the **C$_\sharp$** *vent hole*. Another example is the note F$_3$, where the first open **tone hole** (named B and opened by L2) acts as a register hole. *See also* CROSS-FINGERING (1); *SCHLEIFKLAPPE;* SOUNDING HOLE.

REGULATING SCREWS. Same as **adjusting screws**.

RELATIVE PITCH. The ability to identify a **pitch** based on another reference pitch. Relative pitch can be developed through **ear training** and is quite common. *Cf.* **absolute pitch**.

RENAISSANCE FLUTE. A thin-**walled**, wooden, keyless, **transverse flute** that prevailed from the 16th to mid-17th centuries, when the **one-keyed Baroque flute** was introduced. The Renaissance flute had a narrow **cylindrical bore**, a **cork stopper** in one end, six fairly small **finger holes**, and a small **blowhole** and could be played to the right or left side of the body (*see* LEFT-HANDED FLUTES).

These flutes were made in three graduated sizes—the bass in G, the **tenor** in D, and the **descant** in A—and are mentioned in several 16th-century inventories. Figure 37 shows, from top to bottom, replicas of bass, tenor, and descant flutes made of mountain ash. The tenor flute in D was the most common size and became the size of the standard (**concert**) **flute** from the Baroque period to the present day. Renaissance flutes were made in one piece, except for the largest, the bass, which was usually divided into two pieces or **joints**, probably because it was too difficult to make in one piece and not for **tuning** purposes as would be the case today.

The smaller-size flutes had a **range** of two and a half octaves and were agile and articulate in the higher

Figure 37.   A consort of Renaissance flutes. *Photo courtesy Rick Wilson.*

range, helped by the smaller bore; the bass had a range of only two octaves. Due to the small finger holes and blowhole, the **lowest notes** tended to be quiet, although those on the bass could be heard over the other smaller Renaissance flutes.

The **tenor flute** was said to be in D, because its lowest note was D_1 (see "FLUTE IN . . ." [1]). It had a range from D_1 to A_3. Its best notes were D, E, F, G, A, B♭, B, and C in the **first** and **second octaves**, though E_1 and F_1 were weak. Other chromatic notes could be played, although E♭ was weak and difficult in the first two octaves and some of the other notes were **veiled** or difficult to play **in tune**.

Surviving instruments are commonly **pitched** around A_1 = 410 or 435 Hz and are **tuned** with very **flat** major thirds, especially D to F♯, G to B-natural, and A to C♯. This favors modes with a flat in the key signature such as F major, D minor, and G minor.

Since very little information about the Renaissance flute has survived, along with a limited collection of extant flutes and no surviving descants, a complete history of how the flute was used is not known. One can only surmise that it may have been used by the military in marches and when signaling. Although there is pictorial proof that it was played by cultured musicians in groups of like instruments of different sizes, called *consorts*, and later in mixed consorts where both bowed and plucked string instruments were included, we do not know what sort of music the musicians played. Four-part vocal consort music from the Renaissance period works well with one descant, two tenors and a bass, or three tenors and a bass. Modern Renaissance flute players generally play this music an octave higher than the written pitch.

Renaissance flutes in various sizes and pitches are being made again today for people interested in trying to play older music as it used to be played. *See also* CLASSICAL FLUTE; MEANTONE TEMPERAMENT; NATURAL SCALE; *QUERPFEIFE*; *ZWERCHPFEIFE*.

REPAD. A repair job undertaken infrequently by a professional **flute** repairer when the key **pads** need to be replaced but the flute does not yet need an **overhaul**. During a repad, the flute is completely disassembled; the **key mechanism** is cleaned and **oiled**; all **corks, felts,** and pads in the key mechanism are replaced; the **keys** are adjusted; the flute is played to check the quality of the repairs; and the flute may be left for around a week for the **adjustments** to settle in and then checked again. *Cf.* **clean-oil-and-adjust**, overhaul.

REPERTOIRE. Also *repertoire list.* **1.** A list of **pieces** of music that a musician knows and can play well. *See also* FRENCH FLUTE SCHOOL. **2.** A list of pieces of music that

a musician *should* know well, or possibly a list of pieces to be played in a **master class**.

RESIDUAL TONE. A term coined by renowned flutist **Robert Dick** in 1970 to refer to a **breathy sound** with only a hint of a regular note in the background. The breathy part of the sound can vary widely in dynamics. A residual tone is easily produced by using any **fingering** and directing a more or less unfocused airstream across the **embouchure hole**. An unfocused airstream can be achieved by blowing through a mouth **aperture** that is too large for the note being produced. The larger the mouth aperture, the more unfocused and breathy the tone. **Multiphonics** can be played as residual tones. A residual tone might be notated as:

See also AEOLIAN SOUND; EXTENDED TECHNIQUE; JET WHISTLE; TONGUE CLICK.

RESISTANCE. 1. Something that impedes and makes an action difficult. In acoustics, the term expresses the energy loss in a system, such as a **flute**, that is being driven by an alternating flow, such as air (*cf.* **acoustic impedance**). In the flute, these losses occur primarily in the **bore**, and to a small extent in radiation; the latter may be desirable since more of the energy goes into producing sound. **Flutists** use *resistance* as a subjective term and are not unanimous about its meaning. When they speak of resistance, they are usually referring to how easy a particular flute is to sound. A certain amount of resistance is often said to be necessary to control the **pitch**, to provide a variety of **tone colors**, and to **project** the tone. Flutists often consider that resistance varies with such things as the height of the **embouchure wall** and the amount that a flutist covers the **embouchure hole** with the lower lip. *See also* ACOUSTIC IMPEDANCE; BREATH BUILDER; EMBOUCHURE HOLE; FREE-BLOWING.
    2. *See* RESISTANCE RINGS.
    3. *See* RESISTANCE PLUG.

RESISTANCE PLUG. A term coined in 2001 by renowned flutist **Trevor Wye** to refer to a **cork** with a pencil-size hole in the middle that is placed in the **foot** end of larger **flutes** (e.g., **bass flute, contrabass flute**) to increase **resistance**. The lowest note will be unplayable, but the plug is said to improve the **tone quality** and **resistance** of the **middle** and **low registers**. *Cf.* **resistance rings**.

RESISTANCE RINGS. A term coined in the 1980s by flutemaker **Albert Cooper** to refer to rings of modeling clay that are placed in the larger members of the Boehm

flute family at specific locations to increase the feeling of **resistance**. This allows the player to blow harder and with greater loudness without **cracking** the notes. The rings vary according to preference, but usually have the thickness of a pencil. One can be placed in the open end of any of the flute's **joints**. The idea of inserting rings was taken up by others, resulting in **Olnhausen Rings**, among others. *Cf.* **resistance plug**.

RESIZING HEAD JOINT. *See* HEAD-JOINT REFITTING.

RESONANCE. 1. Acousticians define *resonance* as the capability of many acoustical and mechanical systems to vibrate strongly when driven at certain **frequencies**. Most systems have many **modes** of vibration, each responding to a particular frequency. In most musical instruments, the frequencies of these modes are **harmonically** related, that is, they are close to integral multiples of some basic frequency. **Flute** resonances are approximately 1, 2, 3, 4, and higher integers times the **fundamental** or lowest mode frequency, whereas the first few clarinet resonances are approximately 1, 3, and 5 times the fundamental.

Resonance can be illustrated by listening to ambient noise through the **blowing hole** of the flute (changing **fingerings** makes this more noticeable): the ambient noise appears to be enhanced at the resonance frequencies of the flute, because the **tube** accumulates energy at those frequencies. Resonances are also evident in **key slapping**. The impact of the **key** transfers sound energy to the **bore**. This energy is briefly stored in the different resonances and is radiated away largely at the frequencies of the resonances, thus giving the key slap its **pitch**.

A given fingering on a flute has a number of resonances, of which several are strong enough to be played. In performance, the **air jet** from the player's lips adds a little energy in each cycle to sustain the oscillation in the bore of the instrument. For the **basic fingerings** for the notes b to $C_{\#2}$, the resonances occur reasonably close to the harmonics of the note—see **harmonic series**. For example, the fingering for C_1 has resonances close to C_1, C_2, G_2, C_3, E_3, G_3, very **flat** $A_{\#3}$, C_4, D_4, and E_4.

The resonances for most musical instrument fingerings, including those of the flute, are not in exact harmonic ratios. However, since several of the resonances of the flute are approximately in harmonic ratios for the fingerings of notes in the **low register** (i.e., notes up to $C_{\#2}$), **flutists** commonly use the term *harmonic* to mean a note played using one of the resonances in a harmonic series.

In a plot of the input impedance spectrum (*see* ACOUSTIC IMPEDANCE SPECTRUM) for the flute, the resonances appear as minima (i.e., valleys in the curve of

the graph). Thousands of the possible fingerings on the flute have strongly nonharmonic resonances, and most of these may be used to play **multiphonics**. For example, the fingering

$$\text{T 1 2 3 - / 1 Tr1 - 4D}_\#$$

has easily playable resonances at C_2 and F_2 and allows the flutist to play these notes as multiphonics. *See also* CRACKING (A NOTE); CUTOFF FREQUENCY; EDGE TONE; END CORRECTION; FUNDAMENTAL RESONANCE; HARMONIC (2); "PARABOLIC"; REGISTER (1); REGISTER HOLE; SEAMED TUBING; SOUNDING HOLE; STOPPER; VEILED TONE (1); WHISTLE TONE. For **early flutes**, *see also* BAROQUE FLUTE (2); G$_\#$ KEY (2).

2. Flutists may think of resonance as relating to and sometimes causing the fullness of sound that arises when a sound has been reinforced by its immediate environment. For example, some flutists manipulate parts of their body such as the **larynx**, the throat, and the **uvula** in a particular way, with the aim of changing the **tone color**. *See also* INTERNAL TUNING; NASAL CAVITIES; OPEN THROAT; OVERBLOWING; PALATE; THROAT TUNING; TONGUE CLICK.

RESPONSE. A measure of the ease by which a **flute** responds to the input of the player. This will be to some degree a result of both the quality of its construction and the **head joint**.

Acousticians speak in terms of the *frequency response*, which describes how a system responds to a range of different frequencies. For a flute, they quantify the frequency response by the **acoustic impedance spectrum**. This represents (in simple terms) a measure of how easily the air in the flute vibrates at any given frequency. It determines what notes, **harmonics**, and **multiphonics** are possible and, to some extent, their **timbre**. A database on the Internet at www.phys.unsw.edu.au/music/flute shows the measured acoustic impedance spectra for all standard (and some nonstandard) **fingerings** for a range of different flutes. It also shows the predicted impedance spectra for any of the 40,000 possible fingerings using the **virtual flute**. *See also* AGE-HARDENING; ALTERNATE FINGERINGS; BASS FLUTE (2); BROSSA F$_\#$ LEVER; C FOOT JOINT; CLOSED-KEY SYSTEM; CROSS-FINGERING (1, 2); CUT; DENSITY; D FOOT JOINT; EMBOUCHURE HOLE; EMBOUCHURE RECUT; FAJARDO WEDGEHEAD; FLUTE FAMILY (2); FREE-BLOWING; G/A TRILL KEY (1); HEAD-JOINT CORK; HIGH G$_\#$ MECHANISM/FACILITATOR; LEVELING; LOWER G INSERT; ORCHESTRAL MODEL FLUTE; O-RING (2); OVERCUTTING; PAD; "PARABOLIC"; *SCHLEIFKLAPPE*; SPEAK; STOPPER; STUDENT FLUTE; TUNING RINGS; UNDERCUTTING (1); VENT HOLE (1).

RETAINER. *See* PAD RETAINER; SPUD.

RETUNING. A type of repair job that is done by a tuner (a **professional flute** repairer who specializes in retuning) or other knowledgeable person to improve a flute's **intonation**. This will improve the **tuning** of the notes in the first two octaves, but some errors will remain in the **third octave** from D$_3$ and up, as these **high notes** cannot be entirely corrected by the tuner while maintaining good intonation in the lower octaves, although they can be affected to some extent by changing the position of the **stopper**. Notes lower than D$_3$ are affected only by the stopper position, if it has been drastically altered.

Retuning is usually done only to flutes with **traditional scales**, especially to 19th- and 20th-century metal flutes (e.g., those by **Lot, Bonneville, Lebret, Rive, Buffet, Haynes,** and **Powell**) to bring them up to today's **scale** and **pitch** standards (e.g., taking an old flute that is pitched at A$_1$ = 435 Hz and fixing it so that it will play at A$_1$ = 440 or 442 Hz).

1. For metal flutes, retuning is usually done one of two ways, depending on how permanent the change is to be, how much money the owner of the flute is willing to spend, and the desired quality of the final result. The less expensive, though time-consuming, retuning repair job involves adding a material, such as Plasticine (or toy modeling plastic for a more lasting job) to partially fill the "upper end" of **tone holes** nearest the **head joint** to **flatten** some of the **sharp** notes and improve the intonation (see app. 11 for details about how this is done).

The more expensive and laborious retuning and restorative repair option is usually carried out only on flutes that are made of **silver, gold,** or **brass,** with silver being the easiest to work with and therefore retune. During this type of retuning, the flute is not only **overhauled** (which may involve additional tasks) but also rebuilt in the following way:

- The flute is completely disassembled.
- The tone holes and **ribs** are removed by heating the **tubing** with a blowtorch to unsolder them.
- The **solder** residue is removed and the flute **tube** is completely cleaned.
- The tone holes are repositioned on the flute tube in accordance with the new scale measurements in one of three ways: by **stretching, patching,** or **inlaying,** depending on the distance moved. If the tone hole is being moved just a short distance from its original position, the tubing may be stretched by **burnishing** or by gently hammering in a downward and sideways motion with a planishing hammer (a small flat-faced hammer). This

essentially moves the hole over on one side; the other side is cut out of the tubing. If the tone hole is being moved a distance of more than about 0.06 in. (1.5 mm) from its original position, patching or inlaying is used. For the patching method, the tone hole is **hard-soldered** (or **brazed**) onto a spare piece (or patch) of metal tubing, cut to fit the flute, and **soft-soldered** to the flute in the new location. After the tone hole has been relocated, the inside of the tone hole is cut away, and the tone hole **chimney** is filed where the patch has been soldered to lower the tone hole chimney height. The inlaying method involves putting silver patches into the existing holes in the tubing. After the tone hole has been relocated, the inside of the tone hole is cut away.

- The ribs are repositioned.
- The tone holes and ribs are resoldered to the flute tubing.
- The **body** tubing is shortened (or, in some cases lengthened) to adjust to the new pitch.
- The **key mechanism** is rebuilt to accommodate the new position of the tone holes. This may involve, for example, shortening or lengthening **key tubing** or replacing worn key tubing.
- The key **cups** and **key arms** are cleaned and then resoldered onto the key tubing, which is then fitted with new **steels,** if necessary.
- Any other key components (e.g., B♭ **side lever, clutch, trill keys,** B♭ **thumb key, upper C key**) are rebuilt to accommodate the new position of the tone holes.
- The key mechanism is re-**pinned** onto new steels.
- The flute is reassembled.
- The flute is played to check the intonation and quality of the repairs.
- The flute may be left for a week or so for the **adjustments** to settle in and then checked again.

Flutist **William Bennett** was the first to retune a **silver flute** in the late 1950s. *See also* COLE SCALE.

2. As with metal flutes, the job of retuning pre-**Boehm** wooden flutes is usually done one of two ways: The less expensive but time-consuming retuning option involves adding a material, such as wax, to partially fill holes to flatten some of the sharp notes and improve the intonation. (The process is similar to that for a metal flute; see app. 11.) The more expensive job consists of re-**reaming** the **bore** and/or **undercutting** the tone holes and shortening the **joints**. During this type of retuning, some or all of the following things might be done to the flute:

- The bore, or part of it, is re-reamed, often in order to make it conform better to flutes with known good dimensions.
- The bottom end of the left-hand **section** and/or the top end of the right-hand section might be shortened. This brings all of the right-hand notes and **foot-joint notes** closer to the left-hand notes, thus reducing the scale of the instrument.
- The tone holes that are **flat** in pitch might be enlarged and/or undercut to bring them up to pitch.
- If the foot notes are still flat, the right-hand side of the **foot joint** might be shortened to bring the foot notes up in pitch with the rest of the flute's notes. This may require shortening any key **touches** that, because of the shorter foot joint, are encroaching on the R6 tone hole.

Post-Boehm wooden flutes (from the British high-pitch period) usually suffer the opposite problem in that they are too sharp (short) to play at modern pitch. Retuning these usually requires making up a new body and foot and "transplanting" the mechanism onto the new parts (see www.mcgeeflutes.com/Flute%20Transplant.htm).

REVERSED THUMB KEYS. An option where the position of the B♭ and B thumb **keys** on the flute's **middle joint** are reversed—that is, the B key is set closer to the **head joint** and the B♭ **thumb key** closer to the **foot joint**, rather than the opposite arrangement (see app. 7, fig. 7; for the keys in the regular position, see figs. 8 and 27, and app. 5, fig. 6, for the reverse). **Theobald Boehm**, the inventor of the **concert flute** in 1847, preferred the reversed arrangement, since it is more logical to move the thumb downwards when playing a **lower note** than upwards. The opposite arrangement is most commonly used today, however. Reversed thumb keys are often found on **flutes** with open G♯ **keys**. *See also* CYLINDRICAL BOEHM FLUTE (1, 3); MURRAY FLUTE.

REVERSE TENON. On **one-keyed** and **simple-system flutes**, a **tenon** located where a **socket** is usually the norm (e.g., a *traverso* with a tenon on the **head joint**). Some flutemakers who used reverse tenons are **Thomas Stanesby Jr.** (ca.1692–d.1754), **Tebaldo Monzani** (1762–1839), **Pierre J. Bressan** (1663–1731), and **John Rose** (1793/94–1866). See app. 3, A, fig. 4.

RF (RAYMOND FABRIZIO) MODIFICATION. A modification of the lower **G key** that was exclusive to the Emerson and Koregelos modern **Boehm-system concert flutes** having a closed G♯ **key**. The modification involved omitting the standard lower G key and **duplicate** G♯ **tone hole** and adding a small **vent hole**

just below the upper G key. This vent area was covered by a small **vent key** that was conjointly operated with the opening and closing of the upper G key (see app. 5, fig. 7). There were no changes in **fingering**, added **keys**, or moving parts.

The RF Modification was said by Emerson to allow for an effortless, stable E_3; a centered, accurate $G\sharp_3$ and A_3; and easier **slurring** to and from E_3, $G\sharp_3$, and A_3. It was patented by Raymond Fabrizio in 1983. This modification of the lower G key has essentially been replaced in popularity by either the **lower G insert**, the **split E mechanism**, or a slightly smaller **tone hole** under the lower G key.

RHODIUM-PLATING. A coating of rhodium, a metallic element that looks like **platinum** but is much more expensive. It is occasionally used to cover metal parts of expensive **flutes** for protection against **corrosion**, **tarnish**, wear, and scratches and for hypoallergenic reasons. Since it is a hard type of plating, it is also very durable and easy to care for, but it is more slippery than **nickel-plating** and cannot be repaired or replated. *See also* GOLD-PLATING; SILVER-PLATING.

RIB-MOUNT. A method of supporting the **key mechanism** on **posts** that are first attached to thin and usually long metal strips called *ribs* or *straps* (or often *plates*, if they are short) before being attached to the flute **body**. On metal flutes, the posts are **hard-soldered** or **brazed** onto the ribs, which are then in turn **soft-soldered** to the flute's body. On wooden flutes, the posts are hard-soldered to ribs that are screwed to the wood. Rib-mounting is more common and preferable to **direct-mounting** (see RIBS for reasons why). *See also* POST-MOUNT.

RIBS. Long, thin, flat pieces of metal that are **soldered** lengthwise to the outside of most flute **foot joints** and **middle joints** (see app. 7, fig. 5). They provide a base for the **posts** that hold the **key mechanism**. Having ribbing makes the **flute** more durable in that it protects the **bore** and allows for strong post support. Ribbing is also helpful because it allows the manufacturer to have a reference line for the placement of the **keys**. *Syn.:* straps. Shorter ribs, often seen on **early flutes**, are usually referred to as *plates* (5). *See also* BODYMAKER; COUNTERSINK (1); DIRECT-MOUNT; HANDMADE FLUTE; MODEL NUMBER; POST-MOUNT; RETUNING; RIB-MOUNT; SERIAL NUMBER.

RIGHT-HAND FINGERINGS. The **fingerings** for **right-hand notes**. Usually, this means the fingerings up to $F\sharp_1$, but it may also refer to the fingerings from D_2 to $F\sharp_2$. *See also* CARTE 1867 SYSTEM FLUTE; LEFT-HAND FINGERINGS.

RIGHT-HAND NOTES. Usually, the notes up to $F_{\sharp 1}$, although the term may also refer to the notes from D_2 to $F_{\sharp 2}$. *Cf.* **left-hand notes.**

RIGHT-HAND SECTION. *See* SECTION (2). *See also* BACK-CONNECTOR; BEARING; KING POST; ONE-PIECE CORE BAR.

RIM. 1. Same as **tone-hole rim.** *See also* ROLLED TONE HOLES. **2.** The outer edge of the top of a key **cup** (see app. 7, fig. 8). *See also* BROSSA F♯ LEVER; CHASING; RING (1); ROCKSTRO F♯ LEVER.

RIM FLUTE. *See* END-BLOWN FLUTE (1).

RING. 1. The outer edge or **rim** of the top of a key **cup** on a modern **Boehm flute** (see app. 7, fig. 8), although the term *ring* when referring to **keys** usually means a **ring key.** *See also* CHASING; DAP; ENGRAVING. **2.** A circular piece of metal or other material that encircles a flute **tube** to reinforce, decorate, or protect it. On the modern **concert flute,** these appear at the ends of the **foot joint** and **middle joint** and on the **barrel** of the middle joint (see app. 7, figs. 3 and 12). *Syn.:* **bands,** moldings. *See also* CHASING; COLD DRAWING; DIE (1); ENGRAVING; GOLD FLUTE (1); HYGROMETER; PROFESSIONAL FLUTE; TIP (1–3). On **flutes** in the 17th, 18th, and 19th centuries (or replicas of them), these rings are usually called *mounts, tips,* or *ferrules.* **3.** Tone-hole **chimney** (2). **4.** End protector ring. *See* TENON PROTECTORS. **5.** G donut ring. *See* LOWER G INSERT. **6.** *See* PAD RETAINING RING. **7.** Embouchure ring. *See* EMBOUCHURE-HOLE BUSHING. **8.** *See* FRENCH BUSHING. **9.** *See* O-RING. **10.** *See* OLNHAUSEN RING. **11.** *See* TUNING RINGS. **12.** *See* RISER. **13.** Tone-hole ring. *See* TONE-HOLE BUSHING. **14.** *See* RING-MOUNT; PIN (2). **15.** *See* RING-KEY FLUTE; RING-KEY SYSTEM. **16.** *See* RESISTANCE RINGS. **17.** *See* RING BANDING. **18.** *See* VALGON RINGS.

RING BANDING. A method of **crack** repair more commonly used for clarinets but occasionally seen on wooden flutes. The crack is constrained closed by clamping the outside of the instrument in a metal (usually **silver**) ring. The process is called *flush-banding* if the outside of the ring ends up flush with the outside of the **body** of the instrument. *Cf.* **crack pinning.**

RING KEY. 1. The thin, **padless,** metal **ring** surrounding, and hovering above, a small **tone hole** on some 19th- and 20th-century **flutes** (see fig. 11, *top,* and fig. 12, *left*). When the finger closed the hole, the ring key was also depressed and at the same time activated a **key mechanism** to close or partially close at least one tone hole at another location on the flute. Clarinets today

have this type of **key** design. The first mention of ring keys seems to have been in an 1808 British patent by **Frederick Nolan.** They were later developed by **Theobald Boehm,** who used them on his 1832 **ring-key flute.** *See also* DORUS G♯ KEY; FRENCH-MODEL FLUTE. For **early flutes** or other non-**Boehm-system flutes,** *see also* BRILLE; CRESCENT KEY; FINGER VIBRATO; REFORM FLUTE (1). **2.** Sometimes, the padded **open-hole key** hovering above some large tone holes on the modern **concert flute.**

RING-KEY FLUTE. In general, any **flute** having **ring keys.** More specifically, the term refers to all wooden **conical flutes** based on **Theobald Boehm**'s conical flute of 1832, which was the predecessor of the modern **concert flute** invented by him in 1847. Boehm's 1832 model had three joints: a conical **middle joint** and **foot joint** and a cylindrical **head joint** with a **screw-cork.** It had an **open-key system,** including an open **G♯ key,** and 13 **tone holes** (see fig. 11, *top*), which allowed for a three-octave chromatic scale starting at **low C.** All of the tone holes were relatively large, except for the $C_{\sharp 2}$ tone hole (*see* C♯ VENT HOLE) and a small tone hole which could be used for **trills** that included the note D_2 or D_3. With the challenge of covering 13 tone holes with nine fingers (the 10th "finger," RT, was used for supporting the flute), Boehm designed a **key mechanism** that consisted of **padded** keys and ring keys mounted on interlinked rod-axles (*see* POST-MOUNT). Originally, **flat springs** were used to keep the **key touches** in place until activated. His flute was designed to be played approximately in **equal temperament** with one **fingering** per note. Small **tuning** adjustments could be made by extending the head joint **tenon** slightly from the middle joint **socket** or adjusting the **stopper,** or by changing the playing in some way. There was no **B♭ thumb key** or **B♭ side lever** on the original ring-key flute, both of which are standard on the modern flute; Boehm did not consider these keys an essential part of the mechanism.

Sometime after Boehm's invention of the ring-key flute described above, modifications were made by various makers to his design. These include:

- adding a **trill key** for trills with $D_{\sharp 2}$ or $D_{\sharp 3}$, invented by **Victor Coche** in 1838
- adding needle **springs,** an improvement listed in an 1839 patent by **Auguste Buffet** *jeune*
- moving the axles on the middle joint to the inner side of the flute instead of having them on both sides, thus helping make the flute more comfortable and simplifying the key mechanism
- adding a B♭ thumb key (either the **Briccialdi B♭ thumb** key design or the **reversed thumb keys**) and a B or B♭ side lever

- simplifying the foot joint mechanism by moving the **low C** and **low C**♯ **key** cups to the player's side of the instrument, which allowed for an increase in efficiency and reliability because **articulated keys** no longer needed to be used
- sometimes using two small C holes that were controlled by one key, instead of one small C hole as Boehm had originally designed it, to improve the speech of some **high notes**
- adding a **Dorus G**♯ **key**, designed by **Louis Dorus** (ca. 1838) in collaboration with **Vincent Godfroy** and **Louis Lot**, which helped players of the **old system** adjust to the new

See also app. 4; BOEHM FLUTE; BOEHM SYSTEM; CLINTON, JOHN; CYLINDRICAL BOEHM FLUTE (3); EMBOUCHURE HOLE; FLAGEOLET (1); FRENCH-MODEL FLUTE; GLASS FLUTE; RUDALL, GEORGE; SCHEMA; VAULTED CLUTCH.

RING-KEY SYSTEM. A term that is used on occasion to mean **ring-key flute**.

RING-MOUNT. Similar to a **block-mount**, except that an entire **ring** of wood or **ivory** is left standing after the **turning** of the **body** (see app. 3, B, fig. 2). This type of mount was common in the 17th and 18th centuries. *See also* CHANNEL; POST-MOUNT; SADDLE-MOUNT.

RISER. The metal ring that joins the **embouchure plate** to the **head joint** tube (see fig. 6). Wooden flutes do not generally have risers. The four sides, or **walls**, of the riser are sometimes designated as north, south, east, and west. North is the side the player strikes with her breath and is often referred to as the *blowing wall* or *strike wall*. The height of the riser (measured at the east side of the **embouchure hole** and including the **lip plate** and **tube** widths) varies and affects the ease with which notes are produced in the **low** and **high registers**. A riser with a *medium wall* is from about 4.82–5.08 mm high; a *high* or *deep wall*, from 5.08–5.38 mm; and a *low wall*, anything below 4.82 mm. The average standard wall is around 5.08 mm high.

Makers have different heights for various parts of the riser according to their opinions about the sound the flute should make. *Syn.:* **chimney**, wall, embouchure chimney, and **embouchure wall**, although the meaning of these terms usually also includes the width of the **embouchure plate** and the tubing to which the riser is attached. *See also* AIR REED (2); CUT; EMBOUCHURE HOLE; EMBOUCHURE PLATE; EMBOUCHURE RECUT; FLANGE; HEAD-JOINT MAKER; MODERN HEAD JOINT; OVERCUTTING; PALLADIUM; "PARABOLIC"; PROFESSIONAL FLUTE; RESISTANCE (1); SOLDER; UNDERCUTTING; VOICING.

RITTERSHAUSEN, EMIL (b. Berlin, 1852; d. Berlin, 1927). A **woodwind** maker specializing in **Boehm flutes**. His business thrived in Berlin from 1876 until after 1950. *See also* GOLD FLUTE; SPLIT E MECHANISM.

RIVE, CLAUDE (n.d.). A **woodwind** maker specializing in **Boehm flutes**. His business thrived in Paris from 1877 through at least 1895. *See also* MAILLECHORT; RETUNING.

ROAR-FLUTTER. A term coined by renowned flutist **Robert Dick** in 1969 to refer to an intense, harsh, raspy type of **flutter-tonguing**. It can be produced by placing the tongue far back on the hard **palate**, and then fluttering either the tongue or the **uvula** while blowing across the **embouchure hole** using a regular **embouchure** and strong **breath support**. It is notated in music with the term *roar-flutter* followed by a dotted line, wavy line, or bracket to indicate the length. The roar-flutter is useful in imitating the sound of explosions or animal roars. *See also* EXTENDED TECHNIQUE.

ROBERT DICK GLISSANDO HEADJOINT®. A telescoping flute **head joint** that can be used to gradually lower the **pitch** and make a downward **glissando** on any note on the flute to as much as a major third (see app. 10, fig. 1). The glissando range for each note varies, depending on the length of the vibrating **air column**; **left-hand notes** with a shorter air column, such as C_2, have a longer glissando potential than notes lower down.

The Glissando Headjoint, in its first commercial iteration, consists of a **silver** Brannen Brothers head joint of 0.016 in. (0.41 mm) **wall** thickness that slides inside a silver carrier tube. Self-lubricating plastic seals separate the two tubes and insure that there is no air **leakage**.

When the flute is held in the regular playing position, two adjustable stainless-**steel** wings extend outward from the sides of the **lip plate** to embrace the **flutist**'s cheeks. The wings help to stabilize the **embouchure plate** on the mouth when the flute **body** is being moved by the hands to perform the glissandi. As the flutist moves the flute body to the right, the head joint slides out to the required position.

If an upward glissando is required, the flutist starts with the head joint pulled out—the amount depending on the length of the glissando desired—and slides it gradually back to its **home** position. In its home position, the flute performs normally like a traditional **Boehm flute**.

Robert Dick invented the head joint, his envy of the electric guitar's whammy bar inspiring him to come up with the idea in 1978. Working through a series of prototypes with flutemakers **Eva Kingma**, **Kaspar**

Baechi, and **Bickford Brannen**, the current design evolved over a 12-year period, from the initial Kingma prototype in 1992 to the Brannen production model in 2004. It became available for purchase by the general public in the summer of 2004.

ROCKSTRO, RICHARD SHEPHERD (b. London, 1826; d. Willesden, Middlesex, England, 1906). Originally spelled *Rackstraw*. A British **woodwind** inventor in London. He was also a **flutist**, a renowned teacher, and the author of a famous flute **treatise** (see bib. under "Historical Methods, Treatises, and Tutors"). *See also* BRICCIALDI B♭ LEVER; COCHE, VICTOR JEAN BAPTISTE; EBONITE; ROCKSTRO F♯ LEVER; ROCKSTRO MODEL FLUTE; ROCKSTRO POSITION; WELCH, CHRISTOPHER.

ROCKSTRO F♯ LEVER. An elevated finger-like extension of the F♯ **key** found on some older **flutes** between the E and D keys (see app. 5, fig. 10). It can be easily **fingered** by R3 and allows the player to close the F♯ key without closing the D or E key. It has the same function as the **Brossa F♯ lever**: improved **venting** for the F♯'s and making them more acoustically correct than on the regular **Boehm flute** (*see* OPEN-KEY SYSTEM).

The Rockstro F♯ **lever** was invented by **Richard S. Rockstro** in the mid-19th century. Though it achieves the same purpose as the Brossa F♯ lever, the Rockstro F♯ lever has not been as popular on **standard flutes** because it displaces the D♯ **trill key** to another location (i.e., between the F♯ and F keys instead of between the E and D keys) and because, on **open-hole flutes**, a similar effect (on individual F♯'s) can be partially achieved by depressing the **rim** of the D key. *Syn.*: F♯ lever. *See also* ROCKSTRO MODEL FLUTE; SIMMONS F♯ KEY; SPLIT A KEY (2); SPLIT F♯ MECHANISM.

ROCKSTRO MODEL FLUTE. 1. A modification of the **cylindrical Boehm flute** of 1847 that went through many stages of development starting in 1864 and culminating in 1877. The distinguishing features mentioned by its designer, **flutist Richard S. Rockstro**, in his renowned **treatise** (see bib. under "Historical Methods, Treatises, and Tutors") are as follows:

- A uniform increase to 0.64 in. (1.6 cm) of all the equal-sized **tone holes** (i.e., all those below the C♯$_2$ hole) that improved the **intonation** in the **third octave** and the tone throughout the entire **range**.
- The addition of an F♯ **lever** (now often referred to as the *Rockstro F♯ lever*).
- The placement of the open G♯ **key** and the G key on one rod on the near side of the **flute** in order to facilitate the action of L3 and L4.

- The placement of the tone holes according to what Rockstro thought was the best location according to **equal temperament**.
- The use of a separate lever to close the **G key cup**, so that any accidental bending of the lever would not also bend the actual key cup and cause **leaks**.
- An increase in the size of all **bearing** surfaces of the key **stops** and **clutches**, moving these points of contact to a better location farther from the axles. This improved the leverage and allowed for **cork** to be placed in five locations, instead of two, which made for a quieter key **action**.
- An increase in the length of all key **shanks** (except for the **key** over the C$_2$ hole), which allowed for an increase in the key opening, and an improvement in **venting**, without also causing a simultaneous rising of the front part of the key.
- A modification in the shape of the **key touches** on the **foot joint** keys, except for the already common crescent-shaped D♯ key touch, to allow for easier **slurring** between the **foot-joint notes**.
- An extra B lever for L1 that attached to the key over the C$_2$ hole, allowing for the playing of the note B$_1$ or B$_2$ by using only this finger. This change allowed for easier **fingering** in most keys with sharps.
- An extra-large hole for D$_2$ covered by a **closed key** and attached to the common, and smaller, D$_2$ key. The addition of this larger key facilitated alternating between D$_2$, D♯$_2$, D$_3$, or D♯$_3$ with the lower notes A♯, B, C, and C♯. It also helped some **trills**, the most important of which were C$_2$/D$_2$ and G$_3$/A$_3$, and increased the power mainly of D$_2$ but also of D♯$_2$.
- The addition of a small **vent hole** just above the slightly larger C♯$_2$ hole, which, among other things, improved the stability of the regularly **fingered** D♯$_2$, and the intonation of D♯$_3$ and A$_3$. Special fingerings for D♯$_3$, E$_3$, and A$_3$ were also improved. The C♯ holes were closed or opened together by one double key.
- The addition of a lever at the back of the key of the B♭ hole (not visible in fig. 38) to partially close the C$_2$ hole with L2. This improved the alternation between E$_3$ and F♯$_3$, as in a trill, and the **pitch** of G$_3$ and C$_4$.

The Rockstro model flute was manufactured by the flutemaking company of **Rudall, Carte** & Co. It never really caught on, although some aspects of the **key mechanism** were popular in Britain (e.g., **clutches** against the **body** and **vented** D). Figure 38 shows the Rockstro Model flute as completed in 1877.

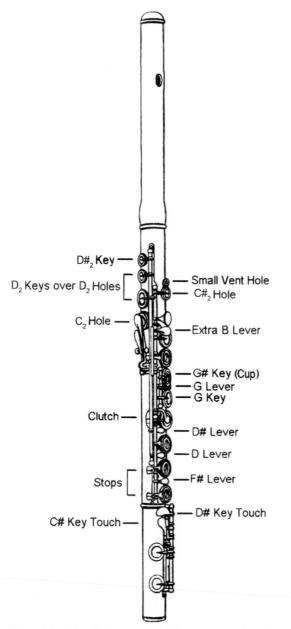

D#$_2$ Key ——

D$_2$ Keys over D$_2$ Holes [

—— Small Vent Hole
—— C#$_2$ Hole

C$_2$ Hole ——

—— Extra B Lever

—— G# Key (Cup)
—— G Lever
—— G Key

Clutch ——

—— D# Lever

—— D Lever

Stops [

—— F# Lever

C# Key Touch ——

—— D# Key Touch

Figure 38. The Rockstro Model flute as completed in 1877. *Reprinted by permission of Boosey & Hawkes, Inc.; key labeling added by Tess Vincent.*

2. The term may refer erroneously to any flute with the large holes of the Rockstro flute described above, regardless of whether they had other features similar to the model or not.

ROCKSTRO POSITION/GRIP. A method of assembling and holding the **flute** that is said to provide for a better balancing of the instrument and to free the fingers, allowing for improved **technique.** The **head joint** and **middle joint** are assembled such that the **blowing edge** lines up inside the center of the majority of key **cups.** With this set-up, and with the head joint and **lip**

plate held in their accustomed position, the main pieces of **key tubing** face the ceiling and cause the weight of the **key mechanism** to be directed downward, thus stabilizing the flute.

For this method, the base of L1 gently pushes the top half of the flute against the lower part of the bottom lip and, with the same amount of force, the tip of RT (which is positioned more or less between R1 and R2 on the near side of the flute) gently pushes the bottom half of the flute outward. Thus the flute is balanced between three points: the lower part of the bottom lip, L1, and the tip of RT.

Although there is evidence that the Rockstro position was used prior to the 19th century, it was not named until after **Richard S. Rockstro** defended it strongly in his famous **treatise** (see bib. under "Historical Methods, Treatises, and Tutors"). The Rockstro position differs from the traditional method where the center of the **embouchure hole** is lined up with the center of the key cups on the middle joint. This approach shifts the weight of the mechanism toward the player, and thus the flute has a tendency to be unstable and roll inward. It also requires a different hand-holding position.

ROD. 1. *See* KEY TUBING. **2.** *See* PIVOT; STEEL. **3.** *See* CLEANING ROD. **4.** *See* VAULTED CLUTCH. *See also* app. 4. **5.** *See* SCREW-CORK ASSEMBLY.

ROD-AXLE. Same as **steels.**

ROD SCREW. A long **steel** with a slot at one end and threads at the other (see app. 7, fig. 14, *bottom two steels*). *See also* PIVOT SCREW.

ROLLED TONE HOLES. A process performed on **drawn tone holes** whereby, after they are **extruded** from the metal **tube,** their **rims** are rounded outward or "rolled" to make them stronger and more durable as well as thicker and smoother so that they will not cut the key **pads,** and to make the **pad seat** more **level,** thus helping to prevent **leaks.** *See also* STUDENT FLUTE.

ROLLER. The part of a **lever** that is shaped like a cylinder with rounded ends and can be rolled by a finger to facilitate movement from one **touchpiece** to another. Rollers are utilized when one finger must operate more than one **key.** The traditional roller is drilled and **counterbored** to accept a **steel** axle that is attached to an **extension arm** with a screw thread. There is a "head" on the axle that fits precisely into the counterbore to allow the roller to turn freely and keep it in place on the axle.

On the **flute**, rollers are used for R4 to facilitate finger movement on the **foot joint**. They are the C roller on the **C** or **B foot joint** and the b roller on the B foot joint (see app. 9, fig. 8). These rollers are often referred to as the **low C key** and low B key, respectively.

Two nonstandard rollers are the D♯ and C♯ rollers. A D♯ roller can be attached to the D♯ key on the foot joint. It helps R4 when sliding from the D♯ key to the low C♯ or C keys. A less common roller, the C♯, can be attached to the low C♯ key and facilitates sliding R4 to the D♯ key. It is rarely seen on American-made flutes, but is more common on German flutes. *Syn.:* touchpiece, **touch**. *See also* ADJUSTMENT; BOEHM FLUTE; EBONITE; PLAY; PROFESSIONAL FLUTE; SPATULA.

ROLL-IN. A **lip plate** that is rolled in toward the lips more than what is considered to be average. If the lip plate is rolled inward, more of the **embouchure hole** will be covered with the lower lip and the tone will be smaller and **flatter**. The reverse will produce a **sharper pitch** and tend to make, or encourage, a bigger tone.

Some **flutists** use a **technique** of rolling in and out (a form of "**note bending**") to help them when they are seeking the correct pitch and **tone quality**. Rolling in and out is also a technique used in contemporary or **extended techniques** to bend notes above or below their normal pitch. *Syn.:* turn-in. *See also* OVERBLOWING; ROLL-OUT.

ROLL-OUT. The opposite of **roll-in**. When used to change the **intonation** of a note, the **flutist** will play **sharper**. *Syn.:* turn-out. *See also* NOTE BENDING.

ROMEI, FRANCESCO (b. Monte San Savino, Italy, 1959). An Italian wooden **simple-system** flutemaker and wood craftsman. *See also* HYPERBASS FLUTE.

ROSE, JOHN MITCHELL (b. Scotland, 1793/94; d. Wolverhampton, England, 1866). A **woodwind** maker whose business prospered in Edinburgh for several years before 1821. He also worked for Wood, Small & Co., pianoforte and organ makers. Rose joined in partnership with **George Rudall** in London from 1821 as Rudall & Rose. *See also* app. 4; BRICCIALDI B♭ LEVER; GOLD FLUTE (1); REVERSE TENON; VAULTED CLUTCH.

ROSEWOOD. A hard, heavy, resinous, dark-reddish or purplish black-streaked hardwood with a pronounced grain and sometimes a roselike odor. It comes from any of various leguminous trees of the genus *Dalbergia* found in tropical or semitropical climates around the world. Brazilian rosewood (*D albergia nigra*) is considered to be the finest type. It may be called *jacaranda* or *cabiuna* by Brazilians.

Older **flutes** made of a dark-reddish wood, easily misidentified as rosewood, are almost always made of **cocuswood**, a much denser wood. However, some feel that certain 18th-century flutes by **Thomas Stanesby Jr.** (1692–1754) and others are in fact made of rosewood. Rosewood is more common for flutes after the wooden flute revival in the 1970s.

ROUGE. 1. A mixture of ferric oxide and a thick, greasy binder used in flutemaking and repair to put the final **polish** on metallic **flute** parts. It comes in reddish powder, cream, and stick forms, the latter softened with kerosene. *See also* BUFFING; FINISH (3). **2.** *v.* To use rouge.

ROUGHING. 1. The process of **turning** away unwanted wood from the **billets** prior to making the parts of a wooden flute. This is done to shorten the time it takes for **seasoning** the wood and is thought by makers to improve the stability. *Syn.:* roughing out. **2.** Setting out the best and matching parts from one or more pieces of wood and cutting the parts to length.

ROUND SHOULDERING. Same as **overcutting**.

ROXBURGH, GRAEME (b. New Zealand, 1952). **Flute** player, computer scientist, and antipodean tinkerer. Has been interested in the **tuning** of **woodwind** instruments for many years, and with Terry McGee (b. 1948) produced a Real Time Tuning Analysis system in 2008. *See also* REAL TIME TUNING ANALYSIS.

RUDALL. 1. Slang abbreviation used by modern Irish players for **eight-key flutes** made by the leading 19th-century London flutemaking company, Rudall & Rose, or any of its successors (*see* RUDALL, GEORGE). These **flutes** are generally regarded to be the best of the Improved-style flutes pioneered by **Charles Nicholson Jr.** and **Sr.** (*see* NICHOLSON'S IMPROVED FLUTE). Although technically superseded by the **Pratten's Perfected**, these continued to be made through the first quarter of the 20th century, more than a hundred years after the company started in 1821. **2.** A modern replica of such a flute.

RUDALL, GEORGE (b. Crediton, England, 1781; d. London, 1871). An English **woodwind** maker, **flutist**, teacher, and musical instrument dealer. Rudall founded the Rudall & Rose instrument-making company in 1821 with **John Rose**. Sometime after meeting **Theobald Boehm** in 1831, he was granted British rights to manufacture Boehm's 1832 **ring-keyed flute** and the 1847 **cylindrical Boehm flute**. **Richard Carte** joined the company in 1850. In 1854, it absorbed a military musical instrument-making company and became Key, Rudall,

Carte & Co. or Key, Rudall & Co. It then became Rudall, Rose & Carte, with Carte as its proprietor, in 1856. In 1871, the firm became Rudall, Carte & Co. Boosey & Hawkes took over the company in the 1940s. *See also* app. 4; BRICCIALDI B♭ LEVER; RUDALL; VAULTED CLUTCH. For Rudall & Rose, *see also* BRICCIALDI B♭ LEVER; RUDALL. For Rudall, Rose, & Carte, *see also* GOLD FLUTE; RADCLIFF SYSTEM FLUTE. For Rudall, Carte & Co., *see also* BASS FLUTE (1); BRÖGGER MEKANIK; BROSSA F♯ LEVER; CARTE 1851 SYSTEM FLUTE; CARTE 1867 SYSTEM FLUTE; FLAT SPRING (1); FMG; HEAD-JOINT LINING; HIGH-PITCHED FLUTE (2); LEFT-HANDED FLUTE; OLD SYSTEM (2); OPEN-KEY SYSTEM; OPEN NOTE; ORDINARY FLUTE (1); PINLESS MECHANISM; PLATINUM FLUTE; RADCLIFF SYSTEM FLUTE; ROCKSTRO MODEL; TREBLE FLUTE IN G; UNIBODY.

RUDALL & ROSE. *See* RUDALL, GEORGE.

RUDALL, CARTE & CO. *See* RUDALL, GEORGE.

RUDALL-CARTE FLUTE. *See* CARTE 1851 SYSTEM FLUTE; CARTE 1867 SYSTEM FLUTE; GUARDS' MODEL FLUTE; RADCLIFF SYSTEM FLUTE.

RUDALL, ROSE & CARTE. *See* RUDALL, GEORGE.

RUN. A musical **passage** that usually consists of a scale, or is scale-like, and is to be played very quickly.

♪

SADDLE. 1. A **tone hole chimney**, usually used only when speaking of **soldered tone holes**. May be so called because it resembles the shape of a horse's saddle when viewed from the side. *See also* COLE SCALE; INTEGRAL TONE HOLE. **2.** *See* SADDLE-MOUNT.

SADDLE-MOUNT. A method of mounting **keys** on **simple-system flutes** and other **wind instruments** that was common in the 19th century. It was similar to the **block-mount**, except that the mount, or **saddle**, was made of metal and attached to the flute's **body** with screws rather than being integral to and of the same material as the body, and usually used a narrow **steel** or **brass** screw for the fulcrum instead of a **pin**. The metal, most often a piece of brass or **silver sheet metal**, was formed into a trough-like shape with a staple-like or U cross-section. The saddle was often made more secure by slightly sinking it into the wood **tube** or by **soldering** it to a curved **plate** that acted as a base (see app. 3, C, fig.

3). *Syn.:* key saddle. *See also* BLOCK-MOUNT; FLAP KEY; POST-MOUNT; RING-MOUNT.

SALT-SPOON KEY. Also *saltspoon key.* A type of **key** found primarily on English flutes that appeared in the earlier part of the 19th century and consisted of an approximately hemispherically shaped **cup**, a **shank**, and a **touchpiece**. The cup was filled with a wool-stuffed leather pad called a *purse pad.* It got its name because the cup looks similar to the back of a salt spoon. A metal **flat spring** was attached to the salt-spoon key at some point on its underside. There was a more or less semicircular **lug** with a hole near the middle of the salt-spoon key's shank. The lug's hole was used to accept a **pin** on which the key was suspended in a wooden or **ivory block-mount**. This type of flute key can be seen today on early 19th-century flutes and replicas, although usually in conjunction with modern-shaped **seats** and fitted with modern **card-backed pads** rather than purse pads (see app. 3, B, fig. 5; app. 6, C, fig. 1). *Cf.* **flap key, pewter plugs**.

SCALE. 1. The *flute scale* usually refers to the size and placement of the **tone holes**, but it may refer to the overall **intonation** of the notes emitted by the flute due to the manufacturer's particular and deliberate construction. When constructing what is in effect an **equal-tempered** scale, manufacturers vary in their efforts at improvements; they experiment with different sizes and positions of the tone holes, or variations in the **key rise** or **head-joint taper**, in an effort to improve the qualities of the flute.

Flute scales are classified as either a **modern scale** or a **traditional scale**. Most flutes produced after about 1980 have one of several versions of the modern scale, although some companies were slow to change. The modern flute scales are simply an update to **Theobald Boehm**'s original **Schema** to raise it from $A = 435$ Hz up to $A = 440$ Hz or above, depending on the common national orchestral **pitch**. In addition, the variations in scales by makers give some extra advantages such as an improvement in **tone quality** of certain traditionally weak notes.

Although all modern-scale flutes have a similar scale design, these variations have different name designations such as **Cooper scale, Bennett scale**, and so forth, commonly taken from the name of the person or flute manufacturer that introduced the scale.

Traditional-scale flutes do not usually have any special scale name designation, but are simply called "traditional-scale flutes." It is generally agreed that these were based on $A = 435$ Hz.

See also BASIC FINGERING; COLE SCALE; CYLINDRICAL BOEHM FLUTE (3); "FLUTE PITCHED AT A = . . ."; FMG; GOLD FLUTE (1); INTERNAL TUNING; MURRAY FLUTE;

OCTAVE LENGTH; OPEN-HOLE FLUTE; RETUNING; SCALE LENGTH; SCALING; SERIAL NUMBER; SHORTENED HEAD JOINT; TUNING (4); TUNING SLIDE (1); TUNING UP (2). For **early flutes,** *see also* PRATTEN'S PERFECTED.

    2. *See* **natural scale.**

    3. *See* **fire scale.**

SCALE LENGTH. Same as **octave length.** *See also* COLE SCALE.

SCALING. The placement of the **tone holes** on the **flute** relative to the **octave length.** This placement will depend on a particular flutemaker's choice of **pitch** for A_1 (e.g., 442 Hz, 444 Hz, etc.) and also on the diameter and height of the tone holes. Flutemakers use a modified version of **Theobald Boehm**'s **Schema** for determining how to **scale** or rescale a flute. *See also* BENNETT SCALE; COLE SCALE; COOPER SCALE; SHORTENED HEAD JOINT.

SCHEMA. A geometrical diagram, made by **Theobald Boehm** (1794–1881), inventor of the modern **concert flute** in 1847 (*see* CYLINDRICAL BOEHM FLUTE), that helps instrument makers determine the **tone hole** positions of **wind instruments** at various **pitches** (e.g., A = 442 Hz) as well as the positions of frets on instruments such as the guitar. When applied to the **flute,** Boehm's Schema uses tone holes of one size on a **closed-hole flute.** In his book *The Flute and Flute-Playing in Acoustical, Technical, and Artistic Aspects* (New York: Dover, 1964), Boehm states that he used a tone hole size of 13.5 mm (0.53 in.) for **silver flutes** and 13 mm (0.51 in.) for wooden flutes, but according to **Dayton Miller,** who translated the book and made comments throughout, the actual measurements of the tone holes on many wooden Boehm and **Mendler** flutes usually show them to be 13.2 mm (0.52 in.) in diameter on silver flutes and 12.8 mm (0.50 in.) on wooden ones.

    A method to determine the change in position for tone holes other than the one size on which the Schema is based is also needed, but Boehm's approach to this is unknown. Since Boehm's Schema was made for a closed-hole flute, further corrections have to be made when applying the Schema to an **open-hole flute.** Boehm published several versions of his Schema, but without the important displacement method.

    The Schema was first exhibited publicly at a London Exhibition in 1862. Figure 39 shows a portion of Boehm's Schema. Many contemporary flute manufacturers have their own versions. *See also* BENNETT SCALE; COLE SCALE; COOPER SCALE; SCALE (1); SCALING; TRADITIONAL SCALE.

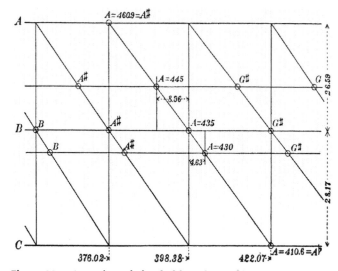

Figure 39.   A portion of Theobald Boehm's Schema. *From Theobald Boehm, "The Flute and Flute-playing in Acoustical, Technical, and Artistic Aspects" (New York: Dover, 1964), 45.*

SCHLEIFKLAPPE. A small closed **vent key** that was invented by **Theobald Boehm** in 1854 for the **alto flute,** and later added to some of his **concert flutes,** with the aim of improving the **intonation** and/or **response** of the written notes $D\sharp_2$ ($E\flat_2$), D_3, $D\sharp_3$ ($E\flat_3$), and A_3. It had a similar shape to the $B\flat$ **side lever** on the standard concert flute of today (see app. 5, fig. 6). The Schleifklappe was opened by rolling the left-hand thumb onto a **lever** situated just above the thumb keys. On the concert flute in C, the **tone hole** operated by this lever was about 0.18–0.20 in. (4.5–5 mm) in diameter and just to the right of the D **trill key cup.** The vent key disappeared from use because it only made a small improvement in some notes. *Syn.:* octave key, Schleif-key, whisper-key. *See also* CYLINDRICAL BOEHM FLUTE (1).

SCHMIDT, JIM (b. Omaha, Neb., 1953). An American flutemaker, jazz **flute** player, flute **pad** designer, and inventor of the new "Schmidt linear **fingering system**" for the flute. *See also* GOLD PADS; SPUD.

SCHNIETZHOEFFER, JACQUES (b. Dunkerque, Nord, France, 1754; d. 1829). A German **flutist** and oboist who played both instruments at the Paris Opéra from 1789 to 1820. Schnietzhoeffer was also **flute** and oboe professor of the **Paris Conservatoire** (flute, 1795–1800; oboe, 1800–1802).

SCHOLARLY EDITION. A modern edition of an earlier **work** that is based on an identified source or sources. Any **editorial** changes are noted either in the text, by means of dotted **slurs,** brackets, and other devices whose use is described in the prefatory remarks concerning editorial policy employed in the edition, or in a critical report at the end of the score. The purpose of both systems is to allow performers or readers to distinguish clearly between what is original to the source and what is not. In addition to a description of the editorial procedure, the preface generally contains a detailed description of the sources and their origin and may contain further information about the composer and the work being studied.

Scholarly editions are generally practical in intent, seeking to present a text that is authoritative, yet suitable for performance. Where something is missing in the source, the editor of a scholarly edition may seek to provide a solution so that the work can be performed. *Cf.* **facsimile, performer's edition,** *Urtext,* **critical edition**.

SCHWEDLER, MAXIMILIAN (b. Hirschberg, Germany, 1853; d. Leipzig, Germany, 1940). A German **woodwind** inventor, **flutist**, teacher at the Leipzig Conservatory from 1908 to 1932, **principal flutist** of the Gewandhaus Orchestra from 1881 to 1917, author, and flute music **editor**. *See also* BRILLE (1); KRUSPE, CARL, JR.; REFORM FLUTE; WINGED LIP PLATE.

SCREW CAP. A small turnable **cap** with extension at the closed end of the **head joint** on some antique **flutes** (or replicas). It has a hole in the center of it, through which the screw of a **screw-cork** was threaded (see app. 3, A, fig. 5). It was the predecessor of the **crown** on modern flutes. *Syn.:* tuning cap.

SCREW-CAP INDICATOR. *See* SCREW-CORK INDICATOR.

SCREW-CORK. 1. A movable cylindrical **cork** plug with an embedded screw protruding out one end and hidden from view inside and near the closed end of the **head joint** on many antique **flutes** (or replicas) (see app. 3, A, fig. 5). The end of the protruding screw fits into a threaded passageway in the center of a **screw cap** and may project through it, in the form of a **pin**, screw, or peg (*see* SCREW-CORK INDICATOR).

The screw-cork was the predecessor of the **head-joint cork** and screw on modern flutes and had a similar purpose. It **sealed** off the end of the flute and could be adjusted to allow for the best balance between the sonority of the lowest notes and the **tuning** of the highest notes. When it was used on a **conical flute**, it had a **stopper**-to-**embouchure** distance greater than used in modern flutes.

The screw-cork was originally invented to make it easier to move the cork when using differently sized up-

per **middle joints** (called *corps de rechange*). Thus, it was invented sometime after the invention of the corps de rechange, which took place around the 1720s (but before 1752, when it was mentioned in the famous **treatise** by **Johann Joachim Quantz**, the *Versuch*). When the length of the upper middle joint was altered, to make the flute play more **in tune** in certain situations, the distance between the **embouchure hole** and the screw-cork was also slightly altered by turning the screw-cap and either drawing the screw out (which also drew the cork out and away from the embouchure hole) or pushing it in (which pushed the cork more inside the head joint toward the embouchure hole). Any projecting part of the screw (or peg) was intended to indicate the position of the inner end of the cork, with respect to the embouchure hole. The protruding part was often marked with numbered rings to make it easier to set.

The screw-cork also appears on flutes with **tuning heads**, where its purpose is still to adjust **intonation** when the flute is tuned. *Syn.:* screw-stopper. *See also* ONE-KEYED FLUTE; TWO-KEYED FLUTE.

2. The modern version of the antique screw-cork above.

SCREW-CORK ASSEMBLY. Same as **cork assembly** (2).

SCREW-CORK INDICATOR. A peg-like part protruding through the **cap** on some antique flutes (or replicas) (see app. 3, A, fig. 5). *Syn.:* **pin**, indicator, indicator rod, screw-cap indicator. *See also* CORK ASSEMBLY (2); SCREW-CORK (1).

SCREW-STOPPER. Same as **screw-cork**. *See also* RING-KEY FLUTE.

SEAL. Usually a reference to how well the **pads** are **seated** on the **tone holes**, but may also refer to how well a **stopper** fits in the **head joint**. An effective hermetic seal is very important for a fully functioning **flute**. *See also* ADJUSTMENT; CLOSED-HOLE FLUTE; FISHSKIN; GARDENER'S FINGERS; HEAD-JOINT CORK; LEAKS; LEVELING; LOST MOTION; PAD IMPRESSION; PAPER WASHER; SHIM (1); TONE-HOLE BUSHING. For **early flutes**, *see also* KEY FLAP; PEWTER PLUGS; SCREW-CORK (1).

SEAMED TUBING. Metal flute **tubing** that is made by wrapping a flat piece of metal around a **mandrel** and then joining the two edges together with a lengthwise seam of **solder**. It was used on metal flutes before about 1898, when **George W. Haynes** and **William Haynes** made the first drawn flute tubes, but is now seldom used. When it is used today, it is seen only on **silver flutes** and not on **gold** or **platinum flutes**, since **gold** is too soft and **platinum** is too hard. Seamed tubing is said to be structurally inferior to **drawn tubing**, because the seam can come apart if the tubing is damaged or expanded, such as when a **head joint** is refitted (*see* HEAD-JOINT REFITTING). Some **flutists** put up with this disadvantage, however, in order to enjoy what they feel is improved **resonance**. *See also* SHEET METAL; SOLDERED TONE HOLES.

SEAMLESS TUBING. Same as **drawn tubing**. *Cf.* **seamed tubing**.

SEASONING. The process of reducing moisture content in wood to a level where it will be in equilibrium with the relative humidity it will encounter in use. Since extremely fine and dense timbers are used in flutemaking, the process of seasoning has to be conducted slowly and very carefully if the timber is not to split due to rapid moisture loss (and therefore shrinkage) on the outside, but slow moisture loss from the inside.

Seasoning methods may vary between flutemakers. Some prefer to **turn** their **billets** round and a little oversize (to remove excess wood) and to bore them undersize (to permit air access to the inside) when delivered, in order to facilitate seasoning with minimum stress to the timber. Even with such treatment, at least several years of seasoning are required if a stable product is to result. *See also* BOXWOOD; BREAKING-IN (PERIOD); ROUGHING; STRESS RELIEVING.

SEAT. 1. The top edge of a **tone hole** that a **pad** contacts. *Syn.:* bed, pad seat. *See also* CHIMNEY (2); LEVELING (1); PATCHING; SEAL. **2.** *See* CHAIR.

SEATING. 1. Placing **shims** of different sizes and thicknesses under a key **pad** to level it and make the pad face match the **tone-hole rim** profile. Also called *leveling* or *shimming. See also* FINISHER; FLOATING; PAPER WASHER; PISONI PADS; PLAYING CONDITION. **2.** The way a key pad rests, or its position, on the **tone hole** or tone hole **chimney** (def. 2). *See also* COVER (1); LOST MOTION; SEAL.

SECOND FLUTE. 1. A **flute** that is **pitched** a minor second above the **standard flute** in use. Since the standard flute today is the **concert flute** in C, the term refers to a **flute in D♭**. (In an older terminology used for **Baroque** and **simple-system flutes**, the standard-size flute was considered to be in D, so a second flute would be said to be in E♭.) This way of naming is rarely used today. For other ways of naming flutes, *see* "FLUTE IN THE KEY OF . . ." and TRANSPOSING INSTRUMENTS. *Cf.* **third flute** (1), **fourth flute** (1). **2.** The second flute **part**. **3. Second flutist**.

SECOND FLUTIST. The **flutist** who plays a supporting role in any **ensemble** that has more than one written flute **part**. The second flutist plays the second flute part, which is usually a subsidiary part containing lower **pitches**, **harmonies** in parallel rhythm, and often fewer melodies than the first flute part. Thus, he usually engages in more of an accompanying role, seeking to match the **intonation**, dynamic level, **articulation** style, note length, note endings, **vibrato** style, and **tone colors** chosen by the **first flutist**. Some composers, however, write equal parts for the first and second flutist. Some examples of orchestral **works** where this occurs are Ravel's "Daphnis and Chloe," Debussy's *"Prélude a l'après-midi d'une faune,"* Prokofiev's "Classical Symphony," Britten's "Young Person's Guide to the Orchestra," Tchaikovsky's Fourth and Fifth symphonies, and Rimsky-Korsakov's "Scheherazade."

In small orchestras, when the music requires it, the second flutist may also **double** on **piccolo**. In larger ensembles, such as large school bands, there can be whole sections of unison second flutists. In some larger bands and orchestras, there are even more subsidiary parts, requiring a **third flutist** and sometimes a fourth. *See also* JUST INTONATION; PRINCIPAL FLUTIST (2); UTILITY FLUTIST.

SECOND OCTAVE. The notes contained in the next octave above the lowest-pitched octave of a musical instrument. On the **flute**, these notes are from C_2 to B_2. *Syn.:* middle notes, middle **register**, middle octave, **second register**. *See also* "Octave Designation" in the introduction; DIFFERENCE TONES; FIRST OCTAVE; FOURTH OCTAVE; MIDDLE C; RANGE; THIRD OCTAVE. For **early flutes**, *see also* RENAISSANCE FLUTE.

SECOND REGISTER. Usually refers to the **second octave**. *Syn.:* middle **register**. *See also* ACOUSTICAL LENGTH (2); FIRST REGISTER; HARMONIC (2); RESISTANCE PLUG; THIRD REGISTER.

SECOND TRILL KEY. Same as the D♯ **trill key**.

SECTION. 1. In an orchestra or band, a group of instruments of the same kind, such as the **flute** section, the clarinet section, the **woodwind section**, or the brass section. *See also* FIRST CHAIR FLUTIST; LEAD (1); PRINCIPAL FLUTIST; SECTIONAL.

2. On the flute with the traditional **pinned mechanism**, a group of **keys** that are held together on the same **steel** by tapered **pins**. There are three main sections on a flute: the left-hand section, the right-hand section, and the **trill-key** section (the left-hand and right-hand sections are sometimes referred to as the **mainline** section).

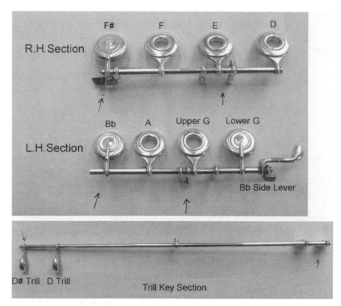

Figure 40. The right-hand *(top)*, left-hand *(middle)*, and trill key sections *(bottom)* of a silver Louis Lot flute, no. 3696, with a traditional pinned mechanism. The arrows point to the pin locations. *Photo courtesy Stephen Wessel.*

They are all on the **middle joint**. Figure 40 shows the sections of a flute with the traditional pinned mechanism. The arrows point to the pin locations.

The trill-key section includes both trill keys (i.e., the D and D♯ trill keys) and trill key **cups**. The left-hand section on a flute with in-line **G keys** includes the B♭ key, the A key, the B♭ **kicker**, the G keys, and the **B♭ side lever**. On a flute with offset G keys, the left-hand section includes only the B♭ key, the A key, and the B♭ kicker. The right-hand section includes the D key, the D **lug**, and the E, F, and F♯ keys.

Syn.: assembly, stack. *See also* BEARING; BRÖGGER MEKANIK; BRÖGGER SYSTEM; COUNTERBORE (1); KING POST; MATIT CARBON-FIBER FLUTE; ONE-PIECE CORE BAR; PINLESS MECHANISM; SQUAREONE FLUTE.

3. *See* JOINT.
4. *See* BEARING.
5. *See* SECTION LEADER.

SECTIONAL. A rehearsal that only involves a **section** (def. 1), or part of the orchestra. For example, a **flute** sectional would be a rehearsal for the flute section alone. *Syn.:* sectional rehearsal.

SECTION LEADER. The main or principal player of any **section** of instruments in a large **ensemble** such as an orchestra. In a **flute** section, this player is the **first flutist** (also called **principal flutist**, **first chair flutist**, or **solo flutist**). Section leaders are responsible to lead, or show through their playing, the style of **articulation**, **phrasing**, interpretation, and so on that the other players are to follow. *Syn.:* **lead**.

SENSITIVE NOTE. Fr. *note sensible*. In music, the leading note of a major scale. The term has also been used to refer to the raised lower note of certain semitone intervals (*see* AUGMENTED NOTES).

SEPTET. An **ensemble** of, or a **piece** for, seven musicians.

SERIAL NUMBER. An identification number (sometimes with a letter prefix or suffix) that is **stamped** or **engraved** on a **flute**, appearing on the **barrel** of the **middle joint**, the **ribbing**, or the **body tube**. It is most often one of a series of sequential numbers and is used to identify the flute from other flutes made by a particular company.

The serial number can be used for registering ownership and to help in tracing a lost or stolen flute. Depending on how the serial number is constructed, it can also be used to gather other information such as the date of manufacture, the craftsperson(s) responsible for making it, and the factory where it was made. These distinctions are important to the manufacturer for determining warranty issues and also for quality control. If good records are kept by the flute company, the serial number can also provide important information about the composition of the metal, the flute's **pitch** and **scale**, and so on. *See also* FACTORY-MADE FLUTE; HANDMADE FLUTE; MODEL NUMBER.

SESSION. A gathering of musicians, at any playing level, who get together to play from memory the traditional music of a particular country (or countries) or genre for their own enjoyment and not for performance purposes. Sessions, which can range from just a few players to dozens, and from highly joyous to very serious, also provide musicians the opportunity to meet with other musicians and to share tunes. Onlookers are welcomed, if they do not distract the musicians. Sessions may be held in public places, such as bars, or in homes and other private places.

Sessions are very popular in many countries. Of note are "Irish sessions," which are famous throughout much of the world. The **"Irish" flute**, the whistle (i.e., **tin whistle**), fiddles, *bohdrans* (traditional drum), button accordion, concertina, and occasionally Irish or *uillean* pipes are instruments commonly seen at an Irish session. Some sessions are accompanied by guitar, *bouzouki*, or piano, but others are not, the musicians preferring to remain unaccompanied to allow the melody players full rhythmic control. Players of other types of instruments are generally not welcomed at Irish sessions because their usage makes it very hard to achieve a harmonious balance of sound and sustain the unique rhythms used in Irish music. The Irish session is based on a large shared repertoire of tunes, accurately played but with some scope for individual variation. The emphasis is on melody and rhythm, not harmony playing and improvisation.

SEXTET. An **ensemble** of, or a **piece** for, six musicians.

SHADING. 1. A **technique** where the **flutist** makes a slight adjustment to the **pitch** or **tone color** of a note in order to play more **in tune** (in the case of a pitch change) or with more expression (in the case of a tone color change). The flutist does this by changing his playing in some way, such as by moving his lips, or by using an **alternate fingering.** *Cf.* **humoring, lipping, note bending. 2.** Partially covering the hole in a **finger hole** or an **open-hole key** in order to achieve a change in pitch or tone color. *See also* CROSS-FINGERING (1); HALF-HOLING; HIGH G♯ MECHANISM.

SHAFFER, ELAINE (b. Altoona, Pa., 1926; d. 1973). An American orchestra **flutist**, recording artist, and music **editor** of **early flute** repertory. *See also* PLATINUM FLUTE.

SHAFT. Same as **steel**.

SHAKE. 1. An older name for **trill. 2.** *See* SHAKE KEY. **3.** Close shake, lesser shake. *See* FINGER VIBRATO.

SHAKE KEY. An older name for a **trill key.** *See also* B♭ SIDE LEVER; B TRILL KEY/LEVER; SIDE LEVER B♭ FINGERING. For **early flutes,** *see also* FIVE-KEYED FLUTE.

SHAKUHACHI. An **end-blown** Japanese **notch flute** with a **conical bore** contracting from the widest part at the **mouthpiece** to an area just past the bottom **finger hole** where the **bore** widens again (see app. 1, fig. 10). The mouthpiece consists of an oblique **blowing edge** with a trapezoidal or curved inlay of water buffalo horn, **ivory,** or, more recently, cell-cast acrylic to preserve it over time. The instrument is made from the root of thick-walled bamboo of the type called *madaké* in Japan and traditionally consists of four finger holes in front and one thumb hole in the back which are **tuned** to a pentatonic (five-note) scale. In the decades following World War II, a seven-hole shakuhachi emerged in response to Western influences.

The sound is produced by resting the top end of the **flute** on the chin and directing an air stream across the blowing edge. Using various **fingerings,** including **half-**holing and quarter-holing, and by controlling the angle of the mouthpiece against the lip, the player can produce not only all 12 tones of the Western chromatic scale but also the swelling or **bending** of notes characteristic of the traditional music. **High notes** can be produced by **over-blowing** and refining the **embouchure**.

The name of the instrument is derived from an ancient Japanese measuring system, "shakuhachi" being the corruption of *i shaku ha sun,* which literally means 1.8 Japanese feet—in Western terms, 21.5 in. (54.5 cm)—the length of the classical-sized shakuhachi in the key of D (named after the **pitch** sounded when all the holes are closed). Even though the name refers to this particular flute, over time it has come to be used generically and applied to many different lengths of instruments that most traditional makers produce.

The origin of the shakuhachi has been traced back as far as ancient China before entering Japan in the sixth century. The instrument reached its final phase of development in the 17th century in the hands of itinerant preachers known as *komuso* ("priests of emptiness and nothingness"). The komuso wore large baskets over their heads to symbolize their detachment from the world. Legend has it that these komuso, forbidden to carry their revered swords, redesigned the shakuhachi from the root of the bamboo, making it longer and stouter for use as a club as well as an instrument for spiritual attainment. Others describe this evolution in design less romantically, ascribing it more to natural than spiritual selection. *See also* AEROPHONE; SHAKULUTE.

SHAKULUTE. A **shakuhachi head joint** for the modern **Boehm flute,** which allows the player to hold the instrument vertically and combine blowing techniques that are normally possible only on the shakuhachi with standard Boehm flute **fingerings.** The head joint was developed by **Monty H. Levenson,** a shakuhachi maker, in 2001.

SHANK. A long, narrow part. On the **flute,** the term most often refers to the narrow part that connects the **tone hole** cover to the part by which it is held or moved (see app. 3, B, fig. 7). On modern flutes, it is usually called the **key arm.** *See also* ARTICULATED KEY; BLOCK-MOUNT; POST-MOUNT; ROCKSTRO-MODEL FLUTE. For **early flutes,** *see also* CHANNEL; FLAP KEY; SHORT KEY.

SHAPING. Same as **phrasing**.

SHARP. Higher than the correct **pitch** for a given note. When an instrument or voice is said to be sharp, most of its notes are sounding higher than their correct pitches. *Cf.* **flat.** *See also* BRILLE (1); BROSSA F♯ LEVER;

COLE SCALE; COOPER SCALE; DENSITY; HALF-HOLING; INTERNAL TUNING; INTONATION; LIP GLISSANDO; MURRAY FLUTE; OPEN-HOLE FLUTE; ORCHESTRAL MODEL FLUTE; PYTHAGOREAN TUNING; RAISING A NOTE; RETUNING; ROLL-IN; ROLL-OUT; SHORTENED HEAD JOINT; SPLIT E MECHANISM; TRADITIONAL SCALE; TUNING SLIDE (1); VIBRATO. For **early flutes**, *see also* AUGMENTED FINGERINGS; AUGMENTED NOTES; *CORPS DE RECHANGE;* ONE-KEYED FLUTE; TUNING SLIDE (2); TWO-KEYED FLUTE.

SHARPEN. *v.* To make a note higher (more **sharp**) in pitch.

SHARPER. Higher (more **sharp)** than another note (i.e., more **out of tune**).

SHEET METAL. Metal that has been rolled into sheets. It is used to make various **flute** parts. Depending on the flutemaker, these parts may include the **embouchure plate**, key **cups, flat springs, pad washers, French bushings, seamed tubing,** and the "dome" of the **crown.** *Syn.:* flatstock. *See also* STAMP. For **early flutes** or other non-**Boehm-system** flutes, *see also* SADDLE-MOUNT; TONE-HOLE BUSHING.

SHEET MUSIC. 1. Musical compositions that are printed or written on unattached and unbound sheets of paper. Sheet music is also available in downloadable digital format or on CDs. *Cf.* **collection. 2.** All printed music, irrespective of the method of binding.

SHIM. 1. A small, thin, flat piece of material used to fill in a small space between parts. For example, a shim of paper may be installed at various places between a large key **pad** and a key **cup** to **level** out the pad and/or to raise it to its correct height. This is done so that the pad will **seal** better with the **tone-hole rim.** *Syn.:* **adjustment** paper, spacer. **2.** A **paper washer.** *Syn.:* full shim, whole shim. A segment of a paper washer is referred to as a *partial shim. See also* ADJUSTMENT SCREWS; CLUTCH (1); GLUE; GOLD PADS; KEY RISE; LEVELING (2); LOST MOTION; PAD IMPRESSION; SEATING (1); STRAUBINGER PADS.

SHIMMING. *See* FINISHER; PISONI PADS; SEATING (1); SPUD.

SHOREY, DAVID (b. Chicago, 1953). A well-known writer, lecturer, historian, dealer in old **flutes**, curator of the **Dayton C. Miller (DCM)** Flute Collection at the Library of Congress in the late 1970s. Declared a Cultural Asset by the Dutch minister of culture in 1999, Shorey was the first foreign flute historian granted Dutch residency. He and his wife Nina currently operate their 28-year-old business—David and Nina Shorey, Antique Flutes—out of Los Angeles. *See also* app. 4; CLUTCH; VAULTED CLUTCH.

SHORT B♭ FINGERING. Same as **thumb key B♭ fingering**. It is probably so called because it is reminiscent of the "short B♭key" on the **simple-system flute** (see app. 2, fig. 4), which was controlled by the LT. *See also* LONG B♭ FINGERING; SHORT KEYS.

SHORTENED HEAD JOINT. A **head joint** that has been shortened by flutemakers or repairers in the erroneous belief that it raises the **pitch** of an otherwise **flat** flute (i.e., raises the pitch of all of the notes). In order to change a flute's pitch, however, not only does the head joint need to be shortened, but the flute also needs to be rebuilt to a **sharper scale** by repositioning the **tone holes.** If the octave length C_1-C_2 has been shortened by one inch (2.5 cm), for example, the **sounding length** to C_2 has been shortened by 1/12, but the sounding length to **low C** has been shortened by only 1/24. The effect of shortening the **head** will be therefore greater for notes nearer the head (**left-hand notes**) than those at the **foot.** If the head joint is only shortened without re-**scaling**, the flute will be **out of tune** with itself (*see* INTERNAL TUNING). *See also* TRADITIONAL SCALE.

SHORT KEYS. Keys on **simple-system flutes** that have keywork or **shanks** that are extra short or within close proximity to the **tone hole** which they control (see app. 2 and app. 3, C, fig. 3, for a short F key). *See also* CARTE 1851 SYSTEM FLUTE; CARTE 1867 SYSTEM FLUTE; CLOSED-KEY SYSTEM; CROSS KEY; DUPLICATE TONE HOLES; EIGHT-KEYED FLUTE; FIVE-KEYED FLUTE; FOUR-KEYED FLUTE; LONG KEY; NINE-KEYED FLUTE; SHORT B♭ FINGERING; SIX-KEYED FLUTE; TEN-KEYED FLUTE.

SHUT G♯ KEY. Same as closed **G♯** key.

SHUT-KEY SYSTEM. *See* CLOSED-KEY SYSTEM.

SICCAMA, ABEL (b. Germany, ca. 1810; d. ca. 1865). A **woodwind** maker whose business thrived in London from 1848 to 1862. He was also a **flute** inventor, classics scholar, language professor, amateur **flutist**, and author. *See also* PRATTEN'S PERFECTED FLUTE; SICCAMA DIATONIC FLUTE.

SICCAMA DIATONIC FLUTE. A modification of the **eight-keyed flute** where the third and sixth **finger holes** were moved farther from the **embouchure hole** to a more acoustically correct position and provided with two open-standing keys so that the fingers could reach

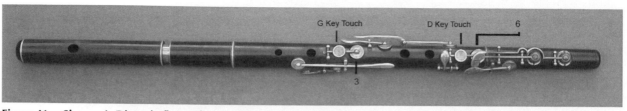

Figure 41. Siccama's Diatonic flute. *Photo courtesy Terry McGee.*

them. Making this change allowed for the other **tone holes** on the **flute** to be moved to better acoustic positions as well. All of these changes resulted in a flute with improved tone and **intonation**. The Siccama Diatonic flute was designed by **Abel Siccama**, an amateur **flutist**, in 1842 and patented in 1845. It was made in London and the United States by a number of different makers over the following 50 years. The term *diatonic* was applied to the flute in order to direct attention to its capability of producing the differences in **pitch** required to produce all the major and minor diatonic scales in perfect intonation. Although Siccama patented three other types of flutes, the Diatonic flute became the most popular, and as a result, it is commonly referred to as the *Siccama flute*. Figure 41 shows the Siccama Diatonic flute, made from stained **cocuswood** with silver **fittings**. *See also* **simple-system flute** (1).

SIDE-BLOWN FLUTE. Any of a family of **flutes** that produce a sound by blowing against the sharp edge of a hole in the side of a **tube**. Some examples include the modern **concert flute** in C, the **fife**, and the **contrabass flute**. *See also* FLAUTO (1); FLUTE FAMILY; TRANSVERSE FLUTE; WALKING-STICK FLUTE. For information about other flute classifications, *see* DUCT FLUTE; END-BLOWN FLUTE; GLOBULAR FLUTE; MULTIPLE FLUTE; NOSE FLUTE; NOTCHED FLUTE; OVERTONE FLUTE; VERTICAL FLUTE; VESSEL FLUTE; WHISTLE.

SIDE EMBOUCHURE. An **embouchure** that has an **off-centered aperture**.

SIDE G♯ KEY. Another name for the closed **G♯ key**.

SIDE HOLE. Usually, same as **tone hole** (1).

SIDE KEY/LEVER. 1. Any **key** that is off to the side of the main keywork on the **middle joint** and is operated by R1. The **B♭ side lever** is the most common side key and is present on all **standard flutes** today. *See also* B TRILL KEY/LEVER; C♯ TRILL KEY; CYLINDRICAL-BOEHM FLUTE (2, 3); G/A TRILL KEY (3); RING-KEY FLUTE; SPLIT F♯ MECHANISM. **2.** The B♭ side lever. **3.** Side or **independent G♯ key**.

SIDE LEVER B♭ FINGERING. A special **basic fingering** for B-flat in the **first** and **second octaves** of the **flute**. This name arose because the **fingering** requires that the **flutist** depress the **B♭ side lever** (along with L1, LT, and R4D♯), distinguishing it from two other basic B♭ **fingerings** in these octaves: the **thumb key B♭ fingering** and the **one-and-one B♭ fingering**. *Syn.:* B♭ lever fingering, B♭ side key/lever fingering, B♭ shake key fingering, B♭ trill key/lever fingering, side lever key fingering, trill-tab fingering.

SIGHT-READING. The practice of reading and immediately playing a previously unlearned **piece** of music. The music is played as though it were being performed. Sight-reading is an integral part of the requirements in many practical flute exams and auditions. To play something "at sight" or "at first sight" means to sight-read it spontaneously. *See also* PARIS CONSERVATOIRE.

SILENCER. Same as **bumper**.

SILENT SINGING. *See* THROAT TUNING.

SILVER. A metallic element and one of the **precious metals**. It is one of the most popular metals used in flute-making, where it is **alloyed** with copper and sometimes other metals in varying amounts to make various parts (*see* SILVER FLUTE). Silver is also used for **plating brass** and **nickel-silver flutes** both for cosmetic purposes and for protection from **corrosion**. It is sometimes used to plate silver flutes to improve the **finish**. Silver naturally **tarnishes** slowly in air, but faster in the presence of sulfur. *See also* BRITANNIA SILVER; COCUSWOOD; COIN SILVER; DENSITY; EBONITE; EMBOUCHURE HOLE; FACTORY-MADE FLUTE; FIRE SCALE; FLUTE FAMILY (2); GOLD; GOLD FLUTE; GS ALLOY; HALLMARK; HANDMADE FLUTE; INTERMEDIATE FLUTE; KEY FLAP; LINING; MODEL NUMBER; NICKEL-SILVER; PCM-SILVER ALLOY; PROFESSIONAL FLUTE; RETUNING; SILVER 900; SILVER 925; SILVER 958; SILVER BRAZING; SILVER-PLATING; SOLDER; SOLID; SOLID SILVER; SPOON FLUTE; STEP-UP FLUTE (1); STERLING SILVER; STRESS RELIEVING; STRETCHING; WALL (1).

SILVER 900. Another name for American **coin silver**, so called because it contains 90.0 percent **silver**.

SILVER 925. Another name for **sterling silver**, so called because it contains 92.5 percent **silver**.

SILVER 958. Another name for **Britannia silver**, so called because it contains about 95.8 percent **silver**.

SILVER BRAZING. In flutemaking, usually the same as **brazing**. Often flutemakers refer to this as **silver soldering**, because the **solder** is made of a **silver alloy**. (Technically, any method of joining parts with solder that runs at temperatures above about 840°F/449°C is known as brazing.)

SILVER FLUTE. 1. A **flute** in which at least the **tube** of the flute is made from a **silver alloy**. The most popular silver alloy used for flutemaking is **sterling silver**, which contains 92.5 percent silver and 7.5 percent copper. The addition of copper content makes the silver harder, stronger, and more practical to work with than pure silver. Other parts are sometimes made from a different metal (e.g., the **keys** may be made of **nickel-silver** or the **embouchure plate** of **gold**). Mechanical parts of the **key mechanism** such as **steels**, screws, and any **pins** are made from mild, carbon, or stainless **steel**. Silver flutes are the most popular type with professional players. A minor drawback of silver is that it **tarnishes**. Silver flutes were introduced by **Theobald Boehm** in 1847. *Syn.:* **solid silver** flute. *See also* BARRÈRE, GEORGES; BRITANNIA SILVER; COIN SILVER; EMBOUCHURE HOLE; FRENCH FLUTE SCHOOL; GOLD FLUTE; HALLMARK; MODEL NUMBER; NICKEL-SILVER FLUTE; PARIS CONSERVATOIRE; PLATINUM FLUTE; RETUNING; SCHEMA; SEAMED TUBING; SILVER-PLATING; SPOON FLUTE; SPRING; THOU; WALL (1).

2. The term may misleadingly refer to a flute of which the **body** tube is of some metal other than silver, but is also silver-plated. Parts other than the tube and **plating** are as described above.

3. Since January 1, 1999, flutes made of silver can only be described as "silver" in the United Kingdom if each part (except the embouchure plate) has passed an assay office test certifying that it is at least 800 parts per thousand silver. If it passes this test, it receives a *hallmark*. If it fails, it cannot legally be sold as "silver," though other parts as defined by the assay office, such as the steels, the screws, and some **solder**, are allowed to be made of other materials. Prior to 1999, the standard for silver was 925 parts per thousand. In the United Kingdom, the **head joint** is treated as a separate instrument from the flute body, and to be legal, a silver head joint cannot be attached to a **base metal** body.

SILVER-PLATING. A coating of **silver** used to cover metal parts. It is commonly used on **brass** or **nickel-sil**ver for protection against **corrosion**. It may also be used to cover silver and improve the **finish** or to cover brass **keys** on an otherwise **silver flute** to keep the cost of the flute down. There is little difference in price between a flute with **nickel-plating** or silver-plating. *See also* FLUTE FAMILY (2); GOLD-PLATING; MODEL NUMBER; NICKEL-SILVER FLUTE; PITTING; PLATING; RHODIUM-PLATING; SOLID SILVER; STEP-UP FLUTE (1); STRIKE PLATE; STUDENT FLUTE; TARNISH.

SILVER SOLDER. Same as hard **solder** or high-temperature solder. *See also* BRAZING (2); FILLER (3); PATCHING; SILVER BRAZING.

SIMMONS F♯ KEY. A modification to the **venting** on the **standard flute** to improve the stability, tone, and **articulation** of F♯₃ (see fig. 42, *bottom*) It enables the same venting as a **split F♯ mechanism** but without actually splitting the A **key** from the B♭ key. This makes it particularly suitable for the **open-hole flute**, as it avoids the mechanical **sealing** of the A key perforation that usually results from the incorporation of a split F♯ mechanism. The modification consists of a new, full-size duplicate B **tone hole** and key, added to the back of the **flute** to the right of the thumb hole for C. The key is opened by leaning with R3 onto a new **lever** to the left of the D key (called the *split F♯ lever*), while simultaneously depressing the D key. Activating this lever while using the normal fingering for F♯₃ and closing the A keys with L2 allows F♯₃ to be played with only the new B tone hole opened, and not the standard in-line B and B♭ tone holes. The Simmons F♯ key was designed and first made by **William Simmons** in December 1995. *Cf.* BROSSA F♯ LEVER; DUPLICATE TONE HOLES; ROCKSTRO F♯ LEVER; SPLIT F♯ MECHANISM.

SIMMONS, WILLIAM (b. Lancashire, England, 1945). Flutist. English maker of **Boehm flutes**, custom keywork including high F♯ key on both **flute** and **piccolo**. Also maker of wooden **whistles**. *See also* SIMMONS F♯ KEY.

SIMPLE-SYSTEM FLUTE. An ambiguous term that, in general, usually refers to a historical form of the **flute** used in the 18th and 19th centuries or to an ethnic or folk flute. More specifically, the simple-system flute may refer to any of the following.

1. As the term is used in this book, and the meaning usually intended by scholars, a development of the **Baroque** and **Classical one-keyed flute** mentioned in definition 3 below, which is a European **transverse conical flute** with six open **finger holes** and a number of **keys** (usually at least four, but sometimes as many as 20), most of which are **closed-standing** on the **body** and **open-standing** on the **foot**. Extra notes can be produced by using **cross-fingerings, half-holing,** and **overblowing.** This is the type of instrument usually meant when the term "pre-**Boehm flute**" or "pre-**Boehm system**" is used, even though they continued to be made well past the introduction of the Boehm flute. Some examples of this type of simple-system flute are the **Meyer-system flute, Tulou** *Flûte Perfectionée,* **Nicholson's Improved flute, eight-keyed Pratten's Perfected, Siccama Diatonic flute,** and **four-, five-, six-,** eight-, **nine-,** and **ten-keyed flutes.** *Syn.:* **keyed flute, multikeyed flute, ordinary flute, old-system** flute (1), old flute. *See also* app. 2 and 3; ARTICULATED KEY; ARTIFICIAL IVORY; BARREL (2); BEAD (3); BLOCK-MOUNT; BODY (2); BREATH VIBRATO; *BRILLE;* BULBOUS HEAD JOINT; CAP; CENTER JOINT/PIECE; CHANNEL; CHARANGA FLUTE; CLOSED-KEY SYSTEM; COCUSWOOD; CONCERT FLUTE (2); CONICAL BORE; CORK ASSEMBLY (2); *CORPS DE RECHANGE;* CROSS KEY; DORUS G♯ KEY; DUPLICATE KEYS; DUPLICATE TONE HOLES; E♭ FLUTE; EXTENDED FOOT JOINT (1); FINIAL; FLAT SPRING (2); FLUTE BAND; "FLUTE IN . . ." (1); FOOT JOINT; FOOT REGISTER; FOURTH FLUTE (1); G/A TRILL KEY (4); GLIDE; G♯ KEY; HEAD-JOINT LINING (1); *KLEINE QUARTFLÖTE;* LEATHERS; LONG KEY; LOWER (MIDDLE) JOINT/PIECE; MEYER, HEINRICH FRIEDRICH; MIDDLE JOINT/PIECE (2); NATURAL SCALE; NICHOLSON, CHARLES, JR.; PEWTER PLUGS; PICCOLO (1); PIN (2); POST-MOUNT; PRINCIPAL RANK; PURSE PADS; RANGE (2); REVERSE TENON; SADDLE-MOUNT; SECOND FLUTE (1); SHORT B♭ FINGERING; SHORT KEY; SIX-FINGERED NOTE; STANDARD FLUTE (1); STOPPER; THIRD FLUTE (1); *TIEFE QUARTFLÖTE;* TONE-HOLE BUSHING; TONE HOLES (1); TULOU, JEAN-LOUIS; TUNING HEAD; TUNING SLIDE (2); UPPER (MIDDLE) JOINT/PIECE. For other non-Boehm-system flutes, *see also* CARTE 1851 SYSTEM FLUTE; CARTE 1867 SYSTEM FLUTE; GUARDS' MODEL FLUTE; RADCLIFF SYSTEM FLUTE; REFORM FLUTE (1).

2. Any non-Boehm-system flute with six open holes and a small number of noninterlocked keys. This seems to be the way the term is used by modern **Irish flute** players.

3. A European transverse conical flute with one key, the common form in the 18th century. *Cf.* one-keyed flute, Baroque flute.

4. Occasionally, almost any keyless flute with six open finger holes. This type of simple-system flute includes many ethnic flutes (e.g., **bamboo flutes,** *bansuri, dizi,* etc.), **fifes,** and **Renaissance flutes.**

SINGING WHILE PLAYING. *See* GLOTTAL STOP; THROAT TUNING; VOCALIZING/SINGING WHILE PLAYING.

SINGLE CASE. A case that holds one instrument. *See also* COMBINATION CASE; FRENCH-STYLE CASE; GLUE.

SINGLE-SKIN. Refers to key **pads** that are covered by a single layer of **fishskin. Skin**-covered pads are normally, and preferably, made with two skins (*see* DOUBLE-SKIN).

SINGLE TONGUING. A type of **tonguing** where only one syllable is used to tongue the notes in a **passage.** The tongue is moved in the same way as if the **flutist** were saying a syllable such as "tu," "thu," or "du" for each note. For *tu,* the tongue is placed forward in the mouth with the tip touching the upper teeth or gum or the space between the teeth. After silently saying the syllable *tu,* the tongue comes slightly away from the upper teeth or gum to release the air to make a sound. Most **flute** notes are started by single tonguing. When the word *tonguing* is used by itself, it generally refers to single tonguing. *See also* DOUBLE TONGUING; MULTIPLE TONGUING; T (2); TRIPLE TONGUING.

SIX-FINGERED NOTE. The note that sounds when the first three fingers of each hand are covering **tone holes** or are pressing **keys** in **home base.** This may also include any thumb tone hole. This term is mainly used when naming **simple-system flutes.** *See also* E♭ FLUTE; "FLUTE IN . . ." (1); PRINCIPAL RANK.

SIX-KEYED FLUTE. A **simple-system** (or **keyed**) **transverse flute** that evolved from, and was similar to, the earlier wooden (or **ivory**), **conical-bored, one-keyed flute** in D except that it had six **keys** and sometimes an **extended foot joint** to accommodate one or two of the extra keys. It has been revived in modern times, and some people play originals or replicas of the instrument for Classical-period music.

There were two common types of six-keyed flutes (see app. 2, figs. 6 and 7). One was an early English type that appeared just after the mid-18th century and was like the **four-keyed flute** with closed-standing keys (i.e., with one key for D♯, the B♭ key, the G♯ key, and a short or **cross F key**), but with an extended foot joint including the open-standing **low C** and **low C♯ keys,** which were operated with R4. The low C key controlled the C♯ hole and, when closed, produced the note **low C;** the low C♯ key controlled the D hole and, when closed, produced low C♯. This is the type of flute that people generally mean when they speak about the six-keyed flute and the flute that was probably intended for Mozart's 1778 "Concerto in C" for flute and harp.

The other type of six-keyed flute appeared after 1800 and had a **D foot joint.** It included the closed-standing keys of the four-keyed flute named above, but with the addition of a long closed-standing C key for C_2 and C_3 that was operated by R1, and a long closed-standing F key, which was a duplicate for the closed-standing short (or cross) F key and was operated by L4 to facilitate playing F when next to D or E♭, or for passing between F and D or E♭. *See also* CHARANGA FLUTE; CLASSICAL FLUTE; EIGHT-KEYED FLUTE; FIVE-KEYED FLUTE; G♯ KEY (2); MULTIKEYED FLUTE; NINE-KEYED FLUTE; TEN-KEYED FLUTE; TWO-KEYED FLUTE.

SIXTH FLUTE. An 18th-century name for a soprano **recorder** in D (named after the seven-fingered note), a sixth above the modern alto (British: treble) recorder in F. *Cf.* **fourth flute** (4), **fifth flute**, **third flute** (2), **octave flute** (2).

SKIN. *See* FISHSKIN. *See also* DOUBLE SKIN; PAD; PISONI PADS; SINGLE SKIN; STRAUBINGER PAD.

SKIP. Same as **leap**.

SLAP TONGUE. Same as **tongue pizzicato** (2).

SLEEVE. 1. Extension sleeve. *See also* B/C CONVERTIBLE FOOT JOINT. **2.** *See* HEAD-JOINT REFITTING. **3.** May refer to **barrel** (1). **4.** May refer to **box**. **5.** May refer to **key tubing**. **6.** May refer to **tenon protector**. **7.** May refer to **tuning ring**.

SLIDE. 1. *See* TUNING SLIDE. *See also* TUNING RINGS. **2.** *See* GLISSANDO. **3.** *See* GLIDE. **4.** *See* HEAD-JOINT LINING. **5.** *See* PORTAMENTO. **6.** *See* FOOT REGISTER. **7.** *See* ROBERT DICK GLISSANDO HEADJOINT. **8.** *See* IRISH FLUTE.

SLIP FIT. The mating of two parts in such a way that the parts can slide together easily. An example of a slip fit is the **head-joint tenon** that slides into the **barrel** of the **middle joint**. *Cf.* **interference fit**.

SLOP. Same as **play**.

SLUR. A sign instructing the player to connect at least two notes that are different in **pitch** by playing them smoothly. The slur is represented by a curved line that is placed above or below the group of notes to be slurred:

Flutists tongue the first note, and the rest of the notes are blown and **fingered** (i.e., slurred).

   The slur naturally emphasizes the first note of a group, but performers may choose to add to this emphasis. In 18th- and early 19th-century music, a slur was thought of as a diminuendo, and there is evidence that it was common to shorten the last note of a two-note slur. Today, apart from a few exceptions, the last note of a slur is held for its indicated time value, though pairs of slurred notes can be shortened depending on the context.

SLURRED. An instruction to **slur** notes. *Cf.* **tongued**. *See also* APPOGGIATURA; DOUBLE TONGUING; *PRALLTRILLER*; ROCKSTRO MODEL FLUTE; SPLIT F♯ MECHANISM; STACCATO; TRILL; TRIPLE TONGUING; TURN. For **early flutes**, *see also* DUPLICATE KEYS; FOUR-KEYED FLUTE; SCHOLARLY EDITION.

SMALL FLUTE. British term for a **recorder** smaller than the alto in the late Baroque.

SMILE EMBOUCHURE. A type of **embouchure** in which the corners of the mouth are pulled back to look like a smile.

SMORZATO. It. dampened, muffled. A special effect produced by repeatedly moving the lower jaw up and down slightly, as if shivering, while the lips are in their normal playing position. The airflow and **pressure** remain constant, but slight changes in **tone color** will be heard. **Flutists** find it easiest to produce this effect in the middle and upper octaves of the flute. *Smorzato* might be notated as:

See also EXTENDED TECHNIQUE; LIP VIBRATO.

SOCKET. Any **flute** part that receives and holds another part. *Syn.:* **receiver, sleeve**. *See also* BARREL; B/C CONVERTIBLE FOOT JOINT; BOX; BULBOUS HEAD JOINT; FIT (1); HEAD-JOINT LINING; HEAD-JOINT REFITTING; LAPPING; LAURENT, CLAUDE; LEAK; OUT OF ROUND; PIVOT SCREWS; TENON; TENON JOINT; THINNED (HEAD OR BODY) JOINTS. For **early flutes** or other non-**Boehm-system** flutes, *see also* HEAD-JOINT LINING; LAPPING; LINING; ONE-KEYED FLUTE; REVERSE TENON; THICKENING; TIP (3); TUNING HEAD.

SOFT MECHANISM. A **key mechanism** made from a metal **alloy** that is too soft. Soft mechanisms are usually found only on cheaply made modern **flutes**, but may sometimes be found on older flutes (e.g., over 35 years old) in any price range. Flutes with these mechanisms have **keys** that are easily bent from playing use and a mechanism that has a tendency to go out of **adjustment** easily. *Syn.:* delicate mechanism.

SOFT SOLDER. Same as low-temperature **solder**. In the past, when soft solder consisted of lead and tin, it was also called **lead solder**. *See also* BRAZING (1); FLUX; PATCHING; POST-MOUNT; RETUNING; RIB-MOUNT.

SOLDER. A nonferrous metal **alloy** that is used in melted form to join metals together. There are two types of solder used in flutemaking: soft and hard, the latter also called **silver solder**. Previously, **soft solder** consisted of **lead** and tin. Nowadays several lead-free alloys are available, and all melt at relatively low temperatures, generally below 600°F (316°C). **Hard solders** are often complex alloys based on **silver**, also containing copper, zinc, tin, or cadmium, although cadmium is very poisonous and not found in the better silver solders used on **precious metals**. The hard solders melt at a higher temperature, generally when the parts to be joined are red hot.

In general, smaller parts such as the **posts**, **lugs**, and **riser** are hard soldered in place for strength, whereas larger surface areas, such as the **ribs** and usually the **soldered tone holes** are soft soldered. Even though soft solder is weaker, it is necessary for the craftsman to use it where he wants to retain the hardness of a part that would otherwise be softened by the use of high-temperature **soldering**. When joining several parts together, the craftsman may use increasingly softer alloys in succession, starting with the highest-melting-point solder. *See also* AURUMITE; BEAD (2); BODYMAKER; BRAZING; HEAD-JOINT MAKER; HEAD-JOINT REFITTING; PATCHING; RETUNING; SEAMED TUBING; SILVER BRAZING; SILVER FLUTE (3); SPUD; STRINGER; SWEAT; UP TONE-HOLE.

SOLDERED TONE HOLES. Tone holes surrounded by short cylindrical tubes that are made separately from **tubing** and then **soldered** onto the flute **body** (see app. 7, fig. 16, *left*). Soldered tone holes in 19th- and early 20th-century France were also **seamed** (e.g., in **flutes** by **Louis Lot** and **Auguste Bonneville**).

Until the invention of **drawn tone holes** in 1898 by **George W. Haynes**, soldered tone holes were the only type of tone hole seen on metal flutes. For quite some time afterward, soldered tone holes were still seen on more expensive **professional flutes** because it was difficult to draw tone holes out of the thin tubing usually found on these high-quality flutes. As the drawn tone hole process became easier and less expensive, more companies were able to offer the choice of a high-quality flute with or without soldered tone holes. *See also* BOEHM FLUTE (1); CHIMNEY (2); FACTORY-MADE FLUTE; HANDMADE FLUTE; HEAD-JOINT REFITTING; SADDLE (1); SWEAT (1); UNDERCUTTING (2); UP TONE-HOLE; WALL (1).

SOLDERING. In metallurgy, the process of joining two or more close-fitting pieces of metal together with **solder**, a nonferrous **filler** metal that has a melting point below 840°F (449°C). *See also* BRAZING; COLE SCALE; CRYOGENICS; FINISHER; FLUX; SADDLE-MOUNT; SOLDERED TONE HOLES; STRESS RELIEVING.

SOLID. To **flutists** in the United Kingdom, the term *solid*, when referring to **silver**, usually means any type of silver **alloy** that has more than 900 parts per thousand silver. *See* SOLID SILVER.

SOLID CUP/KEY. Same as **closed-hole key/cup/key cup.**

SOLID GOLD. Made from pure **gold** or any type of gold **alloy**. In this sense, the term is usually used when comparing a **gold flute** or part with one that is **gold-plated**.

SOLID SILVER. Made from pure **silver** or any type of silver **alloy**. In this sense, the term is usually used when comparing a **silver flute** or part with one that is **silver-plated**. *See also* SOLID.

SOLO. It. alone. **1.** A **piece** of music to be played or sung by one person. Sometimes there is also an accompaniment. Some famous flute solo pieces are Claude Debussy's "Syrinx" and J. S. Bach's "Partita in A minor," both for **flute** alone. **2.** A performance by one person, with or without accompaniment. The player is then called a **soloist**. *See also* SOLO FLUTIST. **3.** A part of a piece or a significant **passage** for one person in a **work** involving other players. See appendix 14 for a listing of orchestra and opera audition **excerpts** and **cues** (1).

SOLO FLUTIST. A **soloist** who is a **flutist**. *See also* PRINCIPAL FLUTIST (1); SECTION LEADER.

SOLOIST. 1. A musician who plays a **solo**. *See* SOLO (2); SOLO FLUTIST. **2.** Sometimes used to mean the same thing as *principal* (*see* PRINCIPAL FLUTIST).

SONORITÉ. *See* DE LA SONORITÉ.

SOPRANO FLUTE. 1. *See* E♭ FLUTE. **2.** *See* TREBLE FLUTE IN G. **3.** *See* SOPRANO FLUTE IN F.

SOPRANO FLUTE IN F. An uncommon member of the **Boehm flute** family (*see* FLUTE FAMILY [2]) **pitched** in F, sounding a fourth higher than the **concert flute** in C. Like the concert flute, the soprano flute is **side-blown**. It uses the same **fingering system** and, except for small playing changes, is played in a similar way. Its **range** is around three octaves, from the note sounding as F_1 to F_4 (written C_1 to C_4; *see* TRANSPOSING INSTRUMENTS). The length of the soprano flute is about 25 in. (63.5 cm).

Little music has been written for the soprano flute, although it may be heard in some **flute choirs** as it can provide another **tone color** in an **ensemble**. Flute players who are interested in playing Latin music *altissimo* will find the soprano flute in F very useful. *Syn.:* **flute in F, flute in the key of F, flute pitched in F,** treble flute in F. *See also* MEMBRANE HEAD JOINT.

SOUNDING HOLE. The open **tone hole** that determines the effective length of the **flute**. It is usually the first open tone hole down from a series of closed tone holes. For instance, for the note F_1 on the **Boehm flute**, the sounding hole is the one operated by R2 (known by most **flutists** as "the F tone hole under the E **key**"). Opening successive tone holes reduces the effective length of the instrument and raises the **pitch**. The terms *effective length* and *sounding hole* are not conceptually useful for the high **range** of the flute because waves of high **frequency** are less well reflected at open holes (*see* CUTOFF FREQUENCY).

The term *sounding hole* can be misleading since it gives the impression that the flute sound emits from only this location, which is not the case. Much of the power in the flute sound is radiated from the **embouchure hole**, less from the sounding hole, and usually still less from any other tone holes and the end of the **foot joint**.

Sometimes keys are opened as **register holes**: these serve not to shorten the effective length but to weaken a **fundamental resonance**. *Syn.:* speaking hole. *See also* ANTINODE; CLOSED-KEY SYSTEM; DUPLICATE G♯ TONE HOLE (1); FINGER VIBRATO; NODE; OPEN-KEY SYSTEM; SOUNDING LENGTH (1); VEILED TONE (1, 2).

SOUNDING LENGTH. 1. *(Of a note)* The length of the vibrating **air column** from the center of the **embouchure hole** to the middle of the **sounding hole** (i.e., the first open **tone hole** that determines the effective length of the flute) when the **joints** of the flute are fully **home**. For example, for the note E_1, the sounding length is from the middle of the embouchure hole to the middle of the E tone hole.

2. *(Of the flute)* The length of the vibrating air column from the center of the embouchure hole to the end of the **foot joint** when the joints are fully home. Physicists and acousticians feel that this meaning (and the one in def. 1) for the sounding length could be misleading since it gives the impression that the air column vibrates only within the sounding length, which is not the case: the air column also vibrates within the flute **tube** above and below the sounding length (how much above or below depends on any note being played, the **stopper** position, and the player's **embouchure**; *see* END CORRECTION). Because of this, they feel that the sounding length cannot be so precisely defined as is suggested in definitions 1 and 2.

3. *(Of the flute)* Because some researchers regard definition 2 above as misleading, they prefer to measure the length of the vibrating air column from the center of the upper C♯ hole to the center of the lower D♯ hole when the joints are fully home. They feel that this method is more accurate because:

- it can be applied equally to **C foot**, **B foot** and **D foot** flutes;
- it doesn't involve the **head**, whose length can be quite arbitrary when a **tuning slide** is fitted;
- it cannot be confused by head shortening (*see* SHORTENED HEAD JOINT), which was not uncommon in the British High Pitch period (second half of the 19th century for philharmonic purposes, and well into the 20th century for military band use);
- it measures the **pitch** at which the flute plays most **in tune**, not the flute's highest achievable pitch, as does the method in definition 2.

For more information, and a listing of differing flute types giving their typical overall lengths, sounding lengths, and C♯-D♯ lengths, see www.mcgee-flutes.com/flutelengths.htm and www.mcgee-flutes.com/CsharpEb.htm. *Syn.:* speaking length, **acoustical length**. *Cf.* **octave length**.

SOUND SPECTRUM. A representation of a sound—often a short sample of a sound—in terms of the amplitude of vibration at each individual **frequency**. It is usually presented as a graph of the microphone voltage as a function of frequency (this voltage is proportional to the sound **pressure**). The voltage or pressure is often presented on a decibel scale, and the frequency is given in vibrations per second (or **Hertz**, abbr. Hz) or thousands of vibrations per second (kilohertz, abbr. kHz). The sound spectrum can be thought of as a sound recipe, the ingredients usually being the **harmonics** (def. 1) in their various proportions that together make up the particular sound. *See also* HARMONIC SERIES; OVERTONES.

SPACER. Same as **shim**.

SPADE. The overlapping sections of a **clutch**, especially when flattened. *See also* app. 4; BACK-CONNECTOR.

SPATULA. Same as **lever**, except that *spatula* is usually reserved for more broad-shaped lever **keys** such as the D♯ or **low C♯ keys** on the **foot joint** and not keys like the D and D♯ **trill keys** on the **middle joint**. *Syn.:* **touchpiece, touch.** *See also* G♯ KEY (1); ROLLER.

SPEAK. *v.* To sound a note, usually with reference to the ease, or otherwise, with which a note can be started. For example, a **flute** might be said to speak very quickly and easily. *See also* RESPONSE.

SPEAKING HOLE. Same as **sounding hole.**

SPEAKING LENGTH. Same as **sounding length.**

SPECIAL EFFECT. *See* EXTENDED TECHNIQUE.

SPECTACLES. *See BRILLE.*

SPINNING. A process used in flutemaking or repair whereby a **flute** part is shaped by rotating it in a **lathe** against a **burnishing** tool. Examples of flute parts that might be shaped using this process are the **head-joint tenon** and the **key tubing** when they need refitting. For hard-to-reach parts that need refitting, such as between two **keys, swaging** is used. *See also* HEAD-JOINT REFITTING; TELESCOPING (1).

SPLIT. *v.* Same as *crack* (*see* CRACKING [A NOTE]).

SPLIT A KEY. 1. Infrequently used term for a **split F$_\sharp$ mechanism,** so called because the normally mechanically connected B$_\flat$ and A **keys** are not connected to each other (i.e., are split), enabling the use of the A key as in a split F$_\sharp$ mechanism (see fig. 42). *See also* BROSSA F$_\sharp$ LEVER; MURRAY FLUTE. **2.** A special A key that can be made for split F$_\sharp$ mechanisms (see fig. 42, *top*), where it is divided into two keys stacked vertically. There is a lower slim key (called "lower A"), which holds the **pad** and is unconnected to the B$_\flat$ key, and another slim key directly on top of it ("upper A") that functions as a **touchpiece** for the note A and is linked to the B$_\flat$ key. Different means have been devised to depress the lower A as part of a split F$_\sharp$ **venting.** *Syn.:* stacked A keys.

SPLIT EMBOUCHURE. Same as **teardrop embouchure.**

SPLIT E MECHANISM. On a **flute** with a closed G$_\sharp$ **key,** a mechanical link from the E **key** that closes the lower of the two normally connected and open-standing **G keys** onto the **duplicate G$_\sharp$ tone hole** when E$_3$ is played (see app. 9, fig. 4). It is an option offered by flutemakers to improve the venting of E$_3$, making it easier to produce and slightly less **sharp.** The split E mechanism is easier to install on flutes with offset G keys, or on flutes with in-line G keys and either a pinless left-hand mechanism or a completely **pinless mechanism.** A disadvantage, noted by some players, is that it isolates the other two difficult nearby notes, F$_{\sharp 3}$ and G$_{\sharp 3}$, but these notes can be similarly improved by having a **split F$_\sharp$ mechanism** and a **high G$_\sharp$ mechanism** fitted. On the other hand, with proper practice, E$_3$ is not a serious problem.

Since some players find that the split E mechanism can make the playing of certain **trills** (in particular, a good G$_3$/A$_3$ trill) and some specialized **fingerings** found in contemporary music difficult or impossible, a few makers offer a split E mechanism with a special **clutch** device that allows the player to engage or disengage the split E mechanism at will (see app. 9, fig. 5). It will also add cost to the flute.

It is generally accepted that the French flutemaker **Djalma Julliot** invented the split E mechanism around 1900 (reportedly after a suggestion by Paul Taffanel), though there may be evidence to the contrary. **Emil Rittershausen** exhibited a **gold flute** in 1896, which has this mechanism, but there is no evidence as to whether it was added on when the flute was made or later. *Syn.:* E assist, E mech/mechanism, high E facilitator, split E, **split G keys.** *See also* BOEHM FLUTE (1); BRIDGE; EXTENSION ARM; G/A TRILL KEY (1); G$_\sharp$ KEY (1); LOWER G INSERT; MODEL NUMBER; ORCHESTRAL MODEL FLUTE; PROFESSIONAL FLUTE; REGISTER (1); RF MODIFICATION; SPLIT MECHANISM; STUDENT FLUTE. For non-**Boehm-system** flutes, *see also* RADCLIFF SYSTEM FLUTE.

SPLIT FINGERING. Same as **fork fingering** or **cross-fingering.**

SPLIT F$_\sharp$ MECHANISM. A nonstandard **key mechanism** that improves the **venting** of F$_{\sharp 3}$ by closing the lower of the normally connected and open B$_\flat$ and A **keys** when F$_{\sharp 3}$ is played. This allows the note to be sustained more securely and **articulated** more easily, and it facilitates secure, even **slurs** between B$_2$ and F$_{\sharp 3}$ and between F$_{\sharp 2}$ and F$_{\sharp 3}$.

There is no standard split F$_\sharp$ mechanism, various configurations having been tried over the past hundred years. For example, flutemaker **Albert Cooper** (b.1924) has designed a split F$_\sharp$ by converting the traditional **B$_\flat$ side lever** into a high **F$_\sharp$ side lever** and replacing the standard A key with stacked A keys (modified key **cups,** one stacked vertically above the other and individually named the "upper A" and "lower A" keys; see fig. 42, *top*). To finger F$_{\sharp 3}$ as a split F$_\sharp$, the player uses the basic **fingering** but depresses the high F$_\sharp$ side lever with R1 (instead of the D key with R3). When the lever is depressed, it closes the **padded** lower A key onto the B$_\flat$ **tone hole** and the F$_\sharp$ key onto the G tone hole. The normal A$_{1/2}$ **fingering** is retained because the upper A key is linked to the B$_\flat$ key and, when activated, depresses this key and the lower A

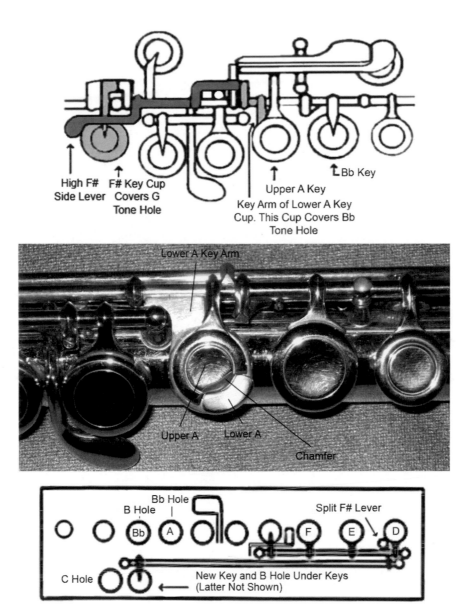

Figure 42. The Split F♯ mechanisms by Albert Cooper *(top)* and William Simmons *(middle)*, and the Simmons F♯ key *(bottom)*. Drawings by Tess Vincent; photo courtesy Andrew Lane.

key. The high $F_\sharp$ side lever may also be used instead of the D key to finger $F_{\sharp_1}$ and $F_{\sharp_2}$ when convenient.

Another example is on the open **$G_\sharp$ keyed Murray flute**, where a special $F_\sharp$ lever between the E and $D_\sharp$ tone holes closes the same tone holes as that of Cooper's high $F_\sharp$ side lever (see fig. 27). For the new $F_\sharp$ fingering in all three octaves, the player uses R4 on the $F_\sharp$ lever. (R4 is not required to open the $D_\sharp$ tone hole for this note on a Murray flute and so is free for the lever.) In the left hand, the player fingers $F_{\sharp_3}$ in the usual way for an open $G_\sharp$ keyed flute.

British flutemaker William Simmons (b. 1945) designed a mechanically simpler split $F_\sharp$ in 2002. As in Cooper's design, it has stacked A keys, but Simmons used a smaller upper A key, leaving room to directly press the raised outer edge of the A key beneath it with L2 (see fig. 42, *middle*). To finger $F_{\sharp_3}$ as a split $F_\sharp$, the player uses the regular fingering but also shuts the lower A key using L2.

Care needs to be taken in choosing the design to incorporate, as its addition may add weight and alter the balance when in playing position. Some designs such as those operated automatically using the standard fingering from the D key, in which the player does not have to learn any new fingering for top $F_\sharp$, may make one or two **trills** or fingerings difficult or impossible and may be detrimental to the tone of those notes (e.g., the **trill fingering** for $F_3/F_{\sharp_3}$ and the **sharper** fingering for $B\flat_3$—i.e., any fingering using the D key that does not need the A key closed). For these designs, a split $F_\sharp$ mechanism **clutch** device can often be ordered, which allows the player to engage or disengage the mechanism at will, thus alleviating any fingering or tonal problems when the mechanism is disengaged.

To achieve the full correction to the traditional venting of $F_{\sharp_3}$, if the chosen split $F_\sharp$ mechanism does not already close the $F_\sharp$ key without having to close the D key, a **Brossa $F_\sharp$** or **Rockstro $F_\sharp$ lever** is also required.

With most split $F_\sharp$ mechanisms, the player will lose the open hole in the A key. However, the **Simmons $F_\sharp$ key** (1995) has been designed to enable the venting of a split $F_\sharp$ without splitting the A key from the $B\flat$ key, thus not losing any **open-hole key** (see fig. 42, *bottom*). *Syn.:* split A mechanism. *See also* BOEHM FLUTE (1); PROFESSIONAL FLUTE; SPLIT A KEY; SPLIT E MECHANISM; SPLIT MECHANISM.

SPLIT G KEYS. For a **flute** with a closed $G_\sharp$ key, a term used infrequently to mean the same thing as a **split E mechanism** and so called because the normally mechanically connected **G keys** can move independently from each other.

SPLIT MECHANISM. A special **key mechanism** designed to eliminate the acoustical problem resulting from the mechanics of double **venting** in the **third register** of the **flute** (i.e., two **tone holes** open between closed tone holes when one open would be better acoustically). Unfortunately, the notes E_3, $F_{\sharp_3}$, and $G_{\sharp_3}$ are double vented on a closed $G_\sharp$ key flute (only $F_{\sharp_3}$ and $G_{\sharp_3}$ on an open $G_\sharp$ key flute) due to the mechanical design that makes other chromatic notes workable. Specialty mechanisms (although sometimes complicated) are required to correct these anomalies with varying degrees of success. On **piccolos** and flutes with a double vented $G_{\sharp_3}$, a nonsplit mechanism called a **high $G_\sharp$ mechanism** can be ordered. *See also* MODEL NUMBER; SPLIT E MECHANISM; SPLIT $F_\sharp$ MECHANISM.

SPLIT TONE. *See* MULTIPHONIC.

SPOON FLUTE. The first **flute** made by flutemaker **Verne Q. Powell** in 1910. It was made from three **silver** watch cases, seven silver teaspoons (hence the name of the flute), and a handful of plugged silver half-dollars. Powell had been motivated to make a flute after hearing **Georges Barrère** perform with the New York Symphony on a silver **Louis Lot** flute in the summer of 1910. Having learned of Powell's homemade silver flute, **William S. Haynes** sent for the flute to examine it and was so impressed that he hired the young Powell to make **silver flutes** for him in Boston. Powell's Spoon Flute has no **serial number** and is currently with his family.

SPRING. A small flexible device fitted to a flute **key** to keep it open or closed until the key is operated. There are two kinds: needle and flat. However, coil springs and even magnetic repulsion (*see* MATIT CARBON-FIBER FLUTE) have been used to produce the same results.

The majority of springs on the **Boehm flute** are of the *needle spring* variety. They look like short needles, and each is attached through a small hole in a key **post**, its other end hooked under a retaining projection called a **spring catch** (see app. 7, fig. 5). Needle springs were invented by **Auguste Buffet *jeune*** just prior to the middle of the 19th century. They are made from carbon **steel** that has been blued by **heat treatment**, stainless **steel**, **white gold**, phosphor-bronze, and beryllium copper, the best material being that which allows a light but positive **action**. Although many flute players prefer the snappy action of blued-steel needle springs, these are not, for the most part, used on modern flutes because they are not rustproof. They also have a reputation for breaking easily when brittle, but this is perhaps undeserved since if they are **tempered** correctly and free of rust, they should not get brittle. **Pitting** caused by rust will often cause failure, but under good conditions, they will last very well. Stainless-steel springs can be designed to have the same snappy action, are rustproof, and can be adjusted easily without breakage. Springs made of white gold are the most expensive type of spring, but they are less likely to break than the other types. Beryllium copper and phosphor-bronze springs are the most common type of springs used for **student flutes** and are inexpensive. *Syn.:* pin springs.

Flat springs operate **one-keyed** and **simple-system flutes** and are still used for the Briccialdi thumb keys (*see* BRICCIALDI B♭ LEVER) on most modern flutes. *Syn.:* leaf spring.

See also BRÖGGER SYSTEM; CLOSED KEY; COLD DRAWING; CYLINDRICAL BOEHM FLUTE (1); DORUS G♯ KEY; FINISHER; GLASS FLUTE; INTERMEDIATE FLUTE; LUG; OPEN KEY; PLAYING CONDITION; POST-MOUNT; PROFESSIONAL FLUTE; RING-KEY FLUTE; SPRING HOOK. For **early flutes** and other non-**Boehm-system** flutes, *see also* BLOCK-MOUNT; POST-MOUNT; REFORM FLUTE (1); SALT-SPOON KEY.

SPRING CATCH/HOLDER. One of the many tiny hooklike parts on the **flute** that holds a needle **spring** (see app. 7, fig. 5). *Syn.:* **lug** catch, **spring hook**, spring holder.

SPRING HOOK. 1. Same as **spring catch. 2.** The tool used to engage or disengage needle **springs** on flute **key mechanisms**, usually made from a small crochet hook.

SPUD. A small postlike fixture that is usually **soldered** to, or integral with, the inside center part of a large **closed-hole key cup** to help hold a **pad** in place in the **cup** and ensure that the center of the pad is airtight (see app. 7, fig. 9). The centers of some pads are held in place by pad snaps, which are snapped through the pad and into a **fluted** spud; others are held in place by screw-over-**washer** combinations that are screwed through the pad and into a threaded spud. *Syn.:* pad nut.

A newer method of retaining the pads has been developed by **Jim Schmidt** in 2002. It consists of one magnet that is permanently fixed to the bottom of the cup. The pad is then held within the cup by a second magnet that is attached to a pad-retaining washer. The second magnet draws the washer tightly against the pad. According to Schmidt, this method gives the pad a uniform amount of pressure, and it is easy for a flute technician to remove and replace for repeated **shimming**. Schmidt calls his contrivance a *magnetic retainer*. For **open-hole key cups,** *see* FRENCH BUSHING.

SQUAREONE FLUTE. The SquareONE flute is a modified **Boehm flute** with square **tone holes** and **keys** designed by **Leonard Lopatin** in 1989. It is his belief that the straight edge of the tone hole on his **flute** provides a better vent than the curved edge of the circular tone hole on the traditional Boehm flute and creates a truly uniform length of **air column**. Lopatin claims that the air column arrives at all points along the **leading edge** of the tone hole at the same time, rather than at different times as it does on the traditional flute. He also feels that this improves the **response** and clarity. The increase in tone hole size or **venting** area for the right-hand **section** and **foot joint** that results when square tone holes are used is said to improve the volume of the **lowest notes**. *See also* TUNING RINGS.

STACCATO. It. detached, separated. Staccato notes are distinctly separated. Staccato is shown by a small dot placed above or below a notehead

and less frequently by the word *staccato* or the abbreviation *stacc.* under the staff. Before about 1800, the staccato dots had a variety of meanings, as did most musical signs, depending on the country and the composer. Staccato is considered to be the opposite of *legato*. Modern staccato has two distinct variants: *mezzo-staccato* and *staccatissimo*.

Mezzo-staccato directs the player to perform notes in a moderately separated manner. When there is only one note to be played mezzo-staccato, it may be shown as a short horizontal line with a dot above or below each notehead:

When there are several notes that are to be played mezzo-staccato, this is shown by dots above or below each notehead and a **slur** over or under the dots:

Some describe this notation as "bell notes" or "**bell tones**." Mezzo-staccato is referred to by many other names: legato-slur, *louré*, half-staccato, non-legato, semi-staccato, slurred staccato, semi-legato, legato-staccato, mezzo-legato, and *portato*.

Staccatissimo is the most emphatic form of staccato. It directs the player to perform notes in as separated a manner as possible. Since around 1800, staccatissimo has been shown by a wedge placed above or below a note:

Overall, the exact length of a staccato, mezzo-staccato, or staccatissimo note depends on the style

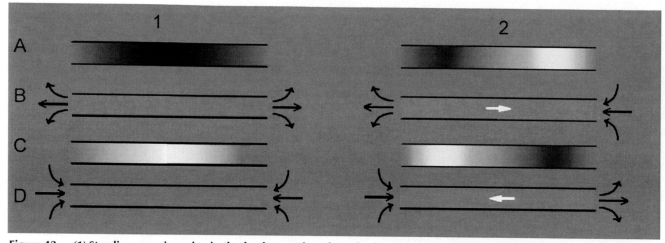

Figure 43. *(1)* Standing wave in a pipe in the fundamental mode at the first resonance or first harmonic frequency. Flutists would usually relate this figure to the notes up to C$_{\#2}$. *(2)* Standing wave in a pipe in the second mode at the second resonance or harmonic frequency. Flutists would usually relate this figure to the notes from D$_2$ to C$_{\#3}$.

and context of the music in which it is found. Staccato may also be referred to as *détaché*. *See also* EXTENDED TECHNIQUE.

STACK. Same as **section** (2).

STAMP. *v.* To shape or cut out a **flute** part by striking **sheet metal** between two **dies**. *See also* HEAD-JOINT MAKER.

STAMPING. A part, such as a key **cup**, that is made by a flutemaker using a stamping process (*see* STAMP). *See also* HEAD-JOINT MAKER; SERIAL NUMBER.

STANDARD FLUTE. 1. As the term is used in this book, the standard **flute** in use at a given time. Today, this flute is the **concert** or **Boehm flute** in C (named after the note that sounds when C is fingered). Historically, it was the **simple-system flute** in D (named after the **six-fingered note**). *Syn.:* **ordinary flut**e. *See also* FOURTH FLUTE (1); MURRAY FLUTE; OCTAVE FLUTE (1); QUINT FLUTE (1); SECOND FLUTE (1); SIDE KEY/LEVER (1). For **early flutes**, *see also* FOURTH FLUTE (1); GERMAN FLUTE (1); OCTAVE FLUTE (1); SECOND FLUTE (1); *TIEFE QUART-FLÖTE;* VOICE FLUTE (2). **2.** Some modern flute manufacturers use the term "standard-model flute" to mean the same thing as a **student flute.**

STANDARD-MODEL FLUTE. *See* STANDARD FLUTE (2); STUDENT FLUTE.

STANDING WAVE. A type of sound wave in which the patterns of sound **pressures** and acoustic or oscillating displacement flows are stationary. This means that the vibration amplitude at any point does not change in time, but depends only on the point's position. Figure 43 shows schematically how the pressures and displacements behave for a standing wave in a **pipe** with two open ends. This corresponds approximately to the situation in the **flute** for a **first-register fingering**, in which the **embouchure hole** provides one open end and the first open **finger hole** the other. In the diagrams, dark shading represents a pressure greater than atmospheric (positive sound pressure) and light shading represents pressure below atmospheric (negative sound pressure). The arrows show the location and direction of the displacement (flow).

Figure 43, #1, shows the standing wave in a pipe in the fundamental **mode** at the first **resonance** or first **harmonic frequency**. Flutists would usually relate this figure to the notes up to C$_{\#2}$. Figure 43, #1A, depicts the moment when all motion has ceased. There is no flow anywhere, but there is positive pressure in the air around the middle of the pipe (dark shading). At this instant, the pressure is exerting its maximum push on the air at either side, which is just beginning to move. A quarter of a cycle later (#1B), the pressure has done its job; it is now everywhere zero, and flow is maximum out either end. Because the air has inertia, it continues to flow, reducing the pressure in the middle so that, by the end of the second quarter cycle, the sound pressure in the middle is at its most negative, as shown by the light shading in #1C. The flow has ceased. The process now reverses, the negative sound pressure sucking the air in so that, by the end of the third quarter-cycle, the flow into the ends is maximum and the pressure is again zero. Then the inward flow continues (#1D) until the situation reverts to that in #1A and the cycle repeats. Notice that there is never any flow in the middle of the pipe; there is a *flow* or *velocity node* at that point. Velocity **antinodes** (maximum flow) are located at the two open ends of the pipe, as shown by the arrows there.

Figure 43, #2, shows the standing wave in a pipe in the second mode at the second resonance or harmonic frequency. Flutists would usually relate this figure to the notes from D$_2$ to C$_{\#3}$. Figure 43, #2A, shows the pattern for the second mode or harmonic. The procedure is the same as in figure 43, #1, except that the frequency is doubled, and two half-size patterns, 180° out of phase in time, occupy the pipe. In #2A, a positive sound pressure appears in the left half of the pipe and, at the same instant, a negative sound pressure in the right half. There is no flow anywhere. In the middle, the pressure is exactly zero, and the sound pressure there will remain zero all during the cycle; there is a *pressure node* at that point. For the notes D2 and D#2 the C# hole is close to this point and flutists take advantage of this by opening it to assure sounding in the second **register**. Other pressure nodes are at the two open ends. Pressure antinodes (maximum pressure) are located where the shading is dark and light. Each half of the pipe proceeds just as in figure 43, #1, through #2B, #2C, and #2D, except that instead of an open end in the middle, each half feeds its flow into the other half.

STANESBY, THOMAS, JR. (b. London, ca. 1692; d. Brompton [now part of London], 1754). An English **woodwind** maker whose business thrived in London from after 1713 until about 1754. Many of his English Baroque woodwind instruments have survived. *See also* FLÛTE D'AMOUR; REVERSE TENON; ROSEWOOD.

STEEL. 1. A hard, tough, malleable metal **alloy** that contains mostly iron with up to about 2 percent carbon, plus other elements such as silicon and manganese. Flutemakers use steel mainly for making axles (called *steels*), **pins**, **pivot screws**, and **springs**.

The properties of steel vary widely according to its constituents, in particular its carbon content. A *low-carbon* or *"mild" steel* might be used on cheaper **flutes** for such parts as pivot screws and steels. A better alternative would be a hardenable *medium-* or *high-carbon steel*. When hardened and **tempered** to a blue color, this has been much used in the past for needle **springs**, whereas nowadays more expensive instruments would make use of *stainless steel* for its resistance to **corrosion**. This contains high proportions of chromium and **nickel**, is extremely tough, and retains its **polish** indefinitely under normal conditions. It is also available as hard wire, suitable for springs. All steels are considerably lighter, tougher, and harder than the **precious metals** used for flute **bodies**.

Stainless steel is used by at least one flutemaker, **Stephen Wessel** (b.1945), to make lighter, more responsive

keys (*see* inlaying [2]) and by another, **Leonard Lopatin** (b.1954), to make **head joints**. *See also* app. 4; BLOCK-MOUNT; FLAT SPRING; NICKEL-SILVER FLUTE; PINNED MECHANISM; QUENCHING; ROLLER; SILVER FLUTE (1); TEMPER (1). **2.** A steel rod or axle. *See also* STEELS.

STEEL ROD. Same as **steels**.

STEELS. The cylindrical steel rods or axles inside the **key tubing** of the flute **key mechanism**. On modern **Boehm flutes** with a **pinned mechanism**, steel pins are used to mount the keywork via key tubing over the **tone holes** (see app. 7, fig. 5). For some keys, the key tubing rotates along with the keys about a stationary steel. For other keys, the steel rotates within the key tubing and connects the movements of keys that are pinned or screwed to the steel. Traditionally, pivot screws are then used to hold this mechanism to the flute using **posts**.

Steels may be made out of mild, carbon, or stainless **steel** (1). Stainless steel is preferable because it is resistant to rust.

There are many designs for ends of steels; see appendix 7, figure 14, for some examples. *Syn.:* axles, hinge-rods, mechanism rods, rods, rod-axles, shafts, steel rods. *See also* app. 4; ALCOHOL; BODYMAKER; BUSHING (1); CLUTCH (1); CYLINDRICAL BOEHM FLUTE (1); FINISHER; G KEYS; GLUE; NICKEL-SILVER FLUTE; ONE-PIECE CORE BAR; PILOT TIP; PIN (1); PINLESS MECHANISM; PIVOT; PIVOT POINT; PIVOT SCREWS; POST-MOUNT; REAM; ROD SCREW; ROLLER; SECTION (2); SILVER FLUTE (1); STRINGER; SWAGING; VERTICAL FLUTE.

STEP. 1. A raised steplike part of the interior tube **wall** of some wooden **flutes**, producing a relatively sudden reduction in **bore** diameter (compared to the more gradual taper of the bore). It is intended to improve the **intonation** and tone of defective notes. *See also* CHAMBERING. **2.** A sudden drop in the bore at the top of the **body** of a wooden **conical flute** when compared to the **head** bore. Conical flutes are traditionally made this way in order to adjust the **tuning** of the **first octave** with the **second octave** notes. **3.** The small but abrupt expansion in the bore below the head-joint **tenon** when the **head joint** is extended out from the **middle joint**. *See* TUNING RINGS. *Syn.:* choke.

STEP-UP FLUTE. 1. The first better-quality **flute** above a standard **student flute**, with some parts made from **silver** instead of the usual **nickel-silver** or yellow **brass** with **silver-** or **nickel-plating**. Depending on the make and model, it may have more options not usually offered with student models, such as the **B foot joint** or **open-hole keys**. **2.** Any flute that is of better quality than the one currently owned, although the term does not usually apply to **professional flutes**. *Cf.* **intermediate flute**.

STERLING SILVER. Silver that contains 92.5 percent silver and 7.5 percent copper (*cf.* **Britannia silver, coin silver**). *Syn.:* **silver 925**, standard silver (after its use as a monetary standard). *See also* AURUMITE; DENSITY; HALLMARK; SILVER FLUTE; SOLID; SOLID SILVER.

STICKY PADS. Key **pads** that have become sticky due to an accumulation of foreign matter on the surface of the pad or **tone-hole rim**. The stickiness makes a clicking sound when the pad is released from the tone hole and, if overly sticky, may even cause technical unevenness. Should the need arise, pads may be cleaned by a competent repairer or by the **flutist** after proper instruction. Note that while some of the pad-cleaning methods usually do work, the more the pads are touched, the more likely that they will be damaged, their life will be reduced, and they will need replacing. *See also* BLIP NOTE.

STOP. 1. *v.* To cover the **embouchure hole** completely with the lower lip, the tongue, or the curved part of the chin directly below the lower lip. Stopping is a flute **technique** used when producing some special effects. For example, when a **flutist** stops the embouchure hole while doing an unblown **key slap**, the **pitch** is lower than what it would be if the embouchure hole were uncovered for that key slap. Another example is when the flutist stops the embouchure hole with the tongue and then opens it to do a **jet whistle**, resulting in a more explosive start to the jet whistle. *See also* TONGUE CLICK. **2. Key** stop. An alternative name for **kicker** (see app. 7, fig. 5). *See also* ROCKSTRO MODEL FLUTE. **3.** The head or top part of a screw. *See* PIVOT SCREW. **4.** An alternative name for **bumper**. **5.** Half-stopped. *See* HALF-HOLING. **6.** *See* DOUBLE STOP; TRIPLE STOP. **7.** *See* TONGUE STOP. **8.** *See* STOPPER. **9.** *See* STOPPER ASSEMBLY. **10.** *See* STOPPER PLATES. **11.** *See* STOP PLATE. **12.** *v.* To cover a **tone hole** with the finger, key, or key **pad**. *See also* PEWTER PLUGS; PURSE PAD. **13.** *v.* To fill a tone hole or other flute part with wax or some other substance. *See also* app. 11; FLAGEOLET (1); *FLÛTE À NEUF TROUS*; PANPIPES.

STOPPER. A plug inside flute **head joints** near the closed end. It is often made of **cork** and is used to create a small volume of air adjacent to the **embouchure hole** (*see* HELMHOLTZ RESONATOR). The **resonance** characteristics of this cavity act to offset the characteristics of the embouchure hole (i.e., as the **frequency** rises, the **impedance** of the stopper cavity drops and offsets the rising impedance of the embouchure hole, which would otherwise cause a **flattening** effect) and so keeps the **third register**

in tune with the lower (i.e., allows an adjustment to the **third octave** notes D_3 and above).

There are several varieties of stoppers. Most modern **Boehm flutes** have a metal-faced cork stopper, often referred to as the **head-joint cork**. Some use alternative stoppers such as a nonelastic material sealed with an **O-ring** (e.g., the "**Bigio Crown and Stopper**"). Early **simple-system transverse flutes** had a simple stopper made of cork. A more elaborate stopper made of cork with an embedded screw, the **screw-cork**, was introduced in the second half of the 18th century. In a **bamboo flute**, a naturally occurring "**node**" of the bamboo is often utilized as the stopper.

For those stoppers that are connected to the **cap** or **crown** with a screw mechanism, rotating the cap or crown alters the volume of the stopper cavity, permitting players to optimize the third-octave **response** to suit their personal **internal tuning** of the instrument's **embouchure** characteristics. A **flutist** whose octaves are narrow can push the cork in a little (and withdraw the **tuning slide** to keep overall **tuning**) to correct the problem. A player with wide octaves can pull the cork out and push the slide in, experimenting until both the overall and internal tuning are correct.

Syn.: end plugs, head stoppers, plugs. Stoppers made of cork may also be called *corks, cork plugs, cork stoppers, end corks, head corks,* or *tuning corks*. *See also* CLEANING ROD; CORK ASSEMBLY (2); CORK PLATES; CORK SCREW; FAJARDO WEDGEHEAD; HEAD-JOINT MAKER; LEAK; OLNHAUSEN RING; "O"-RING (2); RETUNING; SEAL; SOUNDING LENGTH (2); TURNING. For **early flutes** and other non-Boehm-system flutes, *see also* CORK ASSEMBLY (2); ONE-KEYED FLUTE; RING-KEY FLUTE.

STOPPER ASSEMBLY. Same as **cork assembly**.

STOPPER PLATES. Same as **cork plates**.

STOP PLATE. 1. Same as **lug**. *See also* CLUTCH (1). **2.** Same as **cork plate**. *Syn.:* stopper plate.

STRAIGHT-BLOWN FLUTE. Same as **end-blown flute**.

STRAIGHT HEAD JOINT. A **head joint** with no curves, bends, or twists in the **tubing**. It is the most common type of head joint used for **flutes** in the **Boehm flute** family (*see* FLUTE FAMILY [2]). The **concert flute** usually has a straight head joint. *See also* ALTO FLUTE; ANGLED HEAD JOINT; CURVED HEAD JOINT; VERTICAL HEAD JOINT.

STRAP. Same as **rib**. *See also* RIB-MOUNT.

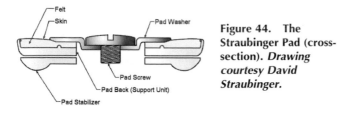

Figure 44. The Straubinger Pad (cross-section). *Drawing courtesy David Straubinger.*

STRAUBINGER, DAVID (b. Macomb, Ohio, 1941). An American maker of **Boehm flutes**, **flute** designer, oboe player, and flute/**piccolo**/clarinet **pad** designer. *See also* STRAUBINGER PAD.

STRAUBINGER™ PAD. A type of modern key **pad** invented and patented by **David Straubinger** as an alternative to the **traditional pad**. It is designed specifically for high-quality **flutes** because of the demands on stability and **adjustment** of the **key mechanism** and because of the expense of the pads and fitting. It consists of a backing disc having an inner and outer rim with a recess between for accommodating the synthetic-fiber **felt cushion**. A sealing **skin** (**fishskin**) is stretched over the entire assembly and is folded around the backside of the backing disc, where it is then glued. The inner and outer rims give support to the skin, and the skin controls the flatness and height of the cushion. Figure 44 shows a cross-section of the Straubinger Pad.

Like the traditional pad, the Straubinger Pad is adjusted and brought to its correct height with **shims**. Unlike the traditional pad, however, the Straubinger Pad rests on a flat plastic stabilizing base, which is secured to the cup with special glue. This adds stability to the pad.

The Straubinger Pad was introduced to the flute world in 1985 and is highly acclaimed for its ability to stay in adjustment once correctly fitted into the key **cup**. According to Straubinger, the improved **seal** of the pad allows the flute to **respond** much more quickly, permits improved finger **technique** since only the lightest **touch** is needed to close a key, and gives more flexibility in dynamics and **tone color**.

To achieve maximum results from the Straubinger Pad, a flute must be in excellent mechanical adjustment. Similar Straubinger Pads have been designed specifically for the **piccolo** and the clarinet.

STRESS RELIEVING. In the metals and wood industries, a process of reducing internal residual stresses in objects. In the metals industry, internal residual stresses in metal objects are relieved by using **heat treatment** or deep-freezing (*see* CRYOGENICS) to restore the grain structure to its usual uniform pattern. During flutemaking or **flute** repair, stress is induced in the metal by **soldering**, bending, hammering, and so on. The stresses will in-

evitably try to equalize themselves if action is not taken, possibly resulting in warping or sometimes metal fracture (especially in **gold**) or in a noticeable flaring of the end of the **tubes** (in both **silver** and gold) when it is cut to length. Metals are stressed-relieved (usually **annealed**) by flutemakers to make them workable and to avoid such problems. Some makers believe that this treatment improves the playing qualities of the **flute**, as well. The specifics of how to stress-relieve a metal part goes beyond the scope of this book. *See also* HEAD-JOINT MAKER.

Shrinkage that takes place as wood dries can leave it with internal stresses that will cause movement or warping once the center of the timber is bored out. For this reason, good flutemakers bore their material months or years ahead of time and leave it for **seasoning** or use artificially induced humidity cycling to speed up the process. Seasoning can thus be seen as a form of stress-relief. But some stresses are not so easily dealt with, particularly those caused by the presence of reaction wood in trees that have not grown vertically. Wooden flutemakers have reported some success in overcoming the tendency of **boxwood** in particular to bend using treatments involving levels of heat and moisture well beyond what would normally be encountered in seasoning.

STRETCHING. The process of extending metal to make it cover an unwanted gap or to partially re-cover a hole. This can be done either by working the metal with a hardened steel **burnishing** tool or gently hammering the edges in a downward and sideways motion with a small flat-faced hammer to make it cover more area. During the stretching process, the worked metal becomes thinner and harder. Flutes are usually made of very malleable metals such as **silver** or **nickel-silver**, but before any working, the metal usually needs to be made more malleable by a process called *annealing*. Stretching may be used when repairing a badly damaged flute, **retuning** a flute, or during **head-joint refitting**. *Cf.* **inlaying** (1), **patching**.

STRIKE EDGE. Same as **blowing edge**.

STRIKE PLATE. An intermediate or **bonding** plate, such as copper, that is applied to a **base metal** and followed by a final **plating** layer. It is used to improve the adhesion of some plating to a base metal. For example, before **silver-plating** can be put on a **nickel-silver flute** tube, a copper strike is applied to the base metal.

STRIKE WALL. Same as **blowing wall**.

STRINGER. The craftsman in a flutemaking company who specializes in making and mounting the **keywork** for a new **flute**. Depending on the company and the materials used, the stringer may:

- cut pieces of **key tubing** to an appropriate starting length
- prepare the **key** parts (key **cups**, **levers**, **arms**, **kickers**, etc.) by filing, bending, and doing some preliminary **polishing**
- **solder** cups to the arms
- solder levers and kickers to the key tubing
- fit the free ends of the arms to the key tubing such that the cups are correctly positioned above the **tone holes** and then solder them in place
- fit the key tubing between the **posts** with the other parts now permanently attached
- make the **steel** rods by taking drill rod of the correct diameter and cutting it to the correct length, threading one end of each steel and slotting the other, or making an external cone on one end and an internal one on the other, as required (see app. 7, #14)
- **ream** out the key tubing to run freely on the **steels**
- pin those keys that need to be pinned to the steels
- solder those keys that need to be soldered to the steels
- make the keys run freely on the steels and the steels run freely between the posts.

The stringer then hands the flute to the **finisher** and repeats the process with another flute. *Cf.* **bodymaker**, finisher, **head-joint maker**.

STUDENT FLUTE. The least expensive **factory-made flute**, designed for beginners. Most of the flute is made from **nickel-silver** or yellow **brass** with **silver-plating** or **nickel-plating**. It usually has **closed-hole keys**, offset G keys, a closed G♯ key, a B♭ **side lever**, Y-arms (*see* KEY ARMS), **drawn** (and **rolled**) **tone holes**, a **head-joint cork**, **adjustment screws**, a **pinned mechanism**, and a **C foot joint**. Optional **keys** and parts, such as **open-hole keys**, in-line G keys, a **split E mechanism**, or a **B foot joint** may be available, depending on the make and model. If there is a B foot, a **gizmo key** is not necessarily present.

Student flutes are designed for easy **response** and durability. Students with a smaller build can obtain a concert flute with a **curved head joint**, which may come without **trill keys** and **low C** and **low C♯ keys** to lessen the weight. *Syn.:* beginner flute, entry-level flute, low-end flute, standard-model flute. *See also* BASE METAL (2); E♭ FLUTE; EMBOUCHURE RECUT; INTERMEDIATE FLUTE; PAD IMPRESSION; PISONI PADS; PLATING; PROFESSIONAL FLUTE; SPRING; STANDARD FLUTE (2); STEP-UP FLUTE.

STUDY. A musical composition that is played in order to learn a certain aspect of music or a musical instrument **technique**. For example, a **flute** study may contain an abundance of notes that involve using R3 and R4 to help the player obtain independence of these fingers. Many studies are meant to be played only for the player's benefit, but some sound so musically satisfying that they are also performed in concerts. A study may be referred to by its French equivalent, *étude*. Some of the most famous flute study books were composed by flutists **Joachim Andersen** and **Marcel Moyse**.

STUFFED PAD. Same as **purse pad**.

STYLED KEY. A **key** with a French-pointed arm. *See* KEY ARM.

SUBBASS FLUTE. Any **flute** that is **pitched** below the traditional **bass flute** in C, although the term is usually reserved for those flutes that are pitched in the octave just below the standard bass flute (e.g., bass flute [def. 4] in F, **contr'alto flute in G**, **contrabass flute** in C) or to those bass flutes whose **range** extends into the octave below the traditional bass flute (e.g., upright bass flute [def. 3] in C until G, **Pinchofon**). The flutes pitched in the octave below the subbass flutes often use the prefix *subcontra-* (see SUBCONTRABASS FLUTE IN C; SUBCONTR'ALTO FLUTE IN G). *See also* FLAUTONE.

SUBCONTRABASS FLUTE IN C. The lowest-pitched, largest, and least common member of the **Boehm flute** family (*see* FLUTE FAMILY [2]), **pitched** in C, sounding two octaves lower than the **bass flute** in C and three octaves lower than the **concert flute** in C. The subcontrabass flute is held almost vertically, but has a horizontal **head joint**. It uses the same **fingering system** as the concert flute and is played in a similar way, though it is more of a challenge to play because more air is required to produce the sound, and **attacks** are delayed. Its **range** is roughly three octaves, from the note sounding as CC to C_1 (written as C_1 to C_4; *see* TRANSPOSING INSTRUMENTS). It is approximately four times the length of the bass flute at about 16.8 ft. (5.12 m) in length, so it is necessary not only for the flute to be held vertically, but for the **tubing** to be bent to make the instrument easier to play (see app. 6, fig. 8). The effective length, or height, is about 7.3 ft. (2.23 m).

The subcontrabass flute was developed in the latter part of the 20th century. It is too soon to say whether it will become a commonly played instrument, as its **projection** is limited without amplification. It has been used in recordings, studio work, and **ensembles** such as **flute choirs**, but it is not a regular member of a band or an orchestra. *Syn.:* double contrabass flute, octocontrabass flute in C. *See also* FLAUTONE; "FLUTE IN . . ."; SUBBASS FLUTE; VERTICAL FLUTE.

SUBCONTR'ALTO FLUTE IN G. An uncommon member of the **Boehm flute** family (*see* FLUTE FAMILY [2]), **pitched** in G, sounding two octaves lower than the **alto flute** in G and two and a half octaves lower than the **concert flute** in C. The subcontr'alto flute is held vertically, but has a horizontal **head joint**. It uses the same **fingering system** as the concert flute and is played in a similar way, though it is more of a challenge to play because more air is required to produce the sound, and **attacks** are delayed. Its **range** is around three octaves from the note sounding as GG to G_1 (written as C_1 to C_4; *see* TRANSPOSING INSTRUMENTS).

It is almost four times the length of the alto flute at about 10.8 ft. (3.30 m), so it is necessary not only for the flute to be held vertically but also for the **tubing** at the head end to be bent into a large figure-4 shape (*see* VERTICAL HEAD JOINTS) to make the instrument easier to play (see app. 6, fig. 7). The height of the instrument, from the open end to the highest point, is about 6.7 ft. (2.05 m).

The subcontr'alto flute was developed in the latter part of the 20th century. It is too soon to say whether it will become a commonly played instrument, as its **projection** is limited without amplification. It has been used in recordings, studio work, and **ensembles** such as **flute choirs**, but it is not a regular member of a band or an orchestra. *Syn.:* subcontrabass flute in G, octocontrabass flute in G, octocontralto flute in G, double contralto flute in G. *See also* FLAUTONE; "FLUTE IN . . ."; QUARTER-TONE FLUTE; SUBBASS FLUTE; VERTICAL FLUTE.

SUPPORT. 1. Same as **breath support. 2.** *See* BO-PEP; CRUTCH; THUMB RESTS; WART.

SUZUKI, SHIN'ICHI (b. Nagoya, Japan, 1898; d. Matsumoto, Japan, 1998). Japanese violinist, violin teacher, conductor, educator, and founder of the **Suzuki method**. *See also* TAKAHASHI, TOSHIO.

SUZUKI METHOD. A famous method of teaching young children, starting at the age of three, how to play a musical instrument such as the **flute**, violin, viola, bass, guitar, **recorder**, piano, harp, or cello. It was originally developed by **Shin'ichi Suzuki** of Japan in the 1940s for the violin and later was developed for other instruments. **Flutist Toshio Takahashi**, at Suzuki's request, developed the method for the flute in 1969.

The Suzuki Method is based on the theory that any child has musical talent and can develop this to a high level of skill. Children are taught music in the same way that they learn their native language, that is, by listening, observing, and imitating. In the beginning of their study, they learn music by imitating it on records. Only after several years of learning in this way (i.e., by ear and memory) do they learn how to read music. Children are given a private lesson once a week and a group lesson with other students once a month. Parents are very involved, attending the weekly private lessons and becoming surrogate teachers at home.

SWAB. 1. A device used to clean moisture out of the **flute** tubing (because, it is generally believed, any moisture left in the flute could damage the **pads**). The swab usually consists of a wire rod, half of which is covered with short pieces of fuzzy stringlike material that projects outward from the rod like a brush (also called a *swab stick*), but it may just be a small piece of material with or without an attached string (see app. 12, fig. 2). *Syn.:* mop. *See also* CLEANING ROD; FLUTE FLAG. **2.** *v.* To clean something out.

SWAB STICK. Same as **cleaning rod**, but may refer to a **swab**.

SWAGING. Also *swedging*. A process that is used in flutemaking to stretch, lengthen, or tighten loose-fitting and/or worn-out and usually clanky keywork, such as **keys** or **key tubing**, by applying pressure with a special pair of pliers that squeeze the tubing against the inner **steel** to make it slightly longer. For example, key tubing may be squeezed with swaging pliers to make it longer and thinner so as to get rid of **play** in the **key mechanism**. *See also* HEAD-JOINT REFITTING; SPINNING; TELESCOPING (1).

SWEAT. *v.* **1.** To heat something, such as **solder**, so that it melts. When solder is sweated, it can be used to join parts, such as a **soldered tone hole chimney** to the **flute tube. 2.** To join metal parts by heating **solder** at the location where the parts meet.

SWEDGING. A misspelling of the word *swaging*, but a more commonly used term in the **flute** world than *swaging*.

SWEET SPOT. The optimum spot for the airstream to strike the **blowing wall** for a clear and **centered** sound.

There is a small range of lip placements that a **flutist** can use to get the same **pitch**, but only one of these placements will produce the clearest and most centered sound. *See also* MOISTURE TRIANGLE.

SYMINGTON, DAVID ARTHUR (b. Miraj, India, 1930). A retired British businessman, amateur **flutist**, and author. *See also* BIGIO CROWN AND STOPPER.

SYNTHETIC PAD. Correctly used, this term refers to a **pad** that consists entirely of synthetic materials, but in the **flute** world, it is used more ambiguously to mean various things, including any pad other than a **traditional pad**, or a pad where the main part—the traditional wool **felt** cushion—has been replaced with a synthetic material. Due to the ambiguity of the term, flutemakers and repairers usually prefer to refer to a particular pad by its trade name.

SYRINX. 1. Same as **panpipes. 2.** *See* PAN. **3.** *See* SOLO (1).

SYSTEM. *See* BOEHM SYSTEM; FINGERING SYSTEM; G♯ KEY (1); KEY SYSTEM; MODE; NEW SYSTEM; OPEN-KEY SYSTEM; QUARTER-TONE FLUTE. For **early flutes** and other non-Boehm-system **flutes**, *see* CARTE 1851 SYSTEM FLUTE; CARTE 1867 SYSTEM FLUTE; CLOSED-KEY SYSTEM; MEYER-SYSTEM FLUTE; OLD SYSTEM; RADCLIFF SYSTEM FLUTE; SIMPLE-SYSTEM FLUTE.

T

T. 1. Abbr. for "thumb." **2.** Abbr. for "tongue." When seen in music, it usually means to tongue the note so labeled (*see* TONGUING).

TABOR PIPE. Also taborpipe, tabor-pipe. A **duct flute** that is usually made in one cylindrical piece from wood or **ivory**, but may taper to the bottom end and have a metal lip. It most often has three (sometimes four) **finger holes**: two in front and one behind—for the index and middle fingers, and thumb, respectively. Despite having so few finger holes, the pipe can produce a one-and-a-half-octave range through **overblowing**, along with **cross-fingering** and **half-holing** for some chromatic notes. Various sizes of pipes provide different ranges of notes.

There is a ridge or ring around the bottom part of the pipe so that it can be held vertically and played with one hand, usually the left. This leaves the other hand free to play the *tabor*, a small drum, either held over the shoulder or strapped to the waist or wrist. The pipe and tabor have long been used to provide music for dancing or marching (see app. 1, fig. 3). They were popular and widespread in the 16th and 17th centuries and have been revived in modern times. *See also* AUTOMATON.

TAFFANEL, CLAUDE-PAUL (b. Bordeaux, France, 1844; d. Paris, 1908). A renowned French flute **soloist** who was a **principal flutist** in various French orchestras, conductor, composer, **flute** professor, and director of the orchestra class at the **Paris Conservatoire** from 1893 to 1908. He is usually considered the founder of the modern **French Flute School**. He created Société de Musique de Chamber pour Instruments à Vent in 1879. Taffanel began writing a history of the flute and a flute **method**, both of which were completed after his death by his pupils **Louis Fleury** and **Philippe Gaubert**. *See also* ALTISSIMO; FRENCH TONGUING; MORDENT (2); SPLIT E MECHANISM; T & G.

TAIL. 1. Same as **foot joint. 2.** Same as **kicker. 3. Back-connector** tails.

TAILLE. German term for tenor **recorder** in the late Baroque.

TAILLE DE FLÛTE. French term for alto **recorder** in the late Baroque.

TAKAHASHI, TOSHIO (b. Tokyo, 1938). A **flutist** who studied with **Marcel Moyse** and **Shin'ichi Suzuki** on Suzuki pedagogy. *See also* SUZUKI METHOD.

T. & G. Literally an abbreviation for (**Claude-Paul**) **Taffanel** and (**Philippe**) **Gaubert**, this term usually refers to the "17 grands exercices journaliers de mécanisme" from the famous *Méthode complète de flûte*, which was started by Taffanel but completed after his death in 1908 by his students Gaubert and **Louis Fleury**. *See also* FRENCH FLUTE SCHOOL; METHOD; MORDENT (2); PARIS CONSERVATOIRE.

TAPER. With regard to **flutes**, usually a reference to the wide-to-narrow **bore** shape of the modern **head joint**. Since the taper is usually slightly curved and not straight, it is sometimes misleadingly referred to as a "**parabolic**" curve. *See also* COLD DRAWING; CYLINDRICAL BORE; DRAWING; FAJARDO WEDGEHEAD; HEAD-JOINT LINING; HEAD-JOINT MAKER; INTERNAL TUNING; SCALE; STEP; TUBE/TUBING (1). For early flutes *see also* head-joint lining.

TARNISH. A film coating on a metal caused when metal reacts with a chemical such as oxygen. **Silver flutes**

are the most prone to tarnish and will be affected when exposed to oxygen, sulfur, or chlorine. The sulfur may derive from the burning of industrial fuels or from certain foods ingested by the player, such as onions, green vegetables, and eggs; chlorine may derive from tapwater. The color of tarnish depends on the metal and what it is reacting with. Tarnish on **silver** that is caused by oxygen is brownish; if caused by sulfur, it is gray or black, but it is the easiest metal tarnish to remove. Some of the more tarnish-resistant metals and their **alloys** that are used in **flute** manufacture are **nickel-silver**, **gold** (14-**karat** or above), **platinum**, **nickel**, **palladium**, rhodium, and **titanium**.

Tarnish cannot be prevented, but it does not harm the flute (since it does not penetrate the surface of the metal) or affect the tone. Nevertheless, it can be unsightly and can be slowed down if **flutists** wash their hands and chin-lip area and brush their teeth before playing. To help prevent tarnish, small strips of chemically treated paper, such as 3M's Silver Protector Strips, specially formulated to reduce tarnish, can be kept at the bottom of the flute case or draped over the flute.

Tarnish can be removed from a disassembled flute by a competent repairer using a nonabrasive silver **polish** or metal cleaner. Alternatively, some flutists use a nonabrasive polishing cloth. *See also* COIN SILVER; FIRE SCALE; GOLD-PLATING; GS ALLOY; OVERHAUL; RHODIUM-PLATING; SILVER-PLATING.

TAUMATA. Short for *Taumatawhakatangihangakoauauotamateaturipukakapikimaungahoronukupokaiwhenuakitanatahu*, which is the name given by the local Maori people, Ngati Kere, to a hill in New Zealand in honor of their ancestor, a famous chief and warrior, Tamatea Pokai Whenua. It is also the world's longest place name. Translated, it means: "The hilltop where Tamatea with big knees, conqueror of mountains, eater of land, traveler over land and sea, played his *koauau* [a Maori **flute**] to his beloved."

TEARDROP EMBOUCHURE/LIP. An **embouchure** where part of the upper lip (usually in the center of the mouth) dips down and divides the **aperture** in half, forming two apertures that are off-center. Having two **off-centered apertures** is usually caused by a characteristic formation of the lips and teeth, with little contribution from habit and playing position. Most teardrops are usually visible whether the **flutist** is playing or not, but for some flutists, the teardrop is noticeable only when they play. A flutist with a teardrop embouchure must eventually learn to close off one aperture and play with the other or to stretch back the part of the upper lip that dips in order to remove it. *Syn.:* split embouchure.

TECHNIQUE. The physical skills necessary for the playing of a musical instrument. These include the skills studied and required for finger dexterity, the **embouchure**, the tongue, and breathing. Specific exercises and **studies** are often used to improve such skills. *See also* ALEXANDER TECHNIQUE; BO-PEP; BREATH SUPPORT; CHOPS (2); CHUNKING; CIRCULAR BREATHING; CROSS-FINGERING (3); CUTOFF FREQUENCY; DIRECTION; DUPLICATE KEYS; EXTENDED TECHNIQUE; FRENCH FLUTE SCHOOL; GLIDE; GROUPING; G♯ KEY (1); HOME BASE; HOMOGENEOUS TONE; HUMORING; LOST MOTION; OPEN-HOLE FLUTE; PERFORMANCE PRACTICE (1); ROCKSTRO POSITION/GRIP; ROLL-IN; SHADING; STOP (1); THROAT TUNING; THUMB REST; TONGUING. For non-**Boehm-system flutes**, *see also* REFORM FLUTE.

TELESCOPING. 1. A method used by flutemakers and repairers to attach replacement **tubing** to **key tubing** when it requires lengthening to avoid end **play**. It is used when other methods of lengthening the tubing by stretching (i.e., **swaging** or **spinning**) will not be sufficient or aesthetically pleasing. **2.** *See* ROBERT DICK GLISSANDO HEADJOINT. **3.** *See* FOOT REGISTER.

TEMPER. 1. A **heat-treating** process used in flutemaking and **flute** repair to bring a metal (especially **steel**) to the required degree of hardness and elasticity. The color of steel can indicate the degree of temper. Blue steel, for example, was often used in the past to make flute **springs**. *See also* FLAT SPRING; POST-MOUNT. **2.** The amount of hardness and elasticity of a metal that is achieved by tempering. **3.** *v.* To harden and improve the strength and structural stability of a metal by a heat-treating process. **4.** *v.* To adjust the **pitch** of a note or **tune** an instrument in a particular **temperament**.

TEMPERAMENT. A method of adjusting the **tuning** of the notes in a scale, and thus the intervals, to accomplish a desired degree of consonance. Most temperaments fall into the classes of **Pythagorean-**, **Meantone-**, **Well-**, or **equal-tempered** scales, though fixed-key instrument **tuners** may depart from these in various subtle ways. A Just scale, which is not **tempered** (def. 4; *see* JUST INTONATION), is considered to be quite consonant in the key for which it has been designed, but if applied to a fixed-keyed instrument, with only 12 pitches, there will be undesirable dissonances when the instrument is played in other keys. The scale must then be adjusted, or *tempered*, using another method so as to achieve a satisfactory compromise in other keys. The scale most widely used in Western music for these purposes is equal temperament, where the octave is divided into 12 equal semitones. Today, **wind instruments** with **tone holes** are manufactured at close to equal temperament, but the player has some flexibility in **intonation** and can, by using the **embouchure** or breathing, adjust intonation while playing and match any of the scales usually encountered. *Syn.:* tempered tuning.

Sometimes "temperaments" are referred to as "tunings" (e.g., "Meantone tuning" rather than "Meantone temperament"). There is an old distinction between these two terms. *Tuning*, specifically, was used only to denote use of the Just scale; *temperament* referred to the slight bending of those pitches into scales that were consonant in several keys. Technically, then, it should be Meantone temperament rather than Meantone tuning. Some find this distinction archaic, while others still observe it. *See also* TUNER.

TEN-KEYED FLUTE. A **simple-system** (or **keyed**) **transverse flute** (or replica of it) that evolved from, and was similar to, the earlier wooden (or **ivory**), **conical-bored**, **eight-keyed flute** in D except that it had 10 **keys** (see app. 2, fig. 12). Both of the two most popular types included the eight keys of the eight-keyed flute and a **B foot joint** with a **low b key**. The 10th key was either a high E_3-D_3 **trill key** or an extra B♭ key/lever. Sometimes all three keys were present, for a total of 11 keys. Ten-keyed flutes appeared in Europe sometime after 1800, although flutes with the B foot joint for **low b** were more common in Germany and Austria than in England and France. Modern replicas are rare. *See also* FIVE-KEYED FLUTE; FOUR-KEYED FLUTE; NINE-KEYED FLUTE; ONE-KEYED FLUTE; SIX-KEYED FLUTE; TWO-KEYED FLUTE.

TENON. An extension at the end of a piece of flute **tube** that fits into a **socket** when the flute is assembled. There are two tenons on the flute: one on the **head joint** (see app. 7, fig. 10) and one on the **middle joint** (see app. 7, fig. 3). It may be called a *pin* when speaking of older flutes. *See also* BURNISHING; CYLINDRICAL BOEHM FLUTE (3); FIT (1); GLUE; HEAD-JOINT REFITTING; HONING; OUT OF ROUND; PLATING-UP; SLIP FIT; SPINNING; TENON JOINT; TENON PROTECTORS; TIP (1); TUNING SLIDE; UNIBODY. For **early flutes**, *see also* BATCH MARK; FOOT REGISTER; HEAD-JOINT LINING; LAPPING; REVERSE TENON; TUNING HEAD.

TENON JOINT. A type of **joint** in which one part, the *tenon*, plugs into another, called the *receiver* or *socket*, with no screw action. There are two tenon joints on the **flute**: one for the **head joint–middle joint** connection and one for the middle joint–**foot joint** connection.

TENON PROTECTORS. Short metal sleeves or **caps** that are placed on **tenon**s. They were previously used to protect the cases from the lubricant used on the **joints** of wooden flutes. Today, most **flutes** are made of metal, so the protectors serve no useful purpose. *Syn.:* end protectors, end protector rings, grease guards, joint caps, joint cap covers, joint covers/protectors, joint protector caps, protective caps, tenon caps.

TENORFLÖTE. Ger. for tenor **recorder** in the late Baroque.

TENOR FLUTE. 1. The most common size of **Renaissance flute**. The tenor flute usually played *cantus*, *altus*, or contratenor and tenor parts in four-part compositions of the time, with the *bassus* taken by a bass flute in G. **2.** Also *contratenor flute*. A **bass flute** in F (def. 4). **3.** An ambiguous term that is sometimes used today for any flute that is **pitched** between the **alto flute** in G and the **concert flute** in C. Since the term *tenor* usually refers to a **pitch** range below the alto, this meaning is felt by many to be erroneous. **4.** Tenor flute in B♭. *See* FLÛTE D'AMOUR.

TENUTO. Abbr. *ten.* A short horizontal dash above a note indicating that the note is to be held for no less than its full value:

A tenuto mark may be interpreted in three ways, depending on the context. **1.** When tenuto follows shorter notes, it indicates that the note should be held for its full value. **2.** When there is a need for *dynamic* stress at some point, tenuto indicates that the note should have dynamic emphasis as well as being sustained, though not as strong as a regular accent. (i.e., >). Some interpreters suggest **leaning** on the note. **3.** When there is a need for *rhythmic* stress, tenuto indicates that the note should be held longer than its value, perhaps emphasizing the note as well (as described in def. 2).

TERZFLÖTE. Ger. for **third flute**.

THEORY. The study of the principles of music. Subjects such as rudiments (or fundamentals), harmony, counterpoint, and analysis are studied. Music students are often required to pass theory exams as a corequisite for practical (i.e., playing) exams. *See also* METHOD (1).

THICKENING. A rarely used term that refers to a raised portion of wood or **ivory** that is purposely left on the **body** of some wooden or ivory **flutes** when it is **turned** in a **lathe**. Its purpose may be to add strength to that part of the flute, to make for wider **sockets**, or for such things as **block-mounting keys**. Thickenings that are small in size may be called *knobs* or *nobs*. *See also* ONE-KEYED FLUTE.

THINNED (HEAD OR BODY) JOINTS. The **heads** and rarely the **bodies** of English wooden **cylindrical flutes** in the post-Boehm period (i.e., after 1847) where the outside of the **head joints** or bodies was turned down to reduce the **wall** thickness, and thus the weight, of the **joints**. Thinning the wood was also believed to increase the vibrancy of the joints and thus the tone.

In order to make a thinned flute head joint or body, extensive work with a **lathe** and careful work by hand was required to cut away much of the wood (reducing the wall thickness to about half that of a regular flute of the time), leaving only **tone hole seatings**, the **lip plate**, and head-joint **socket** standing proud (see app. 5, fig. 2). Since making a flute entirely of thinned wood was a very labor-intensive undertaking, few complete flutes were ever made of thinned wood, and those that were made were very expensive. It was more common to see thinned head joints, which were often metal-lined (*see* HEAD-JOINT LINING).

Today, thinned heads are made by various makers for metal flutes so as to avoid making the flute head-heavy. *See also* BULBOUS HEAD JOINT; FLUTE (4); FMG.

THIRD FLUTE. Ger. *Terzflöte*; Fr. *tierce flûte*. **1.** A **flute** that is pitched a minor third above the **standard flute** in use. Since the standard flute today is the **concert flute** in C, the term *third flute* presently refers to a flute in E♭. (In an older terminology used for **Baroque** and **simple-system flutes**, the standard-size flute was considered to be "in D," so a third flute would be said to be "in F.") This way of naming is rarely used today. (For other ways of naming flutes, *see* "FLUTE IN . . ."; "FLUTE IN THE KEY OF . . ."; TRANSPOSING INSTRUMENTS.) *Cf.* **second flute** (1), **fourth flute** (1), **quint flute** (1). **2.** An 18th-century name for a soprano **recorder** in A (named after the seven-fingered note), a third above the modern alto (British: treble) recorder in F. *Cf.* fourth flute (4), **fifth flute**, **sixth flute**, **octave flute** (2), quint flute (2). **3.** The third flute **part. 4. Third flutist.**

THIRD FLUTIST. The **flutist** who plays a supporting role in any **ensemble** having more than two written flute **parts**. The third flute part is a subsidiary part. In comparison with first and second flute parts, it usually has less independence, more frequent unisons with other parts, more lower **pitches**, and more rests. Thus, like the **second flutist**, the third flutist usually plays an accompanying role, seeking to match the style of the **first flutist**. In large orchestras with four flutists, the third flutist may also **double** on **piccolo** when the music requires it.

Similarly, there may be a part for a fourth flutist. *See also* PRINCIPAL FLUTIST (2, 3); UTILITY FLUTIST.

THIRD OCTAVE. The notes contained in the octave that is two octaves above the lowest-pitched octave of a musical instrument. On the **flute**, these notes are from C_3 to B_3. *Syn.*: **third register**, upper notes, upper octave, upper register, **high notes**, **high register**, **top notes**, **top octave**, top register. *See also* "Octave Designation" in the introduction; app. 11, note 3; B FOOT JOINT; BREATH SUPPORT; CHARANGA FLUTE; CROWN; FIRST OCTAVE; FOURTH OCTAVE; HEAD-JOINT CORK; HIGH (1); OPEN-HOLE FLUTE; PICCOLO (1); RANGE; REGISTER (1); RETUNING; ROCKSTRO MODEL FLUTE; SECOND OCTAVE; STOPPER; TRILL KEYS. For **early flutes**, *see also* FALSET NOTES; FOOT REGISTER.

THIRD REGISTER. Usually refers to the **third octave**. *Syn.*: **high register**, top register, **upper register**. *See also* D FOOT JOINT; INTERNAL TUNING; ORCHESTRAL MODEL FLUTE; REGISTER (1); SPLIT MECHANISM; STOPPER.

THOU. Short for thousandths of an inch. For example, the **wall** thickness of **silver flute tubing** varies from 0.014 in. to 0.018 in. or "fourteen thou" to "eighteen thou."

THROAT TUNING. A term coined by **Robert Dick** in 1978 for the **technique** where the **flutist** silently sings the same note (or if this note is not in his voice range, the same note in another octave) as the note that he is playing on his **flute**. Doing this adjusts the size and shape of the **resonating** spaces in the vocal tract (or "tunes" them) to match the **pitch** that the flutist is playing and thus improves the tone and **intonation** of this note. An effective way to practice this technique is to first play a **passage** normally, then to sing it aloud, then to sing it aloud while playing it, and finally to sing it silently while playing it. *Syn.*: silent singing. *See also* GLOTTAL STOP; MULTIPHONIC; OPEN THROAT; VOCALIZING/SINGING WHILE PLAYING.

THUMB KEY. *See* B♭ FINGERINGS; B♭ THUMB KEY; BRÖGGER SYSTEM; B TRILL KEY; CYLINDRICAL BOEHM FLUTE (1); EQUISONANT FLUTE; FLAT SPRING (1); HIGH G♯ MECHANISM; INLAYING (2); KEY (1); ORCHESTRAL MODEL FLUTE; POST-MOUNT; REVERSED THUMB KEYS; RING-KEY FLUTE; SHORT B♭ FINGERING; THUMB KEY B♭ FINGERING; WATERLINE KEYS.

THUMB KEY B♭ FINGERING. A special **basic fingering** for B♭ in the **first** and **second octaves** of the **flute**. This name arose because the **fingering** requires that the **flutist** depress the **B♭ thumb key** (i.e., the **Briccialdi B♭** lever along with L1 and R4D♯), distinguishing it from two other basic B♭ **fingerings** in these octaves: **side lever B♭ fingering** and **one-and-one B♭ fingering**. *Syn.:* B♭ thumb key fingering, Briccialdi B♭ fingering, **short B♭ fingering**. *See also* CYLINDRICAL BOEHM FLUTE; RING-KEY FLUTE.

THUMBPORT. *See* THUMB REST.

THUMB REST. One of several right-hand thumb (RT) devices that may assist **flutists** in holding their **flutes** with greater control. An improvement in flute balance may help to improve finger **technique** because the flute will be more stable. At the present time, there are several on the market, including the Thumbport, invented by **Ho-Fan Lee** in 2005 (see app. 12, fig. 19); the PRIMA Thumb Rest™, invented by **Ton Kooiman** in 2003 (see app. 12, fig. 16); and the **Bo-Pep** Thumb Guide, invented by **Boleslaw Peplowski** (see app. 12, fig. 18).

TIBIA. Lat. shinbone. **1.** The name the Romans gave to the Greek *aulos*. The word is often mistranslated as "**flute**" in modern sources. **2.** In the Middle Ages, used generally to mean **wind instruments**.

TIEFE QUARTFLÖTE. Ger. low **fourth flute**. An 18th-century name for a **flute** that is **pitched** a perfect fourth below the **standard flute** in use. At this time, the standard-size flute was considered to be a **simple-system flute** "in D" (using the **six-fingered note** name), so a low fourth flute would be said to be "in A." (For other ways of naming flutes, *see* "FLUTE IN . . ."; "FLUTE IN THE KEY OF . . ."; TRANSPOSING INSTRUMENTS.)

TIERCE FLÛTE. Fr., **third flute** (def. 1).

TIMBRAL NOTE/TONE. A note that is played with an **alternate fingering** for a coloristic effect.

TIMBRAL TRILLS. *See* KEY VIBRATO.

TIMBRE. Same as **tone color, tone quality**. *See also* CUTOFF FREQUENCY; *DÉTIMBRÉ*; HARMONIC; RESPONSE; TIMBRAL NOTE; *TIMBRÉ*; VIBRATO; VIRTUAL FLUTE (2). For **early flutes**, *see also* ONE-KEYED FLUTE.

TIMBRÉ. Fr. A sound with more **overtones** than usual. Some **flutists** may describe this sound as "rich." The opposite of *détimbré*.

TIN FLUTE. 1. A British colloquialism that may refer to a **flute** made from a cheap metal such as **nickel-silver**,

German silver, or *maillechort*, but that does not necessarily contain any tin. **2.** Same as **tin whistle**.

TIN WHISTLE. Also *tinwhistle*. A popular type of **duct flute** that is held vertically and has six **finger holes**, a **cylindrical** or **conical bore**, a body commonly made of metal (e.g., rolled tin or **brass**), and either a traditional wooden block inset in a duct-type metal mouthpiece or a mouthpiece made entirely of plastic (see app. 1, fig. 2). It comes in various sizes and keys and has a **range** of at least two octaves. Only those tin whistles with an adjustable mouthpiece are tunable.

Six-hole duct flutes of this type (simple English-style **flageolets**, similar to but simpler than the **recorder**) have a long history. Originally made of wood, they became more popular after an inexpensive tinplate conical version with a wooden block in the mouthpiece was introduced in 1843 by Robert Clarke (1816–1862), a farm laborer in Suffolk. At first Clarke's version was still called a flageolet, but the name "tin whistle" was soon applied to his and other makers' **sheet metal** instruments.

The tin whistle in D, named after its lowest **six-fingered note** D_2 and sounding an octave above the **concert flute**, is the most popular and is the tin whistle that is commonly used for Irish music. The **low D** whistle, a recent innovation, sounds at the same **pitch** as the concert flute and is used mostly for Celtic music (i.e., Irish, Scottish, Breton, Galician, etc.). World-renowned flutist **Sir James Galway** (b.1939) first learned to play music on a tin whistle.

Syn.: **whistle, penny whistle, tin flute**, Irish whistle (the latter name due to its frequent usage to play Irish music). In some places, such as France and Quebec, it is still referred to as a flageolet. *See also* FIPPLE FLUTE; "FLUTE IN . . ."; SESSION.

TIP. 1. A thin metal **ring** that may be found on the **head-joint tenon** that fits into the **middle joint**, and on the **box** part of the **body** that fits into the **foot joint**. It acts as a stop when the **flute** is put together. *Syn.:* rings, moldings. **2.** Same as **mount** (1). **3.** *v.* An 18th-century term meaning "to mount," as in "A flute tipped [tipt] or mounted with **ivory**," which means that a flutemaker has put mounts, moldings, or rings (tips) made of ivory, or other material, on the flute at the ends of the **sockets** on the **joints** and at the lower end of the flute, for protective, decorative, or reinforcement purposes. The term is not used today.

TIPPING. An old term meaning "**tonguing**." The term is not used today.

TITANIUM. A **corrosion**-resistant metallic element with a **density** of 0.16 lbs./in³ (4.5 g/cm³). It is occasionally used to make the **tubing** of expensive **flutes**. Although dark gray in its natural state, it can be colored by anodizing (i.e., coating the metal electrolytically with a decorative oxide). At the moment, **Jonathon Landell Sr.** (b. 1946), who holds the U.S. patent, is the only flutemaker that makes flutes out of titanium. The first one was made in 1996. *See also* MATIT CARBON-FIBER FLUTE; TARNISH.

TOFF, NANCY (b. Greenburgh, N.Y., 1955). A **flute** historian, **editor**, author (see bib. under "History," "Pedagogy," "Biographies and Autobiographies"), and president of the New York Flute Club (1992–1995). *See also* TREATISE.

TONE COLOR. The overall expressive quality of an instrument's sound. For example, a tone color could be said to be pretty, **dark, full,** thin, edgy, **breathy, bright,** forced, open, **hollow,** and so on. Descriptions of tone color such as these can be highly subjective. What might sound like a dark tone color to one listener might not sound so dark to another.

The tone color of a note depends on the amount of breath sound present, the amount of **vibrato,** the starting transient or **attack,** and the **harmonic** spectrum (i.e., the number, selection, and relative strength of the harmonics of which it is composed). For some instruments, such as the flute, the tone of a note can be manipulated by the player so as to produce different colors by changing the **embouchure** (i.e., by blowing higher or lower on the **blowing wall,** changing the lip-to-edge distance, or changing the size of the mouth **aperture**), by blowing more or less hard, or by varying the extent and the time course of the vibrato.

The tone color is, by definition, what allows one to sometimes distinguish the same note played on two different instruments. *Syn.:* **timbre,** tone quality. *See also* ALTERNATE FINGERINGS; *BISBIGLIANDO;* BREAKING-IN (PERIOD); CROSS-FINGERING (1); DIRECTION; FAJARDO WEDGEHEAD; HALF-HOLING; HOMOGENEOUS TONE; OPEN-HOLE FLUTE; PHRASING; PICCOLO (1); PITCH (1); RESISTANCE (1); RESONANCE (2); SECOND FLUTIST; SHADING (1); *SMORZATO;* TONGUE CLICK; WHISTLE TONE.

TONE-COLOR TRILL. *See* KEY VIBRATO.

TONE-HOLE BUSHING. A ring-shaped piece of metal, wood, or **ivory** that has been integrated by the **flute** manufacturer into the part of a wooden or ivory **one-keyed** or **simple-system flute** surrounding the **tone hole** (see app. 2, fig. 14; app. 3, C, fig. 5). Some **bushings** were a **tube** of metal that acted as a **lining** for the **wall** of a tone hole; others were a perforated disk of **sheet metal** that sat on the surface of the tone hole wall. Tone-hole bushings were inserted for various reasons, including preventing wear or damage, creating a sharper edge for tonal improvement, repairing a worn or damaged tone hole, relieving a **flutist**'s allergic reaction to the **body** material, allowing for a more secure **touch** for the fingers due to the sharp bushing edge in the **finger hole,** and as bushings into which a **pewter plug** fits.

Tone-hole bushings are often seen on flutes that have **embouchure-hole bushings.** Placing the bushings under **keys** was very common on Viennese simple-system flutes from at least 1820 on. These bushings extended somewhat from the surface of the flute and made a sharper edge for the **pad** to **seal** against. *Syn.:* bushed finger hole/tone hole, finger-hole bushing, insert, tone-hole ring.

TONE-HOLE CHIMNEY. Same as **chimney** (2). *See also* LEAK; PATCHING; UNDERCUTTING (2); UP TONE-HOLE.

TONE-HOLE COVER. *See* KEY.

TONE-HOLE RIM. The top edge of the short cylindrical tubes (**chimneys**) surrounding **tone holes** on which a key **pad** rests when closing a tone hole. Also called a *bead. See also* FISHSKIN; LEAK; LEVELING; PAD IMPRESSION; PAPER WASHER; PISONI PADS; ROLLED TONE HOLE; SEATING (1); SHIM (1); STICKY PADS.

TONE-HOLE RING. *See* TONE-HOLE BUSHING.

TONE HOLES. 1. The holes in the flute **body,** and/or the **walls** or short cylindrical tubes surrounding them, which may be covered by **keys.** Tone holes directly covered by the fingers, such as those found on many ethnic or **simple-system flutes,** are most often called *finger holes* or *note holes.* All of the tone holes on the flute have note name labels (see app. 8, fig. 3, for the modern **concert flute** and app. 2, fig. 1, for the **one-keyed flute**). The six uncovered holes of the simple-system flute have the same function and names as the six holes of the one-keyed flute. *See also* ALTERNATE FINGERINGS; ANTINODE; BENNETT SCALE; BODY-LINE G♯ TONE HOLE; BODYMAKER; BOEHM SYSTEM; BRÖGGER ACOUSTIC; BROSSA F♯ LEVER; CHIMNEY (2); COLD DRAWING; COLE SCALE; COLTMAN C♯; COOPER SCALE; CROSS-FINGERING; C♯ VENT HOLE; CUTOFF FREQUENCY; CYLINDRICAL BOEHM FLUTE (3);

DRAWN TONE HOLES; DUPLICATE G♯ TONE HOLE; DUPLI-CATE TONE HOLES; EQUAL TEMPERAMENT; FINISHER; FOOT REGISTER; FRAIZING; G/A TRILL KEY (1); HIGH G♯ MECHANISM; HARMONIC (2); INLAYING (1); INTERNAL TUNING; KEY RISE; LEADING EDGE (2); LINING; LOWER G INSERT; MAINLINE; MODERN SCALE; NODE; OCTAVE LENGTH; OIL (2); OPEN-HOLE FLUTE; OPEN-KEY SYSTEM; OPEN NOTE; PAD; PATCHING; PLUG (1); REGISTER (1); REGISTER HOLE; RETUNING; RF MODIFICATION; RING-KEY FLUTE; ROCKSTRO MODEL FLUTE; ROLLED TONE HOLES; SADDLE (1); SCALE (1); SCALING; SCHEMA; *SCHLEIFKLAPPE;* SEAL; SHORTENED HEAD JOINT; SIDE HOLE; SIMMONS F♯ KEY; SOLDERED TONE HOLES; SOUNDING HOLE; SOUND-ING LENGTH (1); SPLIT MECHANISM; SQUAREONE FLUTE; STOP (1, 2); STRINGER; TEMPERAMENT; TONE-HOLE RIM; TUNING (4); UNDERCUTTING (2); UP TONE-HOLE; VEILED TONE (2); VENT HOLE; VENTING; VOICING. For **early flutes** and other non-Boehm-system flutes, *see also* CARTE 1851 SYSTEM FLUTE; *CORPS DE RECHANGE;* CRESCENT KEY; FIVE-KEYED FLUTE; LONG KEY; NICHOLSON, CHARLES, SR.; NICHOLSON'S IMPROVED FLUTE; OLD SYSTEM (2); PRIN-CIPAL RANK; SICCAMA DIATONIC FLUTE; SIX-FINGERED NOTE; TONE-HOLE BUSHING; VEILED TONE (1).

   2. *Mouth tone hole.* An uncommon alternative name for the **embouchure hole.**

TONE HOLE WALL. *See* WALL (3).

TONE QUALITY. Same as **tone color** and **timbre.** *See also* AGE-HARDENING; ALTERNATE FINGERINGS; APER-TURE (1); BAROQUE FLUTE (2); BASIC FINGERINGS; CROSS-FINGERING (1); DENSITY; HARMONIC; LEAK; PICCOLO (1); REGISTER (1); SCALE (1); VEILED TONE; VENT HOLE (1); VOICING. For **early flutes,** *see also* G♯ KEY (2).

TONGUE. *v. See* TONGUING.

TONGUE CLICK. A type of special effect produced by bringing the tongue down quickly from the roof of the mouth in such a way that a type of clicking sound occurs. When producing a tongue click, the **embouchure hole** can be left uncovered or covered (i.e., stopped; *see* STOP [1]) by placing it between the lips. When the em-bouchure hole is uncovered, the tongue-click noise will be heard along with short, extremely soft **residual tones** at the lowest two **pitches** yielded by each **fingering** when **overblown.** When the embouchure hole is covered, the tongue click will be heard along with strong **resonances** that sound from approximately a major third to an octave below the pitch of the fingering used. In the latter case, this drop in pitch cannot be notated, as it varies with the mouth shape of each **flutist.** The pitch and **tone color** re-

sulting from the tongue click are influenced by the vowel shape of the mouth and tongue position.

   There is no standard notation for tongue clicks. It may be notated as a "K" above or below a diamond-shaped notehead, which signifies the note to be fingered:

or

where the brackets indicate a covered embouchure hole.

   The tongue click can be used along with other spe-cial effects such as **key slap.** Sometimes referred to as a *palatal click. See also* EXTENDED TECHNIQUE.

TONGUED. An instruction which means to tongue notes. For example, a **flute** teacher might say: "Play two [notes] tongued, two [notes] **slurred.**" If the word *tongu-ing* or *tongued* is not modified by words such as *single, double,* or *triple,* as in "**triple tonguing,**" then **single tonguing** is implied.

TONGUE OUT. Usually the same as **French tonguing.**

TONGUE PIZZICATO. A type of percussive **tongu-ing** where the tongue makes a hard **articulation** by mouthing the letter *T* against the lips or the **palate.** It can be done in two different ways: **1.** The **flutist** places the tip of the tongue through the lips and, without blowing, withdraws it quickly. Any air that was built up behind the tongue will produce a breathy popping sound. This is also called *lip pizzicato* since the tongue is making a hard articulation against the lips. **2.** The flutist places the tip of the tongue against the roof of the mouth in such a way that it is slightly curled back toward the throat and then brings it down forcefully toward, but not through, the mouth hole while simultaneously forcefully expelling any air that was held back behind the tongue. This is some-times referred to as *palatal pizzicato* since the tongue is making a hard articulation against the palate or as *slap tongue* or **tongue slap,** since the tongue is brought down forcefully.

   There is no standard notation for tongue pizzicato. It may be notated as

or

or

Alternatively, the words *pizz.*, *lip pizz.*, or *palatal pizz.* may appear above the note to be played tongue pizzicato; in the first case, the flutist must decide which kind of tongue pizzicato to use. *See also* EXTENDED TECHNIQUE; KEY SLAP.

TONGUE RAM. Abbr. T.R. Same as **tongue stop**. *See also* EXTENDED TECHNIQUE.

TONGUE SLAP. Also *slap tongue*. Same as **tongue pizzicato** (2). *See also* EXTENDED TECHNIQUE.

TONGUE STOP. A percussive effect produced by surrounding the **embouchure hole** with the lips and rapidly thrusting the tongue into the embouchure hole in a chameleon-like fashion. Some find it helpful to say "Hot" or "ht" when they are doing this. A more powerful sound can be produced if the player blows briefly and forcefully, similar to an **abdomen kick**, into the **flute** just before the tongue thrust. Some **flutists** prefer to produce the effect by thrusting their tongue against the back of the upper teeth or slapping their tongue across the embouchure hole instead of through it.

Tongue stops can be produced using any fingering up to $C\sharp_2$. The note produced on a **concert flute** in C will sound a major seventh below the **fingered** note, but for larger-**bored** flutes, the **flattening** may be less for some notes.

There is no standard notation for tongue stops. It may be notated as

in which the (T) indicates the tongue stop; the diamond-shaped notehead indicates which note is to be fingered. An HT! may appear instead of (T). *Syn.:* tongue thrust (abbr. T.T.), tongue ram (abbr. T.R.). *See also* EXTENDED TECHNIQUE.

TONGUE THRUST. Abbr. T.T. Same as **tongue stop**. *See also* EXTENDED TECHNIQUE.

TONGUING. A **technique** used by **wind instrumentalists** to give a more definite start to a note they have to play. It is accomplished by blocking and then releasing the airflow necessary to produce the note, using a quick movement of the tongue. *Syn.: tipping. See also* ANCHOR-TONGUE EMBOUCHURE; ATTACK; AUTOMATON; DOUBLE TONGUING; FLUTTER TONGUING; FRENCH TONGUING; GLOTTAL STOP; MULTIPLE TONGUING; SINGLE TONGUING; SLUR; T (2); TONGUE CLICK; TONGUE OUT; TONGUE PIZZICATO; TONGUE SLAP; TONGUE STOP; TRIPLE TONGUING; WARM-UP (1).

TOP NOTES. Usually a reference to notes in the **third octave**, but may also refer to notes in the **fourth octave**. *Syn.:* upper note. *See also* HIGH NOTES; LOW NOTES; MIDDLE (NOTE).

TOP OCTAVE. Usually a reference to the **third octave**, but may also refer to the **fourth octave**. *Cf.* **bottom octave**, **middle octave**.

TOP REGISTER. Same as **high register**. *See also* REGISTER (1); THIRD OCTAVE.

TOUCH. 1. Same as **touchpiece**. *See also* LEVER; RETUNING (2); ROLLER. **2.** The amount of effort required to activate a **key** and/or the distance the key has to move. **3.** A player's manner of depressing the keys. For example, someone might say that a **flutist** has a "light touch." *See also* PAD. For **early flutes**, *see also* TONE-HOLE BUSHING.

TOUCHPIECE. Also *touch piece*. Any part of the **key mechanism** that needs to be touched to activate a **key**. For example, the D♯ key may be called a D♯ touchpiece. *Syn.:* key touch, touch. Depending on the shape of the touch piece or how it works, it may alternatively be called by another name such as (key) **cup**, **lever**, **spatula**, **roller**, or **crescent key**.

tr. An abbreviation for **trill**.

TRADITIONAL HEAD JOINT. A **head joint** that, in general, has a smaller, more oval **embouchure hole** than a **modern head joint**, a **blowing edge** not particularly sharp, no **overcut** (or no intentional overcut), and a subtle **undercut**.

TRADITIONAL PADS. Sometimes referred to as **felt pads** or card-backed pads. *See also* CUSHION; GOLD PADS; PAD; PISONI PADS; STRAUBINGER PAD; SYNTHETIC PAD.

TRADITIONAL SCALE. A common modern expression to denote the **scale** on a **Boehm flute** originally designed for $A_1 = 435$ Hz. Sometimes this is mistakenly called a "long scale" to disguise the fact that the manufacturer was in error. In the 1970s, some London **flutists** called for a reassessment of **Theobald Boehm**'s **Schema**, and due to the work of **Albert Cooper** and others, it was found that the "traditional scale" was in fact simply a scale on a **flute** built to play at A = 435 Hz that had not been altered after the international rise in performing **pitch** in the early part of the 20th century (*see* CONCERT PITCH [1]) other than to shorten the **head** (*see* SHORTENED HEAD JOINT). A traditional-scale flute is very difficult to play well **in tune** at A = 440 Hz because the **left-hand notes** are **sharp** and the **foot-joint notes flat**, although some performers have managed by shortening the head and using great skill. Nowadays, players prefer an easier route to perfection by playing flutes with **modern scales**. *Syn.:* old scale. *See also* RETUNING.

TRANSPOSING INSTRUMENTS. 1. As the term is used in this book, instruments that sound at a different **pitch** to that suggested by the music notation. By this definition, all **flutes** in the **Boehm flute** family (*see* app. 1; FLUTE FAMILY [2]) except for the **concert flute** in C are transposing instruments. Their written notes are transposed from the conventional note placement. For example, the **contrabass flute's** written notes are transposed up two octaves, the **bass flute's** by an octave, the **alto flute's** by a perfect fourth, and the **piccolo's** *down* by an octave. This is done for convenience so that the relationship between notation and **fingering** can remain the same as that of the concert flute and also so that the notes are easier to read without using excessive ledger lines. Figure 45 shows the relationship between how music sounds and how it is written for various members of the flute family.

It is important to note that, for simplicity, the names for the **keys** and parts of all the members of the Boehm flute family are not usually transposed, but are named after the similar key or part on the concert flute. For example, using this system, the **foot joint** on the alto flute in G would be called a **C foot joint** and not a G foot and the key **touch** necessary for producing **low C** would be called low C and not low g (see app. 8, note 1). *See also* MURRAY FLUTE.

2. An alternative definition is the same as that above, except referring only to instruments that are *not* in the key of C (*see* "FLUTE IN THE KEY OF . . ."). By this definition, all flutes in the Boehm flute family that are not in the key of C would be considered transposing

instruments (e.g., the alto flute in G, the piccolo in D♭, etc.). Flutes in the key of C sound the note C when any written C is **fingered** and played. Instruments which are **pitched** in the key of C are said to be in **concert pitch**.

TRANSVERSE FLUTE. It. *flauto traverso,* **traverso**, *traversa;* Fr. *flûte traversière, traversière;* Ger. *Querflöte.* **1.** The English translation of the name in various European languages during the 18th century (and French in the 14th century) for the predecessor of the modern orchestral or **concert flute** as we know it today, to distinguish it from the **recorder.** The English language used the name "German flute," and, as it eclipsed the recorder in popularity, simply "**flute**." *Syn.:* cross-blown flute, cross flute. *See also* BAROQUE FLUTE (1); CLASSICAL FLUTE; COMMON FLUTE; EIGHT-KEYED FLUTE; ENGLISH FLUTE; FOUR-KEYED FLUTE; FIVE-KEYED FLUTE; NINE-KEYED FLUTE; ONE-KEYED FLUTE; PICCOLO (1); QUANTZ FLUTE; RANGE (2); SIMPLE-SYSTEM FLUTE (1, 3); SIX-KEYED FLUTE; TEN-KEYED FLUTE; TUTOR (2); TWO-KEYED FLUTE. **2.** Today, the term may also refer to any flute that is held to the side. *See* VERTICAL FLUTE.

TRAVERSA. It. *See* TRANSVERSE FLUTE (1); *TRAVERSO*.

TRAVERSFLÖTE. Ger. *See TRAVERSO.*

TRAVERSIÈRE. Fr. *See* TRANSVERSE FLUTE.

TRAVERSO. Short for *flauto traverso.* **1.** *Flauto traverso, traversa,* and occasionally *traverso* were standard terms for the **transverse flute** in Italy and elsewhere in Europe in the 18th century. *Traversflöte* was a standard term used in Germany in the 20th century. **2.** *Traverso* is used by many today as a synonym for the **Baroque one-keyed flute** or even later 18th-century flutes with more than one key. *See also* EMBOUCHURE HOLE; REVERSE TENON.

TREATISE. An extensive and formal piece of writing on a particular subject, usually containing a discussion of its principles. Four of the most renowned flute **treatises** are those written by **Johann Joachim Quantz** (1752), **Johann George Tromlitz** (1791), **Richard S. Rockstro** (1890), and **Nancy Toff** (1985) (see bib. under "Historical Methods, Treatises, and Tutors" for information about the first three treatises, and under "Pedagogy" for the last). A bibliography of flute **method** books that includes treatises can be found at http//flutehistory.com/Resources/Lists/Flute.methods.php3. *See also* BAROQUE FLUTE (1); CLASSICAL FLUTE; CORPS DE RECHANGE; DOUBLE TONGUING; FINGER VIBRATO; *FLÛTE D'AMOUR* (2); MEANTONE TEMPERAMENT; ROCKSTRO MODEL FLUTE; SCREW-CORK (1); TUTOR.

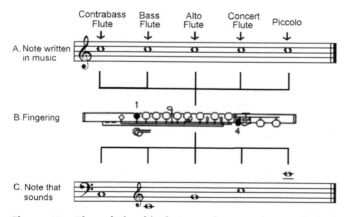

Figure 45. The relationship between how music sounds and how it is written for various members of the flute family. *Flute by Susan Maclagan. Drawing edited and labeled by Tess Vincent.*

TREBLE FLUTE. British term for the alto **recorder** ca. 1700. *Syn.:* treble common flute. *See also* COMMON FLUTE.

TREBLE FLUTE IN G. An uncommon member of the **Boehm flute** family (see FLUTE FAMILY [2]), **pitched** in G, sounding a perfect fifth higher than the **concert flute** in C. The treble flute in G is **side-blown** like the concert flute, uses the same **fingering system**, and, except for small playing changes, is played in a similar way. Its **range** is around three octaves from the note sounding as G$_1$ to G$_4$ (written C$_1$ to C$_4$; *see* TRANSPOSING INSTRUMENTS). The length of the treble flute is about 17.5 in. (44.5 cm). It is likely that **Rudall**, **Carte** & Co. was the first to make the treble flute in G in the late 1800s.

Very little music has been written for the treble flute in G. It may be heard in some **flute choirs**. It is not a regular member of the band or symphony orchestra, although it might be used by **piccolo** players to facilitate the playing of out-of-range **low notes** in some piccolo **parts** (e.g., the *Peter Grimes* part that goes down to **low b**) or to facilitate the playing of some difficult **high notes** in concert flute parts (e.g., Prokofiev's *Classical Symphony*). Students who are too small to hold the concert flute will find the treble flute a suitable beginning instrument.

The treble flute in G is an essential voice in the Northern Irish and Scottish **flute bands**. Music for these bands virtually always includes parts for **solo** treble, first treble, and second treble. The parts are usually played by one person on a part, and the solo treble often carries the principal line of music, often doubling in the same register as the piccolo. Surprisingly, when bands have learning classes or "apprentice bands," they do not use treble flutes. Even when beginners are small (they often begin at age six or seven), they use concert flutes. *Syn.:* G soprano, G treble, treble G, soprano flute in G (*see* "FLUTE IN . . ." for naming information). *See also* app. 1; *FLAUTINO*.

TREMOLO. It. quivering, fluttering, trembling. Abbr. *trem.* **1.** Usually, a rapid repeated alternation of two notes more than a second apart. Special **fingerings** are sometimes necessary to allow sufficient speed. For example, a standard C$_2$ to E$_2$ tremolo fingering is

$$\underline{\text{T}} \ 1 \ \underline{2} \ 3 \ - \ /1 \ 2 \ - \ 4\text{D}_\#$$

(finger E as shown and move the underlined fingers rapidly on and off the **keys** and in unison). Tremolos may be notated in various ways, including

or

The first example indicates that a C$_2$ to E$_2$ tremolo should be played for the length of a quarter note; in the latter example, the tremolo is from C$_2$ to E$_2$ for the length of a half note. *Syn.:* fingered tremolo. *See also* C$_\#$ TRILL KEY; MURRAY FLUTE. *Cf.* trill. **2.** A rapid repetition of one note or chord, usually done on string instruments by using back-and-forth strokes of the bow, the effect being accomplished on the **flute** by rapid **double tonguing** or **flutter-tonguing**. **3.** A **vibrato** that is unpleasant, usually one that is too fast. **4.** A wavering of the tone. This is normally called *vibrato* by modern authorities, but the term *tremolo* was used in the 19th century to describe this effect.

TRILL. Abbr. *tr.* An **ornament** in which two notes a semitone or whole tone apart are alternated in rapid succession. The first note is **tongued** and the rest of the notes are **slurred**. In modern editions of music, it is usually shown by the symbol *tr* OR *tr*⌇⌇⌇ above the note to be trilled, the wavy line indicating the length of the trill. In the 18th century, a "+" above a note indicated an ornament of some kind, including a trill as one possibility.

The note under the trill sign is called the **principal note**, and the other note in the trill is the **upper note**. The upper note is a semitone or a whole tone in **pitch** above the written principal note, according to the key signature and any accidental directly above the trill sign.

The trill is played for a length of time that depends on the time value of the written note under the trill sign. The number of alternations of the trilled notes within this length of time, their rhythmic distribution, their speed, and the way the trill starts and ends varies with the musical context (i.e., the historical period, the tempo, the style of the music, and so on).

In the latter part of the Baroque period, most trills began on the upper note and on the beat. This was done to add dissonance to the music at that point and make it more interesting harmonically. The upper note was usually accented and could be prolonged to bring out the dissonance. The first note or notes on which the trill starts were sometimes shown in the music in the form of small notes. There were two standard endings that could be employed, whether or not they were indicated in the music: a **turn** or a note of anticipation. For the *turned* ending, the last four notes of the trill are those of a turn on the main note and the last two of these are often shown as two small notes, the first a tone or semitone below the main note, and the next, the principal note (see fig. 46, part A). The *note of anticipation* is a note that is played briefly just after the last trilling of the principal note and has the same pitch as the normal note following the trill (see fig. 46, part B).

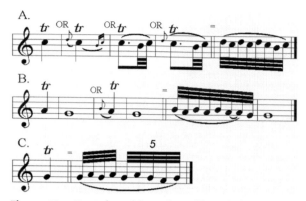

Figure 46. **Examples of how the trill symbols might be written and played.**

The trill changed gradually from the upper-note start to a principal-note start in the first half of the 19th century, since by then the upper-note start was not as important harmonically in the music (see fig. 46, part C). Principal-note starts became more the "rule" after around 1828, when they were advocated by J. N. Hummel in his piano **method**.

Sometimes referred to as a *shake*. See also B/C♯ TRILL KEY; B♭ FINGERINGS; C/D TRILL KEY/LEVER; C♯ TRILL KEY; DORUS G♯ KEY; FINGERING CHART; G/A TRILL KEY; GIZMO KEY; GRACE NOTES; HALF-HOLING; KEY VIBRATO; LEFT-HAND LEVER; MURRAY FLUTE; OPEN-HOLE FLUTE; *PRALLTRILLER*; QUARTER-TONE TRILL; RING-KEY FLUTE; ROCKSTRO MODEL FLUTE; SPLIT E MECHANISM; SPLIT F♯ MECHANISM; *TREMOLO*; TRILL FINGERING; TRILL KEYS; UPPER MORDENT (2); VIRTUAL FLUTE (2). For **early flutes** and other non-**Boehm-system** flutes, *see also* AUGMENTED NOTES; FIVE- KEYED FLUTE; FOUR-KEYED FLUTE; REFORM FLUTE (1); TULOU *FLÛTE PERFECTIONÉE*.

TRILL FINGERING. A combination of two **fingerings** that facilitates the playing of two different but closely pitched notes (a semitone or whole tone apart) several times in rapid succession. Trill fingerings are used mainly to facilitate the playing of **trills**, but they can also be used as **alternate fingerings** for regular note pairs when the speed of the music is too fast to use the **basic fingering** without a great deal of difficulty. For example, the trill fingering for the notes E_2 to $F_{\sharp 2}$ is

$$T\ 1\ 2\ 3\ -\ /\ \underline{1}\ 2\ -\ 4D_\sharp.$$

To perform this trill, the **flutist** puts her fingers on the **keys** shown and then moves R1 up and down on the key that is underlined. Trill fingerings are represented on a trill **fingering chart**. *See also* B♭ FINGERINGS; BROSSA F♯ LEVER; B TRILL KEY; SPLIT F♯ MECHANISM; TRILL KEYS.

TRILL KEYS. **Keys** used to facilitate the playing of certain **trills**. The D and D♯ trill keys are the primary trill keys, used not only to facilitate trills but also in some **basic fingerings** in the **third octave** and in many **alternate fingerings**. R2 usually operates the D trill key and R3 the D♯ trill key. Depending on the **passage**, however, it may be better to use R1 for the D trill key and R2 for the D♯. For example, in order to play from $F_{\sharp 3}$ to B_3, or vice versa, R2 would be used for the D♯ trill key in order to avoid the difficulty of sliding the R3 from the D key to the D♯ trill key. The **flutist** chooses the finger for a trill key that leaves him in the best position to play the notes that follow.

The D trill key was invented by **Johann Nepomuk Capeller** in 1811 and the D♯ trill key by **Victor J. B. Coche** in 1838. The D trill key is sometimes referred to as the *first trill key/lever*, the *upper trill key/lever*, or the *C/D trill key/lever*, and the D♯ trill key may be referred to as the *second trill key/lever*, the *lower trill key/lever*, or the *C♯/D♯ trill key/lever*. Both are sometimes called *shake* keys (*shake* is an older term for a trill).

Other trill keys include the B♭ trill key/lever (*see* B♭ SIDE LEVER), **C♯ trill key**, **G/A trill key**, **B trill key**, and **B/C♯ trill key**.

See also BUFFET, AUGUSTE, JEUNE; BUMPER; CURVED HEAD JOINT; CYLINDRICAL BOEHM FLUTE; FLOATING; MURRAY FLUTE; PIVOT SCREWS; RING-KEY FLUTE; ROCKSTRO F♯ LEVER; SECTION (2); STUDENT FLUTE; WATERLINE KEYS. For **early flutes** and other non-**Boehm-system** flutes, *see also* REFORM FLUTE; TEN-KEYED FLUTE.

TRILL (KEY) SECTION. *Syn.:* trill key assembly. *See* SECTION (2).

TRIO. An **ensemble** of, or a **piece** for, three musicians. A **flute** trio may consist of three **flutists**, or one flutist and two other players. Trio sonatas, a popular form of chamber music in the Baroque period, are played by two **solo** instruments and a keyboard plus a bass instrument reinforcing the bass line. *See also* FLÛTE D'AMOUR (2).

TRIPLE STOP. Three notes sounded together. May sometimes be referred to as a "three-note **multiphonic**." *Cf.* **double stop**.

TRIPLE TONGUING. A type of **multiple tonguing** where three syllables, such as "tu ku tu," "thu ku thu," or "du ku du," are used to facilitate the **tonguing** of notes in fast **passages** where **single tonguing** is not possible (e.g., sixteenth notes). This applies whenever notes are grouped in threes or multiples of three.

For triple tonguing, two parts of the tongue are used alternately to silently pronounce the syllables, one for each note. In each group of three using the pattern *tu-ku-tu*, the first note is played with *tu*, the second with *ku*, and the third with *tu*, for example,

tu ku tu

The position and stroke of the tongue for *tu* and *ku* are the same as for **double tonguing**. The syllables are repeated rapidly for the length of the passage. Some players use and advise double tonguing for triple passages in an effort to smooth out any unevenness.

Note that in certain cases, such as where a rest, a tie, or a **slur** interrupts the normal group of three, some find it easier to double-tongue the two notes after the rest, tie, or slur and then resume the normal triple-tonguing pattern for the following group of three notes.

tu ku tu ku tu

TRIPOLI. A light, porous, sedimentary rock composed mainly of the siliceous shells of diatoms. It may be white, gray, pink, red, buff, or yellow in color. It is used by flute-makers and repairers to **polish** metals. *Syn.:* rotten-stone. *See also* BUFFING; FINISH (3).

TROMLITZ, JOHANN GEORGE (b. Reinsdorf, Germany, 1725; d. Leipzig, Germany, 1805). A German **woodwind** maker and **flute** inventor whose business thrived in Leipzig from before 1753 through 1805. He was also a **flutist, principal flutist** in an orchestra, flute teacher, composer, and author whose works included **treatises** on flute playing and on the **keyed flute** (see bib. under "Historical Methods, Treatises, and Tutors" and "History"). *See also* CLASSICAL FLUTE; MEANTONE TEMPERAMENT (2); TWO-KEYED FLUTE.

TRUMPET-SOUND. Same as **buzz-tone**. *See also* EXTENDED TECHNIQUE.

TUBE/TUBING. The tube-like parts of a **flute**. **1.** Most often, a reference to the **head joint, middle joint**, and/or **foot joint** without any **fittings**. Tubes come in various thicknesses (*see* WALL [1]). Most modern flutemakers who need metal tubing to make flutes get it premade from tube makers or metal suppliers, but usually **draw** the head-joint tube themselves to get the desired **taper**. Wooden flutemakers make their own tubes by **turning** and **reaming billets**, which they get from a wood supplier. *See also* BELL (1); BODYMAKER; BODY TUBING; BORE; BOW; BRIDGE; CROOK; CRYOGENICS; CUTOFF FREQUENCY; DIE (1); DRAWN TUBING; EMBOUCHURE RECUT; END CORRECTION; FOSTER EXTENSION; GLASS FLUTE; GOLD FLUTE; HEAD-JOINT LINING; HEAD-JOINT MAKER; INTERNAL TUNING; LACQUER; MANDREL; MATIT

CARBON-FIBER FLUTE; OCTAVE LENGTH; "PARABOLIC"; PATCHING; PLATINUM FLUTE; RESONANCE (1); RING (2); SEAMED TUBING; SILVER FLUTE; SOLDERED TONE HOLES; SOUNDING LENGTH (2); STEP; STRESS RELIEVING. **2. Key tubing**.

TULOU, JEAN-LOUIS (b. Paris, 1786; d. Nantes, France, 1865). A French **woodwind** maker, **flute** designer, manufacturer, and dealer whose business thrived in Paris from 1829 to 1860. Tulou was also a renowned **simple-system flutist** who was opposed to the **Boehm flute** being used at the **Paris Conservatoire**. He was **principal flutist** in various French orchestras, flute professor at the Paris Conservatoire 1829–1860, a composer, and the author of *Méthode de flûte* (1851). *See also* TULOU *FLÛTE PERFECTIONÉE*.

TULOU *FLÛTE PERFECTIONÉE*. A development of the French **eight-keyed simple-system flute** that usually consisted of four extra **keys** and a **key mechanism** using **post-mounts** to support the keys. The extra keys were:

- a duplicate C key (called *clef d'ut* by Tulou) operated by L3 (in later models by the LT)
- a Tulou F♯ key (*clef de Fa♯*) that was operated by the second joint of R3 or the tip of R4 and designed to slightly raise the **pitch** of the F♯ in all octaves
- a C♯ key (*clef d'UT♯*) operated by R1 and used primarily for the **trills** $C_{\sharp3}/B_2$, D_2/C_2, D_3/C_3, $D_{\sharp2}/C_{\sharp2}$, and $A_3/G_{\sharp3}$
- a D **trill key** (*cadence de Re*) that was operated by R1 and also intended mainly for trills: E_3/D_3, $D_{\sharp3}/C_{\sharp3}$ and F_3/E_3 (see fig. 47).

The *Flûte Perfectionée* was designed by **Jean-Louis Tulou** (1786–1865) and made in the 1840s by **Jacques Nonon**. There were several different versions.

The term *perfectionée* was probably applied to the flute in order to direct attention to its improvements as compared to the basic **five-keyed** and eight-keyed simple-system flutes in use at the time. Tulou's *Flûte Perfectionée* was never very common, but it could be obtained from French makers until the end of the 19th century.

TUNE. *v.* To adjust the **pitch** or pitches of an instrument to an acceptable standard. For example, the **flutist** tries to tune the **flute** by adjusting the **head joint** until the instrument is made to play "**in tune**." *See also* A; CONCERT PITCH (1); DIFFERENCE TONE; EQUAL TEMPERAMENT; "FLUTE PITCHED AT A = . . ."; HIGH-PITCHED FLUTE; INTONATION; JUST INTONATION; LOW-PITCHED FLUTE;

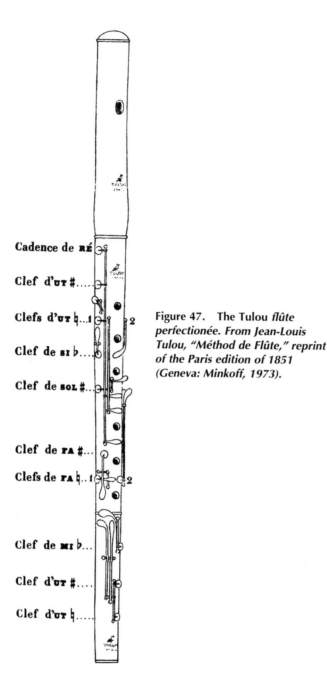

Cadence de **RÉ**

Clef d'**UT** #....

Clefs d'**UT** ♮..1   2

Clef de **SI** ♭....

Clef de **SOL** #...

Clef de **FA** #...

Clefs de **FA** ♮..1   2

Clef de **MI** ♭...

Clef d'**UT** #....

Clef d'**UT** ♮....

Figure 47. The Tulou *flûte perfectionée. From Jean-Louis Tulou, "Méthod de Flûte," reprint of the Paris edition of 1851 (Geneva: Minkoff, 1973).*

MEANTONE TEMPERAMENT (1); MURRAY FLUTE; ONE-KEYED FLUTE; OUT OF TUNE; PYTHAGOREAN TUNING; RENAISSANCE FLUTE; RETUNING; SCREW-CORK; TEMPER (4); THROAT TUNING; TUNING; TUNING NOTE; TUNING SLIDE; TUNING UP.

TUNER. An electronic device used either to determine whether a note is **in tune** or not or to accurately give the **pitch** of a given note. Tuners come with various features and in an assortment of shapes and sizes (e.g., see app. 12, fig. 9).

One feature that tuners always have is visual feedback. They can show, using a graphic display, whether the note that the **flutist** is playing is at the correct pitch. The most important added features that a tuner can have are:

- audio feedback. The pitch of each note in a particular **range** of notes can be sounded. This feature allows flutists to compare the **tuning** of their notes to that of the tuner.
- a control that sets the overall standard reference pitch for A_1 (e.g., $A_1 = 440$ Hz). The range for A_1 on tuners is usually somewhere between 438 Hz and 445 Hz. Most of the time, this control is set to one of these pitches and is thereafter ignored. Once the pitch for A_1 on the tuner is set, all the other notes on the tuner are produced so that they are in tune with that A_1.
- a control that sets the tuner to various **temperaments**, from historic **tunings** such as **Pythagorean**, **Meantone**, and a variety of **Well-temperaments** to the modern-day **equal-temperament** tuning.

On any given tuner, the range of the visual feedback is usually greater than the range of the audio feedback. These ranges may differ from model to model. The best tuner has a visual and audio range that covers as much of the basic range of the **flute** (i.e., up to D_4) as possible. *See also* app. 11; INTONATION; REAL-TIME-TUNING-ANALYSIS; TEMPERAMENT; TUNING NOTE; TUNING SLIDE (1).

TUNE-UP. 1. Same as **tuning up. 2.** Same as **clean-oil-and-adjust.**

TUNING. 1. Adjusting a musical instrument or group of instruments to the desired **pitches.** When done before playing, it may be followed by "up," as in "**tuning up.**" *See also* CONCERT PITCH (1); CYLINDRICAL BOEHM FLUTE (3); HEAD-JOINT CORK; HELMHOLTZ RESONATOR; INTONATION; RING-KEY FLUTE; STOPPER; TUNER; TUNING RINGS; TUNING SLIDE. For **early flutes,** *see also CORPS DE RECHANGE;* FOOT REGISTER; LAPPING; ONE-KEYED FLUTE; RENAISSANCE FLUTE.

2. Adjusting all notes of an instrument to a particular **tuning system,** such as **Meantone** tuning. *See also* DIFFERENCE TONES; BEATS; EQUAL TEMPERAMENT; JUST INTONATION; PYTHAGOREAN TUNING; TEMPER (4); TEMPERAMENT; TUNER; WELL-TEMPERAMENT. **3.** See **tuning note** or tuning system. **4.** The process by which the **tone holes** of a **flute** are moved or altered in such a way as to affect the tuning. *See also* app. 11; RETUNING; SCALE. For early flutes, *see also BRILLE* (1). **5.** *See* INTERNAL TUNING.

TUNING BARREL. *See* BARREL (2); TUNING HEAD.

TUNING CAP. Same as **crown** or **screw-cap**.

TUNING CORK. A **stopper** that is made of **cork** and is part of a **cork assembly**.

TUNING FORK. A two-prong device made of spring **steel** that sounds a note when struck against a semihard object, such as a knee. It looks like a small, two-tine fork (see app. 12, fig. 11). Musicians compare the tuning fork's note with the corresponding note on their own instruments to check whether their note is **in tune**. Tuning forks can be made to sound any note, though the most common ones sound A_1 at 440 Hz, the standard reference pitch for Western music (*see* CONCERT PITCH [1]). The tuning fork was invented by English trumpeter and lutenist John Shore (ca.1662–1752) in 1711. *See also* FREQUENCY; PURE TONE (1).

TUNING HEAD. A two-piece **head joint** that originated in 1785 and was commonly found in wooden or **ivory one-keyed flutes**, **two-keyed flutes**, and **simple-system flutes** by the middle of the 19th century (see app. 3, A, figs. 1 and 2). It had a "head joint proper" with a **screw-cork** assembly (*see* CORK ASSEMBLY [2]) and a **barrel** joint (def. 2) or tuning barrel. On the first models, the head joint proper had a wooden **socket** into which a partially **corked** or thread-covered **tenon** of a barrel joint fitted. The barrel joint functioned as a **tuning slide** (def. 2). **Johann Joachim Quantz** promoted flutes with a tuning head in his 1752 **treatise**, *Versuch* (see app. 3, A, fig. 1).

In 1785, a tuning head was patented by flutemaker **Richard Potter**. Both parts of Potter's head joint were metal lined (see app. 3, A, fig. 2). The **lining** for the head joint proper extended beyond its open end, and when fitted inside a separate extended barrel liner, which was sometimes covered with a thin layer of wood, the whole head was assembled. The fully metal-lined tuning head was common in English and German simple-system flutes by the middle of the 19th century, but was rare in France. *See also* FOOT REGISTER; HEAD-JOINT LINING; SCREW-CORK (1).

TUNING NOTE. A reference note (usually "**concert A**") provided by the oboe for orchestras or, for bands, "concert B♭" provided by an electronic **tuner** or any reliable instrument (*see* CONCERT PITCH [1]) that is played before an **ensemble** plays music together. This is done so that the other members of the ensemble can compare the **pitch** of their own notes (usually also A or B♭) to the reference note. Once compared, the musicians adjust or tune their instruments and/or playing, if required, so that their notes are **in tune** with the reference note. Sometimes more than one tuning note is used.

The tuning note "A concert" has traditionally been used for orchestras because it is easiest to use for string **tuning**. Similarly, "B♭ concert" is traditionally used for bands because it is easiest for the trumpets (which uses no valves for this note) and trombones (which play it in first [or closed] position). *See also* TUNING UP (1).

TUNING REGISTER. *See* FOOT REGISTER.

TUNING RINGS. **Bore**-size wooden or metal rings that were used to fill in the abrupt expansion in the bore that occurred just below the head-joint **tenon** of some 18th- and early 19th-century **flutes** when the **head joint** was extended out from the **middle joint** in order to **tune** the flute. The tuning rings supplied with replicas may be plastic.

The tuning rings were put in by the player during the process of **tuning up**. The number and size of rings that were needed to fill the bore gap depended on the distance the head joint was out from the middle joint. The **flutist** would tune up, measure the distance that the head joint was out, remove it, put in the rings, rejoin it to the middle joint, possibly retune, and then proceed with playing. When tuning rings are used, the average **pitch** is little changed, but the uneven **response** and tuning anomalies that are caused by the abrupt expansion in the bore are alleviated.

Tuning rings were normally only used with those flutes, such as **Baroque flutes**, that did not have **tuning slides**, since when there was a tuning slide, the discrepancy in the bore when the tuning slide was extended for tuning purposes was usually too small to be of concern. Tuning rings were rarely used, if at all, on four-jointed flutes with *corps de rechange*, because the tuning of flutes with these could be adjusted by changing to a longer **upper joint** instead of extending the head joint out from the middle joint, thus avoiding any large expansion in the bore.

Modern flutes do not usually come with tuning rings, although one flutemaker, **Lenny Lopatin** (b.1954), has been experimenting with metal rings of different lengths in his **SquareONE flutes** and has found that they help with smoother transitions between **registers**, give the sound a stronger core, and make it easier to **overblow** the octaves with truer pitch. He has several rings of different lengths so that he can choose the best one for the pitch environment that he finds himself in; if he is playing in a "**sharp** environment," for instance, he will not use a ring. Metal tuning rings may be called *sleeves*. *See also* STEP (3).

TUNING SLIDE. 1. The **tenon** part of the **head joint** that is nearest to the open end (see app. 7, fig. 10). On wooden **flutes**, it is usually made of metal. The tuning slide pushes into the **middle joint** when the flute is assembled. Flutemakers allow for the flute to be **in tune** when the head is pulled out about 0.08 in. (2 mm) or more, depending on the flute make and model. To find this optimal position of the head joint, **flutists** set the **octave length** (*see* TUNING UP [2]). Some feel that pulling out the head joint usually results in a positive effect on the tone.

The tuning slide is used in **tuning** to lengthen or shorten the flute. To play **flatter**, or lower in **pitch**, the head joint is pulled out; to play **sharper**, or higher in pitch, the opposite is done. Flutists try to move the head joint minimally from its original setting, because when it is moved from this position, the **scale** is affected unevenly with the **left-hand notes** being affected more than the right.

If a flutist cannot tune correctly with the head joint adjusted close to the original setting, then something else might be wrong. This usually has to do with the way that the flutist is playing (e.g., he may need to adjust things such as his **embouchure**, or if the problem is in the **upper register**, then the **head-joint cork** may need adjusting). It is also well to verify that the reference note is at the pitch required; checking with a **tuner** rather than another instrument may be more reliable.

When using a different head joint than that which came with the flute, the **head** may need to be pulled out 0.8 in. (2 cm) or even more to set the octave length. *See also* SOUNDINIG LENGTH (3); STOPPER; TUNING RINGS.

2. On some **one-keyed**, **two-keyed**, and **simple-system conical flutes** with two-piece wooden or **ivory** cylindrical head joints—that is, a **barrel** joint and a "head joint proper" with **embouchure hole**, **cap**, and **screw-cork** (*see* TUNING HEAD)—the tuning slide is the wooden or metal extension of one of the head joint parts that joins into the other (see app. 3, A, figs. 1 and 2).

At first, the head joint pieces were wooden and the barrel joint had a long, relatively thin wooden tenon or "tuning slide" that was wrapped with waxed thread or **cork** (*see* LAPPING) and fit into the head joint proper. This type may be found on some flutes made between approximately 1750 and 1820. **Johann Joachim Quantz**, in his 1752 *Versuch*, claims to have invented this type of tuning slide before 1750.

Another type of two-piece head joint incorporating a tuning slide was introduced and patented by **Richard Potter** in 1785. Here the barrel and head joint proper were lined with metal and the metal **lining** of the barrel joint slid telescopically onto the metal lining of the head joint proper, which extended beyond the end. The extended metal part was the tuning slide and became standard on simple-system flutes in the 19th century.

The tuning slide was used to make slight tuning adjustments and gradually replaced the *corps de rechange*, which had been more useful for larger adjustments in pitch. When the tuning slide was lengthened by drawing it out slightly but not completely from the barrel joint, the overall length of the head joint became longer, and the notes of the flute played a bit flatter. When it was shortened by pushing it slightly farther into the head joint, the overall length of the head joint became shorter, and the notes of the flute played slightly sharper. In both cases, the pitches of the **higher notes** in each octave were affected a little more than the **lower notes**.

The tuning slide went through several stages of development, until it gradually evolved into the modern tuning slide of today (def. 1 above).

See also GIORGI FLUTE; SOUNDING LENGTH (3); STOPPER; TUNING RINGS.

TUNING SYSTEM. The set of notes to which some instruments, such as the piano, are **tuned**. *See also* CLASSICAL FLUTE; FINGERING SYSTEM; MEANTONE TEMPERAMENT.

TUNING UP. 1. A procedure undertaken by musicians before they play to ensure they are **in tune**. In a small **ensemble** where no oboist is present, the **flutist** usually leads the procedure. In this situation, the **(first) flutist** plays a reference note or **tuning note** (most often **A** or **B♭**) for a brief time, so that the other musicians may compare the **pitch** of their note to the flutist's and adjust accordingly.

In larger ensembles, bands, and orchestras, an oboist (but occasionally another instrumentalist or a **tuner**) usually produces the reference note. All musicians compare the pitch of their note to the reference note and match the sound of the reference note by adjusting their instrument or their playing. Adjusting the **flute** involves changing the effective length of the flute by pushing the **head joint** into or pulling it out of the **middle joint** (but only if absolutely necessary—see def. 2 below). Adjusting one's playing requires that the flutist change such things as **embouchure** or breathing (*see* INTONATION for more information).

Any procedure may have to be repeated several times before the group is in tune, or if the group has chosen to **tune** to other reference notes as well. *Syn.:* **tuning** (1). *See also* CONCERT PITCH (1); HEAD-JOINT CORK; HIGH (1); LOW (2); LOWERING A NOTE; OUT OF TUNE; RAISING A NOTE; SHARP; TUNING FORK; TUNING RINGS; TUNING SLIDE.

2. The term may also refer to a procedure that should be done by a flutist before playing alone or before tuning with an ensemble as discussed above. It involves establishing the **octave length**, upon which the flute's **scale** is based, by finding the best placement for the head joint on a particular flute. This placement will insure that the flute is set to be played at its best scale and pitch (assuming that the head joint cork is set correctly).

This procedure may require the flutist to move the **foot joint** a short distance out from the middle joint, as some flutes have foot joints that are set slightly sharp. The flutist then finds the best placement for the head joint in the middle joint by playing C_2 as a second **harmonic** of (low) C_1 by using the **fingering** for (low) C_1 and then, without removing the R4 from the (low) C **roller**, comparing it to the pitch of C_2 that is produced when using the otherwise regular fingering for C_2. If the two notes are not exactly in tune, the flutist adjusts the head joint and repeats this part of the procedure until they are. Once these notes are in tune, the octave length is set. It is important that the head joint be left in this position for the best flute scale. If it is necessary to change the setup of the head joint in an ensemble situation, it is critical that it be left as close to the optimum position as possible. If the head joint is changed from this position, the flute will not play in tune with itself (*see* INTERNAL TUNING). *See also* FLUTE FLAG.

TURN. It. *gruppetto* little group. **1.** An **ornament** consisting of a group of four notes that "turn" around the **principal note**. The principal note is notated under the turn sign ∿ or under and slightly to the left of it (see fig. 48). For example, a turn with principal note G_1 might be the group of notes A_1, G_1, $F\#_1$, and G_1. The term is used today for two different ornaments: the upper (or standard) turn and the lower (or inverted) turn. Figure 48 shows examples of these ornaments, labeled as follows:

A. An accented upper turn (i.e., where the turn sign is just above the principal note)
B. An unaccented upper turn (i.e., where the turn sign is above and just to the right of the principal note)
C. An accented upper turn that follows a dotted note
D. An accented lower turn
E. An unaccented lower turn
F. An accented lower turn that follows a dotted note

The *upper* or *standard turn* consists of:

- the **upper note**, which is the note a semitone or whole tone above the principal note
- the principal note
- the **lower note**, which is the note a semitone or whole tone below the principal note
- the principal note again

All four notes are **slurred** together.

During the late Baroque period (ca. 1700–1750), the upper turn was often shown in music by the symbol ∿ above the principal note or above and slightly to the right of it. The upper and lower notes are not shown in the notation. They are in the prevailing key unless there are accidentals applied to the turn sign, which the player has to then apply to the notes. An accidental above the turn sign affects the upper note and an accidental below the turn sign affects the lower note.

The upper turn is performed instead of the notated principal note or after the principal note has been played, depending on the placement of the turn sign. If the turn sign is just above the principal note, then the group of notes is played instead of the principal note. If the turn sign is above and just to the right of the principal note, then the group of notes is played after the principal note has been played. The former type of turn is called an *accented* (or *unprepared*) *turn* since it starts on the beat; the latter is called an *unaccented* (or *prepared*) *turn* since it starts between beats.

The rhythmic execution of the upper turn depends on the length of the principal note, the musical context (particularly tempo), and the effect desired. See A, B, and C in figure 48 for some examples of how the upper turn symbol might be realized.

During the Classical period (ca. 1750–1820), it became common to indicate the exact notes of the turn by small notes, although composers sometimes wrote out turns in ordinary notation or used the sign ∿. All of these methods remain in use today. During this period

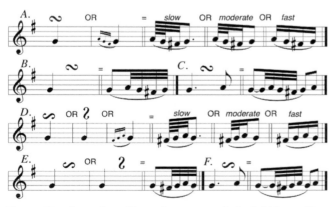

Figure 48. Examples of how the turn symbol might be written and played.

and beyond, the turn was also confusingly indicated by the same signs that are used for the lower turn (see below). One can often tell from the musical context, however, which sign is meant.

The *lower* or *inverted turn* consists of:

- the lower note, a semitone or a whole tone below the principal note
- the principal note
- the upper note, a semitone or a whole tone above the principal note
- the principal note again

Once again, all four notes are slurred together.

The lower turn is most often indicated by small notes, but may be indicated in music with the same symbol as the upper turn except with a vertical line drawn through it, as in ∽, or by the musical symbols ∽ or ?. It is performed in the same ways as the upper turn, but is not as common. See figure 48 D, E, and F for some ways of how the lower turn sign might be realized. *See also* AUGMENTED NOTES; GRACE NOTES; TRILL.

2. A procedure used when making **flutes** to shape a part by guiding a simple cutting tool to the rotating part to create the profile desired. *See* TURNING. *See also* SEASON.

TURN IN/TURN OUT. *See* ROLL-IN; ROLL-OUT.

TURNING. 1. The shaping of a part by guiding a simple cutting tool to the rotating part. Turning can be done by hand (i.e., "hand turning") where the tool is held and guided by the hand on a simple wood **lathe** or by machine (i.e., "machine turning").

Machine turning is similar to hand turning except that the tool is controlled by handwheels. It is much less flexible than hand turning, but more secure and accurate. There are various types of lathes that are used for machine turning: a *copy lathe* duplicates a part from a template; an *ornamental lathe* does decorative turning based on geometric patterns; and a *CNC (Computer Numerical Control) lathe* produces a specified part from a programmed set of instructions.

Turning is used to make anything that is round. This includes such things as **key tubing**, screws, **keys**, the **facing** of the ends of **tubing** on a metal flute, the exterior profiling of a wooden flute, the flute **sections**, the **stopper**, the **cap**, and the troughs at the **joints** for **lapping**. *See also* BAROQUE FLUTE (1); BLOCK-MOUNT; CHAMBERING; FINIAL; FRUITWOOD (1); HEAD-JOINT REFITTING; REAM; ROUGHING; THICKENING; WALKING-STICK FLUTE.

2. The object that is made by the turning method.

TUTOR. 1. Today, usually a private teacher of one or a small group of students. **2.** In the 18th century, a musical instruction book that generally included a **fingering chart**, a few basic ideas on playing the instrument, and a selection of unmethodical tunes. **Jacques Martin Hotteterre** wrote the first tutor for the **one-keyed transverse flute** in 1707. A bibliography of flute **method** books, which includes tutors, can be found at http://flutehistory.com/Resources/Lists/Flute.methods.php3. *See also* BAROQUE FLUTE (1); TREATISE.

TWO-KEYED FLUTE. A **transverse flute** that evolved from, and was similar to, the earlier **conical-bored one-keyed flute** except that it featured two **keys** (see app. 2, fig. 3). In modern times, some types of two-keyed flutes have been revived, and some people play originals or replicas of the instrument.

Probably the most famous type of two-keyed flute was the Baroque period "**Quantz flute**," which was named after **Johann Joachim Quantz** (1697–1773). because of his invention of a second key in 1726. The Quantz flute was distinguished by having two separate keys on the **foot joint** for D♯ and E♭, rather than the one key that served for both notes found on other **Baroque flutes**. Most flutes made by Quantz or under his direction also had a **screw-cork**, a **tuning slide** (said by Quantz to be his invention) in the **head joint**, and as many as five interchangeable **upper middle joints** (*see* CORPS DE RECHANGE). They also had a strong **first octave** compared with other Baroque flutes.

The screw-cork, tuning slide, and set of upper middle joints made it easier for the **flutist** to play **in tune** at the different **pitches** for **A** (e.g., A = 392, 398, 404, 410, or 435 Hz) that existed when he traveled from place to place. The D♯ and E♭ keys, which are sometimes referred to as *enharmonic keys,* made it easier for the flutist to play in tune in the type of Meantone tuning system that was used at the time (*see* MEANTONE TEMPERAMENT [2]). In this system, the **flat** notes were played **sharper** than the sharp notes (e.g., E♭ would be played sharper than D♯). Despite the improvement achieved by these enharmonic keys, they did not catch on with players or many other flutemakers (**Johann George Tromlitz** and **F. G. A. Kirst** being the only two, other than Quantz, that are known), and they disappeared from use before the end of the 18th century.

There were other varieties of two-keyed flutes, three which are worthy of mention. One was the two-keyed flute with a single key for E♭ and D♯ and a **low C key** on an **extended foot joint**. This type of two-keyed flute was the forerunner to the flute with an extended foot joint with a C and C♯ key. The other significant two-keyed flute types were a flute with a single key for E♭/D♯ and a **G♯ key** and a flute with a single key for E♭/D♯ and a low C♯ key. *See also* BLOCK-MOUNT; CONCERT FLUTE (2); EIGHT-KEYED FLUTE; FOUR-KEYED FLUTE; FIVE-KEYED FLUTE; FLAT SPRING (2); KEYED FLUTES (1); NINE-KEYED FLUTE; SIX-KEYED FLUTE; TEN-KEYED FLUTE; TUNING HEAD; TUNING SLIDE (2).

𝒰

UNDERADJUSTMENT. *See* ADJUSTMENT.

UNDERCUTTING. 1. The process of rounding and smoothing the lower edge of the **embouchure wall**. This is commonly only done to the bottom east and west side edges. Figure 49 illustrates a schematic cross-section of a **head joint,** showing the bottom side edges of the embouchure wall as they might look before and after an undercut and the top sides as they might look before and after an **overcut**. The dotted line signifies the placement of the **embouchure plate**. Sometimes undercutting is also done to the bottom south edge of the embouchure wall.

Undercutting is done to make the sound clearer and to improve the **response** of the **low** and **high registers**. Undercutting in general is sometimes referred to as *radiusing*. An undercut edge is sometimes referred to as being *beveled*. *See also* EMBOUCHURE HOLE; EMBOUCHURE RECUT; HEAD-JOINT MAKER; MODERN HEAD JOINT; TRADITIONAL HEAD JOINT; VOICING.

2. The process of rounding and smoothing the edges where the **tone hole chimney** meets the **bore**, although the term *fraizing* is more commonly used for this process. Flutemakers may undercut the entire inside bottom edge of a tone hole chimney or they may undercut only the east and west sides of this edge. Undercutting is most commonly done to **soldered tone holes**, but is occasionally done to **drawn tone holes**, although this can only be minimal since the metal is thin. Undercutting tone hole

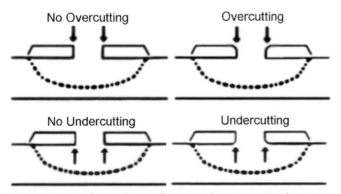

No Overcutting   Overcutting

No Undercutting   Undercutting

Figure 49. Undercutting and overcutting. *Drawing by Susan Maclagan; edited by Tess Vincent.*

chimneys helps the air to pass through more efficiently and produces clearer sounds. *See also* BRÖGGER ACOUSTIC; RETUNING.

3. The angle of the north or **blowing wall** (i.e., from the **blowing edge** to the bottom of the embouchure wall).

UNDERSLUNG. Any part of the flute **key mechanism** that is hidden from view underneath the main body of keywork. *See also* ADJUSTMENT SCREWS.

UNIBODY. A combined **middle joint** and **foot joint,** like that seen on a modern **piccolo**. Some older wooden or metal flutes were made with unibodies. For the player, the main disadvantage of the unibody is that it lacks a separate foot joint part that can be moved to the best position for the player's smallest finger of the right hand. There are two possible advantages to a wooden flute unibody. First, some **flutists** feel that wooden flutes with unibodies sound better. Second, since there is no **joint** in the flute **body,** it is less likely to split and there is no body **tenon** to break off. **Rudall, Carte** & Co. referred to the unibody as "middle and foot in one." *See also* MURRAY FLUTE.

UPPER BODY/CENTER JOINT. Same as **upper (middle) joint/piece**.

UPPER CHAMBER. The inside space of the **head joint** from the center of the **embouchure hole** to the end of the head joint, excluding the **crown**. This space is usually about 2.6 in. (65 mm) in length.

"UPPER" C KEY. An alternative name for the C **key** on the **middle joint** used to distinguish this key from the (**low**) **C key** on the **foot joint**. Often, it is confusingly referred to as the "upper" C♯ key (see app. 8 for an explanation). *See also* FINGER BUTTON; FLOATING; KEY EXTENSIONS; VEILED TONE (2).

"UPPER" C♯ KEY. *See* "UPPER" C KEY.

UPPER G KEY. *See* G KEYS.

UPPER (MIDDLE) JOINT/PIECE. The upper middle part of a four-piece **simple-system flute**. *Syn.:* upper center, upper body/center **joint,** upper joint/piece. *See also* BARREL (2); *CORPS D'AMOUR; CORPS DE RECHANGE;* MIDDLE JOINT (2); TUNING RINGS; TWO-KEYED FLUTE.

UPPER NOTE. 1. Same as **top note. 2.** An **ornamental** note that is higher in pitch by a semitone or whole tone from a preceding or following **principal note**. It occurs in ornaments such as **trills**, **turns**, and upper **mordents**. *Syn.:* upper auxiliary, upper subsidiary note, upper neighbor. *See also* LOWER NOTE (2); *PRALLTRILLER*.

UPPER OCTAVE. Same as **top octave**. *See also* REGISTER (1).

UPPER REGISTER. Same as **high register**. *See also* INTONATION; REGISTER (1).

UPPER TRILL KEY/LEVER. Same as the D **trill key**/lever.

UPRITE® HEADJOINT. A **head joint** invented by **Sanford Drelinger** (b.1943) that has been reconfigured to enable a **flutist** to play on a standard **Boehm-system** flute **body** in a vertical manner (see app. 10, fig. 2). To enable the player to easily hold the flute body, finger and thumb attachments are supplied for providing a five-point suspension system that distributes the weight of the flute equally so that no one area of the holding position is overly stressed. The UpRite Headjoint can be transformed into a transverse head joint, allowing the flutist to also play the instrument transversely. *See also* VERTICAL FLUTE; VERTICAL HEAD JOINT.

UP TONE-HOLE. A **soldered tone hole** chimney having a hole or **leak** in the soldered joint between the flute **body tubing** and the **chimney** (def. 2). Since the soldered joint is not complete, it causes the **tone hole** chimney to be "up" off the surface of the tubing. This can result if the joint is badly soldered or if the **solder** has deteriorated with time.

URTEXT. Ger. original text. **1.** The earliest version of a **piece** of music. **2.** A modern edition of an earlier **work** that is based on the most authentic available text or texts (e.g., in the latter case, the composer may have recomposed the piece). Most Urtext editions are based on the composer's autograph score or on original performing material bearing the composer's holograph corrections. An Urtext edition contains minimal **editorial** intervention, although it may include a detailed critical report. **3.** Loosely, any **scholarly edition**. *Cf.* **critical edition**, **facsimile**, **performer's edition**.

UTILITY FLUTIST. A **flutist** who is prepared to substitute for any of the positions in the **flute** section of an orchestra or band when called upon. Often the utility flutist also has another role, such as **second flutist**. In this case, the title would be "second flute(ist)/utility," and he or she will do mostly second flute playing, but could be asked to play any flute **part**, from **principal flutist** to pic-

colo. Another role that the utility flutist commonly has is as **assistant principal** (*see* PRINCIPAL FLUTIST [3]), which would take the title "assistant principal flute(ist)/utility." If a **work** calls for some other member of the **flute family**, such as a **contrabass flute**, the utility flutist would be called upon to play that part as well. *See also* THIRD FLUTIST.

UVULA. A small, teardrop-shaped extension of the soft **palate** that hangs from the roof of the mouth and is formed from fibers of the soft palate muscles (see app. 13, fig. 4). It is clearly visible on oneself with the aid of a mirror. Its position can influence the "openness" of the throat and the flute tone (*see* OPEN THROAT). The uvula is used in one type of **flutter-tonguing**. *See also* RESONANCE (2); ROAR-FLUTTER.

𝒱

VALGON RINGS™. Ringlike devices that are attached to the outside of each end of a **flute**. They are about 1.16 in. (29.5 mm) long and 1.2 in. (30.5 mm) in diameter and are made from 22-**karat gold** or **sterling silver** (see app. 12, fig. 8). The rings were invented in 1998 by clarinetist **Harold Gomez** and Konstantin Valtchev (1932–), a retired doctor. Gomez claims that the rings strengthen the oscillating **air column** on the outside of the flute, making it easier to play. He believes that all dynamic levels **project** better and the player can hear the sound more clearly. Gomez states that tests at the state-of-the-art D'Addario recording test studios in New York in 2002 showed that the **harmonics** were much stronger when the rings were on the instruments. The rings are also available for the **piccolo**, **bass flute**, and clarinets.

VANOTTI, LUIGI (n.d.). A **woodwind** maker in Milan, Italy, whose business prospered from before 1899 until after 1925. *See also* ALBISIPHON.

VAUCANSON, JACQUES DE (b. Grenoble, France, 1709; d. Paris, 1782). A French engineer who was the inventor of the first true robots. *See also* AUTOMATON.

VAUCANSON'S MECHANICAL FLUTE. *See* AUTOMATON.

VAULTED CLUTCH. A unique **clutch** invented in 1832 by **Theobald Boehm** and his flutemaker **Rudolph Greve** for a one-way connection between flute **keys**, using a curved arm that "vaults" from one side of the flute to close a key attached to the rod on the other side of the flute (see app. 4, fig. 2). This clutch was integral to the functioning of Boehm's ring-keyed 1832 system (*see* RING-KEY FLUTE) and was adopted by **Vincent Godfroy** (1806–1868) and **Louis Lot** (1807–1896) in Paris and by **George Rudall** (1781–1871) and **John Rose** (1793/94–1866) in London, among other makers. The term, coined and first published by **David Shorey** (b. 1953) in his 1983 *Sale Catalog of Historic Flutes*, is now in common use. *See also* app. 4. *Cf.* **back-connector**.

VEILED TONE. 1. On **early flutes**, such as the **Baroque** or **one-keyed flute**, those notes that have a softer and weaker tone because of **cross-fingering** or smaller **tone holes**. For a note to sound **full** and clear, it needs to have adequate **venting**. This includes having the tone holes directly below the **sounding hole** open and large enough to make the **resonance modes** close to **harmonic**. Failure to do this weakens the upper harmonics of the note sounded and affects the **tone quality**.

Notes with a veiled tone contributed to the sound and character of the early **flutes** and were sometimes consciously exploited by the composer for their effect, but in other contexts, where they were not musically satisfactory, they were disguised or worked around by the use of the **embouchure** or **alternate fingerings**. *See also* FOUR-KEYED FLUTE; G♯ KEY (2); RENAISSANCE FLUTE.

2. Veiled tones as described above never occur when using **basic fingerings** on the **Boehm flute**, where the tone holes are large and several are open below the sounding hole. However, a note could be said to have a veiled tone quality if a **flutist** fails to open one or more tone holes necessary for a full and clear sound. For example, it is a common mistake for flute students to play D₂ incorrectly by pressing the **upper C key** (L1) down on its corresponding tone hole, the C♯ **vent hole**:

T 1 2 3 - / 1 2 3 4D♯.

Closing this vent hole permits the sounding of **frequencies** from the octave below and its harmonics, resulting in a somewhat more veiled sound. For a good tone, D₂ needs to have the upper C key unpressed:

T - 2 3 - / 1 2 3 4D♯.

3. A note with adequate venting that is muffled in tone and lacking power due to the flutist purposely, or accidentally, playing it that way or due to **pad leaks**.

VENT HOLE. 1. A hole placed in the **body** of an instrument to improve the **response, intonation**, and **tone quality** of a note. *Syn.:* vent. *See also* COLTMAN C♯; C♯ VENT HOLE; DUPLICATE G♯ TONE HOLE; HALF-HOLING; OPEN-

KEY SYSTEM; QUARTER-TONE FLUTE; RF MODIFICATION; *SCHLEIFKLAPPE*; VENTING; VENT KEY. For **early flutes**, *see also BRILLE* (1). **2.** The same as **register hole**.

VENTING. 1. Generally, the process whereby a path connects the air in a **tube** to air outside. Venting occurs in the **flute** through the **embouchure hole**, the end of the **foot joint**, and the **tone holes**, if completely or partially open. If an instrument has any **leaks**, venting may occur through the leak. *See also* CLOSED-KEY SYSTEM; OPEN-KEY SYSTEM. **2.** The procedure whereby the **flutist** deliberately opens one or more tone holes out of sequence so that the usual covering of tone holes, one after the other, is not followed. *See also* CROSS-FINGERING; FORK FINGERING. **3.** The **technique** of **half-holing**.

See also BROSSA F♯ LEVER; C♯ VENT HOLE; DUPLICATE G♯ TONE HOLE (1); DUPLICATE KEYS; DUPLICATE TONE HOLES; HIGH G♯ MECHANISM/FACILITATOR; KEY RISE; ROCKSTRO F♯ LEVER; ROCKSTRO MODEL FLUTE; SIMMONS F♯ KEY; SPLIT F♯ MECHANISM; SPLIT MECHANISM; VEILED TONE (3); VENT KEY. For **early flutes** and other non-**Boehm-system** flutes, *see also* CARTE 1851 SYSTEM FLUTE; RADCLIFF SYSTEM FLUTE; REFORM FLUTE (1); VEILED TONE (1).

VENTING HEIGHT. Same as **key rise**. *See also* HIGH G♯ MECHANISM/FACILITATOR.

VENT KEY. A **key** that covers a **vent hole**. *See also* RF MODIFICATION; *SCHLEIFKLAPPE*.

VERMEIDEN, PETER (b. Lille, France, 1972). A French master of food science and a **flute** and piano player. *See also* OLNHAUSEN RING.

VERMEIDEN RING. *See* OLNHAUSEN RING.

***VERSUCH*.** An abbreviation for the **treatise** *Versuch einer Anweisung die Flöte traversiere zu spielen* (*Essay of a Method for Playing the Transverse Flute*) by **Johann Joachim Quantz**, first published in 1752. Today, the book is published in English as *On Playing the Flute. See also* BAROQUE FLUTE (1); CORPS DE RECHANGE; DOUBLE TONGUING; FINGER VIBRATO; *FLÛTE D'AMOUR*; SCREW-CORK (1); TUNING HEAD; TUNING SLIDE (2).

VERTICAL FLUTE. A **flute** that is held vertically downwards from the mouth. This is accomplished on **Boehm-system** flutes in one of two ways:

a. Bending the **head-joint tubing** so that the **blowhole** is directly in line with the remainder of the flute **body** (e.g., the Vertical Headjoint by flutemaker **Maarten Visser** and the **UpRite Headjoint** by **Sanford Drelinger**; see app. 10, figs. 3 and 2, respectively). With a **vertical head joint**, the vertical configuration provides the opportunity for the designer to create a more ergonomic and balanced flute than can be obtained with the **transverse flute**, thereby making flutes more comfortable to play due to the shift in weight of the flute and the arms to a lower position in front of the body. This is particularly helpful to those who have neck, shoulder, or back problems.

    b. Bending the body tubing in various ways. This is done with very low-pitched **Boehm flutes**—for example, the **Albisiphon**, **contrabass flute** in C, **contr'alto flute in G**, **subcontrabass flute in C**, **subcontr'alto flute in G**, **Pinschofon**, and **Upright Bassflute in C until G** (*see* BASS FLUTE [3])—because they are too large to be held transversely, so they must have their body tubing bent to enable vertical playing.

See also END-BLOWN FLUTE (2).

VERTICAL HEAD JOINT.

A **head joint** that has its blowhole directly in line with the flute's **body** so that the flute may be played vertically. It is blown in exactly the same way as a **transverse flute**. There are two types of vertical head joints: those that have their **lip plates** directly over one end of the **tube** (e.g., the head joint of the **Boehm-system** Wesley End-Blown Flute™) and those that have a transverse head reconfigured so that the blowhole is directly in line with the remainder of the flute body (e.g., the Vertical Headjoint made by **Maarten Visser** and the **UpRite Headjoint** made by **Sanford Drelinger**; see app. 10, figs. 3 and 2, respectively).

Using a vertical head joint can make flutes more comfortable to play, since there is a shift both in the weight of the flute and of the arms to a lower position in front of the body. It is particularly helpful to those who may have neck, shoulder, and/or back pain while playing. The vertical head joint is not as common as the **straight** or **curved head joint** and must be specially ordered. *See also* ANGLED HEAD JOINT; BOW; VERTICAL FLUTE.

VESSEL FLUTE.

Any of a family of **flutes** in which the **body** is globular or vessel-shaped rather than tubular. Vessel flutes are often made from gourds, fruit shells, or clay. The **ocarina** is probably the best-known example (see app. 1, fig. 15). The sound on a vessel flute is produced when air is blown either across a blowhole edge or through a **whistle**-type **mouthpiece** (*see* DUCT FLUTE for information about the latter). Most vessel flutes have

finger holes that can be opened or closed to play different notes. Raising a finger off a hole raises the **pitch**, regardless of which hole is opened. The amount of pitch change, however, is directly related to the size of the finger holes. Opening two small holes, for example, can give the same pitch as opening one larger hole, which allows for many **alternative fingerings**. Depending on the shape, these may sometimes be referred to as *globular flutes*. *See also* FLUTE FAMILY (1). For information about other flute classifications, *see* END-BLOWN FLUTE; MULTIPLE FLUTE; NOSE FLUTE; NOTCHED FLUTE; OVERTONE FLUTE; SIDE-BLOWN FLUTE; VERTICAL FLUTE.

VIBRATION.
See FINGER VIBRATO.

VIBRATO.
A cyclic variation of the tone produced by a regular variation in the **frequency**, amplitude, and/or **harmonic** content. Thus, over a single cycle of the vibrato, the **pitch**, loudness, and/or **timbre** vary in a periodic way. This effect is used to add musical expression. Players vary in their approach to its production: for some, it is a calculated movement; for others, it can be involuntary.

The **breath vibrato** that gradually became more common after 1800 is a fluctuation in both pitch and loudness as a result of an oscillation of the air **pressure**. In effect, when the air pressure is increased, the note gets **sharper** and louder, and the reverse happens when the pressure drops. The difference between the maximum and minimum frequencies or amplitudes can be called the *width* of the vibrato. The flutist can change the speed and width of the vibrato cycles. Rates of vibrato vary from about four to seven cycles per second.

There are different methods of fluctuating the air pressure. Two of the most common are:

- **abdominal vibrato** (often incorrectly called *diaphragm vibrato*), in which the abdominal muscles are used to regularly vary the air pressure; and
- **laryngeal vibrato**, in which the flutist causes the muscles on either side of the **vocal folds** to move, which in turn fluctuates the air pressure.

In the process of learning vibrato, most agree that the use of the abdominal muscles activates the **larynx** muscles, which allow greater control over its use. The involuntary use of these muscles can lead to what is called *chevrotement* or goatlike vibrato (*see* NANNY-GOAT VIBRATO).

Since vibrato is one of the means of expression, its application is very personal. Its usage also depends on the current fashion during the period of the composition and the country the player lives in. *See also* ABDOMEN KICK; AUTOMATON; *BISBIGLIANDO;* BREATH SUPPORT; DIRECTION;

GLOTTAL STOP; KEY VIBRATO; LIP VIBRATO; PROJECTION; SECOND FLUTIST; *SMORZATO*; TONE COLOR; *TREMOLO* (3, 4). For **early flutes**, *see also* FINGER VIBRATO.

VILLETTE, H. D. (n.d.). A master workman for **Louis Lot** from 1855. Villette took over the business from 1876 to 1882. *See also* app. 4; PINLESS MECHANISM.

VINCENT-JOSEPH VANSTENNKISTE. *See* DORUS, LOUIS.

VIRTUAL FLUTE. 1. A **flute** that was created in a computer virtual reality.

2. A web service at www.phys.unsw.edu.au/flute/virtual that offers **alternate fingerings** for **trills** and awkward passages, for **microtones** and **timbre** effects, and for **multiphonics**. It has a database of the **brightness**, playability, and **intonation** of the notes and multiphonics possible on about 40,000 different **fingerings**. The **flutist** can search for a fingering for a particular note or multiphonic and, to facilitate difficult **passages**, can specify which **keys** must or must not be used. The results may be sorted by intonation, ease of playing, or timbre.

The Virtual Flute is based on a theoretical model of the flute, which in turn is based on a set of careful measurements of how the flute **responds** at different **frequencies**. (Technically, this is the **acoustic impedance spectrum**, which is measured without a player and so depends only on the flute.) It also uses an expert system, based on measurements made using a real expert flutist, to rank playability and timbre.

VISSER, MAARTEN (b. Amsterdam, 1959). A Dutch **flutist**, **Boehm flute** and **head-joint** maker specializing in ergonomic flutes, and adaptive **woodwind** and **flute** repairer. *See also* acknowledgments; ANGLED HEAD JOINT; VERTICAL FLUTE; VERTICAL HEAD JOINT.

VOCAL FOLDS. Two flaps of tissue, mainly muscle, in the **larynx** that vibrate and produce sound when the person speaks, sings, or makes other vocal noises (see app. 13, fig. 13). Looked at from above, they appear as a letter V, joined together at the front behind the Adam's apple, the bulge in the front part of the neck. They come close together in the midline to vibrate. *Syn.:* vocal cords, vocal bands. *See also* ABDOMINAL VIBRATO; GLOTTAL STOP; LARYNGEAL VIBRATO; VIBRATO.

VOCALIZING/SINGING WHILE PLAYING. A **technique** where the **flutist** sings or hums and plays the **flute** at the same time. It is used as a special effect in the playing of contemporary music, but sometimes appears inadvertently from both students and experienced players. For example, the player can sing a melody while playing a sustained note, sing a sustained note while playing a melody, sing a melody while playing the same melody, or sing a melody while playing a different melody.

If the notes being sung and played together are close to, but not exactly at, the same **pitch**—that is, are not **in tune** with each other—**beats** will be heard; if they are not close in pitch, the combined sound may produce a third note called a **difference tone**.

Vocalizing might be notated in music as:

where the S or the X stands for the notes to be sung. *See also* EXTENDED TECHNIQUES; GLOTTAL STOP; THROAT TUNING.

VOICE FLUTE. 1. Fr. *flûte de voix*. A large alto **recorder** in D (named after the seven-fingered note). The origin of the name is obscure, but it may refer to the range of the instrument being in the range of a soprano voice. The instrument is often used today to play **Baroque flute** music, since no transposing is required. Only a little music appears to have been written specifically for the voice flute. **2.** In American sources of the second half of the 18th century, a flute lower than the **standard flute** in D, such as the *flûte d'amour*. *See also* GROSSE TAILLE DE FLÛTE.

VOICING. The regulation of the parameters that affect the **tone quality** (or "voice") of the **flute** in order to produce the best tone. This usually involves making minor adjustments to the **embouchure wall**, the shape of the **embouchure plate**, and/or the **tone holes**. *See also* EMBOUCHURE RECUT; OVERCUTTING; UNDERCUTTING.

VULCANITE. Same as **ebonite**.

W

WALKING-STICK FLUTE. A long **side-blown flute** disguised to look like and serve as a walking-stick. It has a conical-like **bore**, a **blowhole** toward the handle of the flute, at least six **finger holes**, and usually one or more wooden or metal **keys**. Extra length is added to the walking stick at both ends so that it can be used for walking, possibly in the form of a top and/or bottom **joint** that can be removed before playing. When there are no joints, two large opposing holes are added at the bottom end of the flute to terminate the **air column**. Holes near the top of the flute are used for hanging a tassel or other ornament. Any wooden key parts over **tone holes** are **countersunk** and made to look like a knot in the wood.

Walking-stick flutes were fashionable in the latter part of the 18th and the earlier part of the 19th centuries. There are replicas and modern versions of walking-stick flutes being made today. Figure 50 shows a **one-keyed**, two-piece, **boxwood** walking-stick flute in C made by Lambert in Paris during the last half of the 19th century. It is **turned** to look like bamboo and has two holes above an end pin of iron. *Cf.* **cane flute.**

WALL. 1. The **tube** thickness, not including any **plating. Flutes** come in different tubing wall thicknesses. Depending on the type of metal, the flute model, and the manufacturer's preference, there may be a choice of two or three thicknesses: "thin," "medium," or "thick." The standard for each of these thicknesses usually varies from metal to metal depending on the **density** and weight of the material. For example, a **silver flute** with a tube thickness of .014 in. (0.36 mm) is said to be "thin" while one of .018 in. (0.46 mm) is "thick," whereas for **gold,** which is denser and heavier than **silver,** a tube thickness of .011 in. (0.28 mm) would be considered "thin" and one of .014 in. (0.36 mm) "thick." Thicker, heavier tubes are called "thick walls" or "heavy walls" and thinner, lighter tubes are called "thin walls" or "light walls."

For tonal variety or improvement, **flutists** can choose to acquire one or more **head joints** to play with a particular flute **body.** If a certain head joint is different in tube thickness than the body, it will not fit well and may need to be resized (*see* HEAD JOINT REFITTING).

The flutist's choice of tubing wall thickness may affect what type of **tone holes** are available (*see* DRAWN TONE HOLES; SOLDERED TONE HOLES). *See also* AURUMITE; PROFESSIONAL FLUTE; STEP; THINNED (HEAD OR BODY) JOINTS; THOU.

2. An alternative abbreviated name for the **embouchure wall** of any flute, but which may be called the *riser* in a metal flute. *Syn.:* **chimney.** *See also* BLOWING WALL; EMBOUCHURE HOLE; EMBOUCHURE PLATE. **3.** Tone hole wall. Same as tone hole chimney (*see* CHIMNEY [2]). *See also* TONE-HOLE BUSHING.

WARM UP. *v.* To get ready to play.

WARM-UP. 1. An activity in a practice session to help get a musician's muscles flexible. The exercises might be for breathing, tone, rhythm, **tonguing,** or fingers. *See also* LONG TONES. **2.** The act of warming up a **flute** by **fingering** the lowest note and breathing warm air into the **embouchure hole** before playing. *See also* BREAKING-IN (PERIOD); DENSITY. **3.** The time period during which the **flutist** does the warm-up activities defined above.

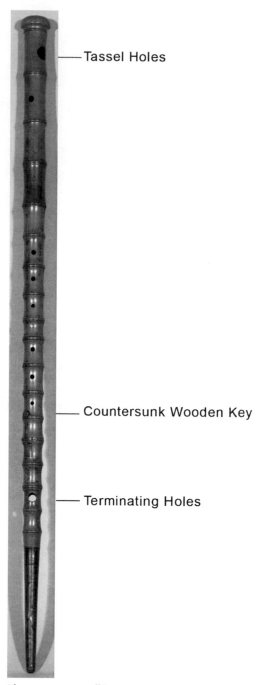

— Tassel Holes

— Countersunk Wooden Key

— Terminating Holes

Figure 50.   A walking-stick flute. *From the Dayton C. Miller Collection, Music Division, Library of Congress, DCM 0908.*

WART. A raised appendage, sometimes seen on older metal **flutes,** that enabled the player to hold the flute more easily with L1. It is often rectangular in shape, with rounded corners and about 0.8 in. (2.0 cm) long, 0.3 in. (0.75 cm) wide, and 0.1 in. (0.25 cm) high (see app. 5, fig. 11). It is **soldered** onto the **middle joint** where L1 meets the flute. The wart builds the **body** of the instrument out, thus reducing tension in L1 and helping the player to support and balance the flute. Another supporting device, called the **crutch**, is usually seen on metal flutes that also have a wart. Modern metal **piccolos** usually have wart attachments. *Syn.:* finger rest, **knob**. *Cf.* **Bo-Pep**.

WASHER. *See* PAD; PAD WASHER; PAPER WASHER; SPUD.

WATERLINE KEYS. The **keys** on the **flute** where moisture has the most tendency to collect on the key **pad**. These keys are the closed **G♯ key cup**, the D♯ key cup, the B thumb key cup, and the **trill key** cups on the underside of the flute. If too much moisture is allowed to collect in these areas, it can render some notes unplayable.

WAVE. Same as **wing**.

WAVE EMBOUCHURE PLATE. Same as **winged lip plate**.

WELCH, CHRISTOPHER (1832–1916). English **flutist** and renowned **flute** historian who wrote two books of note: *History of the Boehm Flute* (1892; see bib. under "History") and *Six Lectures on the* **Recorder** *and Other Flutes in Relation to Literature* (1911). *See* COCHE, VICTOR JEAN BAPTISTE.

WELL-TEMPERAMENT. Any of a number of **temperaments** for keyboards used in the 18th century that could be used to play in all keys, but each key and corresponding scale had a characteristic sound. This is unlike **equal temperament**, where the keys and scales, except for starting on different notes, all sound similar. Examples of Well-temperaments include Werckmeister III, Kirnberger II, and Valotti-Young. These differ in the extent to which the purity of the fifths is compromised to make the thirds more **in tune**, and also in the distribution of compromised fifths throughout the scale. *See also* INTONATION; MEANTONE TEMPERAMENT; TUNER.

WESSEL, STEPHEN (b. London, 1945). A British maker of **Boehm flutes, flute** designer, professional mechanical engineer, and former harpsichord maker. *See also* acknowledgments; INLAYING (2); PINLESS MECHANISM; STEEL (1).

WHISPER KEY. Same as *Schleifklappe*.

WHISPER STOPS/TONES. Same as **whistle tones**.

WHISTLE. 1. Usually refers to a **high-pitched flute** that is short and has either one **finger hole** (e.g., the cuckoo whistle; see app. 1, fig. 8) or none (the slide whistle, sports whistle, etc.). It may also have a small ball, or *pea*, which moves around inside the whistle's body causing a **vibrato**-like sound when the whistle is blown (e.g., sports whistle). Whistles can be made of any material that can hold a shape, and some are even joined together to form a **multiple flute**. They have existed in most cultures since prehistoric times. Depending on the means of sound production, they may also be referred to as *duct flutes, notched flutes*, and other names. Whistles are mainly used for signaling, although in some cultures may also be used for playing music (e.g., slide whistle). For information about other flute classifications, *see* END-BLOWN FLUTE; GLOBULAR FLUTE; NOSE FLUTE; OVERTONE FLUTE; SIDE-BLOWN FLUTE; VERTICAL FLUTE; VESSEL FLUTE. **2.** A **tin whistle**. **3.** *See* WHISTLE FLUTE. **4.** *See* WHISTLE TONES.

WHISTLE FLUTE. Same as **duct flute**.

WHISTLE TONE. A faint **pure** sound sometimes produced by mistake. Whistle tones are produced by blowing a small amount of air, with little but steady breath **pressure**, across the **embouchure hole** using a relaxed **embouchure**.

The regular tone is produced by a mechanism in which the **air jet** wave takes a fraction (from one-half to one-fifth) of a cycle to travel from the lips to the **blowing edge**, arriving at the proper phase to add energy to the vibration in the **flute** column. In a whistle tone, the jet wave travels much more slowly, taking exactly one or two more whole cycles, that is, one or two and a fraction cycles, to cross the space. It therefore arrives at the same proper phase. However, the volume of air carried by the slow-moving jet is much smaller, which is why the whistle tones are relatively faint.

Whistle tones can be produced using any **fingering**. Depending on which fingering is used, it is possible to get from 5 to 14 different whistle tones. Each whistle tone corresponds to a **resonance** of the **fingered** note. The higher whistle tones (i.e., higher resonances) for a given fingered note can be produced by using the same lip-placement **technique** that is used to produce **higher notes** (*see* OVERBLOWING), except that much less blowing pressure is used and a more subtle lip movement, when moving from one note to another, is employed.

Since whistle tones lack the intensity of regularly produced notes, they are infrequently played in music. When they are employed as a special effect because of their unique **tone color**, they need to be electronically amplified in performance as they are difficult to hear unless the listener is at close range. Their main use is in contemporary music, though they are also employed in breathing and tone exercises and for practicing the lip position for **fourth-octave** notes.

Whistle tones are notated in music either as *WT* (for whistle tone) or *WS* (for whisper stop) placed over or under the note, for example,

Since different fingerings can sound the same whistle tone, but with different strengths, a composer may use a notehead in the shape of a diamond to let the **flutist** know which note is to be fingered

With this notation, the actual note that sounds is represented by a normal note written above the diamond-shaped notehead. *Syn.:* whisper stops/tones, **flageolet** sounds. *See also* EXTENDED TECHNIQUE; GHOST TONE; KEY SLAP; RANGE (1). For information about the sounding mechanism for ordinary tones, *see* FLUTE (1).

WHITE. When referring to a metal, *white gold*. White gold **flutes** must be referred to as "white" flutes in the United Kingdom unless they have passed quality tests at an Assay Office and subsequently been **hallmarked**. *Cf.* **red, yellow**.

WIBB. Initials used as a nickname for world-renowned **flute soloist William** (Ingham Brooke) **Bennett** (b. 1936).

WIMBERLY, DAVID M. (b. Safford, Ariz., 1951). A Canadian/American maker of **Boehm flutes** in Halifax, Nova Scotia. *See also* FAJARDO WEDGEHEAD; MURRAY FLUTE.

WIND INSTRUMENT. 1. A class of musical instruments that use air, especially from the breath, to produce their sound. The two main types of wind instruments are the **woodwinds** (i.e., the **flute**, clarinet, oboe, saxophone, and related instruments) and the brass instruments (i.e., the trumpet, trombone, tuba, French horn, and related instruments). *Syn.:* winds. **2.** Any of the instruments named in definition 1. *See also* AEROPHONE; BOEHM SYSTEM; DOUBLING; EMBOUCHURE; FLUTE FAMILY; "FLUTE IN . . ." (2); HARMONIC SERIES; HORN; NATURAL SCALE; OCTET; OVERBLOWING; PISONI PADS; SCHEMA; TEMPERAMENT; TIBIA (2); WIND QUINTET; WINGED LIP PLATE; WOODWIND SECTION.

WIND QUINTET. An **ensemble** of, or a **piece** for, five musicians who play **wind instruments**. It commonly consists of a **flute**, oboe, clarinet, bassoon, and French horn. Sometimes inaccurately referred to as a *woodwind quintet*.

WINDS. Short for *wind instruments*.

WING. 1. One of two raised portions at the side of the **embouchure hole** to either side of the player's lips (see figs. 35 and 36). *Syn.:* cusp, wave, nob. *See also* REFORM FLUTE; *REFORMMUNDLOCH*; WINGED LIP PLATE; **2.** *See* ROBERT DICK GLISSANDO HEADJOINT.

WINGED LIP PLATE. A special type of raised **lip plate** that has a slight ridge (called a "**wing**" or "**cusp**") on both sides of the **embouchure hole** to either side of the player's lips (see fig. 35). Each ridge usually continues, but gradually diminishes, to the side edge of the lip plate opposite the ridge. There may be slight variations between manufacturers. Some **flutists** find that the winged lip plate helps them **focus** the airstream. Others find that, though it helps focus the air stream, it decreases tonal variety.

Since it makes focusing the airstream easier, the winged type of lip plate is popular with musicians who play other **wind instruments**. It is also useful for musicians who have a particular **embouchure** problem that makes playing difficult.

It is uncertain as to when the ridges to either side of the embouchure hole may have first been introduced. Some historical figures who are known to have used them were **Tebaldo Monzani** and **Maximilian Schwedler** (*see* REFORM FLUTE [1]) in the 19th century and **Otto Mönnig** (*see* REFORMMUNDLOCH) in the early part of the 20th century.

Syn.: cusped, high-rise, high-wave, moustache, or **raised embouchure plate**; reformed lip plate; wave **embouchure plate**; winged embouchure; winged embouchure plate; wing lip plate. Some manufacturers have their own specific name for the winged type of lip plate, including some of the names already listed above. *See also* PROFESSIONAL FLUTE; WING-LIP HEAD JOINT.

WING-LIP HEAD JOINT. A **head joint** with a **winged lip plate**.

WOODWIND. 1. A class of **wind instruments** that includes members of the **flute**, oboe, clarinet, bassoon, and saxophone families, whether or not they are made of wood. *See also* AEROPHONE; FINGERING DIAGRAMS; GLASS FLUTE; MULTIPHONIC; QUARTET; REED BOOK; WOODWIND QUINTET; WOODWIND SECTION. **2.** Any of the instruments named in definition 1.

WOODWIND QUINTET. Usually the same as a **wind quintet**. This name is a misnomer, however, because the wind quintet most often contains only four **woodwinds—flute**, oboe, clarinet, and bassoon—along with a French horn.

WOODWIND SECTION. A group of instruments in a band or orchestra that is composed of **woodwind** instruments. In the orchestra, these are most often from the **flute**, oboe, clarinet, and bassoon families. In a band, members of the saxophone family are also included. *See also* SECTION (1).

WORK. Generally a large composition or **piece**. *See also* EXCERPTS; SOLO (3).

WORK-HARDENING. The process of using external force (e.g., hammering or bending) to harden metal.

WS Abbr. for **whisper stop**.

WT Abbr. for **whistle tone**.

WUNDERLICH, JEAN-GEORGES (JOHANN GEORG) (b. Bayreuth, Germany, ca. 1755/56; d. Paris, 1819). Also spelled *Vounderlich, Wonderlich, Wounderlich,* or *Wunderlick*. Wunderlich was active in France from 1775 as a **flute soloist**, composer, and **principal flutist** in various French orchestras. He **edited** a flute **method** (see bib. under "Historical Methods, Treatises, and Tutors") and was a composer and flute professor at the **Paris Conservatoire** 1795–1802 and 1803–1816. *See also* CLASSICAL FLUTE; HUGOT, ANTOINE.

WYE, TREVOR (b. Woking, England, 1935). A renowned British **flute** player, teacher, music **editor**, author (see bib. under "Biographies and Autobiographies," "Intonation," "Pedagogy," and "Repair, Maintenance, and Construction"), and founder of the International Summer School in 1969 and the BFS in 1982. *See also* acknowledgments; app. 11; DIFFERENCE TONES; GARDEN-

ER'S FINGERS; MEMBRANE HEAD JOINT; OVERCUTTING; "PARABOLIC"; RESISTANCE PLUG.

x. In a **fingering diagram**, a closed **finger hole** or **key**, as in xxx ooo, where o means an open finger hole or key.

Y-ARM. *See* KEY ARM. *See also* INTERMEDIATE FLUTE; STUDENT FLUTE.

YELLOW. When referring to a metal, *yellow **gold***. Yellow gold **flutes** must be referred to as "yellow" flutes in the United Kingdom unless they have passed quality tests at an Assay Office and subsequently been **hallmarked**. *Cf.* red, white.

ZAMFIR, GHEORGHE (b. Gaesti, Romania, 1941). An international **panpipes soloist**, recording artist, conductor, composer, and teacher.

ZIEGLER, MATTHIAS (b. Bern, Switzerland, 1955). A Swiss flute **soloist**, professor of **flute** and improvisation at the University of the Arts in Zurich, and designer of special **head joints** (e.g., the Matusiflute; *see* MEMBRANE HEAD JOINT) and electroacoustic flutes. *See also* BASS FLUTE (3).

ZWERCHPFEIFE. One of the two main German terms for the transverse **Renaissance flute**, from the 16th to early 17th centuries, the other being *Querpfeife*.

Appendix 1

Various Flute Classifications

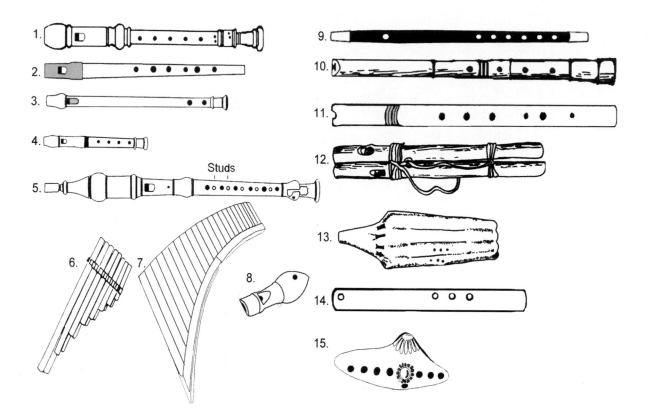

Duct flutes: 1. Recorder. 2. Tin whistle. 3. Tabor pipe. 4. French flageolet. 5. English flageolet.

End-blown flutes: 6. Romanian panpipes. 7. South American panpipes.

Whistle: 8. Cuckoo whistle.

Side-blown flute: 9. Fife.

Notched end-blown flutes: 10. Shakuhachi. 11. Kena.

Multiple flutes: 12. South American double whistle, bone (Gothenburg Museum, Sweden). 13. Mexican quadruple pipe, earthenware, ca. 500 (Museum of the American Indian, New York; based on illustrations from *Musical Instruments of the World*, an illustrated encyclopedia by the Diagram Group, 25; Courtesy Diagram).

Nose flute: 14. *Ohe Hano Ihu* nose flute from Hawaii.

Vessel flute: 15. Ocarina.

Drawing 1 by Susan Maclagan, edited by Tess Vincent; 2–15 by Tess Vincent. Drawings 6 and 7 based on photos from Brad White's pan-flute.com. Other classifications are the overtone flute and vertical flute.

Appendix 2

One-Keyed, Two-Keyed, and Simple-System Flutes

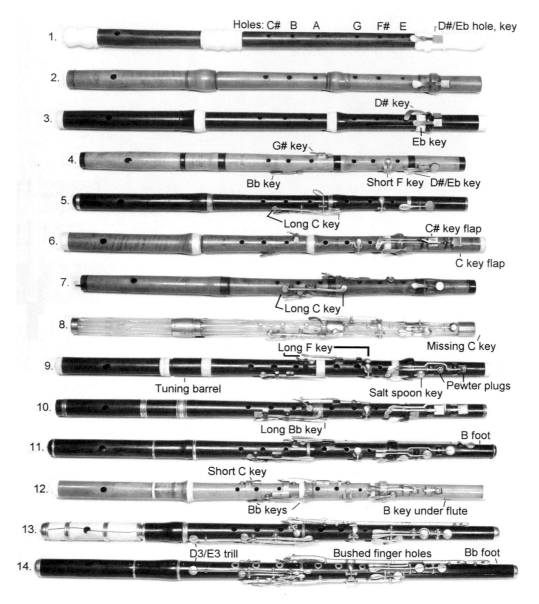

1. One-keyed boxwood flute in three pieces with tone hole names. A modern copy by R. Cameron, San Francisco, after instruments made by Hotteterre, ca. 1700.
2. One-keyed boxwood flute in four pieces, stamped LOTZ. Made ca. 1750.
3. Two-keyed ebony flute. A modern copy by Folkers & Powell, Hudson, N.Y., after an instrument made by J. J. Quantz, ca. 1740. There is a small tone hole under the D♯ key and a larger one under the E♭ key.
4. Four-keyed boxwood flute by J. I. Widmann, Freiberg, ca. 1850.
5. Five-keyed cocuswood flute by J.-L. Tulou, Paris, ca. 1835.
6. Six-keyed boxwood flute by Parker, London, ca. 1800.
7. Six-keyed boxwood flute by W. Liebel, Dresden, ca. 1830.
8. Seven-keyed (originally eight-keyed) glass flute by C. Laurent, Paris, 1834. Broken part of foot covered with a wide metal band.
9. Eight-keyed cocuswood flute by C. Gerock, London, ca. 1830.
10. Nine-keyed cocuswood flute by T. Monzani & Co., London, ca. 1819.
11. Nine-keyed cocuswood flute by A. A. Euler, Frankfurt, ca. 1860.
12. Ten-keyed boxwood flute by S. Koch, Vienna, ca. 1815.
13. Eleven-keyed grenadilla flute by H. F. Meyer, Hanover, ca. 1890.
14. Fifteen-keyed grenadilla flute by Maino e Orsi, Milan, ca. 1900.

Photos courtesy Rick Wilson. Labeling by Tess Vincent.

Appendix 3

One-Keyed, Two-Keyed, and Simple-System Flute Parts

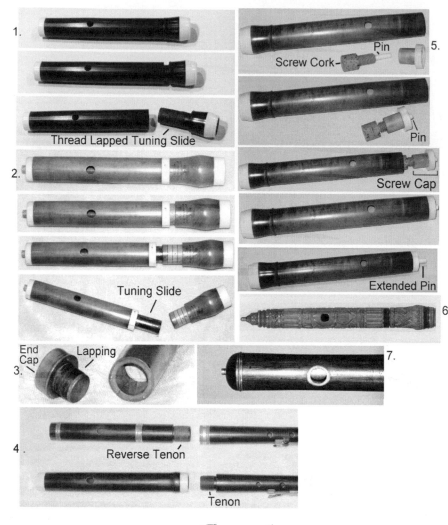

Part A

1. Tuning head of a copy by Folkers & Powell, of a two-keyed flute by J. J. Quantz, ca. 1740, illustrating various positions of the tuning barrel and the head joint proper.
2. Tuning head of a six-keyed boxwood flute by R. Potter, London, ca. 1790, illustrating various positions of the tuning barrel and the head joint proper. Incised lines on the barrel's tenon help the player remember favorite settings. Some of these lines are numbered. Position 6 is when the head is closed up completely, position 5 is the first line, and position 4 is the second line.
3. The end cap and cork of a one-keyed boxwood flute stamped LOTZ, origin unknown, ca. 1750. There is thread-lapping around the cork.
4. *(Top)* Reverse tenon of a nine-keyed cocuswood flute by T. Monzani & Co., ca. 1819. *(Bottom)* Regular tenon of a six-keyed ebony flute by J. G. Braun, Mannheim, ca. 1820.
5. A one-keyed boxwood flute by Rod Cameron after originals by C. A. Grenser, Dresden, ca. 1760, illustrating various positions of the screw-cork. The extended end pin in the last picture indicates that the cork is positioned relatively far from the embouchure hole.
6. Decorative finial on boxwood brass-lined head joint with animal horn ferrules from a C flute by an anonymous maker. Dayton C. Miller Collection, Music Division, Library of Congress, DCM 0414.
7. The ivory bushed embouchure-hole of an eight-keyed grenadilla Nicholson's Improved flute by T. Prowse, London, ca. 1850.

Photos courtesy Rick Wilson. Labeling by Tess Vincent.

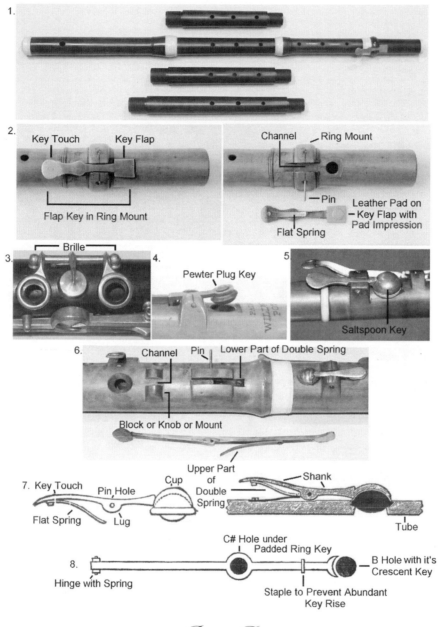

Part B

1. Copy by Folkers & Powell of a one-keyed stained boxwood flute by Jacob Denner, Dresden, ca. 1720. Center joints for A = 415Hz, 400Hz, 392Hz, and a *corps d'amour* joint (a minor third below A = 415Hz).
2. Foot joint and parts from a one-keyed flute stamped LOTZ, ca. 1750, origin unknown.
3. Brille from a grenadilla Schwedler flute by V. Kohlert Sönne, Graslitz, ca. 1910.
4. Pewter plug from a boxwood eight-keyed flute by W. H. Potter, London, ca. 1815.
5. Salt-spoon key from a boxwood eight-keyed flute by W. Bark, London, ca. 1840.
6. Key removed to illustrate double flat spring from an eight-keyed boxwood flute by Clementi & Co., London, ca. 1820.
7. Parts of cupped key and pad.
8. Pottgiesser's ring-and-crescent key.

Photos courtesy Rick Wilson. Line drawings reprinted from *A Treatise on the Flute by Richard Shepherd Rockstro* by permission of Boosey & Hawkes, Inc. Labeling by Tess Vincent.

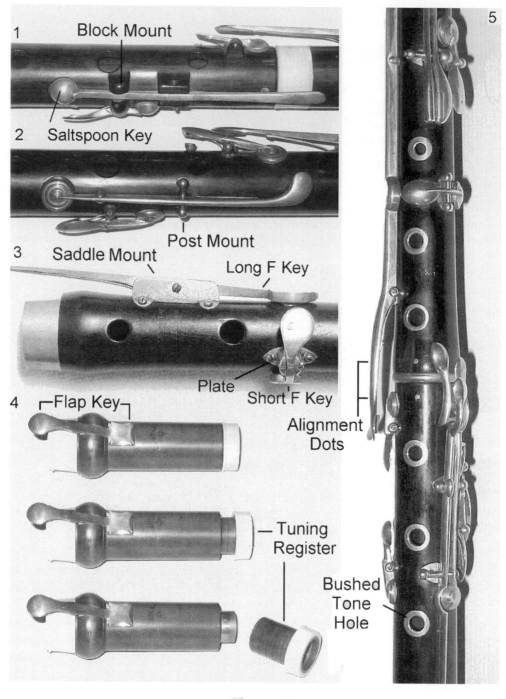

1 Block Mount
2 Saltspoon Key
Post Mount
3 Saddle Mount
Long F Key
Plate
Short F Key
4 Flap Key
Tuning Register
Alignment Dots
Bushed Tone Hole
5

Part C

1. Block-mounted keys on an eight-keyed cocuswood flute by C. Gerock, London, ca. 1830.
2. Post-mounted keys on an eight-keyed cocuswood flute by T. Prowse, London, ca. 1850.
3. Saddle-mounted keys on an eight-keyed cocuswood flute by G. Catlin, Philadelphia, ca. 1830.
4. Foot joint from a Rod Cameron copy of a boxwood one-keyed flute by A. Grenser, Dresden, ca. 1760, illustrating various positions of the foot register. Incised lines on the register help the player remember preferred settings.
5. Tone-hole bushings on a post-mounted 12-keyed grenadilla flute by I. Ziegler, Vienna, ca. 1870. Inlaid metal dots help the player line up the joints.

Photos courtesy Rick Wilson. Labeling by Tess Vincent.

Flute Clutches

David Shorey

The development of the modern flute mechanism is intimately associated with the invention and development of different clutch systems.

A keyed flute with C foot used the most rudimentary clutch, namely, having a bit of the low C key overlap the low C♯ key, so that closing the C meant that both keys closed, while the C♯ was independent.

Theobald Boehm's (1781–1871) 1832 System (ring-key flute) required a more sophisticated clutch to operate both the B♭ and F♯ keys, neither of which had its own special touch. For this task, he and his flutemaker Rudolph Greve (1806–1862) invented what we call the "vaulted clutch," whereby a ring is connected to a solid rod, which in turn is connected to a vaulting arm that crosses the top of the flute to push down a pad, in this case the B♭ or F♯.

Auguste Buffet *jeune* (1789–1864) made an enormous leap in clutches when he invented hollow silver rods (*see* key tubing) with steel inserts (*see* steel, #2). He was able to avoid the vaulted clutches by using overlapping spades that looped around the post. Boehm called these "loop clutches" and used them on his flutes nos. 1 & 2.

Boehm, with his early cylindrical flutes (see cylindrical Boehm flute), continued to struggle with developing clutch designs. His new 1847 mechanism required the right-hand keys to operate independently, yet be clutched to the F♯ and B♭ keys. For this, he used a "split barrel" clutch, which is basically an in-line overlapping spade.

It was Louis Lot (1807–1896) and V. H. Godfroy (1806–1868) who brought all the previous elements together to make the flute design used today. They adopted the hollow tubes and loop clutch of Buffet with a new group of clutches and were thus able to streamline the mechanism into the form used today. The new clutches of Lot and Godfroy are the shoulder clutches for the right hand and the B♭, and the all-important "back clutch" (see back-connector), whereby movement for the F♯ and B♭ keys is made possible. Once Godfroy and Lot designed these clutches, their basic mechanism was adopted by the two other makers of cylindrical flutes, Boehm and the firm Rudall & Rose, although both of these makers continued to modify the Lot-Godfroy model to their own taste.

Lot's successor H. Villette also continued to develop clutches. His most enduring contribution is the "hanging T" clutch, which replaced Lot's two shoulder clutches. Villette also removed the unique loop clutch on the foot joint for low C♯ and replaced it with a pinless foot joint design, reverting to the overhanging keys of the old eight-keyed flute.

Today's flutes are primarily built on the Lot/Villette collection of clutches.

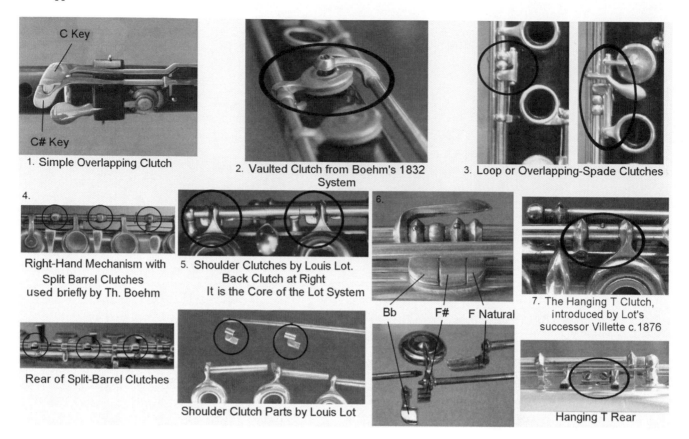

1. Simple Overlapping Clutch

C Key

C# Key

2. Vaulted Clutch from Boehm's 1832 System

3. Loop or Overlapping-Spade Clutches

4. Right-Hand Mechanism with Split Barrel Clutches used briefly by Th. Boehm

Rear of Split-Barrel Clutches

5. Shoulder Clutches by Louis Lot. Back Clutch at Right It is the Core of the Lot System

Shoulder Clutch Parts by Louis Lot

6. Bb   F#   F Natural

7. The Hanging T Clutch, introduced by Lot's successor Villette c.1876

Hanging T Rear

1. Eight-keyed foot joint from Rudall & Rose, flute no. 5389. The overlapping C key is a rudimentary clutch.
2. Vaulted clutch of Theobald Boehm and Rudolph Greve on flute no. 967 by Godfroy *ainé* and L. Lot. The term *vaulted clutch* was coined by David Shorey about 1979.
3. Loop clutch on Buffet Crampon flute no. 104. Auguste Buffet invented the hollow rods and overlapping spades in 1838, which Boehm referred to as loop clutches. At left the B♭ clutch, at right the F♯.
4. Split-barrel clutch of Boehm on flute no. 67. Boehm responded to Buffet's overlapping spades with his split-barrel version. *(Top)* Front view. *(Bottom)* The split in the barrels that forms the clutch. The term *split-barrel* was coined by Shorey about 1981.
5. Shoulder clutch on Louis Lot no. 532, developed by Lot and V. H. Godfroy.
6. Back-clutch on Louis Lot no. 281, developed by Lot and Godfroy. The term *back-clutch* was coined by Shorey about 1979. It is often referred to today as a *back-connector*.
7. Hanging-T clutch on Louis Lot no. 3314. H. D. Villette introduced the hanging-T clutch, replacing the shoulder clutches. The term *hanging-T clutch* was coined by Shorey in 1998.

Appendix 5
Parts from Older or Modified Boehm Flutes

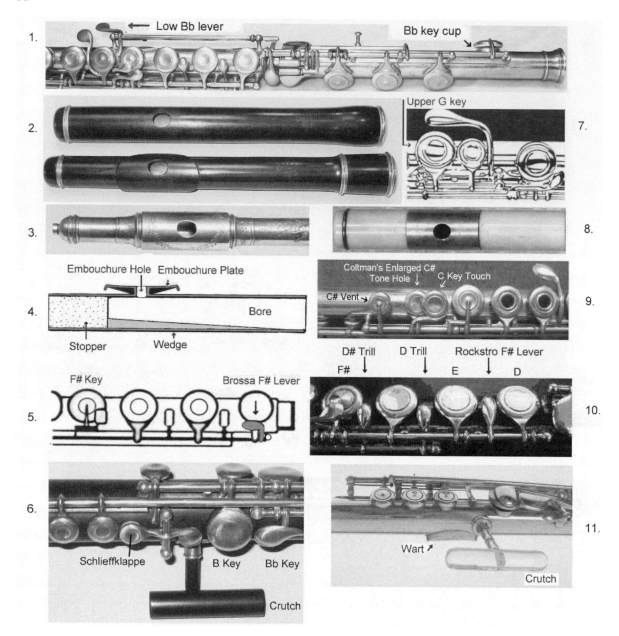

1. Left-hand lever and B♭ foot joint from a silver Boehm flute by A. G. Badger, New York, ca. 1880. Courtesy Rick Wilson.
2. Regular *(top)* and thinned *(bottom)* cocuswood head joints made by Rudall, Carte & Co. in the early 20th century. Courtesy Rick Wilson.
3. Embouchure barrel from the flute described in fig. 1. Courtesy Rick Wilson.
4. Fajardo Wedgehead. Drawing by Tess Vincent, based on U.S. Patent #4,058,046, November 15, 1977.
5. Brossa F♯ lever. Courtesy Tess Vincent.
6. *Schlieffklappe,* reversed thumb keys, and crutch from wooden Boehm flute, ca. 1880. The B♭ thumb key is the type that Boehm & Mendler made. Courtesy Rick Wilson.
7. RF Modification. Drawing by Tess Vincent.
8. Lip plate ferrule. From an eight-keyed flute in C by Chabrier de Peloubet made sometime between 1836 and about 1881. Ivory with a nickel-silver lip plate ferrule. Tuning slide in head. Dayton C. Miller Collection, Music Division, Library of Congress, DCM 0073.
9. Coltman C♯. Courtesy John Coltman.
10. Rockstro F♯ lever. Courtesy John Rayworth.
11. Wart and crutch. Courtesy Joe Sallenger.

Appendix 6

The Family of Boehm-System Flutes

The flutes below use the Boehm System invented by Theobald Boehm in 1832. They are listed in order from the highest to the lowest pitched using their transposing names.[1]

Flutes pitched an octave or more above the concert flute:

Piccoletto in E♭: Each note sounds an octave plus a minor third higher than each corresponding note on a concert flute in C.

Piccolo in D♭: Each note sounds an octave plus a minor second higher than each corresponding note on a concert flute in C.

Piccolo in C: Each note sounds an octave higher than each corresponding note on a concert flute in C; also known as the *octave flute* (see fig. 1).

Flutes pitched less than an octave above the concert flute:

Piccolo in A♭: Each note sounds a minor sixth higher than each corresponding note on a concert flute in C.

Treble flute in G: Each note sounds a perfect fifth higher than each corresponding note on a concert flute in C; also known as the *soprano flute* in G or *G treble*.

Soprano flute in F: Each note sounds a perfect fourth higher than each corresponding note on a concert flute in C; also known as the *treble flute in F*.

E♭ flute: Each note sounds a minor third higher than each corresponding note on a concert flute in C; also known as the *E♭ soprano flute, terzflute, flauto coloratura*, or *treble flute in E♭*.

Concert flute in D♭: Each note sounds a minor second above each corresponding note on the concert flute.

Concert Flute in C (see fig. 2).

Flutes pitched an octave or less below the concert flute:

Flûte d'amour in B♭: Each note sounds a major second below each corresponding note on the concert flute in C. Also called a *tenor flute*, but since the term *tenor* usually refers to a pitch range below the alto, calling the flûte d'amour in B♭ a tenor flute is felt by many to be erroneous.

Flûte d'amour in A: Each note sounds a minor third below each corresponding note on the concert flute in C.

Alto flute in G: Each note sounds a perfect fourth below each corresponding note on the concert flute in C (see fig. 3). Referred to as a *bass flute in G* in the past when the bass flute (in C) was uncommon; this terminology is not used today.

Alto flute in F: Each note sounds a perfect fifth below each corresponding note on the concert flute in C.

Albisiphon in F: Each note sounds a perfect fifth below each corresponding note on the concert flute in C.

Bass flute in C: Each note sounds a perfect octave below each corresponding note on the concert flute in C (see fig. 4).

Big bore bass flute in C: Same as the bass flute in C, but played vertically and having a larger bore.

Upright bass flute in C until G: Same as the traditional bass flute in C, but played vertically and having an extended range to the note g below a regular bass flute's c; also known as the *"Hoover" bass flute in C*.

Pinschofon in C: Same as the traditional bass flute in C, but played vertically and having a narrower bore and an extended range to low G (F with a bell attachment). Except for the bell and two extra low notes, it is essentially the same as the upright bass flute in C until G.

Albisiphon in C: Same as the bass flute in C, but played vertically and having a lowest note of b; also known as the *baritone flute in C*. Referred to as a *contrabass flute* in the past when the alto flute in G was being referred to as a bass flute; this terminology is not used today.

Flutes pitched more than an octave below the concert flute:

Bass flute in F: Each note sounds an octave plus a perfect fifth below each corresponding note on the concert flute; also known as the *subbass flute in F, contratenor flute,* or *contrabassflute in F.*

Contr'alto flute in G: Each note sounds an octave plus a perfect fourth below each corresponding note on the concert flute; also known as the *subbass flute in G* or *contrabass flute in G* (see fig. 5).

Contrabass flute in C: Each note sounds two octaves below each corresponding note on the concert flute in C; also known as the *octocontrabass flute in C* or *octobass flute in C* (see fig. 6).

Subcontr'alto flute in G: Each note sounds two octaves and a perfect fourth below each corresponding note on the concert flute; also known as the *octocontralto flute in G, octocontra-alto flute in G, double contralto flute in G, subcontrabass flute in G,* or *octocontrabass flute in G* (see fig. 7).

Subcontrabass flute in C: Each note sounds three octaves below each corresponding note on the concert flute in C; also known as the *double contrabass flute* or *octocontrabass flute* (see fig. 8).

Note

1. For more flute naming information, *see* "transposing instruments" and "flute in . . ."

The illustration is to scale.

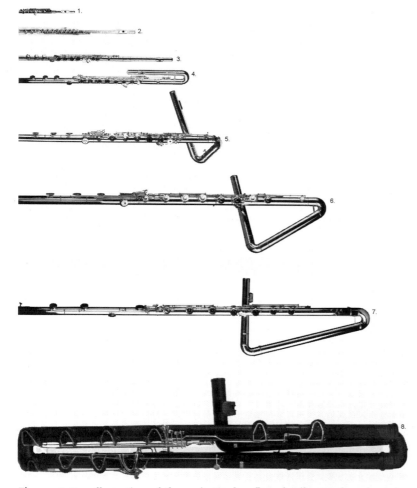

1. Piccolo in C by Hans Reiner, late 1960s.
2. Concert flute in C by Powell, 1969.
3. Alto flute in G.
4. Bass flue in C.
5. Contr'alto flute in G.
6. Contrabass flute in C.
7. Subcontr'alto flute in G.
8. Subcontrabass flute in C by Jelle Hogenhuis.

Flutes 3–7 made by Eva Kingma and photos by Theo Berends. Photos 1 and 2 courtesy Dwight Vincent. Photo 8 courtesy Jelle Hogenhuis.

Figures 1–8.   Illustration of the main Boehm flute family members in order from highest to lowest pitched.

Appendix 7

Basic Modern Flute Parts

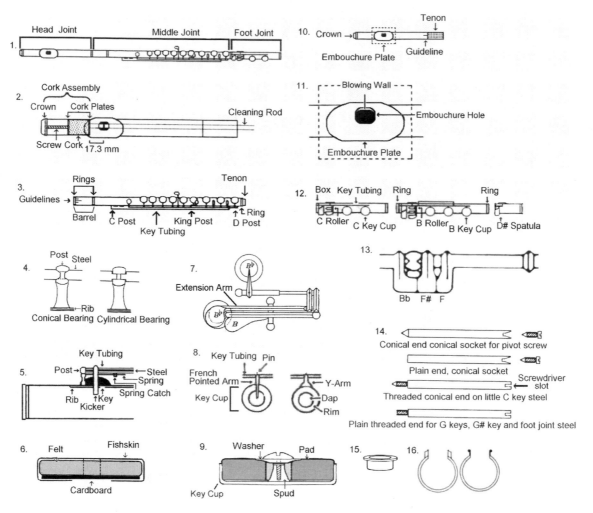

1. Concert flute joints.
2. Inside parts of the head joint and cork assembly. The groove of an inserted cleaning rod is shown in the embouchure hole.
3. Parts of the middle joint.
4. Post bearing types. Drawing by Tess Vincent.
5. Smaller key mechanism parts. The end of a foot joint is shown.
6. Traditional pad and parts. Drawing by Tess Vincent with direction from Stephen Wessel.
7. Briccialdi B♭ lever from the middle joint and the B♭ key cup it activates. From *The Flute and Flute-playing in Acoustical, Technical, and Artistic Aspects* by Theobald Boehm (New York: Dover, 1964), 85.
8. Some key parts.
9. Traditional pad in key cup and parts. Drawing by Tess Vincent with direction from Joe Butkevicius.
10. External head-joint parts.
11. Magnified view of an embouchure plate and parts.
12. Parts of a C foot joint *(left)*, B foot joint *(middle)*, and D foot joint *(right)*; see appendix 9, figure 3, for the B foot gizmo key.
13. Back-connector from the middle joint showing the B♭, F♯, and F lugs. The F lug extends under the other two lugs. Lugs are named for the keys they are connected to and not for the note they produce when activated.
14. Steel types and pivot screws. Drawing by Stephen Wessel, edited by Tess Vincent.
15. French bushing for open-holed keys. Drawing by Tess Vincent.
16. Soldered tone hole *(left)*; drawn and rolled tone hole *(right)*. Courtesy Sankyo Flutes.

Adjusting screws, clutches, plugs and sections are also parts of the flute.

Drawings by Susan Maclagan, edited by Tess Vincent, unless otherwise noted.

Appendix 8

Boehm Flute Key and Tone Hole Names

Key Names

All of the keys on the flute have note name labels.[1] As a general rule, a given key is named after the (usually first-octave) note that sounds when that key is depressed and all the tone holes to the left of this depressed key are closed. Thus, an open-standing key has the name of the note produced when it is closed (e.g., the F key on the modern flute), and a closed-standing key has the same name as the hole it uncovers when opened (e.g., the closed G$\sharp$ and

D$\sharp$ keys on the modern concert flute). The keys that are directly pressed by fingers are named in figure 1.[2]

Note that the C key on the middle joint may be called the C$\sharp$ key in some literature, presumably because of the note that sounds when the tone hole associated with that key is uncovered and all the tone holes to the left of this tone hole are covered. This naming is not consistent with the general rule stated above.[3]

The names of the keys that are not fingered, and only move when other keys are pressed, are shown in figure 2.

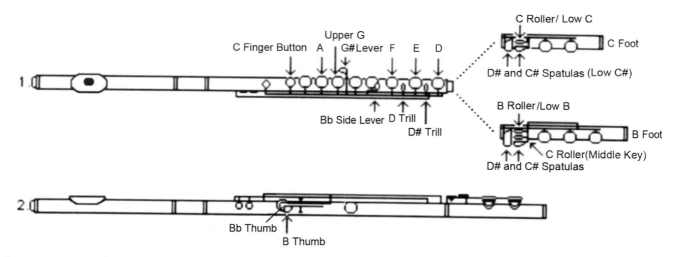

Figure 1. Names of the keys directly pressed by fingers. Some keys on the foot joint are spread out for clarity. Drawings by Susan Maclagan. Edited by Tess Vincent.

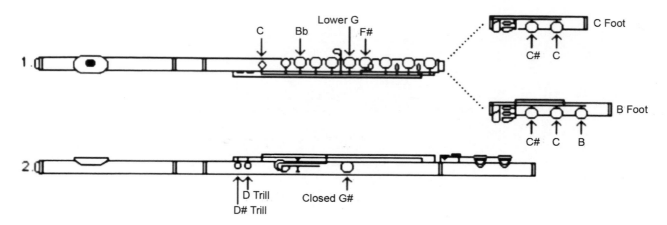

Figure 2.   Names of the keys that are not fingered and only move when others keys are pressed. Drawings by Susan Maclagan. Edited by Tess Vincent.

Tone Hole Names

All of the tone holes on the flute have note name labels. As a general rule, a given tone hole is named after the first-octave note that sounds when all the tone holes above this open tone hole (i.e., toward the crown) are closed and the tone holes below it are open (save possibly a hole or holes that do not significantly affect the pitch). Figure 3 shows the names of the tone holes under the keys shown.[4]

Notes

1. The information about key and tone hole names of the modern concert flute can also be applied to most other members of the Boehm flute family; see the entry on TRANSPOSING FLUTES.

2. Part 1 of fig. 1 shows some of the keys on the foot joint are spread out for clarity. In part 2, it appears that there are three thumb keys on the side of the flute. However, only two of these lever-like keys ever get pressed directly. The third underlying key only moves in response to the movement of the other two.

3. In Theobald Boehm's book *The Flute and Flute-playing*, the keys are named after the note sounded when they are first opened, which results in the key and tone hole names being the same in all cases. Boehm's method of key naming is not frequently used today.

4. In the bottom diagram, two sides of a C foot joint are shown. A B foot joint would also have the D♯ tone hole.

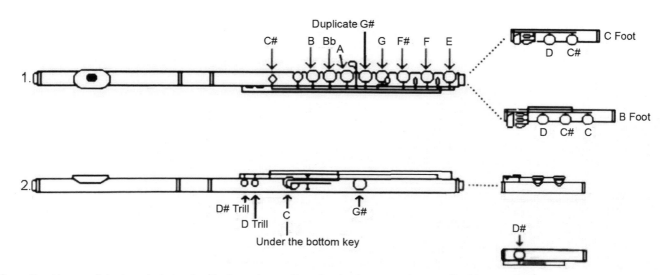

Figure 3.   Names of the tone holes under the keys shown. Drawing by Susan Maclagan. Edited by Tess Vincent.

Appendix 9

Common Modern Flute Options

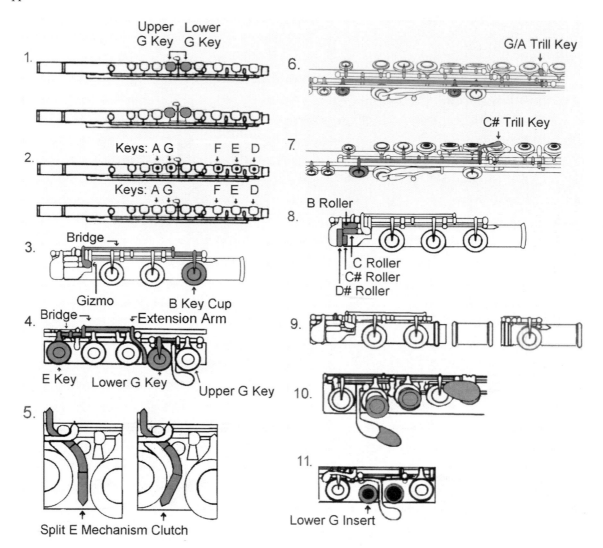

1. G keys: Inline *(top)* or offset *(bottom)* G keys on the middle joint. Drawing by Susan Maclagan, edited by Tess Vincent.
2. Open-holed *(top)* and closed-hole *(bottom)* key cups on the middle joint. Drawing by Susan Maclagan, edited by Tess Vincent.
3. B foot joint with gizmo. The position of the gizmo may vary on different flutes (see the B, C, and D foot joints in app. 7, fig. 12). Drawing by Tess Vincent.
4. Split E mechanism. Drawing by Tess Vincent.
5. Split E mechanism clutch: deactivated *(left)* and activated *(right).* Drawing by Tess Vincent after a photo courtesy John Rayworth.
6. G/A trill key. Courtesy Sankyo Flutes.
7. C♯ trill key. Courtesy Sankyo Flutes.
8. Rollers on a B foot joint. Drawing by Tess Vincent.
9. B/C convertible foot joint. Drawing by Tess Vincent.
10. Key extensions by Brannen Brothers Flutemakers, Inc. The extensions are on, *left to right,* the G♯ key lever, the upper G key, the A key, and the C key. Drawing by Tess Vincent based on a photo courtesy Brannen Brothers Flutemakers, Inc.
11. A lower G insert in the body-line G♯ tone hole. The G keys have been removed in order to show the ring-shaped insert. Drawing by Tess Vincent.

Another fairly common option is engraving. Less common options are: open G♯ key (see G♯ key), split F♯ mechanism, left-hand levers, high G♯ mechanism, and chasing.

Appendix 10

Some Modern Head Joint Options

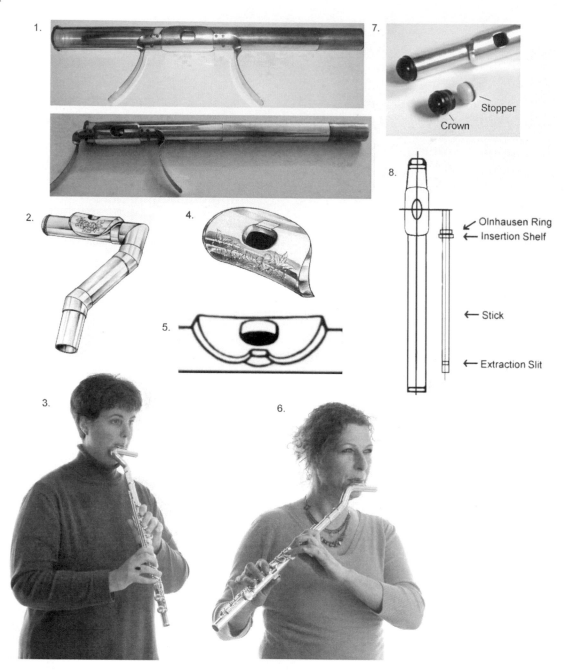

1. Robert Dick Glissando Headjoint® showing telescoping action: head joint within carrier tube fully extended *(top)* and in home position *(bottom)*.
2. UpRite® Headjoint. Courtesy Sanford Drelinger.
3. Vertical Headjoint by Maarten Visser on a regular Boehm flute body. Flutist: Marjan Nieuwenhuizen. Photo by Jeroen Scheelings, courtesy Maarten Visser.
4. Engraved embouchure plate with Platinum-Air-Reed™ or Gold-Air-Reed™. Courtesy Sanford Drelinger.
5. Embouchure plate from Butterfly™ headjoint. Drawing by Tess Vincent.
6. Angled head joint (swan neck) by Maarten Visser on a regular Boehm flute body. Flutist: Yulan Smit. Photo by Jeroen Scheelings, courtesy Maarten Visser.
7. Bigio crown and stopper. Courtesy Mats Möller.
8. Olnhausen ring with insertion tool on the right. Drawing by Tess Vincent, which is based on a drawing from Brooks de Wetter-Smith.

Another modern head joint option is the winged lip plate. One of the first types of winged lip plates is the Reform-mundloch. See figure 36.

Appendix 11

An Easy Guide to Checking Your Flute Tuning and Scale

Trevor Wye

We use octaves and fifths to check flute tuning. Why? Because they are "perfect" intervals. If you are an experienced player, your octaves should be true octaves: check with a tuning meter (*see* tuner). Fifths in our modern equal temperament have been slightly flattened. This variation will still make our tuning check very reliable and useful.

Have a piece of paper and pencil handy. Turn the paper sideways and draw a line to represent the length of the flute body. Make a series of marks along its length corresponding to the names and position of the tone holes. Mark all the tone holes from low C to $C_{\#2}$.

Checking Your Tuning Using Harmonics

Warm up thoroughly and tune carefully with a tuning machine. During this test, make no adjustment to any note to alter its pitch: accept it. Play at the same volume level throughout. Maintain exactly the same embouchure, or covering, throughout the test. Play the harmonic series on low C for at least five minutes to sensitize your ears. Repeat with low $C_{\#}$, D, and $E_{\flat}$. This may seem unnecessary, but as time passes, your ears will be more sensitive to the fine tuning you need to appreciate.

When ready, play low C and, when a good tone is established, without removing your little finger (pinky),[1] play the octave (C_2) with the normal "open" fingering. The two notes should be exactly the same—not nearly, but *exactly*. If they are not, pull out or push in the head joint until they are, even though this is not your usual head joint position. When low C is correct, do the same with low $C_{\#}$. If the result is out of tune (probably a sharp $C_{\#2}$), then either one or the other of these two notes will need adjusting. For the moment, return back to the head position that makes the two C-naturals in tune again.

Play low C and its third harmonic, G_2. Then, without removing your little finger, play the real G_2 and check the pitch with the low C harmonic. There will be a slight difference: the "normal" G_2 should be fractionally sharp.[2] If it is very sharp, make a note of it. Repeat with low $C_{\#}$ and its third harmonic, $G_{\#2}$. Again make note of any problem. Repeat using low D, $E_{\flat}$, E, F, and $F_{\#}$. Make a note of any problems. When you use low C, $C_{\#}$, D, and $E_{\flat}$ and check the third harmonics, you may decide that it is the foot-joint notes that are sharp and not the G_2, $G_{\#2}$, A_2, and $B_{\flat2}$ that are flat!

Low F-natural and $F_{\#}$'s third harmonics (C_3 and $C_{\#3}$) can be swiftly alternated with the fourth harmonic of low C and $C_{\#}$ to check the natural C_2 and $C_{\#2}$ as a further test. Then you may have to make a decision as to whether the low F and $F_{\#}$ are wrong (unlikely) or the C_2 and $C_{\#2}$ are wrong (more likely).

If A_2 and $B_{\flat2}$ are quite sharp, take a moment to read the following: Many flutes have a sharper-than-necessary foot joint. Why? Perhaps the maker has pushed the tone holes closer to the right hand for easier/speedier technique. Who knows? But, if it is sharp, then you will need to pull out the foot joint a little until A_2 and $B_{\flat2}$ are reasonably in tune with the harmonics. You may not get these perfectly correct, but the amount of out-of-tuneness will be better!

Repeat all your checks again starting with low C and its third harmonic, G_2.[3]

How to Fix the Tuning Problem

These are common scenarios: a sharp $C_{\#2}$; a sharp foot joint; and a sharp C2, $B_{\flat1}$, and $C_{\#2}$. Temporary and more permanent solutions are possible.

Temporary Solution

Pull out the foot: about an eighth of an inch (3 mm) is normally enough. If needed, ask your repairperson to tighten the joint, if possible.

Place a strip of transparent tape (e.g., Scotch tape) across the upper part of the $C_\sharp$ tone hole nearest the head so as to cover about a fifth of the hole, sticky side down.[4] It should not affect the pad or cause a leak. Repeat with any other notes.

For an open-hole flute, the notes under the open hole can be effectively flattened by covering the open hole with transparent tape. Covering the open holes has a flattening effect on the pitch equivalent to moving the tone hole down toward the foot by about a 16th of an inch (1.5mm). This is because the open-hole cups (E, F, $F_\sharp$, A, and $A_\sharp$) sharpen the tone hole over which they are placed. (Open- and closed-hole flutes should have a different scale.) Be sure to check that you are flattening the correct note! The names of the keys are not always the same as the notes played! For example, the D key (R3) is over the E tone hole! Placing tape over that open hole will flatten E_1 and E_2, not D_1 and D_2.

Check your results again after a few days.

A More Permanent Solution

Remove the $C_\sharp$ key and place some modeling plastic in the upper part of the hole. At the same time, using a wetted cleaning stick inside the flute, adjust the plastic before it hardens to prevent it from protruding into the tube bore. Carefully clean off the top so that it cannot be touched by the pad (use a modeling blade) and, when dry, replace the key. If you make a mistake, just push the plastic out. If it won't stick easily, then clean the tone hole first.

If you have pulled out the foot, consider placing plastic in the lowest holes, the $E_\flat$ and D tone holes. It is usually unnecessary to flatten the low $C_\sharp$ and C because players most often play them flat anyway!

Notes

1. Moving the little finger onto the $D_\sharp$ key will only marginally affect the result, but the instability resulting from moving it may change the pitch somewhat. It is better to keep it there!

2. It is an advantage to have a slightly sharper G_2 so as to make playing D_3 (a normally flat note) in tune easier in pianissimo.

3. It is foolish to think of tuning the third-octave notes. The notes from D_3 upwards are affected by the cork position. Notes lower than this are affected only if the cork position has been drastically altered.

4. Making a hole smaller will affect the tone—but trying to flatten it also affects the tone! A tone hole made smaller with tape or plastic is the lesser of two evils.

Appendix 12
Tools of the Trade

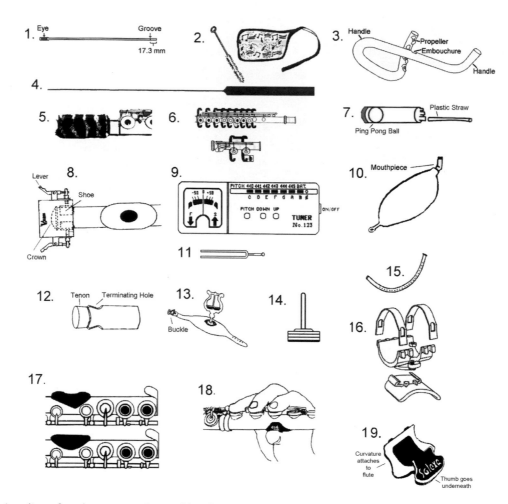

The following is a list of tools commonly used by flute players.

1. Cleaning rod. Drawing by Susan Maclagan.
2. Swabs: wire flute swab *(left)*; pull-through cloth flute swab *(right)*. Drawing by Tess Vincent.
3. Pneumo Pro. Drawing by Tess Vincent.
4. Flute Flag. Drawing by Tess Vincent.
5. HW Pad Saver® for the middle joint. Photo courtesy H. W. Products, Inc.
6. Flute Suit™. Courtesy of Anne Pollack. Created and executed by Megan Reid.
7. Breath Builder. Drawing by Tess Vincent.
8. Valgon Ring™ on the crown end of the head joint. Courtesy of Harold Gomez, edited by Tess Vincent.
9. Tuner. Drawing by Susan Maclagan, edited by Tess Vincent.
10. Breathing Bag. Drawing by Tess Vincent.
11. Tuning fork. Drawing by Susan Maclagan, edited by Tess Vincent.
12. Foster Extension. Drawing by Tess Vincent.
13. Lyre for the wrist. Drawing by Tess Vincent.
14. Flute stand. Drawing by Susan Maclagan, edited by Tess and Dwight Vincent.
15. Dampit. Drawing by Tess Vincent.
16. PRIMA Thumb Rest™. Drawing courtesy of Ton Kooiman.
17. Bo-Pep Finger Saddle *(top)* and Bo-Pep Finger Rest (bottom). Drawing by Tess Vincent, based on a photo courtesy Bob Ford.
18. Bo-Pep Thumb Guide. Drawing by Tess Vincent, based on a photo courtesy Bob Ford.
19. Thumbport. Drawing by Tess Vincent. Based on a photo courtesy Ho-Fan Lee.

The metronome is also a tool of the trade.

Appendix 13

Anatomy of the Human Head, Neck, and Mouth

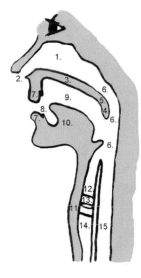 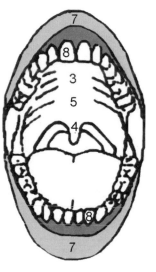

1. Nasal cavity. 2. Nostril. 3. Hard palate. 4. Uvula. 5. Soft palate. 6. Throat cavity. 7. Lips. 8. Teeth. 9. Mouth cavity. 10. Tongue. 11. Adam's apple. 12. Larynx. 13. Vocal folds. 14. Windpipe. 15. Food passage.

Drawings by Tess Vincent.

Appendix 14
Orchestra and Opera Audition Excerpts

Listed below are pieces from which excerpts have often been chosen for orchestral or opera auditions.

Orchestral Excerpts

Bach, Johann Sebastian. No. 58 from *St. Matthew Passion.*

Bartók, Béla. Concerto for Orchestra.

Beethoven, Ludwig Van. Leonora Overture No. 3; Symphony No. 3.

Berlioz, Hector. *Symphonie Fantastique.*

Bizet, Georges. Entr'acte from *Carmen.*

Brahms, Johannes. Symphony No. 1; Symphony No. 4.

Debussy, Claude. *"Prélude à l'Après-midi d'une Faune."*

Dvořák, Antonín. Symphony No. 8; Symphony No. 9 "From the New World."

Gluck, Christoph Willibald. "Dance of the Blessed Spirits" from *Orfeo ed Euridice.*

Hindemith, Paul. *Mathis der Maler: Symphony; Symphonic Metamorphoses of Themes by Weber.*

Mendelssohn, Felix. Scherzo from *A Midsummer Night's Dream.*

Prokofiev, Sergei. *Classical Symphony* (Symphony No. 1); *Lieutenant Kijé Suite; Peter and the Wolf; Romeo and Juliet.*

Ravel, Maurice. *Daphnis et Chloé;* "Bolero."

Rimsky-Korsakov, Nikolai. *Scheherazade.*

Rossini, Gioacchino. *"William Tell* Overture."

Saint-Saëns, Camille. *"Volière"* from *Carnival of the Animals.*

Strauss, Richard. *Death and Transfiguration (Tod und Verklärung);* "Salome's Dance"; "Till Eulenspiegels Lustige Streiche."

Stravinsky, Igor. *Firebird Suite; Petrouchka;* "Song of the Nightingale" *(Le Chant du Rossignol).*

Tchaikovsky. Peter Ilich, Symphony No. 4.

Other Frequently Demanded Orchestral Excerpts

Bach, Johann Sebastian. *St. John Passion.*

Beethoven, Ludwig Van. Symphony No. 1; Symphony No. 6; Symphony No. 7.

Borodin, Alexander. "Polovtsian Dances" from *Prince Igor.*

Brahms, Johannes. Symphony No. 3.

Britten, Benjamin. *Young Person's Guide to the Orchestra.*

Debussy, Claude. "La Mer"; "Nocturnes."

Hindemith, Paul. *Nobilissima Visione.*

Kodály, Zoltán. "Variations on a Hungarian Folksong (The Peacock)."

Mahler, Gustav. Last movement of *Das Lied von der Erde.*

Mendelssohn, Felix. Symphony No. 4 (Italian Symphony).

Mussorgsky, Modest. "Night on Bald Mountain."

Piston, Walter. *The Incredible Flutist Suite.*

Prokofiev, Sergei. Symphony No. 5.

Ravel, Maurice. *Ma Mère l'Oye (Mother Goose);* "La Valse."

Rezniček, Emil Nikolaus Von. "*Donna Diana* Overture."

Rimsky-Korsakov, Nikolai. "*Capriccio Espagnol*"; "Russian Easter Festival Overture" *(Grand Paque Russe).*

Rossini, Giaocchino. Overture to *Il Barbiere di Siviglia (Barber of Seville);* Overture to *Semiramide.*

Schubert, Franz. Symphony No. 1; Symphony No. 5; Symphony No. 6; Symphony No. 10; Symphony No. 15.

Smetana, Bedřich. Overture to *The Bartered Bride.*

Strauss, Richard. *Don Juan; Don Quixote; Ein Heldenleben; Sinfonia Domestica.*

Stravinsky, Igor. *Le Baiser de la Fée (The Fairy's Kiss); Le Sacre du Printemps (The Rite of Spring); Symphony in Three Movements.*

Tchaikovsky, Peter Ilich. *The Nutcracker Suite;* second movement of Piano Concerto No. 1; Symphony No. 6.

Thomas, Ambroise. Overture to *Mignon.*

Wagner, Richard. "Magic Fire Music" from *Die Walküre.*

Opera Excerpts

Bizet, Georges. *Carmen.*

Borodin, Alexander. *Prince Igor.*

Cherubini, Luigi. *Medea.*

Delibes, Leo. *Lakmé.*

Donizetti, Gaetano. *Lucia di Lammermour.*

Gluck, Christoph Willibald. *Alceste; Orfeo ed Euridice.*

Mascagni, Pietro. *Guglielmo Ratcliff.*

Puccini, Giacomo. *La Bohème; Gianni Schicchi; Madama Butterfly; Manon Lescaut; Suor Angelica; Turandot.*

Rimsky-Korsakov, Nikolai. *Tsar Sultan.*

Rossini, Giaocchino. *Il Barbiere di Siviglia (Barber of Seville); Guillaume Tell (William Tell); Semiramide.*

Strauss, Johann, the Younger. *Die Fledermaus.*

Strauss, Richard. *Der Rosenkavalier; Salome.*

Thomas, Ambroise. *Hamlet.*

Verdi, Giuseppe. *Aïda; Falstaff; La Forza del Destino; Rigoletto; La Traviata.*

Wagner, Richard. *Die Meistersinger.*

Wolf-Ferrari, Ermanno. *Jewels of the Madonna (Gioielli della Madonna).*

Selected Bibliography

Acoustics

See also Coltman in "Repair, Maintenance, and Construction."

Benade, Arthur A. *Fundamentals of Musical Acoustics.* New York: Oxford University Press, 1976.

———. *Horns, Strings, and Harmony.* New York: Anchor Doubleday, 1960.

Campbell, Murray, and Clive Greated. *The Musician's Guide to Acoustics.* New York: Schirmer, 1987.

Coltman, John W. "Acoustical Losses in the Boehm Flute." *Flutist Quarterly* 19, no. 1 (Fall 1993): 37–41.

———. "Acoustics of the Flute." 2 parts. *Instrumentalist* 29, nos. 6 and 7 (January and February 1972).

———. "Effect of Material on Flute Tone Quality." *Journal of the Acoustical Society of America* 49, no. 2, part 2 (1971): 520–23.

———. "Flute Scales, Pitch and Intonation."*Woodwind Anthology* (see Journals and Periodicals) (May 1976): 264–68.

Fletcher, Neville H. "Acoustical Correlates of Flute Performance Technique." *Journal of the Acoustical Society of America* 57 (1975): 233–37.

———. "Some Acoustical Principles of Flute Technique." *Instrumentalist* 28 (1974): 57–61.

Helmholtz, Hermann. *On the Sensations of Tone.* New York: Dover, 1954.

Jakeways, Robin. "Hoots, Hertz and Harmonics." *Pan.* 6 parts. (December 1996): 18–23; (June 1997): 20–24; (March 1998): 26–29; (March 1999): 20–27; (September 2000): 26–28; (September 2004): 17–21.

Wolfe, Joe. "Flute Acoustics: An Introduction," n.d. Http://www.phys.unsw.edu.au/jw/fluteacoustics.html.

Wolfe, J., and J. Smith (2003) "Cut Off Frequencies and Cross Fingering in Baroque, Classical and Modern Flutes." *Journal of the Acoustical Society of America* 114 (October 2003): 2263–72.

Wolfe, J., J. Smith, J. Tann, and N. H. Fletcher. "Acoustic Impedance Spectra of Classical and Modern Flutes." *Journal of Sound and Vibration* 243, no. 1 (May 24, 2001): 127–44.

Automatons

Riskin, Jessica. "The Defecating Duck, or, The Ambiguous Origins of Artificial Life." *Critical Inquiry* 29, no. 4 (Summer 2003): 599–633.

Solis, J., K. Chida, K. Suefuji, and A. Takanishi. "The Development of the Anthropomorphic Flutist Robot at Waseda University." *International Journal of Humanoid Robots* 3, no. 2 (June 2006): 127–51.

Solis, J., K. Chida, K. Suefuji, K. Taniguchi, S. M. Hashimoto, and A. Takanishi. "The Waseda Flutist Robot WF-4RII in Comparison with a Professional Flutist." *Computer Music Journal* 30, no. 4 (Winter 2006): 12–27.

Vaucanson, Jacques de. *An Account of the Mechanism of an Automaton or Image Playing on the German Flute (1742): Le Méchanisme du Flûteur Automate (1738).* Facsimile with preface by David Lasocki. Buren, The Netherlands: Frits Knuf, 1979.

Biographies and Autobiographies

Blakeman, Edward. *Taffanel: Genius of the Flute.* Oxford: Oxford University Press, 2005.

Böhm, Ludwig. "Recounting the Wizardry of Theobald Böhm." *Flute Talk* 13, no. 10 (July/August 1994): 21–25.

Dzapo, Kyle Jean. *Joachim Andersen: A Bio-Bibliography.* Westport, Conn.: Greenwood Press, 1999.

Fischer, Penelope. "Philippe Gaubert, French Musician Extraordinaire." *Flutist Quarterly* 14, no. 3 (Summer 1989): 17–24.

Galway, James. *James Galway.* London: Chappell/Elm Tree, 1978.

Goldberg, Adolph. *Biographieen zur Porträts-Sammlung hervorragender Flöten-Virtuosen, Dilettanten und Komponisten.* Berlin: privately printed, 1906. Reprint. Celle: Moeck, 1987.

McCutchan, Ann. *Marcel Moyse, Voice of the Flute.* Portland, Ore.: Amadeus Press, 1994.

Rampal, Jean-Pierre, with Deborah Wise. *Music, My Love.* New York: Random House, 1989.

Scott, Stuart. *Halle Flutes: Flautists of the Halle Orchestra, 1858–1993.* Cheshire, England: SJS, 1998.

Toff, Nancy. *Georges Barrère and the Flute in America.* New York: New York Flute Club, 1994.

——. *Monarch of the Flute: The Life of Georges Barrère.* Oxford: Oxford University Press, 2005.

Wye, Trevor. *Marcel Moyse: An Extraordinary Man.* Edited by Angelita Floyd. Cedar Falls, Iowa: Winzer Press, 1993.

Contemporary Flute

See also Levine under "Flute Family."

Artaud, Pierre-Yves, and Gérard Geay. *Present Day Flutes: Treatise on Contemporary Techniques of Transverse Flutes for the Use of Composers and Performers.* Paris: Éditions Jobert/Éditions Musicales Transatlantiques, 1980.

Averitt, Frances Lapp. "Whistle Tones: Exercises for the *Embouchure.*" *Muramatsu Flute News* (Summer 1978); *Flute Talk* 6, no. 6 (February 1987): 16–19.

Bartolozzi, Bruno. *New Sounds for Woodwind.* Translated and edited by Reginald Smith Brindle. New York: Oxford University Press, 1971.

Cantrick, Robert B. "Buzzing the Flute." *Instrumentalist* 17, no. 9 (May 1963): 53.

Dick, Robert. *Circular Breathing for the Flutist.* New York: Multiple Breath Music Co., 1987.

——. "The Glissando Headjoint." *Flute Focus,* issue 6 (April 2006): 18–19.

——. *The Other Flute: A Performance Manual of Techniques.* 2nd ed. New York: Multiple Breath Music Co., 1989.

——. *The Other Flute: Tone Development through Extended Techniques.* Vol. 1. New York: Edu-tainment Publishing, 1978.

——. *Tone Development through Extended Techniques.* Rev. ed. New York: Multiple Breath Music Co., 1986.

Heiss, John. "The Flute: New Sounds." *Perspectives of New Music* 10, no. 2 (Spring–Summer, 1972): 153–58.

Horne, Robin Mason, with Robert Dick, Sheridan Stokes, Teresa Meeks, Carol Shansky, Helen Bledsoe, Sarah Twichell, and Katherine Kitzman. *Extended Techniques Resource Page.* 2000. Http://www.larrykrantz.com/et/et.htm.

Howell, Thomas. *The Avant-Garde Flute.* Berkeley: University of California Press, 1974.

Levine, Carin, and Christina Mitropoulos-Bott. *The Techniques of Flute Playing/Die Spieltechnik der Flöte.* Kassel, Germany: Bärenreiter, ca. 2002.

Möller, Mats. *New Sounds for Flute.* N.d. Http://www.sfz.se/flutetech/index.htm.

Offermans, Wil. *For the Contemporary Flutists: Twelve Studies for the Flute with Explanations in the Supplement.* Frankfurt am Main: Zimmermann, 1992.

Rich, Alan. "The World of Music." *New York Times,* August 28, 1962.

Stokes, Sheridon W., and Richard A. Condon. *Special Effects for Flute.* Santa Monica, Calif.: Trio Associates, 1976.

Early Performance Practice

See also "Historical Methods, Treatise, and Tutors."

Bailey, John Robert. "Maximilian Schwedler's 'Flute and Flute-Playing: Translation and Study of Late Nineteenth-Century German Performance Practice.'" D.M. thesis, Northwestern University, 1987.

Boland, Janice Dockendorff. *Method for the One-Keyed Flute, Baroque and Classical.* Berkeley: University of California Press, 1998.

Brown, Howard Mayer, and Stanley Sadie, eds. *Performance Practice: Music after 1600.* New York: Norton, 1990.

——. *Performance Practice: Music before 1600.* London: Norton, 1990.

Brown, Rachel. *The Early Flute.* Cambridge: Cambridge University Press, 2002.

Dart, Thurston. *The Interpretation of Music.* New York: Harper & Row, 1963.

Dolmetsch, Arnold. *The Interpretation of the Music of the Seventeenth and Eighteenth Centuries, Revealed by Contemporary Evidence.* Seattle: University of Washington Press, 1974.

Donington, Robert. *Baroque Music: Style and Performance.* New York: Norton, 1982.

——. *The Interpretation of Early Music.* New rev. ed. New York, London: Norton, 1992.

——. *A Performer's Guide to Baroque Music.* New York: Scribner's, 1973.

Haskell, Harry. *The Early Music Revival: A History.* London: Thames & Hudson, 1988.

Lloyd-Watts, Valery, and Carole L. Bigler, with the assistance of Willard A. Palmer. *Ornamentation: A Question and Answer Manual.* Van Nuys, Calif.: Alfred, 1995.

Mather, Betty Bang. *Interpretation of French Music from 1675 to 1775 for Woodwind and Other Performers: Additional Comments on German and Italian Music.* New York: McGinnis & Marx, 1973.

Mather, Betty Bang, and David Lasocki. *The Classical Woodwind Cadenza.* New York: McGinnis & Marx, 1978.

——. *Free Ornamentation in Woodwind Music, 1700–1775: An Anthology with Introduction.* New York: McGinnis & Marx, 1976.

Smith, Edwina. "Revisiting Past Flute Fashions." *Pan* (March 2005): 17–21.

Veilhan, Jean-Claude. *The Rules of Musical Interpretation in the Baroque Era.* Translated by John Lambert. Paris: Leduc, 1982.

Fingerings

Arnold, Jay. *Modern Fingering System for Flute: A New System That Classifies and Demonstrates the Fingerings throughout the Entire Range of the Instrument.* New York: Shapiro, Bernstein, 1963.

Botros, Andrew. *The Virtual Flute.* 2005. Http://www.phys.unsw.edu.au/music/flute/virtual/main.html.

Cavanagh, Jan. "Find 40,000 New Flute Fingerings!" *Pan* 24, no. 2 (June 2005): 14–17.

Herszbaum, Nestor. *Alternative Fingerings for the Flute.* Omaha, Neb.: Nestor Herszbaum, 2003.

———. "A Primer in Practical Alternative Fingerings." *Flutist Quarterly* 30, no. 3 (Spring 2005): 48–51.

Hockley, W. H. "First Principles of Fingering for the Boehm Flute." *CFA [Canadian Flute Association] Journal* 1, no. 1 (August 1980): 8–14.

Mahillon, Victor. "Hints on the Fingering of the Boehm Flute." London: C. Mahillon & Co., 1884. Available at http://www.oldflutes.com/charts/mahillon/thumbnails.html.

Neuhaus, Margaret Newcomb. *The Baroque Flute Fingering Book: A Comprehensive Guide to Fingerings for the One-Keyed Flute Including Trills, Flattements, and Battements Based on Original Sources from the Eighteenth and Nineteenth Centuries.* Naperville, Ill.: Flute Studio Press, 1986. Second edition edited by Ardal Powell. Hudson, N.Y.: Folkers & Powell, 2002.

Pellerite, James J. *A Modern Guide to Fingerings for the Flute.* Rev., enlarged 2nd ed. Bloomington, Ind.: Zalo, 1972.

Reichard, Timothy. *The Woodwind Fingering Guide.* Http://www.wfg.woodwind.org/.

Schaeffer, Burghard. *Annotated Fingering Tables for the Boehm Flute.* Elite Edition 2900. Hamburg: D. Rahter, 1972.

Voorhees, Jerry L. *The Classification of Flute Fingering Systems of the Nineteenth and Twentieth Centuries.* Buren, The Netherlands: Frits Knuf, 1980.

———. *The Development of Woodwind Fingering Systems in the Nineteenth and Twentieth Centuries.* Hammond, La.: Voorhees, 2003.

Flute Collections

See also McGee and Wilson under "History."

Dayton C. Miller Flute Collection, Music Division, Library of Congress. Http://memory.loc.gov/ammem/dcmhtml/dmhome.html.

Dillon, Steve. *Historic Fifes* http://www.dillonmusic.com/historic_fifes/historic_fifes.html

Libin, Laurence, and Robert A. Lehman. *Historic Flutes from Private Collections* [exhibition]. Andre Mertens Galleries for Musical Instruments, Metropolitan Museum of Art, New York, July–August 1986.

Glennis Stout Historical Flute Collection. http://www.i-gadgets.com/flute/gstout/temporary. Collection now dispersed to various new owners.

Sallenger, Joseph. *Joseph Wilds Sallenger's Favorite Flutes Index.* N.d. Http://alpha1.fmarion.edu/goferjoe/flutes.htm.

Seyfrit, Michael, compiler. *Musical Instruments in the Dayton C. Miller Flute Collection at the Library of Congress: A Catalog.* Vol. 1. Washington, D.C.: Library of Congress, 1982.

Simpson, Mary Jean. "Dayton Miller and the Dayton C. Miller Flute Collection." *Flutist Quarterly* 14, no. 5 (Winter 1989): 5–11.

Young, Phillip T. *4900 Historical Woodwind Instruments: An Inventory of 200 Makers in International Collections.* London: Tony Bingham, 1993.

Flute Family

See also Dayton, Dillon, Glennis, Sallenger, and Young under "Flute Collections."

Blumenthal, Amy Rice. "Flute Choirs and the National Flute Association Coming of Age." *Flutist Quarterly* 27, no. 2 (Winter 2002): 48–60.

Clark, Jim. The fife and drum in America. *Pan* 27, no. 4 (December, 2008): 29–34.

Dombourian-Eby, Zart. "A History of the Piccolo." *Flutist Quarterly* 16, no. 1 (Winter 1991): 13–16.

Lane, Andrew. *Piccolo Craft: The Teach-Yourself Piccolo Method: "A Guide to Pleasurable Piccolo Playing for Enthusiastic Flautists."* Birmingham, U.K.: Andrew Lane, 2008.

Lasocki, David, with Robert Ehrlich and Nikolaj Tarasov. *The Recorder.* London: Yale University Press, forthcoming.

Levine, Carin, and Christina Mitropoulos-Bott. *The Techniques of Flute Playing II: Piccolo, Alto and Bass Flute.* Kassel, Germany: Bärenreiter, 2004.

Long, Paige Dashner. "How Low Do They Go?" *Flute Talk* 27, no. 6 (February 2008): 19–22.

Louke, Phyllis Avidan. "Big Flutes." *Flute Talk* 25, no. 3 (November 2005): 12–15.

Miller, Dayton C. "The Contra-Bass Flute and the Albisiphone." *Flutist* (December 1922): 847–50.

———. "The Flute d'Amour and Other Transposing Flutes." *Flutist* (November 1922): 823–27.

Nourse, Nancy. "Flute Choirs Claim the Bottom Line: Big Flutes Now Join American Flute Ensembles." *Flutist Quarterly* (Summer 2003): 52–59.

———. "The Piccolo: An Overview of Its History and Instruction." M.Music thesis, Crane School of Music, Toronto, 1981.

———. "The Piccolo: Examining the Footnotes." *Flutist Quarterly* 15, no. 2 (Spring 1990): 47–49.

Pinschof, Thomas. "The Pinschofon: An Idea and Its Realization." *Flute Notes* (1985): 72–73.

Potter, Christine. *Alto and Bass Flute Resource Book.* King of Prussia, Penn.: Falls House Press, 2005.

Powell, Ardal. Long Military Flutes of the Sixteenth Century. Hudson, N.Y.: www.enterag.ch/anne/renaissanceflute/mfb/militaryflutebasel.html.

Roberto, Richard. "Playing D♭ Repertoire on C Piccolo." *Flute Talk* 11, no. 2 (October 1991): 27.

Stoune, Michael. "The Emerson Treble G Flute." *Emerson Flute Forum* 11, nos. 1 and 2 (1994): 14–15.

———. "An Ulster Experience: Flute Bands in Northern Ireland." *Flutist Quarterly* 33, no. 3 (Spring 2008): 28–32.

Wacker, Therese. "The History of the Piccolo, from Fifes to Intricate Keys." *Flute Talk* 20, no. 9 (May 2001): 8–15.

Walsh, Kate. "The Fall and Rise of the *Flute d'Amore.*" *Flute Focus,* issue 7 (July 2006): 18–21.

Wye, Trevor. "The Flute d'Amour." *Flute Worker* 3, no. 1 (Winter 1985): 3.

Health

Conable, Barbara, and William Conable. *How to Learn the Alexander Technique: A Manual for Students.* 3rd ed., rev. & enlarged. Portland, Ore.: Andover Press, 1995.

Harby, Karla, Kathrin Kucharski, Sarah Tuck, and Julia Vasquez. "Beta Blockers and Anxiety in Musicians." *Pan* 16, no. 4 (December 1997): 32–36.

Levine, John. "Is Flute Collecting a Mental Disorder?" *Pan* 24, no. 2 (June 2005): 38–41.

Matt, Margaret, and Joe Ziemian. *Human Anatomy Coloring Book.* New York: Dover, 1982.

Ogonovsky, Margaret. "Thumb Rests: Do We Need Them?" *Pan* 25, no. 3 (September 2006): 57–58.

Pearson, Lea. *Body Mapping for Flutists: What Every Flute Teacher Needs to Know about the Body.* Rev. & expanded ed. Chicago: GIA, 2006.

Historical Methods, Treatises, and Tutors

Bach, C. P. E. *Essay on the True Art of Playing Keyboard Instruments.* Translated and edited by William J. Mitchell. New York: Norton, 1949.

Devienne, François. *Nouvelle méthode théorique et pratique pour la flûte.* Paris: Imbault, 1794 (maybe earlier ed. of 1792). Facsimile of the original ed. with introduction, annotated catalogue of later editions, and translation by Jane Bowers.

Commentary on the original ed. by Thomas Boehm. Aldershot, England: Ashgate, 1999.

Drouët, Louis. *The Method of Flute Playing.* London: Cocks, ca. 1830. Reprint. Flute Library, vol. 17. Buren, The Netherlands: Frits Knuf, 1990.

Fürstenau, A. B. *Die Kunst des Flötenspiels.* Op. 138. Leipzig: Breitkopf & Härtel, ca. 1844. Facsimile. Buren, The Netherlands: Frits Knuf, 1991.

———. *Flöten-Schule. Anweisung zum Flötenspiel.* Op. 42. Leipzig: Breitkopf & Hartel, 1826.

Gunn, John. *The Art of Playing the German-Flute on New Principles.* London: Birchall, ca. 1793. Facsimile. Hudson, N.Y.: Folkers & Powell, 1992.

Hotteterre le Romain, Jacques. *Principles of the Flute, Recorder and Oboe.* Translated and edited by David Lasocki. New York: Praeger, 1968.

Hugot, A., and J. G. Wunderlich. *Méthode de flûte du Conservatoire.* Paris: Conservatoire de Musique, 1804. Facsimile. Buren, The Netherlands: Frits Knuf, 1975.

Lindsay, Thomas. *The Elements of Flute-playing, According to the Most Approved Principles of Modern Fingering.* 2 parts. London: T. Lindsay, 1828.

Mozart, Leopold. *A Treatise on the Fundamental Principles of Violin Playing.* Translated by Editha Knocker. 2nd ed. Oxford: Oxford University Press, 1951.

Nicholson, C. *C. Nicholson's Preceptive Lessons for the Flute.* London: Clementi & Co.: ca. 1821.

———. *A School for the Flute.* Vols. 1 and 2 combined, 1836. Facsimile. West Somerville, Mass.: P. H. Bloom, 2002.

Quantz, Johann Joachim. *Versuch einer Anweisung die Flöte traversiere zu spielen.* Berlin: Johann Friedrich Voss, 1752. Translated by Edward R. Reilly as *On Playing the Flute.* 2nd ed. New York: Schirmer, 1985.

Rockstro, Richard S. *A Treatise on the Construction, the History and the Practice of the Flute including a sketch of the elements of acoustics and critical notices of 60 celebrated flute players.* London: Rudall, Carte & Co., 1890. 2nd ed. London: Musical Rara, 1928. Reprint. Buren, The Netherlands: Frits Knuf, 1986.

Tromlitz, Johann George. *Ausführlicher und gründlicher Unterricht die Flöte zu spielen.* Leipzig: Adam Friedrich Böhme, 1791. Translated and edited as *The Virtuoso Flute-Player* by Ardal Powell, with introduction by Eileen Hadidian. Cambridge: Cambridge University Press, 1991.

Tulou, Jean-Louis. *A Method for the Flute.* Translated by Janice Dockendorff Boland and Martha F. Cannon. Bloomington: Indiana University Press, 1995.

History

See also "Biographies and Autobiographies," "Early Performance Practice," "Fingerings," "Flute Collections," "Flute Family," "Historical Methods, Treatises, and Tutors," and "Repair, Maintenance, and Construction."

Atema, Jelle. "Old Bone Flutes." *Pan* 23, no. 4 (December 2004): 18ff.

Baines, Anthony. *Woodwind Instruments and Their History.* 3rd ed. London: Faber & Faber, 1967. Reprint. New York: Dover, 1991.

Bate, Philip. *The Flute: A Study of Its History, Development and Construction.* London: Ernest Benn; New York: Norton, 1969.

Bigio, Robert, ed. *Readings in the History of the Flute: Monographs, Essays, Reviews, Letters and Advertisements from Nineteenth-Century London.* London: Tony Bingham, 2006.

Brett, Adrian. "The French Style in America." *Flute Worker* 2, no. 2 (December 1983): 1, 5.

———. "The Other French Players." *Flute Worker* 3, no. 1 (Winter 1985): 1, 6, 8.

———. "300 Years of the French Style." *Flute Worker* 1, no. 2 (November 1982): 1–5.

Colgin, Melissa. "A Century of *Morceaux de Concours.*" *Flute Talk* 20, no. 4 (December 2000): 10–12.

Debost, Michel. "The French School." *Flute Focus,* issue 6 (April 2006): 6–9.

De Lorenzo, Leonardo. *My Complete Story of the Flute: The Instrument, the Performer, the Music.* New York: Citadel Press, 1951.

Dorgeuille, Claude. *The French Flute School: 1860–1950.* Translated and edited by Edward Blakeman. London: Tony Bingham, 1986.

Fitzgibbon, Henry Macaulay. *The Story of the Flute.* London: Walter Scott, 1913. London: W. Reeves, 1928. 2nd ed., corrected & rev., 1919.

Giannini, Tula. *Great Flute Makers of France: The Lot and Godfroy Families, 1650–1900.* London: Tony Bingham, 1993.

Hamilton, Samuel C. "The Simple-System Flute in Irish Traditional Music." *Pan* 26, no. 3 (September 2007): 19–24.

Helin, Matti. *The Flute through the Ages.* Translated by William Dyer and Ilpo Halonen. Helsinki: Oy Atlo Music, 1992.

James, W. N. *A Word or Two on the Flute.* Facsimile of the 1826 1st ed. with new introduction by Stephen Preston. 3rd ed. London: Tony Bingham, 1982.

Johns, Michael. "A History of Woodwind Ensembles." *Flute Talk* 20, no. 4 (December 2000): 18–22.

Lasocki, David. "Lessons from Inventories and Sales of Flutes and Recorders, 1650–1800." Presentation to the XXXIV. Wissenschaftliche Arbeitstagung on "Flötenmusik in Geschichte und Aufführungspraxis von 1650 bis 1850," held at the Musikinstitut für Aufführungspraxis, Kloster Michaelstein, Blankenburg, Germany, March 2006. Proceedings forthcoming.

McGee, Terry. *Terry McGee, Flute Maker: Flutes for Irish, Classical and Early Music.* Http://www.mcgee-flutes.com.

Meylan, Raymond. *The Flute.* Translated by Alfred Clayton. London: B. T. Batsford, 1988.

Montagu, Jeremy. *The Flute.* Buckinghamshire, England: Shire, n.d..

Newcomb, William B. "Flautist vs. Flutist." *National Flute Association* (Summer 1980): 3ff.

Powell, Ardal. *The Flute.* New Haven: Yale University Press, 2002.

———. Flutehistory.com. 2000. Http://flutehistory.com.

Sachs, Curt. *The History of Musical Instruments.* New York: Norton, 1940.

Smith, Fenwick. "Is It a Flautist or Flutist?" *Flutist Quarterly* (Summer 2000): 76–77.

Solum, John. *The Early Flute* (contains a chapter on the Renaissance flute by Anne Smith). Oxford: Clarendon Press, 1992.

Taffanel, Paul. "Great Virtuosi of the Flute." Translated and annotated by John Ranck. *Flutist Quarterly* 17, no. 1 (Winter 1992): 45–61.

Toff, Nancy. *The Development of the Modern Flute.* New York: Taplinger, 1979.

Tromlitz, Johann George. *The Keyed Flute.* Leipzig, Germany: Adam Friedrich Böhme, 1800. Translated and edited by Ardal Powell. Oxford: Clarendon Press, 1996.

Welch, Christopher. *History of the Boehm Flute with Dr. Von Schafhäutl's life of Boehm, and an Examination of Mr. Rockstro's Version of the Boehm-Gordon Controversy.* 1892. 2nd ed. London: Rudall, Carte & Co., 1896. Facsimile of reprint of 1892 ed. New York: McGinnis & Marx, 1961.

Wilson, Rick. *Rick Wilson's Historical Flute Pages.* Http://www.oldflutes.com.

Zhang, Juzhong, Garman Harbottle, Changsui Want, and Zhaochen Kong. "Oldest Playable Musical Instruments Found at Jiahu Early Neolithic Site in China." *Nature* 401 (September 23, 1999): 366–68.

Intonation

See also Coltman, Crabb, and Wye in "Pedagogy," and "Repair, Maintenance, and Construction"

Averitt, Frances Lapp. "An Intonation Method for Flutists (Non-Exclusive of Other Instrumentalists and Singers) Based on the Use of Difference Tones as a Practical Guide to the Achievement of Perfectly Tuned Intervals." D.M. thesis, Florida State University, 1973.

Barcellona, John. "Intonation and Tuning Systems." *Flute Talk* 24, no. 3 (November 2004): 31–32.

———. "Temperaments and Tuning." *Flute Talk* 24, no. 2 (October 2004): 32.

———. "Woodwind Intonation." *Flute Talk* 18, no. 1 (September 1998): 16–19.

Butkevicius, Joseph. "Tuning a Flute." Michael Lange Music Co., 2003. Http://www.langemusic.com/Articles/flutetune.htm.

Coltman, John W. "Flute Intonation in Performance." *Flutist Quarterly* 24, no. 1 (Fall 1998): 42–47.

Cooper, Albert. "Choosing a Pitch (A440, A442, A444, A446)." *Flute Notes* (1985): 3.

Folkers, Catherine. "Playing in Tune on a Baroque Flute." *Traverso* 10, no. 1 (January 1998): 1–3.

Gann, Kyle. "An Introduction to Historical Tunings." 1997. Http://www.kylegann.com/histune.html.

———. "Just Intonation Explained." 1997. Http://www.kylegann.com/tuning.html.

Good, Elizabeth. "Fundamentals of Intonation." *Flute Talk* 25, no. 4 (December 2005): 14–20.

Tipton, Albert. "An Approach to 'Just' Intonation by Employment of Difference Tones." In *The Flutist's Handbook: A Pedagogy Anthology*, 53–58, ed. Michael Stoune. Santa Clarita, Calif.: NFA, 1998.

Wye, Trevor. "Fine Tune Your Intonation." *Pan* 22, no. 3 (September 2003): 32–34.

———. "Intonation: Time for Change." *Flute Talk* (December 2006): 16ff.

———. "Intonation Matters." *Pan* 22, no. 2 (June 2003): 36–37.

———. "The Intonation of the Modern Flute." Presentation at the International Summer School, Ramsgate, 1979; rev. August 1997. Available at http://www.larrykrantz.com/wyept2 .htm#tune.

Journals and Periodicals

Flute Focus. New Zealand. January 2005–present.

Flute Journal. Needham, Mass.: Dorn Publications, 1981–1982.

Flute Talk. Evanston, Ill.: Instrumentalist Co., 1981–present.

Flutemaker, The. Scarborough, Ont.: John Lunn Flutes, Ltd. 6 volumes, 1989–1991.

Flutewise. East Sussex, England. 1988–present.

Flutist, The. Ashville, N.C. 1920–1929.

Key Notes—a publication of the Wm. S. Haynes Co., Boston. 4 issues: 1998–2001.

Marcel Moyse Society Newsletter. Allentown, Penn., 1990–present.

National Flute Association, Inc., Newsletter, The. 1976 to 1984, when it became *The Flutist Quarterly*.

Pan. Journal of the BFS. 1983–present.

Traverso. Historical flute newsletter. 1989–present.

Woodwind Anthology: A Compendium of Woodwind Articles from the "Instrumentalist." Vol. 1: *Flute, General*. Northfield, Ill.: Instrumentalist Publishing Co., 1992.

Orchestra

See also Scott in "Biographies and Autobiographies."

Daniels, David. *Orchestral Music: A Handbook*. 4th ed. Lanham, Md.: Scarecrow Press, 2005.

Del Mar, Norman. *A Companion to the Orchestra*. London: Faber & Faber, 1987.

Kern, Jara. "The Unsung Assistants." *Flute Talk* 24, no. 1 (September 2004): 12–15.

Wion, John. "Orchestral Principal Flutists." 2008. Http:// homepage.mac.com/johnwion/orchestra.html.

Wye, Trevor. "Orchestral Audition Music: Top of the Pops." 1995. Http://www.larrykrantz.com/wyept2.htm.

Pedagogy

See also "Historical Methods, Treatises, and Tutors."

Altès, Henry. *Grand Method for Flute, Boehm System*. Paris: Schoenaers-Millereau, 1880.

Chapman, Frederick B. *Flute Technique*. 4th ed. New York: Oxford University Press, 1973.

Cherry, Anne. *Playing in Colours: Improving Tone for Advanced Players through the Use of Imagery*. London: Paul Rodriguez Music, 2001.

Clardy, Mary Karen. *Flute Fundamentals—The Building Blocks of Technique*. Penn.: European American Music Corp., 1993.

Cohen, Sheryl. *Bel Canto Flute: The Rampal School*. Cedar Rapids, Iowa: Winzer Press, 2003.

Debost, Michel. *The Simple Flute from A to Z*. Oxford:Oxford University Press, 2002.

Delaney, Charles. *Teacher's Guide for the Flute*. Elkhart, Ind.: Selmer, 1969.

Floyd, Angeleita S. *The Gilbert Legacy: Methods, Exercises and Techniques for the Flutist*. Cedar Falls, Iowa: Winzer Press, 1990.

Frederiksen, Brian. *Arnold Jacobs: Song and Wind*. Gurnee, Ill.: WindSong Press, 1996.

Galway, James. *The Flute*. London: Macdonald & Co., 1982.

Gärtner, Jochen. *The Vibrato, with Particular Consideration Given to the Situation of the Flutist*. Translated by Einar W. Anderson (cassette available separately). Regensburg, Germany: Gustav Bosse Verlag, 1981.

Graf, Peter-Lukas. *Interpretation: How to Shape a Melodic Line*. Translated by Katharine Wake. Mainz, Germany: Schott, 2001.

Hahn, Richard, and James Ployhar. *Practical Hints on Playing the Flute*. New York: Belwin Mills Publishing Corp., 1983.

Harrison, Howard. *How to Play the Flute*. New York: St. Martin's Press; London: Elm Tree Books, 1982.

Herbine, Lois. "The Phrasing Styles of Kincaid and Tabuteau." *Flute Talk* 25, no. 3 (November 2005): 22–25.

Hill, Vernon. *The Flute Player's Book*. Rev. 2nd ed. with demonstration CD. Designed and edited by Green Words; printed by National Capital Printers, Fyshwick, 1998.

Hunt, Simon. *Flute Teaching*. London: Pan Educational Music, 1983.

Krell, John. *Kincaidiana: A Flute Player's Notebook*. Malibu, Calif.: Trio Associates, 1973.

Kujala, Walfrid. *The Flutist's Progress*. Vol. 1. Winnetka, Ill.: Progress Press, 1970.

Lindon, Marlee. *FLUTE FUNdamentals*. Glenwood, Md.: Fluteplace Music, 2002.

Lloyd, Peter. *Flute Techniques*. Version #1. CD. Produced at Cola New Media Center, Southern Illinois University, 2001.

Mather, Roger. *The Art of Playing the Flute*. 3 vols. Vol. 1: *Breath Control* (1980), vol. 2: *Embouchure* (1981), vol. 3:

Posture, Fingers, Resonances, Tonguing, Vibrato (1989). Iowa City, Iowa: Romney Press.

Moore, E. C. *The Flute and Its Daily Routine.* Kenosha, Wis.: Leblanc, 1962.

Morris, Gareth. *Flute Technique.* New York: Oxford University Press, 1991.

Nyfenger, Thomas. *Music and the Flute.* Closter, N.J.: Thomas Nyfenger [159 Shore Drive, Guilford, CT 06437], 1986.

Poor, Mary Louise. *Guide to Flute Teaching.* New York: Envolve, 1978.

———. *Guide to Flute Teaching,* rev. ed. Naperville, Ill.: Flute Studio Press, 1983.

———. *The Band Director's Guidebook to Flute Teaching.* Jackson, Tenn.: Flute Studio Press, forthcoming.

Putnik, Edwin. *The Art of Flute Playing.* Evanston, Ill.: Summy-Birchard Co., 1973.

Shephard, Mark. *How to Love Your Flute: A Guide to Flutes and Flute Playing.* Berkeley: Panjandrum Books, 1980.

Soldan, Robin, and Jeanie Mellersh. *Illustrated Fluteplaying.* Minstead, England: London Minstead Publications, 1986.

Stevens, Roger S. *Artistic Flute: Technique and Study.* Edited by Ruth N. Zwissler. Hollywood, Calif.: Highland Music Co., 1967.

Stokes, Sheridon, and Richard Condon. *Illustrated Method for Flute.* Culver City, Calif.: Trio Associates, 1974.

Stoune, Michael C., ed. *The Flutist's Handbook: A Pedagogy Anthology.* Santa Clarita, Calif.: NFA, 1998.

Taffanel, [Paul], & [Philippe] Gaubert. *Méthode complète de flûte.* Paris: Alphonse Leduc, 1923.

Toff, Nancy. *The Flute Book: A Complete Guide for Students and Performers.* New York: C. Scribner's Sons, 1985. 2nd ed. New York: Oxford University Press, 1996.

Weisberg, Arthur. *The Art of Wind Playing.* New York: Schirmer, 1975.

Wilkins, Frederick. *The Flutist's Guide.* 3rd ed. Elkhart, Ind.: Artley, 1963.

Wilkinson, Fiona. *The Physical Flute* and *The Physical Flute: The Exercises.* Self-published, 1982; available through Waterloo Music, Ontario, Canada.

Wion, John. "Vibrato." N.d. Http://homepage.mac.com/johnwion/vibrato.html.

Wye, Trevor. *A Trevor Wye Practice Book for the Flute in 6 Volumes.* Vol. 1: Tone, 1980; Vol. 2: Technique, 1980; Vol. 3: Articulation, 1980; Vol. 4: Intonation, 1983; Vol. 5: Breathing and Scales, 1985; Vol. 6, Advanced Practice, 1987. London: Novello.

———. *Proper Flute Playing: A Companion to the Practice Books.* London: Novello, 1988.

Reference

See also "Flute Collections."

Berdhal, Susan M. B. *The First Hundred Years of the Boehm Flute in the United States, 1845–1945: A Biographical Dictionary of American Makers.* Ann Arbor, Mich.: UMI, 1985.

Blom, Eric. *Grove's Dictionary of Music and Musicians.* 5th ed. in 9 vol., 1954; supplementary vol., 1961.

Diagram Group. *Musical Instruments of the World.* New York: Facts on File, 1976.

Fairley, Andrew. "Flutes, Flautists and Makers (Active or Born before 1900)." London: Pan Educational Music, 1982.

Grove, Sir George. *A Dictionary of Music and Musicians.* 4 vols. London: Macmillan, 1878–1899.

Grove's Music Online. Http://www.grovemusic.com.

Miller, Dayton Clarence. *Catalogue of Books and Literary Material Relating to the Flute & Other Musical Instruments, with Annotations.* Cleveland: N.p., 1935.

Oxford English Dictionary. 2nd ed. Oxford: Oxford University Press, 1989.

Pierre, Constant. *Le Conservatoire national de musique et de déclamation, documents historiques et administratifs recueillis ou reconstitués par l'auteur.* Paris: Imprimerie Nationale, 1900.

Sadie, Stanley, ed. *The New Grove Dictionary of Musical Instruments and Instrument Makers.* 3 vols. London: Macmillan, 1984.

Spohr, Peter. *Transverse Flutes down the Centuries from All over the World.* Frankfurt: Peter Spohr. 1991.

Vester, Frans. *Flute Repertoire Catalogue: 10,000 Titles.* London: Musica Rara, 1967.

Waterhouse, William. *The New Langwill Index: A Dictionary of Musical Wind-Instrument Makers and Inventors.* London: Tony Bingham, 1993.

Woodcroft, R., ed. *Patents for Inventions, Abridgements of Specifications Relating to Music and Musical Instruments, AD. 1694–1866.* Facsimile of the 1871 edition, with abridgements of 740 English patents issued before 1867. London: Tony Bingham.

Repair, Maintenance, and Construction

See also Lunn under "Journals."

Barcellona, John. "Flutes and Their Scales." *Flute Journal* (October 1981): 20–22.

Bennett, Harold. The Permanent Effect of Vibrations on the Musical Instrument." *The Flutist Quarterly* 10, no. 4: summer, 1985: 41-43.

Boehm, Theobald. *The Flute and Flute-Playing in Acoustical, Technical, and Artistic Aspects.* Translated by Dayton C. Miller. New York: Dover, 1964.

Brand, Erick D. *Band Instrument Repairing Manual.* 8th ed. rev. Reprint. Battle Creek, Mich.: Ferree's Tools, 1993.

Brass Bow, The. "Cryogenics." N.d. Http://www.thebrassbow.com/brassbw1.htm.

Britton, Jacqueline Ward. *Dreams to Reality: Designing a SquareONE Alto Flute* [CD]. Photos by Jacqueline Ward

Britton and Leonard E. Lopatin. Lopatin Flute Co., Asheville, N.C., 2005.

Cole, Elmer. "The Elmer Cole Foot Extensions and Trill Key Systems." *Flute Notes* (1985): 30–31.

Coltman, John W. "Designing the Scale of the Boehm Flute." *Woodwind Quarterly* 4 (February 1994): 24–41.

———. "A New C♯ for the Boehm Flute." *Instrumentalist* (May 1977): 64–65.

Cooper, Albert. *The Flute*. 2nd enlarged ed. London: E.B. Reproductions, 1985.

———. "An In-Depth Inquiry into Depth." *Flute Notes* (1985): 41.

———. "Off Set G and A or In Line." *Flute Notes* (1985): 22.

———. "The R.F. Modification." *Flute Notes* (1985): 11.

———. "Splitting Keys." *Flute Talk* 12, no. 8 (April 1992): 21–22.

———. "The Upper Chamber." *Flute Notes* (1985): 65.

Crabb, Nick. "Renovating and Retuning a Flute." *Pan* 16, no. 4 (December 1997): 22–25.

Drelinger, Sanford. *Headjoint Buying Guide and Q&A*. White Plains, N.Y.: Sanford Drelinger, 1978–2008.

Eggs, Les. "Flute Making in a Bygone Age." *Flute Notes* (1985): 61–64.

Giannini, Tula. "An Old Key for a New Flute: The Boehm Flute with Closed G♯: Historical Perspectives." *Flutist Quarterly* 10, no. 1 (Fall 1984): 15–20.

Goodman, Marsha. *Haynes and Powell: The Facts and Figures; A Guide to Their Production and Prices*. Santa Monica, Calif.: Rosewood Press, 1983.

Goosman, Mara. "Annual Flute Maintenance." *Flute Talk* 17, no. 6 (February 1998): 24.

Julliot, Djalma, and F. Borne. *Notice Concernant les Améliorations apportées à la Flûte de Théobald Boehm*. Imprimerie E. Grateau, 1905.

Kaebitzsch, Garry. *Twenty-two Flute Repair Tips for the Player*. Lynnfield, Mass.: Free Bee, 1986.

La Berge, Anne. "The Oston-Brannen Kingma System Flute." *Flutist Quarterly* 20, no. 4 (Summer 1995): 88–90.

Landell, Jonathan A. *The Landell Flute Tune-up Manual*. Vermont Guild, 1983.

———. "Machines and Craftsmanship in Creating Handmade Flutes." *Flute Talk* 22, no. 3 (November 2002): 26.

———. "The Titanium Flute." *Flute Talk* 16, no. 5 (January 1997): 28–29.

Lane, Andrew. "The Toppleless Top F♯ Key." *Pan* 20, no. 2 (June 2001): 29–32.

Lawrence, Eleanor. "Theobald Boehm on the Open G♯ Key." *Flutist Quarterly* 10, no. 1 (Fall 1984): 7–9.

Lopatin, Leonard. "Developing the SquareONE flute." *Pan* 26, no. 2 (June 2007): 51–54.

McCreight, Tim. *Complete Metalsmith: An Illustrated Handbook; Student Edition*. New York: Sterling, 2005.

———. *Complete Metalsmith: Professional Edition*. Portland, Maine: Brynmorgen Press, 2004.

Miyazawa Flutes, Ltd. *Educational Articles*. Http://www.miyazawa.com (select "Educational Articles" from "Media Library" pull-down menu).

Pailthorpe, Daniel. "Why I Play Open G♯." *Pan* (December 1997): 14ff.

Phelan, James. *Flute Fitness: Care and Easy Repair That You Can Do* [video]. Acton, Mass.: Burkart-Phelan, 1992.

———. "How Flutes Are Made." *Pan* 26, no. 3 (September 2007): 25–29.

———. "How Flutes Are Made: Padding and Finishing." *Pan* 27, no. 1 (March 2008): 55–59.

———. "How Flutes Are Made: The Headjoint." *Pan* 27, no. 2 (June 2008): 41–44.

———. "How Flutes Are Made: The Keys." *Pan* 26, no. 4 (December 2007): 37–40.

———. "It's Only Fitting." *Flute Talk* 18, no. 6 (February 1999): 28.

Phelan, J. James, and Lillian Burkart. *The Complete Guide to the Flute and Piccolo*. 2nd ed. Acton, Mass.: Burkart-Phelan, 2002.

Pinksterboer, Hugo, with Gijs Bierenbroodspot. *The Rough Guide to Flute and Piccolo*. London: Rough Guides, 2001.

Powell, Ardal. "Science, Technology and the Art of Flutemaking in the Eighteenth Century." *Flutist Quarterly* 19, no. 3 (Spring 1994): 33–42.

Rayworth, John. *Photographs of Flutes and Their Features*. 2000. Http://www.flute.toucansurf.com/flute/fluteidx.html.

Rees, Carla. "Eva Kingma and the Quarter-tone Flute." *Pan* 26, no. 4 (December 2007): 23–29.

Schmidt, James. "Modifying the Boehm System." *Flute Talk* 12, no. 6 (February 1993): 15–16.

Schwadron, Terry H. *For the Musical Alchemist, a New Tack: Cryogenics*. nytimes.com: Nov. 2, 1999. http://query.nytimes.com/gst/fullpage.html?res=9F03E3D8143BF931A35752C1A96F958260&scp=1&sq=schwadron%20musical%20alchemist&st=cse&scp=3&sq=cryogenics&st=cse.

Smith, Jeff. "The Complete Flute Buyer's Guide." Catalog # 8. Charlotte, N.C.: J. L. Smith & Co., 2003.

———. "Servicing the flute—the companion guide to the Valentino flute fixkit™." J.L. Smith & Co., 2008.

Spell, Eldred. "Anatomy of a Headjoint." *Flute Worker* 1, no. 2 (November 1982): 9.

———. "Louis Lot Flutes: Basic Facts." *Flute Worker* 2, no. 2 (December 1983): 1–2.

———. "Modernizing Old French Flutes." *Flute Worker* 3, no. 2 (Spring 1985): 4–5.

———. "Restoration: Old French Flutes." *Flute Worker* 3, no. 1 (Winter 1985): 4–5.

Symington, David. "Stopper Sounds." *Pan* 22, no. 1 (March 2003): 16–17.

Wimberly, David. "The Murray Flute." *Flute Notes* (1985): 83–84.

Wintizer, Trudy Jo. "The History of the Murray Flute." *Flute Notes* (1985): 85–94.

Wye, Trevor. "The Techniques Used in Retuning Old Silver Flutes." Trevor Wye, 2004, rev., 2006.

Young, Roger W. "Anatomy of a Headjoint." *Flutesmith* 2, issue 1 (March 29, 2004): 1–2.

Zadro, Michael G. "Woods Used for Woodwind Instruments since the 16th Century, Part 1." *Early Music* 3, no. 2 (April 1975): 134–36.

———. "Woods Used for Woodwind Instruments since the 16th Century, Part 2: A Descriptive Dictionary of the Principal Woods Mentioned." *Early Music* 3, no. 3 (July 1975): 249–51.

Singing

Vennard, William. *Singing: The Mechanism and the Technic.* Rev. 5th ed., greatly enlarged. New York: Carl Fischer, 1967.

About the Author

Susan Maclagan is a freelance flutist, flute instructor, and magazine writer who lives in Winnipeg, Manitoba. She has studied the flute for more than 45 years. Her career has included playing in the Calgary Philharmonic and in a flute and harp or piano ensemble called Windsong; teaching privately with a specialty in flute technique and at institutions such as the University of Toronto and Havergal College; and writing for flute magazines and newsletters. Susan has studied at the University of Toronto, the Royal Conservatory of Toronto, the Banff School of Fine Arts, the Aspen School of Music, and Jeunesses Musicales of Canada and has attended many flute master classes and National Flute Association conventions. Her teachers have included Geoffrey Gilbert, Louis Moyse, and Jeanne Baxtresser.